1995

BUSINESS COMMUNICATION

JULES HARCOURT

A.C. "BUDDY" KRIZAN

PATRICIA MERRIER

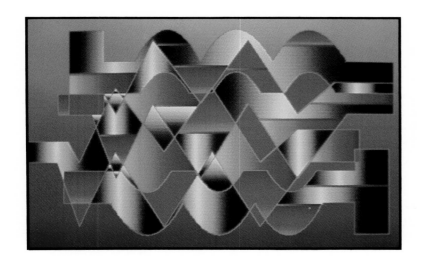

EC42BA
PUBLISHED BY
SOUTH-WESTERN PUBLISHING CO.
CINCINNATI, OH   WEST CHICAGO, IL   DALLAS, TX   LIVERMORE, CA

Library of Congress Cataloging-in-Publication Data

Harcourt, Jules.
    Business communication / Jules Harcourt, A.C. "Buddy" Krizan,
Patricia Merrier. -- 2nd ed.
      p.   cm.
    "EC42BA."
    ISBN 0-538-70093-9 :
    1. Business communication.   I. Krizan, A. C.   II. Merrier,
Patricia.   III. Title.
HF5718.H288   1991
808'.06665--dc20   89-60389
                                                     CIP

1 2 3 4 5 6 7 8 9 D 8 7 6 5 4 3 2 1 0

Printed in the United States of America

CONTENTS

152, 76 2

PART FOUR
WRITTEN REPORT APPLICATIONS

PART FIVE
ORAL AND NONVERBAL COMMUNICATION APPLICATIONS

PART   SIX

SPECIAL COMMUNICATION APPLICATIONS

APPENDIXES

PREFACE

Success in business depends on the ability to communicate effectively more than on any other skill. *Business Communication*, Second Edition, is designed to assist in the learning of this critical skill.

This edition of *Business Communication* retains the flexibility of the first edition. For example, employment communication may be taught in conjunction with persuasive messages or as a separate unit. Research and report writing or business English may be studied as separate units or used as reference. This chapter independence allows a course to be designed to best meet the needs of all students.

In addition to being flexible, *Business Communication* continues to be comprehensive.

Part One introduces communication fundamentals; it presents the principles of business communication, stresses the importance of receiver analysis and message planning, and explains how technology can assist in preparing and transmitting business messages.

NEW   Chapter 3 now includes coverage of ethical and legal considerations in business writing.

NEW   Chapter 4 has been expanded to include information about word processing software (spelling check, thesaurus), computerized style checkers, and oral presentation aids (electronic imagers, desktop slidemakers).

Part Two stresses the importance of correct writing by reviewing parts of speech, sentence structure, punctuation, and style.

Part Three is devoted to building proficiency in writing good news, neutral news, bad news, persuasive, and goodwill messages; letter and memo formats are also presented.

NEW   Letters of inquiry have been included as a separate topic in Chapter 10.

NEW   An example of using the direct plan for bad news has been added to Chapter 11.

NEW   Examples of poor and good business messages are placed on facing pages for easy comparison.

Part Four covers the basics of research and report writing in business. It progresses from proposal writing through the preparation of a formal report;

attention is devoted to selection and preparation of graphic aids. Memo reports are also discussed.

NEW Extensive coverage of proposal preparation has been included in Chapter 14. A poorly written and a well-written proposal are included as examples.

NEW Chapter 15 has been expanded to cover minutes, news releases, and policy statements.

NEW Computer-generated graphics are discussed in Chapter 16.

Part Five focuses on listening and oral communication and relates these important interpersonal skills to success in business.

NEW Listening, previously included in Part Six, is now included with oral communication in Part Five.

Part Six deals with a topic of particular interest to business students—employment communication. Practical suggestions are offered for resume and application letter development, and job interview techniques are presented. International business is also covered in this section of the text.

NEW Employment communication is now covered in *two* chapters. One chapter is devoted to the job search and resume preparation; the other covers application letters, interviews, and other messages related to employment.

NEW Canada is now included among the countries discussed in the international business communication chapter.

Years of studying and teaching business communication have convinced us that students learn best if they are taught general concepts and then given an immediate opportunity for practical application. This learning process is facilitated in the text by providing several examples of poor *and* good messages. In addition, the application exercises and end-of-chapter cases are realistic.

OUTSTANDING FEATURES

Business Communication, Second Edition, contains many features that effectively promote learning and understanding.

LOGICAL ORGANIZATION. Concepts are presented in a simple, straightforward manner and are immediately reinforced with real-life examples of their practical application. Both poor *and* good examples—with analytic comments—are used extensively, so it is easy to fully understand how concepts are applied. All messages are presented in formats commonly found in the world of business.

LIVELY, CONVERSATIONAL WRITING STYLE. The book is written following the principles of business communication it presents. It is written from the you-viewpoint and at a level of readability appropriate for its audience.

CONCEPT-DIRECTED LEARNING OBJECTIVES. Each chapter begins with a concise list of learning objectives that are directed at the most important concepts within the chapter. These learning objectives can be used effectively both for beginning the study of a chapter and for evaluating overall learning in a review of the chapter.

CONCISE PARAGRAPH SUMMARIES. Marginal notes are liberally distributed throughout the book. These notes generally summarize the information contained in the text and are also used to analyze the poor and good examples of business writing. The marginal notes are an effective tool for reviewing important ideas.

EXTENSIVE END-OF-CHAPTER ACTIVITIES. These activities include review questions that cover every major aspect of the chapter. In addition, there are numerous application exercises designed to give practice in applying what has been learned from the instructional material.

When appropriate, chapters include a large number of case problems. These case problems are varied in their subject matter and orientation. There are cases in accounting, marketing, finance, and human resource management. In some cases, students assume the role of business professionals; in other cases, they are individuals writing to organizations.

EXPANDED   The number of case problems at the end of each chapter has been expanded by at least 25 percent; at least half of the end-of-chapter cases are new.

USEFUL APPENDIXES. The most important business communication material is contained within the 22 chapters in the main part of the book. Some topics, however, are more convenient and useful as appendixes. In this edition, the number of appendixes has been expanded from three to seven.

NEW	Word Usage
	Editing Symbols
NEW	Proofreading Procedures
MOVED FROM TEXT	Unbiased Language
	Postal Abbreviations
NEW	Example Proposal
	Example Long Report

ATTRACTIVE, INVITING BOOK DESIGN. Headings, marginal notes, illustrations, and examples are attractively arranged and in color. The wide outside margins provide room for notes and give a feeling of openness. The layout gives the book the uninterrupted coherence essential for ease in learning.

COMPLETE TEACHING-LEARNING PACKAGE

The following items are available as part of the teaching-learning package that supports the Second Edition of *Business Communication*:

INSTRUCTOR'S MANUAL. The comprehensive instructor's manual suggests organizational plans for varying course designs. For each chapter, it contains learning objectives, detailed lecture notes in the form of teaching outlines, suggested classroom strategy, solutions to end-of-chapter activities, suggested chapter test questions (true-false, multiple choice, and essay) and their solutions, and solutions to the learning activities contained in the student supplement.

NEW   Exercises and cases from the first edition that are not included in the second edition have been placed in the instructor's manual as supplemental material.

NEW   Model solutions for selected cases.

OVERHEAD TRANSPARENCIES. Adopters of the textbook will be provided carefully designed overhead transparencies that reinforce the material in the chapters. Transparencies have been prepared to present content, to illustrate good writing, and to provide additional classroom exercises. The lecture notes in the instructor's manual indicate when a supporting transparency is appropriate for use.

NEW   Fifty additional transparencies have been included with the teaching-learning package, bringing the total to 100.

NEW   Model solutions are now presented on transparencies.

COMPUTERIZED TEST BANK. The flexible, easy-to-use test bank contains all test questions included in the instructor's manual. Questions can be modified, and instructor-written questions can be added.

BUSINESS ENGLISH SOFTWARE. For supplemental instruction or for review, the teaching-learning package contains free microcomputer software for programmed instruction on business English. This software is integrated with the textbook and includes references to the appropriate text chapters.

NEW   Coverage has been increased to *12 sections* and *60 screens*.

APPLICATIONS TEMPLATE DISKETTE. This optional diskette can be used with selected commercial word processing software. It contains additional composition and text-editing applications to those contained in the text and student study supplement.

STUDENT STUDY SUPPLEMENT. The completion, true-false, matching, and multiple choice activities as well as the related exercises contained in the student supplement are designed to guide students in their review of text material.

SPECIAL MESSAGE TO STUDENTS

We believe that your study of this textbook and its related materials will improve your ability to communicate. You can learn from *Business Communication* and use it to help you complete assignments in your business communication course. We recommend that you then keep this textbook (along with selected other textbooks in your major) and use it as an effective reference in your other courses and in your future career. Good luck in your business communication study!

ACKNOWLEDGMENTS

Thank you to the following individuals for reviewing the manuscript and offering suggestions for improving *Business Communication*: Mrs. Kathleen Crall, Des Moines Area Community College (Des Moines, Iowa); Mrs. Jean T. Dorrell, Lamar University (Beaumont, Texas); Mrs. Jackye Gold, Southeastern Oklahoma State University (Durant, Oklahoma); Mr. Andrew Halford, Paducah Community College (Paducah, Kentucky); Ms. Joneen Iverson, Aaker's Business College (Grand Forks, North Dakota); Dr. Mary Lou Lamb, Savannah State College (Savannah, Georgia); Dr. Richard B. Larsen, Francis Marion College (Florence, South Carolina); Mr. Andrew Madson, Milwaukee Area Technical College (Milwaukee, Wisconsin); Mr. Ross A. Miller, Milwaukee Area Technical College (Milwaukee, Wisconsin); Dr. Tom Seymour, Minot State University (Minot, North Dakota); Dr. Gayle A. Sobolik, California State University—Fresno (Fresno, California); Ms. Karen Tussey, Southwestern Community College (Creston, Iowa).

Jules Harcourt, A. C. "Buddy" Krizan, and Patricia Merrier

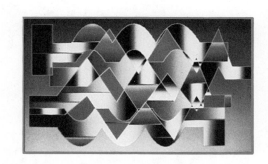

PART ONE

COMMUNICATION FUNDAMENTALS

CHAPTER 1

BUSINESS COMMUNICATION FOUNDATIONS

LEARNING OBJECTIVES

Your learning objectives for this chapter include the following:

- To learn the nature of business communication--its definition, importance, goals, and patterns
- To understand the communication process and your role in successfully using it
- To recognize communication barriers and know how to remove them

Your success depends on your ability to communicate.

You can improve your communication skills.

Materials in this book will be of immediate, practical value to you.

The ability to communicate effectively is the most important skill you can develop. How well you inform, influence, and persuade others determines the progress you make in your career and the quality of your personal relationships. Fortunately, you can make significant improvements in your ability to communicate. You can make these improvements by studying the successful methods and techniques contained in this book.

Included in this book are sections on communication fundamentals, business English, correspondence, written reports, oral communication, employment communication, and other special communication applications. All of these materials are presented in a way that will be of immediate, practical value to you.

THE NATURE OF BUSINESS COMMUNICATION

Your study will begin with a review of the nature of business communication—its definition, importance, goals, and patterns.

DEFINITION OF BUSINESS COMMUNICATION

Business communication can be defined as the transmission of information within the business environment. The information may be transmitted—sent and received—between two individuals or among several individuals. Methods of communicating are speaking, gesturing, listening, writing, drawing, and reading.

> Business communication is the transmission of information within the business environment. Methods of communicating vary.

At times you will be the sender of messages—the speaker or the writer. At other times you will be the receiver—the listener or the reader. In the back-and-forth transmission of information, you will be both a sender and a receiver. You must do both jobs well. When you learn how to be a capable, successful sender of messages, you will understand how to be an effective receiver of messages.

Business communication includes all contacts among individuals both inside and outside organizations—formal as well as informal. These contacts can consist of face-to-face conversations, letters, memos, telephone conversations, reports, speeches, and so on. The word communication comes from the Latin word *communis*, which means common. Individuals strive to transmit information to each other that will establish a commonness of understanding between or among them.

IMPORTANCE OF BUSINESS COMMUNICATION

Effective communication is essential to the success of businesses and individuals.

IMPORTANCE OF COMMUNICATION TO BUSINESSES. Businesses have internal and external communication about short-range and long-range matters. The quality of this communication directly influences the success of the business.

> Businesses depend on communication.

The day-to-day operation of a business depends on the exchange of information among its employees. Information about objectives, job instructions, customer orders, production, problems, corrections, and employee recognition are examples of vital information exchanged daily in the course of business. Long-range planning and decision making are based on research, reports, proposals, conferences, evaluations, and projections—all forms of communication within business organizations.

Equally important to a business is communication with those outside the organization. A business has frequent contact with customers, community members, government officials, or the general public.

Examples of day-to-day external communications are sales calls, sale advertisements, news stories, employment notices, bank transactions, and periodic reports to governments. External communications that have a longer range impact include new product announcements, plant expansion plans, contributions to community activities, and annual reports. Effective communication with those outside the company, which brings orders and builds goodwill, ensures the continued existence and growth of the business.

IMPORTANCE OF COMMUNICATION TO INDIVIDUALS.

The average person spends about 70 percent of his or her waking hours in some form of communication. This communication ranges from conferences and memo writing at work to personal conversations and newspaper reading at home.

The higher the responsibility level to which individuals progress in an organization, the more time they spend communicating. High-level executives in many businesses or nonprofit organizations will spend up to 95 percent of their working time communicating—speaking, listening, writing, and reading. While some persons may spend as little as 10 percent of their work time communicating, it is estimated that an average of 60 percent of employee time is spent in some form of communication.

Research on the opinions of executives and college graduates reveals that the ability to communicate effectively in business is ranked at the top of the skills necessary for promotions and salary increases. In addition, studies show that an individual's communication competence relates directly to his or her job performance and productivity. A satisfactory level of technical skill and knowledge in your field is expected of you. How effectively you communicate that technical expertise determines how successful you will be on your job.

> A man who has knowledge but lacks the power to express it is no better off than if he never had any ideas.
>
> *Pericles, Greek statesman, fifth century, B.C.*

Business communication is vital to both individuals and organizations. Improving your communication skills will be beneficial to both you and your employer.

BUSINESS COMMUNICATION GOALS

The four basic goals of business communication are:

1. The receiver understands the message as the sender intended.
2. The receiver provides the necessary response to the sender.
3. The sender and the receiver maintain a favorable relationship.
4. The sender's organization gains goodwill.

The sender has the responsibility for the achievement of these business communication goals. When you are the sender—when you are initiating messages or responding to messages—you should keep these goals in mind and assume the responsibility for their accomplishment.

RECEIVER UNDERSTANDING. To achieve the first and most important goal of business communication, the sender must transmit the message clearly so that the receiver's interpretation of it will be the meaning that the sender intends. For example, if you want a friend to know that you definitely cannot go to a movie with him Tuesday night even though you would like to do so, you do not want to say, "I probably won't be able to go to the movie Tuesday; I might have to work or something." The meaning you may transmit to your receiver will be that you could go to the movie Tuesday, but you do not want to. It would be better for clarity and understanding to say, "Thanks for asking, but I can't go Tuesday; maybe we can go to a movie some other time."

It is a challenge for the sender to achieve the goal of receiver understanding. The sender may need to plan, research, draft, edit, and revise before the message can be understood clearly by the receiver. To develop a clear message the sender must consider (1) the nature of the receiver, (2) the best form and content of the message, (3) the provision for feedback from the receiver, and (4) the removal of communication barriers. These ideas are discussed in the sections on the communication process and communication barriers later in this chapter.

RECEIVER RESPONSE. The second goal of business communication is that the receiver provides the necessary response to the sender. For example, the response of the receiver could be the simple understanding and acceptance of a message announcing a meeting time to employees. Another example of receiver response could be the placement of a large order for merchandise by a customer after a salesperson's presentation.

The sender should assist the receiver in responding. The wording of the message should encourage response. In a face-to-face conversation, the sender (speaker) can ask the receiver (listener) if he or she understands the message. Furthermore, the sender can ask directly for the response needed. In situations

---

The four business communication goals are:
- Receiver understanding
- Receiver response
- Favorable relationship
- Organizational goodwill

The sender is responsible for the achievement of these goals.

First goal: Receiver understands message as sender intended.

Sending a clear message is a challenge.

Second goal: Receiver provides necessary response.

The sender should encourage and assist receiver response.

where the message is written, the sender can encourage a response by asking questions, providing a return envelope and order form, requesting that the receiver telephone the sender, or any one of many other possibilities for securing the necessary response from the receiver.

For example, suppose your music store has received a mail order for an album; but the customer did not specify whether a record, cassette, or compact disc was wanted. To get the response needed, you should write a letter requesting the information and enclose a postage-paid, addressed reply card on which the customer can simply check the choice desired.

FAVORABLE RELATIONSHIP. The third goal of business communication is that the sender and the receiver maintain a favorable personal relationship. In order to continue doing business together, the sender and the receiver must be able to relate positively to each other. Each will receive benefits from maintaining this relationship. If the sender is the seller, a favorable relationship will probably mean more sales and more profits; if the sender is the customer, a favorable relationship will mean a continued source of supply and possibly better prices. Generally, a favorable relationship will serve the interests of both the sender and the receiver.

It is primarily the responsibility of the sender to provide for the maintenance of a favorable relationship. Some of the ways the sender can do this include using positive wording, stressing the receiver's interests and benefits, and doing more than is expected. For example, suppose you have to refuse overtime work. If you take the initiative in finding another employee willing to work overtime in your place, you would be doing more than your receiver expected you to do.

ORGANIZATIONAL GOODWILL. The fourth goal of business communication is to gain goodwill for the organization. The goodwill of customers or clients is essential to any business or other organization. If a company has the goodwill of its customers, it has their confidence and their continuing willingness to buy its products or services. The more goodwill a company has, the more successful it can be.

Senders of messages have the responsibility to try to increase goodwill for their company whenever they communicate. They do this in much the same way that they maintain favorable individual relationships. The emphasis, however, includes message content and actions that reflect favorably on the quality and dependability of the company's products and services.

An example of how an employee can build goodwill for his or her company is found in the handling of returned merchandise. If it is company policy to accept the return of defective merchandise with few or no questions, the employee should do just that. The returned merchandise should not be accepted grudgingly, but cheerfully. The employee could say with a smile, "It's

Big M Hardware's policy to offer a replacement item or a refund. Which would you prefer?" (Customer answers.) "Okay, we'll take care of that right away!" If the communication situation is handled this way, Big M Hardware will gain goodwill and the fourth goal of business communication will have been achieved.

PATTERNS OF BUSINESS COMMUNICATION

As communicators attempt to achieve the four goals of business communication, they send and receive messages that are both internal and external to their companies. Some of these messages are formal and some are informal; some are work related and others are personal. The wide variations among these patterns of business communication are discussed next.

Communication patterns vary widely.

INTERNAL COMMUNICATION PATTERNS.
Within the business organization, communication flows upward, downward, and horizontally. In the organization chart for a business shown in Illustration 1-1, the lines connecting the employees show these three communication patterns. Messages can flow upward from the workers through the supervisor to the manager. Through the same connecting lines, messages can flow downward. Also, messages can flow horizontally among the A employees and among the B employees—those employees in the same organizational unit. Finally, messages can flow between Unit A and Unit B.

Within a business, communication flows upward, downward, and horizontally.

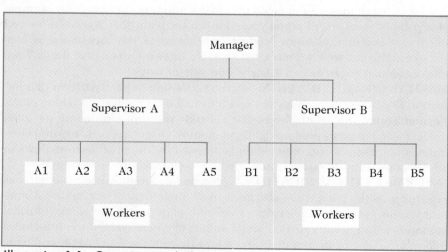

Illustration 1-1 Organizational Chart

Communication also flows diagonally.

In addition, many messages flow diagonally in organizations. **Networking** is the combining of employees from different units and different levels of the organization. Illustration 1-2 shows such a grouping of employees. As shown by the lines connecting each employee with all the other employees in the group, communication flows directly among them regardless of their unit or their organizational level. One of the employees in the network may serve the group as chairperson. In most network communication all participants are equal in status, including the chairperson.

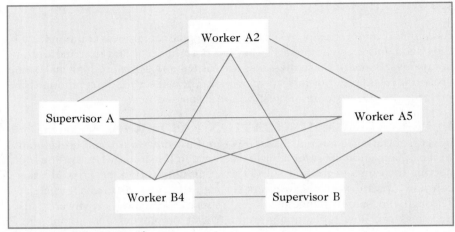

Illustration 1-2   Network

A network may be a planned part of the business operation. An example of a planned network of employees is a project team that has been formed to develop and market a new product. In other cases, the networks may consist of employees who are attracted to each other on a personal basis. They may eat lunch together or be friends outside of work.

FORMAL COMMUNICATION.   In the various directional patterns of information flow, there is both formal and informal communication taking place.

Formal communication is business related.

Formal communication is business related—possibly with some personal touches—and consists predominantly of memos, written reports, and oral communication. Formal communication is planned by the organization, flows in all directions, and is essential for effective operation of the business.

INFORMAL COMMUNICATION.   **Informal communication**—sometimes referred to as the grapevine—also flows in all directions. In fact, informal com-

Informal communication can be either business related or personal.

munication generally has extremely erratic patterns. While some informal communication is work related, much of it is of a personal nature. It includes information ranging from rumors about who the new president of the company will be to a discussion of yesterday's baseball scores. Informal communication is essential for the development and maintenance of human relationships.

SERIAL COMMUNICATION. A great deal of the information flowing within an organization is transmitted through three or more individuals. Employee A will send a message to Employee B who, in turn, will send that same basic message to Employee C. The transmission chain may be longer and include more employees or groups of employees. This type of communication pattern is called **serial communication**. Serial communication is common in downward and upward flows of information. For example, job instructions are developed by managers and transmitted to the supervisors who report to them. The supervisors, in turn, transmit the instructions to the employees under their supervision. Serial communication is usually oral in nature but may include written messages.

In serial communication the messages are usually changed, possibly dramatically, as they are passed from one member of the chain to another. Commonly, details are omitted, modified, or added. Special precautions are necessary to ensure accuracy and understanding in serial communication. Communicators involved in chains should take notes, repeat the message, keep the message simple, and request feedback. These techniques will assist in assuring that the same meaning is transmitted throughout the serial communication.

EXTERNAL COMMUNICATION PATTERNS. Communication that flows between a business organization and society is usually formal in nature. Companies have many external contacts such as customers, suppliers, competitors, the media, governments, and the general public. The information that flows between a business and the public consists primarily of letters, advertisements, orders, shipping and invoicing data, oral communications, and reports.

One example of an external communication pattern begins with a sales letter and an advertisement sent to prospective customers. An interested customer returns an inquiry card requesting that a salesperson call and provide more information about a particular product. The salesperson calls—on the telephone or in person—and makes an oral presentation about the product to the customer. The customer orders the product. When the order form reaches the originating business, it starts a series of internal communications. Appropriate instructions are sent to the sales, production, shipping, and accounting departments. Files are created, reports are issued, and the product is shipped to the customer. Many additional communications may follow this sale. Invoices, payments, reorders, claims, adjustments, service calls, and follow-up visits by a salesperson are some of the possibilities.

A business's success depends on the quality of its external communication. While the products or services of a business firm may be excellent, it is effective communication by salespersons and other personnel that assures the continued existence and growth of the business.

Literally thousands of formal and informal communications take place every day. The success of each individual and the success of a business organization rest on the effectiveness of these messages and their achievement of

Serial communication is chain transmission of information.

In serial communication messages are usually changed.

There are techniques for improving serial communication.

Businesses communicate with many external publics.

Multiple messages are connected with one sale.

The success of a business depends on effective communication.

the four goals of business communication. In the next section the transmission of messages will be analyzed in more detail to assist you in further strengthening your communication ability.

THE COMMUNICATION PROCESS

Understanding the communication process improves your ability to communicate.

One way to help you improve your ability to communicate is to study the process involved in the act of communicating.

A COMMUNICATION PROCESS MODEL

The best way to study the communication process is to analyze a model of it. An understanding of the communication process model shown in Illustration 1-3 will strengthen your performance as a communicator.

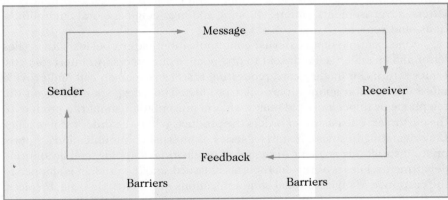

Illustration 1-3   A Communication Process Model

The communication process includes the sender, message, receiver, feedback, and barriers.

The communication environment includes all things perceived.

The communication process model is an open environment that includes the sender, the message, the receiver, feedback, and communication barriers. The **communication environment** includes all things perceived by the participants in that environment; namely, all things perceived by the senses—seeing, hearing, feeling, smelling, and tasting. The communication environment is complex and distracting. Overcoming the distractions is necessary if the goals of business communication are to be met. The components of the communication process model are discussed in the following sections.

The communication environment is complex and distracting.

SENDER'S ROLE

In the communication process the sender initiates the message. The sender may send the message in written, oral, or nonverbal form, or some combination of these forms. The sender, therefore, may be a writer, a speaker, or one who simply gestures.

The sender initiates the message.

As you will recall, the sender has the responsibility for the success of the communication. The sender's role in the communication process includes (1) the selection of the type of message, (2) the analysis of the receiver, (3) the use of the you-viewpoint in composing and sending the message, (4) the provision for feedback, and (5) the removal of communication barriers. How the sender can successfully fulfill this role will be discussed in the following sections.

The sender has the responsibility for the success of the communication.

TYPES OF MESSAGES

The sender chooses the type of message most appropriate for the communication situation.

Message may be:

WRITTEN MESSAGES. Written messages can be memos, letters, notes, reports, telegrams, newsletters, news releases, diagrams, drawings, charts, tables, and so on. Written messages are used when it is desirable to have a record of the communication or when the message is complex.

• Written

ORAL MESSAGES. Oral messages take many forms including face-to-face conversations, telephone conversations, in-person conferences, tele-video conferences, and speeches. Oral messages provide greater opportunity for immediate feedback and confirmation of understanding. In addition, greater speed of transmission of the message is generally possible in oral communication.

• Oral

NONVERBAL MESSAGES. Nonverbal messages can include a nod of the head, a raised eyebrow, a smile, a frown, an extended hand, a pointing finger, and many other gestures and facial expressions. Nonverbal communication usually is used as a supplement to oral communication. However, it can be more powerful than oral communication. When there are conflicting

• Nonverbal

oral and nonverbal messages from a sender, the nonverbal message is believed by the receiver.

COMMUNICATION CHANNELS.   The type of message influences the channel through which the sender chooses to send the message. The channel also is determined by who the receiver is. For memos to employees, the channel usually is the interoffice mailing system. For letters sent outside the business to customers and others, private or public mailing systems are used. Other channels—personal visit, telephone, telegraph, television, computer, and so forth—are chosen for other receivers and other types of messages.

ANALYSIS OF THE RECEIVER FOR THE YOU-VIEWPOINT

The sender's most important task in the communication process is to analyze the receiver for the you-viewpoint. The **you-viewpoint** means composing messages from the receiver's point of view. This is the most powerful concept in business communication. This concept will be discussed in detail later in this chapter. To use the you-viewpoint, you must first analyze your receiver.

ANALYZING THE RECEIVER.   Analysis of the receiver is necessary in order to be certain that the receiver understands the message, gives the response needed, and feels favorably toward you and your company. No two receivers are alike. You must know or learn as much as possible about how your particular receiver thinks and feels. If you have multiple receivers for the same message, such as readers of a form letter or listeners to a speech, you must analyze all members of the group.

It is helpful to analyze your receiver in four areas—knowledge, interests, opinions, and emotional state.

KNOWLEDGE.   The analysis should first include a review of the receiver's education and experience. Attention should be given to the receiver's vocabulary level, general knowledge, and specific knowledge on the subject of the message. What is the capability of the receiver to understand in a given communication situation?

For example, assume you are a public accountant writing a letter to Howard Truster, a contractor who builds homes. Mr. Truster prepares his own tax returns with occasional assistance from your firm. He has had last year's return audited by the Internal Revenue Service (IRS). The IRS did not allow some of the deductions Mr. Truster listed and indicates that he owes $3,750 in additional taxes. Mr. Truster has sent you a copy of the IRS audit report. He asks you to review the report and to give him advice in writing on what he should do.

Your analysis of Mr. Truster's knowledge in this communication situation might reveal the following:

Education:

General—high school graduate; vocabulary approximately tenth to twelfth grade reading level.

About taxes—limited; no formal education on tax return preparation.

Experience:

Has prepared his own tax returns with occasional professional assistance for each of the past ten years.

Has had a good working relationship with you.

Based on this analysis, you will decide (1) to write to Mr. Truster at a level a high school graduate would understand, (2) to avoid using technical tax terms where possible, and (3) to define any technical tax terms that must be used. For any message to be understood, it must be composed at the proper level and be expressed in words that mean the same thing in both the mind of the receiver and the mind of the sender. (Determining the vocabulary level of a message is discussed further in Chapter 3.)

INTERESTS.   Second, the receiver's interests should be analyzed. What concerns, needs, and motivations will the receiver have in this situation? If you are attempting, for example, to show a receiver how your bad news message—a message in which you must give unfavorable news—is of benefit to him or her, you can do this based on an understanding of the receiver's interests.

• The receiver's interests

In the preceeding example you, a public accountant, are writing to Howard Truster, a contractor, about an IRS audit. What are his interests in this situation? Your analysis of him as a receiver shows the following:

Interests:

He does not want to be in violation of the tax laws; he wants to pay only those taxes actually due.

This information about his interests will be helpful to you. You will want to emphasize in your letter the benefits he can receive by following your advice. These benefits include removing the potential tax law violation and paying the amount he actually owes.

OPINIONS.   Third, the opinions of the receiver should be examined. What values, attitudes, biases, prejudices, and viewpoints does the receiver have? What words or symbols will make a positive impression on the receiver? a negative impression? What ideas can be used effectively to communicate with this receiver? The same words and ideas will at times have opposite effects on different receivers. For example, the words liberal, conservative, intellect, abortion, welfare, and wealthy will be received positively by some and negatively by others.

• The receiver's opinions

Let's return to our example. As the public accountant writing to contractor Howard Truster about an IRS tax audit, your analysis of his opinions reveals the following:

Opinions:

Mr. Truster values honesty and free enterprise; he dislikes paperwork and paying taxes.

Based on this analysis of his opinions, your letter should reinforce these facts: (1) the paperwork related to filing an amended return can be handled entirely by you and (2) all he will need to do is sign the amended return.

- The receiver's emotional state

EMOTIONAL STATE. Finally, the receiver's emotional state should be considered. Is the receiver going to receive this message in a happy state, a neutral state, or an angry state? The answer to this question will assist you in determining whether you should use a direct or an indirect approach. In the direct approach you give the main point of your message in your opening. In the indirect approach you provide an explanation, reasons, or other supporting information before you give your main point.

Using the example again, your analysis of Howard Truster reveals the following about his emotional state:

Emotional State:

Disappointment and possibly some anger. These emotions may be mixed with relief that he can turn to you for expert help.

Based on these findings regarding Mr. Truster's emotional state, it is best to provide him an explanation before you give him your recommendation. This will help prepare him for your recommendation and assist him in accepting it.

In any communication situation, an analysis of your receiver will be helpful to you. It will enable you to use effectively one of the most important concepts of business communication—the you-viewpoint.

Using the you-viewpoint will achieve business communication goals.

USING THE YOU-VIEWPOINT. Using the you-viewpoint in your messages means composing your messages from your receiver's point of view. Your receiver's knowledge, interests, opinions, and emotional state are given primary consideration in the development and transmission of the message. To achieve the goals of business communication—understanding, response, favorable relationship, and goodwill—the sender should always use the you-viewpoint.

Your receiver will understand and accept the you-viewpoint message.

Your analysis of the receiver will enable you to use the you-viewpoint. You can use your understanding of the receiver's knowledge to influence your selection of ideas and the amount of explanation to include in the message. In addition, you will be able to use words in the receiver's vocabulary that are understandable and acceptable to him or her.

Also, the message can be directed toward meeting the receiver's interests, that is, his or her concerns, needs, and motivations. Your determination of your receiver's opinions will assist you in avoiding negative situations or, at least, in handling them carefully. Finally, analysis of your receiver's emotional state will influence whether you use the direct or indirect approach in your message.

If you are sending the same message to a group of receivers and you want to achieve the business communication goals with every member of that group, each individual in the group must be analyzed. Then the message must be composed for the member of the group with the least knowledge about the subject, least interest, and most opposed emotionally.

The opposite of the you-viewpoint is the I-, me-, or we-viewpoint. A common error of poor business communicators is that they compose their messages from their own points of view instead of their receivers' points of view. They choose the content for their messages based on their own knowledge, interests, opinions, and emotional states. Most of the time, the we-viewpoint type of message does not achieve the goals of business communication.

The opposite of the you-viewpoint is the I-, me-, or we-viewpoint.

Examine these contrasting examples of sentences from opposite viewpoints:

Contrasting examples of viewpoints are shown here.

We-Viewpoint	You-Viewpoint
We shipped your order Friday.	You will receive your order Monday.
We can sell each unit to you for $10, and you can charge your customers $15.	You can make a $5 profit on each unit when you buy them for $10 each and sell them for $15 each.
I am happy to tell you I have approved your application.	You will be glad to know that your application has been approved.
We manufacture seven different kinds of Haircare shampoo.	So that you may select the shampoo that is just right for your hair, Haircare makes seven special blends.
You simply do not understand what I am saying.	I am not making myself as clear as I should.

As these examples show, the you-viewpoint message is directed toward the receiver's thinking and feelings. It makes the receiver's interests and benefits of prime concern in the message.

The recommendation that you use the you-viewpoint in your messages does not suggest in any way that you ignore basic values. Honesty and forthrightness are basic to all successful business communication.

Be honest and forthright in all your messages.

It will be helpful now to look at two examples of letters that could be sent to Howard Truster, the contractor. As you will recall, Mr. Truster asked you to review the Internal Revenue Service audit of his last year's tax return and to give him advice in writing on what he should do. Illustration 1-4 is an example of a poor letter to Mr. Truster written from the I-, me-, my-viewpoint— the sender's viewpoint. Illustration 1-5 is an example of a good letter to Mr. Truster written in the you-viewpoint. It is the good letter you might have written based on your analysis of Mr. Truster as a receiver.

Illustration 1-4   Example of a Poor Letter to Howard Truster Written from the I-, Me-, My-Viewpoint—the Sender's Viewpoint

Vincent, Allen, Charles, & Riley, CPA's

1000 Kingsway Street • Indianapolis, IN 46001-1234

August 25, 199-

Mr. Howard Truster, President
Best Homes Construction Company
7501 Wilson Brooks Drive
Milroy, IN 46156-1001

Dear Mr. Truster

> I-viewpoint message uses direct approach and words not in receiver's vocabulary.

In regard to my review of the Internal Revenue Service (IRS) audit report dated August 15, 199-, the Audit Division correctly identified several errors you made; and, to avoid violations of the income tax laws and the concomitant potential penalties, an amended return must be filed before the specified IRS deadline.

> Does not consider receiver's interests, is negative, and is too technical.

The errors you made when you prepared your own return involve very technical sections of the IRS Code (particularly Sections 1.000.23.0 through 1.000.45.9 and Section 4.712.11.5) covering provisions of the newly promulgated 199- tax law dealing with partial or complete eliminations of previously allowable deductions for such expenditures as personal interest, state and local sales taxes, and many other deductions. The IRS correctly claims--assuming that your taxes were calculated properly and accurately--that you owe $3,750 in additional taxes.

> Word choice is inappropriate. Sentences are too long and involved.

But the IRS does not and is not required to try to search out in your records other deductions you could have claimed or errors or omissions in your possible favor and to recompute your tax burden. It is my recommendation that you seek professional assistance in the preparation of an amended return for the determination of an accurate specification of your 199- taxes. I and my colleagues at Vincent, Allen, Charles, & Riley, CPA's, can review your records and possibly determine deductions that you failed to claim or otherwise reduce your tax burden. As I will have to accommodate this review in my schedule, please let me know your decision as soon as feasible.

Sincerely

Brett Allen

Brett Allen, CPA

js

Illustration 1-5 Example of a **Good** Letter to Howard Truster Written Using the You-Viewpoint Based on an Analysis of Mr. Truster as a Receiver

Vincent, Allen, Charles, & Riley, CPA's

1000 Kingsway Street • Indianapolis, IN 46001-1234

August 25, 199–

Mr. Howard Truster, President
Best Homes Construction Company
7501 Wilson Brooks Drive
Milroy, IN 46156-1001

Dear Mr. Truster

As you requested, I have reviewed the Internal Revenue Service (IRS) audit of your last year's tax return.

The IRS states that you claimed deductions that are not now permitted under the new 199– law. That tax law did remove or reduce some deductions that were permitted before. These include personal interest, sales tax, and a number of others. The IRS found such items on your return. The IRS further states that you owe $3,750 in additional taxes.

To be sure that the IRS shows all the tax deductions you can claim and the correct amount of your taxes, I recommend that we review your records. We could then file an amended return. This action will assure you that you are obeying the law. Also, you would pay only the taxes that are due.

Please let me know if you have any further questions. If you agree with my recommendation, I will be glad to review your records and prepare the amended tax return for you to sign.

Sincerely

Brett Allen

Brett Allen, CPA

js

You-viewpoint message uses indirect approach and prepares receiver for the recommendation.

Word choice and sentence length appropriate for this receiver.

Receiver's interests are emphasized.

The you-viewpoint message is positive.

PROVISION FOR FEEDBACK

Sender should provide for feedback.

The sender's role in implementing the communication process includes providing for **feedback**—response from the receiver. Providing for the necessary response from the receiver is one of the four goals of business communication. To achieve this goal, you should (1) ask directly or indirectly for the response and (2) assist the receiver in giving that response.

If the sender is applying for a job using a letter and a resume, the desired receiver response is that an interview is granted. In the letter the sender should (1) ask for an interview and (2) provide the receiver with telephone number(s) and address(es) where the sender can be easily reached. In a written sales message, the sender should ask for the order and provide a toll-free telephone number or easy-to-use order form for placing the order.

If the communication is oral, the sender can tactfully ask the receiver if the message is understood or if the receiver has any questions. In critical situations the receiver might be asked to repeat the message and explain his or her understanding of it. If the sender is giving a speech to a group, feedback can be gained by observing the audience, asking questions, or administering an evaluation instrument.

Feedback is essential to confirm receiver understanding.

Since the most important goal of business communication is that the receiver understand the message, feedback from the receiver to the sender is essential to confirm that understanding.

REMOVING COMMUNICATION BARRIERS

Communication barriers interfere with the communication process and must be removed.

Although knowledge of the communication process and skill in implementing it are basic to communicating effectively, the sender must also deal with barriers that interfere with the communication process. **Communication barriers** are any factors that interfere with the success of the communication process. (See Illustration 1-3.) These barriers may occur between any two of the process steps or may affect all steps in the communication process. Being aware of these barriers and removing them is necessary for successful communication to take place. The most crucial barriers are discussed in the next sections.

WORD CHOICE

Choosing words that are too difficult, too technical, or too easy for your receiver can be a communication barrier. As you will recall, the analysis of the receiver should include a determination of the receiver's vocabulary level. The message must then be composed and transmitted at the appropriate level.

Communication Barrier 1: poor word choice.

CONNOTATIONS VERSUS DENOTATIONS

A receiver and a sender may attach different meanings to the words used in a message. Although there is a specific, or denotative, meaning for each word given in the dictionary, these same words may have other meanings in the minds of the communicators. These different meanings are the connotative meanings. Connotative meanings are those other meanings suggested to communicators based on their own experiences, interests, opinions, and emotions. Connotative meanings can also be the result of slang or sarcastic usage.

Communication Barrier 2: differing connotations.

If you as a sender said to one of your subordinates, "Well, that certainly was fast work!" you may have meant the work was completed in less time than you expected. The receiver, however, may attach a different meaning to the statement. This other meaning is the connotative meaning—or the connotation. Based on what he or she is thinking and feeling at the moment, the receiver may connote that you meant the work was slow, was done too quickly, or was done improperly. Other specific examples of connotations versus denotations include the following:

Word	Sender Denotes	Receiver Connotes
cheap	inexpensive	poorly made
liberal	fair	radical
compromise	adjust	give in
determined	committed	stubborn
aggressive	energetic	pushy
proposal	suggestion	decision

Senders should analyze their receivers as thoroughly as possible to determine what connotations those receivers might attach to specific words.

INFERENCES

A sender should guard against a receiver making inappropriate inferences from a message. An **inference** is a conclusion that the receiver may draw from the facts contained in the message. That conclusion may or may not be true,

Communication Barrier 3: inappropriate inferences.

depending on the situation. For example, a manager might say to a secretary, "Please make five photocopies of this memo for distribution to the employees in our unit." The secretary might infer—make an inference—from the facts in the message that the manager not only wanted the copies made but also distributed to the employees. The manager, however, may have wanted the copies to be attached to other material being distributed, held for distribution at a later time, or distributed at the time of a conference with the unit's employees.

Another example of an inappropriate inference is a sender who says, "Be sure to finish this job as soon as you can." The receiver interprets the message as, "work overtime to get this job done" while the sender intended that the job be completed during regular working hours.

Inferences may be drawn from actions as well as words. For example, suppose as a supervisor passes two subordinates, they laugh. The supervisor may infer that they are happy, satisfied employees or that the employees are laughing at him or her. Both inferences may be wrong.

Of course, much business and individual activity is based on inference. Intelligent and appropriate inferences are essential to initiative and follow-through on the job. It is the sender's responsibility to see that the receiver's inferences are appropriate. Inappropriate inferences can be avoided if the sender conveys clear and explicit messages. As with other communication barriers, the barriers caused by unintended inferences can be eliminated by a careful analysis of the receiver.

GRAMMAR, SPELLING, PUNCTUATION, AND SENTENCE STRUCTURE

Communication Barrier 4: poor grammar, spelling, punctuation, and sentence structure.

Incorrect grammar, spelling, punctuation, and sentence structure will hinder the receiver's understanding and acceptance of a message. The sender can lose credibility with the receiver if these communication barriers are permitted to exist.

For example, incorrect sentence construction can cause misinterpretation of the message. If a sender wants to say that there will be a price increase effective January 1 on all product modifications, the sentence should not be constructed "There will be a price increase on all product modifications effective January 1." Is the increase only on product modifications that are effective January 1? That is not the meaning the sender intended the receiver to understand. A better way to structure this sentence would be, "Effective January 1 there will be a price increase on all product modifications."

As another example, assume that employees have requested that they be allowed longer coffee breaks, and management attempts to respond. Note the miscommunication in the following incorrectly punctuated sentence: "For a while longer, coffee breaks will not be permitted." The message management intended was, "For a while, longer coffee breaks will not be permitted."

TYPE OF MESSAGE

Selecting the wrong type of message may lead to communication failure. For example, communicating detailed job instructions orally will most likely fail. A written message is more appropriate for such a complex message. Oral communication, however, is more effective for the resolution of a personal conflict between two employees.

Communication Barrier 5: wrong type of message.

If the message is a report on an evaluation of alternative manufacturing processes, the type of message will depend on who the receiver will be. The message may be written or oral, a long report or a short report, a report with or without technical terms, or a report with or without graphic aids. There often are many choices of types of messages that can be used for any one communication situation.

Generally the higher the level in an organization to which a message is sent, the shorter the message should be. The time of top managers is extremely valuable; therefore, a brief summary is more useful than a long, detailed report. Managers at lower levels, who are close to the actual operational procedures, derive greater benefits from long, technical messages.

APPEARANCE OF THE MESSAGE

The readability and acceptance of a written message will be reduced if its appearance is poor. Communication barriers caused by poor appearance include smudges, poor corrections, light type, wrinkled paper, and poor handwriting. The sender should not allow any messages to contain these types of communication barriers.

Communication Barrier 6: poor appearance of written message.

APPEARANCE OF THE SENDER

The credibility of an oral message can be reduced if the appearance of the sender is unattractive or unacceptable to the receiver. In addition, unintended nonverbal signals can distract a receiver and influence the way an oral message is received. For example, if you smile when you sympathetically give bad news, your motives may be suspect.

Communication Barrier 7: poor appearance of sender of oral message.

If the credibility of the message is questioned, the quality of receiver understanding, acceptance, and response will be reduced. For success in oral business communication, senders should maintain required standards of appearance in dress, cleanliness, and facial and body movements.

ENVIRONMENTAL FACTORS

Communication Barrier 8: distracting environmental factors.

Another common communication barrier is any environmental condition that distracts the sender, the receiver, or both, from the successful transmission and reception of the message.

One such example of a distracting environmental factor is a noisy machine in an area where a supervisor is trying to communicate with an employee. Another example is the boss's desk—a symbol of authority—between a supervisor and a worker. The desk can intimidate the worker and limit his or her ability to respond to a message. Other examples of environmental factors that can serve as barriers to effective communication include room temperature, odor, amount of light, area colors, and distances.

The sender has the responsibility to try to eliminate any environmental factors that are communication barriers. If the room in which an oral presentation is to be given is too warm, the sender should try to get the thermostat turned down or have the windows opened. If the receiver cannot see to read a message because of limited light, the sender should arrange for more light. Environmental factors that are communication barriers can usually be eliminated or adjusted.

RECEIVER'S CAPABILITY

Communication Barrier 9: receiver incapable of receiving message.

If the receiver has a physical or mental limitation that causes a communication barrier, the sender should attempt to assist the receiver in overcoming it. The receiver may have a hearing impairment, a reading disability, or other limitation. The sender can remove or compensate for such barriers in the communication process by carefully selecting the form of the message and providing for appropriate feedback mechanisms. Most of the solutions are clear choices.

For the hearing impaired, the volume of an oral message should be amplified or the message should be in written form. A good example of assisting the hearing impaired is the closed captioning that is now available on many television programs with the use of a special receiver. For the visually impaired, the print of a written message should be enlarged or the message should be orally transmitted.

In recent years considerable progress has been made in providing for full participation of disabled persons in all fields of human endeavor. Effective communicators draw on the resources available or devise their own ways to overcome a limitation of the receiver's capability.

LISTENING

The failure of the receiver to listen is a common barrier to successful oral communication. Listening effectively is not easy. One reason it is difficult for a message receiver to listen is that an average speaker talks at a rate of 100 to 200 words a minute while the average person can listen at a rate of 500 or more words a minute. This difference allows listeners' minds to wander to topics other than the message. In addition, listeners—instead of listening—may be worrying about the type of response that they will make. Listening is a skill, and it must be learned. Some persons have not developed the listening skill as fully as others.

Senders can use several methods to overcome poor listening as a communication barrier. Receivers can be requested to listen carefully, or they can periodically be asked questions to determine the extent of their listening. In some circumstances it may be possible to encourage a poor listener to study and learn improved listening skills. One of the most effective ways to remove poor listening as a barrier to communication is to improve the quality of the message and its conveyance. Short, interesting, clear, organized messages that are presented enthusiastically are more likely to be listened to by receivers.

Communication Barrier 10: poor listening.

OTHER COMMUNICATION BARRIERS

Several of the most important communication barriers and ways to remove them have been discussed in the preceding sections. In attempting to improve your communication effectiveness, you must eliminate other barriers. For example, some receiver-related communication barriers include lack of interest, lack of knowledge needed to understand, different cultural perceptions, language difficulty, emotional state, and bias. You, the sender, will want to do everything possible to remove these receiver-related communication barriers.

Several other barriers exist.

The sender should try to eliminate all barriers.

COMMUNICATION BARRIERS—CONCLUSION

The major way that you as a sender can create a communication barrier is to fail to use the you-viewpoint in your communication. Many of the barriers listed in this chapter can be removed by a careful analysis of the receiver's

You can achieve success in communicating if you use the you-viewpoint.

knowledge, interests, opinions, and emotional state. Based on this analysis, you can achieve effective communication if you use the you-viewpoint in composing and conveying your messages.

DISCUSSION QUESTIONS

1. Define business communication. Explain the definition.
2. Discuss why communication is important to businesses.
3. Discuss why communication is important to individuals.
4. Describe how a sender achieves the primary business communication goal of receiver understanding.
5. The second goal of business communication is receiver response. Discuss techniques the sender can use to achieve this goal.
6. What are the benefits to the sender and receiver of achieving the third goal of business communication, favorable relationship? How can this goal be achieved?
7. What does organizational goodwill mean? How can organizational goodwill, the fourth goal of business communication, be gained?
8. Discuss the nature of internal communication patterns within an organization that represents your major field of study. In your discussion give examples of upward, downward, horizontal, and diagonal flows of information.
9. What is the difference between formal and informal communication? Give examples of each.
10. Explain serial communication. Cite a real-life example of serial communication in action.
11. What is the nature of external communication outside an organization? Give examples of messages to different areas of the general public outside an organization.
12. What is the sender's responsibility in the communication process? Discuss.
13. Give examples of the main types of messages—written, oral, and nonverbal. In what communication situations is it appropriate to use each of these types of messages?
14. Explain why the sender should analyze the receiver. Tell how the analysis of the receiver can improve communication.
15. Discuss analyzing the knowledge of the receiver. Indicate what you can learn from this analysis that is helpful in composing and transmitting a message.
16. Describe the interests of the receiver. Give three examples of receiver interests that would be important considerations in the development of a message by a sender.

17. Explain what the opinions of the receiver are and how they should influence the composition of the message.
18. What is meant by the emotional state of the receiver? How does the emotional state of the receiver help determine the approach that will be used in the message?
19. What is the you-viewpoint? Give an example of the appropriate use of the you-viewpoint.
20. Define feedback. Give three examples of feedback.
21. Discuss the differences between connotations and denotations. Give examples of how senders and receivers attach different meanings to the same words.
22. Define inferences. Describe the appropriate role of inference in business.
23. Describe how the sender's use of incorrect grammar, spelling, punctuation, and sentence structure can interfere with a communication.
24. Explain how environmental factors can be communication barriers. Give three examples of environmental factors and tell how they could be communication barriers.
25. What causes poor listening? How can a sender overcome the communication barrier caused by his or her receiver's failure to listen?
26. What is the major, overriding communication barrier and how does a sender overcome it?

APPLICATION EXERCISES

1. Interview a manager and ask the following questions: (a) How important is communication to the successful performance of your job? (b) What is an example of a successful communication experience you have had? (c) What is an example of an unsuccessful communication experience you have had? (d) What communication barriers do you commonly experience? (e) What does organizational goodwill mean to you? (f) What recommendations do you have for someone who wants to improve his or her communication skills? Share the answers to these questions with the class.
2. Analyze as message receivers the students in your business communication class. Do this analysis on a group basis. Be sure to give attention in your analysis to the students' knowledge, interests, opinions, and emotional states.
3. Select an international leader and describe how he or she communicates. Evaluate the effectiveness of the communication.

152,762

4. Select a poor communicator (you need not name the person) and analyze why he or she is poor. Explain corrective actions this communicator could take to improve.

5. The communication environment was defined in this chapter as including "all things perceived by the participants in that environment." Describe the communication environment in your classroom.

6. Report an example that you have observed of each of the following: (a) an internal communication, (b) an external communication, (c) an informal communication, (d) a formal communication, and (e) a serial communication.

7. Observe and record communication barriers for a 24-hour period. Indicate how each barrier could have been removed.

8. Explain how successful students appropriately use the you-viewpoint in their classwork.

9. Rewrite the following sentences so that they are in the you-viewpoint. Be sure not to change the meaning of the sentences in your revised versions.
   a. We received your order.
   b. I heard you were promoted.
   c. Don't fail to get your report to the corporate office by 19 October.
   d. I have enclosed a post-paid envelope for you to use.
   e. You do not qualify for a loan. Apply later for reconsideration.
   f. I understand that you are telling me that I can interview with the Magnun Corporation.
   g. We have received your application letter and resume that you sent for a job with the accounting department in the Magnun Corporation.
   h. You have failed to meet the job performance standards. Our policy does not permit reevaluation for 90 days.
   i. You will have to pay our costs for the necessary repairs to your car.
   j. The quota for your work is now higher, but the rate of pay per piece is also higher.

10. Describe your personal experiences in (a) a successful communication and (b) an unsuccessful communication.

11. For each of the following words give a denotative meaning and a connotative meaning: (a) fair wage, (b) cautious, (c) clever, (d) thin, (e) hamburger.

12. Bring to class an example of a written message whose poor appearance reduces its readability and acceptability.

13. Bring to class written examples of a sender (a) asking for a response from a receiver and (b) assisting the receiver in responding.

14. Describe three examples of networks in which you personally participate.

15. List the nonverbal messages that are sent and received in a classroom.

16. Give an example of the sender's appearance (a) enhancing an oral communication and (b) interfering with an oral communication.

C H A P T E R   2

PRINCIPLES OF BUSINESS COMMUNICATION

L E A R N I N G   O B J E C T I V E S

Your learning objectives for this chapter include the following:

- To know how to choose words that your receiver(s) will understand and that will gain the receiver reaction you need
- To be able to combine words into clear, concise, and effective sentences
- To be able to form clear, concise, logical, coherent, and effective paragraphs
- To learn to use your own composing style to give uniqueness and life to your messages

The best way to improve your ability to compose effective business messages is to learn and use the principles of business communication. This chapter will provide the principles you need for choosing words, developing sentences, and forming paragraphs.

 The basic principle of business communication is to keep your message short and simple. Some communicators remember this principle by its initials, KISS, which stands for Keep It Short and Simple. Application of this principle means composing your business message using short and simple words, sentences, and paragraphs. Your messages, as a result, will be concise, easy to understand, and straightforward.

Compose effective messages by using the principles of business communication.

Keep business messages **short** and **simple**.

If I'd had more time, I'd have written a shorter book.

Mark Twain (1835-1910)

As Mark Twain implies, it may take extra time to compose the shorter, better message; but it will be worth it to you and your receiver. To be an effective, successful business communicator, you will want to adopt the businesslike KISS principle.

Most of the 15 principles of business communication that are discussed in the following sections apply to both written and oral messages. A few apply only to written messages. As in Chapter 1, readers and listeners will be called receivers.

CHOOSING WORDS

Choose effective words.

Words are the smallest units of messages. You will want to give attention to each word you choose to be sure it is the most effective one. Choosing the most effective words for a business message means selecting words that your receiver will understand and that will gain the receiver reaction you need. You can improve your ability to choose words by (1) using a dictionary and a thesaurus and (2) following some important principles of business communication.

USE A DICTIONARY AND A THESAURUS FOR WORD POWER

The two most valuable resources for the business communicator are a dictionary and a thesaurus.

Use a dictionary to select words.

A dictionary can help you in many ways. You can use it to determine a word's meaning(s), acceptable spelling(s), hyphenation, capitalization, pronunciation(s), and synonym(s). A dictionary is also helpful in choosing correct words. Some words are easily confused and, therefore, at times misused. Examples of such words are effect and affect, capital and capitol, principal and principle, continuous and continual, and further and farther. See Appendix A for an extensive list of easily confused words, and use a dictionary to help you select correct words.

Use a thesaurus to find synonyms.

A thesaurus helps by providing additional synonyms and different shades of meanings. If you have an idea you want to express, you can look up words in a thesaurus that represent that idea and find several alternative words that can be used to express the idea. Each choice usually has a slightly different connotation. This is a way of finding the simplest and most precise words for your message. It is also a way to find synonyms to use so that you can avoid repeating a word.

These two reference tools—a dictionary and a thesaurus—should be at your side when you are attempting to compose effective messages. Your use of them can increase your **word power**—your power to choose the most appropriate words for each of your messages.

In addition to using a dictionary and a thesaurus, you will want to follow some important principles of business communication when you are choosing words for your messages. These principles are discussed next.

PRINCIPLE 1: CHOOSE UNDERSTANDABLE WORDS

The first principle of word selection is to choose words that will be understood by your receiver. Prior to composing your messages, you will have analyzed your receiver's knowledge, interests, opinions, and emotional state. Considering the information you gathered in this analysis and keeping in mind the importance of the you-viewpoint, you will want to choose words that the receiver will understand.

Choose words your receiver will understand.

Choosing understandable words means choosing words that are in your receiver's vocabulary. Consider your receiver's educational level and experience as they relate to your message. The words that will communicate best are those slightly below the receiver's vocabulary level. For most receivers, you should select the more understandable words in the following examples rather than the less understandable ones:

Understandable words are those words in your receiver's vocabulary.

Less Understandable	More Understandable
verbalize	say
utilize	use
facilitate	help
abdicate	resign
equitable	fair
facetious	joking
contemptible	worthless
prognosticate	predict
expeditious	quick
prerogative	right
gesticulate	gesture
oscillate	swing
configuration	shape

Less Understandable	More Understandable
debilitated	weak
emulate	copy
demonstrate	show
finality	end
foremost	first
germinate	sprout
exonerate	clear
perspiration	sweat

Understandable words are generally simpler and shorter.

Notice that the more understandable words are the simpler words normally used in everyday conversations. Also, words that are more understandable are generally shorter.

Appropriate technical words can be efficient.

Using appropriate technical words is a special consideration in choosing understandable words. Technical words—sometimes referred to as *jargon*—are words with special meanings in a particular field. They can assist in conveying precise, meaningful messages among certain receivers and senders. For example, between two accountants the use of the words *accrued liabilities* will be understandable. The use of such technical words for the accountants will be more precise and efficient than using nontechnical language. For most of us, though, *accrued liabilities* is not as understandable as *debts that have not yet been recorded on our books*. Here are some other examples of technical and nontechnical words:

Technical Words	Nontechnical Words
generate	develop
de facto	actual
juried	judged
format	arrangement
brief	summary of legal case
extremity	hand or foot
expectorate	spit
seminar	course
symposium	conference
deciduous	shedding leaves annually

Appropriate technical words are those in your receiver's vocabulary.

You will want to use only those technical words that are in your receiver's vocabulary. To do otherwise reduces the receiver's understanding of your message. If you are not sure whether a technical word is in your receiver's vocabulary, do not use it.

In summary, you can best choose understandable words by selecting simpler words, shorter words, and appropriate technical words. The examples that follow assume that the receiver is a typical high school graduate who has no particular technical knowledge.

Less Understandable	More understandable
The canine pursued the feline.	The dog chased the cat.
The altercation commenced following dissension.	The fight began after a quarrel.
The economic prognosticator speculated that recession was imminent.	The economist predicted that soon there would be a downturn in business.
The cinema was a credible depiction of matriculation.	The movie was a believable story of going to college.
The tabulations of our quantitative measures of refrigerator production reflect increases during the current fiscal year as compared with the immediate past fiscal year period.	Our records show that we are making more refrigerators this year than we did last year.

PRINCIPLE 2: USE CONCRETE WORDS

Use words in your messages that are concrete—words that are specific and precise. Use words that are so clear that there will be no question in your receiver's mind as to the meaning you intended.

Abstract words are the opposite of concrete words. Abstract words are general words. Their meanings are less clear than the meanings of concrete words and are more likely to create wrong or confusing connotations in your receiver's mind. Abstract words are appropriate for literary compositions, but you will want to use primarily concrete words in your business messages. Here are examples of abstract words and ways to make them more specific:

Use concrete words. They are specific and precise.

Abstract Words	Concrete Words
soon	3:00 p.m., Wednesday
most	64.3 percent
often	18 times out of 20
loyal	would give his or her life
fruit	apple
parasite	mistletoe
holiday	Thanksgiving
cold	0 degrees Fahrenheit
good student	Has 3.25 grade point average (4.0 = A)
automobile	Chevrolet Camaro

Notice in the preceding examples that it sometimes takes a few more words to be concrete. These additions to the length of your message are worth the clarity you gain.

PRINCIPLE 3: PREFER STRONG WORDS

Verbs and nouns are strong words. Adjectives and adverbs are weak.

Verbs are the strongest words in the English language. Nouns are next in strength. Adjectives and adverbs, while needed for concreteness at times, are generally weaker, less objective words. You will want to give preference to verbs and nouns in your business messages and avoid the use of subjective adjectives and adverbs. Adjectives and adverbs tend to distract the receiver from the main points of the message. Reducing your use of them will help keep you from overstating a point or position. To have an impact, business messages should convey objectivity by avoiding exaggeration.

Prefer strong words for power and objectivity.

You will recall the following images: person of a few words; strong, silent type; straight to the point; and clear as a bell. These descriptions are often applied to senders who communicate with clarity and forcefulness. The short, powerful message composed of strong words will more likely get the attention of your receiver. Note these examples:

Weak Words	Strong Words
situation	problem
invoice	bill
male parent	father
passed away	died
dismissed	fired
requested	ordered
Following this excellent recommendation will solve all our problems.	Following this recommendation will solve our problems.
A careful study of the market is obviously in order.	A study of the market should be made.

When appropriate, weak words can be used to soften messages.

While Principle 3 advocates a preference for strong words, there will be times when you will want to soften a message with weaker words. This is particularly true for a message that is bad news for your receiver. If you have to discuss a problem with a coworker, it will build better human relations and more acceptance of your message if you use the weaker word, *situation*, instead of the stronger word, *problem*. (This use of weak words is fully discussed in Chapter 11.)

PRINCIPLE 4: EMPHASIZE POSITIVE WORDS

Emphasize positive words and avoid negative words.

A positive, *can do* attitude is one of the most important attributes you can have in business. Possessing that attitude is just the first step; you will want to communicate it to your receivers by selecting positive words and avoiding negative words. Your use of negative words will trigger unpleasant emotional feelings in most of your receivers. A positive approach in a message helps to achieve the business communication goals of securing the needed response, maintaining a favorable relationship, and gaining goodwill. You will want to try to avoid these negative words:

Positive words are more likely to achieve business communication goals.

Negative Words

no	cannot	do not
problem	impossible	never
obnoxious	trouble	complaint
blame	fault	unhappy
apologize	error	mistake
improper	bad	ill timed
discouraging	won't	unfortunate
sorry	delayed	wrong

These examples show that unpleasant and negative words often are strong words. There will be occasions when you will want to use negative words for emphasis. (An example is a claim letter to a vendor to get a piece of defective equipment repaired or replaced; see Chapter 10.)

In some situations, negative words can be used for emphasis.

As the next examples show, however, you will more effectively convey a positive attitude and the you-viewpoint if you emphasize positiveness and what can be done rather than negativeness and what cannot be done.

Negative Phrasings	Positive Phrasings
Do not be negative.	Be positive.
I cannot today.	I can tomorrow.
We can't ship the order until Friday.	You will receive the order Monday.
You will not regret your decision.	You will be happy with your decision.
We close at 9:00 p.m.	We are open until 9:00 p.m.
I am sorry to say that we cannot accept the return of the defective lawn mower.	Please let our expert staff repair your lawn mower at your convenience.

Your professional and personal relationships will both be served well by selecting positive words and avoiding negative words.

PRINCIPLE 5: AVOID OVERUSED WORDS

Some words are so overused in normal conversations or in business messages that they have lost their effectiveness. Their continued use makes the messages less precise and less understandable. Because we have heard them over and

Avoid overused words because they have lost clear meanings.

over, their use makes messages less interesting. Avoid these and similar overused words:

Overused Words and Phrases

good	awful
it goes without saying	below the belt
A Number 1	you know
in due course	turn over a new leaf
sound out	the upshot
very	really
super	by leaps and bounds
adding salt to the wound	right on
straight from the shoulder	manner of speaking
strike while the iron is hot	take the bull by the horns
the bottom line	great

PRINCIPLE 6: AVOID OBSOLETE WORDS

Avoid obsolete words because they are pompous, dull, and stiff.

Obsolete words are those that are out of date, pompous, or dull and stiff. Some of these obsolete words were used years ago in business messages and have been picked up by younger managers and continue to be used. Such words are not normally used in everyday conversation and should not be used in business communication.

Most of us tend to use obsolete words and become formal, stilted, and sometimes pompous when we write messages or speak before groups. We fail to use the desirable conversational language that communicates best with our receivers. Some examples of obsolete words we should avoid are:

Obsolete Words and Phrases

duly	aforementioned
attached herewith	enclosed please find
contents duly noted	pursuant
advised	as per
in closing	perusal
esteemed	enclosed herewith
hoping to hear from you soon	under separate cover
kindly advise	trusting to hear
beg to state	as stated above

As you read through these examples, you quickly realize that most people do not use these kinds of obsolete words in their everyday conversations. Some do, however, in their writing or public speaking. Such obsolete words should be avoided in all business messages.

DEVELOPING SENTENCES

In the first part of this chapter you learned how to choose effective words. Now you are ready to study the principles that will guide you in combining those words into effective sentences.

Businesspersons prefer concise, efficient, effective communication. To be successful, you will want to use clear, short sentences that are in the active voice and that emphasize your most important points. The principles of business communication for developing clear sentences are in the following sections.

Use short, clear sentences that are in the active voice and that have appropriate emphasis.

PRINCIPLE 7: COMPOSE CLEAR SENTENCES

Clear sentences are composed by following the principles for choosing words that were discussed in the preceding sections. Clear sentences use words that are understandable, concrete, strong, and positive. In addition, clear sentences have unity; that is, they normally contain one main idea. Finally, clear sentences are logically composed by keeping related words together.

Compose clear sentences with understandable, concrete, strong, and positive words.

GIVE SENTENCES UNITY. The effective sentence will communicate one main idea—one thought. At times you may want to include in a sentence ideas that support the main idea. The general rule, however, is: one thought, one sentence. If you have two main thoughts, construct two separate sentences. Examine these contrasting examples of sentences without unity and with unity:

Clear sentences have unity.

Lack Unity	Have Unity
The employees were informed that the summer work schedule would be changed from last year and the summer payroll dates would conform to the new summer schedule.	The employees were informed that the summer work schedule would be changed from last year. The summer payroll dates will conform to the new summer schedule.

By separating the two subjects—*summer work schedule* and *summer payroll dates*—each sentence is clearer and is given more emphasis.

KEEP RELATED WORDS TOGETHER. Modifiers should be placed close to the words they modify. Modifiers can be words, phrases, or clauses that describe or limit other words, phrases, or clauses. For the sentence to be clear, the word or words described or limited by the modifier must be obvious.

Related words are together in clear sentences.

Unclear Relationship	Clear Relationship
When I give you the test and raise my hand, *start taking* it.	When I raise my hand, *start taking* the test I have given you.
For last month, the manager discovered that quality control was down.	The manager discovered that quality control *for last month* was down.
I am *immediately* approving your proposal effective so that you can act quickly.	So that you can act quickly, I am approving your proposal effective *immediately*.

USE CORRECT GRAMMAR. Clear sentences are grammatically correct. All parts of a sentence should agree. The subject and verb should agree in tense and number. Pronouns should agree with their antecedents in three ways—number, gender, and clear relationship. Another important form of agreement is parallelism—using the same grammatical form for parts of sentences that serve the same purpose. Correct grammar is discussed in Chapters 5 and 6.

PRINCIPLE 8: USE SHORT SENTENCES

Use short sentences. They are more understandable.

Short sentences are more effective than long sentences. Short sentences generally are easy to understand.

The average length of your sentences will depend on the ability of your receiver to understand. For the middle-level receiver, your sentences should

Sentences should average 15-20 words.

average about 15 to 20 words. Generally, you should use sentences of longer average length for receivers with more education and knowledge about the subject and sentences of shorter average length for receivers with less education and knowledge about the subject.

Vary sentence length for interest.

You will want to vary the length of your sentences, however, in order to provide interest and to eliminate the dull, choppy effect of too many short sentences. You may need a long sentence simply to cover the main idea or the relationship of ideas.

A sentence can be as short as one word; for example, *Yes*. Normally a sentence will have at least two words—a subject and a verb. Any sentence

Examine sentences with 30 words or more for clarity.

that is 30 words or longer should be considered a long sentence and examined for clarity.

Short sentences are preferred because of the following advantages. They are less complex and, therefore, easier to understand. They are efficient, and they take less time to listen to or read. Short sentences are businesslike—concise, clear, and to the point. Sentences can be shortened by omitting unnecessary words and by limiting sentence content to one major idea.

OMIT UNNECESSARY WORDS. Clear and concise sentences are lean. They have only essential words. When composing sentences, attempt to omit all words that are not essential. Compare these examples:

Compose short sentences by omitting unnecessary words.

Wordy	Lean
In the near future, we will meet to confer and establish our goals and aims.	We will establish our goals soon.
In the field of marketing, each and every customer must be given individualized, personalized attention.	Each customer must be given personalized attention.
On the occasion of the company's tenth anniversary, all of its customers were contacted and invited to a gala celebration.	On the company's tenth anniversary, its customers were invited to a celebration.
The accountant is in the process of reviewing the reports.	The accountant is reviewing the reports.
The little personal microcomputer sold for the price of $900.	The microcomputer cost $900.

LIMIT CONTENT. As you will recall, clear sentences convey one main idea. If you have a sentence that is 30 words or longer, you may want to divide it into two or more sentences. Examine the unity of the sentence and see if it is appropriate to divide it further. Remember, you will want just one thought unit for most sentences.

Limiting content is another way to achieve short sentences.

Excessive Content	Limited Content
When the president decided we would purchase a computer, the director of the computer center developed bid specifications; and the company treasurer sent out requests for bids; the vendors who received the bid requests were selected by the purchasing department, which maintains lists of vendors for that purpose.	The president decided we would purchase a computer. As a result of the decision, the director of the computer center developed bid specifications. The company treasurer sent out the specifications with requests for bids. The vendors to receive the bid requests were selected by the purchasing department. The purchasing department maintains lists of vendors for that purpose.
As the current time seems to be ripe for action, it appears it would be a very good idea to make the decision to sell now.	Now is the time to sell.

One technique for developing short sentences from long ones is to change commas and semicolons to periods. In the preceding illustrations you can see that this was done. Many times phrases and dependent clauses can be modified so that they can stand alone as short sentences.

PRINCIPLE 9: PREFER ACTIVE VOICE IN SENTENCES

Prefer active voice. It is clear, concise, and forceful.

Sentences using the active voice of the verb will communicate more clearly, concisely, and forcefully than those in the passive voice. In the active voice the subject does the acting; in the passive voice the subject is acted on. For example, John submitted the report (active voice) versus The report was submitted by John (passive voice). The active voice emphasizes John and the action.

The active voice is more direct, stronger, and more vigorous than the passive voice. The active voice usually requires fewer words and results in shorter, more understandable sentences. You will want to make the active voice predominant in your sentences. Look for the advantages of the active voice over the passive voice in these contrasting examples:

Passive	Active
The principles of business communication were learned by the students.	The students learned the principles of business communication.
The agreement was voted for by the union members.	The union members voted for the agreement.
Applications for the job will be reviewed by a committee.	A committee will review applications for the job.

While these examples clearly show the power, liveliness, and conciseness of the active voice, there are appropriate uses of the passive voice. Use the passive voice when the doer of the action is unknown or unimportant or when you want to de-emphasize negative or unpleasant ideas.

Passive voice can be used for variety and to de-emphasize ideas.

For example, when a customer's order is more important than who shipped it, the passive voice is appropriate:

Active: Aldridge's shipped your order on schedule.

Passive: Your order was shipped on schedule.

In the passive voice, the customer's order is emphasized permitting use of the you-viewpoint; and the doer of the action—the vendor—is de-emphasized and appropriately left unnamed.

In the next example you can see how to reduce a negative impression of a doer by using the passive voice. It permits you to leave the doer unnamed.

Active: Aldridge's shipped your order late.

Passive: Your order was shipped late.

You will also want to occasionally use the passive voice to provide variety and interest to your messages. Because of its many advantages, however, the general principle is to make the active voice dominant in your business messages.

PRINCIPLE 10: GIVE SENTENCES APPROPRIATE EMPHASIS

Giving your sentences appropriate emphasis means emphasizing the important ideas and de-emphasizing the unimportant ideas. Every speaker or writer wants a particular message transmitted to the receiver. As you develop each sentence in the message ask yourself, "Should the main idea of this sentence be emphasized or de-emphasized?" Then design the sentence to give the appropriate emphasis.

Give sentences appropriate emphasis using sentence design.

There are several ways to emphasize or de-emphasize an idea: use length of sentence, use location within sentence, use organization of sentence, repeat key words, tell the receiver what is and is not important, be specific or general, use format, and use mechanical means. Each of these ways is discussed and illustrated in the following sections.

USE LENGTH. Short sentences emphasize content, and long sentences de-emphasize content. Most of the time you will want to use shorter sentences to give your ideas greater emphasis. Compare these examples:

Length: Short sentences emphasize; long sentences de-emphasize.

All of us know that effort will bring success if we are persistent.
Effort will bring success.

The important content of the message—effort brings success—receives far more emphasis in the short sentence. The longer version not only changes the main idea to a dependent clause, but it also surrounds the main idea with excessive, distracting words.

USE LOCATION. Beginnings and endings of sentences are the locations of greatest emphasis. What ideas are stressed in these sentences?

Location: Beginnings and endings emphasize; middles de-emphasize.

Jack received a promotion.
Jack received a promotion from assistant manager to manager.
Outstanding performance resulted in a promotion for Jack.

Jack is emphasized in all three sentences. Jack's promotion also receives emphasis in the first sentence by its location at the end. The fact that Jack is now a manager receives emphasis in the second sentence. Finally, in the third sentence Jack's outstanding performance is emphasized.

Sentence beginnings compete for attention only with the words that follow them; endings compete for attention only with words that precede them. Words in the middles of sentences, however, have to compete with both the preceding and following words and, therefore, are de-emphasized.

If you can emphasize an idea by placing it at the beginning or ending of a sentence, then you can de-emphasize an idea by placing it in the middle of a sentence:

> The new position requires a change in residence, but it affords an excellent opportunity for advancement.
>
> Betty received the stereo; the speakers, which are on back order, will be delivered next Tuesday.

In the first sentence, the *change in residence* is de-emphasized by its location. In the second sentence, *which are on back order* is de-emphasized. Location is an excellent way to give appropriate emphasis.

USE SENTENCE ORGANIZATION. You give the greatest emphasis to an idea by placing it in a short, simple sentence. If you want to show a relationship between ideas, it is possible to emphasize main ideas by placing them in independent clauses and de-emphasize other ideas by placing them in dependent clauses. The independent clause is similar to the short sentence; it can stand alone. Dependent clauses are not complete thoughts; they do not make sense standing alone. The two short sentences that follow give approximately the same emphasis to two main ideas: the finality of the sale and the later delivery of the merchandise:

Organization: Ideas in independent clauses are emphasized; in dependent clauses, de-emphasized.

> The sale is final. The merchandise will not be delivered until later.

If you want the two ideas to share emphasis—each receiving a reduced amount—you can organize them into a compound sentence:

Ideas share emphasis in a compound sentence.

> The sale is final, but the merchandise will not be delivered until later.

However, by organizing these two ideas into one complex sentence, one idea can be emphasized and one de-emphasized. This organizational arrangement is called subordination. Examine the varying emphasis in the following examples:

> While the sale is final, the merchandise will not be delivered until later.
>
> Although the merchandise will not be delivered until later, the sale is final.

In the first example, the idea of later delivery of the merchandise is emphasized by being placed in an independent clause. In the second sentence, the primary idea of the finality of the sale gets the attention as an independent clause.

Organizing your sentences using subordination of ideas gives you flexibility in composing your messages. This is another way to emphasize the important or pleasant ideas and to de-emphasize the unimportant or unpleasant ideas.

REPEAT KEY WORDS.

Main ideas represented by key words can be emphasized by repeating those words within a sentence. Note the emphasis given *defective* and *radio* in this sentence from a customer complaint:

Repeating: Emphasize ideas by repeating key words.

> The radio I purchased from you is defective; please replace this defective radio immediately.

Here is another example of emphasis through repetition of the same root word in different forms:

> Alfredo, who is graduating with honors, graduates in May.

Repetition of key words also provides coherence and movement in a sentence. Coherence and movement will be discussed later in this chapter.

TELL RECEIVER WHAT IS IMPORTANT.

You can tell your receiver that an idea is important or unimportant by your word choice; for example:

Telling: You can tell what is important and unimportant.

> The *most important point* is that the sale is final.
> *Of less concern* is that the merchandise will not be delivered until later.

Of course, there are many words and constructions you can use to indicate the importance of an idea. You can refer to ideas with such words as *significant, of (no) consequence, (not) a concern, high (or low) priority, (not) critical, fundamental, (non)essential.* Your thesaurus will be helpful in choosing words to tell your receiver that one idea is important and another unimportant.

BE SPECIFIC OR GENERAL.

Another way to give appropriate emphasis is to use concrete words (specific words) to emphasize ideas and to use abstract words (general words) to de-emphasize ideas. Here are examples of how this works:

Specifying: Specific words emphasize; general words de-emphasize.

> Specific: Sara bought a new *Sprint convertible.*
> General: Sara bought a new *car.*
> Specific: The employee *suffered from severe heart problems, arthritis, and diabetes.*
> General: The employee *was in poor health.*

Format: Emphasize ideas
with punctuation and
listings.

USE FORMAT. The way you physically arrange a sentence can give emphasis to selected ideas. One way to highlight an idea is to separate it from other information in the sentence. Consider this example:

Marty Brooks—an Olympic winner—has agreed to endorse our products.

"An Olympic winner" stands out because it is set off with dashes. Dashes, colons, and exclamation points are strong punctuation marks and can be used to emphasize ideas. Ideas can be de-emphasized by setting them off with commas or parentheses, weaker punctuation marks.

A vertical numbered or lettered list attracts more attention than a list of items simply set off by commas in regular sentence format. This example shows how you can emphasize points by putting them in a numbered list:

The primary findings of the study reveal the following:
1. Prices are going to increase.
2. Supplies are going down.
3. Demand will level off.

Mechanics: Emphasize
with underlining, type,
color, and other means.

USE MECHANICAL MEANS. There are several ways you can give emphasis to ideas through mechanical means. You can <u>underline</u> or use **boldface** type. You can use a different color to highlight selected ideas. The marginal notes in this book are an example of the effective use of color. Other mechanical means include type size, typefaces, all capital letters, arrows, and circles.

Overuse of format or mechanical means to emphasize ideas will reduce their effectiveness and can be distracting. Their use in letters and memos should be very limited and reserved for special situations. The use of mechanical means to emphasize ideas is more common in advertisements, reports, and visual aids.

There are many ways to emphasize and de-emphasize ideas as you develop effective sentences. You will want to practice and use these techniques to strengthen your business communication skills.

FORMING PARAGRAPHS

Paragraphs organize the
receiver's thoughts.

Combining sentences into paragraphs is an important part of composing a message. Paragraphs help your receiver organize his or her thoughts and see where your message is going. You can form effective paragraphs by following five basic principles of business communication. These principles will guide you in determining paragraph length, unity, organization, emphasis, and coherence.

PRINCIPLE 11: USE SHORT PARAGRAPHS

You will want to use short paragraphs in your business messages. Short paragraphs are easy to understand, help your receivers organize their thoughts more easily, and appear more inviting to the receiver. Receivers are more likely to read them.

Use short paragraphs. They are easier to understand.

Long paragraphs are more complex, appear more difficult to read, and are harder to comprehend. Readers are less likely to read them.

How long is a short paragraph? In business letter and memo writing, paragraphs should average four to five lines. If any paragraph in a letter or memo is eight lines or more, it is long and should be examined carefully to see if it can be shortened or divided. Business letters and memos are likely to be read quickly, and shorter paragraphs will aid receiver understanding.

In letters and memos, paragraphs should average four to five lines. Paragraphs with eight lines or more should be examined.

Business reports are more likely to be studied carefully, and the paragraphs can be somewhat longer, but not much longer. In business report writing, paragraphs can average six to seven lines. Twelve lines or more in any paragraph in a report is a signal that it is long, and its unity should be examined carefully.

In reports, paragraphs should average six to seven lines. Paragraphs with twelve lines or more should be examined.

These guides for the lengths of paragraphs in business messages are recommended averages and maximums. Paragraph lengths can and should vary from one line to many lines. They can consist of one sentence or a number of sentences. The lengths of paragraphs should be varied as necessary to accommodate content and to promote reader interest.

In most business letters, memos, and reports, the first and last paragraphs are shorter than the middle paragraphs. Many times the first and last paragraphs in letters and memos are one to three lines long and consist of only one or two sentences. These paragraphs may be somewhat longer in reports. Short opening and closing paragraphs are more inviting to the reader. They add emphasis to the message's beginning and ending ideas. In Parts 3 and 4 of this book, there are several examples of letters, memos, and reports in which paragraph size can be examined.

Beginning and ending paragraphs are usually shorter for greater emphasis.

PRINCIPLE 12: GIVE PARAGRAPHS UNITY

Paragraphs should have unity. Unity means that all of the sentences in a paragraph relate to one topic. The topic should be covered adequately; but, if the paragraph becomes too long, it should be divided into two or more logical parts.

Clear paragraphs have unity.

Examine these illustrations:

Lacks Unity

Thank you for your order. You will receive the shipment of Everwear shoes before your sale begins on Monday, June 14. At your sale you may want to promote the comfort of these long-wearing shoes. The flex sole design makes Everwears feel like they are already broken in the first time they are worn. In addition, they will feel the same way years later. They do truly seem to wear forever. Good luck with your sale!

Has Unity

Thank you for your order. You will receive the shipment of Everwear shoes before your sale begins on Monday, June 14.

At your sale you may want to promote the comfort of these long-wearing shoes. The flex sole design makes Everwears feel like they are already broken in the first time they are worn. In addition, they will feel the same way years later. They do truly seem to wear forever.

Good luck with your sale!

Giving unity to paragraphs is sometimes more difficult than the preceding illustrations imply. The following example lacks unity. Can you determine why?

Lacks Unity

In order to save money, the Employee Benefits Committee has proposed that a new medical and hospitalization insurance plan be developed for our employees. The new plan should provide essential services our employees need but at a lower cost than the old plan. Consideration also should be given to reducing or eliminating some of the old plan's less essential services. Other savings might be realized through reduction of other fringe benefits such as life insurance, bonuses, and vacation allowances. The development of a new medical and hospitalization insurance plan is important to the company's financial well-being.

Did you note that the fourth sentence did not relate directly to the paragraph's main topic? If you did, you are right. The main topic was saving money with a new medical and hospitalization insurance plan. The fourth sentence shifted the topic to saving money by reducing other fringe benefits. The fourth sentence is a separate topic that requires its own paragraph or paragraphs.

PRINCIPLE 13: ORGANIZE PARAGRAPHS LOGICALLY

Organize paragraphs logically using the direct or indirect plan.

Paragraphs can be organized logically using one of two basic plans: direct plan (deductive approach) or indirect plan (inductive approach). In the direct plan the main idea is presented in the first sentence of the paragraph, and details follow in succeeding sentences. In the indirect plan details are presented first, and the main idea is presented later in the paragraph.

The content determines which plan—direct or indirect—you will use. Good news and neutral news can best be presented using the direct plan. Getting directly to the main point and following it with details helps orient the reader to the content. Bad news or persuasion can best be presented using the indirect plan. This approach enables you to first provide details that pave the way for an unpleasant main point, an unfavorable recommendation, or a request for action.

> Present good or neutral news using the direct plan.
>
> Present bad news or persuasion using the indirect plan.

The sentence that presents the main point of a paragraph is called the topic sentence. The topic sentence will either announce to the reader what the main idea is, or it will summarize the content of the main idea. The topic sentence is, in a sense, like the headline on a newspaper story. In using the direct plan, the topic sentence will be the first sentence as it is in this paragraph. With the indirect plan, the topic sentence will be placed later in the paragraph.

As a general rule, the first sentence in a paragraph should be either the topic sentence or a transitional sentence. How to provide transition (movement) in a first sentence will be explained later under Principle 15. Unless there is an important reason to locate it elsewhere in the paragraph, in business messages the topic sentence should be placed first. Here are examples of the two basic plans with the topic sentences underlined:

> The first sentence should be topic or transitional.

Direct Plan (Topic Sentence First)

<u>Most chief business executives rate business communication as the most important skill a manager can possess.</u> A recent survey of business executives showed that 80 percent of the respondents thought business communication was a manager's most important skill. The remaining 20 percent of the respondents rated business communication second to technical skill. The survey was conducted using a random sample of the presidents of the Fortune 500 companies.

Indirect Plan (Topic Sentence Within)

You are a valuable employee to the manufacturing division. You are the only employee with a high level of expertise in statistical quality control. <u>While I cannot approve your request for transfer to the marketing division at this time, it may be possible to do so soon.</u> The timing of your transfer depends on our success in replacing you by (1) recruiting a qualified new employee or (2) upgrading the skills of a current employee.

Indirect Plan (Topic Sentence Last)

Spring is just around the corner. This means that vacation time is almost upon us. When you think about planning your vacation for this year, think of us. <u>Call the Farlands Travel Agency at (502) 555-1234, and let us send you the "Ideal Vacation Planner's Guide."</u>

In summary, paragraphs can be organized logically using the direct or the indirect plan. Generally, the direct plan is recommended for good news and neutral news; and the indirect plan is recommended for bad news and persuasion.

PRINCIPLE 14: GIVE PARAGRAPHS APPROPRIATE EMPHASIS

Give paragraphs appropriate emphasis using paragraph design.

As you will recall from the section on sentences in this chapter, giving appropriate emphasis means emphasizing the important ideas and de-emphasizing the unimportant ideas. Many of the same ways for giving appropriate emphasis to sentences apply to giving appropriate emphasis to paragraph content. The applicable ways are summarized here:

Design paragraphs using length, location, repeating, telling, format, and mechanics.

Length	Short paragraphs emphasize content and long paragraphs de-emphasize content.
Location	Beginnings and endings of paragraphs are the locations of greatest emphasis. Middles of paragraphs are the locations of least emphasis.
Repeating	Repeating key words throughout the paragraph can emphasize the ideas represented by those words.
Telling	You can tell your reader that an idea is important or unimportant.
Format	The way you arrange a paragraph—set ideas off with punctuation, listings, wider margins, etc.—can give emphasis to selected ideas.
Mechanics	You can emphasize ideas using mechanical means: underlining, boldface type, color, type size, typefaces, all capitals, arrows, and circles.

PRINCIPLE 15: PROVIDE PARAGRAPH COHERENCE

Provide for flow of thought with paragraph coherence.

Providing coherence between and within paragraphs means providing for a flow of thought. You will want to provide for the logical movement of your receiver's mind from one idea to the next. The primary way to assure coherence is to organize paragraphs logically using the direct or indirect plans as discussed in Principle 13.

You can also provide for coherence between and within paragraphs by using transitional words and tie-in sentences. Hints for successfully adopting these latter suggestions follow.

Provide coherence with transitional words.

USE TRANSITIONAL WORDS. Transitional words are helpful bridges from one idea to the next. They help receivers see where you are leading them, why you are leading them there, and what to expect when they get there. Transitional words provide coherence by holding ideas together logically.

For example, suppose you present an idea in one sentence and you want to expand on that idea in the next sentence. By using transitional words such as *in addition*, *furthermore*, and *also* at the beginning of the second sentence, you can help receivers see the relationship between ideas. The following example shows this kind of bridging between two sentences:

Adding Information

Michi is a proficient writer. *In addition*, she is an excellent speaker.

There are other transitional words that provide coherence for different situations. Here are some examples:

Contrasts:	but, however, by contrast, nevertheless, on the other hand, from another viewpoint
Examples:	for example, to illustrate, for instance, that is, as follows, like, in illustration
Sequence:	first (second, third), next, then, finally, last, to sum up, in conclusion
Emphasis:	primarily, most importantly, particularly, especially, in fact, indeed, above all
Conclusions:	therefore, thus, so, consequently, as a result, accordingly, hence
Exclusions:	except, neither . . . nor, except that, all but, except for, all except
Additions:	in addition, furthermore, also, and, similarly, moreover, as well as, too

USE TIE-IN SENTENCES.

USE TIE-IN SENTENCES. Tie-in sentences help your receiver move from one aspect of the subject to the next. When using the tie-in sentence technique for coherence, repeat the same subject one or more times. To develop tie-in sentences, you can paraphrase the subject, repeat key words that describe the subject, or use pronouns that refer to the subject. Examples of tie-in sentences using these approaches are as follows:

Provide coherence with tie-in sentences.

Paraphrasing

The information system in the MNO Company is *used extensively* for decision making. Because of this *high rate of use*, it is imperative that the data in the system are up to date.

Repeating Key Words

Oscar Cruz found that direct mail is a *cost-effective technique* for selling magazine subscriptions. Telemarketing is another proven *cost-effective technique* for promoting subscription sales.

Frank will complete the required research within two months. *He* will report *his* findings no later than December 1.

COMPOSING WITH STYLE

Compose with style—include your personality.

The most effective business communicators use the principles that have been reviewed in this chapter. You, too, should find them effective. There is one other important dimension of your communication—your personality. Your writing and speaking should reflect the interesting, unique person that you are.

Be yourself. Use words and combinations of words that not only are understood by your receiver but also reveal who you are—words that give life and distinction to your message. There are many combinations of words that will send the same basic message to your receiver. Use those words that communicate clearly and concisely and that reflect your personality.

One of America's outstanding orators, Patrick Henry (1736-1799), showed what can be accomplished with style. The first sentence shows how he might have made one of his famous statements; the second sentence is how he did:

Not This

If I can't have freedom, then I would rather not live.

But This

Give me liberty, or give me death!

A great businessperson and political scientist, Benjamin Franklin (1706-1790), had a clear and concrete way of communicating. Compare how he could have written one of his familiar quotations with the way he wrote it:

Not This

In this world nearly everything is uncertain.

But This

In this world nothing is certain but death and taxes.

One of the leaders in advocating full rights for women, Susan B. Anthony (1820-1906), was extremely effective in awakening the American nation to inequities based on gender. Contrast the way she might have expressed her basic belief in equality for women with the way she actually expressed it:

Not This

There is no reason to give women fewer rights than we give men.

But This

Men, their rights and nothing more; women, their rights and nothing less.

Another powerful communicator who moved Americans, Martin Luther King, Jr. (1929-1968), used the principles of communication coupled with his own unique selection of words. What he could have said and what he did say are sharply contrasted in the following illustration:

Not This

It is hard for others to hold you down if you never give them the chance.

But This

A man can't ride your back unless it's bent.

Finally, from an effective writer and speaker, John F. Kennedy (1917-1963), we have this contrast in what could have been said and what was said:

Not This

Do not inquire about what you can get the government to do for you; instead find out what you can do for the government.

But This

Ask not what your country can do for you; ask what you can do for your country.

CONCLUSION

Effective communicators give thought and time to what they say and write. You, too, with study and effort, can improve your ability to be an effective communicator in your professional career and your personal life. Remember to use the you-viewpoint, apply the principles of business communication, and be yourself—you will then be a powerful business communicator.

Be a powerful business communicator. Use the you-viewpoint and the principles of business communication, and be yourself.

DISCUSSION QUESTIONS

1. Define the KISS principle of business communication and discuss the advantages of its use.
2. Explain how the use of a dictionary can help you be a more effective communicator.
3. Discuss how a thesaurus can be helpful when composing messages.
4. How does a sender choose understandable words?
5. Explain how the use of appropriate technical words can assist communicators. Give an example.
6. Discuss the appropriate uses of concrete and abstract words in your business messages.
7. Tell how to implement Principle 3: Prefer Strong Words.
8. What are the relative merits of using positive and negative words in messages?
9. Define overused words. Explain why senders should avoid using them in their messages.
10. Define obsolete words. Explain why senders should avoid their use.
11. Describe briefly each of the following attributes of sentences: (a) unity and (b) related words are together.
12. Explain what must be done to assure that sentences are grammatically correct.
13. Why are short sentences preferred in business communication?
14. In what ways may the content in a sentence be limited?
15. Discuss the advantages of using the active voice and of using the passive voice in sentences.
16. Discuss each of the following ways to emphasize or de-emphasize sentence content (include examples in your discussion): length, location, and repeating key words.
17. Explain how you can give emphasis to sentence content through sentence organization.
18. Give three examples of the ways you can give emphasis to sentence content by telling the receiver what is important and what is not important.
19. Give two examples each of (a) emphasis by the use of specific words and (b) de-emphasis by the use of general words.
20. Discuss the advantages and disadvantages of using format and mechanical means to emphasize message content.
21. Explain why a sender should use short paragraphs in business messages. Tell what the average length of paragraphs should be for (a) letters and memos and (b) reports.
22. What is meant by Principle 12: Give Paragraphs Unity?

23. Explain how to organize paragraphs logically using the direct and indirect plans. Include in your explanation how a sender would decide which plan to use.

24. Discuss using transitional words, paraphrasing, repeating key words, and using pronoun references as techniques for providing paragraph coherence.

25. How can you follow the principles of business communication in your composing efforts and still reflect your own personality in your messages?

APPLICATION EXERCISES

PART A

Instructions: Apply the principle of business communication indicated in the exercises that follow it. Do not change the basic meaning contained in each of the exercises, and do not select the same examples used in this chapter. Use a dictionary and a thesaurus to assist you in these exercises. Assume that your receiver is a high school graduate with a tenth to eleventh grade vocabulary level and no particular technical expertise.

PRINCIPLE 1: CHOOSE UNDERSTANDABLE WORDS.
SELECT SIMPLE WORDS. Select simpler words to replace these difficult words: (a) beguile, (b) impeccable, (c) amass, (d) folio, (e) protocol, (f) illicit, (g) advocate, (h) jeopardy, (i) fortuitous, (j) intrinsic.
USE SHORT WORDS. Select short words to replace these long words: (a) capricious, (b) homogenous, (c) representation, (d) facsimile, (e) reasonable, (f) amalgamate, (g) ambivalence, (h) prerogative, (i) clandestine, (j) gregarious.
USE APPROPRIATE TECHNICAL WORDS. Select nontechnical words to replace each of these technical words: (a) prosthesis, (b) jurisprudence, (c) tabloid, (d) hypothesis, (e) carcinoma, (f) invoice, (g) accounts receivable, (h) system configuration, (i) exempt employee, (j) equity.

PRINCIPLE 2: USE CONCRETE WORDS. Select concrete words to replace these abstract words: (a) bird, (b) factory, (c) office, (d) equipment, (e) computer, (f) tree, (g) soda, (h) afternoon, (i) transportation, (j) periodically.

PRINCIPLE 3: PREFER STRONG WORDS. Select strong words to replace these weak words: (a) suggestion, (b) overdue, (c) decline, (d) request, (e) comply, (f) overlooked, (g) ask, (h) refrain, (i) purchase, (j) resist.

PRINCIPLE 4: EMPHASIZE POSITIVE WORDS. List five positive words that would be good to use in business messages and five negative words a sender should avoid using.

PRINCIPLE 5: AVOID OVERUSED WORDS. List five overused words or phrases a sender should avoid using.

PRINCIPLE 6: AVOID OBSOLETE WORDS. List five obsolete words or phrases a sender should avoid using.

PRINCIPLE 7: COMPOSE CLEAR SENTENCES.
GIVE SENTENCES UNITY. Rewrite the following long sentence. Divide it into a number of sentences each of which possesses unity.

> The planning was to be carried out by the end of October, but the information needed to complete the planning was not available in time; to solve this problem, the vice-president of operations decided to extend the planning calendar through November so that production could continue using the current procedures.

KEEP RELATED WORDS TOGETHER. Revise the following sentences so that there is a clear relationship between the modifiers and the words they modify:
a. The computer needed repair which was purchased recently.
b. A copy was mailed of the article to each manager on May 4.
c. All the reports were submitted promptly from the committees.
d. The employee was too ill to come to work because he sent his report by mail.
e. The information was not available needed to complete the project.

PRINCIPLE 8: USE SHORT SENTENCES. Shorten the following sentences by omitting unnecessary words and limiting content:
a. Be really sure to bring all of your applicable reports to the place where we are holding the meeting of the committee.
b. I was very, very happy about the great decision to go ahead and start right away with the project.
c. The prices which are for the premium grade of gasoline are coming down.
d. The commitment and dedication of most businesspersons lead them to do everything they can to increase productivity.
e. The time of the meeting will be determined, set, and announced soon.

PRINCIPLE 9: PREFER ACTIVE VOICE IN SENTENCES.
Change the following sentences from the passive voice to the active voice:
a. The letter was signed by the manager.
b. Business expenses must be recorded.
c. Telephone calls should not be personal in nature.
d. Income for the quarter has decreased.
e. Reports are to be prepared in duplicate.

PRINCIPLE 10: GIVE SENTENCES APPROPRIATE EMPHASIS.
Following the guideline instructions for emphasis, create one to three sentences for each situation:

USE LENGTH. You want employees to be on time for a meeting. Emphasize this point by the length of your sentence(s).

USE LOCATION. You are approving a promotion for an employee. Emphasize the promotion at the beginning of your sentence(s).

USE SENTENCE ORGANIZATION. You have to say no to a request for a promotion. Use sentence organization to de-emphasize the no in your sentence(s).

REPEAT KEY WORDS. Repeat key words in your sentence(s) to emphasize that a stereo is high quality.

BE SPECIFIC OR GENERAL. Be general in your sentence(s) to de-emphasize the slightly below average miles per gallon rating for a new model car.

USE FORMAT. Use format in your sentence(s) to emphasize the number of games your school's football team has won this season.

USE MECHANICAL MEANS. Use mechanical means in your sentence(s) to emphasize the time of a personnel committee meeting.

PRINCIPLE 11: USE SHORT PARAGRAPHS.
Indicate the recommended average line lengths for short paragraphs in (a) letters and memos and (b) reports. Also indicate the line lengths for paragraphs that are considered long for (c) letters and memos and (d) reports. Finally, indicate (e) the line length of the shortest possible paragraph.

PRINCIPLE 12: GIVE PARAGRAPHS UNITY.
Indicate the sentence that does not belong in paragraphs (a) and (b):

a. Microcomputer education today often begins in the elementary schools. When it starts at that level, high school students are prepared for more sophisticated training in computer usage. Also, today, with lower costs for computers, more people can own them than ever before. Many college students—some with their own microcomputers—are receiving computer education in applications software that is more powerful than mainframe computers were just five years ago.

b. Parents of today's youth are faced with an increasing dilemma: how to pay for the higher education of their children. The cost of college is going up. Over the past five years, this cost has increased 50 percent. Student interest in college is also on the rise. Finding innovative ways to pay the rising cost of a college education is one of today's major challenges.

PRINCIPLE 13: ORGANIZE PARAGRAPHS LOGICALLY.
Using the direct plan, indicate the most logical order of these sentences by listing their letters in that order.

a. The facts in your request clearly supported your position.
b. Your request to attend the conference is approved.
c. Report these expenses to me when you return.
d. Please keep a careful record of your travel expenses.

PRINCIPLE 14: GIVE PARAGRAPHS APPROPRIATE EMPHASIS. Create a paragraph that emphasizes the benefits of purchasing a stereo and de-emphasizes the cost of the purchase.

PRINCIPLE 15: PROVIDE PARAGRAPH COHERENCE. Using the indirect plan, indicate the most coherent order for these sentences by listing their letters in that order:

a. In addition to the kind of handling you want and the high mileage you need, the sale price will fit your pocketbook.

b. The handling is unbelievably responsive.

c. Your new Fastback sports car is waiting for you at your dealer now.

d. And the mileage is great.

PART B

Instructions: Use your creativity in rewriting the following sentences. While retaining the basic meaning of the original version, be sure to draw on your own unique personality in determining the composition of your revised versions.

1. Our division's sales exceed the sales of all the other divisions in the corporation.

2. Communication skills are important for success in business.

3. Since the time has expired, the score has to stand.

4. The book cannot be returned to the bookstore; you have marked in it.

5. We have won.

6. Being ethical is important for many reasons.

CHAPTER 3

DEVELOPING BUSINESS MESSAGES

LEARNING OBJECTIVES

Your learning objectives for this chapter include the following:

- To develop the ability to use a three-step process for planning and composing effective business messages
- To learn how the vocabulary level of business messages can be determined
- To learn how to choose ethical content for business messages
- To understand how to assure the legality of business messages
- To learn how to use available alternatives to assure unbiased language in business messages

The planning and composing process for developing all types of written and oral business messages is the same. The process consists of the following three tasks: (1) determine the message's purpose(s), (2) analyze the receiver(s) for the you-viewpoint, and (3) compose the content of the message. Carrying out this process may take from a few seconds for a simple oral message to several days for a long written report. Following the process is essential for developing effective business messages.

> Use the same planning and composing process for all messages.

Message analysis is a related aspect of developing effective business messages. Control the vocabulary level of your messages so that they fit your

> Analyze your messages.

receivers. In addition, be sure that your messages are ethical, meet legal requirements, and contain unbiased language.

This chapter tells you how to develop effective business messages. It discusses the *how-to* of planning, composing, and analyzing business messages.

PLANNING AND COMPOSING BUSINESS MESSAGES

The process: determine purposes, analyze receiver, and compose content.

The three-step process for planning and composing business messages is simple but critical to your success in communicating. The process incorporates and applies topics in Chapters 1 and 2—communication foundations and the principles of business communication.

STEP 1: DETERMINE PURPOSES

Message purposes will vary.

The primary and secondary purposes for a specific business message will vary depending on the communication situation.

First: Analyze the situation.

ANALYZE THE COMMUNICATION SITUATION. Your first task in determining the purposes of a message is to decide what is involved in a specific communication situation. When analyzing the communication situation, you will want to ask yourself: Who will receive the message? Will the message be good, neutral, bad, or persuasive news for my receiver(s)? On preliminary examination, what will be the main content of the message—the main idea and the supporting ideas? Illustration 3-1 shows the parts of the communication situation analysis.

Who is the receiver? Is the message good, neutral, bad, or persuasive news? What is the main content?

The kinds of specific questions you might ask yourself when analyzing the communication situation could include the following: Can I say yes to an employee's request for a vacation the first two weeks in August? How can I initiate a communication to my customers to promote a summer clearance sale? How do I say no to a customer who wants to return a microcomputer for a full refund of its purchase price?

Analysis may take a few seconds or several days.

The analysis of the communication situation may be done mentally in a few seconds before you dictate a memo or place a telephone call. On the other hand, the communication situation analysis may involve collecting extensive information and may be written down. This would be the case for an involved business report to be submitted to a board of directors.

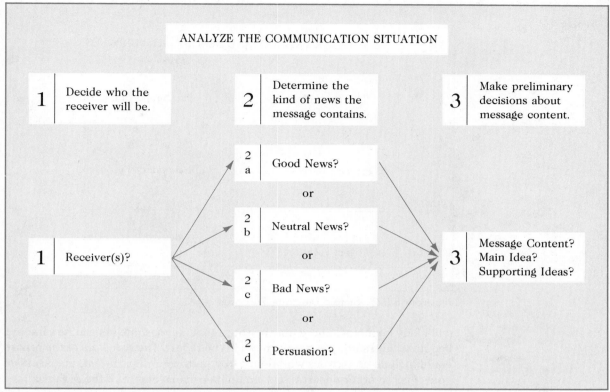

Illustration 3-1 Analyzing the Communication Situation

ESTABLISH PRIMARY AND SECONDARY PURPOSES.

Following the analysis of the communication situation, your second task is to establish the primary and secondary purposes of your message. This will be done within the framework of the four business communication goals of receiver understanding, necessary receiver response, favorable relationship, and organizational goodwill.

Second: Establish purposes within framework of goals.

The message's main idea is the primary purpose, and the supporting ideas are the secondary purposes of the message. For example, assume you can say yes to an employee's request to take a vacation the first two weeks of August. This message can be oral, will be good news, and is being sent to a receiver you know well. Its content will include the yes plus additional information about work priorities—work that should be done before the vacation and work that can wait until afterwards. Illustration 3-2 shows how your purposes might appear for this communication situation if they were written down.

Message purposes: Main and supporting ideas.

Another example shows how establishing primary and secondary purposes for a specific message can be more involved. Assume that the message you are developing is a written annual departmental report. The message category

Purposes can be:

• Simple

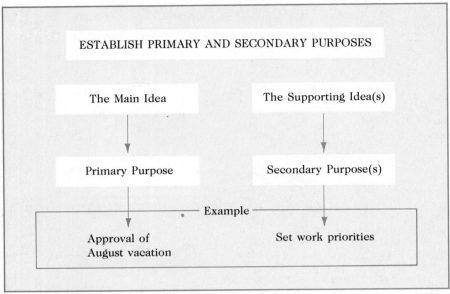

Illustration 3-2   Simple Message Purposes

will likely be mixed. There may be some good news, some neutral news, some bad news, and some persuasive news in the report. The receivers of the report could include employees who report to you in your department, managers at your level in other departments, and upper management of the organization. The primary and secondary purposes for your departmental report might be as shown in Illustration 3-3.

• Involved

INVOLVED MESSAGE PURPOSES

Primary Purposes

1. To document clearly the department's accomplishments for 19--
2. To persuade upper management to meet the department's future needs

Secondary Purposes

1. To instill pride of accomplishment in the department's employees
2. To inform managers at your own level of the department's activities and needs
3. To inform upper management of the contributions your department and its employees have made
4. To convince upper management to finance the department's continuing operation and proposed projects
5. To maintain favorable relationships with others
6. To build organizational goodwill for the department

Illustration 3-3   Involved Message Purposes for Departmental Report

When you have analyzed the communication situation and have determined the primary and secondary purposes of the message, you are ready to analyze your receivers to enable you to use the you-viewpoint.

STEP 2: ANALYZE THE RECEIVER FOR THE YOU-VIEWPOINT

The second step in planning and composing an effective written or oral business message is to analyze the receiver or receivers for the you-viewpoint. Since this step is discussed fully in Chapter 1, only a brief summary of it will be given here.

ANALYZE THE RECEIVER. For some communication situations, you may know the receiver of your message quite well. Little or no analysis of the receiver may be necessary. By contrast, in other communication situations it may be necessary for you to do a careful, detailed analysis of the receiver. Whether your analysis of the receiver requires a limited or an extensive amount of research, the approach is the same. You analyze your receiver in four areas—knowledge, interests, opinions, and emotional state—as shown in Illustration 3-4.

Analyze receiver's knowledge, interests, opinions, and emotional state.

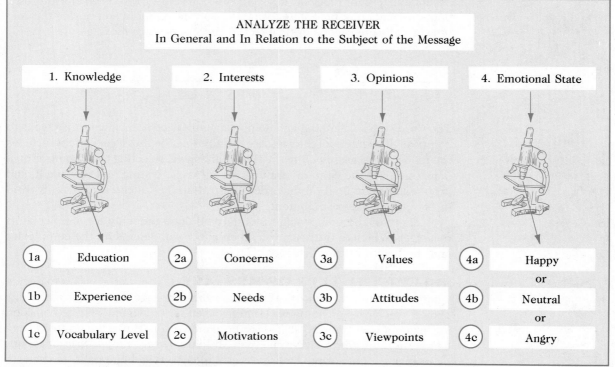

ANALYZE THE RECEIVER
In General and In Relation to the Subject of the Message

1. Knowledge	2. Interests	3. Opinions	4. Emotional State
1a Education	2a Concerns	3a Values	4a Happy
			or
1b Experience	2b Needs	3b Attitudes	4b Neutral
			or
1c Vocabulary Level	2c Motivations	3c Viewpoints	4c Angry

Illustration 3-4 Analysis of the Receiver

If you have multiple receivers of your message, you will need to analyze each receiver in the group. For example, if you are giving a speech to a Rotary Club, you should visualize the various members of the audience. If you are writing a memo to five other people in your office, analyze each receiver. To achieve the goals and purposes of your message with all your receivers, the message must be understandable to the receiver in the group with the least amount of knowledge about the subject, the lowest vocabulary level, and the most emotional opposition to the message.

Your analysis of the receiver will give you better information on the receiver's vocabulary, interests, possible biases, and emotional state. You can determine from your analysis the ideas, words, and approach that will communicate best in each situation. This kind of information is essential if you are to use the you-viewpoint.

USE THE YOU-VIEWPOINT.   Based on the analysis of your receiver, you will be able to use the powerful you-viewpoint in developing your message. When using the you-viewpoint, give highest priority to what you think will be your receiver's perception of the message. You are trying to communicate receiver understanding and to obtain appropriate receiver reaction. The receiver's perception of your message **is** your message.

Using the you-viewpoint means using words that are understandable and acceptable to your receiver. It also means considering the receiver's interests, opinions, and emotional state. Using the you-viewpoint in composing the content of your message is critical to the success of your message.

STEP 3: COMPOSE MESSAGE CONTENT

The third step in planning and composing an effective business message is to compose the content of the message. Composing the message content includes the following tasks: selecting the type of message, selecting the organizational plan, outlining the content, drafting the message, editing and revising it, and proofreading the final product. See Illustration 3-5 for the six tasks involved in composing message content.

Many of the composing tasks may be done mentally for simple, short messages. Which of the tasks you do on paper will depend on the complexity and the length of the message.

SELECT THE TYPE OF MESSAGE.   Your initial task is to decide whether to use a written message or an oral message. Once you make this choice, you have a great many variations of either type of message to consider. For example, written messages can be handwritten, typed, or printed. They can be in the form of electronic mail, diskette, letter, memo, written report, or in many other forms. Oral messages include telephone calls, interviews,

(margin notes)

If you have multiple receivers, analyze each one.

A message must be composed so all receivers can understand it.

Use the **you-viewpoint** for receiver understanding and action.

The receiver's perception **is** the message.

Using the you-viewpoint is critical to success.

Six tasks are involved in composing message content.

Tasks can be done mentally or on paper.

First: Select type of message.

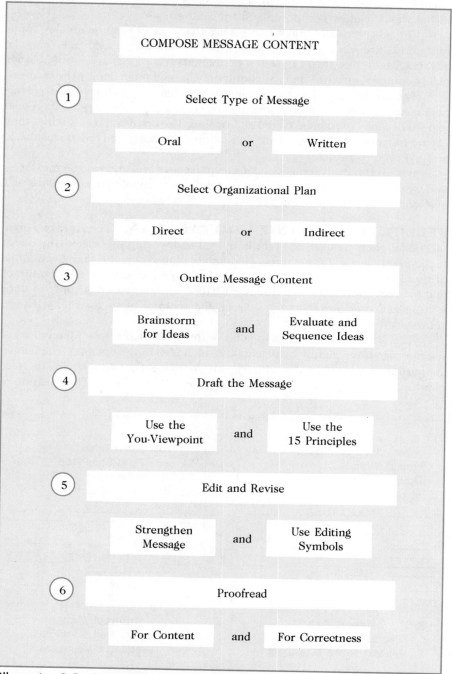

Illustration 3-5 Composing the Message Content

small group presentations, and public speeches. Each of these messages varies in the way it can be composed and transmitted.

Each type of message has advantages and disadvantages.

The advantages of oral messages are that they (1) can be quickly transmitted, (2) are more personal, and (3) allow immediate feedback. The disadvantages are that they (1) lack a permanent record, (2) are unsuitable for highly complex material, and (3) permit only limited reflection by the receiver.

The advantages of written messages are that they (1) provide a permanent record, (2) accommodate lengthy and complex content, (3) can be reread and studied, and (4) can be edited and revised. The disadvantages are that they (1) are transmitted slowly, (2) are more formal, (3) delay and reduce feedback, and (4) require storage.

Select the best type of message for the situation.

Based on the advantages and disadvantages of oral and written messages, you can select the type of message that will best achieve your purposes and best communicate with your receiver.

Second: Select an organizational plan.

SELECT THE ORGANIZATIONAL PLAN. There are two organizational plans that are used for both oral and written messages—the direct (deductive) plan and the indirect (inductive) plan. There are many variations of these two plans. In Part 3 and Part 4, alternative ways to use the direct and indirect approaches are discussed. These alternative ways apply to both written and oral messages. The direct and indirect plans for messages are shown in Illustration 3-6.

Use the direct plan or the indirect plan.

The direct plan attempts to achieve the primary purpose (main idea) of the message immediately by placing the main idea in the opening. The details supporting or explaining the primary purpose follow the opening. The indirect plan opens on neutral ground or on a point of agreement. The opening is

```
    To:   Fred Sheppard                      To:   Ellen Roth
  From:   Ellen Roth                       From:   Fred Sheppard
  Date:   October 1, 199-                  Date:   November 1, 199-
Subject:  Profit Increase               Subject:  Profit Decrease
_____ MAIN IDEA _____          _____
_____         _____
_____         _____
_____         _____ MAIN IDEA _____
_____         _____
_____         _____
```

| Direct Plan | Indirect Plan |
| Use for Good News or Neutral News Messages | Use for Bad News or Persuasive Messages |

Illustration 3-6 Organizational Plans for Messages

followed by supporting reasons or explanation and moves to the primary purpose later in the message. Research has shown that in most situations the direct plan is more effective for good news or neutral news and the indirect plan is more effective for bad news or persuasion.

Direct plan is best for good or neutral news; indirect plan is best for bad news or persuasion.

After selecting the type of message you will use—written or oral—and the organizational plan for your message—direct or indirect—you are ready to outline the message's content.

OUTLINE THE MESSAGE CONTENT.

In outlining message content, you are simply organizing your ideas for the message in your mind or on paper, diskette, or other medium.

Third: Outline the message content.

Start by brainstorming for ideas. Concentrate on both the purpose(s) of your message and your receiver(s), and then note all the ideas that you think should be included in the message. Let this activity take place randomly. Do not evaluate the ideas in detail, just record them. As you do this, you may find it necessary to gather helpful information from files, other employees, or other sources.

Keeping purposes and receiver(s) in mind, brainstorm content.

Assume, for example, that you have received a claim letter from a customer asking for a refund for a ski boat that was bought on sale. Although the customer's letter is not very well written, the message is clear—he wants his money back. You will have to tell him no—send him bad news—because you do not give refunds for items bought on sale. You brainstorm ideas for the content of your response. Your notes, written on the claim letter you received, might appear as in Illustration 3-7.

The second part of the outlining task is to evaluate and sequence the ideas you developed during your brainstorming. You will place the ideas you want to use in a logical order following the organizational plan you chose. In your response to the claim letter, you will want to use the indirect plan because you must give the customer bad news. The order in which you would sequence ideas for the bad-news message is shown in Illustration 3-7 by the number in parentheses following each idea. After completing the sequencing of ideas, you are ready to draft the message.

Evaluate and sequence ideas.

DRAFT THE MESSAGE.

Using your mental or recorded notes, your next task is to draft the message. You may draft the message by dictating, keyboarding, or handwriting. It is important to use the 15 principles of business communication given in Chapter 2 when drafting messages. Also, be sure to use the you-viewpoint. Put yourself in the place of your receiver.

Fourth: Draft the message.

For simple messages your first draft may be the final version of the message. For difficult messages you may have a rough first draft and then one or more improved draft versions of the message. With the development of word processing, it is much easier to have multiple drafts of messages because only the changes need to be keyboarded. Word processing technology and its advantages are more fully explained in Chapter 4.

You may have one or more drafts.

Word processing makes second and succeeding drafts easier to do.

Illustration 3-7   Brainstorming the Message Content on Claim Letter

Purposes of Message:
Reject request for refund on boat.
Maintain customer's business.
Increase organizational goodwill.

Ideas for Content: Express appreciation for purchase. (1)

2300 First Street
Paducah, WI 53001-2783
April 28, 199-

Neutral opening—"do all we can." (2)
Repair at cost or $39.95 kit. (7)

Wish many happy hours of skiing. (8)

Mr. Mario Perez
Store Manager
John Martin Sales Company
577 Linden Street
Cottage Grove, WI   53527-3909

Amount of savings—$2,000. (4)

Dear Mr. Perez

I want my money back on the defective boat I bought
from you during your "Save 33 Percent" Sale. I found a
hole in the hull the first time I put it in the water.

Please send me the refund check for $4,020, and I will
bring the boat back.

Yours truly

John Brame

John Brame

Volume purchases/cut overhead. (5)

Reinforce purchase decision. (3)

No—All sales final during 33% sale. (6)

You may or may not prepare a complete draft for an oral message. You may transmit oral messages from mental notes, or you may use written notes. If you prepare a complete draft of a speech, you should prepare notes for use at the actual presentation of the speech. Reading an oral message from a complete, written draft is not recommended except in circumstances where you must be extremely cautious in what you say. An example of this would be in reading a prepared statement for a news release.

If you are drafting a message that you know you will edit and revise, it is more important to get something down in writing than it is to get the copy perfect. Experienced writers know that the clearest, most effective communication results from editing and revising drafts of messages.

If you can edit and revise, just get something in writing at the start.

Clearest messages come from editing and revising drafts.

You will, of course, prepare complete drafts of your written messages. For example, the first rough draft of the bad-news letter to John Brame about the defective boat is shown in Illustration 3-8.

Upon reviewing a first draft of a message, you decide either that it becomes your final version or that you will edit and revise it. Prior to the advent of word processing equipment, business communicators usually sent first drafts of letters, memos, and reports to avoid the time and cost of retyping. With the advantages of word processing equipment, it is recommended that first drafts of most messages be edited and revised to assure clarity and effectiveness.

EDIT AND REVISE THE MESSAGE.

When editing and revising, keep the primary and secondary purposes of the message in mind. Edit the message from your receiver's point of view using the principles of business communication to guide your improvements.

Fifth: Edit and revise the message.

Keep purposes and receiver(s) in mind while editing and revising.

Editing and revising drafts of messages are composition tasks of the highest priority. Editing and revising are the best ways to strengthen the quality of your messages so that they achieve their purposes in the most effective manner. The results of editing and revising can be seen in Illustration 3-9. Note the clarity, power, and you-viewpoint that have been added in this second draft of the letter.

Standard symbols for editing and revising are shown in Appendix B and used in Illustration 3-9. Editing symbols are helpful communication devices between the originator and the preparer of messages. It is suggested that you learn and use these symbols in your editing, revising, and proofreading efforts.

To aid communication between message preparer and originator, use editing symbols.

Give the editing and revising task the highest priority for important or lengthy, complex messages. This is your opportunity to strengthen your word choice, sentence development, and paragraph formation. You can check that you have used the chosen organization plan effectively. In addition, it will be another chance to add distinctiveness—a part of your personality—to the message.

Give the editing and revising task highest priority.

You may edit and revise some messages many times. Long business reports often are revised three to five times or more. Keep editing and revising until you have a version of the message in the you-viewpoint that is clear, concise, and businesslike.

Illustration 3-8   First Rough Draft of a Bad-News Message

John Martin Sales Company

577 Linden Street, Cottage Grove, WI 53527-3909 (608) 555-8220

April 30, 199-

Mr. John Brame
2300 First Street
Paducah, WI 53001-2783

Dear Mr. Brame

We appreciate your recent purchase of a Blue Waters Ski Boat.
You certainly have bought an extremely high-quality ski boat that
will give you many years of outstanding enjoyment. We want to do
all that we can to ensure that you do have that outstanding
enjoyment.

You made a good decision when you bought your ski boat on sale
during the John Martin Sales Company "Save 33 Percent" sale. The
tremendous savings you got on this sale totaling almost $2,000
were made possible in two ways: We (1) buy merchandise in large
volumes whenever we can, and (2) cut overhead and pass the
savings on to our customers.

One of the ways we cut overhead is to make all sales final on
items purchased during the "Save 33 Percent" sale. We make every
effort to be sure all our customers are aware of this policy by
noting it in all advertisements and posting signs throughout the
store.

You will be very glad to learn that you can easily make the
repair you need on your Blue Waters Ski Boat. It is easy to
make. For $39.95 you can purchase a fiberglass repair kit that
has complete directions and guides for its utilization. You can
either "do-it-yourself" or have our experts in our shop take care
of it for you at cost. Please call us collect at (608) 555-8220
and tell us your preference.

Best wishes for many hours of skiing this summer on the Paducah
Lake.

Sincerely yours

Mario Perez

Mario Perez
Store Manager

bch

Illustration 3-9 Edited and Revised Bad-News Letter

John Martin
Sales Company

577 Linden Street, Cottage Grove, WI 53527-3903 (608) 555-8220

April 30, 199–

Mr. John Brame
2300 First Street
Paducah, WI 53001-2783

Dear Mr. Brame

We appreciate your recent purchase of a Blue Waters Ski Boat. *is appreciated*
You certainly have bought an extremely high-quality ski boat that
can will give you many years of outstanding enjoyment. We want to do
all that we can to ensure that you do have that outstanding
enjoyment *with your new Blue Waters Ski Boat.*

You made a good decision when you bought your ski boat on sale
during the John Martin Sales Company "Save 33 Percent" sale. The
tremendous savings you got on this sale totaling almost $2,000 *that*
was were made possible in two ways: We (1) buy merchandise in large
volumes whenever we can, and (2) cut overhead and pass the
savings on to our customers.

One of the ways we cut overhead is to make all sales final on
items purchased during the "Save 33 Percent" sale. We make every
effort to be sure all our customers are aware of this policy by
noting it in all advertisements and posting signs throughout the
store.

You will be very glad to learn that you can easily make the
repair you need on your Blue Waters Ski Boat. It is easy to
make. For $39.95 you can purchase a fiberglass repair kit that
has complete directions and guides for its utilization. You can
either "do-it-yourself" or have our experts in our shop take care
of it for you at cost. Please call us collect at (608) 555-8220
and tell us your preference.

Best wishes for many *happy* hours of skiing this summer on the Paducah
Lake.

Sincerely yours

Mario Perez

Mario Perez
Store Manager

bch

Sixth: Proofread the message.

Proofread to catch all spelling, punctuation, and grammar errors and to check format.

PROOFREAD THE MESSAGE. The proofreading task is different from the editing and revising task. Proofreading is checking each word to be sure that it is spelled correctly. It is assuring yourself that proper punctuation and grammar have been used, that your sentences are complete and properly constructed, and that your format meets appropriate standards.

Careful proofreading involves (1) reading the message for content and (2) reading it again for correct grammar, spelling, and punctuation. Some proofreaders find that they can find more spelling errors by reading the copy backwards. Errors detract from the clarity of the message and reduce your credibility in the mind of the receiver. Therefore, you or some other competent person should proofread each message carefully. As the one who submits the report or signs the letter or memo, you have the ultimate responsibility for content and accuracy. Several proven procedures and techniques for effective proofreading are given in Appendix C.

Following the planning and composing process will achieve the goals and purposes of your message.

After completing the tasks involved in composing the content of your message, you arrive at its final version. This version should be understood clearly by your receiver, stimulate the action you want, build a favorable relationship between you and the receiver, and increase organizational goodwill. In addition, your message should achieve its specific purposes for the communication situation.

DETERMINING VOCABULARY LEVEL

Message analysis includes determining vocabulary level to assure receiver understanding.

As you know, one of your primary concerns in composing effective business messages is using a vocabulary level that your receiver will understand. Vocabulary level, as used in this book, refers to the level of difficulty of the words and combinations of words in messages.

Readability formulas can be used to check vocabulary levels.

There are several readability formulas that can be used to calculate vocabulary levels for your messages. These formulas—such as the Gunning, Flesch, Dale-Chall, and Fry formulas—are available in most libraries. They generally measure the average length of sentences and the percentage of "difficult" words. While the counting necessary to use the formulas can be done manually, several of the formulas have been computerized and can be easily used with electronic media.

Readability formulas show approximate grade level.

The vocabulary level ratings obtained from readability formulas generally reflect the approximate grade level a person would need to understand the written material. For example, a rating of 12 would mean that a person would have to be able to read at the twelfth grade level to fully comprehend the material.

Readability analysis does not check the actual words you use or the manner in which you combine those words into sentences. An analysis will not show if the writing is accurate or inaccurate, interesting or dull, valuable or not valuable to a receiver. Use readability ratings as guides, and use common sense in their application. A message may have a low readability rating because it uses short words and short sentences even though it uses difficult technical words. By contrast, a message may have a high readability rating because it uses long words and long sentences even though the sentences are easy to understand and the words are familiar. In addition, an appropriate grade level for a message does not necessarily guarantee that the message will communicate effectively. An inappropriate grade level for a message, however, does mean that the message should be examined for word choice and sentence length.

Common sense must be used with readability formulas.

As you compose a message for a given communication situation, keep in mind the estimated vocabulary level of your receiver. A message at too high a vocabulary level will not be understood clearly by your receiver. A message at too low a vocabulary level will insult your receiver or not hold his or her attention and interest.

A message at too high a level will not be understood; too low, insulting.

The middle-level receiver's vocabulary level will fall between grades 8 and 12. Most high school graduates' vocabulary levels will be at grade levels 10 to 12. A rule of thumb: Business messages written at the 8th to 12th grade levels will communicate clearly with most receivers. Readability formulas are important tools for analyzing your messages. It is critical that you use these tools for analyzing the vocabulary levels of form letters or memos, newsletters, speech copy, magazines, books, and similar materials that will be read (or heard) by many receivers. It is also recommended that you use these tools periodically to check the vocabulary levels of your messages to only one receiver.

The middle-level receiver is between grades 8 and 12. Most high school graduates read at grade levels 10 to 12.

BEING ETHICAL

Being ethical in your communication is essential to a successful personal life and business career. Effective interpersonal relationships are built on trust, honesty, and fairness. Promises made are kept. Fair disclosure of information is provided.

Being ethical is essential for success.

> Truth has no special time of its own.
> Its hour is now—always.
>
> *Albert Schweitzer (1875-1965)*

Being ethical is enlightened self-interest. It costs you far more in time, money, and effort to repair the damage caused by false messages than truthful,

Unethical messages are costly.

forthcoming messages would cost in the first place. In addition, it is not always possible to repair the damage caused by an unethical message. Your credibility is lost, interpersonal relationships are destroyed, and your career is impaired.

ETHICS IN BUSINESS TODAY

Unethical behavior receives much publicity.

Today we frequently read in the newspaper or hear on television about unethical behavior in business and government. Insider trading, bribery, misleading advertising, misrepresentation of facts, cover-ups, and stonewalling are seemingly common.

Most people are ethical.

In fact, only a small percentage of business and professional people behave in unethical ways. Those who are unethical do not succeed in the long run, and most of them are not successful even in the short run. Millions of business transactions based on trust and honesty are successfully completed each day. Merchandise is fairly advertised, orders are received, quality products are shipped, and appropriate payment is made on time. If businesses and their customers did not relate this way, businesses could not exist.

Today about 90 percent of large U.S. companies have codes of ethics.

The most successful businesses are managed and operated by ethical employees. Today, about 90 percent of large U.S. companies have codes of ethics to help guide their employees' behavior. Many of these companies have training sessions in which the codes are discussed, and procedures for assuring compliance throughout the company are explained. After a number of years of inattention, most businesses now realize the importance of a strong sense of individual and corporate values.

After years of inattention, businesses are now stressing ethical behavior.

An example of the way a company and its managers faced an ethical situation may make it clearer how most businesses try to operate today. Johnson & Johnson handled the Tylenol tragedy a few years ago with openness, honesty, and positive action. In this crisis situation an unknown criminal poisoned Tylenol capsules resulting in the deaths of seven people. Unaware of the cause of the deaths, Johnson & Johnson managers based their reactions to this crisis on the company's 40-year-old credo.

A company credo guides ethical behavior.

The Johnson & Johnson credo shown in Illustration 3-10 reflects the company's ethical philosophy. It is based on the belief that business is a moral undertaking for the benefit of society with responsibilities that go far beyond sales and profits.

Johnson & Johnson believes it exists to benefit society.

The Johnson & Johnson credo lists the company's first responsibility as being to customers—". . . to the doctors, nurses, and patients, to mothers and all others who use our products and services." The second responsibility is to the company's employees. The paragraph in the credo regarding employees includes the sentence "We must provide competent management, and their actions must be just and ethical." The third responsibility listed is to the communities where the Johnson & Johnson employees live and work. Finally, the responsibility to stockholders to make a sound profit is listed.

Managers' actions must be just and ethical.

Our Credo

We believe our first responsibility is to the doctors, nurses, and patients, to mothers and all others who use our products and services. In meeting their needs everything we do must be of high quality. We must constantly strive to reduce our costs in order to maintain reasonable prices. Customers' orders must be serviced promptly and accurately. Our suppliers and distributors must have an opportunity to make a fair profit.

We are responsible to our employees, the men and women who work with us throughout the world. Everyone must be considered as an individual. We must respect their dignity and recognize their merit. They must have a sense of security in their jobs. Compensation must be fair and adequate, and working conditions clean, orderly and safe. Employees must feel free to make suggestions and complaints. There must be equal opportunity for employment and advancement for those qualified. We must provide competent management, and their actions must be just and ethical.

We are responsible to the communities in which we live and work and to the world community as well. We must be good citizens—support good works and charities and bear our fair share of taxes. We must encourage civic improvements and better health and education. We must maintain in good order the property we are privileged to use, protecting the environment and natural resources.

Our final responsibility is to our stockholders. Business must make a sound profit. We must experiment with new ideas. Research must be carried on, innovative programs developed and mistakes paid for. New equipment must be purchased, new facilities provided and new products launched. Reserves must be created to provide for adverse times. When we operate according to these principles, the stockholders should realize a fair return.

Johnson & Johnson

First responsibility is to customers.

Second responsibility is to employees.

Third responsibility is to communities.

Fourth responsibility is to stockholders.

Printed with the permission of Johnson & Johnson, One Johnson & Johnson Plaza, New Brunswick, NJ 08933

Illustration 3-10 Johnson & Johnson Company Credo

Based on their company's credo, Johnson & Johnson managers reacted to the Tylenol crisis ethically and decisively. Communications were developed to alert the public and medical community. All Tylenol capsules were removed from stores, production was halted, and complete cooperation was given to the media and public health officials. Society was well served by this private company. Its managers' ethical behavior was the foundation for the comeback of Tylenol in new tamper-proof containers. Less than six months after the tragedy, Johnson & Johnson had regained 70 percent of its previous market, and Tylenol—a valuable aspirin-free pain reliever—was again available to the public.

The Tylenol crisis was handled ethically.

The Johnson & Johnson story is a model of ethical managerial decisions and communications. This is just one example of the positive, responsible behavior of most companies today.

HOW YOU CAN BE ETHICAL

How can you be sure you are an ethical communicator? First, you determine exactly what "being ethical" means. Second, you adopt principles or develop systems that work best for you in choosing ethical content for your messages.

WHAT BEING ETHICAL MEANS. Being ethical means doing what is right to achieve what is good. While the meaning of being ethical varies somewhat from culture to culture, what is right and what is good are generally similar worldwide. In business communication, what is right refers to the responsibility to include information in your messages that ought to be there—information that is fully adequate for the circumstance, truthful in every sense, and not deceptive in any way.

What is good refers to the end result of the communication. The ethical ideal is to strive for the highest good attainable for all of those involved in the communication.

Right and good behavior and communication are illustrated in the excellent manner in which the Tylenol crisis was handled. Accurate information freely given to protect society was the hallmark of the Johnson & Johnson managers' actions and communications.

CHOOSING ETHICAL CONTENT FOR YOUR MESSAGES. Choosing ethical content for your messages requires the same analytical and practical skills as does sound business leadership. Being ethical in your communication requires that you determine—from among all the alternatives—the right and good information in given situations.

In many communication situations you will be faced with gray areas. Very few situations in the real world are entirely right or entirely wrong. There may be competing interests among your superiors, subordinates, customers, suppliers, stockholders, and others. To help you make decisions on message content in situations of moral complexity, principles and systems that have worked well for others are provided in the following sections. Choose among these suggestions to find the one or the combination that works best for you. Use the principles and systems you choose on a daily basis to assure yourself that your business messages are ethical.

AN EXAMPLE OF AN ETHICAL SITUATION—A PLANT CLOSING

As you study the principles and systems for making ethical decisions, think about the following example: Assume you are the manager responsible for the development and transmission of messages to various receivers that will

Margin notes:

Being ethical means:
- Doing what is right

- Achieving the highest good

Choosing ethical content requires analytical skills.

You will be faced with gray areas and competing interests.

Reflect on this communication situation as you review the ethical principles and systems.

announce that one of your corporation plants is closing. The plant employs 3,000 people and is one of three major plants in a community of 25,000.

The receivers of your messages will include the plant's current employees, businesspersons in the communities where the plant is located and where the employees live, suppliers to the plant, local and state government officials, managers and supervisors within the corporation, the corporation's stockholders, the corporation's customers, and the general public.

Reflect on the receivers' needs in this communication situation. The employees need to know as soon as possible about the plant closing so they can search for other jobs. The local community and government officials need to know so they can seek other industry to replace the lost jobs and tax income. The suppliers need to know so they can seek replacement customers. The corporate managers and stockholders want a smooth transition and need the plant to be cost-effective until the day it closes. The corporation needs to maintain its good image with its customers and the general public.

How do you decide what is the right information that ought to be in your messages to these receivers? How do you resolve what is the highest good attainable for all those involved? After the following ethical principles and systems have been presented, this plant closing communication situation will be analyzed.

ETHICAL PRINCIPLES AND SYSTEMS

THE GOLDEN RULE. The Golden Rule is "Do unto others as you would have them do unto you." This simply stated, fundamental moral imperative is a helpful ethical principle for many business communicators. They analyze the communication problems facing them. They then analyze the alternative content that they could select for their messages. They choose content based on the full disclosure, honest message they would want to have if they were the receiver(s).

> Do unto others as you would have them do unto you.

THE SOCIAL UTILITY CONCEPT. The concept of social utility provides a higher level system than does the simpler Golden Rule principle. To determine ethical content for a message using this approach, you first list all the alternative content from which you could choose. You then consider the positive and negative impacts of each of the alternatives on all those affected by your message. Those content alternatives that produce the greatest good and the least harm for all affected are chosen for inclusion in the message. Self-interest is overridden using this approach by the requirement that everyone's good be counted equally.

> Choose content that produces the greatest good and least harm.

THE UNIVERSAL LAW CONCEPT. Using the universal law approach, the actions and the alternatives that could be chosen for message content are categorized as good or evil for society as a whole. The question

> Be willing to require everyone to send the same kind of message.

the business communicator asks is, "Would I be willing to require all others in the same circumstances to send the same kind of message I am sending?" The answer has to be yes. You would have to be willing, for the welfare and betterment of society, to establish a universal law requiring all others to behave as you are behaving.

THE FOUR-WAY TEST. Rotary International, a civic club with members throughout the world, has a unique set of questions for promoting ethical decisions, behavior, and communication. The test, referred to as The Four-Way Test of Things We Think, Say or Do, is as follows:

Be sure your content is truthful, fair, friendly, and beneficial to all.

1. Is it the TRUTH?
2. Is it FAIR to all concerned?
3. Will it build GOODWILL and BETTER FRIENDSHIPS?
4. Will it be BENEFICIAL to all concerned?

Printed with the permission of Rotary International, One Rotary Circle, Evanston, IL 60201

This test stresses truth, fairness, goodwill, good interpersonal relationships, and benefits to all concerned. It becomes a helpful, practical way for many for implementing the social utility and universal law concepts.

OTHER PRACTICAL APPROACHES. Two other systems for making ethical decisions—one from the business world and the other from an ethics resource center—may be helpful to you.

Donald V. Seibert of the J. C. Penney Company suggests that the following questions be asked to assure ethical decisions:

1. Am I personally proud of this action?
2. Am I comfortable with this decision?
3. Would I feel comfortable if it were known by my associates, my friends, my family, the public in general?

''Morality Can Be Contagious,'' address by Donald V. Seibert, Chairman of the Board, J. C. Penney Company, Inc., before the Religious Heritage of America, Washington, D. C., October 9, 1978.

Examine your values, conscience, and the potential reactions of others.

These questions help you analyze message content in three important ways. Question 1 helps you apply your personal values to the message content. Question 2 encourages you to examine your conscience. Question 3 enables you to analyze what the reactions of those other than you and your receiver would be if they were to hear or read the message. This simple, straightforward system may work well for you.

Another practical approach has been developed by Ivan Hill of the Ethics Resource Center in Washington, D.C. Hill suggests using this method to analyze situations involving ethics until you get in the habit of telling the truth and trying to be ethical. He offers these four guidelines for dealing with ethical questions:

1. Look at the community in which you live and society in general. What is the normal behavior in this society? Relate your question to this normative standard of conduct. How does it fit the social norms that reflect the ethical principles society has developed as its core guidelines?
2. Now, consider your question again and think about the laws of your community, of your state, and of your nation. How does your question satisfy the laws?
3. Then search out an answer from your conscience. No one knows exactly what a conscience is, but everyone seems to have one.
4. There is still one more step. Most people believe in God, but if you don't, imagine there is a God—ask him your question. He may only give you a hint as to what you should do, but ask Him anyway.

"Common Sense and Everyday Ethics," Ivan Hill, a brochure published by the Ethics Resource Center, Inc., Washington, D.C., 1980, p. 12.

In using this system, first, you make sure your message content meets applicable community and society standards of behavior. Second, you make sure your message is legal. Third, you apply your own personal values to the content. Fourth, you seek guidance from a higher power. This system emphasizes using acceptable standards of conduct in ethical decisionmaking.

Test your content against community standards, the law, your conscience, and a higher power.

AN ANALYSIS OF THE PLANT CLOSING SITUATION

Let's apply the ethical principles and systems given in the preceding section to the communication situation described earlier: You are the manager responsible for the development of messages to various receivers in which you announce a plant closing.

The ethical issues in this communication situation involve competing interests: the corporation's managers and stockholders will want a cost-effective plant closing that does not involve employee turmoil, the plant's employees will need to find other jobs, government officials will be concerned about lost tax income and community development, suppliers will be concerned about replacing lost business, the corporation's customers will need a new source of supply, and the public at large will have a general interest.

The plant closing communication situation involves competing interests.

When do you send the messages? What information do you include in different messages for different receivers? How do you best achieve the highest good for all those involved in the communication?

Seek the greatest good
for all receivers.

The ethical principles and systems can guide you to develop timely, truthful messages. These messages should contain full information and provide the greatest good to all the receivers. With some assumptions about detailed facts in this communication situation, here are logical, ethical decisions regarding your messages:

1. The messages will go out at the same time. They will be sent several months in advance of the closing to give the large number of people who will be hurt time to try to take corrective actions.
2. Information will be provided to the plant's employees and managers that will assist them in the transition. Information will also be provided to the employees to help them find other jobs.
3. Regret that the plant has to be closed will be expressed to all receivers. A truthful, open explanation of why the action had to be taken will be given.
4. The corporation's stockholders and the corporation's managers will be reminded how the timing and content of your messages—to employees, customers, the general public, and others—best serve the corporation's long-term interests. Even if the actions do not result in increased profits, the actions ought be taken because they are the right things to do and benefit the greatest number of people.

A FINAL COMMENT ON BEING ETHICAL

Being ethical is
contagious.

Being ethical in your communication is not only essential and the right thing to do, it is also contagious. Others will follow your lead when they observe the success you experience in interpersonal relationships and in your career. All will benefit from being ethical.

ASSURING LEGALITY

You and your organization could be sued or prosecuted if you violate the law in your business messages. Thousands or even millions of dollars could be lost. Prison terms might have to be served. To assure the legality of your written or oral messages, you must be aware of the law that applies to those messages. Ignorance of the law does not excuse violators.

Learn the legal
requirements that relate
to your work.

You should try to learn the law, court decisions, and administrative regulations that relate to your work. If you are considering content for a message and are not sure about its legality, you should consult with an attorney or other competent authority. Most companies have attorneys who are available to employees. In addition, some company officials—personnel officers, purchasing agents, and others—have specialized knowledge of legal requirements in their areas of responsibility.

A review of some of the most important legal considerations will assist you in assuring the legality of your messages.

CONTRACT COMMUNICATION

The oral and written communication with the customers of your company must meet the requirements of several laws. Among the most important forms of communication is the contract.

PLAIN ENGLISH LAWS. Several states have passed "plain English laws" requiring that contracts be written so consumers can understand them. Some states specify readability levels, average number of syllables per word, layout, size of print, and many other content details. These laws require careful analysis of a contract's content. Other states have more general guidelines such as requiring contracts to contain understandable words, short sentences, and short paragraphs. If the principles of business communication given in Chapter 2 are followed, the requirements of plain English laws would be met.

Plain English laws are common.

WARRANTIES AND GUARANTEES. The Uniform Commercial Code, the Consumer Product Warranty Act, the Federal Trade Commission Improvement Act, and similar legislation cover express warranties (promises made willingly by the seller) and implied warranties (promises created by law). An example of an express warranty is a manufacturer putting in writing the willingness to replace a product during the first year if it proves defective due to quality of construction or materials. An example of an implied warranty provided by law is that the product must be satisfactory for the purpose intended. Promises to consumers and others can be made orally or in writing so be sure you only warrant to the extent you intend.

Warranties can be express or implied.

CREDIT AND COLLECTIONS COMMUNICATION

Many state and federal laws specify the responsibilities of businesses in issuing credit and collecting debts. Here are some of the more important federal laws.

Credit must be equally available.

EQUAL CREDIT OPPORTUNITY ACT. This law requires that credit be equally available to all creditworthy customers. It also covers how credit worthiness is determined. The content of credit applications and any oral questioning of credit applicants must not include references to race, color, religion, or national origin. Credit decisions cannot be based on age, marital status, or future personal plans. The law requires that credit refusals be in writing.

Billing and collection procedures are specific.

FAIR CREDIT BILLING ACT. This law protects credit card users against false charges made to their accounts. It specifies in detail the procedures that consumers and creditors must follow to resolve problems.

FAIR DEBT COLLECTION ACT. This law specifies in detail what bill collectors can and cannot do. What can and cannot be said, how many times you may call the debtor, to whom you may write (not relatives or employers), and other requirements are a part of this law.

Credit terms must be clear.

FEDERAL TRUTH-IN-LENDING ACT. Requirements for full disclosure of credit terms to consumers are stated in this law. Lenders and creditors must clearly disclose service charges, finance charges, and the effective annual interest rate. How the terms and conditions of loans must be specified—such as number of payments and due dates of payments—is covered in this law. It also provides that the borrower has the right to cancel within three business days after signing the contract.

EMPLOYMENT COMMUNICATION

Most managers, supervisors, and employees need to know the legal requirements affecting employment communication. Much of what can and cannot be said or written about employees is specified in the following laws.

Discrimination in employment communication is illegal.

THE CIVIL RIGHTS ACT. This law and its amendments prohibit discrimination in employment. Hiring, firing, compensation, and other conditions of employment cannot be based on race, color, religion, sex, or national origin. This act, first passed in 1964, is landmark legislation and every business communicator should be aware of its requirements. Affirmative Action programs have evolved from the Civil Rights Act, the Equal Employment Opportunity Act, and other extensive federal, state, and local employment regulations.

Communications between labor and management must meet legal requirements.

LABOR-MANAGEMENT RELATIONS ACT. Communications between managers and workers, particularly concerning unions, are guided by this law. Details regarding the implementation of this law are provided by the National Labor Relations Board.

THE PRIVACY ACT. This law gives employees access to information about themselves. It also limits the use of personnel information to the purpose for which it was collected. For example, it is important when serving as a reference that you respond only to specific requests that have been approved by the employee. Further, your comments should relate only to job performance that is documented. Any reference should be objective, given in good faith, and without malice.

Information about employees must be kept private.

OTHER INTERPERSONAL COMMUNICATION

Common law and other legislation cover such important legal considerations as defamation and fraud.

DEFAMATION. The law does not permit you to make statements that injure the reputation or character of another person. Such statements, called defamation, are libel (written) or slander (oral). To be considered defamation, the statements must be false, made to or read by a third person, and cause some injury. True statements can be considered defamation if they are made with the intent of harming the other person.

Libel and slander are statements that injure a reputation.

FRAUD. Lying that causes another person monetary damage is called fraud. Fraud exists when these conditions are proven: (1) a communicator misrepresents or conceals a material fact, (2) the misrepresentation was made knowingly or with a reckless disregard for the truth, (3) the misrepresentation was made with the intention to deceive, (4) the deceived person relied on the false statement, and (5) monetary damage was incurred by the deceived person. Fraud can be committed by words or conduct and includes false advertising and false endorsement of products or services.

Fraud is lying that causes another person monetary damage.

USING UNBIASED LANGUAGE

The use of unbiased language is a final and important consideration in the composition of business messages. Fair and balanced treatment of all individuals regardless of race, creed, sex, age, or socio-economic status is essential in a democracy. Such treatment is vital to the maintenance of favorable human relationships.

    You will want to avoid all words that have unfavorable denotations or connotations in their reflection on any individuals. The use of such language

Message analysis includes assuring unbiased language for fair and balanced treatment of all individuals.

Using biased language not only offends those referred to, but also many others.

The English language structure is biased as to sex stereotyping.

Listeners and readers tend to picture a male when man, he, or chairman is used.

You should avoid these images. See Appendix D for more guidelines.

will not only offend those to whom the references are made, but many other persons will be offended as well. Respect for the dignity and worth of all persons is compatible with being a responsible citizen. To increase your effectiveness as a business communicator, analyze your messages to eliminate any biased language.

Using unbiased language is a special challenge because of the structure of the English language. The English language implies stereotyping of males and females because of (1) the generic use of masculine, singular pronouns—pronouns used to represent both men and women; (2) the generic use of the word *man*; (3) the existence of masculine marker words; and (4) the use of certain words, phrases, and constructions that involve stereotyping. Fortunately, the structure of our language does not stereotype individuals on the basis of race.

Listeners and readers, however, tend to subconsciously picture a male when words such as *man*, *he*, or *chairman* are used. This is true even though such words are used generically—used to represent both men and women. These images should be avoided in your business messages. The examples that follow suggest that many alternatives to language stereotyping are available. Other alternatives are shown in Appendix D.

Biased	Unbiased
businessman	businessperson, business executive, manager
chairman	chairperson, moderator, chair, group leader, presiding officer
cameraman	camera operator
foreman	supervisor
lady or female doctor	doctor
The student should determine which principle of business communication gives him the most difficulty and then practice using it.	The student should determine which principle of business communication gives the most difficulty and then practice using it.
When an individual travels by plane, he is able to work en route.	When individuals travel by plane, they are able to work en route.
If he is not sure he wants what he is buying, he should not buy it.	If you are not sure you want what you are buying, you should not buy it.
the ladies and the men, the girls in the office	the women and the men, the ladies and the gentlemen, the girls and the boys
Gentlemen: Dear Sirs: (letter salutations)	Ladies and Gentlemen: (or avoid salutation by using Simplified Block Letter style shown in Chapter 9)

CONCLUSION

You can develop effective business messages by following the process and guidelines outlined in this chapter. The process for planning and composing business messages—determine the purposes, analyze the receiver, and compose the content—is a proven approach. The recommendations for determining vocabulary level, being ethical, assuring legality, and using unbiased language can assist you further in developing business messages that communicate effectively with your receiver.

You can develop effective business messages by using the planning and composing process, controlling vocabulary level, being ethical, assuring legality, and using unbiased language.

DISCUSSION QUESTIONS

1. Explain the two tasks involved in determining purposes of business messages.
2. Explain how to analyze the receiver for the you-viewpoint.
3. When you have multiple receivers of the same message, for example, a speech to a group, how do you analyze the receiver for the you-viewpoint?
4. Name the six tasks in composing the message content and briefly describe each one.
5. Give the advantages and disadvantages of (a) oral messages and (b) written messages.
6. When should you use the direct plan and when should you use the indirect plan for messages?
7. Describe the two major parts of outlining message content.
8. Discuss how word processing equipment affects the drafting of messages.
9. Discuss editing and revising in the composition of business messages.
10. Explain how readability formulas can be of value in developing business messages.
11. Discuss the status of ethics in business today.
12. What does being ethical mean? Discuss.
13. Describe how you could use the ethical principles and systems given in this chapter in choosing ethical content for your business messages.
14. Describe the social utility and universal law concepts.
15. Explain what plain English laws are.
16. What is the major thrust of the credit and collections laws?
17. Tell how the Civil Rights Act and the Privacy Act affect employment communication.

18. Describe what is meant by defamation and fraud.
19. How is the English language biased in structure? Discuss.
20. Are most people today offended if business communicators continue to use male pronouns, masculine marker words, and language that stereotypes? Discuss.

APPLICATION EXERCISES

1. For years Raymond Bowling has been a regular mail-order customer of Houghton's Big Man's Clothing. Recently he became quite angry at Houghton's and told them so. He had requested that a pair of hiking shoes be special ordered for him (they were not a standard catalog item). Lesley Jones, a new order clerk trying to be efficient, promptly dropped a handwritten postcard to him saying, "The shoes you want are not available; they are not in the catalog." The clerk did not know that Houghton's gladly special orders items for an additional fee. Mr. Bowling wrote to you, Houghton's Marketing Manager, and said, "I have spent over $5,000 with you in the past ten years. If you have quit special ordering, you have just lost a good customer! In fact, you will never hear from me again!"

   a. Analyze this communication situation. What should the primary and secondary purposes be for your response to Mr. Bowling? What would be included in your content outline?

   b. Analyze the receiver, Raymond Bowling, in the four areas of knowledge, interests, opinions, and emotional state.

   c. Specify the type of message—written or oral—that you would send to Mr. Bowling. Give your reasons for your selection.

   d. Select the organizational plan you would use for Mr. Bowling's message and tell why.

   e. Edit, proofread, and rewrite the following message to Mr. Bowling.

   Dear Mr. Boling:

   I am glad to tell you your past business is very much appreciated and I am glad to tell you that Houghton's is steel glad to order special for you. Lesley Jones, a new order clerk, didn't no about our policy and got carried away. She knows now looks forward to getting your next order. The shoes you wanted have been ordered and you can get them sent to you in two weeks. Write us another letter if you still want them. Thank you for your many years of association with Houghton's.

2. Using the principles of business communication, edit and revise the following passage:

   While many hundreds of thousands attend the game of baseball in the major leagues every season of every year, less than 20 percent of these many, many fans see any more than one game a year each year of the season. Repeat business is what the team owners think would increase their business profitability more than any other thing such as trying to get additional new fans who will attend one game.

3. Interview a manager and ask the following questions: (a) When you have to send a message to some person or persons, how do you decide whether to send a written message or an oral message? (b) In what communication situations do you use the direct plan? (c) In what communication situations do you use the indirect plan? (d) How much editing and revising of your messages do you do? (e) Who proofreads the final versions of your messages?

4. Go to a library or other resource center and research material that will enable you to develop a list of (a) various types of written messages and (b) various types of oral messages.

5. Briefly describe (a) five situations in which you would use the direct plan for messages and (b) five situations in which you would use the indirect plan for messages.

6. Edit and revise the following message so that it communicates more clearly and concisely to a middle-level American receiver:

   It is excruciatingly clear that in order to ascend to the new heights of sales to achieve the new sales quotas the salesmen and saleswomen must dramatically and definitely increase their efforts. Here are the things they must do whenever: (a) Get out in the field more of the time (b) practice, practice, practice and improve their presentations that they make. This will ultimately result in more— more commissions for them and more income over expenses, or profit, for the company organization.

7. Write the following paragraph exactly as it is. Use double spacing. Proofread the paragraph by marking errors with the standard editing symbols.

   Proofreadingsymbols air helfull comunikation tech neeks betweeen and orginater of messages and The perparer of the message It is suggested thet you larn and use thes smbols in yer editting revising, and Proofreading efforts

8. Select an ethical principle or system or a combination of them that you think would be helpful to you in choosing ethical content for your messages. Tell how your selection would help you.

9. Report actual examples you have observed of ethical and unethical communication. Do not use real names.

10. Suggest ideas for ethical content for messages for each of the following communication situations:
    a. A department manager is being denied a budget request important to the success of her department.
    b. An employee who does not have the aptitude for the work is being told he is being fired.
    c. A company is developing an advertisement for its newly discovered hair restorer that works for some bald people but not all.
11. Bring to class an advertisement whose content appears to be unethical—not fully truthful or not in the best interests of consumers. Explain why you think the advertisement is unethical.
12. Over a 48-hour period, record all evidences of unethical behavior in business or government that you find in newspapers or magazines or hear on television or radio. Report your findings to the class.
13. Over a 48-hour period, record all evidences of illegal business communication that you find in newspapers or magazines or hear on television or radio. Report your findings to the class.
14. Get together with five or six other students in your class and discuss the topic, "Businesses are more ethical today than they were ten years ago." Appoint one student in your group to report a summary of the group's discussion to the class.
15. Change the language in the following sentences so that it is unbiased.
    a. A manager must inform all his employees of such changes. (*Hint: Eliminate the pronoun.*)
    b. Now is the time for an individual to make his move in the stock market. (*Hint: Change from singular to plural.*)
    c. When he swims, he exercises every muscle in his body. (*Hint: Use genderless words.*)
    d. The salesperson achieved his quota. (*Hint: Change to the passive voice.*)
    e. When an employee retires, he is entitled to full fringe benefits at cost. (*Hint: Repeat the noun instead of using the pronoun.*)
    f. An individual must adjust his thinking to keep up with the times. (*Hint: Include feminine pronoun.*)
    g. All mankind should look to the future. (*Hint: Use an appropriate substitute for the generic man.*)
    h. The insuranceman will call. (*Hint: Use up-to-date substitutes for occupational titles.*)
    i. The laundress provided excellent services. (*Hint: Avoid words that unnecessarily identify gender.*)
    j. This is obviously man's work. (*Hint: Avoid language that is demeaning, patronizing, or limiting.*)

CHAPTER 4

COMMUNICATION TECHNOLOGIES AND TECHNIQUES

LEARNING OBJECTIVES

Your learning objectives for this chapter include the following:

- To identify the need for streamlining the creation and preparation of correspondence
- To recognize the role technology plays in business communication
- To identify the principles used in developing routine and repetitive messages
- To identify the procedures for creating and using guide letters and form paragraphs

STREAMLINING COMMUNICATION

Written communication is an essential but expensive process. The Dartnell Institute of Business Research of Dartnell Corporation conducts an annual survey of correspondence production costs. In 1930, a business letter cost

The cost of producing correspondence is rising.

Labor is the most expensive component of correspondence cost.

30 cents to produce; by 1960, the cost had risen to $1.83; the Dartnell estimate for 1987 was $9.32.[1]

The Dartnell business letter costs are based on seven factors: dictator's time (dictation to secretary), secretary's time, nonproductive labor, fixed costs, materials costs, mailing costs, and filing costs. Illustration 4-1 explains each of these factors. The cost of each factor varies from year to year and from organization to organization; two things, however, do not change—the total cost continues to rise, and labor is the most expensive component.

Dictator's Time

It is assumed that the person creating the correspondence is dictating to a secretary and that it takes eight minutes to complete the dictation of one letter.

Secretarial Time

The recording and transcribing of the dictation, including related activities such as gathering and filing materials and addressing an envelope, is assumed to be 18 minutes.

Nonproductive Labor

The nonproductive labor figure is determined from previous studies and includes absenteeism, interruptions, and time spent waiting for work. In recent years, this portion of the cost has been 15 percent of the labor costs for the two people involved.

Fixed Charges

Fixed charges is a miscellaneous category that includes overhead, depreciation, taxes, fringe benefits, and similar expenses. The current figure is 52 percent of *total* labor costs.

Materials Costs

The costs of stationery, envelopes, carbon paper, copy machine paper, typewriter/printer ribbons or cartridges, and other necessary supplies are reflected in this figure.

Mailing Costs

In addition to postage, this figure includes the cost of gathering, sealing, stamping, and sorting of mail done by personnel other than the secretary.

Filing Costs

Filing costs represent the cost of the time that personnel other than the secretary spend filing and also includes the cost of supplies; equipment costs are prorated.

Source: The Seven Dartnell Factors, Dartnell Institute of Business Research.

Illustration 4-1   Determining Correspondence Costs

---

[1] Dartnell Institute of Business Research

Business communicators must constantly look for ways to halt, slow, or reverse the pattern of increasing communication costs. They must continually try to improve their efficiency in creating and producing written communication without altering the overall effectiveness of the correspondence. Advances in technology can help in this effort.

Technology can help reduce the cost of communicating.

THE DOCUMENT CREATION CYCLE

To fully recognize the impact that technology can have on reducing correspondence costs, a business communicator must understand the document creation cycle (see Illustration 4-2). There are five steps in this cycle: (1) creation; (2) production; (3) reproduction; (4) filing, storage, and retrieval; and (5) distribution.

In traditional offices work is produced manually.

In the traditional office, each of these steps is performed manually. Correspondence and reports are handwritten or dictated to a secretary. They are produced using manual, electric, or limited storage electronic typewriters. If a document contains content or typographical errors, it must be retyped. The retyping portion of the cycle may be repeated several times. The document

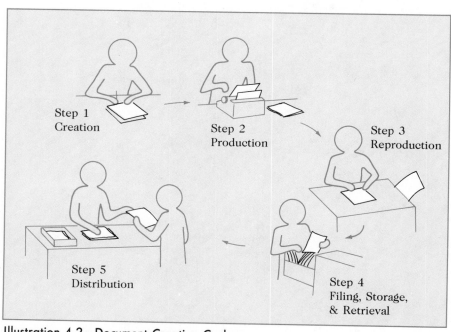

Illustration 4-2   Document Creation Cycle

is then reproduced; carbon paper or photocopiers are used for this purpose. The copies of the document are then filed for later use, usually in a standard filing cabinet. The original document is delivered to the recipient by a messenger (internal distribution) or through the postal service (external distribution). Each of these steps takes time—the longer the time, the higher the cost of the correspondence.

Contemporary offices use electronic equipment.

In a contemporary office the steps of the document creation cycle are performed using electronic equipment. Documents are dictated to a device that stores the message until it can be transcribed. The transcriber listens to each message on the tape and keyboards it using a word processing system. Multiple copies of the document are made by using a high-speed printer or a sophisticated photocopier. The document is stored (filed) on a magnetic medium and is distributed by electronic communication channels. Illustration 4-3 depicts the document cycle in a contemporary office.

An emerging trend is the creation of "hybrid" document creation cycles—those designed to respond to the changing nature of a particular office and to mesh with its resources. For example, a message creator might use a computer and word processing software to prepare a draft version of a document. The

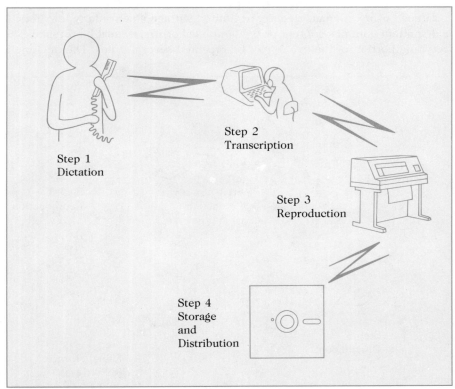

Illustration 4-3   Document Creation Cycle in a Contemporary Office

secretary would also use a computer and word processing software to format the document and to edit it to eliminate grammar, punctuation, and spelling errors. The edited version of the document would then be returned to its creator for revision.

COMMUNICATION TECHNOLOGY

The term **telecommunication** commonly describes any system that sends and receives messages electronically (over wires) or electromagnetically (over optical fibers or by radio waves). Text, data, graphics, voice, and video messages are among the items that may be transmitted. Equipment such as telephones, teletypewriters, word processors, computers, facsimile systems, and video monitors aid in sending and receiving the messages. Items such as text and graphics or video and voice may be combined for simultaneous transmission and simultaneous reception.

With telecommunication technology, neither time nor distance are obstacles to communication. Messages may be created, sent, or retrieved at any time of any day. With compatible equipment at each location, it is possible to send a message to the person seated at the next desk or to someone in a foreign country.

While some organizations own and operate their own telecommunication systems, other organizations use commercial systems owned and operated by service companies or the United States government. Before choosing the most appropriate electronic message systems for your needs, you will want to consult telecommunications experts in your company, professional and trade organizations in the field of telecommunications, and vendors. Some of the more widely used communication technology is described in the following sections.

> **Telecommunication** refers to any system that sends and receives messages electronically or electromechanically.

> Neither time nor distance is an obstacle in telecommunication.

> Telecommunication equipment must be compatible.

> Both private and commercial telecommunication systems are available.

> When choosing electronic message systems, consult with telecommunication specialists.

ELECTRONIC MESSAGE SYSTEMS

Electronic message systems—also referred to as **electronic mail** or **e-mail** systems—are increasingly being used as substitutes for traditional letters, memos, and telephone calls. The sender uses a computer to create a message that is then transmitted to and stored in the receiver's computer. Directories that are customized for each type of technology are helpful in locating the "address" of a receiver.

> **Electronic mail** is used increasingly to replace letters, memos, and telephone calls.

VOICE-MAIL SYSTEMS

Automated **voice-mail systems** eliminate "telephone tag."

Voice-mail systems are automated message systems that combine a computer and a telephone. The automated features of these systems can include voice message storage and retrieval, message forwarding, call placement, group messages, and password protection. Such systems help avoid the "telephone tag" caused by schedule differences between the calling parties. Messages may be left at the convenience of the caller and retrieved at the convenience of the receiver.

TELETYPEWRITER SYSTEMS

Teletypewriter systems can send inexpensive, brief messages quickly throughout the world.

Although they are among the oldest telecommunication technologies, teletypewriter systems are still used extensively and successfully for transmitting brief written messages at costs considerably lower than long distance telephone calls. These systems send and receive messages using **teletypewriters** that are either individually owned or provided by commercial services. Individuals who do not have direct access to a teletypewriter may use the services of the United States Postal Service, Western Union, or another organization to send messages or deliver hard copies of messages to receivers.

FACSIMILE SYSTEMS

Facsimile systems can send accurate copies of original documents.

Facsimile (FAX) systems transmit copies of documents over telephone lines at costs lower than overnight mail, express mail, or messenger service. These systems can send accurate copies of text material, numbers, graph illustrations, photographs, signatures, drawings, or any other original information. Receivers then have a hard copy as a permanent record of the message. Documents may vary in size and may be sent to unattended facsimile equipment.

FAX may soon be found in the personal-use market.

Facsimile equipment is already widely used by businesses: orders are placed and acknowledged; contract proposals are sent, and signed contracts are returned; restaurants accept "FAX-food" orders and deliver them to their customers' offices. Forecasters are predicting a rapid growth of FAX machines in the home- or personal-use market. Industry trends include integration of FAX with personal computer and video technology. Linking FAX with a personal computer will allow users to transmit computer-generated documents without having to print a paper copy and carry it to a FAX machine. The integration of FAX and video will allow transmission of camera images for viewing and, if desired, printing at the receiver's location.

TELECONFERENCING

Teleconferencing is a way for people in different locations to hold a meeting without having to travel. The most common form of teleconferencing is the conference call—two or more people at different locations conferring by telephone.

Video conferencing is the most advanced form of teleconferencing. In video conferencing, not only sounds but also pictures are transmitted. Video cameras enable participants to see one another as well as any visual aids that are used.

Organizations that have implemented teleconferencing report that they have been able to keep travel costs to a minimum while improving managerial productivity and involving more people in the decision-making process.

Teleconferencing permits timely, inexpensive meetings for people who are at different locations.

In video conferencing, both sound and pictures are transmitted.

DOCUMENT CREATION AND PREPARATION

The following equipment and software can help reduce correspondence costs while increasing the efficiency with which documents are created and prepared.

DICTATION EQUIPMENT

Dictation equipment can be categorized as portable units, desktop units, or central recording systems. Portable units are the smallest and least expensive devices. They may be used in an office or at any convenient location. Desktop units are small enough to be located on the desk of the person creating the document. Some desktop units may be converted to transcription units. Central recording systems use central recorders that are permanently installed. Dictation is given through handsets or telephones that are linked to the recording system. These systems provide the greatest efficiency and potential for cost savings in large organizations.

There are three types of dictation equipment.

The dictation is recorded on a magnetic medium—tape or disk. This magnetic medium has the same characteristics as that used on tape recorders. The dictation may be replayed many times or be replaced by new dictation. The originator of a document may review and alter its content as often as necessary to assure accuracy and completeness.

Magnetic media permit recording, replaying, and editing of dictation.

Dictation equipment helps cut the costs of creating correspondence.

Machine dictation is faster than handwriting. It is also faster than dictation to a secretary because only one person is involved in the creation process. In addition, transcribers can keyboard faster from machine dictation than from handwriting or shorthand notes. Accuracy is improved because the transcriber is not interpreting poor handwriting or shorthand symbols. Because labor is the most expensive component of written communication, the time saved by using dictation equipment means that communication costs are lower. Information about the dictation process is presented in Chapter 19.

WORD PROCESSING EQUIPMENT AND SOFTWARE

Using word processing equipment helps cut the costs of preparing correspondence.

Dedicated word processors or microcomputers using word processing software are important forms of communication technology. Material is keyboarded and electronically stored in the unit's internal memory or on external media such as magnetic card, tape, or disk. The material may then be recalled so that revisions can be made or copies printed.

Corrections and revisions are made easily.

Today, most word processing equipment has a screen called a monitor or video display terminal (VDT). The characters that are keyed are displayed on the screen. If an error is made, it can be corrected quickly and easily—without retyping the entire document. Content revisions can be made with the same ease. Thus, the creator of a message can edit its content until the desired effect is achieved. Time is saved, and content is improved. That is a winning combination!

Word processing equipment is helpful in other ways to the person who creates correspondence. Two common features of microcomputer word processing software that benefit business writers are the thesaurus and the spell checker.

Two popular word processing features are

• computerized thesaurus

A software thesaurus is the electronic version of the word-choice book writers use to assist them in document creation. The user may highlight a word within a document or key in a new word and direct the computer to search for and display alternatives on the screen. One of the displayed alternatives may be selected, or one of the alternatives may become the basis for another thesaurus search.

• spell checker

By using a spell checker, a writer can direct the computer to match each word in a document against words contained in a pre-stored software dictionary. If a word in the document is not in the dictionary, the word is highlighted, and a listing of possible alternatives is displayed. The user may choose one of the alternatives, reject all the alternatives, or edit the highlighted word.

The number of words in a spell check dictionary varies among word processing software packages. Most packages, however, offer the flexibility of adding words or creating an additional dictionary. Such features allow the user to customize the dictionary.

Using a spell checker does not eliminate the need for proofreading. Spell checkers are not able to detect a content error. Keyboarding or word choice errors such as using *then* for *than*, *of* for *if*, or *you* for *your* will go unnoticed.

Spell checkers do not eliminate proofreading.

DOCUMENT ANALYSIS SOFTWARE

An innovation useful to business communicators is document analysis software. These programs, often called **style checkers**, use artificial intelligence to help writers improve the quality of their messages. Style checkers detect *possible* errors in grammar, punctuation, spelling, capitalization, abbreviation, and number display. They also detect *possible* violations of the principles of business communication such as the use of weak words or passive voice. (The principles of business communication were explained in Chapter 2.) Possible errors and violations are highlighted, and alternatives are suggested. Summary statistics for items such as readability and tone are presented in numeric and graphic form.

Because of the complexity of the English language and the nature of the software program, some items identified by the software are actually correct. The *writer* must decide if a correction is needed and which, if any, of the suggested alternatives is most appropriate. In addition, the creator of the message must verify that the content of the message is accurate. The software won't know if $150 should be $501 or if December 12 should be December 19.

Document analysis software is continually being improved. Until the software is perfected, however, message creators must remember that the software is not a replacement for good writing skills—it is a powerful supplement to them.

Document analysis software helps writers check for errors in

- grammar
- punctuation
- style
- spelling

DESKTOP PUBLISHING

Desktop publishing is an outgrowth of word processing. When used with a computer linked to a laser printer, desktop publishing software allows users to produce newsletters, brochures, reports, and a variety of other business messages with the quality of a professionally typeset document. Text may be organized into columns of varying length and width. Type styles and type sizes may be varied within or among pages. Charts, graphs, or clip-art illustrations can be used to enhance text. Image scanners allow users to incorporate copies of photographs into their communications.

Industry experts predict that the cost of desktop publishing software will decline and that its capabilities will increase. Some suggest that desktop publishing will replace word processing as the dominant technology.

With desktop publishing, professional quality documents can be created "in-house."

ORAL PRESENTATION AIDS

Technology has helped communicators produce and transmit both written and oral messages; technology is also helping businesspersons give more effective large- and small-group presentations. Two popular aids for oral presentations are electronic imagers and desktop slidemakers.

ELECTRONIC IMAGERS

Computer displays can be projected for viewing by an audience.

By using a special liquid crystal display palette that fits onto the top of a standard overhead projector, a speaker can project images from a personal computer to a display screen. No special software is required, but an interface card is needed. Communication and decision making are enhanced because data can be manipulated while the speaker is with the audience.

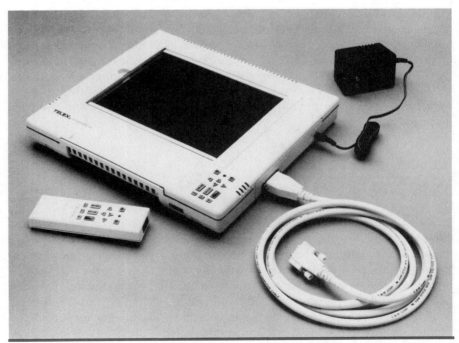

An electronic imager can help a speaker give more effective presentations to large or small groups. The imager is used to project computer images to a large screen, and allows the speaker to manipulate the data that is projected.

DESKTOP SLIDEMAKERS

Images displayed on a computer screen may be duplicated onto 35-mm slides by using a desktop slidemaker. With this equipment, a computer, a camera, and a film recorder are linked. A special computer board is required, and internal storage capacity standards must be met; film is developed by traditional methods. For the most dramatic slides, the computer should have a color display monitor (screen). Image designers should remember to use color for emphasis. By choosing colors carefully and using them wisely, communicators can create slides that are visually appealing and easy to read.

Computer images may be converted into 35-mm slides.

To enhance oral presentations, speakers can use a desktop slidemaker to make 35-mm slides from images displayed on a computer.

SPECIAL COMMUNICATION TECHNIQUES

In addition to effective use of communication technology for your messages, you can increase the cost effectiveness of routine and repetitive messages by adopting the proven techniques described in the following sections.

ROUTINE AND REPETITIVE MESSAGES

Routine messages have a similar content and purpose each time they are created.

A **routine message** is one that is prepared on a regular basis. It has the same or nearly the same content and purpose each time it is sent. A **repetitive message** is one that is sent to many people at the same time. Routine and repetitive messages may be prepared for distribution within an organization or outside the organization.

Virtually every organization has some correspondence that can be classified as routine or repetitive. Perhaps it is a letter to welcome new customers; perhaps it is a postal card notifying clients of an address change. It could be a memo to employees inviting them to the annual company picnic. There are many possibilities. Correspondence creation and preparation costs can be reduced by streamlining the preparation of routine and repetitive messages.

Three preparation techniques are used for routine or repetitive messages:
- form messages
- guide messages
- form paragraphs

Writers should consider using one of three preparation techniques for routine and repetitive documents—form messages, guide messages, or form paragraphs. These preparation techniques make good use of the time of both the message creator and the message preparer. Using form messages, guide messages, and form paragraphs also helps to maintain consistency; similar situations are handled in similar ways. In addition, when form messages are preprinted or when word processing equipment is used to prepare guide messages or form paragraphs, the risk of typographical error is reduced.

Form messages, guide messages, and form paragraphs are all appropriate for good news or neutral messages. Guide messages and form paragraphs are better choices for bad news messages because they can be personalized. Therefore, they have a greater chance of retaining goodwill.

FORM MESSAGES

Form messages are preprinted.

Form messages are preprinted letters or memos. The entire supply may be distributed immediately, or the copies may be kept until needed for routine use. Form messages may be designed in any of four basic styles: plain, fill-in, checklist, or reference.

No additional items are added to plain form messages.

Salutations are very general.

Printing requirements vary.

PLAIN FORM MESSAGES. The plain form message (Illustrations 4-4 and 4-5) is the easiest form message to prepare. The message is completely preprinted—no additional information is filled in at the time the form is used. The salutation is very general: *Dear Customer*, *Dear Subscriber*, and *Dear Friend* are examples. Since plain form messages will probably be sent to both men and women, all gender references are omitted.

Internal plain form messages are generally printed on an organization's interoffice memo stationery. Lengthy external plain form messages are prepared on the company letterhead. The messages are signed before they are

Illustration 4-4   Lengthy External Plain Form Message

THREE CONVENIENT
LOCATIONS

Eastview Bank
452 Stonewall Street
Lancaster, TX 75134-6082
752-555-3520

South Bank
143 Balomede Street
Lancaster, TX 75146-2607
752-555-5144

University Bank
620 Westover Drive
Lancaster, TX 75134-1447
753-555-2711

January 2, 199–

Dear Friend

On December 31, 199–, Acme Bank and First National Bank
merged to become First Acme Bank, the largest independent commercial bank in this area.

There has been no change in ownership; bank policies
that affect you and this community will continue to be
made by people who live and work right here. Likewise,
the same friendly people who have served you as employees of Acme Bank and First National Bank will serve
you at FIRST ACME BANK.

The main benefit to you is **improved service.** The
services which were available to you at each of our individual bank locations are now offered interchangeably
at all three locations of First Acme Bank. Whenever
you wish to make a deposit, borrow money, open an
account, inquire about a balance, or just cash a check,
you'll be able to do it at any of our three convenient
locations. No longer will you have to decide whether
to bank where you live or bank where you work. There
will be an office of First Acme Bank <u>where you need it,</u>
<u>when you need it!</u>

Thank you for your patronage and support; as always, it
is deeply appreciated.

Sincerely

Laurinda K. Frost

Laurinda K. Frost
President

llq

```
Dear Subscriber

Your subscription to Pets has been extended by
ten issues in order to match the rate offered by
Readers' Service.

Thank you for your inquiry; we hope we can
continue to serve you.

M. C. Collier
Subscription Manager

Form 289
```

Illustration 4-5   Brief External Plain Form Message

duplicated. Brief external messages may be printed on a postal card that has the organization's name in the return address area; either a typed or hand-written signature is appropriate. All messages should be carefully proofread before copies are made.

The duplication process varies.

The duplication process for plain form messages depends on the number of copies needed and the quality desired. Photocopying and offset printing are the two most common processes.

Once the plain form messages have been duplicated, they are ready for distribution. If the message is a memo, normal internal distribution procedures are followed. If the document is to be distributed externally, several options exist.

PRESORTED AND THIRD-CLASS VERSUS FIRST-CLASS MAIL.   The United States Postal Service offers four types of service appropriate for form messages: first-class, presorted first-class, carrier route presorted first-class, and third-class mail. First-class mail is the most expensive. The rate per item for first-class business mail is the same as for personal correspondence. In return for the higher rate, mailers receive rapid delivery service. First-class mail to locally designated cities will generally be delivered overnight; first-class mail to locally designated states (usually those within 600 miles) will be delivered in two days. The standard for delivering mail to U. S. locations more than 600 miles from the mailing point is three days.

Bulk mailing is inexpensive.

There are several ways an organization may reduce postage costs. If the items are presorted, the first-class service rate is lowered. Third-class "bulk" mailing service has a much lower rate. Each of these reduced-rate categories has specific quantity, weight, sorting, and coding requirements. A customer service representative of the U. S. Postal Service can provide complete details about these and other services.

Although bulk mail is the least expensive way to mail, there are trade-offs to be considered. First, bulk mail is processed after all forms of first-class mail; therefore, delivery may be delayed. Also, additional labor charges may be incurred in preparing mail to meet the Postal Service requirements. Finally, readers may give less attention to bulk mail; some may even ignore it.

The drawbacks of bulk mailing must be considered.

ENVELOPES VERSUS FOLDED PAPER.   If the sender wishes to create a businesslike impression, the form message is folded and inserted in a No. 10 envelope. For a less formal effect the sender can fold an $8\frac{1}{2}$-inch sheet of paper in half to simulate an envelope and secure the ends with tape or staples. The same effect can be achieved by double folding (the standard fold) an $8\frac{1}{2}$-inch letter size paper and taping or stapling the end. Illustration 4-6 shows the standard fold method. The folding may be done manually or—less expensively—by equipment designed for that purpose. When documents are sent by third-class mail, the bulk mail permit is printed on the form or the envelope before duplication.

Envelopes are not the only way to distribute messages externally.

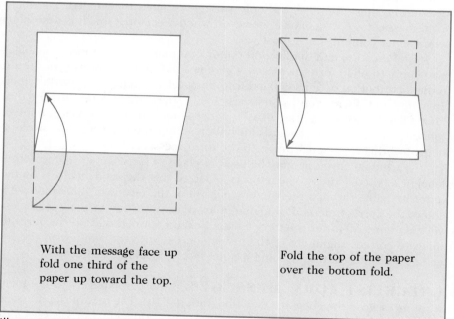

With the message face up fold one third of the paper up toward the top.

Fold the top of the paper over the bottom fold.

Illustration 4-6   Standard Form Simulating an Envelope

INDIVIDUALLY TYPED ADDRESSES VERSUS LABELS.   A personalized appearance will be created by having each mailing address individually typed. This is the most expensive method of addressing envelopes. Individually typed envelopes are, however, more likely to be opened by receivers.

Mailing addresses may be individually typed.

Labels may be prepared.

Prepared labels are an alternative to individually typed addresses. The labels may be prepared from a computer listing or with the aid of word processing or photocopy equipment. Labels may be quickly and easily affixed to envelopes or folded documents by hand or with automated equipment. Prepared labels are less costly than individually typed envelopes; in addition, they may be prepared in ZIP Code sequence thereby reducing the time needed to sort the items for bulk mailing.

Fill-in form messages contain variables.

FILL-IN FORM MESSAGES. The primary difference between a plain form message and a fill-in form message is that the fill-in form message allows the writer to add variables (information that changes). Illustration 4-7 shows a form message that has the date, inside address, and blanks for two content variables as fill-in items. The blank lines shown on the form are optional; if omitted, however, adequate space for the variable must be allowed when the form is designed. A completed fill-in form message is shown in Illustration 4-8.

A fill-in form message is more expensive to produce than a plain form message because each of the variable items has to be individually entered. Unless the date and inside address will be needed in the future, the practice of entering these items as the only variables should be avoided. The fill-in form message is a wise choice, however, when a personal touch is desired or when some content items must vary.

The creation and duplication options outlined for plain form messages also apply to fill-in form messages. There is a difference, however, in the external distribution options. Fill-in form messages are generally inserted in an envelope and distributed by first-class mail. There are two reasons for this. First, fill-in form messages are usually not produced in quantities large enough to meet the minimum standards for bulk mailing. Second, using an envelope helps to bring a personal touch to the form message.

Fill-in form messages may be inserted into window envelopes.

A window envelope may be used in place of a regular envelope with a label or a typed address. The letter is folded so that the inside address on the letter is visible through the window portion of the envelope. Illustration 4-9 shows the correct method of folding a letter for insertion into a window envelope. Some fill-in form letters have a boxed area outlined on the form to indicate correct alignment of the inside address with the window of the envelope. See Illustrations 4-7 and 4-8 for "dot" placement indicators.

CHECKLIST FORM MESSAGES. Another variation of the plain form message is the checklist (see Illustration 4-10). The text of the message is preprinted; the date and the inside address are optional fill-ins. The checklist consists of several items, any or all of which may apply. The person who prepares the message places a checkmark or an X before each item that applies to the receiver of the message. These forms are often completed in handwritten rather than typewritten form. They may be inserted into an individually typed envelope or, if an inside address has been added, into a window envelope. They are mailed first class.

Illustration 4-7   Fill-in Form Message

Robin's Department Store

1032 Fullerton Drive, Detroit, MI   48227-1270   (313) 555-0411

•   •

•   •

Dear

Your check, No. _____ in the amount of $_____,
has been received. It is being returned to you because
the signature has been omitted.

Please sign the check and return it to us in the
enclosed envelope. Your account will then be credited.

Very truly yours

A. C. Carlos
Business Office Manager

kw

Enclosure

BO/665

Illustration 4-8   Completed Fill-in Form Message

1032 Fullerton Drive, Detroit, MI 48227-1270 (313) 555-0411

March 22, 199–

Dominic Valuzio
476 Placid Road
Chicago, IL 60606-2420

Dear Mr. Valuzio

Your check, No. ____3589____ in the amount of $__207.43__ ,
has been received. It is being returned to you because
the signature has been omitted.

Please sign the check and return it to us in the
enclosed envelope. Your account will then be credited.

Very truly yours

A. C. Carlos

A. C. Carlos
Business Office Manager

kw

Enclosure

BO/665

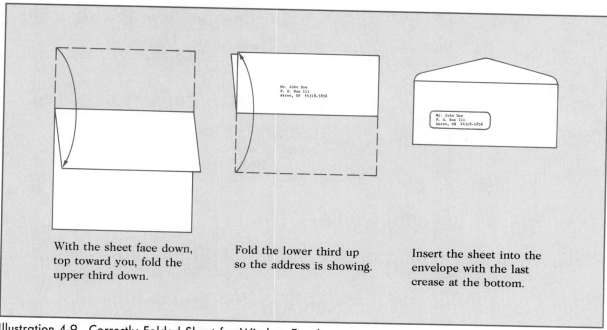

With the sheet face down, top toward you, fold the upper third down.

Fold the lower third up so the address is showing.

Insert the sheet into the envelope with the last crease at the bottom.

Illustration 4-9   Correctly Folded Sheet for Window Envelope

Each checklist form message should be designed to meet one particular need. Separate messages would be created for personnel issues and for customer relations matters. Combining messages into a multipurpose checklist could confuse the reader.

REFERENCE FORM MESSAGES. The reference form message and the checklist form message are similar because they both refer the reader to one or more optional items. In the reference form message, however, the reference numbers or statements are printed on the back of the letter or on a separate sheet (see Illustration 4-11). Readers are asked to match the handwritten or typewritten reference numbers with the appropriate statement(s).

Checklist and reference form messages are similar.

GUIDE MESSAGES

Guide messages (see Illustration 4-12) are used for internal and external routine correspondence that has to be modified to fit special circumstances. A guide message is also used when a writer wishes to personalize a message more than is possible with a preprinted form message.

Illustration 4-10   Checklist Form Message

```
                          ORDER INFORMATION FORM 1




        Dear Customer

        _____    Your order is complete; enjoy your merchandise!

        _____    Item _____ is on special order.  You have
                  been charged for this item, and it will be shipped
                  to you as soon as the merchandise is received at
                  our warehouse.  If it cannot be shipped within
                  three weeks from the date of this letter, a credit
                  memo will be issued.

        _____    Item _____ has been discontinued; a full
                  refund is enclosed.

        _____    Item _____ does not come in the size re-
                  quested on your order.  A credit memo is enclosed;
                  please resubmit your order or request a refund.

        _____    Item _____ does not come in the color re-
                  quested on your order.  A credit memo is enclosed;
                  please resubmit your order or request a refund.

        Thank you for placing your order with us; we hope we may
        serve you again in the near future.

        Very truly yours

        L. L. Lewis

        L. L. Lewis
        Distribution Manager

        ght

        Enclosure
```

Illustration 4-11   Reference Number Form Message

ORDER INFORMATION FORM 2

Dear Customer

Thank you for your recent order; part of your merchandise
is enclosed.

A code letter has been entered on your order form beside
each item we were unable to furnish at this time. Simply
compare each code letter on the form with the items
listed below to determine the status of your order.

It has been a pleasure serving you, and we hope to continue to do so in the future.

Very truly yours

L. L. Lewis

L. L. Lewis
Distribution Manager

ght

* *

Code B   This item is on special order. You have been
         charged for the item, and it will be shipped to
         you as soon as the merchandise is received at our
         warehouse. If it cannot be shipped within three
         weeks, a credit memo will be issued.

Code D   This item has been discontinued; a full refund is
         enclosed.

Code S   This item does not come in the size requested on
         your order. A credit memo is enclosed; please
         resubmit your order or request a refund.

Code C   This item does not come in the color requested on
         your order. A credit memo is enclosed; please
         resubmit your order or request a refund.

Illustration 4-12   Guide Message

```
                            GUIDE LETTER 336


         DATE


         INSIDE ADDRESS


         Dear FIRST NAME

         CONGRATULATIONS!

         You are one of the lucky winners in McGuire's BIG BUCKS
         CONTEST.  Your prize, a $ AMOUNT  gift certificate toward
         your next purchase at McGuire's, is enclosed.

         Thank you for helping to make this year's contest such a
         success.

         Sincerely



         Susan O. Yates
         Sales Promotion Specialist

         gyl

         Enclosure
```

The content of a guide message is prepared in advance, but the document is not preprinted. It is stored in hard copy or magnetic form until needed. At that time the variables are identified, and each piece of correspondence is individually prepared. External correspondence is sent by first-class mail.

Guide messages are individually prepared.

FORM PARAGRAPHS

Form messages and guide messages save time, but they do not offer a great deal of content flexibility. In order to gain more flexibility, a writer may use form paragraphs—a series of paragraphs that are prewritten but not preprinted. They are stored in hard copy or magnetic form until needed. The writer then selects the combination of paragraphs appropriate for the message to be written. Variables are supplied, and each message is individually prepared. Internal correspondence is distributed according to the organization's usual procedure; external correspondence is distributed as first-class mail. Time is saved because the paragraphs do not have to be recomposed each time similar situations arise. Illustration 4-13 contains a sample set of form paragraphs; Illustration 4-14 shows how the paragraphs may be combined to form a message.

Form paragraphs give the message creator flexibility.

PREPARING ROUTINE MESSAGES

Whenever a routine form message, guide message, or set of form paragraphs is created, an identifying number or code should be assigned to it. The creator and the preparer of the correspondence refer to the material by using this number or code.

When routine correspondence is to be prepared, the creator refers to a file or notebook in which a copy of each routine message is kept. The creator may dictate specific instructions for preparation of the correspondence, or the instructions may be written on a preprinted form. Illustration 4-15 shows how a creator might dictate instructions for completion of the guide letter shown in Illustration 4-12; Illustration 4-16 shows a completed work request form for composing letters from the form paragraphs in Illustration 4-13. Similar instructions may be given for completion of a fill-in, checklist, or reference form message.

Code numbers are used to identify form messages, guide messages, and form paragraphs.

Illustration 4-13   Form Paragraphs

```
Number                Paragraph (variables underlined)


  1.    Your copy of the sales report for the  number  quarter is
        attached.  Please review the report and share its contents
        with your staff.

  2.    Congratulations!  Your area was the sales leader for the
         number  quarter.

  3.    The figures for this quarter reflect an increase in sales
        of $_____ for your area.

  4.    Please review the attached sales report for the  number
        quarter and share it with your staff.

  5.    The figures indicate that your area had an increase in
        sales of $_____.  This increase represents a fine
        recovery.

  6.    The sales summary for the  number  quarter has been
        completed,  name of salesperson , and we are concerned
        about what the figures indicate.

  7.    Your area has once again suffered a loss in sales.  The
        figures show that your area experienced a decrease in
        sales of $_____.

  8.    The sales figures for the  number  quarter show that your
        area experienced a decrease in sales of $_____.

  9.    The sales figures for the  number  quarter show that your
        area experienced an increase in sales of $_____.  This
        is the  number  consecutive month in which you have shown
        an increase.

 10.    Thank you!  Keep up the good work.

 11.    Your area has a great sales potential, and you have done
        well with it.

 12.    Your area has a great sales potential, and we want you to
        do well with it.  If there is anything this office can do
        to help you, please let me know.

 13.    There will be a meeting for all sales managers at  time
        on  date  in  location  to discuss sales strategies.
        Please plan to attend.




Form No. 306
```

Illustration 4-14   Interoffice Memo Composed from Form Paragraphs

INTEROFFICE MEMORANDUM

TO: M. J. Daly

FROM: C. P. Zalo *Zalo*

DATE: April 7, 199–

SUBJECT: SALES REPORT

¶ 1   Your copy of the sales report for the first quarter is attached.
Please review the report and share its contents with your staff.

¶ 5   The figures indicate that your area had an increase in sales of
$500,000. This increase represents a fine recovery.

¶ 12   Your area has a great sales potential, and we want you to do well
with it. If there is anything this office can do to help you,
please let me know.

jd

Attachment

Operator, this is Sue Yates of the Sales Department. My extension is 7739. Please make one original and one copy of guide message 336 for each set of variables which follows; use the current date on all letters.

LETTER 1
TO: Mrs. Karen Pearson *(P-E-A-R-S-O-N)*
                             1699 Woodland Avenue
                             Toledo, OH 43607-8845

Variable 1:   Karen
Variable 2:   500
END OF LETTER 1

LETTER 2
TO: Mr. Stanley Gardner *(G-A-R-D-N-E-R)*
                             476 Donora *(D-O-N-O-R-A)* Avenue NE
                             Toledo, OH 43675-2457

Variable 1:   Stanley
Variable 2:   100
END OF LETTER 2

LETTER 3
TO: Ms. Barbara Vincent
                             777 Ada Avenue SE
                             Toledo, OH 43629-1084

Variable 1:   Barbara
Variable 2:   50
END OF DICTATION

Illustration 4-15   Instructions for Completing Illustration 4-12 Guide Letter

The person who is to prepare the routine message refers to the file or notebook where the copies of the guide messages and form paragraphs are kept. Once the correct item has been located, the necessary information is keyboarded. When the variables have been entered or an individually typed document has been created, each item is proofread and then distributed.

In most contemporary offices, copies of all form paragraphs and guide messages are prerecorded on some form of magnetic media. The appropriate messages or paragraphs are recalled from storage, and all needed variable information is added. Since the guide messages were carefully proofread at the time they were composed, only the variables need to be proofread at the time the document is printed. Messages created from form paragraphs should be proofread not only for accuracy of variables but also for paragraph selection and sequence. Using word processing equipment to prepare individually typed routine correspondence increases production speed and minimizes typographical errors while retaining the personal touch of an individually typed document. Illustration 4-17 is an example of a letter produced from form paragraphs.

Variable information must be proofread.

Illustration 4-16   Form for Completing Letters from the Form Paragraphs in Illustration 4-13

```
                        WORK REQUEST FORM


     ORIGINATOR: C. P. Zalo                    PHONE: 555-1718
     FORM NUMBER: 306
     DOCUMENT TYPE:  (circle one)     Letter      (Memo)
     VARIABLES
     DATE: April 7, 199-
     ADDRESSEE: M. J. Daly



      1.  Subject: Sales Report
      2.  #1    first
      3.  #5    500,000
      4.  #12
      5.
      6.
      7.
      8.
      9.
     10.


     COPIES TO:
```

Illustration 4-17   Letter Produced on Automated Word Processing Equipment

DAVIDSON HOTELS

Evelyn S. Miranda
President, Davidson Hotels

November 12, 199–

Dr. Pat Hornsby
University of Minnesota
2400 Oakland Avenue
Duluth, MN 55812-5404

Dear Dr. Hornsby

Thank you for taking the time to fill out our Comment
Card during your recent visit to the Davidson Hotel of
Cleveland. It is comments like yours that are helping
us make the Davidsons your preferred hotels.

I am happy you had an enjoyable stay with us and appreciate your favorable remarks about our hotel.

Your suggestion has been noted and will be taken under
consideration. We welcome the opportunity to receive
ideas from our guests. These ideas will improve our
hotel and help us to better serve your needs.

Enclosed is a list of other Davidson Hotels throughout
the country in case your travels should take you elsewhere. We welcome the pleasure of serving you again at
a Davidson Hotel.

Sincerely

Evelyn S. Miranda

Evelyn S. Miranda
President

ESM/vj

Enclosure

pc Gary Nemeth
   David Dunham

The Miranda Hotel   744 Euclid Avenue   Cleveland, Ohio 44123-4407   (216) 555-7000 TELEX 469567

As an effective business communicator, you should strive to use communication technology to reduce the cost of correspondence and to improve its quality. Your goals should also include using efficient techniques. Managers and administrative support staff should work together to select appropriate communication technologies and to establish cost-effective procedures for their organization.

Increase the cost-effectiveness of your messages by using communication technology and techniques.

DISCUSSION QUESTIONS

1. What are the two most expensive components of correspondence cost?
2. List the different types of information that can be sent through telecommunication systems, and give an example of each.
3. How does telecommunication technology help overcome the communication obstacles of time and distance?
4. Describe the features and benefits of voice-mail systems.
5. List and explain the two forms of teleconferencing.
6. In what ways does a business benefit from teleconferencing?
7. What two word processing features are popular among writers?
8. Explain why spell checkers and document analyzers are not replacements for proofreading.
9. How has technology improved a communicator's ability to make a small- or large-group oral presentation?
10. Explain the difference between a routine and a repetitive message. Give an example of each.
11. What are the steps in the document creation cycle?
12. How does the use of dictation and word processing equipment affect the document creation cycle?
13. How does the creator of a document benefit from the use of word processing equipment?
14. List the four types of form messages. Give an example of a situation in which each might be used.
15. What form message design styles should be used to prepare (a) routine messages and (b) repetitive messages?
16. When should an organization consider using guide messages rather than individually composed correspondence?
17. What are the advantages of using form paragraphs rather than form messages or guide messages?

18. What external distribution options are available for organizations that use form messages?

19. Compare the cost and service differences between first-class and bulk mail.

20. Discuss the differences between preparing routine messages in a traditional office and in a contemporary office.

21. Why is it important to code each form or guide document?

APPLICATION EXERCISES

1. The spell check feature of a popular word processing program was used to search for errors in the following paragraph—no errors were detected. Proofread the paragraph, and circle any errors the spell checker missed.

   Jan was working a lone in the Jewelry department. Three shoppers approached the counter while she was rapping an other customers' package. Jim, the accessory department clerk, was able to assist her and offered to help. Jan eagerly excepted. As a result, all five customers were served quickly.

2. Visit a business that uses an electronic message system. Interview a manager(s) and secure the following kinds of information: (a) benefits derived from the system, (b) system arrangement, (c) system costs, and (d) any plans for changing the present system or installing a new system.

3. Go to a U. S. Postal Service office and collect information on its special electronic message services.

4. Assume that you are a business communication consultant who has been hired by Metropolis University (MU) to make suggestions for streamlining the creation and preparation of the school's routine and repetitive messages. Read each situation below and give advice in the areas outlined. Justify your recommendations.

   a. In August of each year, the school sends a packet of materials about Metropolis to the guidance department of every high school in the state. An explanatory letter accompanies the packet.

      (1) Is the letter routine or repetitive?

      (2) What document preparation technique should be used?

      (3) What would be an appropriate salutation?

b. A representative from MU regularly attends semiannual education fairs held in major cities in this and nearby states. After each fair, the representative writes to each student who stopped at the school's booth.

   (1) Is this a routine or a repetitive message?

   (2) What distribution method should be used?

c. In order to be admitted to MU, students must submit high school transcripts, forward SAT scores, and have a complete physical. The admissions office continually updates each applicant's file and notifies the student of what remains to be done to make the file complete.

   (1) Is this a routine or repetitive message?

   (2) What document preparation technique should be used?

   (3) How should it be mailed?

d. MU is considering the use of a telecommunication system to send monthly reports to the state capital.

   (1) Should it use a commercial or a privately owned system?

   (2) What criteria should be used to make the decision?

5. Business Leaders of the Future, a club for post-secondary business students, will hold its annual state conference in your community next July. As Program Committee Chair, you are responsible for locating and scheduling speakers, introducers, and recorders for each of the ten small-group meetings held during the conference. You have decided that creating guide messages with variables would be the most efficient way to correspond with the individuals who have agreed to participate in the conference.

   Select from the list of variables displayed below those which you feel should be incorporated into a message to be sent to each group. Some items will be used in more than one message; others may not be used in any message.

Group	Variables
Speakers	a. conference registration fee
	b. current date
	c. date of presentation
	d. hotel room rates
Introducers	e. inside address
	f. meal costs
	g. name of speaker
	h. name of introducer
	i. name of recorder
Recorders	j. room in which presentation will be given
	k. salutation name
	l. time of presentation
	m. title of presentation

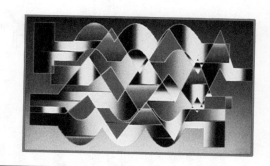

PART TWO

BUSINESS ENGLISH

CHAPTER 5

PARTS OF SPEECH

LEARNING OBJECTIVES

Your learning objectives for this chapter include the following:

— To recognize the eight parts of speech
— To know the purpose of each part of speech
— To use the parts of speech correctly

Knowledge of parts of speech will aid you in communicating.

Every word in a sentence has a use or function. Knowing the functions of words will enable you to select the right word, which in turn will help you communicate your ideas effectively. Your understanding of the parts of speech will aid you in selecting the right word at the right time. The eight parts of speech are as follows:

1. **Verb**—a word or phrase that describes the action or state of being of the subject
2. **Noun**—a word that names a person, place, or thing
3. **Pronoun**—a word that takes the place of a noun
4. **Adjective**- a word that describes or modifies a noun or pronoun
5. **Adverb**—a word that describes or modifies a verb, an adjective, or another adverb
6. **Preposition**—a word that connects a noun or pronoun to other words in the sentence
7. **Conjunction**—a word that connects words, phrases, or clauses
8. **Interjection**—a word that expresses surprise, emotion, or strong feeling and is not related to other words in the sentence

VERBS

The verb is the most important part of speech in a sentence. It expresses an action or a state of being. Every sentence must have a verb. When you are constructing sentences, remember that you should build each sentence around the verb.

A verb is the most important part of speech.

VERB TYPE

The two types of verbs are action verbs and state-of-being verbs.

ACTION VERBS. Action verbs express acts. They add power and precision to your communication. *Audit, negotiate, promote, organize, report, cancel, liquidate,* and thousands of other words are action verbs. The action verb is italicized in the following examples:

Action verbs are powerful.

> The president *promoted* Violeta to manager.
> The marketing managers *organized* their distribution plans.
> Ms. Smith *canceled* her trip to Spain.
> Paul accidentally *erased* the diskette.

STATE-OF-BEING VERBS. State-of-being verbs are also called **linking verbs**. They join or link one part of a sentence to another. State-of-being verbs are less powerful and less precise than action verbs. Verbs that express your five senses (*hear, smell, see, taste,* and *touch*) are state-of-being verbs. Other state-of-being verbs include *is, am, are, was, were, seem, appear, will be,* and *have been.* The state-of-being verb is italicized in the following examples:

State-of being verbs are used to link parts of sentences together.

> The room *smells* of cigar smoke.
> The water *tastes* bitter.
> He *is* a good employee.
> It *will be* fine with George.

VERB TENSE

Verbs appear in six tense forms that indicate time. These six tenses are categorized into two groups—simple tense and perfect tense.

Verb tense indicates the time that action occurs.

The three simple tenses are present, past, and future.

Present tense expresses current and continuing action or general truths.

SIMPLE TENSE.
The simple tenses are present, past, and future. The time of action or state of being of each simple tense is designated by its name.

PRESENT TENSE.
Verbs in the present tense express action that is going on at the present time or action that is continuing or habitual. Present tense verbs may also be used to indicate general truths. Verbs showing present tense are italicized in the following examples:

> The secretaries *are* on coffee break. (present time)
> Dave Wright, our office manager, *edits* all outgoing correspondence. (continuing)
> Computers *reduce* routine and monotonous tasks. (general truths)

Past tense expresses completed action or state of being.

PAST TENSE.
Verbs in the past tense indicate action that has been completed. Verbs in the past tense have two forms—regular and irregular. The past tense of regular verbs is formed by adding *d* or *ed*. The past tense of irregular verbs is formed by changing their root word. Regular and irregular verbs in the past tense are shown in these examples:

> Anne *performed* better than William in sales last month. (regular—perform [root word] + *ed*)
> Anne *sold* more than William last month. (irregular—root word is *sell*)
> Ed *obtained* a microcomputer. (regular—obtain [root word] + *ed*)
> Ed *bought* a microcomputer. (irregular—root word is *buy*)
> Jane *typed* a short letter to Mr. Davis about his indebtedness. (regular—type [root word] + *d*)
> Jane *wrote* a short letter to Mr. Davis about his indebtedness. (irregular—root word is *write*)

Future tense expresses expected action or state of being.

Will is used more than **shall** in business communcation.

FUTURE TENSE.
The future tense is used to indicate actions that are expected to occur in the future. Future tense is formed by using *shall* or *will* before the present tense form of the verb. In the past, distinct rules were adhered to in the use of *shall* and *will*; today, however, most business communicators use *will* to express future tense. *Shall* is used sparingly; it is used mainly to express legal or strong obligation. The following sentences demonstrate verbs in the future tense:

> Eva *will buy* the stock when it drops below $15 a share.
> *Will* you *attend* the convention?
> I *will write* the report on Monday.
> Mr. Clark *will speak* at the political rally.
> You *shall rise* when the judge enters the room.

PERFECT TENSE.
The perfect tense shows action that has been completed at the time the statement is made. This tense requires a form of the verb *have* along with the past participle of the main verb. (Participles are discussed at the end of this section.) The perfect tenses are present perfect, past perfect, and future perfect.

The three perfect tenses are present perfect, past perfect, and future perfect.

PRESENT PERFECT TENSE. Verbs in the present perfect tense refer to an action begun in the past and completed in the present. Present perfect tense may also refer to habitual or repeated past action. It is formed by adding *has* or *have* to the past participle of the main verb. The following examples show how verbs may be used in the present perfect tense:

> Nancy *has repaired* our cash register many times.
>
> Brian *has finished* carving the statue.
>
> Martha and Diane *have dined* here for the past 14 months.
>
> I *have driven* to Arkansas three times this summer.

Present perfect tense = *has* or *have* + past participle

PAST PERFECT TENSE. The past perfect tense refers to an action that was completed before another event in the past occurred. It is formed by adding *had* to the past participle of the main verb. The verbs in the past perfect tense are italicized in the following examples:

> Nancy *had repaired* our cash register before we closed last night.
>
> Brian *had finished* carving the statue before the Arts and Crafts deadline.
>
> Martha and Diane *had dined* here earlier in the week.
>
> I *had driven* to Arkansas before the freeway was completed.

Past perfect tense = *had* + past participle

FUTURE PERFECT TENSE. The future perfect tense is used to express an action that will be completed before a stated time in the future. It is formed by adding *shall have* or *will have* to the past participle of the main verb. Examples of verbs in the future perfect tense are italicized in the following sentences:

> Nancy *will have repaired* our cash register by the time we close.
>
> Brian *will have finished* carving the statue by the Arts and Crafts deadline.
>
> By then, Martha and Diane *shall have dined* here for 14 months.
>
> By September 30, I *will have driven* to Arkansas three times.

Future perfect tense = *shall have* or *will have* + past participle

VERB VOICE

Voice is the term used to indicate whether the subject is doing or receiving the action. Sentence meaning and emphasis are communicated through the proper use of verb voice. The two voices of verbs are active and passive.

The two **voices of verbs** are active and passive.

ACTIVE VOICE. When the subject of the sentence is performing the action, the verb is in the active voice. In business communication the active voice usually is preferred because it is more direct and concise. Sentences

The subject performs the action in the **active voice**.

that use verbs in the active voice identify the one performing the action. The following examples demonstrate how verbs may be used in the active voice:

> Ms. Cortez *hired* Nancy because of her programming skills.
> Julia *is designing* a new office layout for the accounting section.
> Kids Toy Company *will purchase* the rights to manufacture the doll.
> Roberta *will audit* the books at the end of the year.
> Michael *is* energetic.

The subject receives the action in the **passive voice**.

PASSIVE VOICE.　A verb is in the passive voice when the subject of the sentence receives the action. The passive voice is used sparingly in business communication. It is used when the subject is unknown or when the writer wants to soften the message to avoid making an accusation. Another use of the passive voice is to point out the action rather than the person who performed the action. The passive voice can also be used to eliminate a gender pronoun.

Passive voice verbs require a form of *be* as a helping verb along with a past participle of the verb. Uses of verbs in the passive voice are shown in the following examples:

> The office door *was left* open last night. (The person is unknown, or the speaker did not want to accuse anyone. Softened from "One of you left the door open last night.")
> Several suspicious incidents *have been reported*. (Communicator does not want to identify who did the reporting.)
> Progress *was made* by the football team. (Emphasis is on what—progress, not whom—football team.)
> The meeting *was held* in the Oak Room. (A biased statement was avoided by not saying, "He held the meeting in the Oak Room.")

Changing the verb voice from active to passive does not change the verb tense from present to past. The tense in the passive voice is expressed by its auxiliary (helping) verb. The following examples show verbs in the passive voice in several different tenses:

> The museum *is opened* daily at 9 a.m. (*passive voice*, present tense)
> The curator *opens* the museum daily at 9 a.m. (*active voice*, present tense)
>
> The museum *was closed* at 8 p.m. last night. (*passive voice*, past tense)
> The security guard *closed* the museum at 8 p.m. last night. (*active voice*, past tense)
>
> The museum *will be closed* on Labor Day. (*passive voice*, future tense)
> The board of trustees *will close* the museum on Labor Day. (*active voice*, future tense)

VERB MOOD

Communicators use verb moods to express facts, commands, or conditions. The three moods are indicative, imperative, and subjunctive.

The three verb moods are indicative, imperative, and subjunctive.

INDICATIVE MOOD. The indicative mood is used when making statements or asking questions involving facts. Business writers use verbs in this mood more than the other two moods. Examples are:

*Use **indicative mood** to ask questions or make factual statements.*

> Joyce *will represent* us at the meeting.
> Who do you think *will be promoted*?
> How many clients *did* Harry *visit* before taking a break?
> The new employee *appears* to like her job.

IMPERATIVE MOOD. The imperative mood is used to give commands, give instructions, or make requests. Sentences in the imperative mood usually have *you* understood as the subject and, therefore, it is omitted. Verbs used in the imperative mood are shown in the following sentences:

*Commands, instructions, and requests are in the **imperative mood**.*

> *Phone* Mr. Riley before you leave.
> *Send* your payment to the branch office.
> Please *audit* Kane Motors' books before leaving for vacation.
> *Sit* down and *discuss* your problem.

SUBJUNCTIVE MOOD. The subjunctive mood is used to express a wish, a doubt, or a situation that is contrary to fact. This mood is rarely used today. Many people find its use difficult because in the subjunctive mood the verb *were* replaces the verb *was* and the verb form *be* replaces *am, are,* and *is.* Here are some examples; the subjunctive mood verbs are italicized:

*The **subjunctive mood** is rarely used.*

> I wish Kala *were* here. (wish)
> *Should* Kala *arrive*, let me know. (doubt)
> If Kala *were* here, this meeting would adjourn. (contrary to fact—Kala is not present.)
> If I *were* Kala, I would attend. (contrary to fact—I am not Kala.)
> I suggest that this meeting *be* adjourned. (wish—*be* replaces *is*)
> Roy insisted that his hamburger *be* well done. (contrary to fact—*be* is used for *is*)

VERBALS

A verbal is a verb form used as a noun, an adjective, or an adverb. Verbals *cannot* function as verbs and do not express action or state of being. The three verbals are the infinitive, the gerund, and the participle.

The three verbals are the infinitive, the gerund, and the participle.

Infinitive = *to* + present tense

Infinitives are used as nouns, adjectives, and adverbs.

INFINITIVE. The infinitive is formed by placing the word *to* in front of the present tense of the verb. Several examples are *to read*, *to program*, and *to hire*. An infinitive can function as a noun, adjective, or adverb, but it can never be used as a verb. The infinitive is italicized and its use is shown in parentheses in each of the following sentences. (The uses of parts of speech are discussed in Chapter 6.)

> *To hire* an experienced programmer will not be an easy task. (noun—subject)
> Jules likes *to serve* on committees. (noun—direct object)
> Her desire is *to be president*. (noun—predicate nominative)
> Jennifer found paper *to put* in her typewriter. (adjective)
> The Sales Department advertised *to attract new customers*. (adverb)

Gerund = verb + *ing*

Gerunds are only used as nouns.

GERUND. A gerund is a verb form that can function only as a noun. It is formed by adding *ing* to the verb. *Typing, jogging,* and *manufacturing* are examples of gerunds. Gerunds may be used in phrases consisting of a gerund, an object, and words modifying the object. In the following sentences the phrases are in italics, the gerunds are in bold print, and their uses are in parentheses:

> ***Hiring*** *an experienced programmer* will not be an easy task. (subject)
> Jules likes ***serving*** *on committees*. (direct object)
> Cathy's greatest interest in life is ***becoming*** *a musician*. (predicate nominative)
> Don began the meeting by ***tapping*** *the gavel*. (object of preposition)
> Don, ***acting*** *as president*, began the meeting. (appositive)

Participles are used as adjectives or as parts of verb phrases.

Present participle = present tense + *ing*

PARTICIPLE. A participle is a verb form that can be used as an adjective or as part of a verb phrase. The three types of participles are present, past, and perfect.

PRESENT PARTICIPLE. The present participle is always formed by adding *ing* after the present tense of a verb. The verb phrase is in italics, and the present participle is in bold print in each of the following examples:

> Allen owns a ***jogging*** *machine*. (adjective)
> The sales force has a ***driving*** *desire* to be number one in its region. (adjective)
> Mr. Lane, my supervisor, *is **driving** me crazy*. (verb phrase)
> The factory *is **producing** too many defective doors*. (verb phrase)

Past participle usually = present tense + *d* or *ed*

Sometimes the root word is changed.

PAST PARTICIPLE. Past participles are usually formed by adding *d* or *ed* to the present tense of regular verbs. Irregular verbs form their past participles by changing their root words. The past participle is italicized in each of the following examples:

> The horses will be *brought* in air-conditioned trailers. (verb phrase—irregular verb)
> The factory entrance was blocked by the *drifted* snow. (adjective—regular verb)
> Tom has *bought* five copiers from the new office supply store. (verb phrase—irregular verb)
> Charlene delivered the *broken* chairs to the repair shop. (adjective—irregular verb)

PERFECT PARTICIPLE.   A perfect participle is always used as an adjective and is formed by combining *having* with the past participle. The following sentences have their perfect participles italicized:

> *Having called* on eight customers, Joe quit for the weekend.
> Janice, *having completed* the secondary research, began on the survey.
> *Having located* the missing papers, Bob proceeded with the meeting.
> *Having jogged* for five miles, the runners were disappointed that the race was canceled because of rain.

Perfect participle =
having + past participle
The perfect participle is always an adjective.

N O U N S

Nouns name persons, places, and things. The two main groups of nouns are proper nouns and common nouns.

Words that name persons, places, and things are **nouns**.

PROPER NOUNS

Names of particular persons, places, and things are **proper nouns**. Proper nouns are always capitalized. *White House, Lanette Watson, Dallas,* and *The Washington Post* are examples of proper nouns.

Proper nouns are particular.

COMMON NOUNS

Common nouns name general classes of persons, places, things, or ideas. Common nouns are not capitalized. Examples of common nouns are *secretary, console, buildings, stock,* and *deposits.* The three classes of common nouns are concrete, abstract, and collective.

Common nouns are general.

CONCRETE NOUNS.   Concrete nouns name those things that you can see, touch, hear, taste, or smell. Such words as *manager, desk, sandwich, flower, telephone,* and *music* are concrete nouns. Concrete nouns are precise and easily understood, which makes them effective for business communication.

Concrete nouns are precise.

ABSTRACT NOUNS.   Abstract nouns name ideas, emotions, qualities, and beliefs. Abstract nouns are not concrete. Examples of abstract nouns are *courage, disappointment, love, anger, attitude,* and *happiness.* People's

Abstract nouns are not tangible.

opinions and feelings differ in degree; therefore, abstract words are less precise than concrete words. They should be used infrequently in business communication because they are more difficult to understand.

Collective nouns name a group.

COLLECTIVE NOUNS. A collective noun is a group of persons or a collection of things. It is normally treated as a singular noun because the group is acting as one; however, it would be treated as a plural noun if the group members were acting as individuals. Collective nouns include *herd*, *family*, *board of directors*, *team*, *class*, *staff*, and *committee*.

COMPOUND NOUNS

Compound nouns are multiple words used to name singular nouns.

A **compound noun** is two or more words used to name one person, place, or thing. A compound noun may be written as one or more words, or it may be hyphenated. It is best to consult a dictionary for the correct spelling. Compound nouns can be classified under any of the three classes of common nouns. Examples of compound nouns in each class are:

Concrete:	basketball, surgeon general, notebook
Abstract:	self-respect, common sense, goodwill, life cycle
Collective:	book club, air force, civil service

PLURAL FORMS OF NOUNS

A plural noun is normally formed by adding *s* or *es* to a singular noun.

A plural form of a noun is used when naming two or more persons, places, or things. The plural of most nouns is formed by adding *s* or *es* to the singular form of the noun. Because there are so many ways of forming plurals, you should consult a dictionary if a question arises. Examples of different ways that nouns are formed as plurals include document, documents; business, businesses; company, companies; studio, studios; brother-in-law, brothers-in-law; and half, halves.

POSSESSIVE FORMS OF NOUNS

Possessive nouns show ownership.

The possessive form of a noun is used to show possession or ownership. The possessive form of a noun is indicated by using an apostrophe. The following general guidelines will help you correctly form possessive nouns in written communication:

1. The possessive of a singular noun ending in an *s* or *z* sound is formed by adding an *apostrophe s* to a noun with one syllable and by adding only an *apostrophe* to a noun with more than one syllable.

Hawks's notepad   Fairbanks' residents

Placement of apostrophe and addition of **s** *to show possession depends on the noun and the ending sound.*

2. The possessive of a singular noun not ending in an *s* or *z* sound is formed by adding an *apostrophe s*.

driver's truck   accountant's computer

3. The possessive of a plural noun ending in an *s* or *z* sound is formed by adding an *apostrophe*.

two students' classes   all employees' vacations

4. A compound noun has its possessive formed by applying the basic rules and placing the *apostrophe* or *apostrophe s* after the final word or word element.

mother-in-law's hat   all brigadier generals' orders

For compound nouns, possession is shown after the last word.

5. When two or more people share ownership of an object or objects, add an *apostrophe* or *apostrophe s* to the final name.

Bob and Diana's house   Louis and Willis' repair shops

Joint or individual possession of objects influences placement of apostrophe and apostrophe **s**.

6. When two or more people each own separate objects, their possession is indicated by adding an *apostrophe* or *apostrophe s* to each noun.

Bob's and Diana's houses   Louis' and Willis' repair shops

PRONOUNS

Pronouns are used in place of nouns. Pronouns make your writing more interesting because you do not repeat the same noun over and over. There are seven types of pronouns: personal, relative, interrogative, indefinite, demonstrative, reflexive, and intensive. Each type of pronoun performs a different function in a sentence.

Pronouns *replace nouns.*

The seven types of pronouns are personal, relative, interrogative, indefinite, demonstrative, reflexive, and intensive.

PERSONAL PRONOUNS

Personal pronouns refer to specific people or things.

Personal pronouns are substitutes for nouns that refer to specific persons or things. They change their form when they perform different functions and appear in different parts of a sentence. The different forms are called **cases**. The three types of cases are nominative, possessive, and objective.

Nominative case is used when the pronoun is a subject.

NOMINATIVE CASE. The nominative case is used when the pronoun functions as the subject of a sentence or a clause. It is also called the **subjective case**. Singular personal pronouns in the nominative case are *I, you, he, she,* and *it*. Plural personal pronouns in the nominative case are *we, you,* and *they*. The nominative case is also used when the pronoun follows a linking verb. The following sentences illustrate these uses:

> *I* went to the picnic. (subject of sentence)
> If *they* attend the meeting, George will answer the phone. (subject of clause)
> *It* was *she*! (it—subject of sentence; she—follows linking verb)

Possessive case shows ownership.

POSSESSIVE CASE. The possessive case is used to show possession or ownership. It does *not* include an apostrophe. Singular possessive pronouns are *my, mine, your, yours, his, her, hers,* and *its*. Plural possessive pronouns are *our, ours, your, yours, their,* and *theirs*. Several examples of pronouns in the possessive case are:

> Is this paycheck *mine*? (shows whose paycheck)
> *Your* presentation was outstanding. (shows whose presentation)
> If the vase is not *his*, it must be *hers*. (shows whose vase)
> *Our* plane is leaving. (shows whose plane)
> Janet will place *your* reservation for dinner at eight. (shows whose reservation)
> Robert and Leonor were recognized at the banquet for *their* accomplishments. (shows whose accomplishments)
> I would appreciate *your* taking care of the matter by this afternoon. (shows who is responsible for taking care of the matter)

Objective case is used when the pronoun is an object.

OBJECTIVE CASE. The objective case is used when the pronoun functions as an object in a sentence, clause, or phrase. Singular pronouns in the objective case are *me, you, him, her,* and *it*. Plural objective pronouns are *us, you,* and *them*. The following sentences show these functions:

> Cindy hit *me*. (direct object of a sentence)
> The invoice will be sent to *you*. (object of preposition)
> If Dale robbed *her*, why did Roy go to jail? (direct object of a clause)

RELATIVE PRONOUNS

Relative pronouns connect a group of words containing a subject and verb to a noun or pronoun. *Who, whom, whose, which,* and *that* are the relative pronouns. If the word to which the pronoun refers is a person, use *who, whom, whose,* or *that.* Use *which* or *that* if the pronoun refers to a thing. Examples showing the use of relative pronouns are:

> Rhonda, *who* is my boss, can communicate well.
> Each client with *whom* Mr. Anderson serves made money.
> Anyone *whose* ambition is great should run for political office.
> The building, *which* is freshly painted, is ready for occupancy.
> All the cars *that* have over 100,000 miles should be salvaged.

Relative pronouns link clauses to nouns or pronouns.

INTERROGATIVE PRONOUNS

Pronouns used within questions are **interrogative pronouns**. *Who, whose, whom, which,* and *what* are the interrogative pronouns. Pronouns precede verbs when you use them in questions. Like other pronouns within sentences, they function as subjects, objects, modifiers, and subject complements. The following sentences illustrate how interrogative pronouns are used:

> *Who* forgot to turn off the light? (subject)
> *Whose* applications have been rejected? (modifier)
> *Whom* did the company send? (object)
> *Which* way do I turn? (modifier)
> *What* was the cause of the power failure? (subject complement)

Interrogative pronouns ask questions.

INDEFINITE PRONOUNS

Indefinite pronouns are used to make general statements about individuals or things. Indefinite pronouns include *each, anyone, one, anything,* and *nobody.* The indefinite pronouns are italicized in the following sentences:

> *Each* driver passed the test.
> You can give it to *anyone* in the office.
> *One* of the astronauts wore a flannel shirt.
> The new inspector does not pass *anything*.
> *Nobody* leaves until the report is completed.

Indefinite pronouns do not specify a particular person or thing.

DEMONSTRATIVE PRONOUNS

Demonstrative pronouns substitute for specific nouns.

Demonstrative pronouns are used to indicate specific persons, places, or things. The four demonstrative pronouns are *this, these, that,* and *those*:

> *This* is an attractive desk.
> Are *these* the papers that you need?
> *That* is not a worthwhile investment.
> *Those* are the horses that can really run.

COMPOUND PERSONAL PRONOUNS

Compound personal pronouns are **intensive** or **reflexive**.

Compound personal pronouns have the suffix *self* or *selves*. They may be intensive or reflexive pronouns. Intensive pronouns are used for emphasis. Reflexive pronouns reflect the action of the verb back to the subject or to a noun or pronoun in the sentence. Examples of intensive and reflexive pronouns follow:

> He *himself* was as mean as the devil. (emphasizes a pronoun)
> The table *itself* was worth $25,000. (emphasizes a noun)
> The boys saw *themselves* as heroes. (refers back to the subject)
> We think that they have let *themselves* go too far in trying to solve that problem. (refers back to a pronoun)

ADJECTIVES

Adjectives modify nouns and pronouns and make them more precise.

Adjectives provide additional information about nouns and pronouns. They make the meaning of the nouns or pronouns more exact by answering such questions as *which one, how many,* and *what kind*. Adjectives are called **modifiers**.

DEGREES OF COMPARISON IN ADJECTIVES

Adjectives change form to show degrees of comparison of nouns. Adjectives may be regular or irregular. Regular adjectives generally are one-syllable words and add *er* or *est* in making comparisons. Irregular adjectives usually contain two or more syllables and use *less*, *least*, or *more*, *most* in making comparisons. There are three degrees of comparison: positive, comparative, and superlative.

Positive	Comparative	Superlative
smart	smarter	smartest
cruel	crueler	cruelest
generous	more generous	most generous
attractive	less attractive	least attractive

POSITIVE DEGREE. The positive degree is used to describe one item or one group of items. The positive form appears in a dictionary. The adjective in the positive form is italicized in the following examples:

> That computer is *small*.
> Henry is a *capable* manager.
> The red tie is *ugly*.
> Jane is as *bright* as John.

COMPARATIVE DEGREE. The comparative degree is used to show the difference between two items. The comparative degree is formed by adding *er* to a regular adjective or by adding the words *more* or *less* to an irregular adjective. The adjectives shown in the examples under the positive degree are illustrated below in the comparative degree:

> That computer is *smaller* than the typewriter.
> Henry is a *more capable* manager than Rudolph.
> Rudolph is a *less capable* manager than Henry.
> The red tie is *uglier* than the blue one.
> Jane is *brighter* than Opal.

SUPERLATIVE DEGREE. The superlative degree is used in comparing three or more items. It can also be used for emphasis. The superlative degree is formed by adding *est* to a regular adjective or by adding *most* or *least* to an irregular adjective. The following adjectives are now in the superlative degree:

> That computer is the *smallest* one available.
> Henry is the *most capable* manager.
> Rudolph is the *least capable* manager.
> The red tie is definitely the *ugliest* of all!
> Jane is the *brightest* girl in the class.

ABSOLUTE ADJECTIVES

Absolute adjectives are always in the superlative degree.

Absolute adjectives cannot be compared because they are always in the superlative degree. For example, if a set of figures is *wrong*, another set of figures cannot be *more wrong*. Some absolute adjectives are *unique*, *perfect*, *right*, *final*, *full*, *square*, *round*, *correct*, *never*, *dead*, and *empty*.

COMPOUND ADJECTIVES

Two or more adjectives used as one become a **compound adjective**.

A **compound adjective** is two or more adjectives used together to describe a single noun or pronoun. Usually, compound adjectives are hyphenated if they are placed before the noun or pronoun that they modify; they are not hyphenated if they are placed after the noun or pronoun they modify. Both rules are demonstrated in the following sentences:

Yoriko was a *well-known* engineer.
According to all the regional managers, Ramon was *well known*.
State-of-being verbs are less powerful than action verbs.
A verb is a word that expresses an action or a *state of being*.
It is a *low-grade* oil.
This is an oil of *low grade*.

See also "The Hyphen," page 174, where the use of hyphens in compound adjectives (and other compound words) is discussed in detail.

ARTICLES

A, *an*, and *the* are **articles**.
The is specific.
A and *an* are general.

Although classed as adjectives, *a*, *an*, and *the* are called **articles**. The article *the* is used to denote specific nouns or pronouns. Articles *a* and *an* are used to denote general nouns or pronouns. For example:

Marie won *the* championship game.
Marie won *a* game.
Marie won *an* exciting game.

When the word following the article begins with a consonant *sound*, you use *a*; use *an* if the word begins with a vowel *sound*. For example:

The company issued Rosanna *a certificate*.
Jim gave Martha *an hourglass* for Christmas.

Julia earned *an associate* degree.
Rick earned *a degree*.
Leann earned *an A*, *a B*, and *an F*.

ADVERBS

Adverbs are modifiers that restrict, limit, or describe verbs, adjectives, or other adverbs. They answer questions such as *how, when, where, why, in what manner*, or *to what degree*. Many end in *ly*. Adverbs are used as modifiers in the following sentences:

> The contractor *happily* announced the completion of the house. (announced *how?*)
>
> Roger answered the request *promptly*. (answered *when?*)
>
> Bring your complaints *here*. (bring *where?*)
>
> The *extremely* bright student had all A's. (*how* bright?)
>
> Larry works *very* hard. (works *how?* hard; *to what degree?* very)

Adverbs are used to modify verbs, adjectives, or other adverbs.

PLACEMENT OF ADVERBS

An adverb may be a single word (move *slowly*), a phrase (move *in a slow manner*), or a clause (move *as slowly as you can*). A single-word adverb can be placed before or after the word it modifies. Prepositional and infinitive phrases and clauses that function as adverbs usually follow the word they modify. An adverbial clause, which is a dependent clause that acts as an adverb, precedes the independent clause in a sentence. A further discussion of phrases and clauses is on page 146.

DEGREES OF ADVERBS

Some words that are adverbs as well as adjectives have positive, comparative, and superlative degrees of comparison; for example:

Adverbs also have positive, comparative, and superlative degrees.

Positive	Comparative	Superlative
far	farther	farthest
near	nearer	nearest
swiftly	more swiftly	most swiftly
direct	less direct	least direct

PREPOSITIONS

A **preposition** is a connector that needs an object.

A prepositional phrase contains the preposition and its object.

A preposition connects a noun or pronoun that follows it to another part of a sentence. The preposition helps show how the noun or pronoun relates to the other word. The noun or pronoun that follows the preposition is called the **object of the preposition**. A word group containing a preposition and the object of the preposition is called a **prepositional phrase**. The following sentences illustrate prepositional phrases. The prepositions are in italics, and the object of each preposition is in bold print.

> A letter *of* **appreciation** will be sent *to* each **member** *of* the **committee**.
>
> One *of* the most widely written **reports** *in* **industry** is the periodic report *of* **activities**.
>
> Most *of* the **people** you know are happy *with* their **positions**.
>
> The members *of* the **team** rest *between* **games**.

FUNCTIONS OF PREPOSITIONAL PHRASES

Prepositional phrases work as adjectives and adverbs.

Prepositional phrases work as units in a sentence. They perform the functions of adjectives and adverbs and provide variety within the sentence. Examples of prepositional phrases that act as adjectives and adverbs follow:

> An employee *of Bob's* was arrested last night. (The prepositional phrase as adjective modifies the noun *employee*.)
>
> The beauty contestant moved *with grace*. (The prepositional phrase as adverb modifies the verb *moved*.)
>
> The receptionist, apologetic *about the phone call*, continued our conversation. (The prepositional phrase as adverb modifies the adjective *apologetic*.)
>
> The students worked *on the reports*, enthusiastically *for the most part*, *in groups*. (All three prepositional phrases act as adverbs. The first and last modify the verb *worked*; the second modifies the adverb *enthusiastically*.)

OBJECT OF PREPOSITION

Objects of prepositions are nouns or pronouns and can be modified by adjectives.

As previously mentioned, the object of a preposition is a noun or pronoun that follows the preposition. The object of a preposition can be modified by an adjective, such as, "Mary sent a present to the *beautiful* baby." Personal pronouns and *who* have unique objective forms. The objective forms of *who* and personal pronouns are *whom, me, us, you, him, her,* and *them.* The objects of the prepositions are in italics in the sentences below:

> To *whom* are you sending the evaluation?
> Please give the raise to *me.*
> The classes were for *us.*
> The promotional matter is between *you* and *him.*
> I know little about *her.*
> Why must we send it to *them?*

UNNECESSARY PREPOSITIONS

Although prepositional phrases can be used effectively to make communication more interesting, a communicator must be careful to avoid unnecessary and, therefore, incorrect prepositions. Omitting unnecessary prepositions will contribute to precise communication. Use only those prepositions that clarify a sentence. The prepositions *to, of, at,* and *up* are frequently used unnecessarily. Examples of these uses follow:

Omit unnecessary prepositions.

> Where is Ray going *to?* (unnecessary preposition)
> Where is Ray going?
>
> The letters fell off *of* the desk. (unnecessary preposition)
> The letters fell off the desk.
>
> Do you know where my pen is *at?* (unnecessary preposition)
> Do you know where my pen is?
>
> Donna will climb *up* to the top. (unnecessary preposition)
> Donna will climb to the top.

PREPOSITIONS ENDING SENTENCES

Effective business communicators avoid ending a sentence with a preposition; for example:

Normally a sentence should not end with a preposition.

> What is the report for? (incorrect)
> What is the purpose of the report?
>
> Whom did you send the diskettes to? (incorrect)
> To whom did you send the diskettes?

However, it is acceptable to end a sentence with a preposition in oral communication, if rearranging the sentence is awkward:

> Does Alice know about what it is? (awkward)
> Does Alice know what it is about? (preferred)

CONJUNCTIONS

Conjunctions are connectors without objects.

The three types of conjunctions are coordinate, correlative, and subordinate.

Conjunctions connect words, phrases, and clauses. They are also used to introduce clauses. Conjunctions are similar to prepositions in that they serve as connectors but differ in that they do not have objects. The three kinds of conjunctions are coordinate, correlative, and subordinate. The first two join grammatically equal word elements while the last one, subordinate, joins grammatically unequal word elements.

COORDINATE CONJUNCTIONS

Coordinate conjunctions connect elements of equal rank.

A **coordinate conjunction** joins words, phrases, and independent clauses that are of equal importance or rank. Of equal importance or rank means that similar elements are connected; for example, adjectives are connected to adjectives and nouns are connected to nouns. The coordinate conjunctions are *and, but, or, nor, for, as,* and *yet.* The following examples show coordinate conjunctions joining words, phrases, and independent clauses:

> Clara *and* Joe went to the game. (joins nouns)
>
> Hurriedly *but* concisely Suzy audited the books. (joins adverbs)
>
> You can dictate *or* type the letter. (joins verbs)
>
> From Chicago to Cleveland *and* from Cleveland to New York City will be a long drive. (joins phrases)
>
> The workshop was cancelled, *for* the speaker lost her voice. (joins independent clauses)

CORRELATIVE CONJUNCTIONS

A correlative conjunction is a pair of connectors that link sentence elements.

Correlative conjunctions are pairs of words that connect two parallel words, phrases, or clauses. The most common correlative conjunctions are *both . . . and, either . . . or, neither . . . nor, not . . . but, not only . . . but also,* and *whether . . . or.* Examples follow:

> *Neither* Clara *nor* Jack knew about the new truck.
>
> They won *not only* in baseball *but also* in soccer.
>
> *Both* Jill *and* Marie are personnel directors.
>
> Will you *either* repair the stove *or* get Nancy to do it?

A common difficulty with using correlative conjunctions involves **parallelism**. You must be sure that connected elements are equal or parallel in grammatical form or rank. The following sentences demonstrate a few parallelism errors:

Mr. Guzman should *either* sell the car *or* he should get it repaired. (Incorrect—*either* precedes the verb *sell* but *or* precedes the pronoun *he*.)

Mr. Guzman should *either* sell the car *or* get it repaired. (Acceptable—both conjunctions precede verbs.)

Jason plans *either* working at the office *or* to play golf this weekend. (Incorrect—*either* precedes the gerund *working* but *or* precedes the infinitive *to play*.)

Jason plans *either* to work at the office *or* to play golf this weekend. (Acceptable—both conjunctions precede infinitives.)

or

Jason plans *either* working at the office *or* playing golf this weekend. (Acceptable—both conjunctions precede gerunds.)

Ms. Wells *not only* praised the managers *but also* their workers. (Incorrect—*not only* precedes the verb *praised* and *but also* precedes the noun *workers*.)

Ms. Wells praised *not only* the managers *but also* their workers. (Acceptable—both conjunctions precede nouns.)

Be sure that connected elements are parallel.

SUBORDINATE CONJUNCTIONS

Subordinate conjunctions join subordinate clauses to main clauses, that is, dependent clauses to independent clauses. Some subordinate conjunctions are *after, because, before, since, when, while, where, if, whether, though,* and *until*. The subordinate conjunctions are in italics and the main clauses are in bold in the following examples:

Subordinate conjunctions connect clauses of unequal rank.

Because we needed new communication equipment, **we borrowed \$75,000**.
Our production has increased *since* the assembly line has been reorganized.
We will continue operating under these guidelines *until* the new regulations are published.

INTERJECTIONS

Interjections express strong emotions or feelings. They are not related grammatically to any other words in the sentence, and most do not have any meaning if they are taken out of the message context. An interjection is normally

Interjections express strong emotions.

punctuated with an exclamation point. Interjections are seldom, if ever, used in business writing. They are used sparingly in oral communication and in written advertising material. The interjections are italicized in the following examples:

> *Oh!* I forgot to punch the time clock.
>
> *Help!* Our warehouse is full.
>
> *Ouch!* That hurts.
>
> *My goodness!* That's a big desk.

DISCUSSION QUESTIONS

1. List and define the eight parts of speech.
2. Distinguish between the two types of verbs and give an example of each.
3. Describe how verb tense is changed when using passive voice.
4. Explain the difference between verbs in the present tense and verbs in the present perfect tense. Give an example of each.
5. Explain and give an example of each of the three verb moods.
6. Identify and describe the three verbals.
7. Discuss the two main groups of nouns.
8. Distinguish between concrete and abstract nouns.
9. What type of verb should be used with a collective noun? Why?
10. Discuss why pronouns are used to replace nouns.
11. Distinguish between compound nouns and plural nouns and give examples of each.
12. Describe how a singular noun ending in an *s* or *z* sound is changed to show possession.
13. Explain and give an example using each of the three pronoun cases.
14. Describe the three degrees of comparison used with adverbs and adjectives.
15. What are absolute adjectives? Give an example.
16. Compare the uses of the articles *a, an,* and *the.*
17. What is the difference between an adverb and an adjective? Construct a sentence that uses at least one adjective and one adverb.
18. What is an object of a preposition, and what can be used to modify it?
19. What is the primary difference between a preposition and a conjunction?
20. Identify and describe the three types of conjunctions. Give examples of each.
21. What are interjections? Give an example.

A P P L I C A T I O N   E X E R C I S E S

1. Identify each verb and indicate if it is an action or a state-of-being verb. Also indicate if the verb is in active or passive voice.
   a. Will you write the final report?
   b. If we get the contract, we will have to increase our production.
   c. Cattle production increased dramatically during the past two years.
   d. The Cowboys are a good football team.
   e. Tom replaced the broken china before the guests arrived.
   f. The luggage was sent to the wrong city.
   g. There are a number of strategies from which we may choose.
   h. Are you going to the company picnic?
   i. In addition to being a distributor of microcomputers, Ruth developed software programs.
   j. The results of the vote of the union members were taken into consideration by management.
   k. Janet is an honor student.
   l. Ms. Jimenez was recommended for promotion by the committee.
   m. Roxanne began the audit before she left on vacation.

2. Identify each verb and indicate if it is in the indicative, imperative, or subjunctive mood.
   a. Go to personnel on Monday.
   b. Jason will deliver the paper sometime after the parade.
   c. If I were you, I would investigate changing insurance companies.
   d. You will receive a raise after completing six months with our company.
   e. Send my mail to Kerrie while I am attending the convention.
   f. Who bought the computer for Mr. Wright's retirement present?
   g. Should you drop the class, you must repay the tuition.

3. Identify each verbal and state its form (infinitive, gerund, or participle).
   a. Catherine desires to become a musician.
   b. Hiking is a relaxing and healthful pastime.
   c. The tornado left many damaged homes.
   d. The striking clock woke me at midnight.
   e. Studying is important when you are in school.
   f. Adolph is expected to announce his decision.
   g. Instead of studying for finals, Paul went to sleep.

4. Verbs are in italics in the following sentences. Determine the correct verb form and indicate the tense. *Example:* The announcement of the resignation shake the building. *shook—past tense*
   a. He *has came* to this golf course for the past three years.
   b. Bill and Clara *voice* their opinions yesterday.

    c. The boy *say* he *has saw* three deer in his back yard.

    d. The dog *bite* the postal carrier last week.

    e. The dog *bark* each time that a cat *cross* the yard.

    f. By the end of the year, over a million tourists *will have came* to the amusement park.

    g. *Will* you *cut* the orange for my lunch?

    h. As I *speak* on the phone, I *saw* Bill working on his computer.

    i. Tomorrow Betty *will spoke* to our marketing division.

    j. I *have call* my father every day since the first of February.

    k. The workers *will struck* if their demands are not met.

    l. Reed *had call* the insurance adjustor before the police arrived.

    m. The dog *will lay* on the rug in front of the fireplace.

5. Identify each adjective and adverb in the following sentences and indicate how the word is used (*adjective* or *adverb*). Indicate the word that each adjective or adverb modifies.

    a. The video company moved smoothly into modern facilities.

    b. The University's pride was obvious after the overwhelming victory.

    c. Mr. Bardwell announced his annual list of the ten worst dressed people in the United States.

    d. Mrs. Baty's secretary really enjoys using the new laser printer.

    e. Nolan spoke quietly, but his knees knocked loudly.

    f. The most successful managers are those who are most concerned about their employees.

    g. A conscientious manager will always read carefully all contracts and agreements.

    h. Glyn and Sara almost always bring their lunches to work.

    i. The college dropout worked diligently as a dishwasher.

    j. Safety is very important in large factories.

    k. All employees will follow the enclosed schedule for the summer.

    l. Every telephone technician occasionally encounters an irate customer.

    m. The silver market fell rapidly when the tycoon quickly sold his assets.

6. Common errors are found in the following sentences. Find and correct the errors. Explain each correction.

    a. What hotel is the convention held at?

    b. Between the two secretaries, Eddie is the best typist.

    c. The custodian could not remember the room the wastebasket came from.

    d. Leann drove the race car too rapid on the curve.

    e. The secretary either left the door unlocked or she forgot to close it.

    f. The shrub growed well in the open office.

    g. To ensure that the reservations were made correctly, Dale made them himself.

    h. The employee will be expected to create a data base, enter data, save and retrieve files, edit, search, sort.

    i. If I was you, I would apply for the position.

    j. The company president has came by every day this week.

    k. He is gone to the store to purchase the office supplies.

7. Identify the part of speech for each word in the following sentences.

    a. A new employee is expected to read the manual.

    b. Why did Raymond visit only five customers?

    c. Dr. Johnson finished his rounds, and then he went to the spa to jog and to play racquetball.

    d. Jennifer was hired for the position of athletic director.

    e. Hurry! The sale ends Friday.

    f. Our accounting system is ideal for a small business.

    g. Wow! Aren't that deer's antlers magnificent?

    h. You and Bill did really well.

    i. Jim and Kaye did the inventory completely and accurately.

    j. Pat, the new employee, went home because she was ill.

    k. Although the monthly report is accurate, changes have been made recently.

    l. An important step toward investing in silver is an understanding of the commodity market.

    m. If our products sell well, dividends will be distributed to stockholders.

SENTENCE STRUCTURE

Your learning objectives for this chapter include the following:

— To recognize and understand the parts of sentences
— To assure grammatical agreement in sentences
— To know the purposes of sentences
— To recognize and understand the four basic sentence structures

A sentence expresses a complete thought.

A sentence is a group of related words that expresses a complete thought. A sentence always contains a subject and a predicate. It is the basic unit for organizing messages. You can improve your ability to communicate by becoming familiar with sentence construction and by learning how to organize sentences. You do not need to become a grammarian, but you should be able to construct correct sentences. Using correctly constructed sentences in your communications increases the precision and clarity of your messages. In addition, the credibility of your messages will be increased if they are grammatically correct.

PARTS OF SENTENCES

The starting point in developing your understanding of how to structure sentences is to know their two essential parts. These parts are the subject and the predicate.

THE SUBJECT

The subject is the part of a sentence that tells who or what is being discussed.

THE COMPLETE SUBJECT. The complete subject includes all words related directly to the subject. The complete subject is italicized in the following examples:

> *Susan* reads.
>
> *Tall, blond Susan* reads.
>
> *We* left in a hurry.
>
> *The check, which was for over $100,* was received on Monday.

THE SIMPLE SUBJECT. The simple subject is the main noun or pronoun in the complete subject. The simple subject in a sentence is the who or the what that performs the action or is in the state of being described in the sentence. The simple subject is in boldface type in the following examples of italicized complete subjects:

> *Tall, blond **Susan*** reads. (Susan is the *who* that performs the action of reading.)
>
> *The **check**, which was for over $100,* was received on Monday. (The check is the *what* that was received.)
>
> *The football **game*** was most enjoyable. (The game is the *what* that was most enjoyable.)

COMPOUND SUBJECTS. When two (or more) simple subjects are connected by a coordinate conjunction, we have a compound subject. The coordinate conjunctions are *and, or, but, nor, for, yet,* and *so.* The compound subject is in boldface type in the following examples of italicized complete subjects:

> ***Rita and Fred*** went to the dance.
>
> *The **office and plant*** closed for the holiday.
>
> *The **Eagles or** the **Wildcats*** will win the tournament.

THE PREDICATE

The predicate is the part of a sentence that tells something about the complete subject.

The main parts of a sentence are:
• the **subject**

• the **predicate**

THE COMPLETE PREDICATE. The complete predicate, which includes the verb and all the words directly related to it, is italicized in the following examples:

> Susan *reads*.
> We *left in a hurry*.
> The letter *was typed on white paper*.
> Were you *pleased with the gift*?

THE SIMPLE PREDICATE. The simple predicate is the main verb in the complete predicate. The verb expresses action or a state of being. The simple predicate is in boldface type in these examples of italicized complete predicates:

> We ***left*** *in a hurry*. (*left* expresses action)
> The letter ***was typed*** *on white paper*. (*was typed* expresses action)
> They ***seem*** *happy*. (*seem* expresses a state of being)

COMPOUND PREDICATES. A compound predicate is formed when two (or more) simple predicates are connected by a coordinate conjunction. The compound predicate is in boldface type in these examples of italicized complete predicates:

> She ***works*** *hard* ***and learns*** *well*.
> The accounting report ***was prepared, reviewed, and accepted***.

RECOGNIZING SUBJECTS AND PREDICATES

Practice in recognizing subjects and predicates will strengthen your understanding of sentence structure. To analyze sentence structure, start by locating the simple predicate (the verb); then ask *who?* or *what?* to identify the subject. The following examples illustrate this approach:

Analyze sentences by first locating the simple predicate and then finding the subject.

> The bank opened at 9 a.m. (The action: *opened* is the verb. What opened? *The bank* is the subject.)
> Jose manages the jewelry store. (The action: *manages* is the verb. Who manages? *Jose* is the subject.)
> Miss Hart is 20 years old. (The state of being: *is* is the verb. Who is? *Miss Hart* is the subject.)
> The rainbow was beautiful. (The state of being: *was* is the verb. What was? *The rainbow* is the subject.)

Before leaving, Sally and Joyce said goodbye to everyone. (The action: *said* is the verb. Who said? *Sally and Joyce* is the compound subject.)

In the mornings, George rises early and does his exercises. (The action: *rises and does* is the compound predicate. Who rises and does? *George* is the *simple* subject.)

The most common arrangement for a sentence is the subject followed by the verb. In sentences beginning with *Here* or *There*, the subject is placed after the verb. The following examples, in which the subject is shown in bold-face type and the verb is italicized, illustrate this arrangement:

> Here *are* **the papers**.
> There *were* **30 students** in the class.

In the usual sentence arrangement, the subject precedes the verb.

These examples are referred to as inverted sentences—the subject comes after the verb. To locate the subject and verb more easily in these cases, re-state the sentence in the standard order—subject, then verb. For example:

In inverted sentences, the verb precedes the subject.

Inverted order:	Here *are* the papers.
Standard order:	The papers *are* here.
Inverted order:	There *were* 30 students in the class.
Standard order:	Thirty students *were* in the class.

In some of the previous examples, there were words or groups of words that we ignored when we were locating the predicate and subject. We will consider these parts of sentences in the next sections.

OBJECTS AND SUBJECT COMPLEMENTS

Objects and subject complements are important parts of sentences. They help to complete the thought expressed by the subject and the simple predicate. Understanding the functions of objects and subject complements will assist you in avoiding grammatical errors.

Objects and complements help complete the sentence thought.

OBJECTS. Objects are of two types: direct objects and indirect objects. **Direct objects** receive the action of the verb and help complete the thought of the sentence. The direct object answers the *what?* or *whom?* questions raised by the subject and verb. Examine the direct objects that are italicized in the following sentences:

Direct objects receive the action of the verb.

Susan reads the *book*. (Susan reads what?)

If you feel qualified, please enter the *competition*. (You enter what? Note that only action verbs can take direct objects; feel is a linking verb [see page 117].)

He studied *business communication* one semester. (He studied what?)

The training helped *Richard*. (The training helped whom?)

Indirect objects receive the action the verb makes on the direct object.

Indirect objects receive the action that the verb makes on the direct object. Indirect objects are always located between the verb and the direct object. Neither the direct object nor the indirect object ever appears as a prepositional phrase. You can locate the indirect object by inverting the sentence. Here are sentences with their indirect objects in boldface type and with their direct objects italicized:

Susan reads **John** the *book*. (The book was read *to* John.)
We offered the **class** a *free period*. (A free period was offered *to* the class.)

Subject complements rename or modify the subject.

SUBJECT COMPLEMENTS. The subject complement is (1) a noun or pronoun that renames the subject or (2) an adjective that modifies the subject. In both cases, the subject complement follows a linking verb in the sentence. **Linking verbs** (such as *is, was, has been, am, are,* and *seem*) do not show action. In each of the following examples, the subject and the subject complement are italicized and the linking verb is in boldface type:

James Lewis **is** an excellent *communicator*. (*Communicator* is a noun that renames *James Lewis*.)
The *memo* **was** *clear*. (*Clear* is an adjective that modifies *memo*.)
He **is** a powerful *industrialist*. (*Industrialist* is a noun that renames *he*.)
I **am** the *president*. (*President* is a noun that renames *I*.)

PHRASES AND CLAUSES

Recognizing groupings of words—referred to as *phrases* or *clauses*—is also important for understanding sentence structure.

A **phrase** includes either a subject or a predicate, but not both.

PHRASES. A **phrase** is a grouping of related words that functions as a part of speech. Phrases do not contain both a subject and a predicate—just one or the other. Here are some examples of phrases:

Verb phrases:	will be sending have keyboarded is considered
Noun phrases:	the first employee a fast car an excellent proposal
Prepositional phrases:	to the store by the beginning of the class in the morning
Adjective phrases:	better than average brilliant and insightful ready to wear
Participial phrases:	having been promoted seeing clearly keyboarding rapidly being determined early
Infinitive phrases:	to know to have been called to have told to be congratulated

Using phrases as parts of speech—as adjectives, adverbs, and nouns—can make your writing more interesting. They can add variety and color. Phrases are a way to add strong words to your sentences and bring power to your writing. Finally, they can strengthen your writing by providing helpful details and showing relationships. Note how the italicized phrases in the following examples add detail, variety, color, interest, power, and liveliness:

Phrases serve as parts of speech. They help add life to writing.

John manages. (no phrases)
John manages employees *in the plant.* (prepositional phrase)
John manages *better than the average person.* (adjective phrase)
John, *a better than average manager,* oversees *40 employees.* (adjective phrase, noun phrase)
John seems *to have been called to managing.* (infinitive phrase)
A capable manager, John oversees *40 employees.* (adjective phrase, noun phrase)
Managing effectively, John oversees *40 employees.* (participial phrase, noun phrase)

Understanding the purpose served by the phrase in the sentence is also important. For example, prepositional phrases can serve as adjectives and adverbs. If a phrase is serving as an adjective, it should be placed close to the noun it modifies so that the relationship is clear.

Wrong: The members present were of the class.
Right: The members of the class were present.

The phrase *of the class* serves as an adjective and modifies the noun *members.* This relationship is more clearly understood if the modifying phrase is close to the noun.

CLAUSES. A clause is a group of related words that contains both a subject and a predicate. There are two kinds of clauses: independent and dependent. An **independent clause**, sometimes referred to as a *main clause,* can stand alone as a separate sentence because it expresses a complete thought and has a subject and a predicate. In the following examples, the simple predicates are shown in boldface type, and the complete subjects are shown in italics:

A **clause** has both a subject and a predicate.

Independent clauses can stand alone.

the bread and butter **were** on the table
the consumer group **fought** the change

A **dependent clause**, also called a **subordinate clause**, cannot stand alone. It depends on another clause for the thought to be complete. A dependent clause is almost always introduced by a subordinate conjunction (such as *because, as soon as, if,* or *when*) or by a relative pronoun (such as *who,*

Dependent clauses are introduced by subordinate conjunctions or relative pronouns; they cannot stand alone as sentences.

which, or *that*). Look at the subordinate conjunction or relative pronoun (shown in boldface type), the simple subject (underlined), and the simple predicate (in italics) in each of these examples of dependent clauses:

> **if** the <u>order</u> *arrived* by Friday
>
> **that** the <u>report</u> *was* readable

The basic difference between dependent and independent clauses is the subordinate conjunction or relative pronoun. If you add a subordinate conjunction or relative pronoun to an independent clause, you make it a dependent clause. Thus, if you omit the subordinate conjunction and relative pronoun at the beginning of the two previous examples of dependent clauses, those clauses become independent clauses:

> the order arrived by Friday
>
> the report was readable

One other point related to clauses—the word *like* should not be used to introduce a clause. Grammar rules permit using like as a verb, adjective, or preposition, but *as* should be used to introduce clauses.

Wrong:	The message is short, *like* you wanted it to be.
Right:	The message is short, *as* you wanted it to be.

Sentence fragments are incomplete sentences and may or may not have meaning.

SENTENCE FRAGMENTS.   Another name for an incomplete sentence is **sentence fragment**. Sentence fragments are groups of words that may or may not have meaning as shown in the following examples:

> if the vacation is taken early (lacks meaning)
>
> Congratulations! (has meaning in context)
>
> David, having been transferred (lacks meaning)
>
> Best wishes for success. (has meaning in context)

Some writers selectively use sentence fragments; others never use them.

While the use of sentence fragments that have some meaning in context is fairly common in business communication, the acceptability of their usage is debated. Some business communicators think the infrequent, selective use of meaningful sentence fragments gives life and personality to their messages. Other business communicators do not use sentence fragments because, technically, they are grammatically incorrect. You will need to make your own decision on this issue.

SENTENCE PATTERNS

A helpful approach to understanding sentence construction for many students is to examine the most common sentence patterns. While the English language is extremely flexible, these patterns can frequently be noted:

A common sentence pattern is: subject → verb → object or complement.

1. Subject → Verb
   Susan → reads.
2. Subject → Verb → Direct Object
   Susan → reads → a book.
3. Subject → Verb → Indirect Object → Direct Object
   Susan → reads → Joshua → a book.
4. Subject → Verb → Subject Complement
   Ed → is → fine.
5. Here (or There) → Verb → Subject
   Here → is → your order.

SUBJECT AND VERB AGREEMENT

One of the basic rules of sentence construction is that the subject and the verb must agree in number. If the subject is singular—refers to just one person or one thing—then the verb must be singular. If the subject is plural, the verb must also be plural. Your ability to identify the subject is essential to determining whether it is singular or plural. The subject and the verb are italicized in the following examples:

The subject and verb must **agree** in number.

Singular:	The *manager is* attending a meeting.
Plural:	The *managers are* attending a meeting.
Singular:	The *pilot flies* the plane.
Plural:	The *pilots fly* the planes.

Recall that adding an *s* to most subjects makes them plural and adding an *s* to most verbs makes them singular. If you are not sure whether the subject is singular or plural (for example, a word like *data*), look it up in a dictionary. Then use the verb that agrees with the number of the subject. Words between the subject and the verb (intervening words) must be ignored

when determining the correct number of the subject. In the following examples
the subject and the verb are shown in boldface type, and the word or words
to be ignored are in italics:

Singular:	The **man** *with the books* **is** the salesperson.
Plural:	The **men** *with the books* **are** the salespersons.
Singular:	The **ring**, *as well as other valuables*, **was** lost.
Plural:	The **players**, *other than Tim*, **were** on time for the game.

**Compound subjects may
take singular or plural
verbs.**

As you will recall, a compound subject is two (or more) subjects connected by a coordinate conjunction. Some compound subjects take singular
verbs and some take plural verbs. There are three possibilities: (1) When compound subjects are connected by *and*, they are plural and require plural verbs.
(2) When compound subjects are connected by *or* or *nor*, and both are singular, they take singular verbs. (3) When compound subjects are connected by
or or *nor*, and one of the subjects is plural and one is singular, the verb should
agree with the number of the subject which is closer to it. The compound
subjects are in boldface type and their correct verbs are italicized in these
examples:

Plural:	**Antonio and Amelia** *are* students.
Plural:	The **man**, the **woman, and** the **child** *attend* the meeting together.
Singular:	Either **Antonio or Amelia** *is* first in line.
Singular:	Neither **Sheila nor David** *is* going.
Singular:	The **tents or** the **cabin** *is* available for shelter.
Plural:	Neither the **cabin nor** the **tents** *are* available for shelter.

Notice in the last two examples that the plural verb sounds better. In sentences
with both singular and plural subjects, this is almost always true. Thus, it will
be best for you to try to put the plural subject closer to the verb.

**Some subjects appear to
be plural but are
singular.**

Some words used as subjects are singular even though they may give the
appearance of being plural. Examples of these words are *everybody, everyone,
anybody, anyone, somebody, someone, nobody, one, each,* and *neither*. With
these singular subjects, use singular verbs:

Singular:	Everybody is (not *are*) invited.
Singular:	Anyone is (not *are*) welcome.
Singular:	Each of the participants attends (not *attend*) the meetings.
Singular:	Neither was (not *were*) late for the meeting.

Also some words that end in *s* are singular. Use singular verbs with those words:

Singular:	Athletics is an extracurricular activity.
Singular:	Mathematics is my favorite subject.
Singular:	Economics is an important field of study.

The name of one song, book, company, magazine, or article is singular even though the name is plural:

Singular:	*People* is an interesting magazine.
Singular:	Finance Associates, Inc., is the largest lending agency in New York.
Singular:	"Heartaches" is an old song.

Subjects in plural form that are considered as a single unit or as a whole take singular verbs. Amounts, distances, and some compound subjects are examples of this guideline:

Singular:	Thirty pounds is the correct weight.
Singular:	Ten feet is the distance to the end of the walk.
Singular:	Turkey and dressing is a Thanksgiving favorite.

The words *few*, *both*, *many*, and *several* are considered plural and take plural verbs:

Some subjects appear to be singular but are plural.

Plural:	Few are required to take the exam.
Plural:	Both were glad they went.
Plural:	Many select the personal stereo.
Plural:	Several are selling ads.

Collective nouns such as *committee*, *faculty*, and *audience* may be singular or plural. If the group is acting as one, the verb should be singular; if the group members are acting as individuals, the verb should be plural:

Collective nouns may be singular or plural.

Singular:	The faculty has voted its approval of the new course.
Plural:	The faculty are teaching their classes in spite of the noisy construction project.

PRONOUN AND ANTECEDENT AGREEMENT

Pronouns and their antecedents should agree.

Pronouns are noun substitutes.

To be grammatically correct in your communication, there is another form of agreement you will want to know and use—agreement of pronouns and their antecedents. Recall that pronouns are noun substitutes. The pronouns used as subjects, objects, or complements are *he, she, I, we, you, it, they, her, him, me, us,* and *them.* As a possessive, a pronoun is used as a modifier. Examples of possessive pronouns are *my, mine, our(s), your(s), his, her(s), its,* and *their(s).* An **antecedent** is the word, phrase, or clause that is replaced by the pronoun. An antecedent is most likely to be a noun.

Pronouns replace antecedents.

Pronouns and their antecedents must agree in three ways: (1) in number, (2) in gender, and (3) in clear relationship. In the following examples of agreement in number, the antecedent is italicized; the pronoun is in bold-face type:

They should agree in number.

Singular:	The *meeting* was short, and **it** was good.
Plural:	The *meetings* were short, and **they** were good.
Singular:	*Anna* found **her** coat in the conference room.
Plural:	*Anna* and *Frieda* found **their** coats in the conference room.
Singular:	The *Freeline Company* is in **its** fourth year.
Plural:	All Freeline Company *employees* believe **their** company will grow.
Singular:	Either *Fred* or *Jonathan* will take **his** car to the show.
Plural:	*Fred* and *Jonathan* will take **their** cars to the show.
Singular:	The *number* is high; **it** exceeds 100.
Plural:	A *number* of employees have voted **their** convictions.

They should agree in gender.

The next examples of pronouns and their antecedents show agreement in gender. The antecedent is italicized, and the pronoun is in boldface type:

Masculine:	*Alan* will keyboard **his** paper today.
Feminine:	*Nancy* keyboarded **her** paper yesterday.
Mixed:	Every *man* and *woman* must keyboard **his** or **her** paper before Friday.
Neuter:	A *project* is considered complete when a paper has been keyboarded for **it**.

Finally, there must be a clear relationship between a pronoun and its antecedent. Examples of unclear relationships and clear relationships follow:

They should clearly relate.

Unclear:	Anna and Frieda looked and looked and finally found her coat. (Antecedent not clear; whose coat?)
Clear:	Anna and Frieda looked and looked for Frieda's coat and finally found it.
Unclear:	Vincent wrote Adolph when he was in Texas. (Who was in Texas?)
Clear:	When Vincent was in Texas, he wrote Adolph.

PARALLELISM

One other important form of agreement you will want to use in constructing correct sentences is parallelism. **Parallelism** means having balance and consistency between or among parts of sentences that serve the same function.

Sentence constructions should be **parallel**.

Parallelism is achieved by using the same grammatical form for the two or more parts of sentences that serve the same function. Using the same grammatical form means using noun with noun, adjective with adjective, verb with verb, adverb with adverb, phrase with phrase, or clause with clause. Parts of sentences serve the same function if they serve as a part of a series, a contrast, a comparison, a choice, or an expression of equality.

The same grammatical form should be used for parts that serve the same function.

Different types of parallelism are shown in the following examples. The parts of these sentences that are not parallel are shown in boldface type.

1. Series

Parts of series should be parallel.

Not parallel:	Jane is responsible for finance, production, and **to oversee** marketing. (Two parts of the series, *finance* and *production*, are nouns; one part, *to oversee marketing*, is an infinitive phrase.)
Parallel:	Jane is responsible for finance, production, and marketing. (All parts of the series are nouns.)
Not parallel:	He completed the accounting report quickly, accurately, and **with a neat appearance**. (The parts *quickly* and *accurately* are adverbs; *with a neat appearance* is a prepositional phrase.)
Parallel:	He completed the accounting report quickly, accurately, and neatly. (All parts of the series are adverbs.)

Not parallel:	Sheila is a hard worker, **productive**, and a friendly person. (While other parts of the series are adjective-noun combinations, *productive* is an adjective standing alone.)
Parallel:	Sheila is a hard worker, a productive employee, and a friendly person. (All parts of the series are adjective-noun combinations.)

Parts of contrasts should be parallel.

2. Contrast

Not parallel:	The instructor can force a student to attend class but not **think creatively**. (The part *to attend class* is an infinitive phrase, but *think creatively* is a verb-adverb combination.)
Parallel:	The instructor can force a student to attend class but not to think creatively. (Both parts are infinitive phrases.)

Parts of comparisons should be parallel.

3. Comparison

Not parallel:	Gayle persuaded Pat, and Charles **was also convinced** by her. (The part *persuaded* is a verb in the active voice, and the part *was* (also) *convinced* is a verb in the passive voice.)
Parallel:	Gayle persuaded Pat, and she also convinced Charles. (Both verbs are now in the active voice.)
Not parallel:	Your selling season is longer than **the Youngblood RV Center**. (The comparison is not clear—selling season is longer than Youngblood RV Center? The information necessary to complete the comparison is omitted.)
Parallel:	Your selling season is longer than the Youngblood RV Center's selling season. (Both parts of the comparison now contain clarifying adjective-noun combinations.)

Expressions of equality should be parallel.

4. Expression of Equality

Not parallel:	The personnel officer wanted to hire an **aggressive** salesperson and accountant. (The use of the adjective *aggressive* as a modifier for *salesperson* and *accountant* produces the unlikely meaning that one person would be hired to do both jobs.)
Parallel:	The personnel officer wanted to hire an aggressive salesperson and an accurate accountant. (The use of appropriate modifiers in both places clarifies that two people are sought.)
Not parallel:	Julie is **both** responsible for the dinner **and** the entertainment. (The correlative conjunction *both . . . and* is not in a parallel relationship because of the improper location of *both* in relationship to the dinner and the entertainment.)
Parallel:	Julie is responsible for both the dinner and the entertainment. (The correlative conjunction relates to the same parts of the sentence.)

The parallel constructions in these examples are generally shorter, clearer, and stronger than the constructions that are not parallel. Achieving parallelism in your sentences improves their readability and maintains their momentum. Because of their balance and consistency, parallel constructions communicate effectively as well as correctly.

Parallel constructions are both correct and clear.

PURPOSES OF SENTENCES

A sentences can serve one of four basic purposes. These four purposes are as follows:

*Sentences can serve as **statements, questions, commands,** or **exclamations.***

1. To state a fact. A statement or **declarative** sentence is followed by a period. For example:

   The board will meet on Tuesday.
   Thomas referred the matter to Mary.

2. To ask a question. A question or **interrogative** sentence is followed by a question mark. For example:

   Have you finished your report?
   Are you going to the office?

3. To issue a command or make a courteous request. A command or request, also known as an **imperative** sentence, is followed by a period. Usually *you* is understood as the subject in a command or request. For example:

   (You) Please report for work at 8 a.m.
   (You) Make five copies of this memo.

4. To express strong emotion. An exclamation or **exclamatory** sentence is followed by an exclamation point. For example:

   Have a nice day!
   It's snowing!

VARIETIES OF SENTENCE STRUCTURES

Finally, for you to know how to construct correct sentences, it is essential that you know the four basic sentence structures. The technical names of these sentence structures are *simple sentence, compound sentence, complex sentence,*

There are four sentence structures.

and *compound-complex sentence.* Sentence structures are classified on the basis of the number and kinds of clauses they have. The two kinds of clauses—independent (main) clauses and dependent (subordinate) clauses—were discussed in this chapter.

Your messages will be more interesting if you vary the sentence structures you use. You can also emphasize an idea by placing it in an independent clause or de-emphasize it by placing it in a dependent clause. The effective communicator understands and uses all four sentence structures.

THE SIMPLE SENTENCE

Simple sentences contain one independent clause.

The simple sentence contains one independent clause and no dependent clauses. You will recall that independent clauses contain both a subject and a predicate and are not introduced with a subordinate conjunction or a relative pronoun. It should be noted also that simple sentences can have compound subjects or compound predicates and can include phrases. Here are some examples of typical simple sentences:

> Susan reads. (simple sentence)
> Ms. Crawford and Mr. Sams approved the proposal. (simple sentence with compound subject)
> Sales of personal computers doubled last year. (simple sentence with prepositional phrase)
> In the report, Sharon repeated and stressed the importance of planning ahead. (simple sentence with introductory prepositional phrase and compound predicate)
> Mr. Frederickson is the fifth president of the Swanger Company. (simple sentence with prepositional phrase)

You can make your communication of an idea more powerful by using a simple sentence. This sentence structure gives the greatest emphasis to the idea because there are no distracting dependent clauses. The simple sentence is especially effective in composing business messages. It is a clear, concise, and efficient way of communicating—the simple sentence is businesslike. Overuse of simple sentences in a message, however, can result in choppy, sing-song monotony—particularly if the sentences are all short. Note the choppiness in the following paragraph:

> The order was received. We started production. The drilling machine failed. It was not set up properly. The supervisor tried to fix it. The utility engineer tried to fix it. They both were unsuccessful. We missed the delivery date. The customer canceled the order.

To make your writing more interesting and possibly to de-emphasize some ideas, you will want to mix the sentence structures you use.

THE COMPOUND SENTENCE

The compound sentence contains two or more independent clauses and no dependent clauses. In this sentence structure, two or more ideas share emphasis. By pairing the ideas together in one sentence consisting of independent clauses of similar strength, the ideas receive somewhat less emphasis than they would in separate simple sentences.

In the following examples the subjects are italicized, and the simple predicates are shown in boldface type. Note in these examples that the independent clauses in each compound sentence are joined with a coordinate conjunction, a conjunctive adverb, or a semicolon:

> *Victor* **opened** a bank account, and *it* **was** useful to him in transacting business.
> *Birgit* **worked** for International Importing for three years, and *Michele* **worked** for Cosmopolitan Company for five years.
> *Mrs. Franklin* **was offered** the position, but *she* **did not accept** the offer.
> The *first shipment* of appliances **arrived** Monday; however, the *second shipment* **did not arrive** until Friday.
> All the *parts* **are** in stock; the *repair work* **can move** ahead.

Here is a paragraph using compound sentences:

> The order was received and we started production. The drilling machine failed; it was not set up properly. The supervisor and the utility engineer tried to fix it, but both were unsuccessful. We missed the delivery date and the customer canceled the order.

The use of the compound sentence structure enables you to show that two or more ideas are of equal importance. By putting them together in one sentence, you indicate a close relationship that constitutes another, larger idea.

Compound sentences contain two or more independent clauses.

THE COMPLEX SENTENCE

The complex sentence contains one independent clause and one or more dependent clauses. Remember that a dependent clause depends on the independent clause to make a complete thought—hence, the term *dependent clause*. In a complex sentence, one or more ideas are subordinated to the main idea. Less important or negative ideas can be de-emphasized by placing them in dependent clauses; the main idea can be emphasized by placing it in the independent clause. Another advantage of the complex sentence is that

Complex sentences contain one independent clause and one or more dependent clauses.

the dependent clause can be used to further explain, clarify, and strengthen the main idea. The dependent clauses commonly used in complex sentences are:

1. Noun clauses (used as subjects and objects)
2. Adjective clauses (used to modify nouns and pronouns)
3. Adverb clauses (used to modify verbs)

As you know, dependent clauses contain both a subject and a predicate and are introduced with a subordinate conjunction (such as *because, although, while, as soon as, if, whether,* or *when*) or a relative pronoun (such as *who, which,* or *that*). In the following examples the dependent clauses are italicized:

Although we cannot deliver the merchandise until October 14, all the patterns and colors will be included in the first shipment.

While it is important that you be on time for work, you can choose your own starting time.

It is not clear *whether Sally can go.*

All *who are graduating seniors* will be excused from the final exam.

The personnel form should be typed if possible, *although completing it in ink is acceptable.*

Bill Graves is sure *that the sale will go through.*

Here is a paragraph using complex sentences:

When the order was received, we started production. The drilling machine failed because it was not set up properly. Although the supervisor and the utility engineer tried to fix it, they both were unsuccessful. As soon as we missed the delivery date, the customer canceled the order.

Complex sentences are more complicated than simple sentences in that they carry more than one idea. When using this structure, you need to be sure that the idea you want to emphasize is in the independent clause.

THE COMPOUND-COMPLEX SENTENCE

Compound-complex sentences contain two or more independent clauses and one or more dependent clauses.

The compound-complex sentence contains two or more independent clauses and one or more dependent clauses. The compound-complex sentence structure offers a business communicator the advantages of both the compound and complex sentences. Ideas can be related, emphasized, and de-emphasized in this complicated structure. However, the compound-complex sentence structure can become long and cumbersome. Business readers want to be able to understand a sentence on the first reading. For this reason, the compound-complex structure is used infrequently in business messages. In the following examples of compound-complex sentences, the dependent clauses are italicized and the independent clauses are in boldface type:

> *If the fire fighters work quickly,* **they may save the equipment**; *otherwise,* **the fire will cause a total loss.**
>
> *While Mary and Robert are on vacation,* **the work must go on; we know their absence will provide an opportunity for Karen and Will to gain more experience.**

Here is a paragraph using compound-complex sentences:

> When the order was received, we started production; but the drilling machine failed. Even though it was not set up properly, the supervisor tried to fix it and the utility engineer tried to fix it. Because both were unsuccessful, we missed the delivery date; and the customer canceled the order.

In your development of business messages, you have the opportunity to significantly increase your effectiveness by giving attention to sentence construction. In this chapter you have studied material that will assist you in composing correct, interesting, and powerful sentences—sentences that will make you a better business communicator.

DISCUSSION QUESTIONS

1. Describe a sentence.
2. Define the subject of a sentence, and explain the difference between the complete subject and the simple subject.
3. Define the predicate of a sentence, and explain the difference between the complete predicate and the simple predicate.
4. What are compound subjects and compound predicates? Give examples.
5. Create a complete sentence for each of the following thoughts:
   a. A reduction in taxes next year
   b. A salary raise for Tom based on outstanding performance
   c. A bill payment by Mr. Harrison
   d. A high test grade for a student who studied
   e. A curt message tone
6. Describe how to recognize predicates and subjects in sentences.
7. What is an inverted sentence? Give an example.

8. Discuss the sentence functions performed by objects, and give examples supporting your discussion.

9. Discuss the sentence functions performed by subject complements, and give examples supporting your discussion.

10. Define the term *phrase* and give an example of (a) a verb phrase, (b) a noun phrase, (c) a prepositional phrase, (d) an adjective phrase, (e) a participial phrase, and (f) an infinitive phrase.

11. Define the term *clause*.

12. What is the difference between an independent clause and a dependent clause? Give an example of each.

13. Create a correct sentence for each of the following sentence patterns:
    a. Subject → Verb
    b. Subject → Verb → Direct Object
    c. Subject → Verb → Indirect Object → Direct Object
    d. Subject → Verb → Subject Complement
    e. Here (or There) → Verb → Subject

14. What does the term *agreement* in sentence construction mean? In your answer, explain subject-verb agreement, pronoun-antecedent agreement, and parallelism. Give examples of subject and verb (a) disagreement and (b) agreement. Give examples of pronoun and antecedent (c) disagreement and (d) agreement. Also give examples of (e) lack of parallelism and (f) parallelism.

15. What are the four purposes of sentences? Give an example sentence for each purpose.

16. Define and give an example of a simple sentence.

17. Define and give an example of a compound sentence.

18. Define and give an example of a complex sentence.

19. Define and give an example of a compound-complex sentence.

20. Explain why business communicators should vary the sentence structures they use. Be sure to give the advantages and disadvantages of each structure discussed.

APPLICATION EXERCISES

1. Write each of the following sentences. Identify the complete subject by underlining it once and the complete predicate by underlining it twice.
    a. The microcomputer was repaired by Cecil.
    b. Joe sold pencils.
    c. Jean was manager of the plant.
    d. Jan, who was just promoted, is now supervisor of the Information Processing Center.

    e. All the merchandise was replaced.

    f. The sun and the moon were all that he asked for.

    g. Productivity in the plant was up by 55 percent.

    h. There were seven employees on vacation at the same time.

    i. Why can't you return the stereo?

    j. When will the furniture be shipped?

2. For each of the preceding sentences, identify the simple subject and the simple predicate by circling them.

3. Each of the sentences in the following paragraph is identified by a letter preceding it in parentheses. List the letter for each sentence and write the complete subject for that sentence beside the letter.

> (a) Many types of businesses can be profitable. (b) Among the most profitable are restaurants. (c) But they can also be business failures. (d) It comes down to quality—quality food and quality management. (e) Constantine and Norma opened a Greek restaurant. (f) The two of them bought only the best food, and they oversaw its careful preparation. (g) While they charged high prices, many customers were served; and excellent profits were made.

4. For each of the sentences in the preceding paragraph, list its letter and write the complete predicate beside the letter.

5. Name and explain the purpose of the italicized phrase in each of the following sentences:

    a. She *will be sending* the letter tomorrow.

    b. He is known for his ability *to communicate*.

    c. Why is the store *closed so early*?

    d. The supervisor is *an excellent manager*.

    e. All the clerks were tired, *having worked 48 hours straight*.

6. For each of the preceding sentences, identify the direct object or subject complement by listing and naming them.

7. Each of the sentences in the following paragraph is identified by a letter. List the letter for each sentence, and write and explain the purpose of the italicized phrase.

> (a) Several *products* are increasing in popularity. (b) For example, camcorders and VCR's sell *at a faster rate* today than they did a year ago. (c) *To judge* the comparative importance of sales rates, economists analyzed the sales of several products. (d) These *products* included TV's, personal stereos, compact disc players, VCR's, and camcorders. (e) The sales of all of these items increased *over the past year*, but VCR and camcorder sales increased at a faster pace than did the sales of other products.

8. For each of the sentences in the preceding paragraph, list its letter and indicate its direct object, indirect object, or subject complement.

9. For each of the following sentences, list its letter, identify any dependent clause it may contain, and indicate the sentence structure.

    a. The sophomore became a junior after completing the required course work.

    b. Overseas shipments of freight are to be insured for full value.

    c. If managers learn to delegate, they are able to advance more quickly.

    d. When reporting production figures, give the figures in 100-pound units.

    e. I am steadily making progress because I am steadily improving my ability to communicate.

    f. Those who toured the plant were impressed with its efficiency, which is a trademark of Everytime Manufacturing Corporation; on the other hand, they had questions about the human relations practiced there.

    g. If you can, please let me know when the pictures will be ready.

    h. She saw that the problem was solved after the man said that all was clear.

    i. Mildred and Bobby felt that the mill would open after the holiday; but they had not planned on the economic downturn, which surprised everyone.

    j. The horses and cows were grazing in the fields; in addition, the goats and the sheep were in the feeding pens.

10. Write the correct verb form for each of the following sentences, and give the reason for your choice:

    a. Either Paula or Brent (is, are) going.

    b. The committee basically (agree, agrees) with the decision.

    c. Each person on the committee, however, (is, are) waiting for more information.

    d. Errol and Sally (was, were) elected to the ethics committee.

    e. The police (has, have) spoken to the class in the past.

    f. The administrative council, except for the three ex officio members, (establish, establishes) all new regulations.

    g. The woman or the men (is, are) on the council that will vote on the issue.

    h. The *ABC Journal* (publish, publishes) articles on business communication.

    i. Most of the articles (is, are) practical and helpful.

    j. Forensics (is, are) the study of debate.

11. Indicate the correct pronoun in each of the following sentences and give the reason for your choice:

    a. All of the class members had (their, his or her) reports.

    b. Either Melissa or Barbara left (their, her) toothbrush at Bonnie's house.

    c. The college opened (their, its) school year on August 20.

    d. Each of the students introduced (their, his or her) designated partner.

    e. Every woman and man must introduce (their, his or her) partner.

12. Explain how each of the following sentences lacks parallelism. Rewrite the sentence correcting the lack of parallelism.
    a. The firm's quotations were lower than the ABC Corporation.
    b. The manager encouraged the plant employees, and the office employees were motivated by her.
    c. Judy was strong, optimistic, and a woman of courage.
    d. Diane works as a nurse and is volunteering as a firefighter.
    e. The student's paper was brief and clearer.
13. Write a short paragraph in which you illustrate each of the four purposes of sentences—statement, question, command or request, and exclamation.
14. Write a short paragraph on a topic of your choice and use each of the four basic sentence structures—simple sentence, compound sentence, complex sentence, and compound-complex sentence.

CHAPTER 7

PUNCTUATION

LEARNING OBJECTIVES

Your learning objectives for this chapter include the following:

— To review the proper use of terminal punctuation marks—the period, the question mark, and the exclamation point
— To review the proper use of the comma and the semicolon as internal marks of punctuation
— To review the guidelines for using of the following punctuation marks:
The colon
The hyphen
The dash
The apostrophe
Quotation marks
Ellipsis points
Parentheses

Punctuation marks add emphasis and clarity to a message.

When you speak, the tone of your voice, the gestures you make, and the pauses you insert help your listeners understand what you are saying. When you write, punctuation helps your readers understand your message. Punctuation tells your readers where one thought ends and the next begins. Punctuation adds emphasis and clarifies. Writing without punctuation is comparable to traveling from New York to Oregon without road signs.

This chapter reviews the punctuation that occurs most often in business writing. It is not designed to eliminate the need for reference manuals.

Experienced writers freely consult reference sources about punctuation usage. When you have a question about punctuation, do not leave the answer to chance. Take the time to check this chapter, a reference manual, or a similar source. Incorrect punctuation can cause your reader more confusion and frustration than using no punctuation at all.

Check reference sources when you are uncertain about punctuation.

TERMINAL PUNCTUATION

Three punctuation symbols are used to signal the end of a complete thought: the period, the question mark, and the exclamation point. The correct symbol depends on the nature of the thought.

THE PERIOD

The period is the most frequently used ending mark of punctuation. It is used at the end of a **declarative** or an **imperative sentence**:

> Rehearsal will begin at 6 p.m. (declarative)
>
> Chai has decided to campaign for the presidency. (declarative)
>
> Complete and return the survey within two weeks. (imperative)
>
> Take the package to the post office. (imperative)

A request that requires *action* rather than an oral or written response also ends with a period. This type of request is often referred to as a **courteous request**. The writer would rather have the reader devote time to doing what has been requested than to writing or calling to say yes or no:

> Won't you let us know which color you prefer.
>
> Will you please make an appointment with Dr. James.

The period is also used when the writer asks an **indirect question**. A question is indirect when it is a statement about a question:

> I wonder when Beth will call.
>
> Marilyn asked whether you and I are related.

Periods are used to end:

- declarative and imperative sentences

- courteous requests that require action

- indirect questions

THE QUESTION MARK

Question marks are used to end direct questions.

A question mark should be used with an **interrogative sentence**. You will recognize an interrogative sentence because it calls for a response. The response may be a single word, or it may be one or more sentences:

> Do you have a key to the building? (one-word response)
>
> Why were you late? (a response of one or more sentences)

THE EXCLAMATION POINT

Exclamation points show strong emotions.

An **exclamatory sentence** ends with an exclamation point. Although it is not used frequently, the exclamation point can do a great deal to bring life to business correspondence. The exclamation point can help you express strong emotion such as surprise, enthusiasm, or anger:

> Yes! Nikki won the award.
>
> Hurry! Make your reservation today.
>
> Your credit rating is in danger!

Deciding whether to use a period, a question mark, or an exclamation point is easy. Simply ask yourself these questions:

1. Am I expressing a strong emotion? (If you are, use **!**)
2. Am I asking the reader to give me a response? (If so, use **?**)

If your answer to both questions is no, the period is the appropriate mark of punctuation.

INTERNAL PUNCTUATION

Using the appropriate terminal punctuation mark is one step toward achieving message clarity, but appropriate internal punctuation is also important. The comma and the semicolon are the most frequently used internal marks of punctuation. In addition, there are several other symbols that provide clarity, emphasis, and variety in writing.

THE COMMA

The comma plays an important role in business writing. Commas separate items in sentences to help your reader correctly interpret each thought. By learning how commas are used and by mastering the rules for their placement, you will become a more effective business writer.

Commas separate items in sentences.

Using too few or too many commas can hamper communication. Consider these examples:

Too few or too many commas can hamper message clarity.

> After you have eaten the leftover meat, the vegetables and the dairy products should be placed in the refrigerator. (too few commas)
>
> This afternoon, we will meet with the chairman of the board, while staff members, tour the new addition, to the factory. (too many commas)

In the first sentence, the absence of commas makes the reader wonder what is to be eaten and what is to be put into the refrigerator. Confusion results, and additional communication is necessary. The message becomes clear when a comma is inserted after the word *eaten* and between each item in the compound subject:

> After you have eaten, the leftover meat, the vegetables, and the dairy products should be placed in the refrigerator.

In the second sentence, message clarity is lost because four commas were used where none was needed. The sentence should read:

> This afternoon we will meet with the chairman of the board while his staff tours the new addition to the factory.

Although the original versions of these sentences are extreme examples of comma omission and misuse, they illustrate the need for caution in using commas. The best way to assure correct usage of commas is to be able to justify the placement of each comma.

Be sure to justify each comma you use.

APPOSITIVES. An appositive is a word or a series of words that immediately follows a noun and provides additional information about it. Appositives may be essential or nonessential. Only nonessential appositives are separated from the rest of the sentence by commas:

> My oldest sister, Nancy, owns a nursery. (The name *Nancy* is not essential to the meaning of the sentence; only one of the writer's sisters may be the oldest.)
>
> My sister Nancy owns a nursery. (The name is essential; the writer has more than one sister.)

Use commas with
complete calendar dates.

CALENDAR DATES.   A complete calendar date consists of a month, a day, and a year. Whenever a complete calendar date occurs within the body of a sentence, the year is set apart from the rest of the sentence by commas. If the military or international date form is used, however, no commas are needed:

> On *March 1, 1988*, our company served its one millionth customer. (The calendar date is complete.)
>
> In *March 1988* our company served its one millionth customer. (No commas are needed since the date is incomplete.)
>
> On *1 March 1988* our company served its one millionth customer. (The military or international date form does not need commas.)

A calendar date used to clarify the noun that precedes it is also set off by commas. The calendar date may be complete or incomplete:

> On Wednesday, *January 19*, the company will begin its annual Community Share campaign. (The incomplete calendar date *January 19* is needed to clarify Wednesday.)
>
> On Thursday, *November 17, 1972*, two sets of triplets were born at Sidney General Hospital. (The complete calendar date *November 17, 1972* is needed to clarify Thursday.)

Use a comma after a
dependent clause that
introduces an
independent clause.

COMPLEX SENTENCES.   Whenever a dependent clause *introduces* an independent clause in a complex sentence, a comma is used to separate the clauses:

> *Before you leave*, please verify your address. (The dependent clause introduces the independent clause.)
>
> *After we receive your application*, we will review it and notify you of your credit status. (The dependent clause introduces the independent clause.)
>
> Call Zelda Matthews *if you would like to receive a copy of the report*. (No comma is needed; the dependent clause does not introduce the independent clause.)

When two independent
clauses are joined by a
conjunction, place a
comma before the
conjunction.

COMPOUND SENTENCES.   Whenever the independent clauses in a compound sentence are joined with a coordinate conjunction, use a comma before the conjunction:

> The furniture is attractive, *but* it is too large for my patio. (The coordinate conjunction joins independent clauses.)
>
> The audience welcomed the speaker with applause, *and* he responded by giving a dynamic presentation. (The coordinate conjunction joins the independent clauses.)
>
> The letters are for *Mr. Dawson and Ms. Simms*. (No comma is needed because the coordinate conjunction *and* does not connect two independent clauses.)

GEOGRAPHIC LOCATIONS. A complete geographic location consists of a city and a state, province, or nation. Whenever such a geographic location occurs within a sentence, the name of the state, province, or nation is set apart from the rest of the sentence by commas:

> The convention will be held in *Honolulu, Hawaii*, next December. (Honolulu, Hawaii, is a complete geographic location.)
>
> The meeting will be held in our *Alabama* office. (No commas are necessary because the geographic location is incomplete.)
>
> Have you ever visited *London, England*? (The geographic location is complete; the *?* replaces the ending comma because the name of the country is the last item in the interrogative sentence.)

Use commas with complete geographic locations.

NONESSENTIAL ELEMENTS. Words, phrases, or clauses that are not necessary to the meaning or structure of a sentence are considered nonessential elements. These elements take a variety of forms, and each is certain to require one or more commas. If the nonessential element begins a sentence, it should be followed by a comma. If the nonessential element occurs within the body of the sentence, it is preceded and followed by commas. If the nonessential element is the last item in the sentence, it is preceded by a comma and followed by the appropriate terminal punctuation mark.

Place commas before and after nonessential information or transitional words.

To determine if an item is nonessential, omit it from the sentence. If the meaning and structure of the sentence are complete without the item, it is considered nonessential.

INTRODUCTORY WORDS. Introductory words are separated from an independent clause by a comma:

An introductory word is followed by a comma.

> *Yes*, Ms. Armandoza was employed as a clerk in our office. (The introductory word is not essential to the meaning or structure of the sentence.)
>
> *Unfortunately*, the warranty has expired. (The introductory word is not essential to the meaning or structure of the sentence.)

INTRODUCTORY PHRASES. An introductory phrase may or may not be separated from an independent clause by a comma; the deciding factor is readability. If omitting the comma could cause reader confusion, include it. Some writers use a comma after an introductory phrase that has five or more words *or* after one that contains a verb. You, too, may find this technique helpful:

Commas are optional after introductory phrases.

> *To make your reservation* phone Maxine. (No comma is necessary; the message is clear without the comma.)
>
> *By Tuesday morning* she was feeling much better. (No comma is necessary; the message is clear without the comma.)
>
> *Before leaving*, Mildred thanked Ed and Mary for their hospitality. (Message clarity is improved by placing a comma after the introductory phrase. Note that the phrase does contain a verb.)

After signing the letters and inserting them in the envelopes, Madeline realized that she had forgotten to include the checks. (Message clarity is improved by placing a comma after the long introductory phrase.)

Nonrestrictive clauses provide additional information and are set apart by commas.

NONRESTRICTIVE CLAUSES.   A clause that provides additional information or explanation is considered nonrestrictive and is set apart from the rest of the sentence by commas. Nonrestrictive clauses frequently begin with *who* or *which*. Some writers prefer to use the word *which* to begin a nonrestrictive clauses and the word *that* to begin an essential clause.

This facility, *which was built in 1965,* is the largest of its kind in this state. (The clause is not essential to the meaning of the sentence.)

The payment *that was due March 15* is now three weeks past due. (The clause is essential to the sentence.)

The artist *who donated the sculpture* wishes to remain anonymous. (The clause is essential to the sentence; therefore, it is not set apart from the rest of the sentence by commas.)

Please assure Dr. Corey that, *although we have opposed him in the past,* we will support him on this issue. (The clause is not essential to the meaning of the sentence. Note that this nonrestrictive clause does not begin with *who* or *which*.)

Mr. Carlehede, *whose daughter is mayor of Bentley,* has been elected to the school board of Hart City. (The clause does not restrict the meaning of the sentence.)

Parenthetical expressions interrupt the flow of a sentence and are set apart by commas.

PARENTHETICAL EXPRESSIONS.   Words that interrupt the flow of a sentence are called parenthetical expressions. They are separated from the rest of the sentence by commas:

Your refund will, *of course,* be processed immediately. (The words *of course* interrupt the flow of the sentence.)

The white blossom, *although less common,* is as beautiful as the red. (The words *although less common* interrupt the flow of the sentence.)

The show that opened last night, *to say the least,* bombed. (The words *to say the least* interrupt the flow of the sentence.)

Transitional expressions link independent clauses or sentences.

TRANSITIONAL EXPRESSIONS.   A word or phrase that links sentences or independent clauses is a transitional expression. When a transitional expression is used to link two independent clauses, it is preceded by a semicolon and followed by a comma. When a transitional expression is used to link two sentences, it is followed by a comma:

Most of the passengers preferred fast food; *therefore,* the driver stopped at Hank's Hamburger Haven. (A transitional expression links two independent clauses.)

Your newest catalog had not yet arrived when we placed our order. *As a result,* we were unable to use the new price in calculating the total cost of our order. (This transitional expression links two sentences.)

Words such as *however, therefore, of course,* and *as a result* may be either parenthetical or transitional. The key is how they are used in the sentence:

> The check, *however,* will not be mailed until Monday. (The word *however* interrupts the flow of the sentence—it is parenthetical.)
>
> Your request has been granted; *however,* the check will not be mailed until Monday. (The word *however* is used as a transitional word linking two independent clauses.

SERIES.

One of the most frequent uses of commas is to separate items in a series. Whenever three or more words, phrases, or clauses appear in a series and are to be taken as one unit to form a subject, a verb, or an object, they should be separated by commas. The final item is usually set apart from the others by the word *and* or the word *or.* For clarity a comma should be used before the conjunction as well as between each of the items:

Commas separate items in a series.

The final item in a series follows a conjunction.

> *Swiss, cheddar, and mozzarella* are varieties of cheese. (The three names are part of a compound subject.)
>
> Jason bought *markers, pencils, pens, and tablets* for the office. (The items are the direct object of the verb *bought.*)
>
> The contestants *danced, sang, and read* poetry as part of the talent competition. (The verbs describe the actions of the contestants.)
>
> *One and won, their and there, and sum and some* are examples of homonyms. (Each pair of words in the series is part of a compound subject.)

COORDINATE ADJECTIVES.

In the preceding examples, the word *and* or the word *or* was a clue to the presence of a series and the need for a comma. Such conjunctions, however, are generally omitted when the words in the series are used as coordinate adjectives to describe a person or thing. Although the word *and* or the word *or* is not present, the comma is still needed:

A comma replaces the word and between adjectives.

> Sybil is an enthusiastic, dedicated business student.

The adjectives in the series describe Sybil as a business student. The writer could have said:

> Sybil is an enthusiastic and dedicated business student.

This sentence structure is cumbersome. Combining the adjectives is more efficient for the writer and more pleasing to the reader. A good test of the need for commas and where they should be placed is to mentally insert the word *and* between the adjectives. If the word *and* can be inserted without altering the meaning of the sentence, a comma should be used.

Sentence without punctuation:	We arrived on a cold stormy night.
Test:	We arrived on a cold (and) stormy night.
Correctly punctuated:	We arrived on a cold, stormy night.

The following example needs no commas. If we try to insert the word *and* between the adjectives, the sentence becomes awkward.

Sentence without punctuation:	Robert drove a shiny blue sports car.
Test:	Robert drove a shiny (and) blue sports car.
Correctly punctuated:	Robert drove a shiny blue sports car.

The words *shiny, blue,* and *sports* all describe the car.

THE SEMICOLON

Semicolons may be used to separate or to join.

You will recall that the purpose of a comma is to separate. The semicolon is used for the same reason—to separate—but may also be used to join.

COMPOUND SENTENCES. A semicolon is used to join two independent clauses in a compound sentence in two situations:

1. The independent clauses are not joined by a coordinate conjunction.
2. The independent clauses are joined by a coordinate conjunction, but either or both of the clauses contain commas.

Semicolons join independent clauses when no conjunction is used.

In the first situation, the semicolon makes the reader aware of the close relationship between the independent clauses. Although each clause could be written as a separate sentence, a smoother writing style is achieved by joining them with a semicolon:

Please sign and return the enclosed card; it requires no postage. (The clauses are closely related; no conjunction is used.)

Last summer I worked as a cashier; this summer I'll enroll for courses at Mayfair College. (The clauses are closely related; no conjunction is used.)

Semicolons should be used to join independent clauses that contain commas.

In the second situation, clarity is achieved by using a semicolon (rather than a comma) before the conjunction that joins the two independent clauses. In the example that follows, the sentence that uses the semicolon is clearer and easier to read:

Mr. Abelson, Ms. Skurla, and Mrs. Newstrom will leave for Detroit on September 10, but Mr. Yukita, Mrs. Zollar, and Mr. Nelson will not leave until September 12.

Mr. Abelson, Ms. Skurla, and Mrs. Newstrom will leave for Detroit on September 10; but Mr. Yukita, Mrs. Zollar, and Mr. Nelson will not leave until September 12.

SERIES. Using commas to separate items in a series could result in confusion when each item within the series contains a comma. By using semicolons to separate the items in this type of series, the message is easier to interpret. In the example that follows, the second sentence—the one that uses semicolons to separate the series items—is much clearer:

> We have branch offices in Juneau, Alaska, Buffalo, New York, Norman, Oklahoma, and Cheyenne, Wyoming.

> We have branch offices in Juneau, Alaska; Buffalo, New York; Norman, Oklahoma; and Cheyenne, Wyoming.

The comma and the semicolon are two punctuation marks that influence the clarity and readability of a message. Use them effectively to help your reader better understand your message.

Use semicolons to separate long, complex series items that contain commas.

THE COLON

A colon is a clue to the reader that a **listing**, an **explanation**, or an **example** will follow. The words that introduce the listing should contain a subject and a predicate; the items following the colon may be words or complete sentences. The items following the colon may be in paragraph form or in a vertical listing and numbers may or may not be used. The writer makes the placement decision based on the space available and the amount of emphasis to be placed on the items. A vertical listing will receive more attention than items presented in paragraph form.

Items listed in paragraph form are capitalized only if they are complete sentences or proper nouns. Items in vertical list form are always capitalized.

Colons alert the reader that something of importance will follow.

> There are several reasons for our decision: time, distance, and money. (paragraph form)

> There are several reasons for our decision: (1) time, (2) distance, and (3) money. (paragraph form with numbers)

> Our decision was based on the following reasons:
> 1. Time
> 2. Distance
> 3. Money
>
> (vertical list form)

> Our decision was based on time, distance, and money. (No colon is used because the portion of the sentence before the series is not an independent clause.)

THE HYPHEN

Hyphens bring items together.

The hyphen is used to bring things together—to show that two items are related. Hyphens are commonly used in four ways: (1) to form compound words, (2) to join prefixes and suffixes to root words, (3) to join the high and low points in a numeric range, and (4) to indicate where a word has been divided. The first three uses are explained in this section; word division is explained in Chapter 8.

Hyphens form compound words.

COMPOUND WORDS.   The most frequent use of the hyphen is to form compound words—two or more words used as one word. Compound words may be nouns, verbs, or adjectives. Authorities do not always agree on whether compound words should be hyphenated, written as two words, or written as one word; style preferences are continually changing. The best source of information about compound nouns and verbs is a current dictionary. The information presented in this section will help you determine when and how to hyphenate compound adjectives.

Hyphens join some compound adjectives.

Compound adjectives may be formed in several ways. Illustration 7-1 lists the various types of compound adjectives, gives an example of each, and indicates when each should be hyphenated.

Kind of Compound Adjective	Example	When Usually Hyphenated
noun + adjective	*duty-free* souvenir	if listed in current dictionary or before a noun
noun + present participle	*time-consuming* task	before a noun
adjective + participle	*free-wheeling* attitude	before a noun
adjective + noun + *ed*	*able-bodied* person	before a noun
cardinal number + noun	*50-mile* radius	before a noun
adverb + participle	*well-groomed* poodle	only before a noun; only if adverb does not end in *ly*
adverb + adjective	*more interesting* plot	never
participle + adverb	*filled-in* form	only before a noun

Illustration 7-1   Hyphenating Compound Adjectives

The sentences below are examples of how some of the information presented in Illustration 7-1 is applied:

She is a *well-known* author. (adverb + participle before noun)
The author is *well known*. (adverb + participle not before noun)

You are a *well-trained, highly skilled* worker. (coordinate adjectives—adverb + participle and *ly* adverb + participle—before noun)

The new procedure is more *time consuming* and more accurate. (noun + present participle not before noun)

Sometimes two or more hyphenated compound words with the same base word appear in a series. In this case the hyphen is used, but the base word may be omitted in all except the last item of the series:

Your resume should state your *short-* and *long-range* goals. (The word *range* is omitted in the first compound word.)

The dinner will honor *10-, 20-,* and *30-year* members. (The word *members* is omitted in the first two compound words.)

PREFIXES AND SUFFIXES. A prefix is a sound or group of letters added to the beginning of a word; a suffix is a sound or group of letters added to the end of a word. Prefixes and suffixes are generally *not* separated from their root words. There are a few exceptions to this rule, however, and they are explained in this section. The only suffix preceded by a hyphen is *elect*, and it is used only as part of a compound title:

> Hyphens are sometimes used to join prefixes and suffixes to root words.

President-elect Mason

Vice President-elect Marks

Prefixes are followed by hyphens in a variety of situations. Illustration 7-2 lists those situations and gives an example of each.

Prefix/Prefix Ending	Hyphenated	Example
prefix ending in *i*	before word beginning with *i*	semi-interesting
prefix ending in *a*	before word beginning with *a*	ultra-artistic
prefix ending in *e*	seldom; consult dictionary	de-emphasize, deactivate, preelection
prefix ending in *o*	seldom; consult dictionary	coworker, co-official, microchip, microorganism
self	always when a prefix	self-motivated
re (to do again)	to distinguish from word with different meaning	re-form/reform

Illustration 7-2   Hyphenating Prefixes

There is an additional rule of which you should be aware. Whenever a prefix is added to a proper noun, the prefix is separated from the word by a hyphen:

mid-October

trans-Alaska

Hyphens are used between numbers in a range.

RANGES.   A hyphen is used between the high and low numbers in a range. It shows the numbers are related and takes the place of *to* or *through*.

The range of scores on the first test was 51-93.

Read pages 6-10 before Monday.

The reunion will be held August 15-17 in Dallas.

THE DASH

Dashes separate.

Unlike a hyphen, which is used to bring things together, a dash is used **to separate**. A dash shows a sudden change in thought or places emphasis on what follows. There are no spaces before, between, or after the two hyphens that form the dash. Because of the impact it creates, the dash should be used less frequently than other marks of punctuation.

One thing is very clear—without additional funding, the project will fail.

The response to the ad has been excellent—much better than we expected.

THE APOSTROPHE

Apostrophes are used to form possessives and contractions.

As you write letters, memos, and reports, you will use the apostrophe in two ways: to form possessives and to form contractions.

POSSESSIVES.   Possessives show ownership. Both nouns and pronouns may be expressed as possessives. Illustration 7-3 shows the possessive form of several nouns and pronouns. Recall that only nouns use an apostrophe in their possessive forms. The apostrophe is placed either before the *s* ('s) or after the *s* (s') depending on the noun. The context of the sentence will often provide a clue to placement of the apostrophe. Detailed information on forming possessives is in Chapter 5.

Word	Possessive
she (pronoun)	her car
we (pronoun)	our house
they (pronoun)	their class
he (pronoun)	his book
month (noun)	a month's rent
months (noun)	three months' rent
employee (noun)	employee's vacation
employees (noun)	employees' pension fund
Sue (noun)	Sue's memo
window (noun)	window's reflection
Douglas (noun)	Douglas' exam

Illustration 7-3 Possessive Forms

CONTRACTIONS. Contractions are combinations of two words in a shortened form. An apostrophe is used to signal the omission of one or more letters in the contraction. Contractions such as *can't*, *won't*, and *you're* are seldom used in business writing because they lack the formality desired in a permanent record.

Contractions are seldom used in business correspondence.

There are several contractions that, when spoken, sound the same as possessive pronouns. These potentially confusing words are listed in Illustration 7-4.

Word	Meaning
its	possessive form of pronoun *it*
it's	contraction of *it is*
their	possessive form of pronoun *they* (before noun)
they're	contraction of *they are*
theirs	possessive form of pronoun *they* (not before noun)
there's	contraction of *there is*
whose	possessive form of pronoun *who*
who's	contraction of *who is*
your	possessive form of pronoun *you*
you're	contraction of *you are*

Illustration 7-4 Possessive and Contraction Soundalikes

If you are unsure about whether to use an apostrophe, remember this: A contraction *always* has an apostrophe.

QUOTATION MARKS

Quotation marks show exact wording or special emphasis.

Quotation marks serve two different purposes in written messages: (1) They indicate that the writer is using the exact words of another individual, or (2) they emphasize words that are unique or have a special meaning in a particular message. In both cases, the quotation marks are used in pairs—one is placed at the beginning of the quote or item of information, the other is placed at the end.

The length of a quote influences how it is displayed.

QUOTATIONS. The length of a direct quotation determines whether it will be set off by quotation marks or emphasized in a separate, indented paragraph. If a direct quotation occupies less than four lines of type, the copy is placed in quotation marks and is not indented:

> In his inaugural address, Governor Snellgrover told the citizens of the state, "Education, jobs, and the preservation of natural resources are high-priority items."

If the quoted material occupies four or more lines of type, it should not be displayed in quotation marks. A quotation of this length should be displayed as a separate, single-spaced paragraph and should be indented on the left and right sides:

> In his inaugural address, Governor Snellgrover told the citizens of the state:
>
>> During my campaign I promised to work to maintain the quality of life which has made this state such a fine place in which to live. Education, jobs, and the preservation of natural resources are high-priority items. We must not lose what we have worked so hard to achieve; we must strive to make further gains.

This indented format, together with information about the source of the material, makes quotation marks unnecessary.

Notice that the preceding paragraphs have emphasized *exact words* and *direct quotation*. These terms are important because only materials that meet these standards should be included in quotation marks. If you use your own words to describe another person's idea (paraphrasing), quotation marks are not needed; but credit should be given to the originator of the idea. The sentences below illustrate this principle:

> Mr. Adams said, "The report was very well written."
> Mr. Adams said that the report was well written.

Words in quotation marks receive emphasis.

EMPHASIS. Whenever you wish to emphasize a word or phrase, even if it is not part of a direct quote, consider displaying it in quotation marks. Humorous items, definitions, and technical terms used in nontechnical ways are good candidates for this type of emphasis. If words are emphasized with quotation marks too frequently, however, the benefits of this display are lost.

"Shorty" is an unlikely nickname for someone six feet tall!

"Data" is the plural form of the word "datum."

WITH OTHER PUNCTUATION MARKS. Because quotation marks may be used to begin, end, or set off material within a statement or question, some guidelines must be set regarding the use of other punctuation when quotation marks are present. The table in Illustration 7-5 will be a helpful reference.

Punctuation Mark	Placement
period	inside quotation marks
comma	inside quotation marks
colon	outside quotation marks
semicolon	outside quotation marks
question mark	inside *if* quotation is a question
	outside *if* the entire item is a question
exclamation point	inside *if* quotation is an exclamation
	outside *if* the entire item is an exclamation

Illustration 7-5   Quotation Marks with Other Punctuation Marks

There are three additional rules concerning the use of punctuation and quotation marks that business writers should remember:

1. Punctuation may be included in a quotation. If the quote is taken from a printed source, the punctuation should be included where the original author inserted it—even if it is incorrect.
2. Ending punctuation may be placed before *or* after the quotation marks, but never both places.
3. Direct quotes that occur in the middle or near the end of other statements or questions are introduced by either a colon or a comma.

Here are some examples of how the placement guidelines and rules may be applied:

Did the evaluation report contain this statement: "Her work is exceptional; she can be relied upon to complete her work quickly and accurately"? (The entire item is a question.)

He asked: "Where is the Credit Department?" (Only the quote is a question.)

The colonists were warned, "The British are coming! The British are coming!" (Only the quote is an exclamation.)

This badly damaged package was marked "Fragile"! (The entire sentence is an exclamation.)

ELLIPSIS POINTS

Ellipsis points indicate that words have been omitted.

As you work with direct quotations, you may find it necessary to include only part of what another person said or wrote. When this occurs, use ellipsis points. Ellipsis points are a series of three periods separated from the quote and from each other by one space. Ellipsis points are used in advertising and personal business correspondence to indicate a pause. In other forms of business writing, ellipsis points are used to indicate that words have been omitted from a direct quotation:

> In your letter of July 10 you stated, ". . . the deadline for payment was July 7."
> "The contract . . . was ratified by a majority of the members."
> The speaker's opening words were, "I am overwhelmed . . . ."

Notice that in the last example, terminal punctuation has been added after the ellipsis points.

PARENTHESES

Items that are unimportant may be placed in **parentheses**.

Parentheses and commas have one function in common. Either one may be used to separate nonessential information from the rest of a thought. If parentheses and commas were compared according to their strength, however, parentheses would be rated as weaker marks of punctuation. The information they contain may be so unimportant that the writer should consider eliminating it entirely. If an author chooses to use parentheses, certain requirements must be met:

1. Both left and right parentheses must be used.
2. The items within the parentheses are not immune to punctuation. If commas, semicolons, periods, or other punctuation marks are needed, they should be used.
3. The presence of parentheses should not affect the use of punctuation elsewhere in the sentence or question:

After she retired (June 15, 1984), Elsa moved to Idaho.

PUNCTUATION REVIEW

Punctuation helps a writer convey a message clearly and concisely. The chart in Illustration 7-6 contains a list of the punctuation marks discussed in this chapter. It also contains a brief description of how those punctuation marks may be used. Refer to the chart whenever you have a question about punctuation. If more information is needed, review the section of this chapter that discusses the specific punctuation mark.

Punctuation Mark	Use(s)
period	to end a declarative sentence to end an imperative sentence to end a courteous request to end an indirect question
question mark	to end an interrogative sentence
exclamation point	to end an exclamatory sentence
comma	to identify an appositive to separate two independent clauses joined by a coordinate conjunction in a compound sentence to separate an independent clause from the dependent clause that introduces it in a complex sentence with a complete calendar date with a complete geographic location to identify nonessential elements: introductory words, introductory phrases, transitional expressions, nonrestrictive clauses, and parenthetical expressions to separate items in a series to separate coordinate adjectives
semicolon	to join closely related independent clauses when no conjunction is used (compound sentence) to join independent clauses when one or both clauses contain commas (compound sentence) to separate items in a series when those items contain commas
colon	to introduce a listing, an explanation, or an example
hyphen	to form a compound word, especially a compound adjective to join a prefix or suffix to a root word to join high and low points in a numeric range
dash	to add emphasis
apostrophe	to form a possessive of a noun to form a contraction
quotation marks	to identify a direct quotation to highlight an unusual item or word with a meaning unique to the message
ellipsis points	to show that words have been omitted
parentheses	to identify nonessential information

Illustration 7-6   Frequently Used Punctuation Marks

DISCUSSION QUESTIONS

1. What terminal punctuation mark should be used with courteous requests that require action as a response? Why?

2. How can using too few or too many commas hamper communication?

3. What determines whether items in a series should be separated by a comma or by a semicolon? Give an example of each.

4. What determines whether independent clauses in a compound sentence are joined by a comma or a semicolon? Give an example of each.

5. When should a comma be used to separate a dependent clause from an independent clause in a complex sentence?

6. List three nonessential elements and give an example of each.

7. When should a hyphen be used?

8. Distinguish between a direct quotation and a paraphrased thought with respect to the following:
   a. The use of quotation marks
   b. The need to give credit to the originator of the idea.

9. Why would a writer use parentheses rather than commas to separate nonessential elements from the rest of the sentence?

10. How can you distinguish between a contraction and its soundalike possessive pronoun?

11. What is the difference between an essential appositive and a nonessential appositive? Use an example to illustrate the difference.

12. What three items constitute a complete calendar date? How should such a date be punctuated within a sentence?

13. Distinguish between a parenthetical expression and a transitional expression. Using the word *however*, construct a sentence to illustrate each type of expression.

14. Explain how the use of a hyphen differs from the use of a dash.

15. Indicate whether the punctuation marks listed below should be placed *inside* or *outside* an ending quotation mark.
    a. period
    b. comma
    c. semicolon
    d. question mark
    e. exclamation point
    f. colon

APPLICATION EXERCISES

1. Carefully read each item below. Decide which terminal mark of punctuation would be best in each situation.
    a. Thank you for bringing the error to our attention
    b. Is this the Credit Department
    c. Will you please call Mary Jones and cancel our four o'clock meeting
    d. You're our *best* sales representative
    e. Michelle has been hired to fill the vacancy in the communication center
    f. Your order will be shipped on March 27
    g. When will the announcement be made
    h. The alarm is sounding
    i. Mr. Johnson wants to know whether the report is finished
    j. When was Susan promoted to section supervisor
    k. The bids will be opened in my office
    l. Will you please insure the package before mailing it
    m. Act now

2. Read each sentence below and insert commas where necessary in each series or between coordinate adjectives.
    a. The box contained the humidifier an instruction booklet and a warranty card.
    b. The person we hire must be a poised confident individual.
    c. The house has a new roof new carpeting and a fresh coat of paint.
    d. Place an order for two chairs three desks and two magazine racks.
    e. The store is open until 5 p.m. on Monday Tuesday and Thursday afternoons.
    f. FORTRAN COBOL and BASIC are computer programming languages.
    g. The clean basic lines of the design give the garment its appeal.
    h. Mark Abernathy is a witty humorous entertainer.
    i. Jan Jerry or Beth will meet with the television reporter.
    j. Your resume should include information about your work experience your educational qualifications and your service activities.
    k. Mrs. Zimmerman was a lively informative tour guide.
    l. The actors portrayed their characters as warm caring people.
    m. The successful applicant must be a proficient typist an accurate proofreader and a cooperative worker.

3. Locate the dates and geographic locations in the sentences below. Determine if commas are needed, insert them where necessary, and give the reason for their use.

   a. In May the headquarters will be moved from Athens Georgia to Athens Ohio.

   b. The shipment is scheduled to be made on March 17 and should reach you within a week.

   c. Our first after-Christmas clearance sale was held on December 26 1939.

   d. The company is incorporated in Michigan.

   e. The restaurant will be closed for remodeling from June 28 through July 9.

   f. The United States celebrated its bicentennial on July 4 1976.

   g. Martha was born in West Virginia but moved to Tennessee when she was six.

   h. Their journey began in Seattle Washington and ended in Houston Texas.

   i. The board will reconvene at 8 a.m. on Wednesday October 9.

   j. The Made Right Furniture Company has just opened a manufacturing plant in Beijing China.

4. Locate the nonessential elements in each of the following sentences and insert punctuation where needed. Indicate whether the nonessential element is an introductory word, an introductory phrase, a nonrestrictive clause, a parenthetical expression, or a transitional expression.

   a. Mr. Thomas Dailey who is a well-known author and speaker will give the commencement address.

   b. Pradeep said that he would be working late every night this week; he indicated however that he will not be working this Saturday.

   c. You Mr. Tanaka could be one of the lucky winners!

   d. Therefore you will receive an extra 10 percent discount.

   e. Interstate 94 which passes through Chicago is the best way to reach your destination.

   f. Thank you Mrs. Gilbertson for the 25 years of service you have given to Mason Corporation.

   g. For an exciting vacation visit Monterey.

   h. Thomas Hoffman who is well known for his athletic ability is gaining popularity as a portrait painter.

   i. For the past 20 years however there has been a significant growth in the number of unions for clerical workers.

   j. Naturally we will cooperate with you on the project.

    k. The results seem promising; however additional testing will be done.

    l. Your mortgage payment including taxes and insurance will be $670 per month.

    m. No the penalty has not been applied.

5. Insert commas and semicolons where necessary in each of the following sentences. Explain the reason for each punctuation mark you insert.

    a. Calculators were the tools of the 50s computers are the tools of the 90s.

    b. After the report is finished proofread it and deliver it to the vice-president.

    c. Because he did not pay his bill Don's phone was disconnected.

    d. When Catherine Powers phones tell her that Melissa McLean will begin work on July 7.

    e. Word processing has increased our ability to produce written messages rapidly yet the demand for office personnel has not declined.

    f. Do you mean Taylor Texas Taylor Michigan or Taylor Pennsylvania?

    g. The speaker knew the topic and she conveyed her message clearly.

    h. The chairs were the wrong color the style was ideal.

    i. The story captured my attention and when I read the last word I found that I did not want it to end.

    j. Because of the time and money you contributed we were able to reach our goal.

    k. Constance is 18 her brother is older.

    l. Last year the choir toured France this year they will travel through Germany.

    m. The train will arrive at 9 p.m. today it will depart at 4 a.m. tomorrow.

6. Exercises 1-4 focused on a specific internal or terminal mark of punctuation. In this exercise, however, some of the items require no punctuation; others require terminal punctuation, commas, and/or semicolons. Be sure you can justify each punctuation mark you insert.

    a. Sylvan questioned whether Henry had the authority to make the decision.

    b. Mr. Carlysle whose hobby is building model airplanes is our new neighbor.

    c. The price we quoted is correct therefore payment should be made promptly.

    d. He removed his jacket and left it lying on the table.

    e. Juan Ortega our neighbor plants roses mums and geraniums in his garden each year.

f. Have you seen the floppy-eared brown puppy that Samantha recently purchased

g. I enjoyed viewing the film but the book provided more detail about the characters.

h. The sum of 4 8 12 and 24 is 48 the average of the numbers is 12

i. Thank you Mr. Fedora for your kind words of introduction.

j. When the guests had finished eating the band began to play music with a faster tempo

k. This program is designed for persons with no credit questionable credit or bad credit.

l. The United States Hockey Hall of Fame is located in Eveleth Minnesota.

m. Seth is the best candidate because of his previous experience in the field of electronics

n. Neatness accuracy and clarity are important factors.

o. After the instructions were given I started working on the test.

p. Mrs. Adamczak will phone you when she returns from vacation.

q. Todd the tall handsome blue-eyed blond-haired captain of the football team has just been nominated for president of the senior class.

r. You must use a pencil to record your responses otherwise the answers will be marked as incorrect.

s. Meteorologists can't control the weather they simply predict what is likely to occur.

t. The first part of the employment test went fairly well I think but I will need to review my English spelling and mathematics before returning for the next section of the examination.

u. Place the shipment on the truck tonight so it will be ready when the driver arrives in the morning.

v. The new tax laws which were enacted during the current legislative session will take effect on July 1.

w. The price we quoted is therefore correct.

x. The brochure should be redesigned before additional copies are ordered

y. Congratulations Michael

z. Robert Brown president of Brown Brothers Albert Pyroz personnel director at Dataform Sylvia Jacobsen owner of a consulting firm and Amanda Newel records manager at BZP Corporation were all members of the panel discussing mid-life career changes.

7. Insert commas where needed in the following letter. If you think that two
   sentences are closely related, replace the period and the capital letter that
   follows them with a semicolon and a lowercase letter.

May 1, 199-

Mr. Henry Breu
1717 Meadow Lane
Sandusky, WY 94556-3456

Dear Henry

This letter will confirm information shared during our telephone conversation
on April 29.

Your accounting internship will begin on Monday June 4 and conclude on
Friday August 31. For the first part of the summer you will work in the
Payroll Department under the supervision of Darren DeForest. During the last
five weeks of your internship you will work with Janet Lummar in Internal
Audit. Each of these individuals is a dedicated talented accountant from whom
you should learn a great deal.

Please report to our Personnel Department Room 323 at 8 a.m. on June 2.
Stephanie Fritz will explain company rules and procedures as they apply to
your internship.

Henry I'm pleased that you have chosen to spend your summer with Central
Power and Light. By working together we can make the experience pleasant
and beneficial for everyone.

Sincerely

Patrick Hansen
Personnel Specialist

gj

c   J. P. Nichol
       Internship Coordinator
    D. DeForest
    S. Fritz
    J. Lummar

8. Carefully read each sentence below. Decide whether the quotation marks and other marks of punctuation have been used correctly. Make the necessary corrections.

    a. Last night my sister asked me, "When is Lee's birthday"?
    b. A "majority" is one more than half, not simply 51 percent.
    c. According to the minutes, the motion was "tabled" I disagree.
    d. "The day will come, said my mother, when you will be rewarded for your hard work."
    e. The person who said "To err is human" must have been thinking of me!
    f. What did Dad mean when he said the book was a "lulu?"
    g. The police officer yelled, "Get back!"
    h. When she finished the book, Sue said: "Reading that book was as much fun as watching grass grow".
    i. Did the shopper shout "Goodbye! or Good Buy!"?
    j. Everyone at the movie laughed when the toddler yelled, "When will it be over?".
    k. The sign on the door of the restaurant said: Closed until June 1."
    l. Why are people who live in Nebraska called "Cornhuskers"?
    m. Fairy tales usually begin with the words "Once upon a time;" they often end with the words "And they lived happily ever after."

9. Some of the items below contain hyphens; others do not. Your task is to decide if others are needed and if those that are included have been used correctly. Make any changes that are necessary.

    a. The components were broken and had to be refused.
    b. Hans Jensen is best known for the spine tingling mysteries he has written.
    c. Samuel Anderson, who is well-known for his expertise in botany, will be the March speaker at the Lake Shore Garden Club.
    d. The 30 page manual is much clearer than the longer version.

CHAPTER 8

STYLE

LEARNING OBJECTIVES

Your learning objectives for this chapter include the following:

■ To understand the importance of style guidelines in business writing
■ To become acquainted with the suggested style guidelines for:
Expressing numbers
Capitalizing words
Dividing words
Using abbreviations

The word *style* is used in several different ways in business writing. A person's ability to organize and express ideas is called style. The format of a letter, memo, or report may be referred to as style. Reference manuals are sometimes called style manuals. In this chapter, **style** is used to mean the basic rules for the correct use of numbers, capitalization, word division, and abbreviations that apply to business writing.

Writers should be as concerned about correct usage as they are about their basic writing skills. Correct usage—usually called *mechanics*—and good writing skills work together to minimize the number of distractions in a message, bring consistency to communication, reflect well on the writer, and have a positive effect on the reader.

Style may mean different things in business writing.

Here style refers to rules for correct usage.

NUMBERS

General style is used for expressing numbers in business writing.

Numbers have become a major part of our lives. They are used to represent, describe, and locate people and objects. Because numbers are so widely used, attention must be given to expressing them correctly in business writing.

Business writers use **general style** when expressing numbers. General style is a blend of two styles known as *formal* and *technical*. In general style numbers are represented in words when formality is needed and in figures when the clarity of technical style is appropriate.

GENERAL GUIDELINES

There are several guidelines related to the way numbers are expressed. Some of these guidelines are used frequently in business writing, others are rarely used. This section describes those guidelines that have frequent application in business correspondence and reports.

Write whole numbers greater than ten in figures.

FOR WRITING WHOLE NUMBERS. Whole numbers greater than ten are written in figures. This guideline applies only to whole numbers—those that have no decimal or fractional parts.

> Sam purchased *ten* tickets to the play.
> Make *eight* copies of the report and mail them to Rochelle.
> Our destination is *450* miles from here.

Using figures to represent large round numbers draws attention to those numbers.

FOR WRITING ROUND NUMBERS. Round numbers may be expressed in figures, words, or a combination of the two. To reduce the emphasis placed on a round number, words are used. When emphasis is desired, a figure is used. Figures are often used in advertising for emphasis. Since numbers greater than a million may be difficult to read when expressed in figures, a writer may combine words and figures to achieve greater clarity.

> Nearly *6,000* coupons have been redeemed.
> Only *five hundred* tickets are available.
> The population of the country is over *15 million*.

Express numbers that begin sentences in words.

FOR BEGINNING A SENTENCE WITH A NUMBER. Numbers that begin a sentence are expressed in words. If the number is large, rewrite the sentence.

> *Fifty* requests have been submitted.
> *Two thousand* entries have been keyboarded.

Thirteen thousand two hundred seventy-seven people attended the convention. (Awkward. See the following sentence.)

The convention attendance was *13,277*. (Improved version)

FOR WRITING NUMBERS CONSISTENTLY.

Be consistent in expressing numbers, and strive for easy reading. When numbers greater than *and* less than ten appear in the same sentence, use figures. If two numbers are adjacent to one another, as in a series, punctuation and proper spacing are important to make the numbers easy to read. When one of two adjacent numbers is part of a compound modifier, the smaller number is written in words.

Express numbers consistently.

A discount is offered for payment made within *ten* days, and the full amount is due within *30* days. (inconsistent)

A discount is offered for payment made within *10* days, and the full amount is due within *30* days. (consistent)

The following items were ordered: 16 two-drawer chests, 6 four-drawer chests, 7 bookcases, and 1 chair. (adjacent numbers; compound modifier.)

In 1984, 5,668,987 fans attended the games. (easy to read)

FOR PUNCTUATING NUMBERS.

In numbers with four or more digits, a comma is usually used. The comma is optional in round numbers less than 10,000 and is omitted entirely in identification, model, serial, and house numbers.

Use commas in numbers with four or more digits.

1,000,000

5,000 or 5000

6,364

ID No. 76108

7933 West Monroe Avenue

SPECIFIC GUIDELINES

The basic guidelines just presented will help you through many writing situations involving numbers. There are some specific guidelines, too, that should be mastered. As you read the material, you will encounter the term *ordinal*. **Ordinal** words or numbers show position in a series. *First, second, third, tenth,* and *seventy-fifth* are examples of ordinal words; 1st, 2d, 3d, 10th, and 75th are examples of ordinal numbers. Note that *d* is used in place of both *nd* and *rd* in ordinal numbers.

ADDRESSES.

All house numbers greater than one are written in figures. Streets whose names are numbers are written as words if ten or less and as

Use figures for house numbers greater than one.

Use words for street
names of ten or less;
otherwise, use figures.

figures in all other cases. When figures are to be used for both house number and street name, place a hyphen between them.

One George Circle
1015 North Sixth Street
3648 - 41st Street
16 East 12 Street

Notice that in the last two examples the street names are expressed in different ways; one (41st) uses an ordinal ending, the other (12) does not. When a word appears between the house number and street name, the ordinal ending may be omitted.

Use figures for the day
and the year.

DATES.   Figures are used for the day and the year. If the day is used without a month or if the day precedes the month, ordinal numbers or words may be used.

July 4, 1776
August 3
January 1, 2000
the 15th and 31st (ordinal without a month)
the 2d of June (ordinal number)
the second of June (ordinal word)

Some writers use the international (military) date form, but it has not received widespread acceptance in American business correspondence:

15 February 1992
1992.2.15

Use words when a
fraction stands alone; use
figures when a fraction is
part of a mixed number.

FRACTIONS.   When a fraction is used by itself, it is expressed in words. Use a hyphen between the numerator (top number) and denominator (bottom number) of a fraction written in words unless one part already contains a hyphen. When a fraction is part of a mixed number, it is expressed in figures.

one-third of the class (noun)
a one-third share (adjective)
one sixty-fifth
5 1/3

Notice the space in the mixed number between the fraction and the whole number. This space is necessary for readability. Without the space the figure could be misread as 51/3 (fifty-one thirds).

MONEY. Money amounts are expressed in figures. If the money amount is even, the decimal and zeros are omitted. An indefinite amount of money should be written in words.

Express money amounts in figures.

Indefinite money amounts are written in words.

> $5,079.32
> $100
> several thousand dollars
> a few hundred dollars

For amounts of money less than $1, use figures and spell out the word *cents*:

> 5 cents

On orders, invoices, and other business forms, the symbol ¢ may be used. If definite amounts of money greater and less than $1 occur in the same sentence, use the $ symbol and a decimal where necessary:

> We were quoted prices of $1.13, $1, and $.97 per item.

ORDINALS. When an ordinal may be expressed in one or two words, it should be spelled in full. If it exceeds one or two words, the sentence should be rewritten to avoid the need for an ordinal. This restriction applies only to ordinals that appear within the body of a sentence; refer to the sections on addresses and dates for the proper use of ordinals in those items.

Only one- or two-word ordinals should be used in sentences; they should be spelled in full.

> The *first* available date is . . .
> The company's *seventy-fifth* anniversary . . .

PERCENTAGES. In nontechnical business writing, *percent* is spelled out, and the number is expressed as a figure.

Percent is usually spelled out.

> 16 percent
> $18\frac{1}{2}$ percent
> 0.5 percent

At the beginning of a sentence, spell out the number or reword the sentence.

TIME. To designate time with *a.m.* or *p.m.* use a figure; zeros are not needed for on-the-hour times. For formality, use a word before *o'clock*; for emphasis, use a figure before *o'clock*. Approximate time and time on the half hour are expressed in words.

Designate time in figures or words as appropriate to context.

> We are scheduled to leave at *4 p.m.*
> The flight will depart at *6:07 a.m.*
> The doors will be opened at *10 o'clock* each morning. (emphasis)
> The reception will begin at eight o'clock this evening. (formality)

In all cases, be sure the time of day is clear:

The train will arrive at six-thirty. (six-thirty in the morning or six-thirty in the evening?)
The train will arrive at six-thirty this evening. (clear)

To avoid confusion, writers usually use *midnight* rather than 12 a.m. and *noon* rather than 12 p.m.

CAPITALIZATION

In your early education, you were taught to capitalize the first letter of a word that begins a sentence or a direct quotation. In addition, the first letter of a proper noun is capitalized. Few, if any, writers have difficulty with these practices. This section, therefore, will present other basically accepted rules for capitalization.

ACADEMIC COURSES

Capitalize specific academic courses and languages.

When referring to a *specific* course, capitalize the first letter of the main word(s). Do not capitalize general subjects other than languages.

History of Theater is a very popular course on this campus.
Are you taking a *history of theater* course this term?
Dr. Williams teaches *Psychology* 101, 103, and 256.
Dr. Williams teaches *psychology* courses.
Sandra is enrolled in her third *French* class.

COMPASS DIRECTIONS

Compass directions that refer to a specific region should be capitalized.

Specific names of geographic locations (sections, places, continents, countries, states, cities, rivers, mountains, lakes, and islands) are capitalized.

We traveled in the *West* last summer.
Their business will expand to the *Far East*.
Use the entrance on the *east* side of the building. (a direction)
She drove *west* on I-94 to the North Dakota border. (a direction)

GOVERNMENT

The names of domestic and foreign government units, organizations, and agencies are capitalized.

> House of Representatives
> House of Commons
> Committee on Foreign Affairs
> United Nations Security Council

Short forms of national and international government bodies and their major divisions should also be capitalized.

> the House
> the Commons
> Foreign Affair Committee   *but*   the committee
> the Security Council   *but*   the council

The short forms of state and local government bodies are not capitalized.

> the city
> the state
> the department

When in doubt about the capitalization of government and judicial bodies, it is best to consult a recommended reference book such as *The Chicago Manual of Style*, published by The University of Chicago Press.

Full names of governments and their subsections are capitalized.

INSTITUTIONS AND ORGANIZATIONS

The full names of institutions (churches, libraries, hospitals, and schools) and organizations (associations, companies, committees, and clubs) and their divisions or departments are capitalized. The word *the* is capitalized only when it is part of the official title. Follow the style established by the organization or institution as shown on its letterhead or other written communication.

> Memorial Hospital has released the plans for its new addition.
> Temple Israel has been selected as the site for the dinner.
> Are you a member of the Association of Records Managers and Administrators?
> A new business, The Trimmers, will soon be opening in Town Square.
> Publicity Committee   *but*   the committee
> Intensive Care Unit   *but*   the unit
> Accounting Department   *but*   the department

Capitalize the full name of an institution or organization according to its preference.

Capitalize the when it is part of an official name.

TIME

Dates are only one means of expressing time.

Capitalize most references to time.

The most common reference to time in business writing is a date, but time can also be a reference to seasons, holidays, or events. The names of days, months, holidays, religious days, and historical events are *always* capitalized. The names of seasons are capitalized only when they are part of a specific title or are personified, as in poetry.

> Thursday
> February
> Memorial Day
> Yom Kipper
> World War II
> Winter Carnival
> this spring

TITLES

Capitalization of personal titles depends on the title and how it is used.

Titles are divided into two categories—occupational titles and official titles. An occupational title is capitalized *only* when it is a specific job title. An official title is capitalized whenever it comes before a personal name unless the personal name has been added for clarification or description (nonessential element set off by commas). An official title is generally not capitalized when it follows a personal name or is used in place of a personal name. The titles of state, national, and international officials are an exception; these titles are capitalized when they come before, come after, or are used in place of personal names.

> After speaking, President Smith returned to New York.
> The Ambassador hosted the dinner. (international title used in place of name)
> Anthony Mitchell, mayor, reported on economic development. (title following name)
> The treasurer, Myron Backstrom, gave the keynote address. (occupational title)
> Marketing Manager Ellen Francis has announced her resignation. (specific job title)

WORD DIVISION

When traditional typewriters are used to produce business documents, it *may be* necessary to divide a word at the end of a line of type in order to achieve a balanced right margin. Note the emphasis on the words "may be." Word division is an option—not a requirement. Word processors have minimized the need to make decisions about when and how to divide words. These units eliminate manual returns at the ends of lines and have the ability to justify right margins. But even with a word processor, a writer may elect to divide a word. Therefore, it is important for all business writers to know how to properly divide words.

Word division is an option.

There are two reference books that are helpful in deciding where to divide a word: a dictionary and a word book. A word book is a more desirable reference because it shows syllabication and preferred word division points. A dictionary will indicate only syllabication; it is up to you to determine where the word is best divided.

Use a dictionary or word book when you need help in deciding where to divide a word.

If you decide to divide a word, the following guidelines should be used:

1. Divide a word only between syllables.
2. Divide between two vowels if they are pronounced separately, (e.g., punctu-ation, cha-otic, evalu-ation).
3. Divide after a one-syllable vowel unless the one-letter syllable *a* or *i* is followed by *ble*, *bly*, *cle*, or *cal*. When this occurs both syllables should be carried to the next line (e.g., med-ical).
4. Divide before a suffix. (e.g., commence-ment)
5. Divide between two parts of a compound word. If the word is hyphenated, divide at the hyphen. (e.g., well-known)
6. Avoid dividing names, dates, and addresses. If these items must be divided, follow these guidelines:
   a. Do not use a hyphen to show that the item has been divided.
   b. Keep a personal title with the name. (e.g., Mrs. Pat/Jones)
   c. Divide a date between the day of the month and the year. (e.g., June 20,/1991)
   d. Divide an address between the city and the state. (e.g., Cincinnati,/Ohio)
7. No fewer than two letters of the word should be left on the first line, and no fewer than three letters should be carried to the next line. The goal is to give the reader an idea of the word before it is divided. Therefore, if it is possible to divide a word in more than one place, select the division point that places the larger part of the word on the upper line.

The guidelines just listed refer to what should be done when words are divided. There are some times, however, when a word should not be divided:

Not all words should be divided.

1. Words of five or fewer letters should not be divided even if they have two or more syllables.
2. The last word on a page should not be divided. Avoid dividing the last word in a paragraph.
3. Divide as few words as possible; avoid ending two consecutive lines with divided words.
4. Do not divide figures, abbreviations, contractions, or items containing symbols.

ABBREVIATIONS

Use only those
abbreviations that your
reader will recognize.

Abbreviations are a simple way to save space and time in business writing. Their use should be limited, however, to those that the reader will recognize and understand. If an abbreviation is to be used several times within a letter or report, the complete form—followed by the abbreviation in parentheses—should be used at the first instance. The reader will then understand the abbreviation when it occurs again.

The Student Conduct Committee (SCC) has filed its report.

PERSONAL NAMES

Names may be
abbreviated by using
initials or a shortened
form of the name.

Abbreviations for personal names may take the form of an initial or a shortened form of the name. Before abbreviating a person's name, be sure that individual will not object to the use of the abbreviated form.

M. J. Sloan
Patrick D. Seiler
Chas. Johnson

Some of the more widely used abbreviations for names are shown in Illustration 8-1. Personal names should not be abbreviated unless space is limited as in tabulations or enumerations.

Abbreviation	Name
Chas.	Charles
Geo.	George
Robt.	Robert
Thos.	Thomas
Wm.	William

Illustration 8-1 Abbreviated Names

BUSINESS AND ASSOCIATION NAMES

Some business
organizations are known
by their abbreviated
names.

Business firms, government agencies, and professional groups are often known by their abbreviated names. The standard format for such abbreviations is all capital letters, no period or spaces:

IBM (International Business Machines)
AARP (American Association of Retired Persons)

AT&T (American Telephone and Telegraph)
IRS (Internal Revenue Service)

Other commonly used abbreviations are Assn. for Association, Co. for Company, Corp. for Corporation, Ltd. for Limited, and Inc. for Incorporated. These items are generally abbreviated only when they are part of a business name.

PERSONAL TITLES

Personal titles such as *Mr.*, *Mrs.*, *Ms.*, and *Dr.* are abbreviated when they are used before a personal name:

Personal titles should be abbreviated when they occur before a name.

Mr. Juan Estrada
Ms. Edith Owens
Mrs. Barbara Peterson
Dr. Marion Heller

Unless a woman's specific title is known, *Ms.* should be used before her name. It is the woman's responsibility to let her correspondents know her personal preference. When that personal preference is known, it should be used. If a writer's first name may be used by members of either gender, the writer should include a personal title in the signature line. This technique, as well as other options, is illustrated in Chapter 9.

The individual preference of the person should be respected when using titles.

The titles *Jr.* and *Sr.* are abbreviated when they follow a personal name:

Kenneth Langford, Jr.

ACADEMIC DEGREES

Some of the most common academic abbreviations and the degrees they represent are shown in Illustration 8-2.

Abbreviation	Degree
A.A.	Associate of Arts
A.S.	Associate of Science
B.S.	Bachelor of Science
B.S. in Bus.	Bachelor of Science in Business
M.A.	Master of Arts
M.B.A.	Master of Business Administration
Ed.D.	Doctor of Education
Ph.D.	Doctor of Philosophy
M.D.	Medical Doctor
D.D.S.	Doctor of Dental Science

Illustration 8-2 Degree Abbreviations

When referring to a person who has the academic or medical credentials to be addressed as doctor, use either the title or the abbreviation for the degree, but not both. If the title is used, the abbreviation *Dr.* is placed before the name. If the abbreviation for the degree is used, it is placed after the name, and a comma separates the name from the abbreviation.

Dr. James Alexander
James Alexander, D.D.S.

MEASUREMENTS

Measurements may be abbreviated when they occur frequently in tables or business forms. When used, they are displayed in lowercase letters and do not have periods. In most business writing, measurements are spelled out rather than abbreviated.

Measure	Abbreviation
foot	ft
centimeter	cm
pound	lb
kilogram	kg

STATES/TERRITORIES/PROVINCES

The official two-letter postal abbreviations for state, territory, and province names should be used when part of a complete address. In all other cases, the name of the state, territory, or province should be spelled in full. A complete list of the two-letter postal abbreviations is in Appendix E.

MONTHS/DAYS

Each of the months of the year and days of the week has a standard abbreviation. These abbreviations should be used only to save space on business forms; they should not be used in business reports or correspondence.

Sun.	Jan.	July
Mon.	Feb.	Aug.
Tues.	Mar.	Sept.
Wed.	Apr.	Oct.
Thurs.	May	Nov.
Fri.	June	Dec.
Sat.		

SYMBOLS

Symbols are a form of abbreviation. They should be used sparingly in business writing. Only those symbols that are certain to be interpreted correctly should be used. Some standard business symbols, a brief definition of each, and an example of its use are shown in Illustration 8-3.

Symbols are a form of abbreviation.

Use only those symbols that your reader will recognize and understand.

Symbol	Definition	Example
&	ampersand (meaning *and*)	Jones & Buntley
*	asterisk (usually refers to a footnote)	Current prices*
@	at, each, per	17 @ $2 each
©	copyright	© South-Western Publishing Co.
®	registered trademark	Kodak®
°	degree	68°
/	diagonal, slash	and/or, 2/3, 12/31/99
¢	cents	95¢
$	dollars	$10
′	feet (apostrophe)	6′
″	inches (quotation mark)	2″
:	ratio (colon)	3:2
#	number (before figure)	#3
#	pounds (after figure)	16#
%	percent	6%
×	by or times (lowercase *x*)	2 × 4, 5 × 7
K	thousand	256K, $10K

Illustration 8-3   Standard Business Symbols

DISCUSSION QUESTIONS

1. Why are style guides important to a business writer?
2. What style is used to represent numbers in business correspondence? Explain this style.
3. List three of the five general guidelines for writing numbers. Give an example of each.

4. What technique should a business writer use to *emphasize* a round number? To *de-emphasize* a round number?

5. What advice would you give to a writer about using numbers greater and less than ten in the same sentence?

6. What are the guidelines for using figures to display house numbers and street names?

7. When should dates be expressed in figures? in words? Give an example of each.

8. When should fractions be expressed in figures? in words? Give an example of each.

9. Explain and give an example of how each of the following money amounts should be expressed:
   a. A definite amount
   b. An indefinite amount
   c. An amount less than one dollar
   d. Money amounts less than and greater than one dollar that appear in the same sentence

10. What are ordinals? When should they be spelled in full?

11. Explain how percentage figures should be written in nontechnical business documents.

12. Give an example of how each of the following should be written:
    a. Time expressed with *a.m.* or *p.m.*
    b. Time expressed with *o'clock*
    c. Approximate time and time on the half hour

13. When should each of the following be capitalized?
    a. Academic courses
    b. Compass directions

14. When should the short form of a government agency or its divisions be capitalized?

15. When should the word *the* be capitalized in the name of an institution or organization?

16. In what ways may time be expressed other than a date? Which, if any, should be capitalized?

17. When should titles of international, national, and state government officials be capitalized?

18. List the seven guidelines for word division.

19. When should a word not be divided?

20. Explain where you would divide the following items:
    a. A name preceded by a personal title
    b. A complete calendar date
    c. A complete geographic location

21. In what two ways may a personal name be abbreviated?

22. Assume that you wish to use the abbreviation CBEC to represent Columbia Business Executives Club within the text of a message. How and when would you introduce the abbreviation?

23. Give two examples other than those in the text of businesses that are known by their abbreviated names.

24. When should the title *Ms.* be used?

25. Pat Carter and Gayle Jorgenson want to know how to ensure that receivers of the messages they author know they are men. What advice would you give them?

26. Give three examples of abbreviated academic degrees.

27. Is it permissible to use both the title *Dr.* and the abbreviated form of the academic degree with the same personal name?

28. When should measurements, months, and days of the week be abbreviated?

29. When should the two-letter postal ZIP Code state abbreviation be used within business messages?

30. List three symbols that are commonly used in business and give their meanings.

APPLICATION EXERCISES

1. Select the appropriate expression for each number in the items below:
   a. (Sixteen/16) ounces equal (one/1) pound.
   b. We expected to pay less than ($500/$500.00/5 hundred dollars).
   c. Effective July 1, your salary will be increased by (fifty dollars/$50/ $50.00) a month.
   d. The (first/1st/1) (100/one hundred/1 hundred) people to arrive will receive a gift.
   e. Be sure to have a dental checkup every (six/6) months.
   f. (Fifty/50) percent is ($\frac{1}{2}$/one-half), but it is not a majority.
   g. Will the contract take effect on May (31/31st/thirty-first) or on the (1/1st/first) of June?
   h. Since it was nearly (eleven/11/11:00) o'clock, the meeting was adjourned.
   i. Please change my address from (763 - Fifth Avenue/763 - 5th Avenue/ 763 5th Avenue/763 Fifth Avenue) to (376 - Fifth Avenue/376 - 5th Avenue/376 5th Avenue/376 Fifth Avenue).
   j. Bobby has grown almost (two/2) inches since his last visit.
   k. The entire process will take only (10/ten) or (15/fifteen) minutes.
   l. The average price was (93¢/93 cents/$.93).

m. Officials estimate that more than (2,000,000/2 million/two million) people will attend the (three-/3-) day event.

n. The auto dealer reported that there were (fifteen/15) (two-door/2-door) sedans left in stock.

o. Their grandchildren's ages are (2, 6, 10, 13, and 19/two, six, ten, thirteen, and nineteen/two, six, ten, 13, and 19).

p. Our forwarding address is (710/Seven Ten/Seven Hundred Ten) West (Six/6/Sixth) Street.

q. We have a (one/1) in (1,000,000/1000000/a million) chance of winning the sweepstakes.

r. Model (1,613/Sixteen Thirteen/1613) was our most popular product last quarter.

s. Minnesota has about (twenty-five percent/25%/25 percent/twenty-five %) of the nation's peat supply but less than (five percent/5%/5 percent/five %) of the growing market.

2. Each sentence below requires corrections in capitalization. Some words shown in lowercase should be capitalized; some shown in capital letters should be in lowercase. Locate and correct the errors.

a. according to a recent Report from the American Council on Science and Health, fluoridation of drinking water is a very effective weapon against tooth decay.

b. The applicant earned a master's Degree in geology at Albrook college in New Mexico.

c. The department of Pubic Works is located in city hall.

d. The Civil war pitted the North against the south.

e. The vice president will represent the President at the Nato meeting.

f. The department of the navy has given the science research Institute a grant of $600,000.

g. Have you taken an Introduction to Business course?

h. The "Real Estate report" is available from the Cove chamber of commerce.

i. The Internal Revenue Service will process your Income Tax return.

j. The Commencement speaker will be Mayor Bhagwan Pandy.

k. Roman P. Quirk, the treasurer of the Association, received the Group's annual distinguished service Award.

l. the senate has adjourned for its Holiday break; sessions will resume in four weeks.

m. The article has been translated from English into spanish, french, and german.

n. The west end Summer spree will begin Sunday, august 3.

o. the director's comments were well received; her Staff applauded.

p. A recent issue of *the News-Tribune* contained a blazing story about personality conflicts among members of the City's Convention Center Committee; the Chair of the committee refuted the statements.

3. Indicate **if** and **where** each word below should be divided. Some words may be divided in more than one place; indicate *all* acceptable dividing points.

   a. filed
   b. urgency
   c. three-fourths
   d. different
   e. Robert
   f. booklets
   g. regulation
   h. predicts
   i. required
   j. mortgage
   k. original
   l. billing
   m. mechanical
   n. inventory
   o. discuss
   p. recreation
   q. interest
   r. events
   s. conversation
   t. optional
   u. supervisory
   v. benefits
   w. monthly
   x. variable
   y. compartment
   z. dials

4. Each item below contains at least one abbreviation. Decide if each has been used correctly. If the abbreviation is incorrect, change it.

   a. Mr. @ Mrs. George Addams
   b. Dr. Karl Ives, Ed.D. was the instructor.
   c. The Buffalo team outscored its opponents 3/2.
   d. The maximum weight is 5,000#.
   e. Hotels were recently opened in St. Paul, MN; Montgomery, Alabama; San Diego, CA; and Calgary, Alberta.
   f. Tms. G. Galdwin will replace M.S. Sloan as our representative in your area.
   g. MS Edith Port has been named ceo at Player, ltd.
   h. The new pc has 640K of memory.
   i. Ron Zefirov, Jun., recently visited the Soviet Union.
   j. You and-or your representative should attend the meeting.
   k. Is it G.M. or Chrysler that will open an assembly plant in Kapus?
   l. On a Fahrenheit scale, the freezing point is 32° and the boiling point is 212°.
   m. Mr. Milo Carver, Mrs. Niko Osi, and Doctor Tim. O'Donnell will be our representatives.

PART THREE

CORRESPONDENCE APPLICATIONS

FORMATS OF LETTERS AND MEMOS

Your learning objectives for this chapter include the following:

- To understand how to construct a letter using the seven standard parts of a letter
- To know when it is appropriate to use each of the supplementary parts of a letter
- To recognize each of the different acceptable formats for business letters
- To understand how to construct a memo properly
- To recognize the characteristics of appropriate stationery for letters and memos

Your reader's first impression of your letters and memos has a lasting effect.

The initial impression made by your letters or memos will have a lasting effect on the receivers of your messages. The energy expended in writing good letters or memos will be well spent when you select appropriate stationery and formats. The reader will assume that you care and that you are knowledgeable about letter and memo writing. It is important that you select the correct stationery and format for your message.

LETTERS

Letters communicate formal written messages. The appearance of a letter is important because it will make the first impression on the reader; the content is important because you want to ensure that the reader clearly understands and accepts your message. The appearance of a letter depends on the parts of a letter, the punctuation style, the letter format, and the stationery. In this chapter, you will be shown how to improve the appearance of a letter; you will be taught how to organize and write the content of a letter in Chapters 10, 11, 12, 13, and 22.

Letters are used to transmit written messages.

USES OF LETTERS

Letters are used to communicate written messages to individuals outside an organization. Letters are also used to communicate formal written messages to employees within an organization.

Letters are used for both internal and external communication.

STANDARD PARTS OF A LETTER

The number of letter parts and their location depend on the format you select. As shown in Illustration 9-1, most letters contain seven standard parts: heading, letter address, salutation, body, complimentary close, signature block, and reference initials.

Letters normally contain seven standard parts.

HEADING. The first standard part of a letter is the heading, which consists of the letterhead and a date or the return address and a date. All business organizations should use letterhead stationery for the first page of a letter. The letterhead should always contain the name of the company and its complete address. The amount of information in a letterhead will depend on the type of organization sending the letter. It may contain a phone number, originating department, originator's title, establishment date, organizational emblem or logo, and other information that the organization deems appropriate. The letterhead should use no more than 2 inches of stationery space. Organizations today normally place the letterhead at the top of the page but may place part of the information at the bottom of the page. The letterhead may contain more than one color. Examples of letterheads are shown in Illustration 9-2.

Date and letterhead make up the heading.

The letterhead should be limited to 2″ of vertical space.

Illustration 9-1 The Seven Standard Parts of a Letter

PARENTS FOR IMPROVED EDUCATION
P. O. BOX 1006
ANNISTON, ALABAMA 32061-1006
(205) 555-4158

1. (Heading)

XXXXX

2. **LETTER ADDRESS**
XXXXXXXXXXXXXXXXXX
XXXXXXXXXXXXXXXXXX

3. **SALUTATION:**

4. **BODY**

5. COMPLIMENTARY CLOSE,

6. **SIGNATURE BLOCK**
XXXXXXXXXXXXXXXXXX

7. **REFERENCE INITIALS**

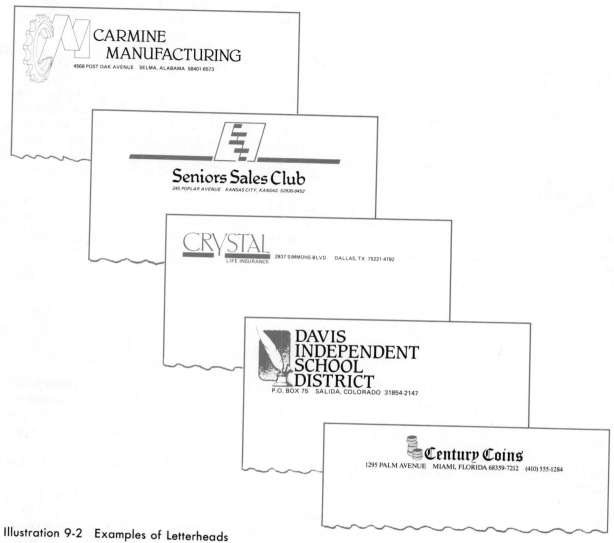

Illustration 9-2   Examples of Letterheads

The heading also contains the date that the letter is written. The dateline should contain the day, month, and year. The month should be spelled out. Figures should not be used for the month (e.g., 2/10/90) because there is no universal agreement as to whether the day or month appears first. The dates may be written in the following two styles:

The date of the letter is part of the heading.

May 11, 199–
11 May 199–

Notice that there is no punctuation when the day appears before the month in the date. Placing the month before the day is the style used by most business organizations. Placing the day first is the preferred style for international and military use.

The vertical placement of the date will vary depending on the length of the letter. The date will usually be two or more lines below the printed letterhead. When a typewritten return address appears at the top of a personal business letter, the date is placed immediately below it. When the return address appears below the signature block of a personal business letter, the date is usually placed between lines 10 and 15. The horizontal placement of the date (or the type-written return address and date) depends on the letter format that is used.

Letterhead stationery should be used only for the first page of a letter. The same color and quality of stationery without the letterhead should be used for continuation pages. Each additional page should contain a heading that begins on line six. The continuation page heading should contain the first line of the letter address, the page number, and the date. Two popular formats for continuation page headings are:

Mr. Royce Scurlock   2   September 3, 199–

or

Mr. Royce Scurlock
Page 2
September 3, 199–

The body of the letter should continue on the second line below this heading. There should be at least one complete paragraph of the letter on a continuation page. A paragraph should be divided only if you can leave at least two lines on the preceding page and carry over at least two lines to the following page.

LETTER ADDRESS.   The letter address includes the addressee's courtesy title (Ms., Miss, Mrs., Mr., Dr., etc.), name, street or mailing address, city, state, and ZIP Code. The two-letter abbreviation for the state should be used in complete mailing addresses. A list of the state abbreviations is in Appendix E. The ZIP Code should be placed one or two spaces after the state abbreviation.

The ZIP Code is a five-digit code that identifies areas within the United States and its possessions. In 1985 the United States Postal Service introduced the ZIP + 4 system. This system uses the original ZIP Code plus a hyphen and four additional numbers. This expanded code enables the Postal Service to sort mail on high-speed automated equipment for specific streets, specific buildings, or even to specific floors within buildings. The ZIP Code for an address can be obtained from a ZIP Code Directory provided by the United States Postal Service.

The letter address is always flush with the left margin. The first line of the letter address is at least four line spaces below the date.

SALUTATION. The salutation is the greeting that begins a letter. Examples of correct and incorrect salutations in writing letters to specific individuals include:

The salutation is the greeting of the letter.

Correct	Incorrect
Dear Ms. Hawks:	Dear Nancy Hawks:
Dear Nancy:	Dear Ms. Nancy:
Dear John and Nancy:	

Examples of correct and incorrect salutations in writing the same letter to many people include:

Correct	Incorrect
Dear Customer:	Dear Gentlemen:
Ladies and Gentlemen:	Dear Ladies and Gentlemen:

The content of the salutation depends on the first line of the letter address. When a letter is addressed to a company and contains an attention line, the salutation is directed to the company and not to the person in the attention line. The formality of the salutation depends on the relationship between the sender and the receiver of the letter. A general guide is to use the name that you would use if you met the person or persons face to face. If the first line of the letter address is singular, the salutation must be singular; if it is plural, the salutation must be plural.

The salutation should be flush with the left margin and placed two line spaces below the last line of the letter address. A colon is placed after the salutation in a business letter if mixed punctuation is used; no punctuation is placed after the salutation if open punctuation is used. The salutation is omitted in the simplified block letter format (see page 219).

The salutation begins two lines below the letter address at the left margin.

BODY. The body is the message section of the letter. It begins on the second line below the salutation. The body is single-spaced within paragraphs and double-spaced between paragraphs. The paragraphs may be indented or blocked depending on the letter format selected. Normally the first and last paragraphs of a letter are shorter than the other paragraphs.

The message is contained in the body of the letter.

COMPLIMENTARY CLOSE. The complimentary close is a phrase used to end the communication that began with the salutation. Frequently used complimentary closes include:

The complimentary close ends the letter.

Sincerely,   Sincerely yours,   Yours truly,   Cordially,

The complimentary close should be typed two lines below the last line of the body of the letter. The first character of the close should begin at the same horizontal point as the first character of the date. Only the first character of the first word in the complimentary close is capitalized. The complimentary close should be followed by a comma if mixed punctuation is used and no punctuation if open punctuation is used. The simplified block letter omits the complimentary close.

SIGNATURE BLOCK.   The signature block should contain the typed name and position title of the sender. The name should be placed four lines below the complimentary close. The typed name does not include the courtesy title of a man but may include that of a woman if she has a courtesy title preference, e.g., Ms., Miss, or Mrs., or if the name could be mistaken as a man's name, such as Pat, Kim, or Lynn. The position title of the sender should be placed immediately after or directly beneath the typed name. If on the same line, the name and position title are separated by a comma. The sender of the message should sign the letter in the space between the close and the typed name.

REFERENCE INITIALS.   The initials of the message originator and the keyboarder make up the reference initials. If the originator is the same person who signs the letter, his or her initials are optional. If the originator's initials are given, they are separated from those of the keyboarder by a colon or a diagonal. The originator's initials should be capitalized and the keyboarder's lowercased. The reference initials are placed flush with the left margin two lines below the sender's position title. Examples of reference initials are:

bc   BGH:da   SMH/reh

SUPPLEMENTARY PARTS OF A LETTER

In addition to the seven standard parts, letters may contain one or more supplementary parts. These parts include the attention line, subject line, company name in signature block, enclosure notation, copy notation, and postscript.

ATTENTION LINE.   When a company name is used as the first line of the letter address, the attention line can be used to direct the letter to a person, position title, or department within the company. Today the attention line is not commonly used because using a person's name in the first line of the letter address is preferred.

When used, the attention line should be the second line of the letter address. It may be typed with initial capitals or with all capitals. The word *Attention* should not be abbreviated, and it should not be separated from the rest of the attention line with a colon. An example of an attention line is:

Schroeder's Plumbing Company
Attention Warehouse Manager
3592 Pecan Street
Chandler, TX 75758-3291

The sender's name and title appear in the signature block.

Reference initials are those of the keyboarder and the writer.

The attention line is part of the letter address.

SUBJECT LINE. The subject line immediately identifies the content of the letter to the reader, and it assists the secretary in filing the letter. It is considered part of the body of the letter. The subject line should be short—less than one line—and it should not be a complete sentence.

The subject line should be placed on the second line below the salutation. It may be centered, flush with the left margin, or indented the same amount as the paragraphs. It may be typed in all capitals or typed with initial capitals. If the word *Subject* is used, it should be followed by a colon. A letter that includes a subject line is shown in Illustration 9-3.

A *reference line* is sometimes used instead of a subject line. It is intended to cite a previous letter, policy, contract, etc., that is discussed in the present letter.

> The subject line is a synopsis statement of the message.

COMPANY NAME IN SIGNATURE BLOCK. The name of the company may be typed in all capital letters on the second line after the complimentary close. This practice is not common when letterhead stationery is used. The first character of the company name is aligned with the first character of the complimentary close. An example of this supplementary part is:

Sincerely,

BENTON FINANCE, INC.

Pauline E. Conners
Executive Vice President

ENCLOSURE OR ATTACHMENT NOTATION. Any item included in the envelope other than the letter, such as a check, invoice, or photograph, is considered an enclosure. Whenever an enclosure is included with a letter, an enclosure notation should be typed a single or double space beneath the reference initials (flush with the left margin). The enclosures may be identified, or the number of enclosures may be put in parentheses. Examples of enclosure notations are:

> Enclosure notation is used when an item accompanies a letter.

Enclosure: Check   enc   Enclosures (3)   Enc. 3

The word *Attachment* may be used in place of *Enclosure* when an item is stapled or fastened in some way to the letter.

COPY NOTATION. A copy notation is used when a copy of a letter is being sent to someone other than the addressee. The copy notation should be flush with the left margin and two line spaces below the reference

> Copy notations list persons in addition to addressee who will receive letter.

Illustration 9-3   Block Style, Mixed Punctuation

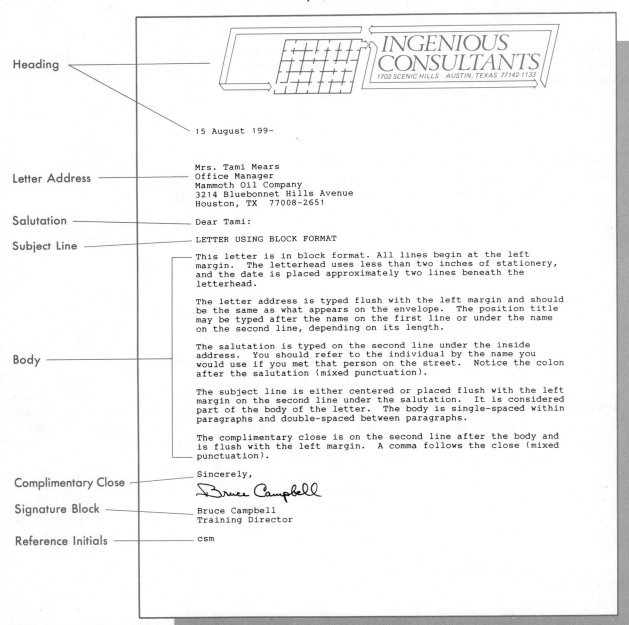

initials (or enclosure notation if used). The copy notation may be a *c* (copy), a *cc* (carbon copy), or a *pc* (photocopy); however, many organizations use *c* regardless of how the copy was made. The names of the individuals to receive the copies should be typed after the notation. Examples of copy notations include:

> c Jerry Crum
>   Anna Greer
>
> cc David Watkins
>
> pc Alice Rath
>   Jim Thomas

POSTSCRIPT.   A postscript may be used to add a personal comment or to emphasize an important point discussed in the body of the letter. It should *not* be used to add an important point omitted from the body of the letter. The postscript should follow the last notation and be displayed in the same style as the paragraphs of the message. If the paragraphs are indented, the postscript should also be indented. A postscript may be handwritten. The notation *P.S.* is usually omitted.

Postscripts are used for personal messages or points needing reemphasis.

PUNCTUATION STYLES

The two styles of punctuation commonly used in business letters are mixed and open. The most popular style is mixed punctuation. **Mixed punctuation** requires a colon after the salutation and a comma after the complimentary close.

Open punctuation is becoming more popular but is still less popular than mixed punctuation. Letters using **open punctuation** omit the colon after the salutation and the comma after the complimentary close.

Punctuation styles are mixed and open.

LETTER FORMATS

The format is part of the reader's first impression of your letter. Organizations usually designate the format of their letters, but in some circumstances they may permit the originator to select the format. The most frequently used formats are block, modified block, and simplified block.

Letter formats include block, modified block, and simplified block.

Letters in block style are fast to keyboard.

BLOCK. The block format is becoming very popular. It is economical to keyboard because none of the parts of the letter is indented. Illustration 9-3 and Illustration 9-4A show a block format letter.

Modified block style has two versions.

MODIFIED BLOCK.   The date (or the return address and date), complimentary close, and signature block begin at the horizontal center of the page in the modified block format. There are two versions of the modified block format: (1) body of the letter with block paragraphs and (2) body of the letter with indented paragraphs. Letters using the modified block format are shown in Illustrations 9-4B and 9-4D.

Simplified block is a modern format that eliminates the salutation and complimentary close.

SIMPLIFIED BLOCK.   The simplified block is a modern, efficient letter format similar to the AMS Simplified Letter that was developed several years ago by the Administrative Management Society. The simplified block letter eliminates the use of a salutation and a complimentary close. Illustration 9-4C shows a letter in the simplified block format.

PLACEMENT

The margins should frame the letter.

A carefully arranged letter resembles a picture in a frame. The letter should have a border of blank space to form a frame. The width of this frame will vary with the length of the letter, but it should normally be at least one inch on each side. Today, with many offices using word processing equipment, a letter can be easily adjusted to give it an attractive appearance. Some organizations are justifying their line lengths (making the right margin even). This gives an attractive but very formal appearance.

PERSONAL BUSINESS LETTERS

There is no specific format for a personal business letter, but standard parts and placement are the same as in a business letter.

Personal business letters are those written by individuals in conducting business of a personal nature. An application for employment, a request for information, and a comment about services received are examples of personal business letters. A good grade of paper should be used for this type of letter. A block style or modified block style with mixed or open punctuation is suitable. The trend is to place the sender's address immediately under the signature block; traditionally the return address is part of the heading. The simplified block letter format is not recommended for application letters because many individuals interpret the lack of a salutation as being impersonal. Illustration 9-4D shows a personal business letter.

15 August 199-

Mrs. Tami Mears
Office Manager
Mammoth Oil Company
3214 Bluebonnet Hills Avenue
Houston, TX 77008-2651

Dear Tami:

LETTER USING BLOCK FORMAT

This letter is in the block format. All lines begin at the left
margin. The letterhead uses less than two inches of stationery,
and the date is placed approximately two inches beneath the
letterhead.

The letter address is typed flush with the left margin and should
be the same as what appears on the envelope. The position title
may be typed after the name on the first line or under the name
on the second line, depending on its length.

The salutation is typed on the second line under the inside
address. You should refer to the individual by the name you
would use if you met that person on the street. Notice the colon
after the salutation (mixed punctuation).

The subject line is either centered or placed flush with the left
margin on the second line under the salutation. It is considered
part of the body of the letter. The body is single-spaced within
paragraphs and double-spaced between paragraphs.

The complimentary close is on the second line after the body and
is flush with the left margin. A comma follows the close (mixed
punctuation).

Sincerely,

Bruce Campbell

Bruce Campbell
Training Director

csm

Letter A

458 Office Plaza Grand Forks, North Dakota 58201-4818

November 18, 199-

Commonwealth Insurance
Attention Office Manager
2207 Harlan Park Freeway
Bismarck, ND 58501-7291

Ladies and Gentlemen

     You asked for information about the modified block letter
format. This letter is in the modified block format with indented paragraphs. A pamphlet with additional information about
letter formats is enclosed.

     Notice the date in the heading begins at the horizontal
center of the page. The inside address is flush with the left
margin. The addressee's name is unknown so an attention line
is used. The salutation is plural since the first line of the
inside address is the name of a company; the use of a singular
title in the attention line has no effect on the salutation. No
punctuation is used after the salutation since this letter is
using the open punctuation style.

     The body of this letter uses indented paragraphs, but could
have used blocked paragraphs. As in most letters, the body is
single-spaced within paragraphs and double-spaced between paragraphs.

     The complimentary close begins on the second line after the
body and at the horizontal center of the letter. Notice that it
is in line with the date and is followed by no punctuation (open
punctuation).

     The reference initials contain the originator's and key-
boarder's initials since the individual signing the letter did
not originate the document. The enclosure notation is used to
ensure that the person mailing the letter includes the pamphlet
and that the person receiving the letter is aware that it was
included.

     The modified block is a well-accepted format that is popular
in many organizations.

                              Cordially

                              Raquel Silva

                              Ms. Raquel Silva
                              Consultant

KW:mb

Enc.

Letter B

3368 LINCOLN ROAD
CINCINNATI, OHIO 45227-2121

May 11, 199-

DR SALLY MILLS
EDUCATION COMPUTING
428 BYTE AVENUE
CLEVELAND OH 44106-3728

SIMPLIFIED BLOCK LETTER

This letter form, Dr. Mills, is in the Simplified Block Letter
format. It is modern and time saving. The letter should be constructed using these guidelines:

1. Use block format.

2. Omit the salutation and complimentary close. Use the addressee's name in the first sentence to personalize the message.

3. Always use a subject line typed in all capitals or cap-and-
lowercase letters. The subject line should be double-spaced below the address and the body should be double-spaced below the
subject line.

4. When listing items, do not indent enumerations.

5. The originator's name and title may be typed in all capitals
or cap-and-lowercase letters flush with the left margin and four
lines below the body of the letter.

6. Place the keyboarder's initials in lowercase letters two
lines below the originator's name. Enclosure notations and copy
notations are placed under the keyboarder's initials.

Dr. Mills, you will enjoy using this format once you become familiar with it. An enclosed brochure describes future writing
workshops which will give you practice in creating letters in
different formats.

Ronald Schroeder

RONALD SCHROEDER, COMMUNICATION SPECIALIST

sj

Enclosure

c Rhonda Young

Letter C

                              1520 Quail Run
                              Billings, MT 59103-8641
                              January, 12, 199-

Mr. Stanley Purcell
Individual Investments
7345 Skiers Road
Denver, CO 80202-4784

Dear Mr. Purcell:

     This is a personal business letter typed in modified block
format with indented paragraphs. The personal business letter
may use any of the three accepted formats.

     The heading contains the sender's address immediately above
the date. This address is typed and not printed as is letterhead
stationery. Notice that the individual sending the letter omits
his or her name in the heading. A general guide is to place the
heading on lines 10-12, but this varies with the length of the
letter.

     The letter address is flush with the left margin about four
to six lines below the dateline. The letter address is the
receiver's address which appears on the envelope.

     The salutation is placed on the second line after the letter
address. Place a colon after the salutation since this letter is
business and not personal in content.

     You may use supplementary parts (attention lines, subject
lines, enclosures, etc.) as in regular business letters. The
body of the letter contains the message that the sender is transmitting to the receiver. The body should be single-spaced within
paragraphs and double-spaced between paragraphs.

     Sign your name in the space between the complimentary close
and the signature block. Normally a personal business letter
does not contain reference initials since the sender types the
letter.

                              Yours truly,

                              Joyce Manvil

                              Joyce Manvil

Letter D

Illustration 9-4   Four Business Letter Formats

ENVELOPES

The envelope should be appropriate for the letter.

Envelopes should be the same color and quality as the stationery. The envelope must be of adequate size to hold the letter and any enclosures or attachments without unnecessary folding. The return address, mailing address, and envelope notations are the three things that may be included on an envelope. Correctly addressed envelopes are shown in Illustration 9-5.

Return address goes in upper left corner.

RETURN ADDRESS.   The return address is printed or typewritten in the upper left corner of the envelope. It should contain the sender's address as shown on the letterhead. Often the sender's name will be typewritten immediately above a printed business address. For personal business letters, return addresses should be typewritten on plain envelopes.

The envelope address should be the same as the letter address.

MAILING ADDRESS.   The mailing address should contain the receiver's name and address as shown in the letter address. The address should not exceed five lines, and all lines should be blocked. The ZIP Code or ZIP + 4 should be used in all addresses. Although the letter address is prepared in uppercase and lowercase, the Postal Service recommends using all capital letters and no punctuation on the envelope to facilitate use of optical scanning equipment.

The first line of the address should be typed seven spaces to the left of the horizontal center of the envelope and on line 14 of a No. 10 envelope or on line 12 of a No. 6$\frac{3}{4}$ envelope.

Envelopes may have two types of notation.

ENVELOPE NOTATIONS.   Two types of envelope notation are used. Special mailing instructions should be in all capital letters below the postage stamp and at least three lines above the address. These Postal Service requirements permit electronic scanning and sorting of mail. Mailing instructions include *SPECIAL DELIVERY, SPECIAL HANDLING, REGISTERED, AIR MAIL, CERTIFIED,* and so on.

Instructions for individuals handling the receiver's mail should be in all capital letters three lines below the return address. These notations may be *CONFIDENTIAL, HOLD FOR ARRIVAL,* or *PLEASE FORWARD.*

MEMOS

Memos are the primary form of internal written communication.

The most common form of written message for communication within an organization is the interoffice memorandum, or **memo** as it is usually called. Memos have grown in popularity as organizations have become larger and as communications within organizations have become more complex. They are normally less formal and shorter than letters.

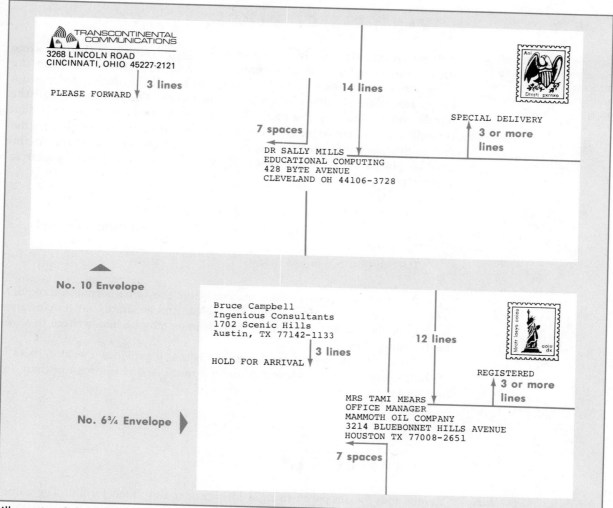

Illustration 9-5   Correctly Addressed Envelopes

USES OF INTEROFFICE MEMOS

Memos are used in a variety of ways. They may be used to communicate upward to superiors, downward to subordinates, laterally to peers, and diagonally to other members of a network. Information of all kinds can be conveyed from one department to another through the use of memos. They are used to announce such things as times and dates of upcoming meetings as well as results of previous meetings, proposed or actual changes in policies or procedures, reports of activities, and instructions.

Memos have a wide variety of uses.

ADVANTAGES OF MEMOS

The use of memos has several advantages. One advantage is that the same memo can be addressed to several individuals. If you want to send the same memo to specific employees, you can list all the names and place a check mark after a different name on each copy. Or, you can list all the names and request that the memo be "routed" from the first-named person through the last-named person. Entire groups can be addressed in a memo and individual copies given to each member of the group, or the memo may be placed on a bulletin board. Examples of ways to properly address memos are:

Specific Individuals	Entire Groups
TO: Emi Ayako, Jacqueline Nelson, and Mary Williams	TO: Personnel Department Employees
TO: See Distribution List Below	

A second advantage of using memos is that they are informal and require less time to compose. Memos should be clear and accurate, but they do not have to be as polished as formal letters. Memos may be handwritten to save keyboarding time.

Another advantage of using a memo is that it provides a written record of the message. Written messages make a more lasting impression than do oral messages.

FORMAT OF MEMOS

Memos may be prepared using a formal or a simplified format. The same organization may use more than one format for its memos, or it may specify the format that will be used throughout the organization.

Formal memos may be prepared on printed forms that contain the headings *To, From, Date* and *Subject.* **Simplified memos** are prepared on plain paper or letterhead stationery. The format of a simplified memo is the same as a simplified block letter except the address is omitted.

Standard size paper ($8\frac{1}{2}'' \times 11''$) and half-sheet paper ($8\frac{1}{2}'' \times 5\frac{1}{2}''$) are the two most common sizes of paper used for formal memos. The paper-saving advantage of using half sheets is often outweighed by the disadvantage of locating the smaller sheet when it is filed with standard size paper. Simplified memos are prepared on standard size paper. An example of a formal memo is shown in Illustration 9-6 and of a simplified memo in Illustration 9-7.

Illustration 9-6   Format of Formal Memo

INTEROFFICE COMMUNICATION

COMMUNITY SERVICE INSURANCE

TO: All Employees

FROM: Sara Jackson, VP for Administration *sj*

DATE: March 1, 199-

SUBJECT: Characteristics of Formal Memos

———— Heading

Many questions have arisen concerning proper construction and use of formal memos. The following guidelines should answer these questions.

Formal memos contain several characteristics which are unique. Some of these characteristics are

1.   A printed memo head consisting of <u>TO</u>, <u>FROM</u>, <u>DATE</u>, and <u>SUBJECT</u>.

2.   The individual sending the memo may or may not use a business title. The sender normally does not use a complete signature. An individual's first name or initials are usually written after the typed name on the FROM line in the heading.

3.   The memo is not centered vertically as is a letter.

4.   Memos, whether formal or simplified, are normally short and contain only one topic; that topic is indicated in the subject line. If more than one topic is needed, separate memos are sent.

5.   The body of the memo is in block style beginning a double space below the heading. The body is single-spaced.

6.   Informal writing style is appropriate for memos. First person, I, is commonly used along with inferences and jargon.

7.   Reference initials, enclosure notations, copy notations, and second page headings are used as in letters.

Remember that memos should be concise and easy to read and should not contain any irrelevant information. Please let me know if you think of any other characteristics of formal memos.

gs

———— Body

———— Reference Initials

Illustration 9-7   Format of Simplified Memo

March 1, 199–

All Employees

CHARACTERISTICS OF SIMPLIFIED MEMOS

Many questions have arisen concerning proper construction and use of memos. The following guidelines should answer these questions.

Simplified memos contain several characteristics which are unique. Some of these characteristics are

1. Full sheets are used to prepare simplified memos, whether plain paper or letterhead stationery.

2. All spacing guidelines for a simplified block letter also apply to the simplified memo. The only difference is that no address is used in the simplified memo.

3. Personal titles are not used but a business title or department name may be used.

4. Memos, whether formal or simplified, are normally short and contain only one topic; that topic is indicated in the subject line. If more than one topic is needed, separate memos are sent.

5. Informal writing style is appropriate for memos. First person, I, is commonly used along with inferences and jargon.

6. Reference initials, enclosure notations, copy notations, and second page headings are used as in letters.

Remember that memos should be concise and easy to read and should not contain any irrelevant information. Either the formal memo or simplified memo format is acceptable for our interoffice communication.

Sara Jackson
Sara Jackson, VP for Administration

gs

SPECIAL FORMS OF MEMOS

Business firms have developed various kinds of memo forms to perform specific functions within an organization. One is a **round-trip memo**, which is also called a *message-reply memo*. It usually consists of multiform paper, carbon or carbonless, on which the sender can complete the heading and the message portion. The sender can then remove a carbon copy for her or his files before sending the memo. The receiver may add a reply and remove a copy before returning the memo to the original sender. An example of this kind of memo is shown in Illustration 9-8.

Special forms of memos exist for specific functions.

To	From
	Robert Rinner The Webster Corporation Grand Forks, North Dakota 58201-3452

MESSAGE

SUBJECT   DATE

SIGNED

REPLY

DATE

SIGNED

Illustration 9-8   Round-Trip Memo

Another frequently used special memo form is a **telephone memo**. It is designed so that minimal effort is needed to relay a telephone message. An example of a telephone memo is shown in Illustration 9-9.

```
To_____
Date_____ Time_____
       WHILE YOU WERE OUT
M_____
of_____
Phone_____
        Area Code    Number    Extension
┌─────────────────────┬──────────────────────┬──┐
│ TELEPHONED          │ PLEASE CALL          │  │
├─────────────────────┼──────────────────────┼──┤
│ CALLED TO SEE YOU   │ WILL CALL AGAIN      │  │
├─────────────────────┼──────────────────────┼──┤
│ WANTS TO SEE YOU    │ URGENT               │  │
├─────────────────────┴──────────────────────┼──┤
│          RETURNED YOUR CALL                 │  │
└─────────────────────────────────────────────┴──┘
Message_____
_____
_____
_____
_____
_____
                    Operator
```

Illustration 9-9   Telephone Memo

STATIONERY

The purpose of the message must be determined so the proper stationery can be selected.

Stationery that is used for letters or memos will influence the impression formed by the receiver of the message. The type of stationery that is used will be determined by the purpose of the message. For example, the stationery used for closing a major business transaction should be of a higher quality than the stationery used for announcing an upcoming sale to credit card customers.

WEIGHT

The weight of the paper is a factor in selecting stationery.

The most common weight is 20-pound paper.

The weight of paper plays a part in impressing the receiver of your message. The most common stationery for business letters is 20-pound bond. The weight measurement is determined by the weight of four reams of $8\frac{1}{2}'' \times 11''$ paper. One ream equals approximately 500 sheets.

SIZE

Letters are normally prepared on $8\frac{1}{2}'' \times 11''$ paper.

Most business letters are prepared on standard size stationery, $8\frac{1}{2}'' \times 11''$. Letters from business executives are sometimes placed on $7\frac{1}{2}'' \times 10''$ high-quality stationery called *executive stationery*. Memos are placed on various sizes of stationery, but the most common sizes are $8\frac{1}{2}'' \times 11''$ and $8\frac{1}{2}'' \times 5\frac{1}{2}''$.

Memos are prepared on various sizes of paper.

COLOR

Color is another important consideration in selecting business stationery. White is the most popular color and is acceptable in all circumstances. Recently, there has been a trend toward using other colors. Selecting the appropriate stationery color is extremely important to the image of the company. The type of industry certainly must be a determining factor in selecting paper color. For example, a cosmetics company that caters exclusively to a female clientele may effectively use a pastel pink, while a lumber company may very effectively use light wood-grained stationery. Some companies use different colored memos to identify originating departments.

White stationery is always appropriate; other colors may be used.

QUALITY

The quality of stationery is determined by the amount of rag content in the paper. The *rag content* is the amount and type of fiber (usually cotton) used in the composition of the paper. High-quality stationery usually has 25 percent or more rag content. High-quality stationery also has a watermark showing the name of the company that manufactures the paper or the emblem of the organization that uses the stationery. Letters should be prepared on high-quality stationery; all pages should be of the same weight, color, quality, and size. Memos should be placed on less expensive grades of paper. The advantages of using high-quality stationery for letters include superior appearance, excellent texture, neat corrections, and long life without chemical breakdown.

High-quality stationery has high rag content and a watermark.

Paper used for second and successive pages should match the letterhead stationery.

SPECIAL CONSIDERATIONS

While the foregoing factors are important, they do not represent the end of the stationery selection process. Envelopes, too, must be given consideration. They should be of the same color and quality as the stationery. Also, envelopes should be in proportion to the size of the stationery. For example, standard $8\frac{1}{2}'' \times 11''$ stationery requires No. 10 ($9\frac{1}{2}'' \times 4\frac{1}{8}''$) envelopes; executive stationery is $7\frac{1}{4}'' \times 10''$ and requires No. 7 ($7\frac{1}{2}'' \times 3\frac{7}{8}''$) envelopes.

Envelope paper should match the stationery.

An organization may convey a positive or a negative image by its written messages. The stationery selected to carry these messages should share importance with the composition of the messages.

DISCUSSION QUESTIONS

1. List and explain the seven standard parts of a business letter.
2. Distinguish between the use of memos and the use of business letters.
3. List and describe five supplemental parts of a letter.
4. Distinguish between a subject line and an attention line as concerns their use and location.
5. When should the word *attachment* be used as a notation in a business letter?
6. Identify information that is essential and information that is optional in a letterhead. Explain why information included in a letterhead may vary among organizations.
7. In what type of situation is it appropriate to use a postscript in a letter and in what type of situation is it inappropriate?
8. Compare the two punctuation styles that may be used in letters.
9. Describe a situation where simplified block format is more appropriate than block or modified block letter format.
10. Compare the three most frequently used letter formats.
11. What is meant by "framing" your letter?
12. Describe the most important format features of a simplified block letter.
13. Distinguish between the two types of envelope notation and give examples of each.
14. Explain why most personal business letters are not written on letterhead stationery.
15. Discuss format differences between formal and simplified memos.
16. List three advantages of using memos.
17. List the parts that normally comprise the heading of a formal memo.
18. Describe two types of special form memos.
19. What is rag content? How does it affect stationery?
20. Describe the four characteristics that should be considered when selecting stationery.

APPLICATION EXERCISES

1. Visit two business firms and obtain copies of memos used in their organizations. Describe the formats of the memos.
2. Bring to class two business letters. Identify their various parts.
3. Write a memo to your instructor explaining the advantages of using the simplified block letter format when the name of the addressee is unknown.
4. Bring to class three envelopes that you have received from business organizations. Explain the different ways in which envelopes are addressed.

5. Visit your Postal Service office and obtain information about addressing envelopes and using ZIP Codes. Write a memo to your instructor conveying this information.

6. Obtain three or four samples of business letterheads. Explain the characteristics of the paper. Describe the differences in the letterheads.

7. Correct the following personal business letter headings.

   a. Mr. Robert Clay
      3728 Landeco Ln.
      Coralville, Ia. 52241-4322
      15 August, 199-

   b. Oct. 7, 199-
      812 Walnut Street
      Kearney, Nebraska 68847

8. Correct the following formal memo headings.

   a.　　TO: Deanna Adamson,
      FROM: Kevin Olson
      DATE: May 5 199-
      Request for Vacation

   b.　　　TO: Sales Managers
      FROM: Roxanne Meyers
      SUBJECT: Fall Sales Conference

9. Correct the following business letter addresses and salutations (assume mixed punctuation).

   a. Dr. Kirk Fountain, M.D.
      Mental Health Center
      2912 Belmont Road
      Las Cruces, N.M. 73417

      Dear Mr. Fountain:

   b. Silverman's Farm Supply
      1240 Cotton Ave.
      Pine Bluff, Ark. 33477

      Attn: Bookkeeper

      Dear Sir,

   c. Ms. Janice Kraig
      609 McNair St.
      Delta, Ohio 43515

      Dear Janice Kraig;

10. Correct the following business letter headings, letter addresses, salutations, and complimentary closes (assume mixed punctuation).

    a.
    　　　　　　　　　　　　　　　　January 3, 199-

    Ms. Teri Stephens
    1817 Cherry Circle
    Houston 74623-4455

    Dear Ms. Teri;

    Sincerely

    b. 530 Tulane Drive
       Lafayette, LA 55327
       9 October, 199-

       TO: Kim Warren
          1114 Campbell Drive
          Richmond, Virginia 32461

          Dear Ms. Warren

          Sincerely Yours

CHAPTER 10

GOOD NEWS AND NEUTRAL NEWS MESSAGES

L E A R N I N G   O B J E C T I V E S

Your learning objectives for this chapter include the following:

- To understand the nature of good news and neutral news messages
- To appreciate the advantages of using the direct plan for effective communication of good news, inquiries, and claims
- To understand the four specific guidelines of the direct plan
- To recognize the differences between poor and good examples of messages
- To use the direct plan competently for a variety of different kinds of good news, inquiry, and claim messages

Good news messages and neutral news messages give favorable or neutral information.

A good news or a neutral news message conveys pleasant, favorable, or neutral information to the receiver. Such a message may inquire about a service, a product, or a person; it may grant a request that has been sent to you or your organization; it may announce an upcoming sale or a new product; or it may be used in internal communication to announce promotions, expansions, salary increases, or improvements in fringe benefits. The receiver will be getting news that is favorable or neutral and will accept the contents of the message easily. The message should be constructed using the direct plan so the receiver can readily see the benefits gained.

Claim messages will be discussed in this chapter because they follow a plan similar to that used for good news. Although claim messages may be considered to convey bad news—the sender is indicating that he or she has been wronged—receivers should welcome claim messages because they assist in improving products or services. Claim messages are strengthened when written in the direct plan format.

USE THE DIRECT PLAN FOR GOOD NEWS AND NEUTRAL NEWS

The direct plan should be used in conveying all good news and neutral news messages. The direct plan will immediately give the good or neutral news to the receivers; they will then respond favorably to the remainder of the message. One of the advantages, therefore, of using the direct plan to convey good or neutral news is that receivers will know at once that the message is conveying information that is going to be beneficial to them (or at least not harmful). If the good or neutral news—the purpose of the message—is not at the beginning, the receivers may lose interest and may not finish the message.

Another advantage of giving the good or neutral news at the beginning of the message is to put receivers in the proper frame of mind before presenting the conditions under which the good or neutral news will be carried out. The explanation will have a much better chance of acceptance if receivers are in a good mood rather than in an apprehensive state.

> The **direct plan** gives receiver good news or neutral news immediately.

> Direct plan increases chances that reader will read entire message.

> Direct plan gets receiver in positive frame of mind.

HOW TO USE THE DIRECT PLAN

You should incorporate into your good news and neutral news messages the effective business communication fundamentals that were presented in the first three chapters. In particular, analyze your receiver and use the you-viewpoint in these messages. The four stages in the direct plan for presenting good or neutral news are detailed in Illustration 10-1.

The direct plan is used for a variety of good news messages—adjustment grants, approved requests, approved credit applications, approved employment applications, favorable decisions, or any other favorable information. The direct plan is also used for neutral information and claim messages. The content of the message must be decided before the direct plan can be implemented.

> There are specific steps in the direct plan.

> Direct plan should be used for messages presenting good news, neutral news, and claims.

I. The Good or Neutral News **Opening**
   A. Give the good or neutral news at the start.
   B. Be positive.
   C. Provide unity.
   D. Use emphasis techniques.
   E. Stress the interests of and benefits for the receiver.

II. The **Explanation**
   A. Present related information.
   B. Make it objective.
   C. Keep it concise.
   D. Be positive.

III. **Sales Appeal** (if Appropriate)
   A. Make it personal.
   B. Suggest alternatives if needed.
   C. Aim for quick action from the receivers.

IV. The **Friendly Close**
   A. Build goodwill.
   B. Keep it short.
   C. Be positive.
   D. Express your appreciation for the receiver's business.
   E. Point out that other services can be provided.

Illustration 10-1   Direct Plan Outline

DETERMINING CONTENT

Content of message is developed after objective is determined.

The situation must be analyzed and the objective of the communication determined before any message can be composed. If the objective is transmitting good or neutral news, the direct plan should be used in organizing the message. Before composing a good or neutral news message, the following questions on content must be answered: What is the most favorable news? How will this news benefit the receiver? What additional information should be explained to the receiver? Would a convincing sales appeal in this message be appropriate? What friendly message can be transmitted in the close to build goodwill?

Once you have determined the content, you are ready to organize your message. The parts of the direct plan outline are discussed in the following sections, and the most important considerations are reviewed.

GOOD OR NEUTRAL NEWS

In the direct plan, the memo or letter should begin with the main idea—the good or neutral news. Give the good news immediately, be positive, provide unity, use emphasis techniques, and stress receiver interests or benefits.

The first sentence of the first paragraph should contain the news that will be most beneficial to the receiver. Only positive words should be used in describing the news. The paragraph should be short for emphasis. The receiver's interest will be aroused if the benefits of the good news are stressed in the first paragraph. For unity, information should be provided so that the receiver will know which request, order, contract, or previous transaction you are discussing. This identification may be placed in a reference line.

> In the direct plan, messages begin with the good or neutral news.

EXPLANATION

The second paragraph of a message using the direct plan should contain the explanation. The explanation presents any additional information that relates to the good or neutral news that was presented in the first paragraph. The explanation is factual and, therefore, needs to be presented in an objective manner. It should be concise but still contain all the details the receiver needs. The explanation should be written in a positive manner.

> The supporting explanation should follow the good or neutral news paragraph.

SALES APPEAL

A sales appeal can be effective in many good news and neutral news messages but is not appropriate in all of them. Situations in which a sales appeal should be used include letters approving charge accounts, letters informing students that they have been accepted into a program, and messages approving claims. Situations in which a sales appeal would not be appropriate include claim letters and messages agreeing to speak at a meeting.

The sales appeal, if used, should follow the explanation. It may be placed in a paragraph by itself or combined with the closing paragraph. It should be adapted to the situation and may provide alternatives for the receiver. The sales appeal may tell about an upcoming sale or a new product. It should be personalized to convince the receiver that it is in his or her best interest to take immediate action.

> The sales appeal should be used if it is appropriate.

FRIENDLY CLOSE

A properly written close builds goodwill.

The primary purpose of the friendly close is to build goodwill. Goodwill is built by being personal, positive, and optimistic. The close may express appreciation for an employee's past service or for a customer's business. The close may move to a topic-related subject, or it may unify the message by referring to the good news given in the first paragraph. The close in a good or neutral news letter normally is short and avoids cliches.

IMPLEMENTING THE DIRECT PLAN

A communication case will help illustrate how to compose good news messages.

The direct plan will be illustrated through the development of a good news letter to a customer. Here are the details of the communication situation:

> You are vice president of customer services for Valley National Bank in Kingsville, Texas. Robert Herrera, an entrepreneur, has requested that your bank loan him $125,000 to open a hardware store. Robert worked as a salesclerk in a hardware store before moving to Kingsville. He has good credit references and also has saved $25,000 for a down payment. You will write a letter to Robert informing him that his loan application for the $125,000 has been approved. He will need to repay the loan in 20 years at a variable interest rate. The rate for the first year will be $12\frac{1}{2}$ percent, and the rate for subsequent years will be $\frac{1}{2}$ percent above the average treasury rate set by the federal government. You want to express appreciation for his business and invite him to conduct all his financial transactions with Valley National Bank.

DETERMINE APPROPRIATE CONTENT

The first step in writing a message is to analyze the situation and determine the message content that will most effectively accomplish the objective of the communication. In the Robert Herrera letter the objective is to transmit good news—the approval of a loan—so the ideas should be developed and organized using the direct plan. The following sections illustrate how the content for the good news letter may be developed. Each section discusses a stage of the direct plan and presents an example of *poor writing* and then an example of *good writing*.

PRESENT THE GOOD NEWS

A **poor** first paragraph presenting the good news is:

> It has come to my attention that you will need to stop by my office to sign the necessary papers for your loan. Our credit committee approved it yesterday in its weekly meeting.

The **poor** example lacks you-viewpoint.

This poorly written opening paragraph stresses the writer's interest instead of the receiver's interest and benefits. Note that the good news, the loan approval, is not given until the second sentence and the loan is not clearly identified. The paragraph is also written in a stiff, impersonal manner rather than in a positive, friendly style. After reading the first paragraph, Robert will be neither excited nor eager to read the explanation giving the conditions of the loan.

The following would be a **good** opening paragraph for this case problem:

> Your application for a $125,000 loan has been approved. This money should provide the necessary capital for you to open your hardware store.

The **good** example meets all requirements for presenting good news.

In contrast to the poorly written opening paragraph, this paragraph meets all the requirements of properly presenting good news in a message. It gives the good news immediately and positively. The you-viewpoint is emphasized—the benefit that the receiver will realize from the loan is given. The loan is specifically identified in the two sentences. Because this first paragraph has a positive, personal tone, Robert should have an open mind toward Valley National Bank.

PROVIDE AN EXPLANATION

The next step in composing a message using the direct plan is presenting an explanation of the conditions under which the good news—the loan approval— will be carried out. A **poor** way to present an explanation to Robert is:

> The loan is for a 20-year period. Valley National Bank makes loans only at a variable interest rate because of the uncertainty of inflation rates. The interest rate for your loan for the first year will be 12.5 percent, but the rate will probably be higher for subsequent years. The monthly payment is due by the fifth day of each month. There is a 1 percent penalty for late payments.

The **poor** explanation lacks you-viewpoint and is negative.

The style of this explanation is similar to the style of the first paragraph in that it stresses the writer's interests rather than the receiver's benefits. Lack of a you-viewpoint and the negative tone of the message make the paragraph negative. The explanation should contain all relevant facts so that the receiver will not have any questions. In this **poor** example, no information is given concerning how the monthly payments are to be made or when the money will be available. The explanation could have been made more concise by stating that the details of the loan would be furnished when Robert came in and signed the loan agreement.

In contrast, a **good** explanation follows:

The **good** example meets all requirements for a good explanation.

> This loan is for a 20-year period. The rate for the first year is the lowest available from any local financial institution—12½ percent. The interest rate on your loan after the first year is at a low ½ of 1 percent above the average treasury rate set by the federal government. We can arrange the payment dates and method of payment when you come in to sign the loan agreement and pick up your check. At that time I will also discuss with you other agreement details.

This explanation presents the facts in an objective way and answers the receiver's questions. The paragraph is written positively. It contains enough information so that the receiver understands the conditions of the good news, yet it remains concise by indicating that details of the loan will be furnished at a later time. After presenting the explanation the writer should consider using a sales appeal.

CONSIDER SALES APPEAL

A sales appeal should be used whenever the writer is attempting to obtain additional business from the receiver. In this case the following is a **poor** example of an appeal for additional business from Robert:

The **poor** example of a sales appeal is cold and impersonal.

> I want to invite you to use our bank for all your financial business. We will consider giving you additional loans as soon as you have more equity in your store.

Note the impersonal tone of the message. There is no you-viewpoint in the sales appeal and the second sentence is more likely to discourage than encourage additional business.

The following is a **good** example of a sales appeal for this case:

The **good** example of a sales appeal is positive and personalized.

> Mr. Herrera, you are on your way to becoming a successful businessperson. You may be interested in using all the financial services offered by Valley National Bank. Your preferred customer rating entitles you to free checking if you maintain a $1,000 balance in your passbook account, a low-interest revolving credit account, preferred status on additional loans, free photocopying, and other banking services. Please ask about these benefits on your next visit to Valley.

This example of a sales appeal is written in a personalized way; it encourages Robert to use other financial services at Valley National Bank. It mentions additional services that Robert can receive at the bank, and it encourages quick action on Robert's part without appearing pushy.

The sales appeal may be written as a separate paragraph or as part of the final paragraph of the letter.

END YOUR LETTER WITH A FRIENDLY CLOSE

A good or neutral news message should conclude with a friendly close that builds goodwill. A **poor** close, on the other hand, will guarantee ill will:

> Don't forget to come to Valley and sign the loan papers. We cannot release the money until the paperwork is completed and signed. Thanks for doing business with us. If there is anything else I can do, please call.

The **poor** example of a close is negative and does not build goodwill.

A **good** example of a friendly close that will do much to establish goodwill follows:

> You may stop in at your convenience and complete the necessary paperwork for your loan. Your business is certainly appreciated, Mr. Herrera; our staff is available to help meet all your financial needs.

The **good** example of a close is friendly and builds goodwill.

This friendly close is written in a positive, personalized, and optimistic way and it is short. Appreciation is shown for Robert's business. It casually implies that other services can be provided.

SUMMARY—POOR AND GOOD MESSAGES TO ROBERT HERRERA

Poor and good examples have been shown to demonstrate how effective good news messages are written. The **poor** example paragraphs are combined as a letter in Illustration 10-2. This **poor** example fails to use the direct plan for good news, and it also fails to incorporate the communication fundamentals that were presented in Chapters 1, 2, and 3.

Customer goodwill is promoted in the complete good news letter shown in Illustration 10-3. This letter combines the **good** example paragraphs. It integrates communication fundamentals into the direct plan message to produce an effective business communication.

An approval of a loan request has been used to illustrate how the direct plan is used to communicate a good news message. To further demonstrate

Contrasting poor and good letters to Robert Herrera are presented in Illustrations 10-2 and 10-3.

Illustration 10-2 Poor Example of a Good News Message

❸❸ Valley National Bank

P. O. Box 75
Kingsville, Texas 78363-7742
(512) 555-4802

May 23, 199-

Mr. Robert Herrera
1678 Scenic Drive
Kingsville, TX 78363-6686

Dear Mr. Herrera

It has come to my attention that you will need to stop
by my office to sign the necessary papers for your
loan. Our credit committee approved it yesterday in
its weekly meeting.

The loan is for a 20-year period. Valley National Bank
makes loans only at a variable interest rate because of
the uncertainty of inflation rates. The interest rate
for your loan for the first year will be 12.5 percent,
but the rate will probably be higher for subsequent
years. The monthly payment is due by the fifth day of
each month. There is a 1 percent penalty for late
payments.

I want to invite you to use our bank for all your
financial business. We will consider giving you additional loans as soon as you have more equity in your
store.

Don't forget to come to Valley and sign the loan
papers. We cannot release the money until the paperwork is completed and signed. Thanks for doing business with us. If there is anything else I can do,
please call.

Sincerely

Paul Simmons

Paul Simmons
Vice President

ah

Margin annotations:

Weak good news.

Explanation is impersonal and negative.

Sales appeal lacks you-viewpoint.

Impersonal close.

Illustration 10-3 **Good** Example of a Good News Message

88 Valley National Bank

P. O. Box 75
Kingsville, Texas 78363-7742
(512) 555-4802

May 23, 199–

Mr. Robert Herrera
1678 Scenic Drive
Kingsville, TX 78363-6686

Dear Mr. Herrera

Your loan for $125,000 has been approved. This money
should provide the necessary capital for you to open
your hardware store. — Positive good news.

This loan is for a 20-year period. The rate for the
first year is the lowest available from any financial
institution in town--12 1/2 percent. The interest rate
on your loan after the first year is at a low 1/2 of
1 percent above the average treasury rate set by the
federal government. We can arrange the payment dates
and method of payment when you come in to sign the loan
agreement and pick up your check. At that time I will
also discuss with you other agreement details. — Facts presented in positive manner.

Mr. Herrera, you are on your way to becoming a successful businessperson. You may be interested in using all
the financial services offered by Valley National Bank.
Your preferred customer rating entitles you to free
checking if you maintain a $1,000 balance in your pass-
book account, a low-interest revolving credit account,
preferred status on additional loans, free photocopying, and other banking services. Please ask about
these benefits on your next visit to Valley. — You-viewpoint used to sell additional services.

You may stop in at your convenience and complete the
necessary paperwork for your loan. Your business is
certainly appreciated, Mr. Herrera; our staff is avail-
able to help meet all your financial needs. — Friendly close expressing appreciation.

Sincerely

Paul Simmons

Paul Simmons
Vice President

ah

how the direct approach is used in actual business correspondence situations, several other good and poor examples of good news and neutral news messages are presented in the following pages.

INQUIRIES

Businesspersons periodically make routine requests for information. These inquiries may be about a product, a service, or a person. Routine inquiries are neutral news messages that require no persuasion and, therefore, should be written using the direct plan.

Use direct plan with inquiries because persuasion is not needed.

A message of inquiry must be written so that the writer will obtain all the information necessary to make a decision about a product, service, or person. Consider what you or your company needs to know and ask specific questions. Your letter of inquiry should be written so that the receiver can reply easily, quickly, and completely.

Inquiries should ask specific questions.

An inquiry about products or services should make the receiver of the message happy to respond. The inquiry may be very short and include only one sentence requesting a pamphlet or catalog; or it may have several paragraphs in which questions are asked. If several questions are asked, numbering them will aid the receiver in responding. Use the direct plan outline by presenting your request and stating the reason for it (if necessary) in the opening paragraph. In the second paragraph give enough information so that the receiver can respond intelligently. Close your message by requesting action.

Message receiver should be happy to receive inquiry about products or services.

An inquiry about a person must be made carefully to protect the rights of the individual. You should ask only questions that are relevant to the situation. Information obtained should be kept confidential. State whether or not the person about whom you are inquiring authorized your request. Begin your inquiry by clearly identifying the person and stating your need for the information. The explanation should contain relevant facts—pertinent information that the individual shared with you, requirements that must be met (job, loan, award, etc.), or questions that you need answered. Close by stating that you would appreciate the receiver's sharing the information and by promising to keep the information confidential.

Inquiries about persons should ask only relevant questions and should promise that responses will remain confidential.

Illustration 10-4 is a **poor** example of an inquiry requesting details about information processing workshops. The inquiry is not specific enough to enable Mr. Whitfield to send the information Mr. Barnett needs to make a decision. It would be difficult for Mr. Whitfield to answer the two questions unless he knows what types of software programs would need to be taught, the location of the training, the number of hours of training that would be needed, etc.

The letter in Illustration 10-5 is a **good** example of an inquiry about a service. The letter starts by presenting the reasons for the request. Sufficient information is provided to Mr. Whitfield so that he can provide the necessary details in his reply. The numbered questions make it easier for Mr. Whitfield to respond to all of them. The close is positive and encourages a prompt reply.

REQUEST APPROVALS

Managers of business organizations receive requests from their customers, their employees, and others. These requests may include, for example, a request from an employee for six months' parenting leave or a request from a civic organization for the manager to speak at a conference. These requests should be carefully considered and granted whenever feasible.

Businesses receive many requests.

Most requests are approved.

The proper handling of a request can build goodwill for an organization. For instance, approval of a parenting leave will gain goodwill for the organization. The employee taking the leave will have a sense of obligation to the company and will return refreshed and enthusiastic about the job. Goodwill, no doubt, will spread throughout employee groups when they observe the company's humanistic philosophy. Accepting an invitation to speak at a meeting of a civic organization can build goodwill for the company among those attending the meeting. The acceptance letter should convey enthusiasm about the prospect of appearing before the group; it should in no way indicate a duty to perform a community service. The acceptance letter should emphasize the good news of accepting the invitation to speak.

Goodwill can be improved with proper handling of requests.

To illustrate how the direct plan can be used in a good news message communicating approval of a request, assume that you are the human resource manager of Clark Manufacturing Company. Kathy Gibson, an assembly line worker, has requested a change from the day shift to the night shift. This change will allow Kathy to eliminate baby-sitting services and enable her husband to take care of the children while she is at work. Because you want to build goodwill and because there is a shortage of workers on the night shift, you would write a memo to her approving this change and giving her the good news.

Request approvals should stress the good news.

A **poor** approval memo for this request is shown in Illustration 10-6. It does little to build employee morale and goodwill for the company. Note the absence of the you-viewpoint. Also, notice that the good news is not given until the second paragraph.

The **good** memo in Illustration 10-7 uses the direct plan and should positively influence Kathy's attitude toward the company. It gives Kathy the good news in the first sentence. The second paragraph presents an explanation that is factual, positive, and concise. A friendly close is given in the final paragraph. A sales appeal—the optional third step in the direct plan—is not appropriate for this situation.

Illustration 10-4 **Poor** Example of an Inquiry

Barnett's Insurance _____

2136 Clover Lane
Raleigh, NC 27610-1200

August 15, 199–

Mr. Thomas Whitfield, Manager
Innovative Software Trainers
3646 Boulder Drive
Asheville, NC 28802-1122

Dear Mr. Whitfield

Barnett's Insurance has been serving eastern North
Carolina for 50 years. We have agents in more than 100
communities.

Last year we started modernizing our branch offices.
We put computer systems in each office. Now we must
teach the personnel how to use the equipment. Can your
company provide training for our personnel? How much
will it cost?

I am looking forward to your reply.

Sincerely

William Barnett

William Barnett
Owner

ls

The **poor** opening does not present the request.

The explanation does not provide the receiver with necessary information.

Weak close.

Illustration 10-5 **Good** Example of an Inquiry

Barnett's Insurance _____

2136 Clover Lane
Raleigh, NC 27610-1200

August 15, 199-

Mr. Thomas Whitfield, Manager
Innovative Software Trainers
3646 Boulder Drive
Asheville, NC 28802-1122

Dear Mr. Whitfield

Barnett's Insurance is modernizing its operation and
needs computer training for its personnel.

Approximately 125 employees will need training on word
processing, spreadsheet, and marketing software programs. Our personnel would be available for training
between November 1 and February 1. Specifically, we
need answers to these questions:

1. What would be the optimum size for each class section?
2. Would the instruction be more effective if taught
   at your location or in one of our regional offices?
3. On what software packages can you provide training?
4. How many hours of instruction would be necessary
   for each software package?
5. Could your organization provide this type training?
6. How much would this type of training cost?

Your prompt reply to the above questions would be
appreciated so that we may begin planning an effective
training program.

Sincerely

William Barnett

William Barnett
Owner

ls

The **good** opening
presents reason for
request.

Facts are given to
permit reader to
respond properly.

Specific questions
will aid receiver in
providing the
necessary
information.

Closes with request
for prompt reply.

Illustration 10-6 **Poor** Example of a Request Approval Memo

CLARK MANUFACTURING COMPANY

C M C

Interoffice Communication

TO: Mrs. Kathy Gibson

FROM: Tania Silverton *TS*

DATE: November 12, 199–

SUBJECT: Request for Shift Change

I have received your request dated November 7 to change from the day shift to the night shift.

I have approved the request effective November 20. I will have everyone notified by then so you can start the late shift on that day.

I hope this allows you to work out all your problems.

Approval is not given in first paragraph.

Explanation is not clear.

Negative close.

Illustration 10-7 **Good** Example of a Request Approval Memo

CLARK MANUFACTURING COMPANY

C M C

Interoffice Communication

TO: Kathy Gibson

FROM: Tania Silverton *TS*

DATE: November 12, 199–

SUBJECT: Request for Shift Change

Your transfer to the midnight shift has been approved. I am sure you will enjoy working with Beth Nugent, your new shift leader.

You begin working the night shift (midnight to 8 a.m.) on Monday, November 20. Please continue working the day shift through Friday, November 17.

Kathy, you are a valuable asset to our company, and we are pleased to approve this change which will assist you in your baby-sitting arrangements.

Good news given immediately.

Clear explanation stressing receiver's interests.

Friendly close builds goodwill be being personalized and positive.

CLAIMS

Claims include requests for merchandise exchange, for refunds on defective merchandise, for refunds for unsatisfactory service, and for correction of work. Generally, the receiver wants the claim information so that he or she can make necessary corrections as soon as possible. For this reason and to give strength to your claim, use the direct plan. This plan gives your complaint greatest emphasis by making it the first item in the message.

The plan for claim messages can easily be adapted from the direct plan used for good news and neutral news given in Illustration 10-1 on page 232. The claim should be presented in an objective way without a display of anger. The *opening* should present immediately the claim and its impact. The impact could include the inconveniences suffered and identification of specific damages. The *explanation* should provide any necessary additional background that relates to the claim. In this section you could provide facts supporting the claim and describe actions that have been taken. In addition, you should specify actions that you want the receiver to take; and set a deadline by which corrective action should be taken. There would be no *sales appeal* in a claim letter. Finally, the *friendly close* should be optimistic and positive.

Illustration 10-8 is a **poor** example of a claim letter from a jewelry store that received some broken china in a shipment from a wholesaler. Note that the main objective of the letter—notification that china was received in un-satisfactory condition—did not appear until the second paragraph. Also note that the letter implies blame; the claimant should avoid accusing the receiver because the receiver will only be angered by this approach. The claim was not clearly identified—how many and which pieces of china were broken? The receiver needs this information but is not interested in sender-related details such as the claimant's order number. And lastly, this letter is not written in a considerate tone.

A far superior letter for the same situation is shown in Illustration 10-9, a **good** example of the use of the direct plan for a claim. This letter is ob-jective and courteous. The wrong and its impact are specified in the opening. The damaged items are clearly identified. A concise explanation of the known circumstances is given in the second paragraph. A deadline as to when re-placement china is needed is given politely in the third paragraph. The close is friendly and optimistic.

ADJUSTMENT GRANTS

Business firms that receive claim messages should respond to them quickly in order to maintain the goodwill of the customer. The response to a claim is known as an **adjustment**. If there is any doubt about the legitimacy of a claim, the customer usually receives the benefit of the doubt.

A letter granting an adjustment is good news and should use the direct plan. The letter should begin with the good news—the adjustment. This immediate good news will aid in eliminating any customer negative feelings toward the company. The explanation should be convincing to regain the customer's confidence. An effective, personalized sales appeal gives the company an opportunity to emphasize to the customer the quality of the product or service. To avoid ending on a negative note, an adjustment letter should never close with an apology.

A **poor** example of an adjustment response to the claim letter about the broken china is shown in Illustration 10-10. This letter does not get to the good news until the third paragraph. The explanation places the blame on the delivery company and is not convincing. The repeated references to the trouble and inconvenience caused continually remind the receiver of the negative aspects of the situation. Details as to when the replacement items are to arrive are omitted. The hollow apology in the close does not build the goodwill of the customer. The you-viewpoint is absent from the letter.

A **good** example of a letter granting an adjustment is shown in Illustration 10-11. Note that this letter goes directly to the good news. The explanation emphasizes not the wrong itself but what was done to correct the wrong. This explanation should regain the customer's confidence. In the third paragraph, the writer uses a personal approach when describing an item that Mr. Glenn may be interested in selling. The close ends the letter on a happy, positive note.

Use direct plan for **adjustment letters**.

UNSOLICITED GOOD NEWS MESSAGES

Many times organizations will initiate a good news communication. Such good news messages are referred to as *unsolicited*. Unsolicited good news messages to customers may announce new products or services, reductions in prices of merchandise, relocation to a new building, or employment of new customer representatives. Unsolicited good news messages to employees may announce new fringe benefits, an unscheduled pay increase, a promotion, or some other good news.

Unsolicited good news messages should employ the direct approach. In the **poor** example, Illustration 10-12, Mr. Gomez misses an opportunity to build on the goodwill that was gained when he gave Ms. Murphy the $500. The letter is written from the savings and loan's viewpoint rather than from Ms. Murphy's.

In the **good** example of an unsolicited good news letter in Illustration 10-13, Mr. Gomez increases Ms. Murphy's enthusiasm for doing business with Cavalier Savings and Loan. Note how the you-viewpoint is used to enhance the good news.

Businesses send both internal and external **unsolicited good news messages**.

Illustration 10-8 **Poor** Example of a Claim Letter

Glenn's Jewelry

Midwest Mall   Topeka, Kansas 66601-4252
                                              (913) 555-8788

September 12, 199-

Sparkler Wholesale Supplies
4764 Industrial Road
San Diego, CA 92118-2405

Ladies and Gentlemen

As your records will show, on August 3 I ordered three
complete sets of Corigan China (my Order 4398). The
units were shipped to me by Fleet Van Lines (your
Invoice 854H) and arrived at my store September 2.

At the time of delivery the receiving clerk noticed
that two of the boxes were smashed in on the side.
Further inspection showed that your organization used
cheap cartons to ship expensive china. As a result of
the inferior cartons and the rough handling of the
china, over half of it is broken.

It is hard for me to understand how a wholesaler who
handles china could permit such inadequate treatment of
its products. I do not accept this shipment of china.
Further, I want this broken china taken off my hands
and replaced with new pieces. Because I will be holding my annual autumn sale in October, I insist that the
replacement Corigan China reach me by September 25.

Sincerely

Harry Glenn

Harry Glenn
Owner

rw

While providing transition, the **poor** opening does not clearly identify the damages.

The explanation is not written in considerate tone.

Negative and demanding close.

Illustration 10-9 **Good** Example of a Claim Letter

Glenn's Jewelry
Midwest Mall   Topeka, Kansas 66601-4252
(913) 555-8788

September 12, 199-

Sparkler Wholesale Supplies
4764 Industrial Road
San Diego, CA 92118-2405

Ladies and Gentlemen

Damage to Corigan China, Your Invoice 854H

Much of the shipment of Corigan China received on September 2 was broken and, therefore, is not available for our upcoming sale. Below is a list of the broken items

16 Dinner Plates	2 Platters
9 Salad Plates	1 Salt Shaker
13 Saucers	1 Ash Tray
19 Coffee Cups	15 Cereal Bowls
3 Gravy Boats	17 Dessert Bowls

At the time of the delivery, the condition of the shipping containers was called to the attention of the Fleet Van Lines driver by the receiving clerk. Upon inspection, the receiving clerk found that two cartons had been smashed and their contents broken. It appears that a prong from a forklift had been driven through the two cartons. The china in the two undamaged cartons was not broken.

Since our store has advertised an autumn sale, please ship the replacement merchandise by September 25. Also, will you please instruct me about disposition of the broken china and the damaged cartons.

I am aware, of course, that accidents such as this occur in spite of all precautions. I am confident that you will make the necessary adjustment with your usual courtesy.

Sincerely

Harry Glenn
Harry Glenn
Owner

rw

The wrong and the impact of the wrong are specified.

Damages are clearly identified.

Explanation is given without a display of anger.

Gives demands in considerate manner.

Friendly, optimistic close.

Illustration 10-10 **Poor** Example of an Adjustment Letter

SPARKLER WHOLESALE SUPPLIES

4764 Industrial Road
San Diego, California 92118-2405
(714) 555-1496

September 17, 199–

Mr. Harry Glenn, Owner
Glenn's Jewelry
Midwest Mall
Topeka, KS 66601-4252

Dear Mr. Glenn

We have received your September 12 claim reporting that
our shipment of china was damaged. We regret the inconvenience caused you and understand your unhappiness.

Following our standard practice, we investigated the
situation thoroughly. We found that a forklift operator had driven a fork through the cartons when loading
the cartons into the delivery truck. We can assure you
that Fleet Van Lines will not be used to deliver any
more of our merchandise.

I am pleased to report that we are shipping replacement
items. The shipment will be made using Speedy Delivery
Service.

Again, we regret the trouble that the damaged china has
caused you.

Sincerely

Catherine Holmes

Catherine Holmes
Shipping Manager

gb

Negative opening
that does not give
good news.

An impersonal,
non-convincing
explanation.

Good news should
be in first paragraph
and should use
you-viewpoint.

Negative final
apology.

Illustration 10-11 **Good** Example of an Adjustment Letter

SPARKLER WHOLESALE SUPPLIES

4764 Industrial Road
San Diego, California 92118-2405
(714) 555-1496

September 17, 199-

Mr. Harry Glenn, Owner
Glenn's Jewelry
Midwest Mall
Topeka, KS 66601-4252

Dear Mr. Glenn

Your replacement china will reach you by September 23 in time for
your annual autumn sale. This fast delivery of the replacement
china is our way of proving to you that we value your business. ——— Gives good news immediately.

Because your continued business is important to us, we have carefully examined the handling of your order. It was determined
that a forklift operator for Fleet Van Lines accidentally drove a
fork through two of the cartons. The manager of the van lines
assures me that the forklift operator has been given additional
training and will be more careful in the future. ——— Convincing explanation.

Mr. Glenn, jewelry stores throughout the United States are having
excellent sales with our new add-a-pearl necklace. The necklace
chain is made of 14-karat gold and comes in 16-, 18-, 24-, or
30-inch lengths. The pearls are white and of highest quality. A
sample necklace containing six pearls is enclosed. Also enclosed
is a convenient order form listing prices for your use. Why not
order now so you will have this new profit-making item in your
store for your sale? ——— Announces a new item for sales appeal.

Best wishes for your upcoming autumn sale. ——— Positive close.

Sincerely

Catherine Holmes

Catherine Holmes
Shipping Manager

gb

Enclosures

Illustration 10-12 **Poor** Example of an Unsolicited Good News Letter

Cavalier Savings and Loan

386 Main Street
Cavalier, North Dakota 58220-0020
(701) 555-4497

April 23, 199-

Ms. Sara Murphy
1270 Snowy Lane
Cavalier, ND 58220-0020

Dear Sara

Cavalier Savings and Loan opened its third branch
office last week. We have grown substantially during
the past five years. This growth is a direct result of
the good service that we provide our customers.

I was pleased to learn that you attended this grand
opening and registered for our drawing of $500. I know
that you will be happy to learn that you won this drawing. The $500 has been credited to your savings
account.

Congratulations on your winnings. We would like you to
make your savings grow with weekly deposits.

Sincerely

Fred Gomez
Fred Gomez
President

rht

Opening does not
use you-viewpoint.

Good news needs to
be in first paragraph
and should stress
receiver interest.

Should
de-emphasize
benefits to bank.

Illustration 10-13 **Good** Example of an Unsolicited Good News Letter

Cavalier Savings and Loan

386 Main Street
Cavalier, North Dakota 58220-0020
(701) 555-4497

April 23, 199–

Ms. Sara Murphy
1270 Snowy Lane
Cavalier, ND 58220-0020

Dear Sara

Congratulations! You have won $500 in a drawing held
at the grand opening of our third branch office.

The $500 has been deposited in your savings account and
has begun earning you interest at an 8.5 percent annual
rate. At your earliest convenience, please come into
the branch office and have the $500 recorded in your
passbook.

Thank you, Sara, for participating in our grand opening. Staff at each of our three locations will be
happy to serve your banking needs.

Sincerely

Fred Gomez

Fred Gomez
President

rht

Positive,
you-oriented, strong
beginning.

Stresses benefits to
customer.

Continues building
goodwill.

Use of direct plan in good news messages increases their effectiveness.

Skillfully used, the direct plan is appropriate for messages that request information, convey favorable news, convey neutral news, or make or settle claims. With the direct plan, effective messages can increase employee morale, promote customer goodwill, and positively affect those who receive them.

DISCUSSION QUESTIONS

1. Identify a bad news message that should use the direct plan. Explain why this message should be constructed using the direct plan.
2. Explain why a good news message should use the direct plan.
3. Discuss four characteristics of the good or neutral news section of a direct plan.
4. Discuss three characteristics of the sales appeal section of good or neutral news messages.
5. What is the purpose of a friendly close? How is this purpose accomplished? Give an example of an effective friendly close.
6. Identify several types of good or neutral news that could use the direct plan.
7. Discuss five characteristics of an inquiry.
8. Discuss five communication fundamentals presented in Chapters 1 through 3 that should be used in good or neutral news messages.
9. Identify several types of good news that would be referred to as unsolicited. Use examples other than those in the text.

APPLICATION EXERCISES

1. Describe the various types of information that a customer would like to receive other than notification that his or her claim has been approved.
2. Visit two retail stores in your community and ask how they handle adjustment messages. Get copies, if possible, of their letters and share this information with the class.
3. Obtain an example of a good news message used by a business in your community. Present an analysis of this message to the class.
4. Visit several business firms in your community and discuss with their administrative officers the various situations in which they use good news messages. What organizational plan do they use for presenting the good news?

5. Develop a form letter that could be used as an inquiry for obtaining information from prospective members of a student organization. Assume that this student organization requires a 3.0 GPA, completion of 45 semester hours of general education courses and 15 semester hours of business courses, and two recommendations from instructors.

CASE PROBLEMS

INQUIRIES

1. You own a video recorder that was given to you upon graduation from high school. You are interested in purchasing a camcorder so you can take movies. Write a letter to Video World requesting information about the camcorders it sells so that you can make an intelligent purchase. You want to know if the equipment Video World sells has features such as wide angle lens, telephoto lens, warranty, rechargeable batteries, etc. Supply details to make a complete letter.

2. Your garden club is sponsoring a community-wide symposium on wild flowers. Mr. David Minulcik, a noted horticulturist, will conduct several of the sessions. You are responsible for preparing the promotional material about the activities. Write a letter to Mr. Minulcik requesting information about his background. The deadline for delivering the brochure to the printer is approaching. It is important that all necessary data are obtained with this one letter to Mr. Minulcik.

3. The director of personnel at Thompson and Miller's Accounting Services is developing a vacation schedule for the next six months. No more than two individuals can be on vacation at one time. Develop a memo that could be used to determine the employees' vacation time preferences.

4. The Executive Club is planning a cruise on the Brazos River for its spring social activity. As vice president for programs, you are responsible for planning this event. You need to contact Texas Queen Lines for information about its cruises. Write a letter that will obtain the pertinent information. Be sure to include necessary details to make this a complete inquiry.

5. As a recent college graduate entering the business world, you are interested in building an investment portfolio. Many of your friends recommend Southland Investments. Write a letter to Southland asking about its investment programs. You would like information about minimum initial investment, types of investments (stocks, bonds, mutual funds, etc.), withdrawal penalties, tax shelters, etc.

6. As human resources manager of Joshua's Electronics, you frequently must obtain information about prospective employees from their references. You must gather sufficient information on each individual to enable your company to make hiring decisions. Develop the body of a form letter that could be used to obtain the necessary information.

REQUEST APPROVALS

7. You are the supervisor at the Safety Tire Company responsible for approving employee vacations. Bill Barnett works on the assembly line and is entitled to two weeks of vacation each year. He has been planning a one-week wedding trip in August but had to use his two weeks of vacation in March to settle an uncle's estate. Bill has requested an additional week of paid vacation. You are restricted by company policy from granting this request; however, because the company's fiscal year begins September 1, you can allow Bill to draw on one week of his next year's vacation.

   Write a memo informing Bill of your decision. You want Bill to accept this compromise without bitterness toward the company. He has been a faithful, loyal employee for the past five years; it is your wish that he continue to be a good employee.

8. You are the credit manager for Underwood Used Cars in Dallas, Texas. Dorothy Stratemeyer has applied for a $4,750 loan to purchase a used car. Write Dorothy a letter granting her request and explain the details of the loan. Add the necessary facts to make the letter complete.

9. As director of customer service for Treetop Airlines, you receive the following letter from Rosanna Simpson:

   I purchased a round-trip airline ticket ($250) from Nashville, Tennessee, to Houston, Texas. While in Houston, an emergency caused me to change my plans for returning on your airline.

   I am returning the unused portion of my ticket. I would appreciate a $125 refund.

   Write a letter to Rosanna and grant her request for a refund. Be sure to thank her for using Treetop Airlines.

10. You are vice president of your college's Future Business Leaders student organization. One of your responsibilities is to coordinate the organization's public service activities within your community.

    Jeremy Cole is organizing the Special Olympics for the region. He has asked your organization to provide seven members to assist in judging events. Future Business Leaders normally does not commit itself to activities that are not directly related to business; however, the Special Olympics is very important to the community, and your organization will receive excellent exposure. You believe that your organization should participate in this activity. Write Mr. Cole a letter expressing appreciation for being considered to participate in such a worthwhile cause. Tell him that you will have seven individuals there and can assist with more persons if necessary.

11. You are the Pulaski County judge and have the authority to perform marriage ceremonies. However, the large number of time-consuming duties of a county judge has forced you to initiate a policy of not performing marriage ceremonies. Mr. and Mrs. Carl Thompson, strong supporters of your last campaign, have requested that you officiate at their daughter's upcoming wedding. You will make an exception to your policy and perform the ceremony. Write a letter to the Thompsons and inform them of your decision. Supply necessary details to make your message complete.

12. Your company owns a beachside condominium. You receive many requests from customers and employees for the use of this facility. Develop a form letter that could be used to grant permission for these individuals to use the facility. Include approved dates of use, rules of occupancy, and other pertinent details.

CLAIMS

13. Mr. Al Sams was vacationing in Milroy, New York, when he had tire trouble and purchased four blemished tires from Browning Tire Sales, Inc., in Milroy. Blemished tires are usually perfect except for some small defect that does not affect their usability. The defect could be a misprint on the labeling of the tire, imperfect whitewall coloring, or irregular tread pattern.

   When driving home (about 600 miles), Mr. Sams began experiencing tire trouble. The tires caused his car to handle improperly because they are out-of-round. Mr. Sams is upset with Browning Tire Sales. He is aware that the sales agreement stipulated that all sales are final and that no adjustments will be made, but he is convinced that an exception should be allowed since the tires have less than a thousand miles on them.

   Write a claim letter for Mr. Sams requesting an adjustment on the tires. Organize the letter in a polite way so as not to antagonize anyone at Browning Tire Sales, Inc.

14. You are the manager of Boyd's Office Supplies, Inc. For many years you have ordered the majority of your merchandise from Wholesale Office Supplies, Inc.

    Recently, you were speaking with a competitor and learned that the competitor receives a 45 percent discount from Wholesale Office Supplies, Inc. This competitor has been in business for only one year.

    Write a claim letter to Wholesale Office Supplies, Inc., requesting that your discount be increased from 40 to 45 percent and that the new rate be applied on your last purchase of $3,167.83. Add facts necessary to make your letter complete.

15. You are the manager of Chuck May's Music Store. Two months ago you received four musical instruments—a clarinet, an oboe, a trumpet, and a flute. You inspected the instruments on their arrival, and all of them seemed to be in excellent condition. Yesterday as you were showing the clarinet to a customer, you noticed a crack in the wood.

    The warranty for the clarinet states that the instrument is guaranteed against cracking for six months from the purchase date. You would like a replacement clarinet as quickly as possible. Write a letter to Music Instruments, Inc., that could be included with the instrument. Make the claim message complete by adding necessary facts.

16. You are the director of Westside Shopping Mall. This mall was built by Perrin Construction Company and completed nine months ago. Last week the roof of the mall was damaged by a severe hailstorm. It is your opinion that the roof should have been sturdy enough to withstand the storm. Insurance on the building covers this type of claim, but you do not want your premiums to be increased and the damage appears to be due to poor workmanship on the part of the construction company. Write Perrin Construction Company a claim letter requesting that the roof be repaired immediately to avoid further damage to merchandise in the stores.

17. The Better Health Insurance Company held its annual employees' appreciation dinner at a local convention center and had its meal catered. A previous arrangement had been made to serve pheasant as the main course, but two days before the function the catering service called and said that only Cornish hens were available. It was understood that the Cornish hens would be provided for $2 less than the pheasants. However, the bill did not include the $2 discount. Write a letter to Chuck's Catering Service requesting the $850 discount ($2 each for 425 dinners). Supply any additional details that are necessary to make a complete claim letter.

18. You are the administrative manager of Robert's Lamp Post, a retail store specializing in lighting fixtures. Frequently, you receive shipments of lamps in which several of the fixtures are broken. You would like to develop a claim form letter that could be stored in your word processor and used when returning damaged merchandise. Write this form letter.

ADJUSTMENT GRANTS

19. You are the service manager for Bates Heating and Air Conditioning Co. You have just received a letter from Brian Davis, 3197 Poplar Street, Marvell, Arkansas, stating:

    > I purchased an 11,000 BTU air conditioner from your company two months ago. This unit was guaranteed to cool a 500-square foot room. I am trying to get it to cool a 12- x 20-foot room and have been unsuccessful.
    >
    > I paid over $475 for this unit, but it will not do the job. I want you to immediately send someone to pick up the unit. Credit my account for the purchase amount.

    Write a letter to Mr. Davis informing him that you will have the unit picked up. Explain that next Friday is the earliest date the truck can be there. Because Marvell is 95 miles away, deliveries and pickups are made there only once a week. Express disappointment that the air conditioner did not work, but remind Mr. Davis that at the time of the sale you mentioned that he may need to have his home insulated in order to obtain maximum service from the unit.

20. Carol Goings bought a registered Siamese cat for $275. Within two months of the purchase, the cat died. Carol has written requesting a full refund for the purchase price of the cat. As owner of Noah's Pet Shop, grant Carol's request for the $275. In addition, you should ask Carol if she is interested in purchasing another animal, mentioning that all pets are on sale for 40 percent off the regular price.

21. You are a branch manager for Andre's Jewelry Store. Betty Graves lives in Spokane, Washington, but purchased an expensive necklace at your store when she was visiting an aunt in your town. Ms. Graves has requested that you replace her necklace with one that contains less gold. Such a necklace would be more durable than the one she originally purchased.
    Write a letter to Ms. Graves granting her request and informing her that she is entitled to a $27 credit that may be used to purchase merchandise from the catalog you are enclosing.

22. Westrup's Nursery landscaped Pat Freeman's home last fall. Four beautiful 15-foot trees were planted for $575 per tree. A winter storm broke three of the main branches on one of the trees. Pat has requested a replacement tree or a refund for one tree.
    As manager of Westrup's Nursery, write a letter to Pat stating that a replacement tree will be planted for her this fall. Suggest that she stop at the nursery and look at a different variety of tree that can withstand more weight on its branches. Of course, there will be no charge to her for the replacement tree.

23. You are Chuck Morgan, operator of Chuck's Catering Service. Recently, you catered a dinner for the Better Health Insurance Company. Pheasant had been ordered for the main course, but influenza struck your supplier's farm and killed all the pheasants. The company agreed to accept Cornish hens as a substitute. There was no difference in the cost of the two entrees. Better Health Insurance Company has now requested an adjustment of $2 a dinner ($850 total) because it believes the Cornish hens were of lesser value.

    Write a letter to Better Health Insurance Company granting the claim for $850. Enclose a check with your letter. Explain the circumstances that led to the change in the entree.

24. Hermitage Coins of Nashville, Tennessee, conducts most of its business by mail order. Periodically, customers return coins stating that the coins do not meet their specifications. This is understandable since grading of coins is an inexact science. You need to prepare a form letter that could be used in processing these adjustment grants. Hermitage is willing to make refunds, but would prefer to send customers replacement coins.

UNSOLICITED GOOD NEWS MESSAGES

25. You are initiating a new program to try to reduce the number of sick days that your employees use each year. Employees who complete the year without missing work will have their names entered for a drawing in which one person will win a five-day cruise for two to the Caribbean. Write a memo that could be sent to all employees announcing this program. Add necessary information.

26. Educational Computers, Inc., manufactures microcomputers for educational institutions. The costs of components used in its computers have been reduced due to technological advances. You, the director of sales, have decided to pass these savings on to your customers.

    Compose a letter to educational institutions informing them that the price of your microcomputers has been reduced 15 percent. Include in your letter a sales appeal for related computer equipment and supplies.

27. You were the chairperson of the fund-raising committee of Ranch for Teens, a nonprofit recreational facility. This year's fund-raising drive collected $100,000 more than the previous year's drive.

    Because of this highly successful effort, the directors of the ranch approved the building of an additional bunkhouse that will allow ten more teenagers to use the facility. Write a letter to the major contributors informing them of this good news.

28. The Watertown Civic Club had a successful chili supper. It would like to donate some of its profits to a worthwhile cause within the city. The Civic Club has decided to give the Watertown High School Band $3,000 for its upcoming trip to the Cherry Blossom Festival in Washington, D.C. As the Civic Club treasurer, write a letter donating the money to the band.

29. All-Wood Furniture Company makes a line of fine furniture for home use. The company was forced to lay off 34 employees one year ago due to lack of sales. During the past 60 days sales have improved, and warehouse inventories have decreased. This condition has made it possible to recall the 34 employees effective the first of next month. Write a letter to the employees informing them of their recall.

30. Parker Super Mart is a thriving food store with very civic-minded management. It would like to give a free turkey to every senior citizen for Senior Citizen Week. A list of the town's senior citizens has been obtained from the Senior Citizen Organization.

    A form letter needs to be written that will announce the program. Write the letter telling each senior citizen that he or she may come in to pick up the turkey or call to have it delivered. Add any necessary information.

CHAPTER 11

BAD NEWS MESSAGES

Your learning objectives for this chapter include the following:

- To understand the nature of bad news messages
- To appreciate the advantages of using the indirect plan for effective communication of bad news
- To know when it is appropriate to use the direct plan for bad news messages
- To use the indirect plan competently for a variety of bad news messages
- To recognize the differences between poor and good examples of bad news messages

Bad news messages give unfavorable information.

Bad news messages are those that are likely to be viewed as unpleasant, disappointing, or unfavorable by the receiver. These messages, for example, may refuse a request that has been made of you or your organization. The messages may provide information about a change in policy that employees do not particularly favor or a price increase that customers prefer to avoid.

A bad news message is a challenge to compose. At the same time, it is an opportunity for you as a writer or speaker to successfully resolve a common business problem. You can even win a friend for yourself or a customer for your organization with an effectively conveyed bad news message.

USE THE INDIRECT PLAN FOR BAD NEWS

The general strategy for conveying all types of bad news is to use the indirect plan. With the indirect plan, the sentence or the section of the message that conveys the disappointing idea follows reasons that explain why you must refuse a request or why you must provide unfavorable news. This plan of presenting information prepares your receivers for the bad news. Research has shown that preparing receivers to receive bad news will assist them in accepting such news.

> The **indirect plan** prepares receiver for bad news.

> Research supports effectiveness of indirect plan.

IS THE DIRECT PLAN EVER APPROPRIATE FOR BAD NEWS?

You are already familiar with the direct plan for message preparation; that is, the main idea of the message is conveyed in the first sentences. There are occasions when the direct plan is used for bad news messages—when the bad news is given first. Your analysis of the situation and the receiver will help you determine when you can use the direct plan.

> The direct plan gives bad news *first*.

You may use the direct plan when you know your receiver prefers to learn the bad news first and the good news later. For example, if your receiver's personality is the type that prefers directness, use the direct approach.

> The direct plan may be used for some receivers.

You may also use the direct plan when the negative information is routine and will not be upsetting to your receiver. For example, a receiver will not be upset to learn that a nonessential meeting has been canceled.

In another situation, ethical behavior may be the issue and directness would strengthen a disappointing message. Chrysler Corporation's disconnected odometer problem is a good example of this situation. The corporation dealt directly and ethically with this bad news by having open letters to the public printed in several newspapers (see Illustrations 11-1A and 11-1B).

(Page 1 of a 2-page open-letter advertisement that appeared in the Tuesday, July 7, 1987, edition of the LOS ANGELES TIMES.)

"Testing cars is a good idea. Disconnecting odometers is a lousy idea. That's a mistake we won't make again at Chrysler. Period."

(signed) Lee Iacocca

Illustration 11-1A Bad News Message Using the Direct Plan, Page 1.

(Page 2 of a 2-page open-letter advertisement that appeared in the Tuesday, July 7, 1987, edition of the LOS ANGELES TIMES.)

LET ME SET THE RECORD STRAIGHT.

1. For years, spot checking and road testing new cars and trucks that come off the assembly line with the odometers disengaged was standard industry practice. In our case, the average test mileage was 40 miles.

2. Even though the practice wasn't illegal, some companies began connecting their odometers. We didn't. In retrospect, that was dumb. Since October 1986, however, the odometer of every car and truck we've built has been connected, including those in the test program.

3. A few cars—and I mean a few—were damaged in testing badly enough that they should not have been fixed and sold as new. That was a mistake in an otherwise valid quality assurance program. And now we have to make it right.

WHAT WE'RE DOING TO MAKE THINGS RIGHT.

1. In all instances where our records show a vehicle was damaged in the test program and repaired and sold, we will offer to replace that vehicle with a brand new 1987 Chrysler Corporation model of comparable value. No ifs ands or buts.

2. We are sending letters to everyone our records show bought a vehicle that was in the test program and offering a free inspection. If anything is wrong because of a product deficiency, we will make it right.

3. Along with the free inspection, we are extending their present 5 year or 50,000 mile protection plan on engine and powertrain to 7 years or 70,000 miles.

4. And to put their minds completely at ease, we are extending the 7 year or 70,000 mile protection to all major systems: brakes, suspensions, air conditioning, electrical and steering.

The quality testing program is a good program. But there were mistakes and we were too slow in stopping them. Now they're stopped. Done. Finished. Over.

Personally, I'm proud of our products. Proud of the quality improvements we've made. So we're going to keep right on testing. Because without it we couldn't have given America 5 year 50,000 mile protection five years ahead of everyone else. Or maintained our warranty leadership with 7 year 70,000 mile protection. I'm proud, too, of our leadership in safety-related recalls.

But I'm not proud of this episode. Not at all.

As Harry Truman once said, "The buck stops here." It just stopped. Period.

CHRYSLER	7/70
MOTORS	LIMITED WARRANTY
CHRYSLER · PLYMOUTH · DODGE CARS · DODGE TRUCKS	

We just want to be the best.

Illustration 11-1B   Bad News Message Using the Direct Plan, Page 2.

Another instance in which the direct plan may be used is if you want to emphasize how sorry you are about the bad news. An example of this situation is a sympathy note sent regarding a death or tragedy.

Another situation in which the direct plan may be used for bad news messages is when the bad news needs to be emphasized. Maybe you have previously told your receiver that you could not continue to sell to him or her if past-due invoices are not paid, but the message was misunderstood or not accepted. The direct plan will emphasize the negative message you must send in this situation.

The direct plan may be used for additional emphasis.

In most bad news situations, however, you will want to use the indirect order of presentation because of its many advantages.

ADVANTAGES OF INDIRECT PLAN

Important advantages of the indirect plan are that it enables receivers (1) to accept the bad news you must give them and (2) to maintain a satisfactory relationship with you.

The indirect plan has these advantages because it maintains calm through its gradual approach. It gives time for the receiver's anxiety to subside. The indirect plan affords the opportunity for reason to prevail and for understanding to develop. If the bad news is given first, the receiver may ignore the rest of the message; even a fair, reasonable explanation following the bad news may never be accepted.

If your message is written thoughtfully and carefully in the you-viewpoint, the receiver may even agree that the negative decision is the right one. An effective presentation of the message may clearly show that the bad news is, in fact, in the best interest of the receiver. It may represent a decision that benefits the receiver. The achievement of a positive receiver reaction is your goal in preparing bad news messages.

The indirect plan enables receivers to accept bad news and maintain their relationship with you.

*The **indirect plan**:*
- *Maintains calm*
- *Permits reason to prevail*

- *Changes a negative situation to a positive one*

HOW TO USE THE INDIRECT PLAN

In this section specific guides for using the indirect plan for writing bad news messages will be given. In addition, you will want to use the fundamentals of effective business communication that were presented in Chapters 1, 2, and 3.

There are specific steps in the indirect plan.

Illustration 11-2 outlines the steps and specific guides for using the indirect plan to present bad news.

I. The **Opening Buffer**
   A. Provide coherence.
   B. Build goodwill.
   C. Be positive.
   D. Maintain neutrality.
   E. Introduce the explanation.

II. The **Logical Explanation**
   A. Relate to opening buffer.
   B. Present convincing reasoning.
   C. Stress receiver interests/benefits.
   D. Use emphasis techniques.
   E. Be positive.

III. The **Bad News**
   A. Imply or give bad news explicitly.
   B. Relate to logical explanation.
   C. Use de-emphasis techniques.
   D. Give bad news quickly.
   E. Be positive.
   F. Say what can be done (not what cannot).
   G. Avoid an apology.

IV. The **Constructive Follow-up**
   A. Provide alternative solution and/or
   B. Give additional reasoning.

V. The **Friendly Close**
   A. Build goodwill.
   B. Personalize the close.
   C. Stay off subject.
   D. Be warm.
   E. Be optimistic.

Illustration 11-2   Indirect Plan Outline

The indirect plan can be used effectively for a variety of different kinds of bad news messages—refused claims, refused requests, refused credit applications, unfavorable decisions, or any unpleasant information.

DETERMINING CONTENT

Each communication situation must first be analyzed to determine the basic content of the message. The following questions on content must be answered for bad news messages: What ideas can I use in the opening to establish coherence and build goodwill in this particular situation? Why is it in the receiver's interest for me to refuse the request or present the unfavorable news? Is there an alternative course of action that I can recommend to this receiver? What friendly message can I convey in the off-subject close?

Once you have determined the content of the bad news message, you are ready to implement the indirect plan. To successfully implement the indirect plan, there are general principles and ideas that should be followed. In the following pages each section of the indirect plan outline is discussed, and the most important considerations are reviewed.

The situation must be analyzed before the indirect plan is implemented.

OPENING BUFFER

In the indirect plan, the opening buffer should meet the following requirements: provide coherence, build goodwill, be positive, maintain neutrality, and introduce the explanation. The opening buffer will usually consist of one to three sentences. It will serve as the first paragraph in a memo or a letter.

To provide coherence, the opening buffer puts you and your receiver on the same wave length. The bad news message is tied to some common ground—a previous conversation, a point of agreement, a memo or letter received earlier, a prior transaction, or some other common ground.

You will want to build goodwill by using courteous, polite words such as *thank you*, *please*, and *appreciate*, and by keeping the receiver's interests central to your opening buffer. Use positive words; avoid negative words. This helps set a favorable tone and makes your message more acceptable to the receiver. It is possible, in fact desirable, to compose bad news messages without using a single negative word.

The two final requirements for a good opening buffer—maintain neutrality and introduce the explanation—are closely related. You will want your receiver to read through the opening buffer into the logical explanation that follows. You do not want to give away the bad news in the opening. Therefore, the opening buffer should not imply either a yes or a no. It should not lead the receiver in either direction; it should be neutral.

The final requirement of the opening buffer is to set the stage for the explanation, that is, introduce the explanation. In the last sentence of the buffer, give your receiver some indication of the thrust of the explanation. In effect, give the receiver the "headline" for the explanation that follows in the next paragraph(s). This sets up the strategy for the logical explanation, which is the next part of your message, and it assists in providing coherence.

*Use **opening buffer** to:*

- *Provide coherence*

- *Build goodwill*

- *Be positive*

- *Maintain neutrality*

- *Introduce the explanation*

LOGICAL EXPLANATION

Logical explanation
follows the opening
buffer and precedes the
bad news.

The second part of the indirect plan is the logical explanation. In a memo or letter, the logical explanation usually begins after the opening buffer and can often be handled in one paragraph. If the explanation is short, the bad news may be included in the same paragraph. In some situations the constructive follow-up can immediately follow the bad news in the same paragraph. This buries the negativeness of the bad news in the middle of a paragraph. In other written message situations the logical explanation may be so long that it requires two or more paragraphs.

The logical explanation:
• Justifies the bad news

One of the most important aspects of the indirect plan is that the reasoning that justifies the bad news is presented *before* the bad news. After the opening buffer, you present the reasons explaining why you must convey the bad news. If at all possible, these reasons should show how the bad news will be in the best interest of your receiver. This reasoning, in order to be effective, must be presented in a calm, convincing, and pleasant manner using the you-viewpoint.

The specific requirements for the logical explanation are that it coherently relates to the opening buffer, presents convincing reasoning, stresses receiver interests/benefits, uses emphasis techniques, and is positive.

• Provides coherence

The opening buffer will have introduced the explanation. The beginning of the logical explanation should use coherence techniques to relate it to the opening and facilitate the flow of thought. You may use repetition of key words, a tie-in sentence, or some other coherence technique to ensure that the logical explanation follows the opening.

• Presents convincing reasoning

The convincing reasoning, which supports the unfavorable news, should be composed with the receiver's interests or benefits as the focal points. The receiver's favorable reactions to the words you choose will be your goal. In fact, if at the end of the reasoning the receiver agrees that the bad news is the best alternative in this situation, you will have composed the ideal bad news message.

Although the ideal logical explanation presents the reasoning in terms of receiver benefit, circumstances will not always permit you to compose the ideal message. You may have to base your reasoning on what is fair for all concerned. Also, there may be occasions when confidentiality precludes giving any specific reasons. In these situations, you will want to communicate convincingly and persuasively that in the interest of the receiver the matter was carefully considered before the decision was reached.

• Uses rules of emphasis

You will want to use rules of emphasis in the logical explanation. Start with the points that are most favorable to your receiver; and, as you move deeper into the paragraph, deal with the least favorable aspects of your reasoning.

• Accents positiveness

Finally, the logical explanation should be positive. Avoid all negative words, if possible. For example, use *situation* instead of *problem* and *needed change* instead of *correction*. In referring to the problem, avoid such words as *failure*, *cannot*, *trouble*, *inadequate*, and *defective*.

BAD NEWS

After the opening buffer and the logical explanation, you are ready to present the bad news. This step in the indirect plan consists of the request refusal, unfavorable decision, or other disappointing information. If the opening buffer and the logical explanation have been effective, receivers will be expecting the bad news. In fact, in most circumstances, it is possible for you to prepare your receivers so well that they will easily accept the information, refusal, or decision.

The **bad news** follows the logical explanation.

The primary goal in presenting bad news is to be sure that the receiver clearly understands this part of your message. You will want to clearly imply or explicitly state your decision. Wording such as "...therefore, it would seem better for you to follow the company policy" may leave a question in the mind of your receiver. With this lack of clarity, the receiver may think that the decision is still up for discussion or that he or she could decide what to do.

Be sure bad news is clear.

If it is possible to clearly imply the bad news, this is desirable in most circumstances. It softens the bad news and permits you to present negative information in a positive manner. For example, "Smoking is permitted in the hallways only" is much more positive and acceptable to most people than "Smoking is prohibited in the classrooms and offices." These statements both say basically the same thing; the first just says it positively. For effective communication of bad news, it is better to say what can be done rather than what cannot be done.

It is best to imply the bad news.

Stress what can be done (not what cannot be done).

There are situations when the bad news should be given in explicit terms. These are the times when you believe that an implied refusal would not be strong enough or might be misunderstood by your receiver. In the case of rejection of admission to a college, for example, it may not be possible to imply the refusal. In this type of situation, it is better to present the logical explanation and then explicitly state the refusal in clear terms: "...therefore, the committee has disapproved your application for admission." This wording can leave no doubt in the receiver's mind. In most cases, though, you will want to imply the bad news in order to play down its negativeness.

The recommended placement of the bad news section of the message is immediately following the logical explanation. In a written message, never place the bad news in a separate paragraph which then emphasizes it. In order to de-emphasize the bad news, it should be in the middle of a paragraph. The bad news may be followed by an additional reason or suggested alternative(s). This placement would tuck the bad news inside the paragraph and de-emphasize it.

De-emphasize the bad news by placing it in the middle of a paragraph.

The bad news should be given quickly in as few words as possible. Ideally, you can further de-emphasize the unfavorable news by placing it in a dependent clause. As in all sections of a bad news message, you will want to use positive words and avoid negative words—say what can be done and not what cannot be done. Also, avoid negative apologies throughout the message because they only call further attention to the negativeness of the situation. Do not use apologies such as, "I am sorry I must refuse your request."

State bad news quickly.

Be positive.

Avoid an apology.

In summary, bad news is clearly implied or explicitly stated, follows the logical explanation, uses techniques to de-emphasize it, is given quickly, is positive, says what can be done, and avoids apologies.

After giving the bad news, your next step in the indirect plan is to provide constructive follow-up.

CONSTRUCTIVE FOLLOW-UP

Constructive follow-up consists of other solutions or additional justification.

In the constructive follow-up section of a bad news message, you provide other solutions to the problem or, if that is not possible, you give an additional reason justifying the unfavorable news.

For example, one good way to strengthen your communication and to build improved human relations is to do more than is expected by offering an alternative or solution to the receiver. If you were asked to return to your high school on October 24 to speak to seniors about attending college and your schedule would not permit you to do so, you could suggest an alternative speaker or an alternative date. Even though you have to refuse the request, your suggested alternative may solve the problem and maintain effective human relations. In the case of adjustment refusals, you can make a special offer or resell the customer on the product or service.

If you cannot suggest an alternative or offer a solution to the problem, it will be important for you to save part of the logical explanation and place it following the bad news. This helps the receiver accept the bad news by de-emphasizing its importance and giving him or her additional justification for it.

FRIENDLY CLOSE

The **friendly close**:

The friendlly close moves the receiver's mind away from the problem—the bad news—and provides an opportunity to build goodwill. If you must refuse a customer credit, you will want him or her to continue to buy with cash. If you have to refuse an employee's request, you will want to maintain good human relations and not reduce the employee's productivity.

• Builds goodwill

You can build goodwill in the friendly close by ensuring that it is personalized, off the subject, warm, and optimistic. The wording of the friendly close should fit the receiver and the particular situation. It could make further reference to the constructive follow-up, or it could express appreciation to a customer for his or her business.

• Is off subject

The friendly close should not include anything that reminds the receiver of the bad news you have given. It should be off the subject of the bad news. The friendly close should not include a final negative apology such as, "Again, let me say how sorry I am that we cannot honor your claim." This only reminds the receiver of the problem. Off-subject possibilities can include any friendly remark appropriate to your receiver. The prime requirement for the friendly close is to regain the goodwill that may have been lost due to the bad news.

IMPLEMENTING THE INDIRECT PLAN

The step-by-step development of a memo to an employee who must be given bad news shows clearly how the indirect plan works. Here are the details of a communication situation:

> Donna Riley, an interoffice courier under your supervision, has written you a memo requesting that she be permitted on a regular basis to arrive for work at 9 a.m.—an hour late. She is having problems securing baby-sitting services for her two children. An important part of Donna's job is regular courier service throughout the office. Since it is critical to the operation of the office that her first run start at 8 a.m., you must refuse her request. Your task is to write a memo conveying the bad news to her and, at the same time, to make that news acceptable and maybe even desirable for her. Donna is an excellent worker. You want her available during the regular working hours.

A communication situation will help illustrate ways to compose bad news messages.

DETERMINE APPROPRIATE CONTENT

The first step in writing a message is to determine its appropriate content. For the bad news message to Donna Riley, the ideas must be developed and organized for each step in the indirect plan. Poor and good examples of content you could decide to use are illustrated in the following sections.

WRITE EFFECTIVE OPENING BUFFER

The five qualities of a good opening buffer described previously can best be illustrated for this communication situation through contrasting examples. An example of a **poor** opening buffer for a memo in response to Donna's request is as follows:

> It would be very inconvenient for the company for you to come in late. Please make arrangements to be on time.

In analyzing this poor opening buffer, note the lack of you-viewpoint and absence of goodwill. Also, receiver interests are ignored. This poor example provides coherence in a negative way by referring to Donna's request as one "...to come in late." Finally, this opening buffer reveals the negative answer

*The **poor** example starts with bad news and lacks the you-viewpoint.*

to the request immediately. There is no motivation for Donna to read the logical explanation which is to follow the opening.

An example of a **good** opening buffer for this situation is:

The **good** example meets all requirements for an effective buffer.

> Donna, thank you for your memo about your work schedule. You have been doing an excellent job as a courier, and resolving your situation so you can continue your effective service is important to all of us.

In contrast to the poor opening buffer, this paragraph effectively meets all the requirements of a good buffer for a bad news message. It provides coherence by concretely acknowledging Donna's memo and its subject matter. It does this in a positive, appreciative way by thanking her for sending the "... memo about your work schedule."

Goodwill is further built through commending her for her work in the company. This good opening buffer is neutral—it does not say yes or no to her request. It introduces the logical explanation by suggesting that a discussion of Donna's situation and service will follow.

PROVIDE A CONVINCING LOGICAL EXPLANATION

The next step in the indirect plan is to build on the opening buffer with a logical explanation justifying the bad news. A **poor** logical explanation to Donna might read as follows:

The **poor** logical explanation fails to justify the bad news.

> Company policy requires that all employees report to work at 8 a.m. Your pay would be docked if you were to come in late; and eventually you might be the subject of punitive action. We need you to be here on time.

This logical explanation shows—as did the poor example of the opening buffer— a lack of positiveness and you-viewpoint. This poorly worded explanation illustrates a basic error commonly found in bad news messages: it resorts to hiding behind company policy. In a bad news message involving company policy, the justification for the policy and its existence should be stated as a part of the reasoning. Finally, the most positive part of this poor logical explanation "We need you ...," is stated in the we-viewpoint!

Conversely, a **good** logical explanation for this communication situation could read as follows:

The **good** example meets all requirements for a good logical explanation.

> The high quality of your work as a courier has been possible for at least three reasons: (1) your interest in and enjoyment of the work, (2) your commitment to promptness and thoroughness during your rounds, and (3) the scheduling of your work at the time it is most needed—during regular working hours. The flow of work in the office depends on this kind of courier service.

This logical explanation coherently follows the good example of an opening buffer by picking up on the ideas "...doing an excellent job..." and "...continuing your effective service..." This good logical explanation concentrates on Donna's commitment to doing a good job and the need for her to be there during regular working hours. The most positive ideas are presented early in the paragraph with a gradual movement to less positive ideas. This is an effective use of the rules of emphasis. It is important to note that not a single negative word was used in this example.

After reading this logical explanation, Donna may feel that it is in her interest for you to tell her she has to be at work at 8 a.m. regularly so that she can continue to do a good job. At least, she will believe you have presented her with a fair, logical explanation. She will be prepared for the bad news that will be presented to her next.

GIVE BAD NEWS POSITIVELY

A **poor** way to tell Donna that you must refuse her request follows:

> I am sorry that I am forced to tell you that you have to be at work at 8 a.m.

The **poor** example states the bad news explicitly.

This is an explicit rather than an implied statement. It is written in the "I-viewpoint" rather than the you-viewpoint and has overemphasized the problem by using negative words (*sorry, forced,* and *have to*) in an apology.

A **good** way to refuse Donna's request is:

> Since your continued excellent performance requires that you be at work at 8 a.m., I want to assist you in any way I can in making the necessary arrangements to do so.

The **good** example implies the bad news and stresses what can be done.

This presentation of bad news clearly implies the refusal. It also builds on the quality of Donna's work and your interest in helping continue her service to the company. The refusal is de-emphasized by being placed in a dependent, introductory clause. The emphasis is on what can be done (not what cannot)—you are willing to assist her in making the arrangements to be on time. Instead of an apology, which would emphasize the negativeness of the situation, positive words express optimism that the problem can be solved.

Because you prepared Donna to receive bad news, this refusal will likely be acceptable to her. In fact, as suggested earlier, she may prefer the decision you have given her instead of the decision she originally requested. You have told her she is doing a good job, she is important, and she is needed at a particular time so that the work flow can function properly. She also knows you respect her because you took time to explain your refusal.

ASSIST RECEIVER WITH CONSTRUCTIVE FOLLOW-UP

Is there an alternative solution you can suggest to Donna Riley in the communication situation? The following is a **poor** example of what you might say in the constructive follow-up section of your memo to Donna:

The **poor** example of constructive follow-up does not really help, while the **good** example does more than is expected.

> I hope you can get your baby-sitting problems worked out.

A **better** constructive follow-up section would be:

> Betty Marine, my secretary, uses the ABC Child Care Center in the building next to ours. She said it is highly respected, and her child likes the Center very much. Betty checked and found it has openings for additional children now.

This constructive follow-up suggests a possible solution for Donna Riley. If it is not the permanent solution she wants, it is at least one she could use temporarily. You will note the better suggested alternative is longer than the poor suggested alternative. This is often true of you-viewpoint writing or speaking. In order to achieve the overall goal of effective business communication, the additional effort and additional words are worthwhile.

BUILD GOODWILL IN FRIENDLY CLOSE

The last part of the indirect plan is the friendly close. A **poor** friendly close for Donna's memo might read this way:

The **poor** example of a friendly close contains a negative final apology.

> Again, Donna, let me say I am sorry I have to require you to be at work at 8 a.m. If I can be of any further help, please let me know.

Obviously, the apology serves no purpose other than to remind Donna of the bad news she has received. In fact, it reemphasizes that bad news; and you do not want to do that. Also, the last sentence in the poor example appears to offer the kind of help she really does not need.

A **good** friendly close for Donna's memo is as follows:

The **good** example is in the you-viewpoint and builds goodwill.

> Please contact Betty if you would like further information on the ABC Child Care Center. It appears to be a good alternative for you.
>
> Your excellent work is appreciated, and I hope you stay with Murphy Universal for many years to come!

This friendly close meets all requirements. It builds goodwill. It is personalized, warm, and optimistic. It also meets the important requirement of being off the subject—it does not refer to the bad news.

SUMMARY—POOR AND GOOD NEWS MEMOS TO DONNA RILEY

In reviewing how to write effective bad news messages, two example memos—one poor and one good have been presented. Both of these memos carry the bad news refusal in response to Donna's request to begin work at 9 a.m. instead of 8 a.m. The **poor** example (see Illustration 11-3) shows a failure to use proven communication guides that enhance understanding and acceptance of bad news messages. Also, the poor example fails to use the indirect plan of presentation of the message.

The **good** example of the bad news message for Donna shown in Illustration 11-4 incorporates recommended guides for effective business communication. The good example memo shows how the indirect plan, properly implemented, builds goodwill and improves human relations.

The communication guides for composing a bad news message using the indirect plan apply to both written and oral messages. To further illustrate how the guides apply to actual business correspondence situations, several other examples of poor and good bad news messages will be examined in the following pages.

Contrasting memos to Donna Riley are presented in Illustrations 11-3 and 11-4.

REQUEST REFUSALS

Business firms frequently receive requests—for example, a request from a senior citizens' organization for a contribution to its greenhouse project or a request from a local Boy Scout troop to use a bank's community meeting room on the first Wednesday night of each month. Many of these requests are reasonable, and companies will want to respond positively.

Sometimes, however, it is not possible to grant a request, and a bad news message must be sent. For example, the company receiving the senior citizens' request may budget all charitable contributions once a year; therefore, no allocation is available at the time of the request. The company must then refuse this worthy request—at least at this time. The constructive follow-up in this bad news message might be that the company will be glad to consider the request when the next budget is planned.

In the case of the local Boy Scout troop's request to use the bank's meeting room, this may be exactly the type of use the bank intended for the meeting room. However, if the room is scheduled for use by the League of Women Voters on the first Wednesday night of each month, the bank must refuse the request. The bank, if possible, will suggest an alternative night for the Boy Scouts.

*Businesses receive many **requests**.*

Some requests must be refused.

Illustration 11-3 **Poor** Example of a Bad News Message

MU   Murphy Universal

Interoffice
Communication

TO: Donna Riley, Courier

FROM: Brian Nichols, Administrative Manager *Brian*

DATE: March 1, 199-

SUBJECT: Request to Come in Late

Negative reference.

Poor buffer.

It would be very inconvenient for the company for you to come in late. Please make arrangements to be on time.

Explanation lacks
receiver benefit;
negative refusal.

Company policy requires that all employees report to work at 8 a.m. Your pay would be docked if you were to come in late; and eventually you might be the subject of punitive action. We need you to be here on time. I am sorry that I am forced to tell you that you have to be at work at 8 a.m. I hope you can get your baby-sitting problems worked out.

Negative final
apology.

Again, Donna, let me say I am sorry I have to require you to be at work at 8 a.m. If I can be of any further help, please let me know.

dfm

Illustration 11-4 **Good** Example of a Bad News Message

MU **Murphy Universal**   Interoffice
                                           Communication

TO: Donna Riley, Courier

FROM: Brian Nichols, Administrative Manager *Brian*

DATE: March 1, 199-

SUBJECT: Your Work Schedule —————————————————— Positive reference.

Donna, thank you for your memo about your work schedule. You
have been doing an excellent job for us as a courier, and resolv- ———— Good opening
ing your situation so you can continue your effective service is   buffer.
important to all of us.

The high quality of your work as a courier has been possible for   You-viewpoint is
at least three reasons: (1) your interest in and enjoyment of   reassuring.
the work, (2) your commitment to promptness and thoroughness
during your rounds, and (3) the scheduling of your work at the
time it is most needed--during regular working hours. The flow
of work in the office depends on this kind of courier service.
Since your continued excellent performance requires that you be   Bad news is
at work at 8 a.m., I want to assist you in any way I can in   de-emphasized.
making the necessary arrangements to do so. Betty Marine, my
secretary, uses the ABC Child Care Center in the building next to   Alternative
ours. She said it is highly respected, and her child likes the   suggested.
Center very much. Betty checked and found it has openings for
additional children now.

Please contact Betty if you would like further information on the
ABC Child Care Center. It appears to be a good alternative for
you.

Your excellent work is appreciated, and I hope you stay with   Goodwill and
Murphy Universal for many years to come!   off-subject close.

dfm

Use the *indirect plan* for refusals.

In any request refusal situation, it will be important to a business to maintain goodwill. At the same time, the business has to send a message that the receiver does not want to receive. Effective use of the indirect plan will make the refusal more acceptable.

Here is another situation that illustrates the use of the indirect plan for a request refusal: Assume you are a program coordinator of the Northfield Center at your school. The center sponsors educational seminars. A seminar entitled "Improving Your Business Writing Skills" is scheduled for the 15th of next month. The number of participants is limited to 25; more than 40 registrations have been received. You must write to those whose registrations cannot be accepted. A form letter is the easiest way to accomplish this task. Illustration 11-5 shows a **poor** form letter for this situation.

The **good** form letter for this request refusal shown in Illustration 11-6 builds goodwill by explaining the situation and suggesting alternatives to the registrants.

ADJUSTMENT REFUSALS

Handling customer claims is a common problem for business firms. These claims include requests to exchange merchandise, requests for refunds, requests that work be corrected, and other requests for adjustments. Most of these claims are granted because they are legitimate. However, some requests for adjustment must be refused, and these refusals are bad news for the customer. Adjustment refusals are necessary when the customer is at fault or the vendor has done all that can reasonably or legally be expected.

Businesses **try to retain customers** when refusing adjustments.

An adjustment refusal message requires your best communication skills because it is bad news to the receiver. You have to refuse the claim and at the same time retain the customer. You may refuse the request for adjustment and even try to sell the customer more merchandise or service. All this is happening when the customer is probably angry or at least inconvenienced.

You will want to use the indirect plan effectively for the presentation of this bad news. As a case in point, consider a customer who wants to return a defective boat that he bought on sale. Illustration 11-7 shows a **poor** letter in which the boat dealer fails to implement the indirect plan and probably makes an enemy.

On the other hand, the same basic message can be written using the indirect plan and result in keeping a good customer. Illustration 11-8 is a **good** example of how this letter refusing the return of the boat should have been written. (This is the letter that was developed in Chapter 3 on pages 60-68.)

CREDIT REFUSALS

Buying on credit is common today. Most businesses permit and even encourage qualified customers to buy on credit. It is a strategy that increases sales.

Customers who have good credit ratings or who have sufficient assets for collateral will be granted credit. Customers who have problems paying their bills or who own nothing of sufficient value to use as backup may be refused credit. They may be offended when they are refused.

Business firms attempt to communicate credit refusals in a manner that makes the answer acceptable and helpful to the customer. Businesses want to do this out of common decency and also because they want to continue to serve the customer on a cash basis if possible.

Credit refusals are communicated in the following four basic ways: (1) personalized letters, (2) form letters, (3) telephone calls, or (4) face-to-face conversations. In all these cases the indirect plan is used for communicating the credit refusal.

Illustration 11-9 is a **poor** example of a personalized letter in which a department store refuses to issue a customer a credit card. The indirect plan is not used in this letter.

An improved letter for this circumstance is shown in Illustration 11-10, a **good** example of the use of the indirect plan for a credit refusal. A mutually satisfactory business relationship could develop from this credit refusal. The customer should not be offended by the credit refusal in Illustration 11-10.

> Buying on **credit** is common today.

> Some customers must be refused credit.

> Credit refusals usually are in the customer's interest.

UNSOLICITED BAD NEWS MESSAGES

Not all bad news messages are in response to a request or an inquiry. Some of these messages are initiated by the businessperson. Examples of such unsolicited bad news messages include communications about price increases for products or services, budget reductions, and staff reductions (layoffs). These messages are especially difficult to compose because they initiate the bad news.

In Illustration 11-11, you can feel the negative impact of the **poor** interoffice memo informing employees of a reduction in their insurance benefits. The indirect plan and the guides for its implementation were not used.

Notice in Illustration 11-12, how the same information can be conveyed in a more acceptable manner. Employees are not going to be happy about the reduction, but at least the situation is more acceptable when the indirect plan is used. There is no need for a communicator to anger, disturb, or hurt receivers—intentionally or inadvertently—through poorly conveyed messages.

> Sometimes businesses must initiate bad news messages.

Illustration 11-5 **Poor** Example of a Request Refusal (Form Letter)

Poor request refusal
lacks coherence and
clearness.

Explanation not
logical or
meaningful.

Suggested
alternative not
helpful.

UNION
HILL
UNIVERSITY

College of Business and Public Affairs
Northfield Center of Business and
Governmental Research
Union Hill, NY 14563-6437
(516) 555-1418

March 1, 199–

Dear Registrant

Your check to cover the cost of registering for our
seminar, "Improving Your Business Writing Skills," is
enclosed. The check arrived after the class limit was
reached.

Thank you for your interest in this program; we hope
you will try to register for this seminar the next time
it is offered.

Sincerely

Edward Simmons

Edward Simmons
Program Coordinator

dfm

Enclosure

Illustration 11-6 **Good** Example of a Request Refusal (Form Letter)

UNION
HILL
UNIVERSITY

College of Business and Public Affairs

Northfield Center of Business and
Governmental Research
Union Hill, NY 14563-6437
(516) 555-1418

March 1, 199–

Dear Registrant

Thank you for the interest you have shown in our seminar entitled, "Improving Your Business Writing Skills." The seminar is an extremely popular one; over 40 people have submitted registration forms.

One of the reasons this seminar is so popular is that the leaders believe in giving each participant individual attention. To be sure this occurs, seminar enrollment is limited to 25 participants. Registrations were processed on a first-come, first-served basis, and the 25-person class size limit was reached before your form and check arrived. Your check is, therefore, enclosed with this letter. Your name and phone number have been placed on our waiting list; if an opening becomes available, we will notify you immediately.

The Northfield Center is committed to providing seminars which meet the needs of the business leaders in this area. The enclosed brochure lists the courses which will be offered during the next three months. If you would like additional information about any of them, please call collect (516) 555–1422.

Sincerely

Edward Simmons

Edward Simmons
Program Coordinator

dfm

Enclosure

Good request refusal has coherence and a neutral opening.

Logical explanation stresses receiver's interests and benefits.

Bad news implied.

Helpful alternative suggested.

Off-subject, friendly close.

Illustration 11-7 **Poor** Example of an Adjustment Refusal Letter

John Martin
Sales Company

577 Linden Street, Cottage Grove, WI 53527-3909 (608) 555-8220

April 30, 199–

Mr. John Brame
2300 First Street
Paducah, WI 53001-2783

Dear Mr. Brame

We are sorry we cannot honor your request for a refund
for the defective boat you recently purchased from us.
Our sales policy, widely known in this area, has always
been to refuse refunds for any items sold on sale.

It would cut our profit if we were to give refunds on
sale items. We are always willing to give refunds on
non-sale items. We have signs posted throughout the
store on our sales policy. Also, our clerks are sup-
posed to use our rubber stamp which says "Sorry, no
refunds on sale items" on each sales slip during sales.

Again, let us say we are sorry that you didn't notice
our policy and that we can't refund you for the defective boat. We would encourage you to come in and buy a
repair kit from us.

Sincerely yours

Mario Perez

Mario Perez
Store Manager

bch

Poor letter gives bad news first (direct approach), is negative, talks down to receiver.

Explanation not in you-viewpoint; not logical.

Negative final apology; constructive follow-up poorly written and out of proper sequence.

Illustration 11-8 **Good** Example of an Adjustment Refusal Letter

John Martin Sales Company

577 Linden Street, Cottage Grove, WI 53527-3909 (608) 555-8220

April 30, 199–

Mr. John Brame
2300 First Street
Paducah, WI 53001-2783

Dear Mr. Brame

Your recent purchase of a Blue Waters Ski Boat is appreciated. You have bought a high-quality ski boat that can give you many years of enjoyment. We want to do all that we can to ensure that you do have that enjoyment with your new Blue Waters Ski Boat.

You made a wise decision when you bought your ski boat on sale during the "Save 33 Percent" sale. The tremendous savings of almost $2,000 that you realized on this purchase was made possible in two ways: (1) We buy merchandise in large volume, and (2) we cut overhead and pass the savings on to the customer. One of the ways we cut overhead is to make all sales final on items purchased during the "Save 33 Percent" sale. We make every effort to be sure all our customers are aware of this policy by noting it in all advertisements and posting signs throughout the store.

You will be glad to know that the repair needed on your Blue Waters Ski Boat is easy to make. For only $39.95 you can purchase a fiberglass repair kit that has complete directions for its use. You can either "do-it-yourself" or have our expert shop take care of it for you at cost. Please call us collect at (608) 555-8220 and tell us your preference.

Best wishes for many happy hours of skiing this summer on Paducah Lake.

Sincerely yours

Mario Perez

Mario Perez
Store Manager

bch

Good letter has coherence; builds goodwill.

Positive.

Neutral opening introduces explanation.

Convincing reasoning positively presented; receiver benefits stressed; bad news implied and de-emphasized.

Alternative solution suggested; writer does more than expected.

Goodwill, off-subject close.

Illustration 11-9 **Poor** Example of a Credit Refusal Letter

Payne and Johnson

215 Howard Street
Glendale, CA 91206-7211
(213) 555-3554

March 1, 199—

Ms. Claudia Hess
1042 Pebble Hills Lane
Cavalier, CA 40986-0488

Dear Ms. Hess

Poor letter's negative opening gives bad news; not in you-viewpoint.

I am sorry to inform you that Payne and Johnson cannot issue a credit card to you at this time. We would like to issue a credit card to you, but our store policy does not permit us to issue credit to college students.

Not personalized or in you-viewpoint; negative.

College students do not have full-time employment and may not be able to pay their bills at the end of the month. The majority of students are temporary residents, and we cannot take a chance on someone leaving town with unpaid bills. We know that you may not be this type of individual, but we cannot take a chance.

No constructive follow-up to the bad news; negative final apology; poor reselling.

Again, let me say that I am sorry that we cannot issue credit to you. If you are in need of school clothing or supplies, please stop at Payne and Johnson to do your shopping.

Sincerely

Nancy Nelson

Nancy Nelson
Credit Manager

htc

Illustration 11-10 **Good** Example of a Credit Refusal Letter

Payne and Johnson

215 Howard Street
Glendale, CA 91206-7211
(213) 555-3554

March 1, 199–

Ms. Claudia Hess
1042 Pebble Hills Lane
Cavalier, CA 40986-0488

Dear Ms. Hess

Your interest in obtaining a Payne and Johnson credit card is sincerely appreciated. Our aim is to give you the best service possible.

Because your satisfaction is most important to us, your credit application was processed immediately. While processing your credit application, our credit department learned that you are a full-time student at California State University. The credit reference portion of your credit application was left blank. Payne and Johnson grants credit to individuals who are employed and who can provide a minimum of two good credit references. When you obtain part-time employment and resubmit an application listing two credit references, your request will be re-evaluated.

Payne and Johnson is always in touch with the latest in college fashions. A large shipment of the newest Easter fashions will be arriving next week. Please stop in to select a special dress for the spring festivities.

Congratulations on being selected a cheerleader for California State. Your performance must be one of the reasons that CSU's football team has such an outstanding record.

Sincerely

Nancy Nelson

Nancy Nelson
Credit Manager

htc

Good opening buffer builds goodwill; is neutral.

Explanation logical; stresses receiver interests.

Bad news implied.

Alternative solution.

Resells.

Friendly, off-subject close; warm and personalized.

Illustration 11-11   **Poor** Example of an Unsolicited Bad News Memo

MAJOR PRODUCTS MANUFACTURING COMPANY
6400 WEST EUCLID AVENUE, MILWAUKEE, WISCONSIN 53219-7648

MICHAEL TOWNLEY, President

Interoffice Memorandum

TO: Employees of Major Products Manufacturing Company

FROM: Sarah Lewis, Personnel Manager *SL*

DATE: January 23, 199–

SUBJECT: Reduced Insurance Benefits

It is my unfortunate duty to inform you that insurance benefits for employees' dependents will be eliminated as of March 1.

I know that this reduction comes at a bad time since inflation is eating up so much of our paychecks. We must cut your benefits in order for our company to make a profit for our shareholders. This benefit reduction will reduce the company's insurance costs $50,000. This will give us the opportunity to pay higher dividends to our stockholders.

Again, let me say that I am sorry that you will have to provide your own insurance coverage for your dependents. If you need help in finding an insurance company that can provide you with coverage, please contact me.

hkm

Opening gives bad news explicitly and negatively.

Lacks you-viewpoint (receiver's interest ignored); negative.

Close not off-subject; limited offer to help.

Illustration 11-12 **Good** Example of an Unsolicited Bad News Memo

MAJOR PRODUCTS MANUFACTURING COMPANY
6400 WEST EUCLID AVENUE, MILWAUKEE, WISCONSIN 53219-7648

Interoffice Memorandum

MICHAEL TOWNLEY, President

TO: Employees of Major Products Manufacturing Company

FROM: Sarah Lewis, Personnel Manager *SL*

DATE: January 23, 199–

SUBJECT: Your Insurance Benefits

The insurance benefits that you receive are superior to those of employees of most manufacturing companies in this area. Since the fringe benefits that you receive are tax free, you have more take-home pay. In your interest, Major Products plans to maintain this competitive position.

The nation's economy, however, is currently in a fluctuating period. Our company is facing the challenge of maintaining our quality products at a competitive price while providing adequate salaries and security for employees. To maintain our current number of employees and continue paying competitive wages, the dependents' hospitalization coverage must be discontinued. All employees will continue having the $20,000 life insurance policy and the $50 deductible hospitalization plan.

Dependent hospitalization coverage will still be available from our same insurance company at a 25 percent savings for Major Products' employees. An insurance representative will be available in the conference room all day on Thursday, January 30, to answer any questions you may have.

There are optimistic signs that the nation's economy is turning around. By working together we can all look forward to good years ahead.

hkm

Good opening buffer builds coherence; is positive, neutral, and sets stage for explanation.

Convincing logical reasoning precedes bad news.

Bad news de-emphasized by position in paragraph and by being followed with good news.

Receiver's interests stressed in helpful alternative solution.

Friendly close is warm and optimistic.

CONCLUSION

You can be a successful business communicator even when the message contains bad news. By effectively using the indirect plan presented in this chapter, you will be able to handle these challenging messages.

DISCUSSION QUESTIONS

1. What are bad news messages?
2. Explain why a bad news message usually should be prepared using the indirect plan.
3. When is it appropriate for a bad news message to be prepared in the direct plan?
4. Discuss how you think readers reacted to the Chrysler Corporation open letter about the disconnected odometers.
5. Discuss the importance of using the you-viewpoint for successfully communicating bad news messages.
6. What are key questions to be asked when you are determining appropriate content for a bad news message that will use the indirect plan?
7. What are the requirements for an effective opening buffer in a bad news message that follows the indirect plan?
8. What are the benefits of following the guidelines for developing the logical explanation section of a bad news message?
9. Give contrasting examples of giving bad news (a) by saying what can be done and (b) by saying what cannot be done. What are the relative benefits of each way?
10. Give an example of doing more than is expected for a message receiver. Discuss the advantages and disadvantages of doing more than is expected.
11. List several examples of content for off-subject, friendly closes for bad news messages.
12. Why does a business concern itself with building goodwill?
13. What is an adjustment refusal?
14. How can a company keep a customer's cash business after having to turn him or her down for credit?
15. What is the difference between solicited and unsolicited bad news messages? Give an example of an unsolicited bad news message.

16. Review the essential concepts for effectively sending bad news to a receiver. Include in your discussion the role of the indirect plan, the goals of business communication, the importance of an analysis of the receiver, and the use of the you-viewpoint.

APPLICATION EXERCISES

1. With four students on each side of the issue, debate the use of the indirect plan versus the direct plan for bad news messages.

2. Observe and record over a 48-hour period those oral and written communications that can be classified as bad news messages—messages that are unpleasant, disappointing, or unfavorable to the receiver. Report those observations to the class so that the members can analyze the effectiveness and success of the communications. Use the indirect plan and its benefits as criteria for this analysis.

3. Visit a business in your community and obtain an example of a written bad news message. Present an analysis of this message using the indirect plan approach explained in this chapter.

4. Discuss your personal experiences in receiving bad news. Analyze the strengths and weaknesses of the quality of these messages.

5. Change the following statements to reflect what can be done instead of what cannot be done:
   a. Students are prohibited from lounging on the sidewalk in front of the Student Center.
   b. No hunting is permitted in the camping area.
   c. Sick leave cannot be used for personal business.
   d. Refunds will not be made without the sales slip.
   e. Merchandise may not be returned unless the request is approved by the Customer Service Manager.
   f. You do not have sufficient collateral, so we cannot allow you credit.

6. Interview a manager who supervises employees and ask (a) what is the most common bad news he or she has to give employees and (b) what is the most effective way he or she has found to convey this bad news. Share your findings with the class.

7. Discuss the most effective ways you have observed for instructors to convey low grades (unfavorable news) to students.

8. List the names of three major retail stores in your community. Analyze each of these stores in regard to its merchandise return and exchange policies and performance.

CASE PROBLEMS

REQUEST REFUSALS

1. You own approximately 100 acres of undeveloped land just north of a college campus. A student organization has asked your permission to hold a rock concert on your land. You must refuse this request because your land does not have developed roadways, connections to sewer systems, or liability insurance coverage.

   Refuse the student organization's request in a manner that will maintain goodwill and show the receivers how your denial benefits them. Supply any additional details that are necessary to make a complete letter.

2. Write a form letter that can be used to reject applications for employment at the Island River Mine, Bellville, Montana. The Island River personnel office is being deluged with letters of application, requests for application forms, and phone calls about employment possibilities. More than 50 percent of the miners in the area are currently unemployed. There is a need for a brief, courteous letter that maintains goodwill but refuses applications. Make this bad news as acceptable as possible for these persons who so desperately need and want work.

3. You are the information processing manager for ABC Sales Corporation in Miami, Florida. One of your supervisors in the information processing center, Terry Forest, has just given you a memo in which he requests permission to attend a three-week seminar on personal computers in Hawaii. It is important for this supervisor to be well aware of how the personal computer operates and the extent of its capability. You are in the process of buying 32 new PCs for use in the information processing center.

   You must write a memo to Terry refusing his request. Keep in mind two considerations: (1) Terry attended a similar conference about six months ago and (2) there is a considerable amount of programmed self-instruction that can be used on the PCs once they are received in the information processing center.

   Write the memo so that you will maintain Terry's goodwill and productivity but will refuse his request to attend the seminar in Hawaii. Incidentally, you are concerned about Terry's sincerity in his request. Is he really interested in the seminar, or is he anticipating a vacation in Hawaii?

4. You have been out of school five years; they have been good years for you. You are now successfully established in your own computer service agency. Business is good; in fact, it is so good that you find it difficult to keep up with all of the requests for your services.

   One of your best clients, the Matsumi Engineering Company, has just asked you to do a roadbed analysis for a new three-mile section of Interstate I-674 through the mountains. It is a huge project—enough work to keep your whole facility busy for three months. However you have other commitments; you must refuse this request from Matsumi for your services.

   Think through the indirect approach for refusing a request. Provide convincing reasons that the owners of Matsumi will understand and that will show the benefit to them of your decision not to undertake this particular project. You can commit your agency to complete other current projects for them in your usual quality fashion. One of the things that you refuse to do is accept more work than you can handle in an efficient, effective way for your clients. Write a letter to Matsumi telling them no and suggest an alternative that will possibly solve their problem.

5. A group of employees under your supervision has requested that you extend the number and length of their coffee breaks from two 10-minute breaks to four 15-minute breaks. Refuse their request. The additional coffee breaks would significantly lower production rates. Lower production rates would also mean lower bonuses for employees at the end of the year. Add any necessary details.

6. You have just received a telephone call from the nominating committee for the local chapter of the Information Administration Society. They want to enter your name into nomination for the presidency of the chapter for next year. They request that you not give an immediate response but "sleep on your answer and write us a letter indicating your willingness to accept this nomination."

   As you reflect on the responsibility of being the president of the local chapter of the Information Administration Society, you decide that your heavy schedule will not permit you to do the high-quality job the chapter needs.

   Write a letter to the nominating committee that will show its members how your refusal is really in their best interest. Indicate your perception of the responsibility required to lead the chapter successfully during the next year. Further, indicate how your schedule will not permit you to spend the time necessary for the leadership required. Do this in convincing you-viewpoint writing so that you can maintain positive relationships with the members of the nominating committee as well as the rest of the chapter members. Add any necessary details to make this a complete request refusal letter.

7. You are a student at the Rushville Academy in Arlington, Vermont. It is final examination time. Your employer has written you a memo requesting you to work overtime during the week of finals.

   This is a very serious situation. You need the job desperately to enable you to continue your education. Also, you especially need to study this week so that you can do well on the final examinations in your courses. It would be a wasted investment of time, having worked all semester long, to be unable to perform effectively on the final examinations. You could possibly lower your grade or even fail a course if you do not study for finals.

   Your employer has implied to you on several occasions that once you graduate he will be interested in continuing your employment. Maybe this is one of the bases for your logical explanation as to why you must tell him you cannot work overtime during finals week.

   Write your boss a memo that will convince him it is important to him (and to you) for you to study for finals and not work overtime this coming week. Also add any details that will make this a complete indirect memo that refuses a request. Be sure to include suggested alternative(s) for your boss.

8. You are the manager of a franchise for Pizza Stores, Inc. You have been asked by an executive of a manufacturing plant near your restaurant if he could have his employees attend a pizza party at your restaurant at 9:00 p.m. Thursday. You would have to close your restaurant two hours early to accommodate the large number of his employees. You do not feel it is possible for you to close your restaurant to the public two hours early so you will have to turn the request down. You would be glad, however, to cater a pizza party at some other location. You can do this in the manufacturer's plant, at the community center, or at some other location of the executive's choosing. Write a letter to the executive that will turn down his request and keep the business. Add any neccessary details.

ADJUSTMENT REFUSALS

9. You are sales manager for Browning Tire Sales, Inc., in Milroy, New York. Your most popular line of tires is the one that is rated "blemished." Blemished tires have some small defect that does not affect their usability. The defect may be a misprint on the labeling of the tire, imperfect white-wall coloring, or irregular tread pattern. In some instances, however—and these are rare—blemished tires may also have serious defects such as

being out-of-round. These tires do not ride well and may cause vibration inside the car.

You sold some blemished tires to Al Sams when he was vacationing in Milroy. He has now returned to his home state, almost 600 miles away, and has written you that he wants a full refund on the blemished tires. Your policy and the standard policy throughout the United States on blemished tire sales is that there will be no refunds. The retail prices of blemished tires are considerably below those for unblemished tires. The fine print in the sales agreement with the customer specifies no refunds on blemished tires.

Mr. Sams has stated in his letter that he intends to destroy the tires as soon as he receives your refund. He further states that all four tires seem to be out-of-round and that they cause his car to handle improperly. This, you believe, is an overstatement. In a threatening tone Mr. Sams tells you that he has several friends in the Milroy area to whom he will write to encourage them to discontinue their business with your company. In addition, he will ask them to encourage others to discontinue their business if a refund is not forthcoming promptly.

You need to write a courteous adjustment refusal letter to Mr. Sams. The purposes of this letter will be (1) to resell Mr. Sams on the tires that he now has, (2) to convince him that it is to his benefit to continue to use those tires, and (3) to generally calm him down. His tires are obviously out-of-round. Equipment is available in almost every community to shave tires to correct such a problem. Could Mr. Sams take care of this locally? Suggest an alternative that might help him see that his problem is not hopeless. Furnish any necessary details to make this a complete adjustment refusal letter.

10. You are the warranty manager for a manufacturer of miniature vacuum cleaners. Since you warrant these mini-cleaners to the first owner only, one of the conditions of the sale is that the customer who originally purchases the cleaner must register the warranty with you. A number of customers who bought the mini-cleaners failed to register their warranties and are now seeking warranty work. You are going to have to refuse these requests for warranty repair. Suggest as an alternative (to prove that they are the first owners) that they send the warranty registration card and their sales receipt to you. Upon receipt of this evidence, you could then approve warranty repair on their vacuums. Write a form letter that will cover all of these customer claims. Be sure to maintain goodwill for your company.

11. You are the claims manager for USA Airline whose headquarters are in Atlanta, Georgia. You have just received a claim from Mrs. Norma

Lawson, 123 Magnolia Drive, Jackson, Mississippi. Mrs. Lawson says in her claim letter:

... I am angry. I just opened my suitcase upon arriving home after flying on Flight 270 from Paris, France, to Atlanta, Georgia. Guess what I found? My $250 bottle of perfume was crushed. The perfume had soaked throughout my clothes and into the suitcase lining.

Had your luggage handlers been more careful, this would not have happened. I would still have my $250 bottle of perfume and many other happy memories of my trip, but your airline ruined this for me with the unhappy ending I experienced. Also, I would not have had the $75 clothes cleaning bill and $125 suitcase repair bill.

I want the $450 by return mail.

Sincerely,

You investigated carefully what might have happened in this situation by talking with experienced luggage handlers at the Atlanta airport. What you found is what you suspected; for the perfume bottle to have broken, it must have been unprotected and probably near an outer cover of the suitcase. The airline does not take responsibility for glass items that are not packaged according to instructions and inspected prior to the flight. This policy is printed on the back of all tickets.

You must refuse this angry customer's request for an adjustment. Be sure to justify your airline's policy on glass items. At the same time you will want to encourage her to continue to fly on USA Airline. Your check of her flight record reveals that she has been a customer many times on the airline.

As a constructive follow-up, does she have personal property insurance coverage in a homeowner's insurance policy which may cover this loss?

12. A baseball team ordered uniforms from your sporting goods store. The team coach specified the colors and seemed satisfied with the uniforms when they were delivered. After three games (which the team lost), the players voted to return the uniforms for replacement because the "color wasn't just right." Write a letter refusing the adjustment. Add any additional details needed.

13. As manager of Acme Landscaping Service you have just received a claim letter from one of your largest accounts—the Paris Country Club Golf Course. The letter reads as follows:

Dear Mr. Butterworth:

The replacement sod you placed on Greens 13, 14, and 15 is dying and is unsuitable for championship golf. I know that we have had an unusually hot and dry summer, but this grass should have survived it. Please make arrangements with me immediately to resod these greens. Of course, I expect this to be done at your expense in accordance with your warranty.

Sincerely yours,

Robert Ryan
Golf Pro

You will have to refuse this claim. First, the warranty Mr. Ryan refers to specifies that any claim must be entered within 90 days of purchase. The warranty expired 32 days ago. Second, the warranty also called for "adequate watering." There are generally recognized standards of what adequate watering means to golf greens keepers. In fact, during the warranty period you became concerned about the limited watering being done by Gus Blakely, Paris's greens keeper. As you passed the golf course on your way home each day, you noticed that he was not providing adequate watering. You finally made a special point to stop and give him specific advice on how much additional watering he needed to do.

Refuse the adjustment request. Provide the logical reasoning that justifies your refusal.

14. You are the owner and operator of a small gift shop with a policy of no refunds. You are glad to give credit toward another purchase if a customer wants to return an item. You have three signs that are clearly visible in your store which cite your no-refunds policy. Mildred Brown, a good customer who lives out of town, has written you asking for her first refund on a $125 vase. She believes the vase does not complement her decor. Refuse the adjustment. In your letter to Ms. Brown explain and justify your policies on refunds and credits. Can you suggest an alternate solution? Add any necessary details.

15. You have just received a letter from Sally DeFord who recently purchased a microcomputer from your store. Sally's letter to you is as follows:

Dear Mr. Martinson:

When you sold the Model IX Microcomputer to me, you said that there would be no strain on my eyes from looking at the screen. I have not found this to be the case. I find, instead, that after working three or four hours at the computer, my eyes begin to water and burn.

I must request that you permit me to return this microcomputer to your store for a full refund. It is just not satisfactory for my purposes.

Please let me know when I can return the microcomputer to you and pick up my refund check.

Yours truly,

Sally DeFord

You don't want to lose this sale. In fact, even though your warranty says that you will refund the money for any microcomputer which is not completely satisfactory to the customer, you have decided to refuse this particular request. It will be necessary in your logical explanation to convince the customer that she should keep the microcomputer. After all, there were several good reasons on which she based her decision to buy the microcomputer. Resell her on its benefits.

However, you still have the problem of Sally's eyestrain. Suggest to her that you can correct the problem. You can do this by attaching to the front of the microcomputer screen a green Plexiglas eye ease cover at a cost of $14.95. In most cases this cover has solved the problem of eyestrain suffered by people using a computer. Do your best with this letter. If this bad news message does not change the customer's mind, you will have to take the microcomputer back and refund her $1,800.

16. It is spring. Sales of your leading fertilizer, Evergreen Brand, are at an all-time high. One of your recent customers, Mr. Harold Brown, has written to you saying that the Evergreen Brand fertilizer is not all that it is cracked up to be. His letter follows:

Dear Mr. Flintrock:

Recently, I purchased ten bags of Evergreen Brand fertilizer for use on my lawn. That was one of the biggest mistakes I ever made in my life. I spent more than 100 hours preparing the lawn bed for new seed and fertilizer. All that work was lost.

Your fertilizer killed my grass.

I am requesting that you reimburse me for the following items: 100 hours of labor at $10 an hour, $1,000; 10 bags of Evergreen Brand fertilizer at $8 a bag, $80; 5 bags of Evergrow grass seed at $20 a bag, $100; total $1,180.

Let me tell you this story. After preparing the lawn bed, sowing the grass seed, and watering it faithfully for five days, I then put what I thought was the finishing touch on it. I applied your fertilizer. It was, in fact, the finishing touch—it killed all my grass. Not only did your fertilizer not help my grass grow, it terminated its very existence.

Isn't my claim reasonable?

Sincerely,

Harold Brown

No, Mr. Brown's claim is not reasonable, and you must refuse it. Your warranty, which appears on every bag of Evergreen Brand fertilizer, warns that refunds will not be made if the fertilizer is applied to grass seed recently sown. In fact, the fertilizer warranty indicates that the grass should be at least an inch high and ten weeks old prior to the application of the fertilizer. Fertilizers that can be applied earlier than this are weaker and do not have the long-term value of Evergreen Brand.

Explain and justify your policy to Mr. Brown. Restore his goodwill so that he will come back to your store and buy additional grass seed to replace that which he has lost. The fertilizer that he placed on his lawn is still good, and it will have settled into the grass bed sufficiently by this time so as not to damage any newly sown grass seed. Write an adjustment refusal letter that assures the sale of additional grass seed.

CREDIT REFUSALS

17. You are the loan officer for the First National Bank of Bloomington, Ohio. You have just been approached by Sandra Morales who lives on a small farm at the edge of town. Her intent is to borrow money from the bank, buy 25 head of cattle, and make a little extra money on them. Her case to you is that she has plenty of land for grazing the cattle, and her job will permit her to feed them and care for them adequately.

    Her request for credit must be refused. First, she has had no experience in raising cattle. It is difficult, at best, for an experienced farmer or rancher to be successful at raising cattle and to make a profit in so doing. Second, the livestock market does not look good to you at this time. The costs of feed are excessive, and the market price for cattle is in a long downward trend. Write a letter that will maintain this customer's business with the bank but will refuse this particular loan.

18. Write a letter to the credit customers of your grocery store telling them that you are changing to a cash only policy. This will enable you to effect significant savings in record keeping, bad debt losses, postage, etc. You plan to pass a major share of the savings to your customers. You have studied this matter carefully; be concrete in your explanation.

19. You are manager of Chapman's Fine Carpet Warehouse, Inc., in Sandusky, California. You have just received a letter from Fred Langemo, manager of the Triangle Restaurant in Grand Rapids, California, placing a large order for carpeting for his restaurant. In fact, this is the largest order you have received this month: more than $10,000 of commercial carpeting! You want this order very much.

    Unfortunately, Mr. Langemo has requested unreasonable credit terms. He suggests that he will pay you $500 down at the time the carpeting is satisfactorily installed. He wants to pay you the balance of approximately $10,000 (including a low rate of interest) over a ten-year period in installments of $1,000 a year. In an installation such as a restaurant, carpeting wears out in two to four years. It is important, therefore, that the carpeting be paid for within three years. Also, it is your standard practice to require that approximately one half of the order be paid for before the carpeting is installed. This enables you as a supplier to obtain the carpeting and pay for it prior to installation.

Write a credit refusal letter to Mr. Langemo that will keep his business. Explain the credit terms that you are willing to provide once his credit application has been approved.

20. A 17-year-old college student has requested that your credit union provide her with a $3,000 line of credit. State laws governing lines-of-credit do not permit granting such requests, so you will have to refuse. As an alternative you could suggest the possibility of a qualified co-signer. Add any necessary details.

21. You are the credit manager for Buckley Buick in Racine, Nebraska. You have just received a note from Joel Sullivan, a young college student who is attending an out-of-state university. Joel writes that he has picked out a convertible model that he would like to buy from you. He tells you that he has a $200 down payment. The problem is that he needs at least a $1,200 down payment. With a cost of almost $12,000 for the convertible, the minimum down payment that you can accept is 10 percent. This is true for all the cars on your lot.

Your objective is to ensure a sale to Joel. But the car he chooses must be a much less expensive car than the convertible. You can give Joel credit for 90 percent of the cost of any car in stock. That means that $2,000 is the maximum amount that Joel can afford to spend for a car.

Write Joel telling him that you must refuse his credit request on the $12,000 car. Be sure to attempt to maintain Joel's business by showing him the advantages of buying a car that costs $2,000 or less.

22. You are one of the credit rating officers in the InternationalCard credit department. You have just received an application for a credit card from Joe Seymore, a college student at Brenham State College.

Your policy covering the granting of credit cards is that the card holder must be employed full time in a permanent position. Furthermore, an applicant's current financial condition must show assets exceeding liabilities at a ratio of at least 2 to 1.

Joe Seymore's application reveals that he has half-time employment and virtually no assets. Refuse his application at this time, but be sure to do so in a way that ensures his business in the future.

23. Fred Bowling is a young businessman who is really on the go. He is running several different enterprises—an ice cream store, an apple orchard, and a fishing bait business.

Fred has come to your bank with a plan for establishing yet another enterprise. He has submitted to you, along with his plan, his current financial statements including a balance sheet, a profit-and-loss statement for the past year, and related documents. His plan is to build a new apartment complex that would cost $450,000. He has requested that you provide him with the entire financing for this project. His reasoning for this request is based on his success in all his other enterprises.

What Fred says is true to a degree. He does show an excellent profit picture on the small capital investment that he has in his various business projects; but therein lies the problem—his small capital investment capability. Joe currently has an overall 1-to-2 ratio of assets to liabilities. At least a 2-to-1 ratio of assets to liabilities is required for any given project. Fred does not have that ratio on any of his current projects; therefore, you must refuse his request for credit because of insufficient capital.

Write a credit refusal letter that will maintain your relationship with Fred. He will be a good customer for the bank within the next few years. In fact, his current success in business indicates to you that he may very well qualify for the kind of loan he desires within three to four years. The rate of profit growth that he is showing in his current statement supports this analysis.

24. As manager of Wholesale Plumbing Company, you sell supplies to contract and home service plumbers. Many of these plumbers have established a line of credit with you that enables them to charge their purchases. You bill them once a month. A young woman who is new to your area and who has just opened a plumbing service business has asked you to establish a $3,000 line of credit for her. You must refuse this request for credit because she has not yet achieved a credit worthy record with your company. As an alternative arrangement, you can suggest that you could permit her purchases up to $300. These purchases would be paid for on a weekly basis. If you have a favorable experience with her over the next three months, you could establish a higher line of credit for her that could be paid on a monthly basis.

UNSOLICITED BAD NEWS MESSAGES

25. As plant manager for the Vanderbilt Toy Company, you have the unfortunate responsibility to let your 56 employees know that there will be no holiday bonus this year. Your company has consistently given generous bonuses for each of the past five years since the plant opened.

Provide convincing reasoning in a memo to your employees that will show them how they benefit by this bad news. The $38,000 that your company will save this holiday season by not giving the bonuses will be the difference between letting two employees go and keeping them on the payroll for the next year. You will admit, and you are proud of it, that the company has given each employee at least $500 for each of the past five holiday seasons. However, the economy is such this year that you are not going to be able to do it. Toy sales are down.

Convince the employees that your message is one they really want to receive. They have been depending on this $500. Add any additional details that will make your unsolicited bad news message complete.

26. Write a form letter to the students at your college telling them that beginning next year there will be a $50 parking charge per term. In addition, reserved parking slots will be assigned. There has not been a charge for open parking privileges in the past. The income from the new parking fee will be used to repair the parking lots and improve security. Add any additional details to make your letter complete.

27. Write a memo to Marvin Boles telling him that he will be terminated as of March 1. The corporation has made a 10 percent across-the-board reduction in the number of employees, and your department's share of this is one employee. Terminations were based on length of employment. Marvin is an excellent employee. Maintain goodwill for the corporation and a favorable relationship for yourself with Marvin. You would like to see him come back to work for you when economic conditions permit. Add any necessary details to make this a complete memo.

28. As marketing manager for the Red Arrow Office Supply Company, you have had the good fortune of having customers buy paper from you on a regular basis. In fact, you have several standing orders for large quantities of paper. These orders are delivered monthly as part of your standard routine.

Now you are faced with a problem. There has been a significant increase in the cost of paper—15 percent to be exact. In order to continue serving your customers effectively with quality paper, you must pass along to them this cost increase.

In addition, you have experienced several other increases in operating costs. Gasoline prices for your delivery trucks continue to rise. The rent on your warehouse has gone up. You have had to pay higher salaries to keep your delivery personnel. In fact, you must not only pass the 15 percent cost increase along to your customers, but you must also increase the price of paper an additional 5 percent in order to cover your pyramiding operating costs.

Write the form letter that will maintain the goodwill of your customers, keep their business, and help them accept your bad news. Add any additional details to make your letter complete.

29. Picture yourself as an insurance agent in Hopkinsville, Virginia. You have an affluent clientele of senior citizens in this retirement community. Many of these senior citizens have expensive jewelry collections. Insuring these collections has been an excellent source of income for your agency for many years.

Just today, however, you received a letter from the home office of your company. This letter indicates that the increased crime rate in Hopkinsville and similar metropolitan areas makes it necessary for your company to discontinue this type of coverage. This will be bad news to many of your clients. It is bad news, of course, to you as well.

Write an unsolicited letter to your many senior citizen customers explaining the situation to them. Be sure that you do not alienate them from your insurance company. They will be disappointed. They may think immediately about shifting all their insurance to another company that will offer them jewelry insurance. Convince them through logical reasoning that they should stay with you as their agent and stay with the Reliable Insurance Company for all coverage except jewelry. Can you suggest to them an alternative source of coverage for their jewelry? Can you assist them in any way in obtaining this coverage? Use the indirect plan in a letter that will achieve your objective. Add any necessary details to make the letter complete.

30. As sales manager for Old English China, Inc., you have the sad duty of informing several hundred customers that your company is going out of business. Replacement dishes in various patterns have been available from Old English China for more 82 years. Closing the business means these patterns will no longer be available from any source. The company's owner, Mr. Rudolph Budweiser, recently died. The heirs have decided that the patterns and manufacturing techniques used at Old English China all these years will not be sold to any other china manufacturer.

You do have one happy piece of news to convey. There is still a supply of almost all patterns, which will probably meet most customers' needs for the next four to five years.

Write to your customers explaining the circumstances and encourage them to order within 90 days to fill their anticipated needs for the next few years. Maintain the goodwill of your customers toward the Budweiser family because this family has several other enterprises from which these customers buy various kitchen and household items.

31. As a graduate of Murphy State College, you know the value of cooperative education. In fact, as a student, you participated in cooperative education for three years while you earned your degree. Now you employ Murphy State College co-op students in your Christmas tree farm business. But, with the popularity of artificial Christmas trees, you are practically out of

business. Twenty-five cooperative education slots that you have provided to Murphy State College will have to be discontinued.

Write the letter to the Murphy State College Cooperative Education Director, Dr. Ann Thompson, giving her the bad news. It will be important for you to maintain your relationship with the co-op education office because you may have other needs in the future as you develop other business interests. Also, as an alumnus of Murphy State College, you are interested in continuing friendly relations.

Write this unsolicited bad news message in a manner that will (1) maintain goodwill and (2) provide some direction to the cooperative education office for placement of the students you can no longer hire. Compile the necessary facts for a complete letter.

32. You are the public relations manager for a large manufacturer of breakfast cereals. It has just been learned that a batch of your leading brand, Fiber Munchies, was processed improperly. Due to a combination of machine failure and an inexperienced quality control inspector, this batch of Fiber Munchies has too few raisins and nuts and does not meet your high quality standards. You must write to all the grocery stores that have bought Fiber Munchies and ask them to take the cereal off the shelf. Further, the store managers should return the cereal to you at your expense. Use the direct approach for this bad news letter and express your apologies up front. Most importantly, regain the confidence of these grocers. Assure them that there is nothing harmful in the cereal and that there is no need to recall the cereal from customers. Remind them that complaints should be graciously handled with replacement cereal and a discount-on-future-purchases coupon that you are providing the grocers. Your approach to handling this problem has been cleared with the National Public Health Service.

CHAPTER 12

PERSUASIVE MESSAGES

LEARNING OBJECTIVES

Your learning objectives for this chapter include the following:

- To understand the nature of persuasive messages
- To appreciate the advantages of using the indirect plan for persuasion
- To recognize the difference between poor and good examples of persuasive messages
- To use the indirect persuasive plan competently for different kinds of persuasive messages
- To recognize the types of messages that should be written at the various stages of collection

Persuasive messages are (1) requests for action when you believe the receiver may be unknowing, disinterested, or unwilling or (2) communication trying to change the opinion of a receiver. These messages will be viewed as neither good news nor bad news by the receiver.

Persuasive messages are used in both internal and external communication. Examples of persuasive messages in internal communication include a speech asking employees to volunteer to work on upcoming weekends, an employee's memo to a manager requesting that the organization initiate a flex-time policy, an employee's recommendation or proposal to establish a day care center, and a letter to employees requesting donations for a charity that has just been endorsed by the company.

Persuasive messages are used to convince receivers to take action.

Persuasive messages are used for a variety of purposes in internal and external communication.

Sales messages are the most common persuasive messages in external communication. Other examples of persuasive messages used in external communication include a telephone call to the manager of another company requesting that she be the keynote speaker at an annual banquet and a letter persuading readers to respond to a questionnaire. Persuasive messages also include application letters requesting employment with the company.

Persuasive messages have to be designed to convince receivers that taking the requested action is in their best interest. The supporting facts in the message must be presented as useful or profitable to the receiver. Persuasive messages should be presented using an indirect approach.

Receivers will have to be convinced that it is in their best interest to take action.

USE THE INDIRECT PLAN FOR PERSUASIVE MESSAGES

The indirect plan assists in convincing a receiver to take action.

The indirect plan conditions a receiver to accept the message.

The indirect plan should be used for messages that attempt to convince the receiver to take an action. The advantage of using the indirect plan for persuasive messages is that it enables the sender to first present the benefits that receivers may gain from fulfilling the request. This puts receivers in the proper frame of mind to consider the request. If the request were given prior to the explanation, the receiver might form objections that would be difficult to overcome. The receiver also might not read the part of the letter that contains the benefits. The indirect plan does require the use of more words than the direct plan, but the result is worth the additional words.

You-viewpoint should be used.

If the message is positively constructed in the you-viewpoint, the receiver will more likely be in a positive mood to consider the value of the entire message and will more likely agree with its contents. An effective presentation will associate the message with the motivating factors in the receiver's mind.

HOW TO USE THE INDIRECT PLAN

Carefully analyze receiver to determine motivational factors.

Analyzing your receiver is especially important when planning a persuasive message. You will have to anticipate what motivates the receiver—his or her goals, values, and needs. You must then build your message around these factors.

You must also use the you-viewpoint when constructing your persuasive message. Do this by stressing the receiver's interests and benefits.

The two primary purposes for the originator of a persuasive message are to get the receiver to read or listen to the entire message and then to have the receiver react positively to the request in the message. These purposes are more easily achieved when the indirect plan is used in constructing the message. The specific guides for using the indirect plan to construct persuasive messages are shown in Illustration 12-1.

Purposes of persuasive message are to have receiver consider entire message and then to take requested action.

I. **Attention**
   A. Attract receiver's attention in the opening sentence.
   B. Cause the receiver to read or listen to the rest of the message.
   C. Be positive and brief.

II. **Interest**
   A. Build on the attention gained in the opening.
   B. Show benefits to the receiver.
   C. Increase receiver's desire to continue reading.

III. **Desire**
   A. Continue to build on receiver's attention and interest by providing proof.
   B. Reemphasize the benefits to the receiver.
   C. Downplay any negative points or obstacles.

IV. **Action**
   A. Motivate the receiver to take immediate action.
   B. Be positive.
   C. Make action easy.
   D. Be optimistic.

Illustration 12-1   Indirect Plan Outline for Persuasion

The indirect plan can be used for a variety of persuasive messages—requests, recommendations, special claims, sales, collection, and employment. The organization and development of the first five persuasive messages will be discussed in this chapter, and employment messages will be covered in Chapter 22. An analysis of the indirect plan for persuasion will be helpful prior to discussing the construction of five sample persuasive messages.

Persuasive messages include requests, recommendations, special claims, sales, collection, and employment.

ATTENTION

The opening in any persuasive message must gain the receiver's attention. A persuasive message is successful only when the desired action is taken by the receiver. The desired action is not likely to be taken unless the receiver is motivated to read or listen to the entire message. An attention-getting opening increases the chances that the receiver will read or listen to the entire message and then will take the desired action.

A receiver's attention must be gained to ensure message is read or heard.

The receiver's attention must be captured in the opening sentence. It is important that the opening be concise and positive. In a well-planned

Get receiver's **attention** immediately.

persuasive message, the receiver's curiosity is aroused when a message opens with an interesting point. When a positive emotion is aroused, the reader will continue reading.

Many different methods have been successfully used by communicators to capture the receiver's attention. These methods include mechanical devices (such as color or drawings), using of the receiver's name in the sentence, rhetorical questions, and interjections. The you-viewpoint must be considered when organizing the content of the message. Any method that gets the receiver's attention can be used if it is relevant to the topic of the message and is not trite or high pressured. Gimmicks may be used but should not give the receiver the impression that an attempt is being made to mislead him or her. For example, beginning a letter with, "Your investment of $10 may grow to a million by the end of the year," will probably cause the reader to read no further because the message is unrealistic.

Senders use different techniques to gain receivers' attention.

INTEREST

The receiver's interest must be held after his or her attention is gained in the first paragraph. The topic of the first paragraph is expanded while maintaining the interest of the receiver. Interest will be maintained when benefits to the receiver are shown. When taking the action will result in several benefits to the receiver, the benefits may be emphasized by listing and numbering them. The receiver may hesitate to take the desired action unless he or she clearly sees the value of taking such action.

*To hold **interest**, the receiver must be made aware of the benefits of taking the action.*

DESIRE

Once you have the receiver's attention and interest, proof of the benefits that the receiver can gain should be given so that he or she will be motivated to take the requested action. Remember, the purpose of the persuasive message is to move the receiver to take the desired action. Details of the message are used to intensify the interest and create desire within the receiver. Anticipate the receiver's negative reactions to taking the desired action; attempt to overcome these feelings by pointing out proof of the benefits to the receiver.

*Providing proof of the benefits and values increases a receiver's **desire** to take action.*

ACTION

You are ready to ask the receiver to take *immediate action* once you have built his or her interest and desire. The action you request the receiver to take should be a logical next step. This action should be requested in a direct and positive manner.

*The receiver should feel that taking the **action** is a logical conclusion.*

The message sender must ensure that a minimum of effort is required for the receiver to take the necessary action. It is easier to ask for an action such as checking a choice and returning an enclosed card than to ask the receiver to write an entire letter.

Make it easy to take the action.

When the desired action is required by a certain date, be sure that this date is clearly stated. If no time limit is involved, encourage the receiver to make a quick decision.

If deadline date is necessary, give it.

Many techniques can be used to influence the receiver to take the desired action immediately. A sales letter can offer coupons that can be redeemed, specify a date that the offer ends, or suggest that supplies are limited. Collection letters can offer assurance that the receiver's credit will not be damaged if payment is received by a certain date. Including the receiver's name in a drawing for a free prize if he or she returns a questionnaire can be used with requests. All these techniques are effective if the receiver feels no undue pressure.

There exist various methods of getting the receiver to take action.

IMPLEMENTING THE INDIRECT PLAN

The use of the indirect plan for persuasion will be illustrated through the development of a request to a fellow member of a professional organization. Here are details of the communication case problem:

A communication case will help illustrate ways to compose persuasive messages.

Charla Stafford has been a loyal member of the Society of Professional Managers (SPM) since her graduation from college eight years ago. She served as treasurer two years ago. Recently, she has been promoted to administrative manager of the home office of Security Insurance Company. In this position she is responsible for 225 office employees. Write her a letter informing her that she has been nominated president-elect for SPM. You realize that Charla is busy in her new position at Security but is highly deserving of the office in SPM. This position involves much public relations work. As benefits you may remind Charla that she will have a year to prepare for the presidency and that officers do not pay dues. You must write a letter to Charla convincing her that she should accept the nomination.

DETERMINE APPROPRIATE CONTENT

As is the case in developing all business messages, you must first analyze the situation to determine the content that will best accomplish the purpose of the communication. The following sections show how the content of the Charla

Stafford letter may be developed. Each section discusses a stage of the indirect plan for persuasive messages and presents an example of *poor writing* and then an example of *good writing*.

CAPTURE THE RECEIVER'S ATTENTION

The first step in writing a persuasive message is to grab the receiver's attention. A **poor** way of gaining Charla's attention is shown here:

*The **poor** example is negative and impersonal.*

> The nominating committee has selected you as president-elect for the coming year. You would serve in this position for one year and next year would assume the duties of president.

This poorly written opening paragraph begins by immediately telling Charla that she has inherited another responsibility. It may get her attention but not in a positive way. The paragraph is impersonal and shows a lack of appreciation for Charla's previous service. She may be reluctant to continue reading the letter because she immediately senses that this is just another job rather than an honor.

In contrast a **good** opening to gain Charla's attention follows:

*The **good** example is positive and personal.*

> Your dedication and hard work over the past eight years have been among the principal reasons for the outstanding growth of the Society of Professional Managers. The nominating committee, therefore, shows its appreciation to you for this service by nominating you president-elect.

This good opening gains Charla's attention by recognizing her longtime dedication to the organization. This paragraph uses both a positive approach and the you-viewpoint. It should interest her because it praises her for her previous service. Everyone likes to receive recognition, and this acknowledgement of her efforts should motivate Charla to read the remaining portion of the letter with an open mind.

BUILD THE RECEIVER'S INTEREST

After you have captured the receiver's attention, you must concentrate on building interest in the receiver to accept the request. A **poor** way of building Charla's interest is:

*The **poor** example lacks a you-viewpoint.*

> This responsibility should not be taken lightly since it will take many hours each week to carry out all the duties. I know you are busy with your new position at Security Insurance Company, but all of us have a lot of work. One of the primary functions of the office is to improve the public relations between our organization and the community. I know you can do an effective job with this.

This poor attempt to build the receiver's interest is similar to that of the poor opening in that it is impersonal and negative. The paragraph is cold and lacks a you-viewpoint—it is of no help in building Charla's interest in accepting the nomination.

A **good** paragraph, which should build Charla's interest, follows:

> As president-elect you would be able to observe the operation of the presidency and also would be able to assist the president with various duties. You might be asked to attend a few activities that the president could not attend; these functions would prepare you for assuming the position of president next year. As you are aware, the organization does not pay its officers; but the officers are exempt from paying dues.

The **good** example aids in building receiver's interest.

This good paragraph outlines the duties and one benefit of the office in a positive manner. Charla's interest, now aroused, will peak in the next paragraph.

STIMULATE DESIRE IN THE RECEIVER

In this section, reemphasize the benefits that Charla would receive by taking the requested action. An attempt should be made to overcome any negative thoughts that Charla may have. A **poor** attempt to stimulate desire is illustrated here:

> I know you are a busy person, but we certainly need someone to guide our organization. I feel you are the person who can do it. Our membership has grown significantly in the past two years; we feel you can maintain this growth pattern.

The arguments in this **poor** example are presented from a selfish point of view.

This approach will do little to motivate the reader to accept the nomination. It is written from the sender's point of view—not from the receiver's. Charla will look at the nomination as nothing more than additional work with no corresponding benefits.

A **good** attempt to stimulate Charla's desire to accept the nomination follows:

> You would be consulted by the business leaders in the community. Promoting SPM would take some of your time, but this time would be well spent. Three of the last four presidents of SPM have been promoted to high-level management positions in their companies.

This **good** example points out the proof of the benefits to the receiver.

The benefits that Charla can gain from the position are clearly explained in the good example. Proof of the benefits that can result from being president are also shown. The negative aspect of the job—that it is time-consuming—is handled in a positive way. Charla should now be looking forward to accepting the nomination.

REQUEST ACTION FROM THE RECEIVER

Once Charla has been motivated to accept the nomination, request that she do so immediately. Charla's action of accepting the nomination should be made as easy as possible for her. A **poor** example of requesting action is shown here:

*This **poor** request for action is presented in a negative manner.*

> Charla, if you feel that you can spare the time to be president-elect, I would appreciate your writing a letter stating so. Make sure that you let me know because if you don't accept, I will have to find someone else.

This paragraph does little to motivate Charla to accept the nomination. The you-viewpoint is absent. The paragraph is negative; it emphasizes the alternative that she does not have to accept the position.

A **good** example of requesting action may be written as follows:

*The sender of this **good** example makes it easy for receiver to take action.*

> Please accept the nomination for president-elect of the Society of Professional Managers. Call me at 555-8701 with your decision by October 10 so that I may place your name on the ballot.

Notice the direct, positive approach used in this paragraph. Accepting the nomination is made easy for Charla simply by telephoning her acceptance.

SUMMARY—POOR AND GOOD MESSAGES TO CHARLA STAFFORD

Good and poor examples of constructing a persuasive message have been illustrated. The **poor** example paragraphs are combined as a letter in Illustration 12-2. This poor example of a persuasive request does not follow the guidelines for constructing persuasive messages.

The chances of Charla's accepting the president-elect nomination are improved in the **good** example shown in Illustration 12-3. This effective persuasive message follows the guidelines described earlier in this chapter.

This case problem shows how the indirect plan can be effective in communicating persuasive messages. To further assist in understanding the use of the indirect plan in organizing persuasive messages, several other examples of both good and bad messages will be illustrated in the following pages.

PERSUASIVE REQUESTS

Organizations use both simple requests and complex requests. The simple request was discussed in Chapter 10 and should be constructed with the direct plan. The complex request will have to convince the receiver to take a requested action and, therefore, uses the indirect plan.

In this section we will be concerned only with requests that require persuasion. Examples of persuasive requests are those that seek an increase in a department's budget, want a donation to a community organization, look for participants for a research project, desire a change in a work schedule, and want volunteers.

Illustration 12-4 is a **poor** example of a persuasive request for employees to donate to a company-sponsored charity. This example does not create any receiver interest. The memo is written from the writer's point of view rather than the receiver's. The employees will have little motivation to support this year's fund drive.

Illustration 12-5 is a **good** example of an interoffice memo that creates receiver motivation for the same situation. The memo gains attention, builds interest, stimulates desire, and makes taking action easy.

Organizational plans for **requests** may be:

- simple—*direct,* or
- complex—*indirect*

RECOMMENDATIONS

Individuals in business, government, and civic organizations periodically submit recommendations to receivers who are above, below, and at their same organizational levels. These written recommendations involve persuading the receiver to take an action proposed by the sender. They are most effective when the indirect persuasive plan is employed. Examples that should use the indirect plan include recommendations to a professional organization to endorse a political candidate, to a company officer to advise the firm to replace obsolete equipment, to a manager to change a company policy, and to a civic leader to use a tract of land for a city park rather than a housing project.

Illustration 12-6 shows a **poor** example of a recommendation from Mike Lynch, a supervisor, to Mindy Latimer, the manager, attempting to persuade her to give his division responsibility for manufacture of a new product. Mike probably will not be successful in his recommendation if the poor memo is submitted. This memo is aimed at Mike's desire to increase the size of his division rather than at the advantages to the company of his division

Recommendations are submitted at all organizational levels.

Recommendations are best when submitted in the indirect persuasive plan.

Illustration 12-2 **Poor** Example of a Persuasive Message

Society of Professional Managers
741 Braemar Blvd., Minneapolis, Minnesota 55435-2729
(612) 555-9201

September 12, 199–

Ms. Charla Stafford
Administrative Manager
Security Insurance Company
Minneapolis, MN 55440-6486

Dear Charla

Gains attention negatively.

The nominating committee has selected you as president-elect for the coming year. You would serve in this position for one year and next year would assume the duties of president.

Fails to show benefits.

This responsibility should not be taken lightly since it will take many hours each week to carry out all the duties. I know you are busy with your new position at Security Insurance Company, but all of us have a lot of work. One of the primary functions of the office is to improve the public relations between our organization and the community. I know you can do an effective job with this.

Emphasizes obstacles.

I know you are a busy person, but we certainly need someone to guide our organization. I feel you are the person who can do it. Our membership has grown significantly in the past two years; we feel you can maintain this growth pattern.

Fails to motivate receiver.

Charla, if you feel that you can spare the time to be president-elect, I would appreciate your writing a letter stating so. Make sure that you let me know because if you don't accept, I will have to find someone else.

Sincerely

Rick Suggs

Rick Suggs, Chairperson
Nominating Committee

jb

Illustration 12-3 **Good** Example of a Persuasive Message

Society of Professional Managers

741 Braemar Blvd., Minneapolis, Minnesota 55435-2729

(612) 555-9201

September 12, 199–

Ms. Charla Stafford
Administrative Manager
Security Insurance Company
Minneapolis, MN 55440-6486

Dear Charla

Your dedication and hard work over the past eight years have
been among the principal reasons for the outstanding growth of
the Society of Professional Managers. The nominating committee,
therefore, shows its appreciation to you for this service by
nominating you president-elect.

As president-elect you would be able to observe the operation of
the presidency and also would be able to assist the president
with various duties. You might be asked to attend a few activities that the president could not attend; these functions would
prepare you for assuming the position of president next year. As
you are aware, the organization does not pay its officers; but
the officers are exempt from paying dues.

You would be consulted by the business leaders in the community.
Promoting SPM would take some of your time, but this time would
be well spent. Three of the last four presidents of SPM have
been promoted to high-level management positions in their companies.

Please accept the nomination for president-elect of the Society
of Professional Managers. Call me at 555-8701 with your decision
by October 10 so that I may place your name on the ballot.

Sincerely

Rick Suggs

Rick Suggs, Chairperson
Nominating Committee

jb

Focuses attention on receiver.

Continues interest and keeps attention that was gained in first paragraph.

Emphasizes proof of benefits to receiver.

Motivates receiver while making action easy to take.

Illustration 12-4 **Poor** Example of a Persuasive Request

HUTCHINS ❧ CHEMICAL SUPPLY   Interoffice Memorandum

TO: All Employees

FROM: Robert McCann, Personnel Director *RM*

DATE: October 25, 199–

SUBJECT: Mountaintop Children's Home

The committee for selecting a charity for Hutchins to sponsor has chosen Mountaintop Children's Home this year. We need you to send your donation no later than November 15.

We need to beat the $8,700 that we gave to Needline last year. We think that Mountaintop is in more of a need than was Needline. This year's goal is $10,000.

If you need more information, read the enclosed brochure that gives all the details.

hf

Enclosure

Impersonal—does not gain attention.

Selfish—does little to build interest.

Vague—difficult for receiver to take action.

Illustration 12-5 **Good** Example of a Persuasive Request

HUTCHINS✿✿
CHEMICAL SUPPLY   Interoffice
                                       Memorandum

TO: All Employees

FROM: Robert McCann, Personnel Director ℛℳ

DATE: October 25, 199-

SUBJECT: Mountaintop Children's Home

Imagine Thanksgiving without turkey or Christmas without Santa ————————— Gains attention.
Claus.

The Mountaintop Children's Home makes sure this is not a reality
for the 45 children who live there. Mountaintop is a nonprofit
organization which provides care for children who have lost their ————— Builds interest.
parents. A brochure is enclosed describing the facilities and
services provided at the home.

Each year Hutchins Chemical Supply sponsors a charity selected
by a committee consisting of one member from each department.
This year we have pledged our support to Mountaintop. Last year
the employees of Hutchins generously gave $8,700 to Needline, ————— Provides details that
and we know that you will help us meet this year's $10,000 goal   stimulate desire.
for the Mountaintop Children's Home. Your contribution is tax
deductible.

Please return the enclosed pledge card by November 15. The
amount you select will be deducted from your paycheck. Feel free ——— Makes taking action
to call me for additional information.   easy.

hf

Enclosures

producing the new product. The memo is not written with the you-viewpoint, and it displays bitterness, which hinders communication. In addition, the memo is not written using the indirect plan—the key to successful persuasive messages.

The **good** memo in Illustration 12-7 should increase the chances of Mike's division gaining responsibility for the new product. Note how the indirect persuasive plan presents the advantages (of having Mike's division produce the telephones) before the recommendation. This memo gains the manager's attention in the opening, uses the you-viewpoint in presenting the reasons supporting the recommendation, and presents the recommendation in a positive, professional manner. Note that this memo does not question the manager's decision to give another division responsibility for the telephones. Furthermore, it does not imply that another division is favored.

SPECIAL CLAIMS

Special claims requiring persuasion should be written using the indirect plan.

Claims which are unique should use the indirect persuasive plan. Routine claims use the direct plan and were discussed in Chapter 10. Special or non-routine claims may require convincing the receiver that you are entitled to an adjustment or a refund.

Examples of special claims that should be organized as persuasive messages include the following: You want a roofing contractor, who has guaranteed his work, to replace the shingles on your office building because they are not aligned properly. A transportation company has purchased a fleet of 25 trucks, 20 of which have had to have their transmissions replaced in the first six months. The company wants the manufacturer to absorb the cost of the transmissions. A work of art (which was purchased for $50,000) was found to be a forgery; the buyer demands reimbursement from the gallery that sold it.

Illustration 12-8 is a **poor** example of a special claim letter from Frank Edwards, owner of Edwards' Tower. Frank contracted to have wallpaper hung in the fifth floor office suites of the tower, but the contractor hung the wrong pattern. It is easy to see that the writer of this letter is upset. The receiver's attention may be gained in the opening paragraph, but not in a way that will get the desired reaction. The writer does not clearly give the necessary details. The entire letter is negative, which will irritate the receiver and hinder getting the desired action—new wallpaper.

The letter in Illustration 12-9 covers the same situation but is a **good** example. Notice how the writer shows the receiver the benefits he can gain by replacing the wallpaper. The writer of this letter remains calm and explains the necessary details for the receiver. The positive tone of the letter will encourage cooperation from the receiver. The writer is courteous through-out the complaint but emphasizes that the contractor rehang the wallpaper and absorb the cost. Notice that a deadline for the completion of the job is given.

SALES MESSAGES

Sales messages come in many different forms, such as letters, brochures, leaflets, catalogs, radio and television commercials, and billboards. Most of these messages are prepared by professionals; however, you may one day be asked to compose one.

Before you compose a sales message, know the product or service you are going to sell. Know its strengths, its weaknesses, its competitors, and its market. As you compose the message, emphasize strengths and omit any mention of weaknesses. Your market should be carefully researched to deter-mine how to appeal to your customers and get their business.

Various techniques are used in sales messages to gain the receiver's attention: color, sentence fragments, catchy slogans, famous quotations, testi-monials from celebrities, and descriptions of benefits. A salutation is frequently omitted from the message.

Once you gain the receiver's attention, you must maintain his or her interest to ensure that the entire message is read or heard. A careful analysis of the receiver is critical in preparing the message from the receiver's point of view. Extra care must be taken in the analysis of the receiver because sales messages are usually prepared for multiple receivers.

A **poor** example of a sales message to retailers who may purchase from The Wizard Corporation is shown in Illustration 12-10. This message is not written from the you-viewpoint. The letter fails to point out the benefits of the product. The microcomputer's features are given, but the writer does not explain why it is good that the machine has these features. The request for action is weak. How should the customer "let us know"?

A **good** example of a sales letter is shown in Illustration 12-11. Note how this letter stresses the benefits that retailers will receive if they purchase the Little Wizard. The subject line is effective in gaining the reader's attention. Mentioning the dealer's profit will build interest. Notice how the letter inter-sperses benefits and proof of those benefits. It not only points out the capa-bilities of the microcomputer but also explains how these capabilities will benefit the purchaser. Notice how the postscript is used to emphasize an additional benefit for the receiver.

Most **sales messages** are prepared by professionals.

A careful analysis of the product or service should be considered before composing the sales material.

Receiver's attention is gained through different techniques.

An interested receiver will hear or read all of the message.

Illustration 12-6 **Poor** Example of a Recommendation Memo

ELECTRONICS, INC.

Interoffice
Memorandum

TO: Mindy Latimer, Manager

FROM: Mike Lynch, Product Supervisor *ML*

DATE: February 13, 199-

SUBJECT: Responsibility for Cordless Telephones

Uses selfish —————————— You are still not giving my division an opportunity to expand by
approach.   allowing it to produce the new cordless telephones.

Displays anger. ——————— I cannot believe that you selected Fred's division to develop the
                                  product. It seems that his division is always getting the
                                  breaks. His division already has responsibility for eight prod-
                                  ucts while mine only has four.

Demands action. ——————— You need to reconsider your decision. I would like to supervise
                                  the production of the new telephones.

                                  lw

Illustration 12-7 **Good** Example of a Recommendation Memo

ELECTRONICS, INC.

Interoffice
Memorandum

TO: Mindy Latimer, Manager

FROM: Mike Lynch, Product Supervisor *ML*

DATE: February 13, 199-

SUBJECT: Responsibility for Cordless Telephones

As you know, Division C has been a leading profit center for
Electronics, Inc., for each of the last three years. The four
products that it produces are in the top six of our most profitable products. One of the reasons that it is so profitable is
that Division C produces its products in less time than our competitors do, putting us in a favorable cost position.

Mindy, you realize that there will be high demand for Electronics' new cordless telephones. It will be critical that we mass-
produce these products quickly but with high quality. Division C
had the lowest quality-control rejection rate of Electronics'
four divisions during the last three years.

Another advantage of assigning Division C responsibility for
cordless telephone production is that it could assume this task
with only five new employees--three temporary and two permanent.
The other divisions would have to hire five permanent employees.
As you know, the installation of the new equipment will be completed by April 1, reducing Division C's personnel requirements.

I recommend that you give Division C responsibility for producing
the new cordless telephones.

lw

— Gains the manager's attention.

— Builds interest.

— Stimulates desire.

— Gives a recommendation.

Illustration 12-8 **Poor** Example of a Special Claim Letter

Edward's Tower
1355 Southfield Avenue
Lincoln Park, Michigan 48146-6430
(313) 555-2904

March 2, 199–

Mr. Ted Winklemann
Ted's Interior, Inc.
One Woodward Street
Detroit, MI 48229-7258

Dear Mr. Winklemann

Is negative. ——————— You need to replace the wallpaper in Edward's Tower
because it is not what I ordered.

Shows anger. ——————— I did not pay $8,600 to redecorate and then not have
the wallpaper properly match the carpeting. The tenant
is threatening to leave due to your careless error.

Demands action
rather than making ——————— I intend to have you replace all the paper on the fifth
a request. floor without charging me one dime. I need you to
replace it promptly before the tenant leaves, creating
another problem for me.

Sincerely

Frank Edward

Frank Edward
Owner

ns

Illustration 12-9 **Good** Example of a Special Claim Letter

Edward's Tower
1355 Southfield Avenue
Lincoln Park, Michigan 48146-6430
(313) 555-2904

March 2, 199-

Mr. Ted Winklemann
Ted's Interior, Inc.
One Woodward Street
Detroit, MI 48226-7258

Dear Mr. Winklemann

You were selected to redecorate my fifth floor office
suites because of your reputation as the best paint
contractor in Detroit.

You assisted me in selecting the wallpaper that would
match the new carpet on the fifth floor. In fact, I
paid an extra $4 a roll just to get perfect color
coordination.

On the day we finalized the arrangements, I told you I
would be out of town the week you would hang the paper.
We agreed that this should create no problem, but it
seems this was not true. Upon my return, I immediately
noticed that the wallpaper that had been hung was not
the color upon which we had agreed.

Because the paper is not the color that I had selected
and it does not match the new carpeting, please rehang
the wallpaper using the proper color. The occupant of
the suite needs the work completed by April 1.

Sincerely

Frank Edward

Frank Edward
Owner

ns

— Attracts attention
with praise.

— Gains interest by
giving details.

— Additional details
are given.

— Request is polite and
gives a deadline.

Illustration 12-10 **Poor** Example of a Sales Message

THE WIZARD CORPORATION   3370 Geary Blvd.
San Francisco, California 94118-8709
(415) 555-0447

June 9, 199–

Bob's Computers
1487 Huntington Avenue
South San Francisco, CA   94080-1614

Gentlemen

Opening is not from the you-viewpoint.

The Wizard Corporation has lowered its wholesale price on the Little Wizard microcomputer from $1,199 to $999.

Receiver's benefits are not pointed out.

The Little Wizard comes with two single-sided disk drives and 640K RAM. It has a 12-inch monochrome monitor which displays 25 lines of 80 characters. The monitor is available in green phosphor or amber. The Little Wizard uses the 8086 microprocessor.

The receiver's benefits are not reemphasized.

The Little Wizard is a good portable microcomputer. It is compatible with all software packages for the IBM Personal Computer. Another good feature is that it can be expanded with a 20Mbyte or a 40Mbyte hard disk drive.

The request for action is not positive.

Let us know if you want any Little Wizards at this reduced price. Remember our policy of an additional 5 percent discount if you order ten or more machines.

Sincerely

Lisa Downs

Lisa Downs, President

gv

Illustration 12-11 **Good** Example of a Sales Message

THE WIZARD CORPORATION 3370 Geary Blvd.
San Francisco, California 94118-8709
(415) 555-0447

June 9, 199–

Bob's Computers
1487 Huntington Avenue
South San Francisco, CA   94080-1614

LITTLE WIZARD REDUCED TO $999

You can now purchase the Little Wizard microcomputer with two
single-sided disk drives and 640K RAM for only $999. This low
price allows you to earn $250 if you sell it at the suggested
retail price of $1,249.

The 12-inch monochrome monitor of the Little Wizard is small
enough to make it portable but large enough to display 25 lines
of 80 characters. The monitor is available not only in green
phosphor but also in amber. The Little Wizard's 8086 microprocessor ensures that the computer can outperform any 8088-based
machine. The 8086 can process data several times faster than the
8088 can.

The Little Wizard's storage capacity can easily be expanded with
a 20Mbyte or 40Mbyte hard disk drive. The wholesale price of the
20Mbyte drive is only $675, and the 40Mbyte is only $1,075. This
expansion will allow customers to have the same capabilities that
they would have with regular-size microcomputers.

All software packages designed to run on the IBM Personal Computer will operate on the Little Wizard. This compatibility
allows the customer wide selection of programs. In addition,
many programs designed only for the Little Wizard are available.

Please place your order for these versatile machines by calling
our toll free number, 1-800-555-9675.

Lisa Downs
Lisa Downs, President

gv

P.S. You earn the 5 percent discount by ordering ten or more
machines.

Mention of profit gains attention.

The value of the characteristics is given.

Ease of expansion will interest some readers.

The availability of software will build desire to purchase computer.

Action can be taken easily.

COLLECTION MESSAGES

Collection messages are designed to collect money and build goodwill.

Collection messages are written in three stages.

Collection messages are used by business firms to collect overdue accounts. The two purposes of collection messages are to collect the money due and to retain goodwill with the customer.

Collection messages are written in several stages—reminder, appeal, and warning. Each stage is progressively more persuasive, and each stage has several steps within it. The number of steps in each stage will vary according to the type of business involved and the credit rating of the customer.

REMINDER STAGE

The *reminder stage* is for customers who forgot to pay.

This stage is for customers who intend to pay but just need a reminder. Collection messages in this category are not considered persuasive. These messages are normally only short notes or simply a sticker on a bill (see below).

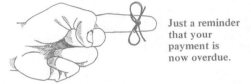

Just a reminder that your payment is now overdue.

Examples of collection messages in the reminder stage include:

Past Due
Reminder
Please Remit

Messages in the reminder stage are very courteous because failure to make a payment is often only an oversight. A harsh reminder may well alienate a customer who had intended to pay on time. If the reminder fails, the collection process will proceed to the appeal stage.

APPEAL STAGE

The *appeal stage* must effectively persuade the receiver.

A letter in the appeal stage is stronger than a reminder because the customer has failed to heed the reminder notice. You need to carefully analyze the customer before writing a letter in this stage. You will have to select the type of appeal that will persuade the customer to pay. You may appeal to the customer's pride, credit rating, morality, or reputation. Once you have selected the type of appeal to use, construct the message using the indirect persuasive outline.

A **poor** example of a collection letter in the appeal stage is shown in Illustration 12-12. This letter is too harsh. It is written from the writer's point of view and will cause anger, which will reduce rather than increase the chances of collection. Necessary details such as the amount due are not furnished.

The **good** collection letter in Illustration 12-13 is recommended for the appeal stage. It is written in a positive, courteous tone. The opening paragraph will get the customer's attention by appealing to his pride. The customer should feel that the store is trying to help him maintain his excellent credit reputation. The store's chances of collecting are greatly increased with this letter.

WARNING STAGE

Reminders and appeals may not succeed in extracting payment for all past due bills. When these efforts fail, you must move into the final stage—warning. Until now you were interested in maintaining the customer's goodwill while trying to collect. When the warning stage is reached, you are interested only in collecting the past due amount.

*The **warning stage** is used only when other stages have failed.*

This final collection attempt is a last chance warning to a customer to pay an account before it is transferred to a collection agency, a credit bureau, or an attorney. Use the direct plan in this stage.

A **poor** example of a collection message in the warning stage is shown in Illustration 12-14. The customer will be inclined to resist because of the anger shown here. The writer does not get directly to the warning in a firm manner without displaying anger. Notice that the amount is never given. The use of threats will not increase the writer's chances of collection and is illegal.

Illustration 12-15 is a **good** example of how a collection letter in the warning stage should be written. This letter gets directly to the main idea—the customer's account is past due and no attempt is being made to correct the problem. This letter does not show any sign of anger but gives the facts in a positive tone. In the last paragraph the customer is told exactly what must be done to avoid legal action.

Finally, let's summarize the approach that is used in each stage of collection messages.

Stage	Approach
Reminder	Direct
Appeal	Indirect
Warning	Direct

Your use of the guidelines and examples in this chapter will enable you to compose effective persuasive messages. The ability to do so will serve you well throughout your career.

Illustration 12-12 **Poor** Example of a Collection Message—Appeal Stage

---

KLAUSNER'S
Big & Tall Men's Store

2525 Far Hills Avenue, Dayton, Ohio 45419-3791, (513) 555-4678

---

21 September 199–

Mr. William Dumas
4726 Sycamore Drive
Dayton, OH 45432-8241

Dear Mr. Dumas

I am totally disappointed with you for not making a
payment on your overdue account. We must have our
money now.

We were generous with you by extending credit to you,
but then you let us down. I will have to inform the
Credit Bureau if I don't receive a payment in ten days.

Once again I appeal to you to make an immediate payment
so I don't have to destroy your credit reputation. I
am expecting payment by return mail.

Sincerely

Rebecca White

Rebecca White
Credit Manager

mf

Attacks the receiver too severely.

Written from the writer's point of view.

Too demanding.

Illustration 12-13 **Good** Example of a Collection Message—Appeal Stage

KLAUSNER'S
Big & Tall Men's Store

2525 Far Hills Avenue, Dayton, Ohio 45419-3791, (513) 555-4678

21 September 199-

Mr. William Dumas
4726 Sycamore Drive
Dayton, OH 45432-8241

Dear Mr. Dumas

It is clear that you take a lot of pride in your appearance because you selected our suits for your ward-
robe. Surely this pride extends to other aspects of
your life. — Uses pride appeal.

You have been a valued credit customer of ours for many
years, and we would like this relationship to continue.
For some reason you have not responded to the reminders
which were sent on August 10, August 25, and September
10. Your account is three months overdue. — Courteously reviews past actions.

Please send a check for $725.90 in the enclosed enve-
lope so that your credit reputation can remain highly
regarded. — Motivates receiver to take action.

Sincerely

Rebecca White

Rebecca White
Credit Manager

mf

Enc.

Illustration 12-14 **Poor** Example of a Collection Message—Warning Stage

KLAUSNER'S
Big & Tall Men's Store

2525 Far Hills Avenue, Dayton, Ohio 45419-3791, (513) 555-4678

November 15, 199-

Mr. William Dumas
4726 Sycamore Drive
Dayton, OH 45432-8241

Dear Mr. Dumas

We have been trying for five months to get you to pay
the balance due on your account. We can no longer
tolerate your getting by without paying when all the
rest of our customers pay promptly.

We are going to turn your account over to our attorney
if we do not get the money by November 22. You will be
sorry when this happens because we are giving the
attorney all authority to do anything to collect the
money.

Sincerely

Rebecca White

Rebecca White
Credit Manager

mf

Neglects the
you-viewpoint.

Threatens receiver.

Illustration 12-15 **Good** Example of a Collection Message—Warning Stage

KLAUSNER'S
Big & Tall Men's Store

2525 Far Hills Avenue, Dayton, Ohio 45419-3791, (513) 555-4678

November 15, 199-

Mr. William Dumas
4726 Sycamore Drive
Dayton, OH 45432-8241

Dear Mr. Dumas

Your account balance of $725.90 is five months past
due, and you have ignored all our collection attempts.   ——— Gains reader's attention.
This leaves us no choice but to turn the account over
to our attorney.

This is not a pleasant action for either of us but one
that has to be taken because of your negligence to   ——— Reminds reader of past actions.
respond to our previous notices. This action will be
expensive and embarrassing to you.

Our attorney assures us that if your account balance,
$725.90, is paid by November 22 no legal action will be   ——— Motivates receiver to take immediate action.
taken and your credit reputation will be maintained.
Please send the check in the enclosed envelope prior to
November 22 to avoid this action.

Sincerely

Rebecca White
Rebecca White
Credit Manager

mf

Enc.

DISCUSSION QUESTIONS

1. What are the two primary purposes of a persuasive message?
2. Describe three characteristics of the interest section of an indirect plan for persuasion.
3. Describe how an effective communicator builds desire in a persuasive message.
4. Identify the organizational plan that should be used in recommendations, and explain why it should be used.
5. Discuss the circumstances under which a claim message should be written using (a) the direct plan and (b) the indirect plan.
6. Discuss the analysis that should be completed before a sales message is composed.
7. Explain why the following paragraph would be ineffective in opening a sales message. Rewrite the paragraph to be more effective.

    We need to sell many Executive Typewriters. Our warehouse is full, and bills need to be paid.

8. Why is it especially important that a writer carefully analyze a customer before writing a collection letter in the appeal stage?
9. Identify and discuss the three stages of collection messages.

APPLICATION EXERCISES

1. Analyze a sales letter that has been received in your household. Identify the parts of the message that correspond to the parts of the organizational plan of persuasive messages.
2. Visit a business in your community and request copies of the various collection letters that it uses. Compare the approach used by the business and the approach discussed in this chapter.
3. Outline the ideas to include in the interest and desire sections of a message to send to your school's administration recommending that final examinations be eliminated.
4. Collect and review several advertisements from newspapers and magazines. Write a memo persuading your instructor to teach the approach of the ad that you believe is most effective.
5. Visit either an insurance agency or a real estate agency and ask what persuasive techniques have been most successful in selling policies or properties in the community. Lead a class discussion comparing the methods.

CASE PROBLEMS

PERSUASIVE REQUESTS

1. Cleo's Barbecue was established as a restaurant three years ago. Since the opening of the first restaurant, 26 additional establishments have been started in your state. As marketing director of Cleo's you are interested in determining whether Cleo's can expand to three neighboring states. Prepare a cover letter to send with a questionnaire designed to determine consumer support in these three states if the restaurants are opened. Your letter should persuade the individuals receiving the survey instruments to return them.

2. You feel that you have earned an A (or a B or C) in your Business Communication class. Your teacher would like you to convince him or her that you deserve the grade you selected. Write a persuasive memo; supply the necessary details.

3. Ann Jacobs has been working for your organization for five years and has been doing an outstanding job. In fact, she has been doing such an excellent job that you immediately granted the vacation dates she requested. Since granting that request, you have learned that the company auditors have scheduled their annual audit during the period that Ann would like her vacation. You need Ann in the office during the auditors' visit, and the visitation date cannot be changed. Write Ann a memo requesting that she change her vacation dates. If she changes her plans to a future date, you will grant her one additional week of paid vacation.

4. You are program director for the accounting organization on your campus. You have done an outstanding job which has resulted in your being asked to obtain the keynote speaker for this year's state conference. Mr. John Thompson, a local CPA, has spoken to your local chapter and has done an excellent job. Write a letter to Mr. Thompson requesting that he speak at no cost, except travel expenses, at the state conference. Add any details needed to make this a complete request.

5. You are the director of a wellness clinic at a local hospital. Doctors in the clinic wish to do a research project to help people lower blood pressure and cholesterol levels through diet and exercise rather than medication. Volunteers are needed to participate in the program. Write a personalized form letter to be sent to patients persuading them to volunteer for the project. Note that no monetary compensation will be given but that the weekly check-ups are provided without cost.

RECOMMENDATIONS

6. You are the Administrative Office Manager of the Professionals Insurance Company (PIC) home office. The company has outgrown its present facilities. You would like the company to construct a new building that would be designed specifically for PIC. The present facility could be remodeled and expanded for less money, but it would not be so luxurious, functional, or efficient as a new building. Write a memo to the company's president recommending the building of a new office headquarters. Include necessary details to increase the chances of your recommendation being approved.

7. You recently saw an educational display of coins and stamps in another city. You learned that this display can be brought to a city for three days at a cost of $5,000. You feel that the display would be of value to the students in your city. Write a memo to your supervisor recommending that she authorize your company to sponsor this display. Add any details to make the memo complete and persuasive.

8. Becky Wolf is an excellent clarinetist. She received many honors in high school. She is now working in Memphis, Tennessee, and has been identified as a potential member of the city's symphonic orchestra. She needs a personal letter of recommendation. Write a letter to the Memphis Symphony Orchestra Board of Directors telling them what an asset Becky would be.

9. You are the personnel director for Scurlock Department Store. It has been determined that employees of your organization are in need of communication training. Izumi Mori, the training director, has informed you that she has two options for providing this training. She can conduct the training using personnel in her division, or she can hire an outside consulting firm. You have not been particularly pleased with the in-house training in the past and would like her to hire Communicators, Inc. Write a memo to Izumi giving her your recommendation. Add any details to make the memo complete.

10. Bellville Savings and Loan has a policy that customers may borrow money only for a home in which they will reside. Many customers would like to purchase other property such as rental houses or weekend homes. Bellville Savings and Loan cannot loan the money but is willing to recommend them for credit at another financial institution. Write a personalized form letter that could be used to recommend these individuals. Supply necessary details.

SPECIAL CLAIMS

11. Rhonda Ragan bought her father an 1876 twenty-cent piece for $1,250. The coin was purchased from Ted's Numismatics as Uncirculated (MS-60). The coin showed wear on Liberty's kneecaps and hair, and there was wear on the eagle's breast on the reverse. Her father, an avid coin collector, graded the coin as Extremely Fine (XF) to About Uncirculated (AU). This coin in Grade XF-AU sells for about $275. Write a letter to Ted's Numismatics requesting a replacement coin or a check for $975. Add necessary details to make the letter complete.

12. You were recently involved in an automobile accident. As you were going to work early one morning, a deer jumped in your path. You were traveling at such a high rate that you could not avoid hitting the animal. Your damages are estimated at $1,495. An accident report was filed, and you did not receive a ticket. Your insurance company will only pay $800; it feels you were partially responsible because you were traveling too fast. Write a letter to your insurance company asking it to pay the full amount.

13. Your accounting firm purchased an accounting software package from Wizards Software, Inc., for $3,800. This package was advertised to be capable of handling up to 2,000 entries each month, handling up to 500 accounts, and providing graphs with periodic reports. The package does not measure up to what was advertised. You need to write a letter to Wizards informing them that you would like a refund. Its address is 320 Software Lane, Dallas, Texas 75227-0391.

14. Bill Porter owns an orchard containing 1,000 peach trees. This spring Bill purchased 100 peach trees that were later found to be diseased. These trees not only died but caused 500 other trees to die. Write a letter for Bill to Greenbriar Nursery requesting replacement trees or a $12,000 refund to cover the cost of the trees and the labor.

15. Holiday Tours is an agency that arranges package tours for clients. Often clients return from a tour and complain that accommodations did not meet the standards described in the brochures. Prepare a personalized form letter that could be sent to hotels and motels asking for a refund for a dissatisfied customer.

SALES MESSAGES

16. You are treasurer of your student business organization and have made arrangements with a local nursery for your organization to receive $2 for

each mum corsage sold for homecoming. Write a form letter that could be sent to students promoting the sale of these corsages. Add the necessary details to make the letter complete.

17. You work at Video Sounds. You have been asked to write a VCR advertisement. The ad will be distributed as a flyer in the school paper. All VCRs will be marked down 20 percent during the last week of the month. Features of the VCRs include 4 heads, on-screen programming, 8-event timer, and 30-function remote. VCRs permit students to attend classes without missing their favorite television programs.

18. Ralph Dupont is building a new home in an exclusive neighborhood in New Orleans, Louisiana. Most homes in this neighborhood have tennis courts, swimming pools, sauna rooms, and hot tubs. Write a sales letter to Ralph convincing him to purchase a hot tub from your company, Relaxation Experts. Add the necessary details.

19. Reed's Furniture has been operating as a retail furniture store in your hometown for 25 years. It has recently decided to expand its stock to include waterbeds. The Comfort Sleep, which Reed's will sell, offers standard-, queen-, and king-size waterbeds. A complete waterbed with mattress, heater, and bed frame will start at $199.99. Write a letter to your customers announcing the addition of waterbeds to your inventory. Add details to make the letter complete and to gain the reader's attention.

20. Greek Publications is a magazine sales clearinghouse that offers sororities and fraternities an opportunity to make money through sales projects. The clearinghouse has a publication list of 300 nationally known magazines and a selection of more than 500 records and tapes. The organizations earn 30 percent of the total proceeds from the drive. Develop a form letter that could be sent to the presidents of professional and social Greek organizations on college campuses throughout the country.

COLLECTION MESSAGES

21. St. Anthony Laundry permits its commercial customers to pay monthly. The Scenic Hills Lodge is four months past due in its payments. This has just been brought to your attention. You would like to keep Scenic Hills as a customer, but you need to collect the past-due balance of $735. At a meeting with Scenic Hills' manager, Debbie Kramer, it was agreed that the motel would pay $50 per month on the past-due balance and cash for the laundry delivered each month. Since the meeting with Debbie, the motel has operated on a cash basis for each month but has made no payments on the past-due balance. Write a letter to Debbie reminding her of the agreement to make payments on the past-due account.

22. Dee Grayson bought a watch from Diamonds Unlimited for $429.35. She has a balance due of $310.15 and has not made a payment in four months. She has been a faithful customer in the past, and Diamonds Unlimited does not want to lose her business. However, Diamonds' manager is concerned because Dee has not responded to four collection letters. Write a letter to Dee that will convince her to resume paying on her account and that will maintain her goodwill.

23. You are the branch manager of Northern Optical Center. Nine months have passed since you sold George Huckabay a pair of Softezee contact lenses for $275. George made a down payment of $50 and has not made any additional payments. You sent him four reminders and five letters appealing for your money. You are no longer interested in maintaining a good customer relationship with Mr. Huckabay; you simply wish to collect your $225. Write a warning collection letter to Mr. Huckabay requesting immediate payment. If this payment is not received within 15 days, you will forward the account to a collection agency. Add details to the letter to make it complete.

24. Cosmetology Supplies Company sells beauty supplies to hair care shops in a six-state area. Credit is extended to each business after a credit check is conducted. Nanci's Salon accumulated a credit balance of $736.89 over a six-month period before Cosmetology Supplies revoked Nanci's credit privileges. Nanci's has been sent six collection letters to which no response has been obtained. Write a letter for the collection office informing Nanci's that it must pay the $736.89 balance within ten days or the account will be forwarded to an attorney.

25. Acme Finance Company's primary business is loaning money to individuals for purchasing used cars. Often individuals will make payments for a period of time and suddenly stop paying on their accounts. Sometimes a reminder will get them to continue their payments, while sometimes it will not. Write a form letter that could be individualized for each customer requesting payment to update the account. Add necessary details.

GOODWILL MESSAGES

L E A R N I N G   O B J E C T I V E S

Your learning objectives for this chapter include the following:

- To understand the nature of goodwill messages
- To recognize the six common uses of goodwill messages and know how to compose each
- To understand the three styles of goodwill messages and the criteria used in selecting each

The purpose of some messages is to promote goodwill.

Previous chapters have stressed the use of the you-viewpoint and the creation of goodwill. It has been suggested that you maintain good relationships with receivers by personalizing good news, bad news, and persuasive messages. Certain messages have only one purpose, however, and that is to convey goodwill.

Goodwill messages are written to communicate your concern and interest. Sending a goodwill message shows that you care about the receiver.

Positive opinions are formed by goodwill messages.

Avoid canceling the positive effects by inserting statements that will cause the receiver to think you are simply trying to further a business relationship. Your goodwill messages should cause your receiver to form a positive opinion of you—the sender of the message. Timeliness is of utmost importance; goodwill can be lost if a message is received six weeks after an event.

USES OF GOODWILL MESSAGES

Goodwill messages may be sent for various reasons: congratulations, condolence, appreciation, invitation, holiday greetings, and welcome.

Certain occasions call for goodwill messages.

CONGRATULATIONS

Everyone enjoys receiving praise. One of the reasons that congratulatory messages are so effective in building goodwill is that organizations and businesspersons do not use them very often. Congratulatory messages may be as formal as a typewritten letter or as informal as a handwritten note attached to a newspaper clipping of a birth announcement.

*Timely **congratulatory messages** are effective.*

Congratulatory messages are sent to both individuals and organizations. The occasion that warrants such a message may be either personal or business in nature. A congratulatory message may be sent to an individual on the occasion of a business related accomplishment such as attaining the highest sales for the month, retiring after 30 years of service, or receiving a promotion. You also may send a congratulatory message to an individual for a personal event such as a birthday, an engagement, a marriage, a birth, or an election to office in a social or civic organization. A business firm could receive a message of congratulations for expansion of its company, relocation to a new building, announcement of a new product, or celebration of an anniversary.

Congratulatory messages are sent for accomplishments or special occasions.

Congratulatory business messages should be written in a personal, sincere manner. A direct approach should be used by immediately mentioning the honor or accomplishment. The message should focus on the receiver from start to finish. A closing that refers to the writer's help or assistance diminishes goodwill. A congratulatory letter to an individual for being elected to an office is shown in Illustration 13-1.

*A **direct approach** should be used in composing a congratulatory message.*

CONDOLENCE

Letters of condolence or sympathy are difficult to write because they deal with misfortune; but when written properly, they should leave no doubt about your empathy and, more importantly, should help ease the pain of the receiver.

*Messages of **condolence** must be sincere.*

Messages of sympathy may be sent for an illness, death, natural disaster, or other misfortune. They may be typewritten or handwritten, or they may be in the form of a printed card. Handwritten messages are by far the most personal and will be the most appreciated.

Illustration 13-1 Congratulatory Letter

Broadwerth Enterprises, Inc.

8823 Outhaul Lane
Cheyenne, Wyoming 82001-3252
(307) 555-0708

April 17, 199-

Ms. Sarah Lewis
Seashells Galore
561 Ocean Drive
Charleston, SC 29404-1354

Dear Sarah

Offer
congratulations. ——————— Congratulations on being elected president of the
Eastern Retailers Association. The association will
benefit greatly from your leadership.

Give compliments. ——————— By electing you to this high office, members of the
association are showing their recognition of your
ability to lead and your dedication to the profession.
You should be proud of the confidence that they place
in you.

Use friendly close. ——————— If I can assist you during your presidency, please call
on me.

Sincerely

Ralph Woods

Ralph Woods
President

dk

The direct approach should be used for condolence letters. Begin with the purpose of the message—conveying sympathy. Only the necessary details need to be mentioned, and these should be treated positively and sincerely. For example, in a letter of sympathy prompted by the death of a loved one, rather than eulogizing the deceased person, it is better to assure the survivor that she or he was appreciated and loved by the deceased person.

Make a sympathy letter short and positive.

If appropriate, a letter of condolence can offer assistance. Your message may be concluded by referring to the future in a positive way. Illustration 13-2 shows a letter sent to a business friend whose building was destroyed by a tornado.

APPRECIATION

Most people do not expect rewards for acts of kindness or thoughtfulness; however, we all enjoy knowing that our efforts are appreciated.

Letters of appreciation may be sent for longtime thoughtfulness or for a onetime favor. Some examples of individuals who have shown sustained thoughtfulness are a long-standing, loyal customer; a faithful employee for many years; a friend who has consistently recommended a company and brought it many customers; and a volunteer who has generously contributed time and effort to charitable causes. Letters expressing thanks to such persons are always appropriate. Some examples of letters of gratitude for onetime favors are a complimentary letter from a customer to a service department, a letter to a guest speaker who has given an excellent presentation, a letter to a new customer, a letter to a new member of an organization, and a letter to someone who has found a lost article and returned it to the owner.

*Messages of **gratitude** show your appreciation.*

Letters of appreciation should follow the direct approach. The good news—the expression of gratitude—should be given in the first paragraph and be followed by supporting evidence in a second or succeeding paragraphs. The letter should conclude with a comment of appreciation in the final paragraph. The thought of the letter, not the length of the letter, is the important consideration. A letter thanking a client for recommending a prospective home buyer to a realtor is shown in Illustration 13-3.

Thank the receiver in the first paragraph.

INVITATION

Business invitations are used in various situations. Inviting employees to a small social gathering, asking prominent community members to attend a fund-raising event, inviting civic leaders and selected customers to a company open house are all examples of invitations that are currently used in

Illustration 13-2 Condolence Letter

Sommers Printing

839 Powder Circle
Lexington, Virginia 24450-3223
(804) 555-8072

November 11, 199–

Mr. Richard Whitehead
The Bedford Gazette
105 Printers Alley
Bedford, VA 24523-3004

Dear Dick

Convey sympathy.

The people in our organization were disturbed upon
learning that yesterday's tornado caused much destruc-
tion in your community and to your building. We express our sympathy to all of The Gazette's employees.

Offer assistance.

You are welcome to use our facilities, at no cost, to
print your newspaper until your facility has been
restored. We are interested in helping you maintain
the 75-year tradition of uninterrupted service to your
community. If you need further assistance, please let
me know.

Use positive close.

Dick, The Gazette will overcome this disaster and continue providing the excellent news service to the Bedford area that it has provided for so many years. Best
wishes to you for a quick return to normal operations!

Sincerely

Viola Sommers

Viola Sommers
Owner

hj

Illustration 13-3   Letter of Appreciation

PERRIN REALTY

145 Rocky Lane
Stillwater, Oklahoma 74074-5557
(918) 555-5856

June 6, 199–

Mr. Bill Barnett
975 Langdon Drive
Stillwater, OK 74074-4759

Dear Bill

Thank you for recommending Perrin Realty to Ms. Carol Richerson. You can be sure that we are doing our best to locate a home for Carol in which she will be comfortable and proud to live.   — Say thank-you.

Carol is a welcome addition to our community. I know that you must be most pleased to have hired a person of such caliber.   — Give supporting comments.

Bill, your confidence in Perrin Realty is appreciated. We welcome seeing any clients that you can send us and will do everything we can to locate a residence which is right for them.   — Express appreciation.

Sincerely

Robert Perrin

Robert Perrin
President

ad

the business community. A form letter inviting selected local citizens to a
$15-a-plate dinner recognizing honor students is shown in Illustration 13-4.

An invitation may be
formal or informal.

An invitation may be handwritten, it may be typed on company stationery, or it may be a formal, printed invitation. It should include all the
necessary details such as the date, time, place, and suggested dress. In order
to plan efficiently, an invitation should include an *R.S.V.P.*; that is, a request
for a reply to the invitation.

HOLIDAY GREETINGS

Holiday greetings may
be sent to celebrate
festive seasons.

Holiday greeting messages can be sent before or during any festive season.
New Year's Day, Easter, Labor Day, Thanksgiving, Hanukkah, and Christmas
are holidays generally celebrated in the United States. Businesses participating
in international trade should be aware of and acknowledge appropriate holidays
in those countries where they have employees, customers, or suppliers.

A greeting card is often
used.

Many companies send season's greetings cards to customers or suppliers.
These greetings usually have the company name printed on the card. Executives and sales representatives may use a different kind of company card on
which they can write personalized greetings to business friends and colleagues.
Some companies send distinctively designed cards that bear the company
name and logo. This type of card is impressive because it is unique to the
organization sending it. Individualized holiday greeting letters are sent by
some business firms.

Illustration 13-5 shows a company letter to employees that contains
a holiday greeting and includes a token of appreciation for the employee's
efforts during the past year. Along with wishes for a happy holiday season, the
letter anticipates a prosperous year ahead.

WELCOME

Welcome letters are
appropriate for new
employees, new customers,
or new community
members.

Welcome messages build goodwill for a company. Such messages may be
used to greet new employees and to familiarize them with the company. Many
cities have organizations, such as the Welcome Wagon, that send welcome
letters to persons moving into the community. These letters usually include
special offers, coupons, small gifts, and other enticements from business firms
wishing to attract new customers.

Welcome letters are frequently sent to new customers, particularly to
those who are establishing credit with the store. These messages are used to
congratulate the customer on opening a charge account with the store and to
offer an incentive to the new customer to use the store's facilities in the near
future. Illustration 13-6 is an example of such a letter.

Illustration 13-4   Letter of Invitation

PARENTS FOR IMPROVED EDUCATION

P. O. BOX 1006
ANNISTON, ALABAMA 32061-1006
(205) 555-4158

April 15, 199–

**(Individualized
Inside
Address)**

Dear **(Name)**

You are invited to join PIE for dinner at the Country
Steak House on May 12 at 6:30 p.m. to honor the out-
standing May graduates from Anniston High School. ———————— Extend invitation.

The $15 price per plate includes a steak dinner (with
all the trimmings) for you and your guests and helps to ———————— Give details.
provide complimentary dinners for the honor students.

Through your commitment to the community, you have set
a fine example for the students of Anniston High
School. Your participation in this important community
function will make possible the recognition of these
students' high academic achievements.

Please send your reservations for yourself and your
guests by April 29. Checks should be made payable to ———————— Request reply.
Parents for Improved Education.

Sincerely

Thomas Seymour

Thomas Seymour
President

Illustration 13-5   Seasonal Greeting

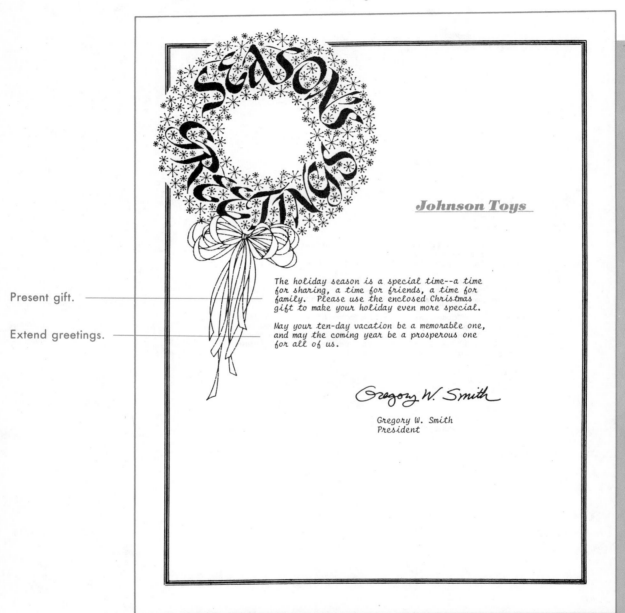

Johnson Toys

Present gift.

Extend greetings.

The holiday season is a special time--a time
for sharing, a time for friends, a time for
family. Please use the enclosed Christmas
gift to make your holiday even more special.

May your ten-day vacation be a memorable one,
and may the coming year be a prosperous one
for all of us.

Gregory W. Smith

Gregory W. Smith
President

Illustration 13-6   Welcome Letter for New Credit Customer

SCOTT AND TOM'S FURNITURE
1710 Eudy Drive
Vicksburg, Mississippi 39180-9512
(601) 555-3904

October 12, 199-

Ms. Helen Underhill
856 War Road
Vicksburg, MS   39180-6296

Dear Helen

Welcome to the convenience of credit card buying at
Scott and Tom's Furniture. You will find this service   ———— Welcome customer.
an easy way to purchase home furnishings.

The credit agreement for your account is enclosed.
Please take a moment to read it. If you have any questions, please call me. I will be happy to help you.

Scott and Tom's is pleased to have you as a charge
customer, and it truly appreciates your business. To   ———— Show appreciation.
show its appreciation, you will receive a 15 percent
discount on your first credit purchase within 30 days.

Sincerely

Scott Eudy

Scott Eudy, Finance Manager

mi

Enc.

STYLE IN GOODWILL MESSAGES

A goodwill message is an effective way to build a positive relationship with a customer, an employee, or a supplier. Style is important in accomplishing the purpose of the communication.

HANDWRITTEN VERSUS TYPEWRITTEN VERSUS PRINTED MESSAGES

A goodwill message may be handwritten, typed, or printed.

You must decide whether a goodwill message should be handwritten, typewritten, or printed. A handwritten note is appropriate in times of sorrow; but a printed invitation to a social function is preferred whether it is for a small wedding or a dinner and dance for several hundred people. A typewritten message is normally used to welcome a customer or employee to a business. The form that is most effective for conveying your message should be the basis of your decision.

CARD VERSUS LETTER

Whether to select a card or a letter depends on the occasion.

A commercially produced card is less time consuming and frequently is more suitable than a typed letter. A short, handwritten note on a holiday greeting card or a card of sympathy may mean more to the receiver than a long, formal letter. However, a typewritten welcome letter to a new credit customer is the preferred business procedure.

FAMILIARITY VERSUS FORMALITY

How well you know the receiver dictates the formality of the message.

The formality of a goodwill message depends on the type of message you are sending and on how well you know the receiver. Put yourself in the place of the receiver and write a letter that you would like to receive—whether the message must of necessity be phrased in formal language or whether the nature of the message permits you to be relaxed and informal.

DISCUSSION QUESTIONS

1. Explain why a business or a businessperson should send goodwill messages.
2. Describe how a congratulatory message should be composed.
3. Briefly discuss the different ways that an organization may transmit holiday greetings to its customers.
4. Describe the approach that should be used in composing a thank you letter.
5. Describe how welcome messages to new customers are different from welcome messages to new employees.
6. Cite three factors that must be considered in selecting the style to use in goodwill messages.

APPLICATION EXERCISES

1. Visit a business in your community and determine the types of goodwill messages it uses. Obtain copies of the messages if possible. Report your findings orally to the class.
2. Describe to the class any unique holiday greetings that you have received from business firms. Discuss the effectiveness of these greetings in gaining your goodwill and encouraging you to patronize the company.
3. Design a birthday card that can be printed and used by a business in your community.
4. Design an ad that could be placed in your school paper welcoming new students to campus on behalf of your student organization. This ad also needs to inform the students of your student organization.

CASE PROBLEMS

CONGRATULATIONS

1. You work for a restaurant supply company. Recently, one of the restaurants in your territory has been awarded a five-star rating by a dining

association. Prepare a letter that can be sent to this restaurant congratulating it on the accomplishment. Add any necessary details.

2. Gerald Hoskins is the information processing supervisor for your employer, Brown and Wentworth, Legal Associates. He has recently completed the requirements for the Certified Administrative Manager (C.A.M.) designation. Compose a message congratulating Gerald on his accomplishment. Add any necessary details to make this a complete message.

3. Reed Cothern has recently driven his one-millionth accident-free mile for Sunnyvale Bus Lines and, thus, will receive the Master Driver's Award from the bus line. Fewer than 10 percent of the drivers achieve this status. You are the public relations officer for the United Bus Drivers (a nationwide union). Write a letter to Reed congratulating him on his accomplishment. Add any necessary details to make this a complete letter.

4. You are production manager for Mathis Electronics Supplies. Each year several employees in your department have children graduate from high school. You try to generate goodwill by sending these graduates a congratulatory message. Prepare a form letter that could be sent to these graduates congratulating them on their accomplishment.

CONDOLENCE

5. A friend of yours, Natalie Hobbs, does not attend your school. She has just completed a national campaign for president of a student organization at her school. She lost the election by a close margin. Write Natalie a letter expressing your sorrow at her loss.

6. The Doe Run Farm operates a breeding and horse-racing business. Today in the Kentucky Open, Quick Buck developed a fracture that will cause him to be retired to stud service. As a racing enthusiast, write a letter to Dan Whitney, the manager of Doe Run Farm, expressing condolences for the misfortune. Add any necessary details to make this a complete message.

7. David Travis is executive director of your community's industrial foundation. He has been trying for more than six months to get a company to relocate to your community. Yesterday, this company announced that it was relocating to another city. David is extremely dejected and is giving consideration to resigning his position as executive director. Compose a condolence letter to David that will show your support for him.

8. You are president of a financial institution in a small community. Earlier this week a school bus transporting students to a conference in a nearby town was involved in an accident in which 14 children died. Many of the parents of these school children were customers of your organization. Write a letter that can be sent to the parents expressing your sorrow.

APPRECIATION

9. The photographer for your local newspaper took pictures at a handicapped children's field day that your student organization sponsored. Yesterday, the newspaper had an entire page devoted to this event. You feel that the photographer was instrumental in getting this event so well publicized. Write the editor of the newspaper expressing your appreciation for the photographer's excellent work.

10. Jane Sickle has been a faithful volunteer with the Hospice Program for five years. She has given freely of her time and energy. Write a letter to Jane thanking her for her contribution.

11. Florence Simmons works as an adjustor for LMO Insurance Company. She is retiring after 38 years of service. Florence is a conscientious employee who has performed admirably. Write a letter thanking her for her dedication and service. Add any necessary details to make a complete message.

12. Many individuals donate their time as volunteers to the public library in your town. Eight of these individuals have been volunteers for more than ten years. You are the publicity chair for the Community Volunteer Association and would like to send each of them a letter showing your appreciation for their services. Compose a form letter that can be sent to each volunteer.

INVITATION

13. Your company owns a condominium on Mount Royale Island. Each year you invite several of your better customers to spend a week at the condominium. You would like to invite Cathy Maddox and her family to spend a week at the condominium during the month of July. Write a letter inviting Cathy and her family, and ask her to select the week that she would like to use the condominium.

14. You are the department manager at Vance Appliances and are having an informal dinner in your home for your employees. Each employee may bring a guest. Write an invitation that can be duplicated and given to each employee.

15. The computer club at your school is displaying its programming projects for the past year. Write a memo that the school can send to all parents inviting them to this computer fair.

16. You belong to a community service organization that is sponsoring a fish fry to raise money to send underprivileged children to summer camps. You are responsible for sending personalized invitations to businesspersons in your community inviting them to the fish fry. Prepare this invitation adding necessary details to make it complete.

HOLIDAY GREETINGS

17. Hi-Tech Communications is renting a boat for its employees for a Fourth of July celebration. The company will provide refreshments and a live band as the boat cruises for five hours on the river. Prepare a memo that can be sent to the employees informing them of this holiday activity.

18. White Heating and Air Conditioning is providing an old-fashioned family picnic at Wildcat Lake on Memorial Day. All the employees are invited and are encouraged to bring their families or guests. You are the personnel manager for this organization. Write a memo announcing this picnic and wishing the employees a happy holiday. Include all necessary details.

19. Barrett's Insurance Agency would like to extend holiday greetings to its customers for the new year. Prepare a letter that Barrett's can send to express New Year greetings to its clients.

20. The Hermann Furniture Store wishes to express its appreciation to its customers by presenting them with carving sets for Thanksgiving. It is your responsibility to compose a letter that a customer can present in exchange for a carving set. This is the store's way of wishing customers a happy Thanksgiving.

WELCOME

21. You are the personnel manager for Integrated Computer Services. Felicia Johnson recently was hired as a systems analyst. Felicia was an honor graduate of a prestigious university; she was highly recruited. You want to make Felicia feel at home and consider ICS her place of employment for many years. Write a letter welcoming Felicia. Add necessary details.

22. Sharon Knight has opened a checking account at your financial institution. Write a letter to Sharon welcoming her as a customer.

23. The local Neighbor's Watch Committee is interested in the security of the neighborhood. It is planning to have a block party next Friday to meet residents who have recently moved into the neighborhood. The party will be held at the Community Center on Martin Street at 7:30 p.m. Soft drinks and snacks will be available. A representative from the local police force will give a presentation on home security at 8 p.m. Write a message welcoming newcomers to the neighborhood and inviting them to attend the party.

24. You are a part-time employee for Ken's Seafood. Prepare a letter to be sent to incoming freshmen at your school welcoming them to your community. In the letter invite them to Ken's for a free lunch.

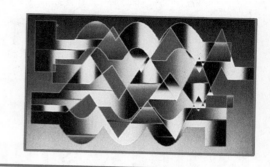

PART FOUR

WRITTEN REPORT APPLICATIONS

BUSINESS STUDIES AND PROPOSALS

LEARNING OBJECTIVES

Your learning objectives for this chapter include the following:

- To understand and appreciate the importance of business studies and proposals
- To learn how to use the five steps for conducting a business study
- To learn how to write a successful proposal

Conducting studies and preparing proposals are frequent tasks in business.

Frequently, managers and employees in business conduct studies or prepare proposals. The systematic procedures used to conduct a business study are called *research methods*. These methods will be discussed in the first part of this chapter. The last part of this chapter provides guidelines for preparing proposals. Report preparation and graphic aids for reports and proposals will be covered in Chapters 15 and 16.

BUSINESS STUDIES

Studies are made to solve problems and make improvements.

Business studies are conducted and reports written for many reasons. Such studies may result in new procedures, new products, new markets, or other new ways to increase profits. Studies are conducted to determine solutions to problems, make recommendations for improvements, or offer proposals for actions. From these studies, reports are written for the consideration of management. Such reports contain solutions, recommendations, and proposals developed through the business studies. Conducting a study is a common activity, and everyone in business should know how to complete a study and record the results in a report.

CONDUCTING A STUDY

The five steps in conducting a business study are:

1. Plan the study.
2. Gather information.
3. Analyze the information.
4. Determine solution(s).
5. Write the report.

There is a common, overall approach for conducting business studies.

Steps 1 through 4 are discussed in the next four major sections of this chapter. As mentioned previously, Step 5 is discussed in Chapters 15 and 16.

PLANNING THE STUDY

Planning the study includes stating the problem of the study, setting the boundaries of the study, determining the readers of the report, and deciding on the procedures to be followed in completing the study.

The first major step is to **plan the study**.

STATING THE PROBLEM. A clear, accurate written statement of the problem of the study can serve as an agreement about what is to be studied. Prior to arriving at this statement, there may be discussions within the organization about what the study should accomplish. A preliminary investigation of the situation that prompted the study may be made to help define the problem of the study. You may look at files, talk to employees, read other similar reports, talk to vendors, or make any number of preliminary inquiries to help you clarify what needs to be studied.

Start planning by stating the problem.

After this preliminary consideration, you can develop a statement of the problem of the study. Here are examples of problem statements for studies:

1. To determine ways to improve the morale of ABC Company employees.
2. To design a new procedure for the company's annual inventory.
3. What is the best store location for cash registers?
4. Should microcomputers be purchased to replace the typewriters in the Information Processing Center?

Problem statements can
use either the infinitive or
the question form.

Next, set the study
boundaries.

What factors will you
study?

What time schedule will
you follow?

How much will the study
cost?

Notice that the first two examples are infinitive statements while the last two examples are presented as questions. Either form is appropriate.

SETTING THE BOUNDARIES OF THE STUDY. A study needs to have boundaries. These boundaries are determined by defining the scope of the study, setting up a time schedule, and estimating budget allowances.

DEFINING THE SCOPE OF THE STUDY. The scope of the study is defined by determining the factors that will be studied. It will be best to limit the amount of information you will gather to the most needed and most important factors. The factors for one of the problem statements given previously might look like this:

Statement of Problem: To determine ways to improve the morale of ABC Company employees.

Factors:
1. Salaries
2. Fringe benefits
3. Work assignments
4. Work hours
5. Evaluation procedures

You could study many other factors relative to improving employee morale. Some may be important, and you may want to consider them later. For any one study, however, a reasonable scope must be clearly defined by determining what factors will be included.

SCHEDULING THE STUDY. An agreement should be made on when the report of the study is needed or when it will be possible to complete the report. Working back from the report deadline, a time schedule should be set for the study indicating when each step is to be completed. Using the steps for conducting a business study, a time schedule could look like the one in Illustration 14-1. The time schedule shown there is called a **Gantt chart**. It shows clearly when each major task will be worked on and completed. It also shows that some tasks can be worked on at the same time. For example, it is possible to write preliminary parts of the report while you are completing the analysis of the information. Time schedules should be as detailed as necessary so everyone understands exactly what is to be done and when.

BUDGETING THE STUDY. All studies cost money. Even studies that are conducted within an organization will have some costs above normal operating costs. A large organization may use a charge-back system to bill one department for having work done by another. For example, if you are doing a study for the personnel department, the computer department may charge the personnel department for processing the survey results. In addition, the printing department may charge the personnel department for printing the report. There may be other study costs for such items as personnel time, supplies, and postage. All costs should be estimated and a budget approved before the study officially begins.

Tasks	Time								
	May					June			
	1	8	15	22	29	5	12	19	26
Plan Study	▬								
Collect Information		▬▬▬▬▬▬							
Analyze Information					▬▬▬				
Determine Solutions							▬		
Write Report								▬▬▬	

Illustration 14-1   Time Schedule

DETERMINING THE READERS OF THE REPORT.

Effective communication depends on using the you-viewpoint in all written and oral messages. This is certainly true for written reports. The way in which you write the results of your study should be determined by your readers' knowledge, interests, opinions, and emotional states—the key factors in analyzing readers. When there will be primary and secondary readers of the report, both should be analyzed. If, for example, you are a financial manager writing a report for which colleagues in the field are primary readers, you can use the technical language of finance because it will be understood by other financial managers. If members of the general management staff, members of the production management staff, general employees, or stockholders are secondary readers, you may want to define your terms the first time you use them or include a list of terms and definitions as an appendix.

Analyze the receivers of the report.

DECIDING ON THE STUDY PROCEDURES.

You need to determine the procedures to follow in completing each step in the overall study. A comprehensive study will result if these procedures are carefully planned. You may want to seek the advice of a professional consultant. If, for example, you are going to use statistical procedures to analyze the information you gather, be sure the procedures selected will give you valid and reliable results. A professional statistician can help with the selection of appropriate procedures. Some questions that must be answered may be: Will I use information about the topic that is already printed? Will I survey employees? Will I seek information from outside the company? Will I use a computer to analyze the information? Will the report be typed or printed?

Finally, in planning the report, decide on procedures.

Deciding on procedures for each step in your study simply means deciding exactly how to carry out that step. The procedures you actually select will vary from study to study.

GATHERING INFORMATION

You may gather information for your study from one or more sources.
There are two basic types of information sources: secondary and primary.
Secondary sources of information are the published materials on the topic.
Primary sources include individuals, company files, observations, and
experiments.

SECONDARY SOURCES OF INFORMATION. Published
materials on most topics are readily available in company, public, and
college libraries. Experienced reference librarians can provide valuable assistance in finding published information that will be helpful in your study.
They can direct you to indexes, catalogs, reference books, government
documents, computer data bases, and other helpful secondary sources of
information.

Of particular value to businesspersons today are computerized searches
of published information on a given topic. Most reference librarians can assist
you in searches that quickly give you an up-to-date bibliography of reference
materials on your topic and sometimes abstracts of the materials. With this
information you can go to microfilm files, book stacks, or other appropriate
locations to examine the available information in greater depth.

If your study requires gathering information from both primary and
secondary sources, you should gather secondary source information first. The
published information may contain good ideas on what primary information
you should gather and how you can gather it.

PRIMARY SOURCES OF INFORMATION. Your study may
require gathering original information—information that has not been previously published on your topic. This primary information may come from an
examination of original company records, a survey of knowledgeable individuals, an observation of an activity, or an experiment.

Examining original records and files is an obvious source of historical
information that may be helpful to you. The other ways to obtain primary
information—surveys, observations, and experiments—are not such obvious
sources of information.

SURVEYS. To get firsthand information from individuals, you can survey
them. The basic ways to survey people are by mail, telephone, or face-to-face
interview. As compared with other surveys, mail surveys are less expensive;
the percentage of responses, however, will likely be lower. Telephone surveys
will cost more than mail surveys, but they will get a higher percentage of
responses. The most costly surveys are face-to-face interviews. They are a way,
however, of assuring responses; the responses can be in greater depth than
in surveys by mail or telephone.

Questionnaires are developed and used to obtain information by survey. With questionnaires you can obtain opinions and facts from individuals. Here are some important guidelines to follow when developing questionnaires:

1. The survey questions should be developed from the factors being studied. In a survey of employees on employee morale, you might develop questions to seek opinions or facts about employee salaries, fringe benefits, work hours, etc.
2. The questions should be clear. They should mean the same thing to everybody. A question such as "What kind of car do you own?" is not clear. Based on the respondents' interpretations, the answers could be convertible, Chevrolet, sports, foreign, etc. An example of a clearer way to obtain specific information is: "Please indicate the name of the manufacturer of your car."
3. Avoid leading questions. Leading questions influence readers to give one answer. Questions such as "Would it be a good idea to improve the arrangement of our work hours?" will likely be biased toward a yes answer. A better version of this question is:

The present arrangement of our work hours is:
_____ very satisfactory
_____ satisfactory
_____ unsatisfactory
_____ very unsatisfactory

4. Avoid skip-and-jump directions such as: "If your answer to Question 9 is no, skip Questions 10, 11, 12 and go directly to Question 13. If your answer to Question 9 is yes, also answer Question 10 but skip 11 and 12 if you do not have children. . . ."
5. Choose the form of the questions carefully. The two basic types of questions are open-ended and forced-answer. Open-ended questions let respondents answer in their own words. These kinds of questions must be very carefully worded in order to receive comparable answers. If at all possible, use forced-answer questions. In this type of question you provide the possible answers to the questions, and the respondents choose among the alternative answers given. More comparable and useful information can be obtained with forced-answer questions than with open-ended questions.
6. Sequence questions appropriately. Start your questionnaire with easy questions that will encourage respondents to continue. Group similar topics together. For example, put all questions on salaries in the same section of the questionnaire. Arrange questions in logical order—the way people commonly think of the topics.

Forced-answer questions are commonly used in mail and telephone surveys. Open-ended questions are more likely to be used in surveys conducted by personal interviews.

Questionnaires are used in surveys. They should be developed carefully.

The two basic types of questions are **open-ended** and **forced-answer**.

In designing forced-answer questions, be sure the "stem"—the question—is clearly worded. There should be no overlap in the possible answers, i.e., use 25-29, 30-34, 35-39 instead of 25-30, 30-35, 35-40. Provide lines or boxes for easy check mark answering. The lines or boxes for the responses should precede the possible answers.

Sample forced-answer questions are shown in Illustration 14-2.

---

1. Please check your age:
   - _____ Under 25
   - _____ 25-29
   - _____ 30-34
   - _____ 35-39
   - _____ 40-44
   - _____ 45-49
   - _____ 50-54
   - _____ 55-59
   - _____ 60-64
   - _____ Over 64

2. Please check your department:
   - _____ Accounting
   - _____ Computer Center
   - _____ Finance
   - _____ Personnel
   - _____ Production
   - _____ Purchasing
   - _____ Sales
   - _____ Shipping and Receiving

3. I favor the idea of a four-day workweek:
   - _____ Strongly Agree
   - _____ Agree
   - _____ Undecided
   - _____ Disagree
   - _____ Strongly Disagree

4. If a four-day workweek were implemented, which day would you want off? Mark that day 1, then mark the next best day off for you 2, etc.
   - _____ Monday
   - _____ Tuesday
   - _____ Wednesday
   - _____ Thursday
   - _____ Friday

5. How do you value the company newsletter as a source of information about company matters? Circle the most appropriate number.

   Valuable   Not Valuable

     1   2   3   4   5

Illustration 14-2   Sample Forced-Answer Survey Questions

Examples of open-ended questions that may be asked in a personal interview are:

1. What do you think are the most important qualities a supervisor should have?

2. What do you think of the idea of a four-day workweek?

You will receive narrative-type answers to these questions. For several respondents, the answers will vary considerably and will be difficult to tabulate. However, if you interview only a few people and want to get all their ideas on selected topics, the personal interview approach, using open-ended questions, is best.

Questionnaires should be designed attractively to encourage response. A questionnaire should be accompanied by a covering letter or statement that explains it and motivates the recipient to fill in the questionnaire and return it to you.

Questionnaires should encourage response.

To save time and money, surveys are usually sent to a few people who are representative of a larger group. This type of survey is called a *sample survey*. Such surveys must be designed carefully so that the information gathered is reliable and valid. Unless you are an expert in survey design, it is recommended that you consult with a statistician on any sample survey you may be planning.

Surveys are usually conducted using samples.

OBSERVATIONS. Observation is another way to gather primary information for a study. This technique involves one or more observers watching and recording facts about an activity. While the observation technique can incur high personnel costs, it is a way to obtain precise information. A common use of the observation technique is to gather information on a worker-machine operation in a factory. The worker's repetitive movements might be timed for a number of operations, production records maintained, and conclusions drawn about the efficiency of the procedures. Similarly, observers might be posted in selected areas of cities to count out-of-state cars in order to get a measure of tourist traffic.

Observations may be used to gather primary information.

It is important that the observation technique be carefully controlled. All observers must look for exactly the same thing and record their observations in the same way for the information to be of comparative value. Many managers and employers use *informal observation* to obtain information that is helpful to them in performing their jobs. This kind of information, while not scientifically obtained, can be of value in a limited way.

The observation technique must be carefully controlled.

EXPERIMENTS. The last way to gather primary information for a business study is the experiment. Experiments in business are usually used to compare two ways of doing something in order to determine the better way. For example, employees in one plant might be placed on a four-day workweek while employees in another plant would be kept on a five-day workweek. The employees in the two plants would then be observed and surveyed periodically to determine their productivity and their satisfaction with work hours.

Experiments may be conducted to gather primary information.

Another approach would be to have a presurvey and postsurvey of a group of employees that you plan to change from a five-day workweek to a four-day workweek. In this approach, employees who are on a five-day workweek could be asked a series of questions about the effect their work schedule has on their productivity and job satisfaction. Then their five-day workweek would be changed to a four-day workweek. After three months have passed, the employees would be asked the same set of questions they were asked before their work schedule was changed. Then the two sets of answers would be compared.

Experiments are a good way to make comparisons.

Experiments are not as common in business as they are in scientific laboratories, but experiments do have their uses. You can easily compare the old way with the new way or Method A with Method B in an experiment. Experiments can be expensive. Carefully designed and controlled experiments, however, have provided businesspersons with much valuable information.

ANALYZING INFORMATION

The third major step is to **analyze the information.**

Once you have planned your study and gathered information, you are ready to begin your analysis. The analysis may take only a few minutes. The information you gathered may speak for itself. It may clearly say "yes" to adopting a new procedure or product. The information you gathered may clearly say that employees overwhelmingly prefer the four-day to the five-day workweek. On the other hand, you may have gathered a great amount of complex information. It may take you days, weeks, or months to complete the analysis.

Analysis should be objective.

To analyze means to look at the parts by comparing and contrasting them.

The purpose of the analysis is to make sense, objectively, out of the information you have gathered. You will not want personal bias of any kind to enter into the analysis. Use your brain power—objectively and unemotionally. The word **analysis** means to look at the parts of things separately or in their relationship to the whole. The various parts of your information are compared and contrasted in an effort to try to develop new or better ideas. Separate facts and figures are interpreted by explaining what they mean—what significance they have.

For example, if you were doing a study to determine which microcomputer to buy for your office, you would collect information on the type of work you are currently doing and the kinds of work you want to do. Then you would gather information on microcomputers including cost, software compatibility, speed of operation, machine capacity, machine dependability, maintenance availability, potential for upgrading, and other factors. Then you would compare and contrast (analyze) the different machines to determine how well they can do what you want done, what their potential is, how dependable they are, and so on. Once the analysis has been completed—you are ready to determine solutions.

DETERMINING SOLUTIONS

Based on your analysis, you will be ready to offer a solution or solutions to the problem you have been studying. Depending on your position in the organization and the particular business study, the solution you determine will be either the answer that you will use or a recommendation to someone else who will make a decision on its use.

The fourth major step is to **determine solutions**.

For formal studies and reports, you may draw conclusions from your analysis and state them separately from the recommendation(s). A conclusion is an inference—a reasoned judgment—you make from your analysis. If you were to select the most important ideas suggested by your analysis, these ideas would be your conclusions. Based on your conclusions, you could state the study answer or recommendation(s)—the study solution. The conclusions and recommendations must be based on the findings and your objective analysis, not your personal opinion of what a good solution would be. Your conclusions and recommendations for a report might look like this:

Solutions may consist of conclusions and recommendations.

Conclusions:
1. Procedure B appears significantly more cost-effective than Procedure A in the two installations studied.
2. Dependable equipment for implementing Procedure B on a wide-scale basis is not currently available.
3. The XYZ Manufacturing Company currently has in stock 20 Model 3CA machines that can be used to implement Procedure B.
4. The XYZ Manufacturing Company projects that they will have 500 Model 3CAs available within six months.

and

Recommendations:
1. Immediately lease the 20 Model 3CAs from XYZ and continue the comparison study of Procedure A and Procedure B for three more months.
2. Enter an option to purchase 500 Model 3CAs from the XYZ Manufacturing Company.
3. If the additional study continues to show that Procedure B is significantly more cost-effective than Procedure A, exercise the option with XYZ to purchase the 500 Model 3CAs.

WRITING THE REPORT

The final step in a business study is to write the report. It is an important step; you will want to present your results effectively. How to write a successful report is discussed in detail in Chapter 15, "Report Preparation," and Chapter 16, "Graphic Aids."

The fifth major step is to **write the report**.

PROPOSALS

Developing and writing proposals is a way to achieve success.

Recognition, professional gains, millions of dollars, and personal rewards will be won today by successful proposal writers. These writers will persuasively propose a solution to a problem, and the reader will accept the proposal and provide the necessary support to carry out the solution. You, too, can develop successful proposals and benefit from their approval by following the recommendations in the remainder of this chapter.

DEFINITION OF A PROPOSAL

Proposals analyze problems and provide solutions.

A proposal is an analysis of a problem and a recommendation for a solution. The problem may be a need for equipment, services, research, a plan of action, or a variety of other needs. The recommended solution may be products, personnel, a business study, a description of work to be performed, or any of several other ways of solving a problem.

THE NATURE OF A PROPOSAL

A proposal is a persuasive message designed to win a reader's approval of the writer's recommendations. Proposals are common in business.

Writing proposals is a common way to improve productivity and profitability.

A proposal is a gamble.

Businesspersons look for initiative. They welcome suggestions of ways to change things for the better. Customers and suppliers want to receive proposals that will mutually benefit them and you. Successful organizations depend on the creation of ideas that will improve productivity and profitability.

Proposals are gambles. They take time to develop, and many times they are rejected. Some proposal developers believe that they are doing well if they win acceptance of one of every ten proposals. Successful proposal writers are risk takers. They will assess the probability of their being successful, and then decide whether to develop a proposal. If a large organization is considering developing a proposal involving millions of dollars in contracts, that assessment will involve many people and departments.

Proposals may be:

Another dimension of proposals is the variety of ways to categorize them. Proposals can be external or internal, solicited or unsolicited. Understanding these categories will be helpful to you in writing proposals.

• *External*

EXTERNAL PROPOSALS. Proposals that go to those outside an organization are external proposals. These messages include proposals to supply products or services at given prices—to construct buildings, to provide equipment, to perform research, to design roads, to provide paper, to perform audits, and on and on. Receiving approval of external proposals is essential to the success of many organizations.

INTERNAL PROPOSALS. Proposals sent to others within an organization are internal proposals. These can be proposals to solve problems or meet needs by improving procedures, changing products, adding personnel, conducting studies, reorganizing departments, increasing facilities, reducing budgets, or making other changes. Ideas for internal improvement, creatively developed and convincingly presented, are the lifeblood of organizations.

- Internal

SOLICITED PROPOSALS. Proposals initiated by a person or an organization with a specific problem or need are solicited proposals. These are requests to others for a solution to that problem or a recommendation for meeting the need. Such a request is called a Request for Proposal or RFP. The form of the solicitation may be a face-to-face request, a telephone call, or a written 1-page, 50-page, or 500-page RFP. When responding to solicited proposals, it is essential to provide the information requested in the format specified.

- Solicited

UNSOLICITED PROPOSALS. Proposals initiated by an individual or an organization that are not in response to an RFP are unsolicited proposals. They represent an independent analysis of another's problems or needs and the creation of proposed solutions.

- Unsolicited

QUALITIES OF A SUCCESSFUL PROPOSAL

Successful proposals have qualities that separate them from unsuccessful proposals. While success sometimes depends on factors such as luck, politics, timing, and reputation, most proposals must have excellent content clearly presented to be accepted. The following qualities are usually required for a successful proposal:

Successful proposals have excellent content clearly presented.

1. The purpose of the proposal is clearly stated.
2. The problem or need is clearly understood and defined.
3. The solution is innovative and convincingly presented.
4. The benefits outweigh the costs.
5. The personnel implementing the solution are qualified.
6. The solution can be achieved on a timely basis.
7. The proposal is honest, factual, realistic, and objective.
8. The presentation is professional and attractive.

To convey these qualities in the proposal, the writer must carefully analyze the situation and the receivers, use the you-viewpoint, and apply the principles of business communication. The proposal should be a powerful

Proposals should be
powerful persuasive
messages.

persuasive message. The receivers are going to be looking for the benefits to them, their department, the company, the community, society, or some other group to which they belong. The proposal should get the receivers' attention, show clearly the benefits of accepting the proposal, give proof of those benefits, and motivate favorable action.

THE ELEMENTS OF A PROPOSAL

Successful proposals
contain specific elements.

A successful proposal contains essential elements or parts. In solicited proposals, the elements are specified in the RFP. All of the elements requested in the RFP should be responded to carefully and fully. If you think elements necessary to the acceptance of your proposal are missing from the RFP, then you should try to work those parts into the specified format.

In unsolicited proposals, you must decide which elements to include. For elaborate, detailed proposals you will likely include all of the elements listed in this section. For short proposals you will select those elements that you think are essential for the success of the proposal. The order of presentation of the elements may vary based on the situation.

A comprehensive list of common proposal elements includes the following:

1. Cover Letter or Memo
2. Title Page or Cover
3. Reference to Authorization
4. Table of Contents
5. List of Illustrations
6. Proposal Summary
7. Purpose
8. Problem or Need
9. Background
10. Benefits of the Proposal
11. Description of the Solution
12. Evaluation Plan
13. Qualifications of Personnel
14. Time Schedule
15. Cost
16. Glossary
17. Appendixes
18. Bibliography

While all of these elements are important for many large proposals, the key elements are the Purpose, Problem or Need, Benefits of the Proposal, Description of the Solution, Qualifications of Personnel, Time Schedule, and Cost. The proposal elements are described in the following sections.

COVER LETTER OR MEMO. The cover letter or memo, also referred to as a transmittal message, introduces the proposal to the reader. A letter is used for an external proposal and a memo for an internal proposal. The cover letter or memo should include content that provides coherence for the reader, reviews the highlights of the proposal, and encourages action.

The cover letter or memo highlights the contents and encourages action.

TITLE PAGE OR COVER. The information contained on the title page or cover of a proposal can include: title of proposal, name and location of receiver, name and location of submitter, date of submission, principal investigator, proposed cost, and proposed duration of project. The title should answer all of the appropriate six "W and H" questions—What? Where? Who? When? Why? How? The title of the proposal should attract the reader's attention and, because it will be used to identify the proposal, it should be easy to remember.

The title page or cover includes essential information.

REFERENCE TO AUTHORIZATION. If the proposal is solicited, the request should be noted in a reference to authorization. The information contained in the reference to authorization depends on the RFP. For an informal or short RFP, it could be as simple as listing the RFP number on the cover or including a line in the cover letter or memo that says "This proposal is in response to your telephone call of May 5, 199–." For a formal RFP, it should include a separate page or a number of pages following the title page or cover. A lengthy RFP may require an abstract as a reference to authorization.

If the proposal is solicited, its authorization should be noted.

TABLE OF CONTENTS. The table of contents should list the titles and page numbers of all the major sections of the proposal. It will assist in orienting readers and will serve as a reference to aid them in quickly locating specific information. The names and page numbers of the appendixes also are included in the table of contents.

The table of contents orients the reader and serves as a reference.

LIST OF ILLUSTRATIONS. The titles and page numbers of any tables, figures, graphs, or other illustrations are placed in a List of Illustrations immediately following the table of contents.

The list of illustrations contains the names and locations of graphic aids.

PROPOSAL SUMMARY. The proposal summary is the proposal in capsule form. This section must be written after the proposal is complete. It contains the most vital information in each of the major sections of the proposal. It should be short. The summary is designed to quickly give busy people a complete overview of the proposal. For short proposals the summary may be just a paragraph. For a long proposal of 100 to 500 pages, the summary might be 1 to 10 pages long.

The summary provides an overview of the proposal.

PURPOSE. Following the summary, the actual proposal begins. The proposal's purpose should be stated first. This helps the reader understand

The purpose clearly
describes reason for and
nature of the proposal.

clearly (1) the reason you are making the proposal and (2) the nature of the proposal—how it will accomplish the purpose. Example purpose statements are:

This is a proposal to reduce manufacturing costs 10 percent by replacing Assembly Line A's conveyor system.

The purpose of this proposal is to increase sales by adding commission sales personnel.

These purpose statements may stand alone or they many be followed with brief explanations. The amount of explanation given depends on the reader's knowledge and his or her need for information.

State the problem being
solved or the need being
met.

PROBLEM OR NEED. The next section should describe the problem being solved or the need being met. This section should use coherence techniques so it relates to the section in which the purpose of the proposal was given. For example, the first purpose statement given in the previous section might be followed by a problem statement such as this:

Manufacturing costs for the second quarter are up 5 percent over the first quarter. Most of this cost increase can be attributed to the new labor agreement that became effective March 1. To meet competition, we must find new ways to reduce manufacturing costs.

BACKGROUND. If necessary for your reader's complete understanding, you should provide background data on the problem. This section may be combined with the section on Problem or Need; or it may, if both sections are long, be a separate section. In the background section, you may explain the problem—how it developed, its magnitude, and the consequences if nothing is done.

BENEFITS OF THE PROPOSAL. The benefits of the proposal are important. They represent the outcomes of the implementation of the proposed solution. The benefits must be in the you-viewpoint; they must clearly serve the interests of the reader and/or his or her organization. The benefits

must outweigh their cost. (The cost data will be given later in the proposal.) If your proposal is competing with other proposals, the benefits you cite must be more cost-effective than your competitors' benefits for your proposal to be the winning one.

When presenting the benefits of the proposal, use the emphasis techniques given in Chapter 2; but be careful not to overstate the benefits. Make them concrete, realistic, and honest.

DESCRIPTION OF THE SOLUTION. The description of the solution is the most important section in the proposal. It will likely be the largest section. It contains the solution to the problem or the way you recommend meeting the need.

Depending on the proposal, the description may consist of subject matter similar to the following:

New information system design
Products to meet a need
Complex business study plan
New job descriptions
New organizational arrangement
Personnel qualifications for new employees
Budget reduction plan
Building construction plans
Revised fringe benefits program
Road design project
Corporation expansion plan
Equipment acquisition plan
Product development plan

The description of the solution section must tie coherently to the information given previously in the proposal. References must be made in this section to the proposal purpose, the problem or need, and the benefits of the proposal. From the description of the proposal section, your readers must understand your solution clearly and be convinced that it achieves the purpose, solves the problem, and provides the benefits cited earlier.

Be sure the description is realistic and persuasive.

The description of the solution should include specifically what you are proposing be done, who will do it, when it will be done, where it is to be done, how it will be done, and why it should be done. If you are responding to an RFP, your response must carefully provide the information called for in each item of the description section.

You will want to stress the innovative aspects of your proposal, the special nature of the resources you are recommending, and the strength of your solution's rationale. Show how these features of your proposal fit your reader's needs. A good way to do this is to relate your solutions directly to each of the benefits given earlier. Those benefits might be individually relisted followed by an appropriate part of the description. The intent is to show clearly that you have carefully thought through all aspects of the proposed solution and that it represents a realistic, feasible, and desirable way of solving the problem or meeting the need.

EVALUATION PLAN. If appropriate for your proposal, you will want to include an evaluation plan. This plan would be a way to judge the degree of success achieved if your proposal were implemented. The evaluation plan could consist of a record keeping system; a review by a panel of experts; statistical analysis procedures; a reporting system; or any number of control, analysis, measurement, or judgment techniques.

An evaluation plan provides a way to judge success of proposal implementation.

An evaluation plan is a major element in proposals for research studies. In other proposals, such as increased staffing proposals, the evaluation system might be an employee performance review procedure already in place. In this case, only a brief reference to the existing plan would be needed.

QUALIFICATIONS OF PERSONNEL. In the qualifications of personnel section you provide biographical information about each key participant involved in implementing the proposal. You show his or her qualifications to provide the services proposed. The information should include the education, experience, accomplishments, successes, and evidences of achievement that directly relate to each participant's involvement in the proposed solution. You are, in this section, justifying to the reader that these persons are fully qualified to serve in their assigned roles. The types of data that are appropriate are discussed in detail in Chapter 21, "The Job Search and Resume."

The personnel qualifications section shows ability to provide proposed services.

Depending on the nature of the proposal, the length of the data presented for each individual will vary from a few lines to several pages. In some proposals, brief summaries are presented in the qualifications of personnel section and full resumes are provided in an appendix. If you are responding to an RFP, provide exactly the amount and type of personnel information specified.

TIME SCHEDULE. The time schedule shows when activity is to start and when it is to be completed. For simple proposals, the time schedule may consist of a listing of activities and beginning and ending dates. For elaborate proposals, it may be necessary to use more complex task-time analysis charts such as Gantt (see page 355), PERT (Program Evaluation Review Technique), Milestone, or other scheduling techniques. If you need assistance in selecting a time schedule format, most libraries have good reference materials you can use. Your responsibility in this section is to clearly show the reader a realistic time schedule.

The time schedule shows when activities begin and end.

COST. The cost or the price of the proposed solution is shown next. This section may be labeled Cost, Prices, Budget, or another appropriate title. The cost may be presented in logical parts such as personnel, supplies, equipment, facilities, etc.; or it may be shown by benefit, description part, time phase, or other appropriate category. The cost of the proposed solution must cover your expenses and desired profit. It also must be reasonable in relation to the benefits and products or services to be provided. If you are following the guidelines in an RFP, the format for the cost section will likely be specified and should be used.

The cost section shows cost of proposed solution.

GLOSSARY. Based on a careful analysis of your readers, you may decide to include a glossary in your proposal. A glossary lists alphabetically the unfamiliar terms used in the proposal and gives their definitions. A glossary is

The glossary defines unfamiliar terms.

included only when many unfamiliar specialized or technical terms have to be used. When there are only a few such terms, they should be defined the first time they are used.

APPENDIXES. To keep the body of the proposal as short and readable as possible, it is sometimes appropriate to place complex supporting information in an appendix. It was suggested earlier that resumes of key personnel might appropriately be placed in an appendix. Other information that might be placed in appendixes includes your organization's history, product specifications, records of past successes with similar projects, letters of support, details further supporting information in the description section, questionnaire to be used for the proposed research, or other supporting and reference materials. An RFP may specify what appendixes are to be included. Be sure to include only those appendixes essential to the reader's understanding and decision making. If the proposal becomes too bulky, it will be less acceptable to a potential approver, funder, or purchaser.

> Complex supporting information is shown in the appendixes.

> Limit appendixes to information that is essential to reader's needs.

BIBLIOGRAPHY. If you think it strengthens your case to indicate your knowledge of important reference materials, include a bibliography in the proposal. If you have footnoted material in the proposal, you must include those sources in a bibliography.

> The bibliography contains appropriate reference sources.

WRITING A PROPOSAL

For a long, complex proposal, a writing team may be formed. Sections of the proposal may be assigned to different individuals for writing. In this case, it is important to have one chief writer to assure consistency throughout the proposal and to tie all the parts together coherently. For short proposals normally one person is responsible for the writing. It may or may not be appropriate for that writer to ask others to read his or her proposal before it is finalized and submitted.

> A proposal may be written by a team or by an individual.

Illustration 14-3 is an example of a **poor** short proposal in which a personnel manager is recommending to the president that the company change its medical insurance carrier. The suggestions in this chapter for writing successful proposals are not implemented in this memo.

An improved proposal for the same situation is shown in Illustration 14-4. This example of a **good** short proposal follows the guidelines for developing and writing successful proposals.

Appendix F (pages 583-590) is an adaptation of an actual proposal for a pilot study designed to test an expanded employee screening system. It shows most of the proposal elements commonly used in long proposals.

Illustration 14-3 **Poor** Short Proposal

Subject line is not specific.

Purpose is not clearly stated.

Problem statement is not clear, concise, or concrete.

Background information is not logically organized. Some is not helpful.

Benefits are not emphasized or clearly presented.

The proposed action is not clear.

To: Mr. Brett Randolph, President

From: Katrin Herbig, Manager *KH*
         Personnel Services

Date: September 15, 199-

Subject: Medical Insurance

For the past five years we have had deteriorating service from and paid increasing medical insurance premiums to the ABC Insurance Company. The premiums have gone up more than 10 percent, and the processing turn-around time has doubled. Because of the severity of these problems, we decided we should take action to try to solve them by taking bids. We went out on bids to a number of companies in July, and the USM Health Insurance Group was the low bidder.

I hope you will take this information into consideration as you plan for the next Board of Directors' meeting. We need to take action soon as our contract with ABC, which has a 30-day notice of contract cancellation provision, has an expiration date of December 31. A significant amount of money--in excess of $200,000--could be recaptured by transferring our medical coverage to USM. USM is offering some unique provisions that, if implemented, promise further benefits to us. For example, they will hold the line on premiums in the future and cut processing time significantly. I believe the advantages of transferring our coverage far outweigh the disadvantages.

mre

Illustration 14-4 **Good** Short Proposal, Page 1

To: Brett Randolph, President

From: Katrin Herbig, Manager *KH*
         Personnel Services

Date: September 15, 199-

Subject: Proposed Change in Medical Insurance Carrier

The Proposal

This proposal is to reduce medical insurance costs and improve
employee services by changing NESCO's medical insurance carrier
from the ABC Insurance Company to the USM Health Insurance Group.

The Medical Insurance Problem

The cost for NESCO's medical insurance with the ABC Insurance
Company for last year was $890,000 and for this year will be
$1,005,700—a 13 percent increase. ABC now requires six weeks
turn-around time on processing employee claims. Both the insurance cost and the processing time have increased each of the five
years we have had ABC as our medical insurance carrier. Costs
have increased an average of 11 percent per year, and the processing time for employee claims has doubled from three weeks to
six weeks. As compared to industry standards, both the current
cost of coverage and the processing time appear to be excessive.

To attempt to solve our medical insurance problem, we sought bids
from the 12 leading carriers; and the USM Health Insurance Group
was low bidder.

The Benefits of Implementing the Proposal

If we were to change our medical insurance coverage from the ABC
Insurance Company to the USM Health Insurance Group, NESCO would
benefit in the following ways:

1. Insurance costs would be reduced by 20 percent ($201,140)
    next year over this year.

2. USM would commit to maximum premium increases of no more than
    6 percent per year for the next two years regardless of medi-
    cal cost increases.

3. If medical cost increases are less than 6 percent in each of
    the next two years, our premium increases will be identical
    to the actual percent of the medical cost increases.

4. USM would commit, for the three-year term of the contract, to
    a maximum employee claim processing time of four weeks.

The subject is clear.

Headings orient reader.

The purpose is given first.

The problem is stated concretely.

Helpful background information is provided.

Benefits are clearly and emphatically stated.

Illustration 14-4 **Good** Short Proposal, Page 2

Brett Randolph
Page 2
September 15, 199-

5.   Medical Insurance Rating, Inc., an independent medical insurance carrier rating service, rates USM more highly than
ABC--98.7 to 96.3, a significant rating difference.

6.   Our medical insurance coverage with USM would be identical to
the coverage we currently have with ABC.

Recommended Action

To change NESCO's medical insurance carrier from ABC to USM, we
must give ABC notice of our cancellation by December 1.   This
gives us adequate time to negotiate a contract with USM prior to
canceling our current coverage.

I propose that you recommend to the Board of Directors at its
September 30 meeting that NESCO's medical insurance carrier be
changed from the ABC Insurance Company to the USM Health Insurance Group, Inc.

mre

The proposed action is clearly and concretely presented.

A CONCLUDING COMMENT ON PROPOSALS

Proposals are the ways that new ideas are conveyed to decision makers. Most of the recommendations in this section on proposals apply to both written and oral proposals. Some proposals will be accepted, but many will be rejected. Successful businesspersons develop and submit many proposals in their careers. They are not deterred by rejections. They keep developing and submitting proposals and realize the professional and personal gains when their proposals are accepted.

Write proposals; they are an important way to succeed in your career.

DISCUSSION QUESTIONS

1. Discuss the importance of conducting studies and writing reports in business.
2. Describe the overall approach for conducting a business study.
3. Explain how you determine the problem of a study; indicate two ways of stating the problem.
4. What are factors in a study?
5. Explain what a Gantt chart is.
6. Why is it important during the planning step to determine who will read the final report?
7. What are study procedures?
8. Explain the two basic kinds of information sources—secondary and primary.
9. Name the three major ways to obtain primary information and describe each one briefly.
10. What is meant by "analyze information"?
11. Describe the conclusions and recommendations in a report.
12. Explain the role and nature of proposals in business.
13. Discuss the qualities of successful proposals.
14. Describe the proposal summary or abstract.
15. What are the two most important parts of the purpose of the proposal?
16. Discuss what is meant by the benefits of the proposal.
17. Describe the content that should be contained in the description of the solution section of a proposal. Give examples of the types of subject matter that might appear in this section.
18. Give three examples of evaluation plans that might be a part of a proposal.

19. What kind of information should you include in a proposal to show that the personnel you are recommending are qualified to carry out the solution or meet the need?

20. Indicate the key proposal elements that might precede a lengthy, formal proposal.

21. Indicate the key proposal elements that might follow a long, involved proposal.

22. Discuss the purpose of including appendixes in proposals and give three examples of content for appendixes.

APPLICATION EXERCISES

1. Do a study to determine students' attitudes toward midterm grades. In your study, implement all the major steps in conducting a business study except writing the report.

2. Indicate what would be (a) an appropriate statement of problem and (b) an appropriate list of factors for a comparative business study of two procedures for processing employment application forms in a personnel office.

3. You plan to determine why students prefer the "fast food" option over the "balanced meal" option in the college cafeteria. State the problem, list the study factors, and indicate the way you would gather data for such a study.

4. Develop a questionnaire that could be used to survey student opinion on one of the following topics:
   a. Work ethic
   b. Coeducational housing
   c. Four-day school week
   d. Required class attendance
   e. Establishment of pass/fail system
   f. Year-round school

5. Administer the questionnaire developed in Application Exercise 4 to the students in one of your classes. Tabulate the students' responses and analyze the information you have secured.

6. Contact a local businessperson and seek permission to survey the organization's employees on a mutually agreeable topic. Once the topic is chosen, complete all five steps in conducting a study. Possible topics for your study could be:
   a. The importance of communication in a business organization
   b. Whether or not continuing education is desirable for full-time employees
   c. The advantages and disadvantages of flex-time work schedules
   d. The most important motivators of employee performance
   e. Other topic negotiated with the businessperson

7. Seek the cooperation of a local restaurant to perform a study that will evaluate customer reaction to the food, service, environment, and other appropriate factors. As a class project, develop a questionnaire that can be left in quantity on the tables, completed by customers, collected by restaurant personnel, and returned to the class for tabulation and analysis. Report the findings and appropriate recommendations to the restaurant manager.

8. Develop a proposal on one of the following topics. The proposal is to be sent to the dean of your college.
   a. Elimination of final examinations
   b. Development of an honors system for examinations
   c. Optional class attendance for all classes
   d. Increased summer school offerings
   e. Advanced course in business communication

9. Write a proposal to your instructor in which you recommend ways to strengthen one of the following aspects of your business communication course:
   a. Testing
   b. Outside assignments
   c. In-class writing activities
   d. In-class oral communication exercises
   e. Student involvement in class discussions
   f. Student attendance

10. Develop and write a complete proposal using all 18 proposal elements discussed in this chapter. The subject of your proposal is the initiation of a pass/fail grading system for 25 percent of the non-major courses required for graduation at your college. The receiver of your proposal will be the president of your college. Keep in mind that the president will likely ask several other individuals and groups to review your proposal.

11. Write a short proposal on subject matter appropriate to your major. For example, if your major is accounting, write a proposal to your manager recommending that your company change auditing firms, fiscal year, reporting system, banks, inventory accounting, or some other such topic. Select a topic with which you are familiar and limit the length of your proposal to two pages. Include the following sections in your proposal: purpose, problem, benefits, description of solution, time schedule, and cost.

12. You are the new assistant personnel manager for the Sonta Corporation. Your manager has asked you to propose an extensive seminar that she is calling "Communication Skills for Managers." Using all the proposal elements you think are appropriate, write a long proposal that solves the problem that your manager has specified as "poor communication in the corporate headquarters that interferes with effective operations." You can draw on the table of contents in this textbook to assist you in the design of the proposed program.

REPORT PREPARATION

Your learning objectives for this chapter include the following:

- To understand the advantages of correct report formatting
- To understand when to use a long, formal report and when to use a short, informal report
- To learn how to write an informal report
- To learn how to write a formal report
- To learn how to report proceedings of a meeting effectively through the use of minutes
- To learn how to develop policy statements
- To learn how to write a news release

The report writer will first conduct a business study, as described in Chapter 14. After this research is completed, the writer must present the resulting information in an accurate, objective manner and in a usable, readable format.

The time and effort spent in researching and writing a report are wasted unless the report is read and understood. The probability that a report will be read and understood is increased when certain principles of formatting are followed. These principles should be applied regardless of the length or formality of the report. This chapter discusses the formatting principles for effective report preparation.

Formatting is important to the acceptance and understanding of a report.

376

ADVANTAGES OF CORRECT REPORT FORMATTING

It is just as important to select the proper format for reports as it is to select the proper format for letters and memos. The reader's first impression of the report will be based on its appearance. A negative first impression may increase the time it takes for a reader to gain confidence in the report writer's credibility.

The credibility of the content depends, in part, on the appearance of the report.

Formatting a written report properly will improve its readability. Paragraphs averaging six to seven lines make it easy for the reader to concentrate on the written material. Proper spacing between paragraphs and correct margins make it easy for the reader to follow the material. Thus, attractive formatting improves the readability of a report.

Properly formatted reports help the reader follow the organization of the material by using appropriate headings. Headings lead the reader from one section to the next by announcing the next topic.

Headings make it easy for a reader to understand a report.

TYPES OF WRITTEN REPORTS

Written reports vary from long, formal reports to short, informal reports. An informal report may consist of a body and a title page or of a body only. A formal report may consist of all or some of the following parts: title page, title fly, letter or memo of authorization, letter or memo of transmittal, table of contents, list of illustrations, abstract, body, glossary, appendix, and bibliography.

The two types of written reports are **formal** *and* **informal**.

Informal reports are normally written in first person (I recommend that . . .); formal reports are usually in third person (It is recommended that . . .). Recent trends, however, lean toward informality in both formats; many formal reports are now written in the first person. The degree of formality is determined after an analysis by the report originator of the report receiver.

MECHANICS OF WRITTEN REPORTS

The mechanics of a written report—format, spacing, footnotes, etc.—are as important as the mechanics of a letter or memo in that they make the first impression on the reader. The writer must consider general guidelines of report

The appearance of the report influences the reader of the report.

mechanics as well as the guidelines and policies of the organization for which the report is being prepared. The primary consideration in the physical presentation of a written report is that the mechanics improve the readability of the report.

COVER

The cover of a written report is normally a light, cardboard material that protects the contents of the report. It should include the title of the report and the author's name or have a cutout section through which the title and author's name on the title page may be seen. Many organizations have preprinted covers on which the author only has to place the title and his or her name. Normally the title is in uppercase letters, and the author's name has initial capital letters. The cover should be attractive and may contain an appropriate picture or drawing that will add to its attractiveness. Covers are usually used only on long, formal reports.

The cover should be attractive, should include the report title and the author's name, and should protect the report.

MARGINS

Proper margins in a report are important because they create the white space that makes the report visually appealing to the reader. As a general rule, report margins should be 1 inch on each side and the bottom and $1\frac{1}{2}$ inches on top. However, reports that are bound at the left should have a $1\frac{1}{2}$-inch left margin, and reports that are bound on the top should have a 2-inch top margin. One-inch margins can be created by using a 65-character line with pica type and a 78-character line with elite type.

Margins add to the attractiveness of a report and range from 1 to 2 inches.

SPACING

Reports may be single-spaced or double-spaced. The trend in business organizations is toward single spacing to reduce the number of sheets of paper that have to be handled. Single-spaced reports should be doubled-spaced between paragraphs. In reports using double spacing, paragraph indentions should be five spaces from the left margin; no space is added between paragraphs.

Most reports are single-spaced, but double-spacing is acceptable.

HEADINGS

Appropriate headings help the reader follow the report organization and enable him or her to refer quickly to specific sections within the report. Sections that are of little interest can be skipped or quickly scanned.

Headings may be either informative or structural. An informative heading indicates the content of a forthcoming section and orients readers so that they can more easily understand the material. Structural headings emphasize the functional sections within the report. Once the type of heading is selected, it should be used consistently throughout the report. An example of each is shown below:

Informative heading:

EMPLOYEES' OPINIONS CONCERNING CHANGE IN
INSURANCE BENEFITS

Structural heading:

FINDINGS

The ways headings are presented vary according to the reference manual used by the organization. Regardless of the method selected, consistency of presentation is vital. An explanation of one widely accepted method follows:

First-level headings (main headings) are centered on the page in uppercase letters. Second-level headings (side headings) begin at the left margin, and the first letter of each important word is capitalized. Side headings are often underlined for emphasis. The third-level heading (paragraph heading) begins five spaces from the left margin, is underlined, and has the first letter of important words capitalized. An example of this method is shown in Illustration 15-1.

The headings at each level must be constructed so that they are grammatically parallel. Headings do not have to be parallel from level to level. For example:

INCOME FOR OCTOBER

Sales
Interest

WAYS THAT OCTOBER INCOME IS SPENT

Salaries
Rent
Supplies

The second-level headings are parallel, but the first-level headings are not. This example could be corrected by changing "Income for October" to "Ways That October Income Is Earned." A better way to correct the example would be to change "Ways That October Income Is Spent" to "Expenses for October."

All headings within a report should be typed or printed a double space below the last line of the text in the preceding section. Text for sections with first- or second-level headings begin a double space below the heading. Text for sections with third-level headings begin two spaces after the period in the heading. This method of heading organization is shown in Illustration 15-1 and in the sample report in Appendix G.

> Structural or informative headings may be used.

> Headings must be used consistently.

> Headings are placed on the second line below the preceding section.

Illustration 15-1   Levels of Headings

FIRST-LEVEL HEADING

Xxxxxxxxxxxxxxxxxxxxxxxxxxxxxxxxxxxxxxxxxxxxxxxxxxxxxxxxxxxxxxxxx
xxxxxxxxxxxxxxxxxxxxxxxxxxxxxxxxxxxxxxxxxxxxxxxxxxxxxxxxxxxxxxxxxxxxx
xxxxxxxxxxxxxxxxxxxxxxxxxxxxxxxxxxxxxxxxxxxxxxxxxxxxxxxxxxxxxxxxxxxxx
xxxxxxxxxxxxxxxxxxxxxxxxxxxxxxxxxxxxxxxxxxxxxxxxxxxxxxxxxxxxxxxxxxxxx
xxxxxxxxxxxxxxxxxxxxxxxxxxxxxxxxxxxxxxxxxxxxxxxxxxxxxxxxxxxxxxxxxxxxx
xxxxxxxxxxxxxxxxxxxxxxxxxxxxxxxxxxxxxxxxxxxxxxxxxxxxxxxxxxxxxxxxxxxxx

<u>Second-Level Heading</u>

Xxxxxxxxxxxxxxxxxxxxxxxxxxxxxxxxxxxxxxxxxxxxxxxxxxxxxxxxxxxxxxx
xxxxxxxxxxxxxxxxxxxxxxxxxxxxxxxxxxxxxxxxxxxxxxxxxxxxxxxxxxxxxxxxxxxxx
xxxxxxxxxxxxxxxxxxxxxxxxxxxxxxxxxxxxxxxxxxxxxxxxxxxxxxxxxxxxxxxxxxxxx
xxxxxxxxxxxxxxxxxxxxxxxxxxxxxxxxxxxxxxxxxxxxxxxxxxxxxxxxxxxxxxxxxxxxx
xxxxxxxxxxxxxxxxxxxxxxxxxxxxxxxxxxxxxxxxxxxxxxxxxxxxxxxxxxxxxxxxxxxxx

    <u>Third-Level Heading</u>. Xxxxxxxxxxxxxxxxxxxxxxxxxxxxxxxxxxxxxxx
xxxxxxxxxxxxxxxxxxxxxxxxxxxxxxxxxxxxxxxxxxxxxxxxxxxxxxxxxxxxxxxxxxxxx
xxxxxxxxxxxxxxxxxxxxxxxxxxxxxxxxxxxxxxxxxxxxxxxxxxxxxxxxxxxxxxxxxxxxx
xxxxxxxxxxxxxxxxxxxxxxxxxxxxxxxxxxxxxxxxxxxxxxxxxxxxxxxxxxxxxxxxxxxxx

    <u>Third-Level Heading</u>. Xxxxxxxxxxxxxxxxxxxxxxxxxxxxxxxxxxxx
xxxxxxxxxxxxxxxxxxxxxxxxxxxxxxxxxxxxxxxxxxxxxxxxxxxxxxxxxxxxxxxxxxxxx

    <u>Third-Level Heading</u>. Xxxxxxxxxxxxxxxxxxxxxxxxxxxxxxxxxxxx
xxxxxxxxxxxxxxxxxxxxxxxxxxxxxxxxxxxxxxxxxxxxxxxxxxxxxxxxxxxxxxxxxxxxx
xxxxxxxxxxxxxxxxxxxxxxxxxxxxxxxxxxxxxxxxxxxxxxxxxxxxxxxxxxxxxxxxxxxxx
xxxxxxxxxxxxxxxxxxxxxxxxxxxxxxxxxxxxxxxxxxxxxxxxxxxxxxxxxxxxxxxxxxxxx

    <u>Third-Level Heading</u>. Xxxxxxxxxxxxxxxxxxxxxxxxxxxxxxxxxx
xxxxxxxxxxxxxxxxxxxxxxxxxxxxxxxxxxxxxxxxxxxxxxxxxxxxxxxxxxxxxxxxxxxxx
xxxxxxxxxxxxxxxxxxxxxxxxxxxxxxxxxxxxxxxxxxxxxxxxxxxxxxxxxxxxxxxxxxxxx

<u>Second-Level Heading</u>

Xxxxxxxxxxxxxxxxxxxxxxxxxxxxxxxxxxxxxxxxxxxxxxxxxxxxxxxxxxxxxxx
xxxxxxxxxxxxxxxxxxxxxxxxxxxxxxxxxxxxxxxxxxxxxxxxxxxxxxxxxxxxxxxxxxxxx
xxxxxxxxxxxxxxxxxxxxxxxxxxxxxxxxxxxxxxxxxxxxxxxxxxxxxxxxxxxxxxxxxxxxx

FIRST-LEVEL HEADING

Xxxxxxxxxxxxxxxxxxxxxxxxxxxxxxxxxxxxxxxxxxxxxxxxxxxxxxxxxxxxxxx
xxxxxxxxxxxxxxxxxxxxxxxxxxxxxxxxxxxxxxxxxxxxxxxxxxxxxxxxxxxxxxxxxxxxx
xxxxxxxxxxxxxxxxxxxxxxxxxxxxxxxxxxxxxxxxxxxxxxxxxxxxxxxxxxxxxxxxxxxxx

Xxxxxxxxxxxxxxxxxxxxxxxxxxxxxxxxxxxxxxxxxxxxxxxxxxxxxxxxxxxxxxx
xxxxxxxxxxxxxxxxxxxxxxxxxxxxxxxxxxxxxxxxxxxxxxxxxxxxxxxxxxxxxxxxxxxxx
xxxxxxxxxxxxxxxxxxxxxxxxxxxxxxxxxxxxxxxxxxxxxxxxxxxxxxxxxxxxxxxxxxxxx

FOOTNOTES

Footnotes must be used to give credit to the source of quoted or paraphrased material. Reports in the business community do not contain as many footnotes as reports in other fields because business reports usually contain only information that is based on data gathered through primary research. Two commonly used methods for citing sources of information follow.

The traditional method of footnoting is convenient for the reader when a report contains information gathered from a number of sources. Material to be footnoted has an Arabic numeral that is raised one-half line and is placed at the end of the quoted material. The footnote numbers begin with 1 and are consecutive throughout the report. The footnote is separated from the text by a $1\frac{1}{2}$-inch rule beginning at the left margin one line below the last line of the text material. The footnote is typed or printed on the second line under the rule; it is single spaced with the first line indented five spaces from the left margin.

Information contained in traditional footnotes varies depending on the source—book, periodical, encyclopedia, governmental publication, newspaper, or unpublished material. For a book, the footnote contains the author's complete name, title of the publication, city in which published, publishing company, year published, and page number. An example of a traditional footnote for information taken from a periodical follows:

The number of new oil wells being drilled has decreased by 10 percent from the number drilled last year.[1] There will be a shortage of oil products if the trend of drilling fewer wells continues for the rest of this decade.

---

[1]J. D. Bassell, "Oil Production in 1989," Texas Oil Monthly (March 1990), 4.

A contemporary method of footnoting information is more appropriate for reports that contain information from only a few sources. These sources can be easily documented by placing the information (name of author, date of publication, and page number) in parentheses at the end of the sentence relating to the citation. For information about the source, a reader would refer to the bibliography. An example of this method is:

The number of new oil wells being drilled has decreased by 10 percent from the number drilled last year (Bassell, 1990, p. 4). There will be a shortage of oil products if the trend of drilling fewer wells continues for the rest of this decade.

An authoritative reference manual should be consulted before constructing footnotes or other citations.

Information obtained from secondary sources must be footnoted.

Commonly used footnoting methods are:

• Traditional

• Contemporary

NUMBERING OF PAGES

Reports containing more than two pages should be numbered.

Short reports of one or two pages do not have to be numbered. Long reports should have their pages numbered consecutively. Preliminary pages (pages prior to the body of a report) should be numbered by placing small Roman numerals (ii, iii, iv, etc.) at the center, one inch from the bottom of the page, beginning with the second page. The title page is considered page i, even though no page number is given.

The body of the report should begin as page one, identified with Arabic numerals (1, 2, 3, 4, etc.). The page number should be centered and one inch from the bottom edge on each section or chapter that is started on a separate page. On all other pages of unbound or left-bound reports, the number should be placed on the fourth line from the top of the page at the right-hand margin; on top-bound reports the page number should be centered and one inch from the bottom edge of the page.

FORMAL REPORTS

A formal report is normally written for upper management.

A formal report normally contains many pages, usually is written in third person, contains several sections or chapters, utilizes graphic aids, and is read by individuals in top levels of management and possibly by individuals outside the writer's organization. It may take from several weeks to several months to research and write the report. This research and writing may be accomplished by one person or by a team of several individuals.

A formal report generally contains three main sections.

A formal report may be divided into three major divisions: the preliminary section, the body, and the supplementary section. A formal report may contain all or some of the following parts.

1. Preliminary Section
   a. Title Page
   b. Title Fly
   c. Letter or Memo of Authorization
   d. Letter or Memo of Transmittal
   e. Table of Contents
   f. List of Illustrations
   g. Abstract
2. Body
   a. Introduction
   b. Procedures
   c. Findings
   d. Analysis
   e. Conclusions
   f. Recommendations

3. Supplementary Section
   a. Glossary
   b. Appendix
   c. Bibliography

PRELIMINARY SECTION

The preliminary section contains all the parts of a report that precede the body. The preliminary pages will vary from report to report according to the formality of the report. A discussion of the individual parts follows.

TITLE PAGE. A title page normally contains the following: the title of the report; the name of the person or organization receiving the report; the writer's name, title, and department; and the date of submission. The title should indicate the purpose and content of the report.

> All formal reports should contain a **title page**.

Many organizations have specific guidelines for the preparation of title pages. When they exist, the company guidelines should be followed. If specific guidelines do not exist in an organization, each line on the title page should be centered, and there should be equal vertical spacing between each item. The title should be all capitals; other lines may be either all capitals or initial capitals. A courtesy title should be placed before the name of the person to whom the report is addressed but not before the name of the report writer. A title page taken from the sample report in Appendix G is shown in Illustration 15-2a.

TITLE FLY. The title fly may be either a blank sheet of paper or a sheet of paper with the report title centered horizontally and vertically. It is used to make the report more formal. The title fly may be placed immediately before or immediately after the title page. A title fly taken from the sample report in Appendix G is shown in Illustration 15-2b.

> A **title fly** makes a report more formal.

LETTER OR MEMO OF AUTHORIZATION. This message is written before the study begins by the person giving permission for the study. It is included in the final report by the writer of the report. The document will be a letter if the authorization is from an agency outside the organization and a memo if from within the organization. The document gives any relevant information necessary to accomplish the study, such as statement of the problem, amount of money available to support the study, personnel to assist in the study, and due date. A memo of authorization is included in the sample long report in Appendix G and is shown in Illustration 15-2c.

> A **letter or memo of authorization** gives the researcher permission to do the study.

LETTER OR MEMO OF TRANSMITTAL. The letter or memo of transmittal is written by the report writer and is used to introduce the report to the reader. A report to readers outside the organization would contain a letter, while reports for internal use would contain a memo. In more formal reports, a preface or foreword may be used.

> A **letter or memo of transmittal** contains items you would tell the reader if you were to hand deliver the report.

OPINIONS OF YOUNG ADULTS

ON TELEVISION VIOLENCE AND ITS

EFFECT ON CHILDREN

Prepared for

Dr. Anna Hess

Department of Management

Prepared by

Robert Vineyard

MGT 215-02

School of Business Administration
Tripp Long-Creek College
Forney, Idaho 83115-7201

April 12, 199-

Illustration a

OPINIONS OF YOUNG ADULTS

ON TELEVISION VIOLENCE AND ITS

EFFECT ON CHILDREN

Illustration b

To: Business Communication Students

From: Anna Hess, Professor *ah*

Date: January 3, 199-

Subject: Authorization for Study on Television Violence

You are authorized to study how young adults perceive television
violence affects children. Survey a random sample of Tripp Long-
Creek College students to obtain your data.

Your study will be discussed on the university television channel
this summer. A copy of your report will be sent to Idaho's Commission on Improving the Quality of Living. Your report may be
used as a basis for determining if further studies on television
programming are warranted.

There has been no budget allocation for this project. I recommend that you use telephones to conduct the survey. You may
use the telephone in my office if you do not have one readily
available.

Your report needs to be in my office by April 15 so that I will
have time to review it and forward it to the commission no later
than May 1. You may contact me at any time at extension 4196 for
assistance or further guidance.

gb

Illustration c

Box 1123, University Station
Forney, ID 83115-1123
April 12, 199-

Dr. Anna Hess
Department of Management
School of Business Administration
Tripp Long-Creek College
Forney, ID 83115-7201

Dear Dr. Hess

Here is the report you requested on the opinions of young adults
regarding the effect that television violence has on children.

The purpose of this study was to provide you and Idaho's Commission
on Improving the Quality of Living with young adults' opinions
about the effects television violence has on children. To get this
information, a random sample of 434 Tripp Long-Creek College students (about 6 percent of TLC students) were surveyed by telephone.

The survey results were divided into two groups--students with a
child or sibling under 12 and those not having a child or sibling
under 12. The majority of both groups thought that television has
both positive and negative effects on children and that television
violence does reinforce violence in children's lives. The respondents also thought that parents have the major responsibility for
controlling the child's exposure to television violence.

Based on these findings, I recommend that parents and their children jointly plan a schedule of television programs for viewing. I
also recommend that the commission begin a campaign (1) to inform
parents of the destructiveness of television violence and (2) to
convince networks to limit the amount of violence on television.

Thank you for the opportunity to study this problem. If you need
any additional information, I can be reached at extension 2357.

Sincerely

Robert Vineyard

Robert Vineyard
MGT 215-02

Enc.

Illustration d

Illustration 15-2   Example Preliminary Pages

The letter or memo of transmittal may be subjective in that the writer may offer a suggestion or opinion not supported by data. It may contain personal comments. The letter or memo may also refer readers to parts of the report of special interest or suggest special uses of the information. In general, any item worthy of discussion may be included in the letter or memo of transmittal. A letter of transmittal is included in Appendixes F and G and is shown in Illustration 15-2d.

TABLE OF CONTENTS. A table of contents should follow the letter of transmittal and should list all major sections that follow it. Its purpose is to aid the reader in quickly locating specific information in the report. A table of contents is normally not used in reports of fewer than five pages.

The table of contents is double-spaced between major sections; subsections are single-spaced. Section heads should be listed exactly as they appear in the body and should be connected to the page number by dot leaders (horizontally spaced periods). Page numbers are optional for subheadings. The table of contents is normally prepared after the report is typed or printed in final form. A combined table of contents and list of illustrations taken from the sample report in Appendix G is shown in Illustration 15-3a.

> The **table of contents** lists all major items of the report.
>
> A table of contents should be used only when a report exceeds four pages.

LIST OF ILLUSTRATIONS. Graphic aids are identified in a list of illustrations. The list may be on the same page as the table of contents, or, if the report contains more than four illustrations, it may begin on the page following the table of contents. The list of illustrations uses the same format as the table of contents, with illustration heads instead of section heads. A report may group all graphic aids into one list of illustrations, or it may group each type of graphic aid (chart, graph, etc.) separately. This section is normally prepared after the report is typed or printed in final form. See Illustration 15-3a for a combined table of contents and list of illustrations taken from the sample report in Appendix G.

> A **list of illustrations** indicates the graphic aids in the report.

ABSTRACT. An abstract is a brief version of the formal report; it restates each section of the report in miniature form with an emphasis on findings, conclusions, and recommendations. Other common names for an abstract are *summary*, *executive summary*, and *synopsis*. Busy executives who do not need to read an entire report are provided vital information in a capsule form. An abstract also provides an overview to readers of the report so that they will have a general idea of what the study is about prior to reading the entire report.

The maximum allowable length of an abstract will vary among business organizations. A general rule is that it should be approximately 10 percent as long as the report but should not exceed one or two single-spaced pages. A sample abstract taken from the long report in Appendix G is shown in Illustration 15-3b.

> An **abstract** is a capsule form of the report.

TABLE OF CONTENTS

LIST OF ILLUSTRATIONS

v

Illustration a

ABSTRACT

The purpose of the study was to determine how young adults perceive the effects of television violence on children. A
telephone survey was administered to 434 of the 7,400 Tripp Long-
Creek students to obtain the data.

The related literature shows that television definitely affected
children's behavior. Several studies point out the violent content of children's programs. The research of secondary sources
revealed that parents are in the best position to control what
their children view on television and should assume this responsibility.

The survey revealed that 52.5 percent of the students with a
child or sibling under the age of 12 felt television had a
moderate effect on children, and 84.9 percent felt it had both
positive and negative effects. Of the students without a child
or sibling under the age of 12, 56.6 percent felt television had
a moderate effect on children, and 88.1 percent felt the effect
was both positive and negative. The majority of both groups felt
that television does reinforce violence in children's lives and
that parents have the major responsibility for controlling the
amount of violence that their children see.

An analysis of the primary and secondary findings leads to the
conclusion that viewing television violence reinforces violent
behavior in children. In addition, parents--not governmental
agencies--should control the amount of violence viewed by their
children.

Based on these findings, it is recommended that parents monitor
the amount of violence their children see on television and inform television programming personnel about their opinions concerning the programs shown. It is also recommended that another
survey be conducted to determine how parents should control the
amount of violence that their children see on television.

vi

Illustration b

I. INTRODUCTION

Background

Children spend much of their free time watching television. Some
of the viewing time is spent on educational programs, and some of
the viewing time is spent watching programs containing violence.
In recent years there has been much controversy over the amount
of television that a child should watch and the types of programs
that the child should view. Another area of concern is who has
primary responsibility for children's television viewing habits.
The opinions of young adults with recent television viewing experience as children should be helpful in studying these problems.

Statement of the Problem

The problem of this study was to determine the attitudes of young
adults regarding the effects of television violence on children
under the age of 12.

Purpose of the Study

The purpose of this study was to provide parents, teachers, adult
family members, and other interested parties with young adults'
opinions on the effects of television violence on children. The
study was also conducted to see if young adults think legislators
should take action to control the amount of violence that television stations broadcast.

Scope

The scope of the study included the effects of television on
children, the value of regulations to control violence on television, and the responsible parties for controlling television
violence.

Limitations for this study include (1) only Tripp Long-Creek
College students were surveyed, and (2) time permitted no testing
and revising of the questionnaire.

II. RELATED LITERATURE

Violence on television has been a concern for many years. When
research about television began, three positions became popular.
The first position was that television violence was beneficial
because it helped vent hostilities symbolically, and so young
viewers were less likely to act violently in real life. The
second position was that television violence had no effect. The
third position held that television violence could lead to subsequent aggression. Even today, it is considered questionable as
to which position is correct.

1

Illustration c

2

In 1990, the National Advisory Committee on Social Behavior
submitted a report to the Surgeon General regarding the effect of
television violence on children. The basic conclusion of the
report was that television violence does have measurable effects
on children. Many young children cannot distinguish between
fantasy and reality, and violence they see on television has the
same psychological effect as violence they see in the real world.
Viewing violence on television has been linked with violent
behavior subsequent to viewing. The report concluded that the
only way for parents to significantly influence the effect television violence has is to watch television with their children
and help them distinguish between fantasy and reality (Gibbs,
April 1990, 121).

In a 1989 study by Nathan Goff, it was noted that an average
viewer saw violence in seven of every ten programs and eight of
every ten cartoons. Mr. Goff felt that parents must be aware of
the role television played in their children's lives and act
according to their children's best interests (Goff, October 1989,
72).

Some interesting conclusions were drawn by Krause about what
types of television violence seem to cause violent behavior in
children. Programs that contain more real-life violence have a
greater impact on the child's behavior. Programs that do not
seem to promote violent behavior include comedies, cartoons, and
science fiction. Krause was of the opinion that whether programs
do incite violence depends on how deeply they penetrate the
child's personal value system (Krause, March 1987, 42-43).

Child Psychology took a nationwide survey entitled, "Does Television Affect Your Child?", which was published in its June
issue. The survey received over 5,000 responses from parents;
68 percent of the parents are under 34 years of age. The majority of these parents felt that changes in television violence
should be made by the public by deciding whether or not to watch
the program (McCann, June 1989, 55).

Although most of the parents felt it was the public's responsibility (contrasted with only 11 percent indicating that it was
the federal government's responsibility), 52 percent would have
the government offer incentives to stations to keep up the number
and the quality of children's programs. Forty-eight percent also
believed that children's programs were much too violent.

Studies done on who has the major responsibility for controlling
the amount of television a child views all seem to agree that
parents are in the best position to monitor their child's viewing
habits.

The Television Viewer published the conclusions made from a study
conducted by Sara Williams. The study concluded that parents are
the single most important contributor to a child's development

Illustration d

Illustration 15-3 Example Preliminary and Report Body Pages

BODY

Most formal reports will contain all the information presented in the following sections; however, some of the sections may be combined. The material in the body may be presented using the direct or the indirect approach. In the direct approach the conclusions, recommendations, or both come at the beginning of the body. They come at the end of the body in the indirect approach. The sample report in Appendix G presents the material using the indirect approach. Appendix G also illustrates many of the sections that will be discussed in the following paragraphs. See Illustrations 15-3c and 15-3d for the first two pages of the body.

The body of a report may use the direct or indirect plan.

INTRODUCTION. The introduction provides an adequate background concerning the study so that the reader can understand the remaining parts of the report body. Material for this section will be similar to what is included in a proposal. (Proposals are discussed in Chapter 14.) The specific parts to be included in this section depend on what is necessary to assist the reader in understanding the scope and sequence of the report.

The introduction will assist the reader in understanding the rest of the report.

BACKGROUND. The introduction often begins with a general description of the problem that was studied and the main issues involved in it. The background leads to more specific details that develop into the statement of the problem.

STATEMENT OF THE PROBLEM. The statement of the problem clearly identifies the specific problem that was researched. The statement of the problem should be brief but informative. It may be followed by the purposes of the study, which indicate why the study was conducted.

The specific topic of the study is given in the statement of the problem.

SCOPE. The scope of the study is defined by the main factors that were studied and generally appears next in the introductory section. It lets the reader know the extent of the study. The limitations over which the researcher had no control are also listed in this section of the introduction. These limitations may include lack of resources, lack of time, or geographic boundaries.

The scope lets the reader know the extent of the study.

RELATED LITERATURE. A review of related literature may be included in the introduction when a limited amount of literature is available about the topic. A separate section should be used when extensive amounts of related literature are reviewed.

GLOSSARY. Definitions of terms unfamiliar to the reader may be included in the introductory section. When many terms need to be defined, however, a glossary should be included in the supplementary section.

PROCEDURES. The procedures, or methodology, section describes the steps that were taken in conducting the study. One purpose of this section is to allow readers to determine whether or not all aspects of the problem were adequately investigated. This section can also be used by another researcher to conduct a similar study that could validate or disprove the results of the original study. Appendix G has an example of a procedures section for a formal report.

The steps used in conducting the study are described in the procedures section.

The results of the study
are presented in the
findings section.

FINDINGS. This section should be presented in a factual and objective manner without personal opinions or interpretations. All findings—positive and negative—are presented in this section. Graphic aids may be used to assist the writer in communicating the findings of the study. An example of a findings section can be found in Appendix G.

Significant relationships
are discussed in the
analysis section.

ANALYSIS. An analysis is conducted using the findings presented in the previous section. Findings in related studies should be compared with the findings of the current study. This analysis permits the reader to determine which relationships are significant. The report in Appendix G contains an analysis section.

Conclusions are drawn
from the findings of the
study.

CONCLUSIONS. Conclusions are statements of reasoning that a researcher makes after a thorough investigation. All conclusions should be made using the findings of the study and should be based on the analysis section of the report. In many studies, conclusions are summary statements of the content of the analysis section. No new data should be presented in this section. A study may have one or several conclusions. The conclusions are the bases for the writer's recommendations. A combined conclusions and recommendations section is shown in the report in Appendix G.

Recommendations are
based on conclusions.

RECOMMENDATIONS. This section may be combined with the conclusions section. Recommendations are the writer's suggestions to the reader as to the action(s) that should be taken to solve the problem that was studied. They should develop logically from the findings and conclusions of the study. A single recommendation or several recommendations may be presented in one study. If more than two recommendations are presented, they may be listed and numbered. This section may contain only the recommendations, or it may contain both the recommendations and the supportive reasoning for their development. A combined conclusions and recommendations section is included in the report in Appendix G.

SUPPLEMENTARY SECTION

The final section of a written report contains material that is indirectly related to the main topic of the study. This section may consist of a glossary, an appendix, and a bibliography.

Unfamiliar terms are
defined in the **glossary**.

GLOSSARY. A glossary lists alphabetically terms used in the report with which the reader may be unfamiliar and gives their definitions. It is used only when numerous unfamiliar terms are included in the text. When there are only a few specialized terms, they should be defined in the introduction or where they are first used in the text.

APPENDIX.   An appendix contains items that are indirectly related to the study but that have been excluded from the body to improve readability. When there is more than one item, each should be labeled as a separate appendix. Each appendix is identified with a capital letter:

> Appendix A: Employee Questionnaire
> Appendix B: Letter to Supervisors

All appendixes will be referred to in the body of the report. If the material is not referred to in the body, it is not relevant enough to be included as an appendix. Some items commonly included as appendixes include:

> Questionnaires
> Computer printouts
> Follow-up letters
> Reports of similar studies
> Working papers
> Intricate tables
> Supporting material

Indirectly related material is placed in an **appendix**.

BIBLIOGRAPHY.   A bibliography is an alphabetical listing of all references used as sources of information in the study. All footnoted sources must be included in the bibliography; however, it may also contain a source not footnoted in the body. A bibliography may also be labeled "references" or "sources." A bibliographical reference for a magazine article includes the author's name, title of the article, name of the publication, date of publication, and page number(s):

> Jackson, Mark. "Education in Records Management." Records Management, October 1989, 52-55.

All references are listed in a **bibliography**.

Different types of sources are arranged differently in bibliographical entries. Reference manuals should be used to ensure proper construction of bibliographical entries. An example of a bibliography is shown in the report in Appendix G.

INFORMAL REPORTS

An informal report does not contain all the parts of a formal report. As the name indicates, informal reports may be written informally using first person. Most of the time this type of report will not contain graphic aids or material from secondary sources.

Informal reports *do not contain all the parts of formal reports.*

In business, the informal report is used much more frequently than the formal report. There are many different types of informal reports; five of the most common—letter, memo, progress, periodic, and technical—are discussed in the following sections.

LETTER REPORTS

A **letter report** is used to communicate with people outside an organization.

Letter reports use a letter format to communicate to individuals outside an organization. A letter report uses a subject line and has headings for sections within the report. The personal style using first person pronouns (I, we, and you) is common in letter reports. Letter reports are often used for submitting annual reports, giving recommendations, and presenting information. A letter report giving a recommendation is shown in Illustration 15-4.

MEMO REPORTS

A **memo report** is used for informal communication within an organization.

Memo reports are used to communicate information to individuals within an organization. They are used primarily for reporting routine information concerning day-to-day operations. Memo reports may be used to provide a written record; they are less formal than letter reports.

A memo report uses standard memo headings and no salutation, complimentary close, or signature. The originator should initial the memo report next to his or her typed name in the heading. Topic headings are frequently used for easy reading. The progress report in Illustration 15-5 is written as a memo report.

PROGRESS REPORTS

Significant changes in a project are reported in a **progress report**.

A progress report is used to inform readers about the status of a particular project. It assists managers in monitoring and making decisions about the project. The report should inform the reader about the work that has been accomplished, the work that is currently being done, and the work that is scheduled to be done in the upcoming reporting period. Any significant progress or problems should be discussed in the report.

Progress reports may be written daily, weekly, monthly, or quarterly. The frequency of the reports will depend on the type or nature of the project being discussed. An example of a progress report is shown in Illustration 15-5.

Illustration 15-4 Letter Report

Pauley Foods Company

1100 Ohio Drive S.W., Washington, D.C. 20242-3988
Telephone: 202-555-6706

February 10, 199-

Dear Stockholder

SUBJECT: PROPOSED MERGER OF PAULEY FOODS AND KRIZCO

You are being asked to consider and vote upon a proposal to adopt and approve a merger agreement. If the
merger is approved, all of the issued and outstanding
shares of the company's common stock will be cancelled
and all stockholders will receive $24 cash for each
share of common stock.

In making a determination to recommend the offer of the
merger, the board of directors considered, among other
things, the marketplace's acceptance of the new company
on the American Stock Exchange. During the past ten
years, the price of our common stock has not reached
$24, and our stock has generally shown little activity
and low volume.

The nature of our company's business is such that predicting the degree of profitability of the company is
extremely difficult. Its profits are significantly im-
pacted by factors beyond the control of our company.

As a result of these factors, Pauley Foods' board of
directors believes it would be in the best interest of
all stockholders to vote for the merger. We recommend
that you sign and return the enclosed computer card
voting for the merger by March 1, 199-.

Sincerely

James Pauley
James Pauley
Chairman of the Board

hv

Enclosure

Illustration 15-5   Progress Report in Memo Format

DATA CONSULTANTS, INC.   Interoffice
                                                              Memorandum

TO: President Curry

FROM: Anne Crum, Director of Computing *A.C.*

DATE: April 5, 199–

SUBJECT: Quarterly Progress Report on Microcomputers

Introduction

All employees will have microcomputers on their desks at the completion of this project. The employees will also receive forty
hours of instruction on the use of word processing, data management, and spreadsheet software.

Work Completed

This project was started on September 25, 199–. During the first
quarter, we purchased 40 personal computers and 10 printers. We
trained 5 managers, 20 middle managers, and 15 supervisors during
the first three months.

During this past quarter, we purchased 120 microcomputers and 30
printers. Since January 1, 8 managers, 7 middle managers, 12
supervisors, and 63 secretaries have completed training.

Work Remaining

We have to purchase 160 microcomputers and 40 printers to complete this project. During this quarter we will purchase 120
microcomputers and 30 printers; the rest of the equipment will be
purchased during the last quarter of the year.

Only 3 managers and 6 supervisors yet need to be trained. All 9
will receive their instruction this quarter. We have 30 secretaries who currently need 15 more hours of training to complete
their education. The remaining 151 secretaries needing instruction will receive training in the next two quarters.

Conclusions

This project of purchasing 320 microcomputers and 80 printers is
on schedule with no foreseeable problems. We should have all 320
employees trained on applications software by the end of the
fiscal year.

br

PERIODIC REPORTS

Periodic reports provide managers with statistical information at regularly scheduled intervals. These intervals may be daily, weekly, monthly, quarterly, or annually. Periodic reports follow no set formats, and many organizations place them on preprinted forms. A form used to report the number of hours that a part-time employee worked in a month is shown in Illustration 15-6.

MONTHLY TIME REPORT
MID-TEX CATTLE

Month of _____ , 19_____

Name of Employee _____

Soc. Sec. # _____

Week	Daily Number of Hours Worked							Weekly Totals
	Mon	Tues	Wed	Thur	Fri	Sat	Sun	
1								
2								
3								
4								
5								

TOTAL HOURS

I hereby certify that the above reported hours are the correct number I have worked during the month herein reported.

_____
Signature of Employee

_____
Date

I hereby certify that the above is a true statement of the hours worked by this employee and that the work was performed in a satisfactory manner.

_____
Signature of Supervisor

_____
Department

Illustration 15-6   Periodic Report

TECHNICAL REPORTS

Technical reports, as the name implies, convey specialized or scientific information. There are no standard formats or organizational plans for technical reports. However, organizations will often specify particular formats and plans to be used for reports within their business. Standardization of formats makes it easy for readers to scan reports for information of particular interest to them. Some companies limit the number of pages that a report may contain. An example of a technical report is shown in Illustration 15-7.

Technical terms must be defined if they may be misunderstood by the reader.

Technical terms need not be defined when a technical report is prepared for someone familiar with the terminology. If the reader of the report does not have the technical expertise, words used in the report must be clarified. A good rule to follow is to remember the principles of business communication discussed in Chapter 2.

SPECIAL REPORTS

Some business reports require special content or format considerations. Three common special reports are minutes, policies, and news releases.

MINUTES

Minutes serve as the official report of a meeting.

Minutes are an official report of the proceedings of a meeting. They should be concise, accurate, and well-organized. Minutes serve as an official record, assist in refreshing memories of participants, provide information to individuals who were not present, and assist in preparing members for upcoming meetings.

Only pertinent information should be included in minutes.

Minutes should be brief and should include only pertinent information that accurately summarizes the meeting. All motions and resolutions should be recorded word-for-word as presented. Individuals presenting motions and resolutions should be identified by name in the minutes. It is important to indicate that a motion was seconded, but the name of the individual who seconds a motion need not be recorded. The outcome—approval or defeat—should also be included.

The parts that are normally included in minutes are: name of the committee or organization conducting the meeting; date, time, and location of the meeting; listing of members present and absent; approval of the minutes of the previous meeting; record of the meeting in chronological order; time of

Illustration 15-7   Technical Report

INTEROFFICE
MEMORANDUM

TO: Kevin Moore

FROM: Paul Catanzarite *PC.*

DATE: October 12, 199–

SUBJECT: Temporary Steam Valve Substitution for Ethylene Plant Equipment

As you requested, a check has been made to determine whether a spare TLE shell steam relief valve (SV-906S) may be temporarily used on the steam drum (TK-101C) that serves the two large vertical ethylene furnaces. This substitution would prevent a shutdown of the steam drum due to a broken spring in its relief valve. A new valve spring will not be available for at least eight weeks.

Our records and visual examination of the spare relief valve and the relief valve (SV-1204C) presently serving the steam drum indicate that the valves are identical with respect to inlet, outlet, and orifice size. Our findings show that the only differences between the valves are manufacturer and inset pressure, which is slight.

Based on this investigation, I believe the spare TLE steam relief valve may be substituted for the relief valve serving steam drum TK-101C. Resetting of the set pressure on the spare valve may be done since it falls well within the 10 percent range allowable for the valve spring.

tg

cc B. Cory
   F. Schroeder
   G. Twain
   D. Mathis

Not all minutes will contain the same parts.

adjournment; and signatures of the secretary and/or chairperson. These parts will vary depending on the purpose and formality of the meeting. Illustration 15-8 shows an example of minutes for a committee planning a company-sponsored Labor Day picnic.

POLICIES

Policy statements serve as guidelines for operation of a business.

Policy statements in business organizations serve as guidelines that employees must follow. Policy statements normally will be assembled into a policy manual. This manual can be used to orient new employees and can serve as a reference for long-time employees.

Policies should be broad for managerial personnel and specific for nonmanagerial personnel.

Policy statements should be written in the third person and should be clear, concise, and complete. Policies written for managerial personnel are broad guides that allow flexibility while policies for nonmanagerial personnel are more narrow and restrictive. An example of a policy statement is shown in Illustration 15-9.

NEWS RELEASES

News releases build good public relations.

News releases are special business reports containing information that will be of interest to the public. News releases need to be newsworthy, accurate, timely, concise, and positive. Common subjects for news releases include promotions, business expansion, employee layoffs, and introduction of new products.

News releases should be written in the inverted pyramid format.

The inverted pyramid format should be used for news releases. The inverted pyramid format begins with a summary lead that tells who, what, where, when, and sometimes why or how. The body of the release should be developed by giving details in descending order of importance—most important facts first and least important facts last. A news release should not contain a conclusion. The advantages of using the inverted pyramid format are (1) the release can be shortened easily by cutting from the end without rewriting, and (2) the release satisfies reader curiosity by getting to the main idea quickly.

News releases should end with **-30-** or ###.

The news release should be double spaced with the company's name and address typed or printed at the top. The contact person's name and telephone number should be shown on the news release. Special instructions to the newspaper staff (FOR IMMEDIATE RELEASE, FOR RELEASE ON JANUARY 12) should be typed in all capital letters at the top of the news release. The release text is immediately preceded by city, state, and date. A news release should end with a **-30-** or a ### under the last line; if it is longer than one page, **-more-** should be printed on the bottom of each page that is to be continued. Illustration 15-10 shows a sample news release about an employee promotion.

Illustration 15-8   Minutes

                                    MINUTES
                           Labor Day Picnic Committee

The meeting was held in the conference room on August 25, 199-, at
3 p.m.

Members Present: Cox, Harris (Chairperson), Jackson, Miller (Secretary), Thomas, and Williams

Member Absent: Hunt

The minutes of the previous meeting (August 2, 199-) were approved as
distributed.

<u>Selection of Caterer</u>

Ms. Jackson reported that J. R.'s Barbeque would cater the event for
$4.25 per person and Donna's Catering would charge $4 per person.
Each firm would furnish meat, beans, potatoes, and soft drinks for
these prices. Ms. Jackson moved and it was seconded that Donna's
Catering be hired for the picnic. Motion passed.

<u>Picnic Announcement and Reservations</u>

Mr. Cox reported that announcements of the picnic had been sent to
all employees with instructions to respond by August 26 and to state
how many people from their families would be attending the picnic.
By noon today, responses indicated that 220 individuals would be
attending. Ten employees had not yet responded. Tomorrow the number of attendees will be forwarded to Ms. Jackson so she can notify
Donna's as to the number of people who will be at the picnic.

<u>Softball Equipment</u>

Mr. Thomas reported that softball equipment had been obtained from
the local American Legion post. He would draft a letter for Ms.
Harris' signature thanking the post for the use of its equipment.
This letter should be sent within a couple of days after the picnic.

<u>Pony Rides for Children</u>

Ms. Williams reported that she had checked with Gordy's Riding
Stables, and the cost of having two ponies at the picnic for chil-
dren's rides would be $80. Children's safety was discussed. Ms.
Williams moved and it was seconded that $80 be allocated to Gordy's
Riding Stables for furnishing free pony rides to children. The
motion carried.

The meeting was adjourned at 3:40 p.m.

Respectfully submitted,

Roy Miller

Roy Miller
Secretary

Illustration 15-9   Policy Statement

POSTAL SERVICES POLICY

The following policies have been established for the operation of
the company postal service:

1. The Company Post Office, located in room 2104, provides mail
   service from 8:00 a.m. to 4:30 p.m. weekdays and is closed on
   Saturdays and Sundays. The service window is closed each day
   from 9:00 a.m. to 10:00 a.m. and from 2:30 p.m. to 3:15 p.m.
   for mail sorting prior to delivery.

2. United Farmers Mutual Postmaster will be the source of
   approvals and advice for all on-site and off-site mailing
   services. The vice president for administrative services has
   the responsibility for implementing company mailing policies
   and the authority to approve any exceptions to these
   policies. Any request for deviation from the stated policies
   and procedures should be submitted in writing. The vice
   president for administrative services will function as the
   liaison between the U.S. Postal Service and United Farmers
   Mutual.

3. All company budget units are eligible to use the company mail
   service for official mail pertinent to the function and operation of United Farmers Mutual.

4. United Farmers Mutual mail carriers deliver and pick up mail
   from designated mail stops. Company mail carriers are not
   authorized to change the location of the mail stop within an
   office, to delete a mail stop, or to add a new mail stop on
   their route. Written requests for changes or additions to
   mail delivery routes should be submitted to United Farmers
   Mutual Postmaster.

   It is the responsibility of each office or department to distribute mail to the employees served by each mail stop. Each
   office or department should notify the United Farmers Mutual
   Postmaster of all changes in both personnel and personnel
   location.

5. United Farmers Mutual Postmaster is charged with the responsibility for coordinating all mass mailings. Offices and
   departments should contact the Postmaster for technical assistance and scheduling information.

Illustration 15-10   News Release

NEWS
RELEASE

2110 Industrial Road • Kansas City, MO 64105-3101

CONTACT:

FOR IMMEDIATE RELEASE

> Dwain McIntosh
> (606) 555-3740

Kansas City, MO, April 15, 199- -- Ms. Yolanda Flores
has been promoted to Mid-West Regional Sales Manager
for Bellaire Air Products. She will now have responsibility for 15 sales representatives in eight states.

Ms. Flores joined Bellaire Air Products as a sales representative in 1978 after graduating Summa Cum Laude
from Kansas State University. Since her employment
with Bellaire, she has twice been named the Outstanding
Salesperson for the company.

Flores is very active in professional organizations.
She is immediate past president of the Missouri Mar-
keting Association and has held two offices in the
Kansas City Chamber of Commerce.

Ms. Flores, her husband, Lewis, and their two children,
Roberta and William, reside in Spanish Oaks.

-30-

DISCUSSION QUESTIONS

1. What are the advantages of correctly formatting a report?
2. Describe the two types of headings that may be used in written reports.
3. Describe two methods of footnoting sources of information in reports and give reasons for the use of each.
4. Compare a title fly to a title page.
5. What is the general purpose of placing an abstract at the start of a report?
6. How do conclusions and recommendations differ?
7. What is a bibliography? List the items that may be included in a bibliographical entry.
8. Compare a letter report with a memo report.
9. Briefly describe a technical report.
10. Discuss two advantages of using the inverted pyramid format for composing news releases.

APPLICATION EXERCISES

1. Your student government association is investigating student reaction to midterm grades. It has asked that all students write a report giving their thoughts on the subject. Write a report to the president of the student government association that will convince him or her to support your convictions.
2. Presume that your aunt is willing to loan you money to open a restaurant in the town where you go to school. Using the information that you learned in Chapter 14, devise a questionnaire to survey students and faculty to determine the type of facility that should be most successful. Write a formal report using the results gathered in the survey which can be presented to your aunt to convince her that she will be making a sound investment.
3. You are the secretary for a student organization in your business department. Your organization is planning to send eight members to a national conference in Houston, Texas. Your organization needs its faculty adviser to attend this conference but has insufficient funds for travel expenses. Gather facts and write a report to the appropriate administrator requesting that the institution pay for your adviser's travel expenses.
4. You have learned that a local civic organization has decided to give grants to students with financial need who make above average grades. You can

demonstrate your need by preparing a report describing your past year's income, expenses, and academic achievements. Be sure to include in your report justification for why you deserve the grant.

5. It seems that your school is lacking in school spirit. You have been asked by your school's vice president for student affairs to investigate ways to improve school spirit. Study the problem and report your findings and recommendations to the vice president in a letter report.

6. Your school has received a large monetary gift that can be used for whatever purpose the administration wishes. The Student Government Association has been assigned the task of determining how students would like to spend the money. Some ideas that have been suggested are: purchasing classroom equipment, creating student scholarships, building additional recreational facilities, and providing for faculty development. Develop a questionnaire to determine what the students want. After completing the secondary research and the survey, write a formal report that will inform the administration of the desires of the students.

7. A copy of Butler Insurance's Fringe Benefit Committee minutes is shown below. List the items that have been omitted from the minutes.

MINUTES
FRINGE BENEFIT COMMITTEE
BUTLER INSURANCE

The meeting was called to order at 10:30 a.m. on April 18, 199-.

Copies of the last meeting's minutes were distributed.

Ms. Carson presented a proposal on the new procedures for vacations. Mr. Wilson moved that the proposal be approved. The committee unanimously approved the motion.

The proposal for adding dental insurance to the family policy was defeated by a 5 to 2 vote.

The president appointed Mr. Thomas to gather information on eye care insurance. He was directed to report his findings at the next committee meeting.

The meeting was adjourned at 11:15 a.m.

CASE PROBLEMS

1. The employees of Seymour Tires have asked about the possibility of classes being offered on-site. Upon inquiring at Belmont College, it was learned that up to three classes could be taught if enough students would enroll to make the classes cost effective. A survey was taken;

78 employees responded. The results are given below. Write a memo report to the personnel director, Susan Driskell, giving the results of the investigation and your recommendations.

1. What courses would you be interested in taking? (Give your top 3 choices as 1,2,3.)

	1	2	3
Business Communication	13	21	17
Human Relations	5	3	3
Spreadsheets	22	14	13
Word Processing	15	17	11
Database Management	12	9	2
Desktop Publishing	9	6	19
Programming	2	8	13

2. What would be the best day for the class?

Monday	7
Tuesday	29
Wednesday	17
Thursday	24
Friday	1

3. What would be the most convenient time for the class?

4-7 p.m.	21
5-8 p.m.	42
6-9 p.m.	15

2. You are an instructor at Gimbell's Business College. Ms. Beverly Petry, the vice president for academic programs, has asked you to survey businesses in the area to determine to what extent dictation is used. You develop a questionnaire and mail it to 50 managers of area businesses. Usable responses are received from 34 managers. The number of responses for each question is as follows:

1. Age:

less than 25	1
25-34	3
35-44	6
45-54	12
55-64	9
65 or older	3

2. Number of employees under your direct or indirect supervision:

less than 5	7
5-24	18
25-99	6
100-499	2
500 or more	1

3. Classification that best describes the business or organization in which you are presently employed (check only one):

Construction/Engineering	3
Education	1
Insurance	4
Finance	7
Government	2
Manufacturing	4
Sales	9
Utilities/Energy Diversified	4
Other	0

4. Show the amount of time (in percentages) that you spend each day originating written messages by each method.

	None	less than 10%	10-25%	26-50%	51-75%	76-100%
Dictation	8	5	2	6	7	6
Handwriting	0	3	6	9	6	10
Keyboarding	13	6	10	5	0	0
Other	31	1	2	0	0	0

If your answer does <u>not</u> include dictation as a method of originating messages, go to Question 8.

5. Show the division of time (in percentages) that you spend dictating to a secretary and/or a machine.

	less than 10%	10-25%	26-50%	51-75%	76-100%
Secretary	1	2	4	2	12
Dictation Machine	2	3	3	5	7

6. Types of messages you dictate (check all that apply):

Memos	24	Reports	5
Letters	25	Other	2

7. For each of the following types of messages, indicate the average number you <u>dictate</u> per day:

	less than 3	4-6	7-10	more than 10
Memos	15	6	1	2
Letters	12	7	3	3
Reports	5	0	0	0

8. Is it important that students in a business communication class be taught how to dictate?

Yes	28	No	1	Don't Know	5

Write a report to Ms. Petry giving your recommendations on the inclusion of dictation in the business communication course. Your report should include appropriate report sections and appropriate graphic aids to complement the text of your findings.

3. Beyers Manufacturing's contract with an insurance company elapses in four months. It is trying to determine its employees' attitudes toward medical coverage. Listed below are the results of a survey to which 134 of the 180 employees responded. The responses have been grouped into three groups—single persons, individuals with one dependent, and individuals with two or more dependents. Use these data to prepare a report that could be sent to the company's president.

	Single	1 Dependent	2+ Dependents
1. Which type of coverage is best?			
a. Employee only	43	4	5
b. Family plan	8	14	60
2. Which coverage should be available?			
a. Basic medical	51	18	65
b. Major medical	49	18	62
c. Hospitalization	51	18	65
d. Dental	13	10	44
e. Optical	14	11	46
f. Prescriptions	20	9	50
3. What limit should policy place on out-of-pocket expenses?			
a. $500	25	10	32
b. $1,000	7	4	19
c. $2,000	15	3	6
d. $5,000	4	1	8
4. Should the company offer a menu insurance program where employee can choose type of coverage desired?			
a. Yes	45	16	61
b. No	6	2	4
5. Which would you prefer?			
a. Minimum coverage—company pays premium	38	9	21
b. Increased coverage—employee shares in paying premium	13	9	44
6. What should be the maximum premium that the employee must pay each month?			
a. 0	38	9	21
b. $25	9	4	8
c. $50	4	2	16
d. $100	0	3	20

4. Hodde, Miller, and Tate is a corporate law firm with more than 200 attorneys. The firm's volume of work has increased 10 percent per year for the past three years. The number of attorneys has increased 20 percent; however, the administrative staff has not been increased. The administrative staff includes 18 word processors, 130 legal secretaries, and 35 paralegal clerks.

You, the personnel manager, must prepare a report using the data shown in the table below to convince the senior partners that 25 new administrative personnel (word processors, legal secretaries, and paralegal clerks) must be hired. The hiring of these individuals would reduce overtime pay and would improve the quality of work. Your report should recommend the number of administrative personnel that would be hired in each category (word processor, legal secretary, paralegal clerk). Address the memo report to William J. Hodde, Senior Partner.

Hours Worked for First Quarter of 199-

Divisions	Word Processors			Legal Secretaries			Paralegal Clerks		
	Jan	Feb	Mar	Jan	Feb	Mar	Jan	Feb	Mar
Real Estate	332	431	438	2,410	3,130	3,169	653	751	838
Litigation	534	466	365	3,837	2,408	2,641	1,048	626	698
Bankruptcy	831	738	730	6,006	5,298	5,283	1,615	1,251	1,397
Corporate	465	399	438	3,351	2,891	3,170	908	751	838
Tax	399	565	840	2,812	4,095	4,494	896	1,439	1,606
Criminal	540	463	542	3,854	3,371	3,968	1,032	938	1,048
Probate	233	256	291	1,687	1,927	2,119	439	500	559

CHAPTER 16

GRAPHIC AIDS

LEARNING OBJECTIVES

Your learning objectives for this chapter include the following:

- To understand the purpose of graphic aids in written reports
- To decide where to place a graphic aid within a report
- To understand how to label graphic aids properly
- To select the appropriate type of graphic aid to present data most effectively
- To use tables to present statistical information
- To use the three types of charts that commonly appear in business reports
- To understand how miscellaneous graphic aids are used to communicate in a report
- To recognize when graphic aids are being used to deceive a reader

Graphic aids make a report more understandable.

A **graphic aid** is any illustration used to assist a reader in understanding the text material in a report. These illustrations are used to complement the communication. Graphic aids may reduce the volume of text, but they do not eliminate the written material completely. Graphic aids may be in the form of tables, graphs, charts, drawings, photographs, diagrams, or maps.

Various graphic aids accomplish different objectives.

Graphic aids can complement your communication by summarizing complex figures in charts and graphs, by identifying your company through the use of a drawing or photograph for a logo, by showing relationships in a chart, by indicating trends in a graph, or by presenting in a table details that are too cumbersome for written text.

GRAPHIC AIDS USAGE

When they are used properly, graphic aids can be helpful in effectively communicating ideas in written reports. Modern technology makes graphic aids easier to construct. Appropriate placement and identification of graphic aids will enhance the effectiveness of your communication.

COMPUTER-GENERATED GRAPHIC AIDS

Graphic aids are extremely powerful tools for supplementing written text. They are becoming more popular because they are easy to construct using computers. Many programs are available that can integrate graphics software with word processing software to develop an easy-to-read and informative written report.

Graphic software programs are easy to use. The report writer only has to enter the raw data and select the type of graphic aid desired. The computer will create the chart or graph selected. These graphic aids may be printed using several colors depending on the type of software and printer.

The report writer can produce graphic aids from the simple to the sophisticated. Simple graphic aids that can be produced include bar graphs, line graphs, and pie charts. Most software programs permit the creation of several variations of each type of graphic aid, such as stacked bar graphs or exploded pie charts. More sophisticated software programs have additional options: photographs may be printed in a report; the size of graphic aids may vary; lines, curves, and geometric shapes may be created instantly; key headings and captions with special fonts may be inserted; and color and patterns may be added.

An advantage of using a simple graphic software program is that little training is required to produce a graphic aid. A disadvantage of using a simple program is that the graphic aid produced may not be exactly what is desired. For instance, pie charts should begin at the 12 o'clock position with the largest piece and continue in a clockwise direction. Most simple graphic software programs do not follow this pattern. Also, a simple program may limit the number of characters that may be included in the titles or captions of the graphic aids. Care should be taken in selecting a graphic software program so that it will meet the report writer's needs.

Computers have simplified the creation of graphic aids.

Many types of graphic aids may be generated using computer software.

Consideration should be given to the advantages and disadvantages of each program when selecting computer graphic software.

PLACEMENT OF GRAPHIC AIDS

Reports are improved
when graphic aids are
placed in proper
locations.

Graphic aids (also referred to as *illustrations*) must be placed in appropriate locations to enhance the written message of the report. Illustrations that directly relate to the topic should be placed within the written text. A small illustration, less than one-half page, should be placed after the first reference to the aid, preferably on the same page. A large illustration, one-half to one page, should be placed on the page following the first mention of the illustration. Avoid dividing a graphic aid onto two pages. It is more desirable to place the entire illustration on one page, separate from the copy, than to divide it.

Illustrations that indirectly relate to the copy may be of interest to only a few readers. These illustrations will add unnecessary bulk to the main body of the report and should be placed in an appendix.

Illustrations should be
referred to in a report
before they appear.

You should refer to a graphic aid within the written text of the report *prior* to its appearance. This reference is a powerful tool—it guides the reader to the items you want to stress. The reference may be nothing more than telling the reader, "as shown in Graph 2," or "(see Table 3, page 12)." A reference to a graphic aid should be casual and not distract the reader's attention from the material being read.

IDENTIFICATION OF GRAPHIC AIDS

Illustrations must be
titled.

All formal graphic aids within a written report should be identified by appropriate titles. The title of a graphic aid should describe its contents. The title should contain enough detail so that the reader can understand the graphic aid without reading the text of the report, but it should not be extremely lengthy. You should consider the five W's (Who, What, When, Where, and Why), and use those that will make the title most clear.

The report writer must
determine the method of
numeration for the
graphic aids.

Methods of numbering graphic aids vary. One method is to label all graphic aids *Illustrations* and number them with either Arabic or Roman numerals. A second method is to divide the graphic aids into two categories and use Roman numerals for *Tables* and Arabic numerals for *Figures* (all other illustrations grouped together). A variation of that method is to categorize and number each type of figure separately (*Chart, Diagram, Graph*, etc.) but again use Arabic numerals for identification.

Illustrations must be
numbered in a consistent
manner.

Graphic aids should be numbered consecutively; however, if there is only one graphic aid in a report, it need not be numbered. If the report contains more than one section or chapter, the illustrations may be numbered consecutively throughout the report (Figure 1, Figure 2, etc.); or they may be numbered consecutively by sections or chapters (Figure 1-1, Figure 1-2, Figure 2-1, etc.). The most important consideration in numbering illustrations is consistency.

Illustration titles may be printed in either uppercase or uppercase and lowercase letters. Traditionally, titles are placed above tables and below all other illustrations. Today, businesses place the titles either above or below an illustration. As in the numbering of illustrations, consistency is the important guideline in title placement.

Titles may be placed above or below illustrations.

IDENTIFICATION OF GRAPHIC AIDS SOURCES

The same consideration for acknowledging sources of text material should be used in acknowledging sources of graphic aids. If the content of an illustration is originated by the writer, no source note is required. Source notes are used whenever content is obtained from another source. The source note normally consists of the word *source* in uppercase letters followed by a colon and the source. An example of an illustration using material from a report written by Walter Lippman is:

Source notes have to be used for illustrations obtained from others.

SOURCE: *Walter Lippman Report*, May 2, 1990, p. 21.

A source note is normally placed a double space below the illustration, or it may be placed under the title of the illustration.

GRAPHIC AIDS DEVELOPMENT

Effective communication may depend on the selection of the most appropriate graphic aid for a specific situation. You must be knowledgeable about the various illustrations so you can select the one that will most effectively convey information under specific conditions. The most frequently used graphic aids in business reports are tables, charts, and graphs.

Selecting the right graphic aid improves communication.

TABLES

Tables are typed or printed displays of words and numbers arranged in columns and rows. The data in tables should be presented in an orderly arrangement for easy and clear reference. In addition to the title, a table includes headings for the columns and the rows. These headings need to identify the data clearly but should be short so they do not detract from the data.

Tables show data arranged in rows and columns.

Statistical information can be presented more effectively in a table than in text material. To illustrate this point, consider the following information:

The number of calories used depends on the activity in which an individual is engaged. A 200-pound person involved in one hour of the following activities would use the indicated number of calories: sleeping uses 80; standing uses 140; walking uses 300; and running uses 750. This information was obtained from *Dr. Ryan's Exercise Report*, which was published in April 1989.

This statistical information would be communicated more effectively if presented in a table, as shown in Illustration 16-1.

According to information contained in *Dr. Ryan's Exercise Report*, the number of calories used depends on physical activity. The table below shows calories burned by a 200-pound individual involved in one hour of activity.

TABLE 1: CALORIC REQUIREMENTS FOR ONE HOUR OF ACTIVITY

Activity	Calories Used*
Sleeping	80
Standing	140
Walking	300
Running	750

*Calculated for a 200-pound person.

SOURCE: *Dr. Ryan's Exercise Report*, April 1989

Illustration 16-1   Table

When information to be presented in a table requires numerous columns, the table may be constructed vertically on the page rather than horizontally. Illustration 16-2 is a table constructed vertically.

CHARTS

Pie charts, flowcharts, and organization charts are commonly used.

The three types of charts commonly used in business reports are organization charts, flowcharts, and pie charts. None of these charts needs lengthy text interpretation. The first two types, organization charts and flowcharts, clearly present relationships and procedures. The pie chart is used to illustrate the proportion of a part to the whole.

1a
The keyboard is used to input data. The software uses the data to produce pie charts or other types of graphic aids.

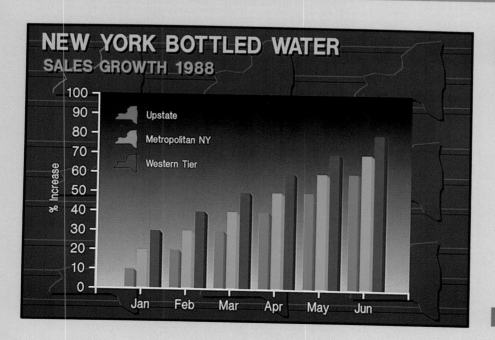

NEW YORK BOTTLED WATER
SALES GROWTH 1988

Upstate

Metropolitan NY

Western Tier

% Increase

100
90
80
70
60
50
40
30
20
10
0

Jan Feb Mar Apr May Jun

1b
Bar graphs effectively illustrate changes in monthly sales.

2a

Once data has been entered it can be easily modified by using the keyboard.

2b

Computers can be used to make realistic estimates and to present these estimates in attractive illustrations.

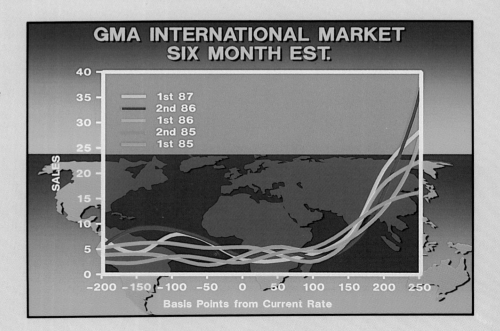

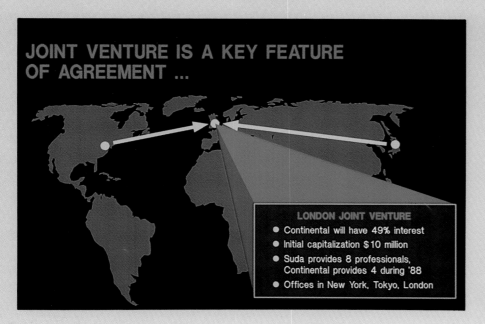

3a

Key points may be projected for emphasis.

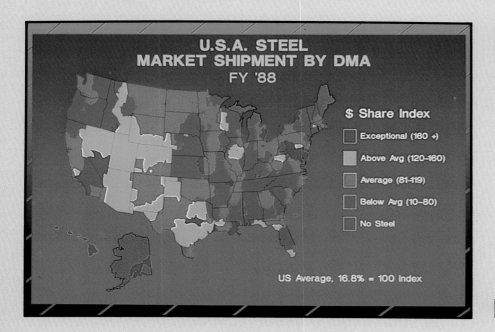

3b

Using color in maps can assist the reader in visualizing geographic locations.

4a

Effective use of color in a graphic aid can help receivers understand such topics as soil composition.

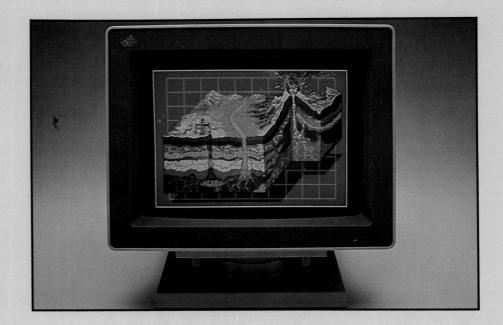

4b

A complicated assembly is easier to understand when drawings are used to explain its construction.

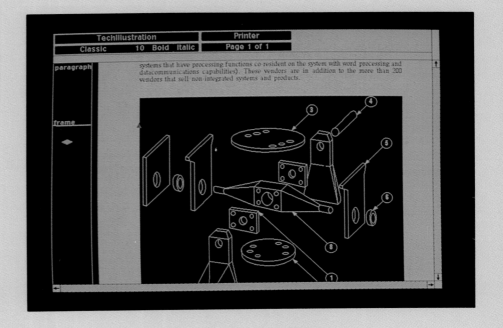

EMPLOYEE ABSENTEE REPORT—DAYS ABSENT FOR 1990

Employee	Jan.	Feb.	Mar.	Apr.	May	June	July	Aug.	Sept.	Oct.	Nov.	Dec.	Total
Lynne Adams	0	2	1	0	3	0	6	2	0	1	0	4	19
John Burkeen	2	1	0	1	0	3	1	0	2	1	0	1	12
Tom Cope	3	0	0	0	0	0	0	2	0	0	4	2	11
Clara Davis	0	0	3	4	0	0	0	0	0	2	0	0	9
Julia Elliot	0	1	0	3	0	2	0	0	2	0	1	1	10
Larry Goff	1	1	1	1	1	1	1	1	1	0	1	1	11
Julio Martinez	0	0	2	0	0	0	0	1	0	0	2	0	5
Nell Neumann	0	0	0	0	0	0	2	0	0	0	0	0	2
Ray Osborne	0	0	1	0	3	0	0	2	0	0	7	0	13
Kim Ott	0	0	0	0	0	0	0	0	0	0	0	0	0
Ann Parker	0	4	0	2	0	1	0	3	0	1	1	2	14
Scott Schroeder	1	0	0	0	2	0	0	0	1	0	0	0	4
Jay Winters	0	3	0	0	0	0	2	0	0	1	0	2	8
Totals	7	12	8	11	9	7	12	11	6	6	16	13	118

Illustration 16-2 Lengthwise Table

Lines of authority and relationships within an organization are shown in an organization chart.

ORGANIZATION CHARTS. An organization chart shows lines of authority among the various positions within an organization. This type of chart illustrates the relationships among departments and the personnel within the departments. The chart may depict the entire organization or a selected portion of the organization. The senior position is placed at the top of the chart. Other positions are placed on the chart in descending order of authority. These positions are connected by solid lines if they are in line positions with authority over other positions and by broken or dotted lines if they are in advisory roles. An example of an organization chart is shown in Illustration 16-3.

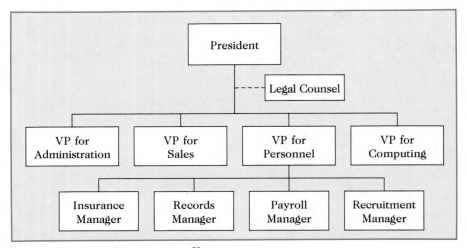

Illustration 16-3 Organization Chart

Flowcharts simplify the interpretation of complicated procedures.

FLOWCHARTS. Flowcharts may be used to illustrate complicated procedures. Such procedures could include the steps needed to manufacture a product, the route that a form follows when processed in an office, or the steps in a computer program.

    Complicated written instructions are more easily understood when accompanied by a flowchart. Each step of the procedure needs to be included, but the chart should not be so detailed that it becomes difficult to understand. Boxes of various shapes are connected by arrows to illustrate the direction that the action follows during the procedure. The size of a box is determined by the number of words in the label and does not indicate the importance of that particular portion of the procedure. A flowchart for preparing an order in a fast-food store is shown in Illustration 16-4.

A pie chart is a circle; its slices show the relationships of the parts to a whole.

PIE CHARTS. A pie chart can be used to show how the parts of a whole are distributed and how the parts relate to one another. To make the chart easy to read, you should begin slicing the pie at the 12 o'clock position and continue in a clockwise direction. The pieces should be arranged in descending

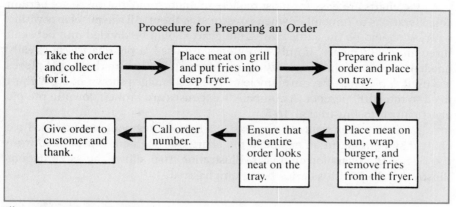

Illustration 16-4 Flowchart

order of size. If several smaller pieces are combined into an "Other" category, this piece should be placed last. "Other" should never be the largest segment. Individual pieces should be labeled by showing the quantity, or percentage, of each piece as in Illustration 16-5.

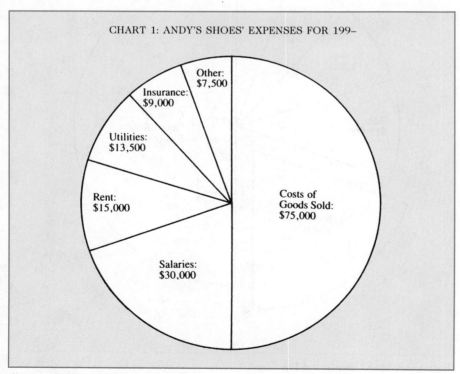

Illustration 16-5 Pie Chart

Certain principles should be followed when constructing pie charts.

Pie charts are easy for most readers to understand, but there are certain considerations to remember when constructing them. All the pie charts within a report should be the same size. A pie chart should be divided into between three and eight pieces. If only two pieces are used, a pie chart is not really needed because of the simplicity of the information; if more than eight pieces are used, a pie chart becomes unclear. The percentages shown in a pie chart need to total 100 percent. A company's expenses are broken down in the pie chart shown in Illustration 16-5.

An exploded pie chart is used to emphasize one segment.

When a writer wants to emphasize a specific segment, an exploded pie chart may be used. In an exploded pie chart, one segment is separated from the rest of the chart for emphasis. Illustration 16-6 shows the same data as Illustration 16-5 with salaries being emphasized.

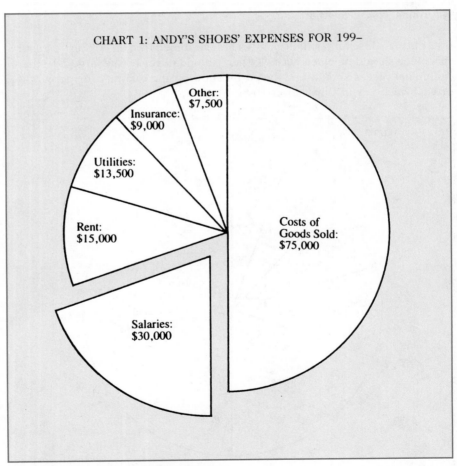

Illustration 16-6 Exploded Pie Chart

GRAPHS

A graph is a drawing that represents the relationships of quantities or qualities to each other. It provides a convenient medium through which data can be compared. Graphs should use a simple design so the reader can interpret the information easily. Using complex graphs to impress readers will only confuse them. The most frequently used graphs in business organizations are bar and line graphs. These types of graphs have several variations.

Graphs show relationships between variables. They should not have a complex design.

BAR GRAPHS. Bar graphs are effective for comparing differences in quantities. These differences in quantities are illustrated through changes in the lengths of the bars. Bar graphs may be constructed either horizontally or vertically. The most widely used bar graphs include simple, broken, multiple, stacked, and positive-negative. All bar graphs except the positive-negative one should begin with zero at the bottom or extreme left.

Comparisons of quantitative differences can be shown in bar graphs.

In a *simple bar graph*, the length or height of a bar indicates quantity. You should use a bar width that makes a good visual impression. The width of individual bars should not vary within a graph. A simple vertical bar graph is shown in Illustration 16-7, and a simple horizontal bar graph is shown in Illustration 16-8.

The length or height of a bar indicates quantity in a simple bar graph.

Graphs depicting large amounts make it impractical to include the entire amounts, so a *broken-bar graph*, as shown in Illustration 16-9, may be used.

Multiple bar graphs are used to compare several quantitative areas at one time on a single graph. Cross-hatching, shading, or color variation can be used to distinguish among bars representing different areas. Bars should be labeled, or a legend should be included on the graph to identify the different cross-hatching, shading, or color variations. The graph will become cluttered and difficult to read if more than four areas are compared on one graph. Illustration 16-10 shows a multiple bar graph.

Several quantitative variables can be compared on one multiple bar graph.

Elements within a variable may be illustrated in a *stacked bar graph*. This type of graph is useful in demonstrating differences in values within variables by dividing each bar into its parts. Values should be included for each part, and the parts should be differentiated and identified as in multiple bar graphs. A stacked bar graph is shown in Illustration 16-11.

A stacked bar graph shows differences in values within variables.

A *positive-negative bar graph* shows plus or minus deviations from a fixed reference point. The bars go up or down from this fixed reference point. Relationships between positive and negative values can be illustrated clearly using a positive-negative bar graph as shown in Illustration 16-12.

A comparison of variable values that fall above or below a reference point can be shown on a positive-negative bar graph.

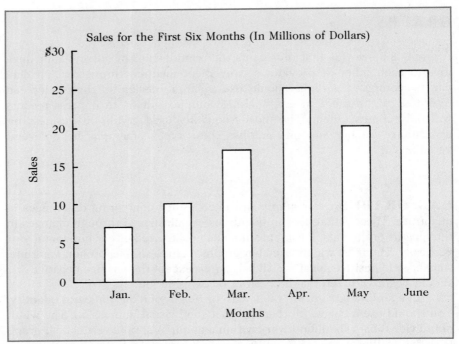

Illustration 16-7   Simple Vertical Bar Graph

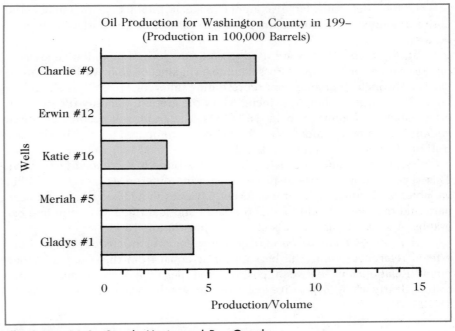

Illustration 16-8   Simple Horizontal Bar Graph

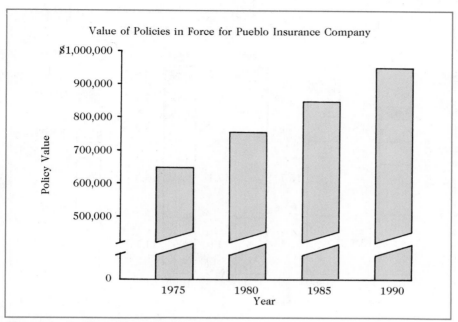

Illustration 16-9   Broken-Bar Graph

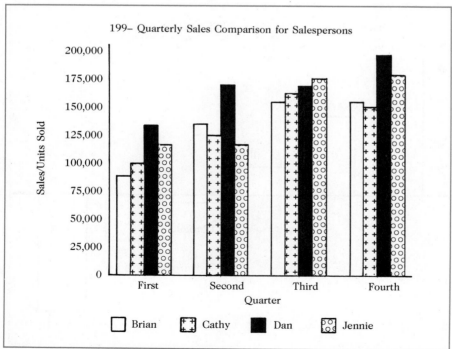

Illustration 16-10   Multiple Bar Graph

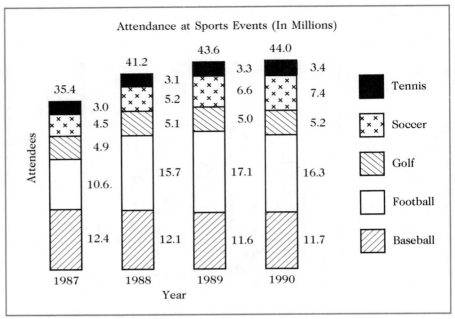

Illustration 16-11   Stacked Bar Graph

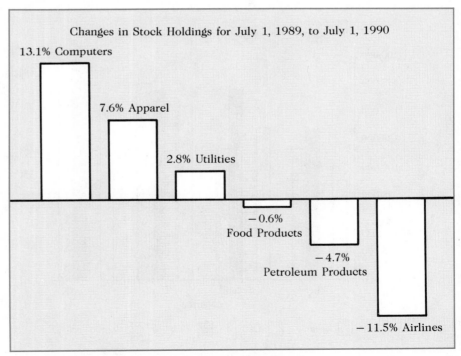

Illustration 16-12   Positive-Negative Bar Graph

LINE GRAPHS. Line graphs are used to illustrate changes over time. Trends can be effectively portrayed by showing variations within each time period.

Line graphs show changes over time.

A line graph is constructed by drawing a line on an equally divided grid with the horizontal reference line called the X-axis and the vertical reference line called the Y-axis. The interval between each vertical and horizontal line depends on the data being illustrated. The grid lines may or may not appear on the finished version of the line graph. All the data needs to be included to give an accurate and informative illustration. If the data is so excessive that it becomes unwieldy, the grid may be broken by slash or wavy lines as shown in Illustration 16-13.

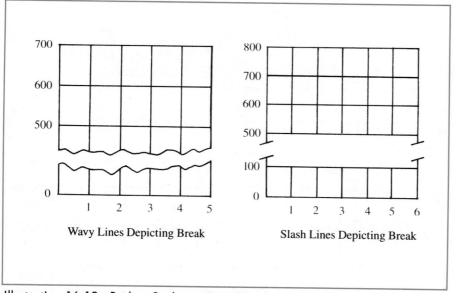

Illustration 16-13   Broken Scales on Line Graphs

A line graph can include either a single line or multiple lines. A *single line graph*, which is shown in Illustration 16-14, depicts movement of one variable. Shading may be used in a single line graph to add emphasis.

A *multiple line graph* is used to illustrate changes in more than one value. The lines can be differentiated easily by using dotted, broken, or solid lines. Some writers prefer using different colors for each line; however, this technique requires that the report be printed using several colors, which will increase the printing costs. Regardless of the method used to differentiate the lines, a legend should be shown to identify lines that are ambiguous or difficult to interpret. A multiple line graph is shown in Illustration 16-15.

Changes in several values can be shown at one time on a multiple line graph.

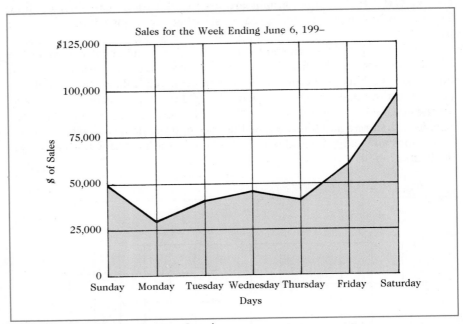

Illustration 16-14   Single Line Graph

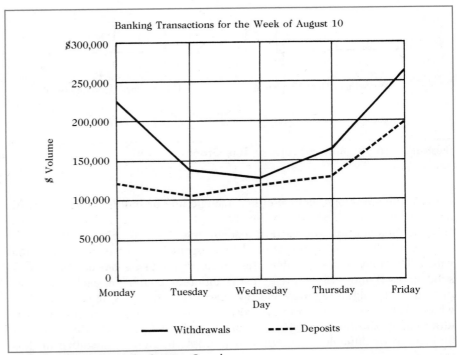

Illustration 16-15   Multiple Line Graph

MISCELLANEOUS GRAPHIC AIDS

Although the most commonly used graphic aids are tables, charts, and graphs, these are not the only effective graphic aids that can be used in reports. Graphic aids such as maps, photographs, pictographs, and drawings are used infrequently but can be extremely effective in conveying specific messages at appropriate times. Any relevant graphic aid that clarifies and strengthens the written text should be considered for use in a report.

Maps can be effective in helping a reader visualize geographic relationships. The complexity of maps ranges from simple sketches to detailed, multicolored presentations. The content of the map determines the size of the graphic aid. Notice how easy it is to identify the locations of the four factory sites shown on the map in Illustration 16-16.

> Any illustration that complements the written text should be considered for use.
>
> Maps can help the reader understand geographic details.

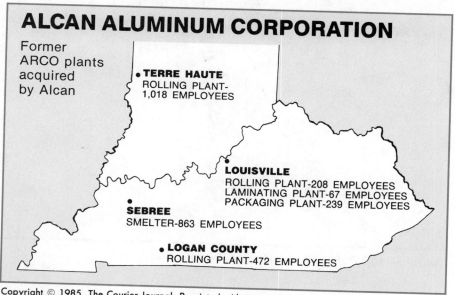

Copyright © 1985. The Courier-Journal. Reprinted with permission.

Illustration 16-16 Map

A personal touch can be added to a business report by including a **photograph** of a facility, product, or employee. In order to enhance communication, a photograph must be clear and well planned. A mistake often made in the use of photographs is including too much material. If a photograph shows something extremely large or extremely small, a reference point should be included. A coin or a pin can be a useful reference point for small items, and a person can be a good reference point in a photograph of a large item. Illustration 16-17 shows how a photograph can be used to stimulate interest in vacationing at a resort.

> Photos used as graphic aids should not contain too much material.

Illustration 16-17   Photograph Used to Promote Resort

Pictographs use images to emphasize differences in quantitative data.

Pictographs are similar to bar graphs in that they emphasize differences in statistical data but differ in that they use images of items or symbols instead of bars. All the images or symbols should be the same size to avoid distorting their values. The pictograph in Illustration 16-18 graphically accentuates the increase in microcomputer sales for a period of time.

Drawings can be used to emphasize one point within a procedure.

A **drawing** may be the most effective means of communicating a complicated idea or procedure. A photograph may not be desirable because it would contain clutter that would distract from the idea to be communicated. A drawing will omit the clutter and emphasize the desired details in an idea or procedure. A drawing depicting the process for making aluminum is shown in Illustration 16-19.

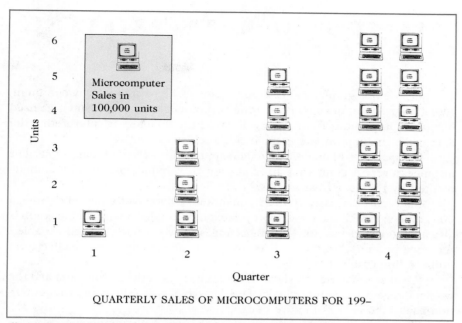

Illustration 16-18 Pictograph Showing Microcomputer Sales

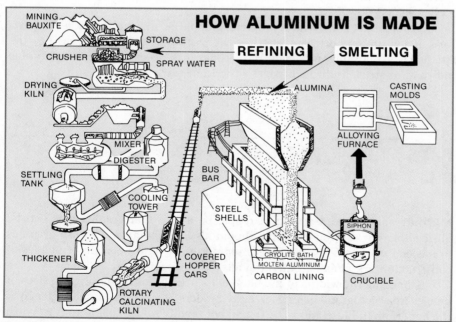

Illustration 16-19 Drawing of Aluminum Process

SELECTION OF APPROPRIATE GRAPHIC AIDS

Selecting appropriate illustrations is critical for effective communication in a report.

The purpose of a graphic aid is to complement the written text by communicating information quickly. Presenting accurate data in a clear and organized manner is important. The reader will have little difficulty in interpreting the data when the appropriate graphic aid is selected.

Compare *quantities* in bar graphs.

Comparisons of quantities in data are best illustrated by bar graphs. For instance, a report comparing fixed costs with variable costs can be complemented by the use of bar graphs.

Illustrate *trends* in line graphs.

If a report discusses trends in quantitative data over a period of time, a line graph would be the most appropriate graphic aid. A multiple line graph is also an effective device for showing changes in two or more related variables. A company comparing the sales trends for its four salespersons can effectively utilize a line graph.

Show *relationships* with pie charts.

Pie charts are used to show the relationships between the parts and the whole. Budgets are commonly displayed in pie charts to illustrate the proportion each item is to the entire budget.

Illustrate *steps* with flowcharts.

Flowcharts illustrate steps within a procedure. A new employee can easily learn the flow of a work order within an organization by carefully studying a well-designed flowchart.

Careful selection of the appropriate graphic aid may enhance the effectiveness of a written report. The length of the written text can be reduced by the use of a well-chosen graphic aid. Many times it is easier to interpret a graphic aid than to struggle through pages of written text.

POSSIBLE DECEPTION IN GRAPHIC REPRESENTATION

Graphic aids can mislead a reader.

Not only should the reader of a report be aware that graphic aids can be misleading, but the report writer should also be careful not to use graphics to mislead readers. This misrepresentation may occur if certain principles of construction are violated—intentionally or unintentionally.

Bars should be of the same width.

Changing the widths of the bars in a bar graph or increasing the sizes of images in a pictograph can deceive the readers of a report. A quick glance at the bar graph in Illustration 16-20 may not readily reveal that item A is worth half the value of item B. A reader hurriedly reading a report containing the pictograph in Illustration 16-20 may interpret Group II to be of more value

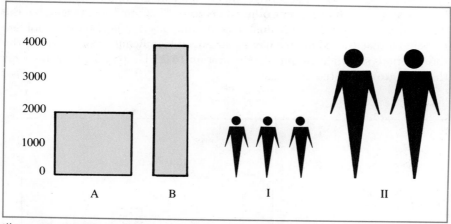

Illustration 16-20   Deception Caused by Changing Width or Size

than Group I; in fact, Group I is 50 percent larger than Group II. Specific principles must be followed in creating and interpreting bar graphs and pictographs. In a bar graph, the height or length of the bar—not the width—determines the value; and in a pictograph, the number of images—not their size—determines the value.

A report writer could deceive a reader into thinking Item A in the pie chart shown in Illustration 16-21a is one-third of the whole; it is actually one-fourth. Each piece of a pie chart must be of the same proportionate size as the part that it represents is to the whole pie (see Illustration 16-21b).

Pieces of pie charts need to be drawn to correct proportions.

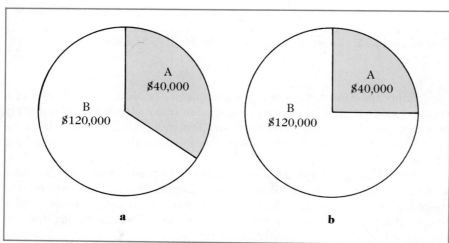

Illustration 16-21   Pie Charts Showing Disproportionate and Correct Division

The reference point of all bar graphs should be zero.

Another method of deceptive illustration is beginning the bottom of the bars in a bar graph at a point other than zero. This method exaggerates the differences between the individual bars. A company can lead its stockholders to believe that the company has experienced significant growth during the three periods shown in Graph A of Illustration 16-22; Graph B better represents the true growth of the company.

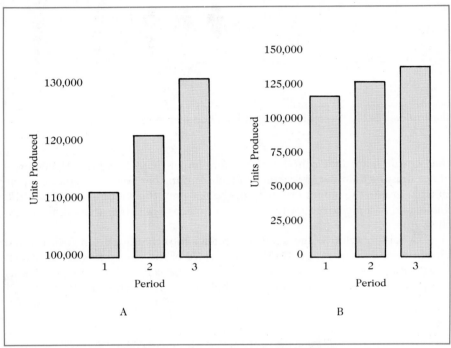

Illustration 16-22   Deception Caused by Not Starting Baseline at Zero

Grid increments should be of consistent value throughout a line graph.

Improper construction of a line graph can also deceive the reader of a report. Inconsistent values between grids can make changes appear greater or lesser than they actually are. Notice in Illustration 16-23 how the increase from Period 2 to Period 6 appears four times greater than the decrease from Period 1 to Period 2.

The labels of a graphic aid should also be critically evaluated. A reader looking at the bar graph in Illustration 16-24 should question why the odd years have been omitted. Is the report writer attempting to make the reader believe that there has been a steady increase in the values throughout the period? What happened in 1987 and 1989?

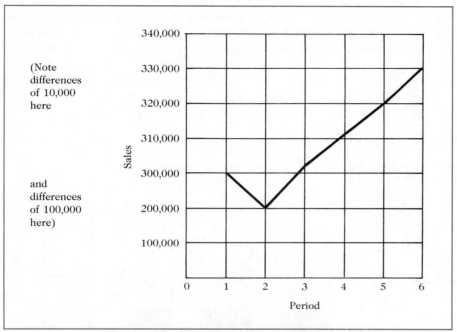

Illustration 16-23   Inconsistent Increments on a Line Graph

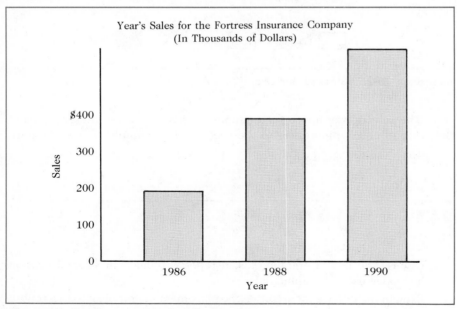

Illustration 16-24   Intentional Omission of Data

Text references to graphic aids should be considered, too. Suppose a report reads "Sales, as shown in Illustration 16-25, have grown steadily during the four periods." Would the reader assume that all three types of sales have grown or would the reader assume that only catalog sales have grown?

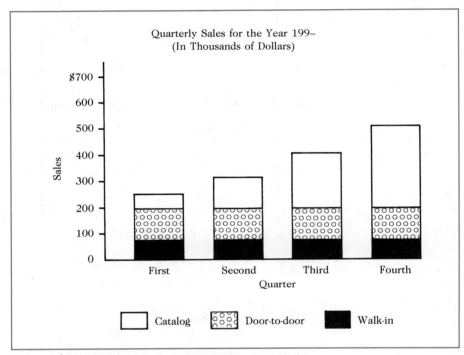

Illustration 16-25   Stacked Bar Graph Showing Sales

The written text must accurately describe the graphic aid.

The selection of appropriate graphic aids and accurate descriptions of them are of equal importance to the successful communication of a report.

DISCUSSION QUESTIONS

1. Discuss the use of graphic aids in reports. Include in your discussion improper uses of graphic aids.
2. Explain the criteria for selecting the placement of graphic aids in a report.
3. Discuss the proper method of identifying graphic aids.

4. Describe the three types of charts commonly used in business reports.
5. Compare a simple bar graph with a multiple bar graph.
6. Why would broken scales be used on line graphs?
7. Distinguish between a single line graph and a multiple line graph.
8. Describe four miscellaneous graphic aids that can be used in a report.
9. Give four examples of how graphic aids can be deceptive.

APPLICATION EXERCISES

1. Collect five magazine or newspaper articles that contain illustrations. Analyze the graphic aids. Include in your analysis the placement of the aids, their labels, references to them in the text, and how they can be improved.

2. Prepare a graphic aid that will illustrate each step of the procedure you follow from the time you awaken to the time you leave for your first class.

3. Construct a graphic aid that illustrates the grades you have made in this course.

4. Select the most appropriate graphic aid to illustrate each of the following. Give justification for each of your selections.
   a. The average weekly temperature for a three-month period
   b. Damage to a house from a tree blown down during a tornado
   c. The number of freshmen, sophomores, juniors, and seniors in an institution
   d. Monday gold, silver, and platinum prices (individually shown) in relation to interest rates for a one-year period
   e. Procedure that students must follow to register for classes
   f. The dollar amounts of loans that specific bank branch offices have made each month for a year
   g. Monthly change in fish population for a lake after an antipollution plan is put into effect
   h. Comparison of weekly absences of company personnel during the first quarter of 1989 and the first quarter of 1990
   i. Correct placement of fingers on home row keys of a microcomputer
   j. Low temperatures of major cities in the United States

5. Construct the graphic aid that best illustrates the data for each of the following situations. Create your own titles and labels. Write the introduction to the aid. Be sure to direct your reader to some aspect of the data and refer to the illustration by number.

   a. Grocery list: eggs—75 cents, bacon—$2.19, crackers—79 cents, beans—32 cents, liver—$1.54, apples—75 cents, macaroni—42 cents

   b. Number of employees:
      1987: laborers—32, supervisors—5, managers—2
      1988: laborers—34, supervisors—6, managers—4
      1989: laborers—36, supervisors—8, managers—6
      1990: laborers—40, supervisors—11, managers—8
      1991: laborers—41, supervisors—12, managers—8

   c. Times for three-mile jog:

      April 2:   Ann—18 min 37 sec   April 21: Ann—18 min 17 sec
                 Bob—19 min 43 sec   Bob—18 min 57 sec
                 Tom—23 min 12 sec   Tom—21 min 49 sec

      April 9:   Ann—18 min 21 sec   April 25: Ann—18 min 20 sec
                 Bob—19 min 30 sec   Bob—18 min 59 sec
                 Tom—22 min 37 sec   Tom—21 min 33 sec

      April 15: Ann—18 min 28 sec   April 29: Ann—18 min 15 sec
                 Bob—19 min 18 sec   Bob—18 min 55 sec
                 Tom—22 min 03 sec   Tom—20 min 58 sec

   d. Composition of 24-hour viewing day:
      1989: news—3 hr 30 min   1990: news—5 hr
             sports—4 hr 15 min   sports—2 hr 30 min
             movies—4 hr   movies—6 hr
             weekly series—8 hr   weekly series—9 hr
             other—4 hr 15 min   other—1 hr 30 min

   e. Number of customers for each day of the week:
      Monday—321
      Tuesday—290
      Wednesday—354
      Thursday—311
      Friday—298
      Saturday—391
      Sunday—277

6. A student's expenses for a semester may consist of the following:

Tuition	$4,500
Room and Board	2,100
Clothing	450
Entertainment	1,825
Other	1,325

   Construct a graphic aid that most effectively illustrates how each expense compares with the other expenses.

7. Construct the most appropriate graphic aid to compare the monthly rainfall for the three years.

	1988	1989	1990
January	2.1 inches	3.9 inches	1.1 inches
February	2.4	3.3	1.9
March	3.4	4.0	1.7
April	2.4	2.6	2.8
May	1.1	1.6	0.7
June	0.7	1.1	0.0
July	0.5	0.6	0.2
August	0.0	1.2	0.8
September	1.4	1.3	2.1
October	1.9	2.0	2.4
November	2.2	2.4	3.2
December	2.7	1.9	3.4

PART FIVE

ORAL AND NONVERBAL COMMUNICATION APPLICATIONS

LISTENING AND NONVERBAL MESSAGES

L E A R N I N G   O B J E C T I V E S

Your learning objectives for this chapter include the following:

- To understand the four elements of the listening process
- To learn the guidelines for effective listening
- To distinguish among the three modes of listening
- To recognize barriers to effective listening and know how to overcome them
- To understand the advantages of effective listening
- To identify different types of nonverbal messages and their impact on the communication process
- To understand the importance of nonverbal communication

Listening and nonverbal communication are important.

The significant roles of written communication have been stressed in the preceding chapters of this book. The importance of listening, nonverbal communication, and oral communication in the business environment should not be overlooked. This chapter will discuss listening and nonverbal communication. Chapters 18 and 19 discuss oral communication.

LISTENING

There are various reasons for listening. Some common ones are to enjoy entertainment, to gain information, to receive instructions, to hear complaints, and to show respect. For each reason for listening, there are various situations in which listening takes place. For example, information may be acquired in several types of situations: listening one-on-one over the telephone or in face-to-face conversation; listening in a small group, such as a few supervisors receiving instructions from their manager; and listening in a large group, such as hearing a keynote speaker at a conference.

Information is acquired through listening.

HEARING VERSUS LISTENING

You may have attended a class and heard the teacher give instructions for completing a report or project. Later, as you began preparing the assignment, you realized that you could not recall the details needed to complete the work. Consider another situation where a painter was told to go to a resort area and paint the weekend home of a client. After spending a week completing the work, the painter was informed that he had painted the wrong house. These are two examples in which hearing occurred, but the entire listening process was not utilized.

Hearing is not the same as listening.

THE LISTENING PROCESS

The listening process consists of four elements. Hearing is only one of these elements; the other three are filtering, interpreting, and recalling. Illustration 17-1 shows the four elements of the listening process.

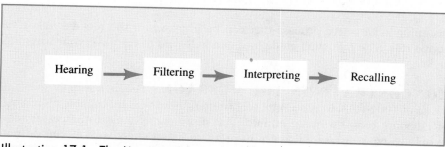

Illustration 17-1   The Listening Process

HEARING. The first element in the listening process, hearing, involves the physiological process of the auditory nerves being stimulated by sound waves. Everyone hears sounds unless he or she has a hearing impairment.

FILTERING. The second element in the listening process, filtering, is the elimination of unwanted stimuli. Filtering allows a listener to focus on stimuli that are of specific interest. Consider an example illustrating both unwanted and wanted stimuli: Suppose someone attending a meeting on insurance benefits is seated by a window through which the aroma from a nearby fast-food restaurant is making the listener hungry. The unwanted stimuli is the food aroma, and the wanted stimuli is the speaker's information about the insurance. An individual has difficulty concentrating on an oral message when the filtering process is incapable of eliminating or at least minimizing distracting stimuli.

INTERPRETING. The third element of the listening process is interpreting. When interpreting stimuli, the listener's mind assigns meaning to the stimuli. This assignment of meaning is done through the use of the person's mental filters. As pointed out in Chapter 1, it is important for the receiver to interpret the stimuli in the way the sender intended.

RECALLING. The fourth element, recalling, involves remembering at a later time the information that was interpreted earlier. The success of this element depends heavily on the association (relationship) placed on the stimuli during the interpretation phase.

SUCCESSFUL LISTENING. The success of the listening process depends upon all four elements. If one of the elements is omitted or fails to function properly, the entire listening process is jeopardized. To ensure that the listening process is carried out properly, certain guidelines need to be followed.

GUIDELINES FOR LISTENING

Listening is an active process that can be improved if the receiver takes an active role. The following guidelines can help you to improve your listening skills.

CONCENTRATE ON THE MESSAGE. People normally speak at a rate of 100 to 200 words a minute. Listeners, however, are capable of hearing at rates up to 500 words a minute. This discrepancy makes it necessary for people to concentrate diligently in order to listen effectively. If you do not concentrate intensely, your mind may wander to another topic.

Margin notes:

Hearing is a physiological process.

Filtering eliminates unwanted stimuli.

Stimuli are interpreted and assigned meanings by the receiver.

Proper association improves recall ability.

Listening is an active process and can be improved.

You can hear at a faster rate than you can speak.

To be a successful listener, you need to take an active role in the listening process.

One concentration techinque is to mentally summarize the message. This technique is especially important when the speaker has not organized the speech well. Also, you should concentrate on the main points the speaker is trying to convey, look for hidden messages, and determine if the speaker is using facts, opinions, or inferences. Do not allow the speaker's physical appearance, manner of speaking, or manner of dress to distract you from concentrating on what is said. Concentrating on the message will assist you in overcoming barriers such as these that may interfere with your hearing the entire message.

DETERMINE THE PURPOSE OF THE MESSAGE. Messages presented orally have purposes, as do written messages. You, as a listener, need to determine the purpose of the oral message so that you can decide on the mode that you will use to listen to the message. The three modes that are commonly used to listen to messages are cautious listening, skimming, and scanning.

CAUTIOUS LISTENING. This mode is used when you need to understand and remember both the general concept and all the details of the message. This mode requires more energy than the other modes because of the amount of spoken material on which you must concentrate. When listening in this mode, your mind does not have any time to relax.

SKIMMING. You can skim the spoken material when you only need to understand the general concept of the message. When using this mode for listening, your mind has time to relax because you do not need to remember all the details being presented. Think of your mind as a computer. The amount of storage is vast but not limitless. Cluttering your mind with insignificant matter causes it to tire, which could cause you to forget the important facts.

Concentrate on the main concepts, but be aware of hidden meanings.

Block distractions and concentrate on the message.

The three modes of listening are cautious listening, skimming, and scanning.

Cautious listening is when you attempt to remember concepts and details.

Skimming is used when you need to remember only the general concept.

Scanning is the least careful type of listening.

SCANNING. When scanning, you concentrate only on the details that are of specific interest to you, instead of on the message's general concept. No energy is wasted trying to retain information that is not of specific interest. One shortcoming in using this mode is that your mind may wander, and you may miss material that is important.

Don't allow biases to influence listening.

KEEP AN OPEN MIND. The speaker is presenting the message from his or her viewpoint. Respect this viewpoint by not allowing your biases to block out what is being said. Your listening ability may be impaired when you are not receptive to the message being presented. When you listen with an open mind, both you and the speaker will benefit. The speaker will believe that what he or she is saying is worthwhile, and you may acquire valuable information. Evaluations of a speaker's message should be made after the entire message is heard. *Frozen evaluations*—judgments made early on and often rigidly set—benefit no one.

Positive feedback will improve the communication process.

USE FEEDBACK. Feedback is important. It is your response to the speaker. The speaker may volunteer more information if positive feedback is received. For instance, a worker describing a problem in the office may expand on his or her comments when you offer feedback such as "Tell me more" or "Yes, but . . ." or "Uh-huh." Some listening situations are not conducive to giving any type of feedback to the speaker. These situations include radio, television, and video presentations. Large group presentations lend themselves best to oral feedback. Each situation should be analyzed as to its appropriateness for providing feedback.

Taking notes may interfere with the listening process.

MINIMIZE TAKING NOTES. It may be wise to record complicated presentations for later review; however, the amount of recording should be kept to a minimum so that you are not distracted from listening. You will not be able to concentrate on listening if you attempt to record everything that is said. In oral communication situations that are not complex, just the major points should be recorded; notes should only be used to refresh your memory. Try to remember what is said without using notes.

Facial expressions and voice tones can change the meaning of a message.

ANALYZE THE TOTAL MESSAGE. Watch the speaker's actions and facial expressions and also listen to his or her tone of voice. A speaker can change the entire meaning of a message by raising an eyebrow or by changing the inflection of his or her voice. Such cues as these enable the listener to understand hidden messages.

Talking and interrupting interfere with listening.

DO NOT TALK OR INTERRUPT. An individual cannot talk and effectively listen at the same time. When you are talking, you cannot use all the elements of effective listening. Interrupting a speaker at inappropriate times or talking to others while the speaker is speaking is rude and reduces the effectiveness of the communication.

BARRIERS TO LISTENING

Barriers are any obstacles that interfere with the listening process. You should be aware of barriers so that you can avoid letting them interfere with your listening. Some of the more important barriers to listening are discussed here.

PHYSICAL DISTRACTIONS.   The individual responsible for setting up the meeting place in which the listening will occur is primarily responsible for minimizing physical distractions. However, you can take actions to limit this barrier such as sitting at the front of the room if you have a hearing impairment, not sitting near a corridor or open window, or not sitting next to an individual who will talk or whisper during the presentation.

Be aware of physical distractions.

MENTAL DISTRACTIONS.   You have a responsibility as a listener to give your undivided attention to a speaker. You should avoid daydreaming or allowing your mind to wander. You can think about four times faster than a speaker can talk, so it is easy to begin thinking about other business or personal interests instead of paying attention to the speaker.

Don't let your mind wander when listening.

A very common distraction is mentally constructing a question to ask rather than concentrating on what is being said. A related mental distraction is forming an opinion or rebuttal during a presentation. To listen effectively, keep an open mind—that is, hear what is said before making judgments.

NONVERBAL DISTRACTIONS.   A listener may give a speaker negative nonverbal feedback. Facial expressions—frowning, yawning, raising an eyebrow, or closing the eyes—can convey a message of disinterest or disapproval. Glancing at a watch or a clock may tell the speaker that you are ready for the presentation to be terminated. The lines of communication will remain open when these nonverbal distractions are avoided.

Give the speaker positive feedback by avoiding negative nonverbal actions.

INAPPROPRIATE TIMING.   A listener should ensure that a speaker can present his or her message at an appropriate time. A listener often knows if the time is appropriate. For example, a manager going through a plant may casually ask a worker, "Any problems?" It may seem to the worker that the manager does not really want to listen to him or her. The manager has asked the question at an inappropriate time if a supervisor is standing nearby and the manager is aware that the worker would be reluctant to complain in front of the supervisor. A more appropriate comment from the manager would be, "If you have any problems, I have an open door policy and have reserved Wednesday afternoons to listen to employees." This would allow the speaker (the worker) to present his or her message at an appropriate time.

The timing of the communication is important.

An individual presenting a message should be given adequate time so that he or she does not have to rush. It is the listener's responsibility to ensure that the speaker will have enough time to present the entire message.

A listener should give a speaker adequate time to present a message.

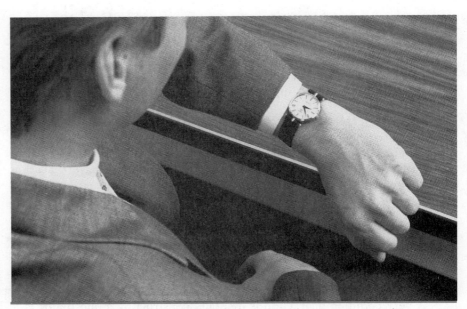

A nonverbal distraction, such as glancing at your watch, can give a speaker negative feedback and interfere with the listening process.

For example, if a manager has to leave for a meeting in 5 minutes and a supervisor enters the office to discuss a problem that will take 15 minutes, the manager should make an appointment to hear the supervisor at a later time. The manager should not expect the supervisor to condense the presentation into 5 minutes.

INEFFECTIVE SPEECH CHARACTERISTICS. A listener must be able to hear and understand a speaker in order to interpret the message. If the words are spoken at insufficient volume or at such a high pitch that the listener has trouble hearing the words, listening will be difficult, if not impossible. Other speech characteristic barriers include dialects, unusual pronunciations, jargon, regional speech patterns (accents), and speech impairments. These barriers are difficult to overcome because a listener cannot review a spoken message the same way as a written message. Careful concentration may help a listener deal effectively with speech characteristic barriers.

Speech barriers are difficult to overcome.

ADVANTAGES OF EFFECTIVE LISTENING

Effective listening will enable you to be more successful.

One of the best ways to acquire information is through effective listening. Effective listening will help you develop better attitudes. Also, it will improve your relationships with others because they will realize that you are interested in them. Interested individuals will work diligently in communicating with you. This, in turn, will allow you to do a better job because you will have the support of the people around you. Effective listening will encourage individuals to relate minor problems to you before they become major problems.

NONVERBAL COMMUNICATION

Communication that is not written or spoken is considered nonverbal. Nonverbal messages can add to, or detract from, communication. Nonverbal messages may be delivered in various ways.

Nonverbal communication is a message without words.

As an example, suppose every day on your way to work you meet the same person at the same place. Each morning as you pass each other you exchange greetings. Suddenly, one morning your greeting is met with indifference; the person does not acknowledge your presence. Later in the day someone asks you if you saw the passerby this morning, and you recall your earlier encounter. Would you have been so aware of your recollection if the passerby had spoken to you earlier in the day? Was the passerby's nonverbal message stronger than a verbal communication would have been?

We are constantly communicating—either consciously or unconsciously— through nonverbal messages. These messages are an important part of the communication process. Here is another example of how nonverbal messages affect other forms of communication: A prospective customer receives a sales letter announcing a gigantic clothing sale, and the letter is filled with typographical errors. The presence of typographical errors is a nonverbal message suggesting carelessness. How quickly will the customer rush to the store for the sale? Which message is more effective—the written or the nonverbal?

Nonverbal messages are important.

TYPES OF NONVERBAL COMMUNICATION

Nonverbal messages come in various forms. Some of the common types of nonverbal communication will now be considered.

PHYSICAL APPEARANCE. Physical appearance is an important type of nonverbal communication. It may cause the receiver of a written message to form a frozen evaluation about the subject. An individual will form a first impression from a letter's envelope, stationery, letterhead, format, and neatness. This first impression will definitely influence the reaction of the receiver to the letter.

The physical appearance of a written message influences its first impression.

The physical appearance of a speaker influences an oral message as much as the appearance of a letter influences a written message. A sloppily dressed salesperson will find it difficult, if not impossible, to sell expensive clothes.

Manner of dress
communicates a
nonverbal message.

People oftentimes judge the status of others by the appearance of their possessions. For instance, an individual who wears designer clothes, custom-made shoes, and expensive jewelry will transmit a nonverbal message. This nonverbal message will be perceived differently depending on the occasion for which the individual is dressed. If the individual is going to lunch or dinner at an elegant restaurant, most people would perceive the person to be wealthy and successful. If the individual is washing a car or mowing a lawn, many people would perceive the person to be a show-off or to be lacking in common sense.

The meaning of verbal
messages may be changed
by body language.

BODY LANGUAGE.   Nonverbal messages are constantly being transmitted through the actions of our bodies. These messages may be intentional or unintentional. Body language may change the meaning of a verbal message.

People transmit nonverbal messages through the actions of their bodies.

Researchers have studied body language extensively in recent years and have developed body language dictionaries such as Bauml and Bauml's, *A Dictionary of Gestures*. A body language gesture such as crossing the arms over the chest usually means that one's mind is made up and is not open to change. Tapping a foot usually indicates impatience.

An advantage of using body language to respond with nonverbal messages is that it conveys instant feedback to the sender of a message. A smile indicates satisfaction, a frown shows disagreement, and a raised eyebrow communicates uncertainty on the part of a receiver of a message. An instant message is communicated by an individual's eye contact during a conversation. Failure to look a person in the eye when speaking may indicate shyness, dishonesty, or embarrassment. Eye contact may indicate confidence, agreement, or interest

Body language may give instant feedback.

Crossing the arms over the chest usually means that a person's mind is made up.

A person's posture while sitting is another form of body language that communicates a nonverbal message. By sitting erect, a person conveys confidence and pride; by slumping, a person conveys tiredness and depression.

Nonverbal messages are communicated through a person's posture.

in the subject of a conversation. An individual glancing around while speaking exhibits nervousness or lack of interest.

Other forms of body language include postures and gestures. The way a person sits or stands communicates a nonverbal message. An individual standing or sitting erect conveys confidence and pride, while a person slumping over may be perceived as being tired or depressed. If an individual leans toward another person during a conversation, body language indicates that the person likes or is interested in the other communicator. If the person leans away from the other person, the posture shows a dislike or disinterest in the other individual.

A nonverbal message can be communicated by the way a person shakes hands. Confidence, aggression, or insecurity may be conveyed.

A handshake also communicates a nonverbal message. A person who firmly grips your hand demonstrates confidence, while an individual who squeezes your hand so tightly that it causes pain gives the impression of being overly aggressive or inconsiderate.

Handshakes communicate messages.

Gestures are an integral part of nonverbal communication.

It is practically impossible to communicate without some use of gestures. A gesture may be as simple as thumbs-up to signify approval or thumbs-down for disapproval. A gesture may be used to emphasize a critical point in an oral presentation. How interesting would a speech be if the only communicative motion was the opening and closing of the speaker's mouth? Care should be taken in using gestures because, as will be pointed out in Chapter 20, different cultures interpret gestures in different ways. For instance, if a woman in southern Germany tilts her head to the side and leans forward to listen she is considered attentive, but in northern Germany she would be perceived as cringing and timid. To be considered attentive in northern Germany, she would sit up straight and look the speaker directly in the eye (which in southern Germany would indicate that she is angry). Similar cultural differences apply to other nonverbal messages.

SPACE. Communication is influenced by space. Space as used in nonverbal communication includes the size of a physical area, proximity to another person, and obstacles between you and the person with whom you are speaking.

The amount of space in an office or home indicates the status of the occupant.

Space transmits a nonverbal message.

The size of a person's office is an indication of importance within the hierarchy of an organization. The larger the office, the higher the position. People in our society are influenced by sizes and locations of homes. The amount of space people possess influences our attitudes and, therefore, inadvertently is a form of nonverbal communication.

A person in charge wants to keep his or her most trusted aide nearby. Therefore the proximity of an employee to a supervisor communicates nonverbally the importance of this employee within the organization. The employee's importance may be nonverbally indicated by location of parking space, by location and size of office, or by seating location at meetings.

Research has shown that eliminating obstacles such as desks, chairs, and tables will improve oral communication between individuals. The communication will improve if both communicators are on the same level—sitting or standing. The distance between the communicators will also affect the communication. This distance will vary with individuals from different cultures.

Emphasis on time transmits a message.

TIME. As communicators, we must be aware that the amount of time devoted to a subject transmits a nonverbal message. If the president of a company, for instance, meets with one manager for ten minutes and another manager for two hours, a nonverbal message is unintentionally being transmitted.

Punctuality relays a nonverbal message. A person who is always on time is perceived as well organized. A person who is always late transmits a message that he or she is unorganized or that the appointment is unimportant. For instance, if two people of equal credentials were interviewing for a job and one arrived 15 minutes late for the interview, it is more likely that the punctual applicant would be hired.

THE IMPORTANCE OF NONVERBAL COMMUNICATION

A person should be aware of the impact of nonverbal communication. Nonverbal messages may not always be intended; nevertheless, they clearly communicate with and influence people. Nonverbal messages may aid or hinder communication. The following summarizes the more important characteristics of nonverbal communication:

Nonverbal communication is an important part of the communication process.

1. The nonverbal communication can be unintentional. The sender may be unaware that he or she is nonverbally sending a message and, consequently, may not be aware of the impact that message may have.
2. A nonverbal communication can be more honest than a verbal one. Since the message may be unconsciously transmitted, the sender will not have planned it. Therefore, a nonverbal message can be more reliable than a verbal or a written one, which can be thought out ahead of time much more easily.
3. Nonverbal communication makes, or helps to make, a first impression. At times this first impression can result in the recipient of the message forming a frozen evaluation of the sender, and this frozen image may be very difficult for the sender to alter.
4. Nonverbal communication is always present. Neither verbal nor written communication exists without nonverbal communication being present.

DISCUSSION QUESTIONS

1. Describe the difference between hearing and listening.
2. Explain the listening process.
3. How do hearing and speaking rates affect listening concentration?
4. List and describe the three modes of listening.
5. How can a listener keep an open mind?
6. Describe five barriers to listening.
7. How can effective listening improve your communication?
8. What are various ways that appearance communicates nonverbal messages?
9. Describe several forms of body language, and explain how they transmit nonverbal messages.
10. How do time and space communicate messages?

APPLICATION EXERCISES

1. Watch the President of the United States give a speech or conduct a press conference. Record nonverbal messages that are transmitted. Be prepared to discuss the effects of the nonverbal messages on the presentation.

2. After the class has been divided into at least two teams, take turns acting out, without speaking, roles presented by the teacher.

3. Visit a shopping mall or large department store and observe customers and salespersons. Record the nonverbal messages that each presents. Describe the messages that are transmitted.

4. Visit offices of different levels of managers in a business and write a short report on how the use of space communicates a message in the organization.

5. Observe students' and instructors' body language on Monday and Friday. Record the differences in the communication for the two days. Are the differences easily apparent?

CHAPTER 18

IMPROVING YOUR ORAL COMMUNICATION

LEARNING OBJECTIVES

Your learning objectives for this chapter include the following:

- To appreciate the role and the importance of oral communication in business
- To learn how to improve the basic quality of your voice
- To develop the ability to use your voice effectively
- To develop the ability to strengthen your personal presence

Most of your communication in business will be oral. Your personal success and achievement, therefore, will depend primarily on the effectiveness of your oral communication. The effectiveness of your oral communication relates directly to your understanding of the principles, processes, and goals of business communication. All that you have learned about written communication—grammar, direct and indirect approaches, message development, and graphic aids—can be of value to you in oral communication.

Most business communication is oral.

If you want to provide leadership to others, your degree of success will relate directly to your ability to speak clearly, intelligently, and persuasively in a confident, convincing manner. Your effectiveness will depend on the quality of your voice and the strength of your presence.

Leadership depends on oral communication ability.

In this chapter, the role of oral communication in business, the improvement of your voice qualities, the effective use of your voice, and the strengthening of your presence are the major topics.

COMMUNICATING ORALLY IN BUSINESS

Business success depends on communication.

A business that provides products or services needed by customers possesses the basic requirement for success. How successful the business is, however, depends on the quality of its internal and external communication. In other parts of this textbook, you have studied the general foundations and principles of written business communication. This section concentrates on oral business communication. Both forms—written and oral communication—are vital to success. Oral communication is critical to the success of a business because it is used so extensively.

USES OF ORAL COMMUNICATION IN BUSINESS

Businesspersons may spend up to 95 percent of their time in oral communication.

Depending on your position and level of responsibility in an organization, the amount of time spent in oral communication can vary from 10 to 95 percent of your day. Generally speaking, the higher the level to which you are promoted in an organization, the greater the amount of time you will spend in oral communication. Also, there are certain jobs that especially require a high level of oral communication.

MANAGERIAL USES OF ORAL COMMUNICATION.

Supervisors, managers, and executives spend most of their time communicating orally. They must be skilled in receiving oral communication—hearing and listening effectively—and sending oral communication—speaking effectively. They must be able to instruct, inform, persuade, inspire, convince, and correct others. They are required by their positions to give leadership to others through the strength and forcefulness of their oral communication.

Managers lead through oral communication.

Supervisors, managers, and executives must communicate orally downward. They are responsible for the morale, productivity, and quality of performance of their subordinates.

Supervisors, managers, and executives spend most of their time communicating orally.

Supervisors, managers, and executives also communicate orally both upward and laterally. They are responsible for making effective oral proposals, recommendations, and reports to their peers, superiors, boards, and stockholders, as well as to the public.

EMPLOYEE USES OF ORAL COMMUNICATION.

Certain jobs in business require extensive oral communication. The most extensive oral communication is required of people in marketing. The primary requirement for any salesperson is skill in the effective use of oral communication—the ability to convince customers to buy a business's products or services.

Many other positions in business firms require extensive oral communication. These positions include receptionist, purchasing agent, union negotiator, customer relations agent, accountant, bank teller, budget director, union official, public relations specialist, office manager, secretary, and loan officer. The list could go on at great length. Because the use of oral communication in business is extensive, the importance of oral communication to the success and achievement of individuals and business firms is paramount.

Some jobs require extensive oral communication.

The most extensive oral communication in business is required of people in marketing.

TYPES OF ORAL COMMUNICATION IN BUSINESS

There are many different types of oral communication in business. Three categories of these types are one-to-one, one-to-small group, and one-to-large group. Within each type, there can be different forms and methods of oral communication.

ONE-TO-ONE ORAL COMMUNICATION. One-to-one oral communication can be face-to-face conversation, dictation to a secretary or a machine, telephone conversation, video conversation, or communication

There are three **categories** of oral communication.

• *One-to-one:* Talking to one other person.

through other various electronic devices for voice transmission. Face-to-face conversation can include conferring with a subordinate about work plans, performance evaluation, or non-work related topics. One-to-one oral communication includes the dictation of letters, memos, and reports. Businesspersons also frequently talk with each other, customers, and members of the public on the telephone.

To be effective, one-to-one oral communication requires intelligent word choice, clarity of enunciation, variety in voice inflection, and conveyance of positive personal feelings.

ONE-TO-SMALL GROUP ORAL COMMUNICATION. It

is common in business for three or more persons to meet and talk. Small groups—usually fewer than 20 persons—meet to solve problems, to develop policy, to develop new products, to hear progress reports, and for many other reasons. For example, a committee may be formed to consider an employee tardiness problem, to determine a pricing policy, to decide on a new product line, or to hear a report on the past quarter's sales.

In addition to the requirements for effective one-to-one oral communication, effective one-to-small group communication requires understanding group dynamics, increased voice volume, and the use of special techniques to facilitate group effort.

- *One-to-small group:* Speaking to fewer than 20 persons.

ONE-TO-LARGE GROUP ORAL COMMUNICATION. One-

to-large group oral communication is commonly referred to as making a speech. For most purposes, a large group can be defined as 20 or more people. Large groups can be huge. Businesspersons may find themselves speaking to as many as 100 or more employees or attendees at a professional conference. The main speaker at a general session of a meeting may speak to 500, 5,000, or more people at one time. Of course, television and radio enable some individuals to speak to millions of people at one time.

- *One-to-large group:* Speaking to 20 or more persons.

Specific examples of types of speeches can be quite varied. You may be called on to give a speech to your company's employees in which you report last year's financial activities. You may speak to a college class on your profession, or you may speak to a community service club on the need for support of a community activity.

Having to give a speech makes most people somewhat anxious. It is, however, a unique opportunity to inform or persuade a group of people on a topic. It is an opportunity for you to be in the spotlight and on center stage for a time. It can be an extremely rewarding experience. Later in this chapter, we will discuss methods that you can use to overcome the anxiety you may feel in one-to-large group oral communication.

In addition to the requirements for effective one-to-one and one-to-small group oral communication, one-to-large group oral communication requires particular considerations of body movements, voice volume, audience analysis, and visual aids.

Improving your voice quality and personal presence will improve your oral communication.

Improving your oral communication—whether to one person or to several persons—involves improving the quality and effectiveness of your voice and strengthening your personal presence. These topics are covered in the remaining sections of this chapter. Chapter 19 discusses successful techniques for planning and presenting oral communications.

IMPROVING YOUR VOICE QUALITIES

Because the use of oral communication is extensive and its effective use is so important to you and your organization, it is vital that you do all you can to improve the quality of your voice. The starting point for improving your oral communication, then, is to improve the physiological aspects of your speaking voice.

PROPER BREATHING CONTROL

Quality sound depends on proper use of air.

High-quality sound with adequate volume depends on the proper use of the raw material of air. You use air for speaking in two basic ways. First, with two or three deep breaths you can relax your sound-producing organs and prepare them for speaking. Second, with sufficient inhalation of air and proper control of exhalation of air while speaking, you can improve the quality of the sounds you make.

Inhale deeply to fill the lungs with ample air for speaking.

Controlled deep inhalation of air fills your lungs and provides ample air for speaking. When you inhale deeply, you should not raise your shoulders, you should extend your abdomen. The air should go all the way to the diaphragm—a muscle between the chest and the abdomen. When you get nervous, you tend to breathe shallowly and not fill your lungs, thereby not providing enough air for rich and full sounds.

Exhale air past vocal cords to fill the head cavities for full, rich sounds.

The exhalation of air as you make sounds should come from your diaphragm. With a sufficient amount of air, you can bring the air up from the diaphragm past your vocal cords to fill the orifices in your head with enough force to cause the sound to be rich and full. The orifices in your head—mouth, nose, and sinuses—are like echo chambers and enrich the sound of your voice.

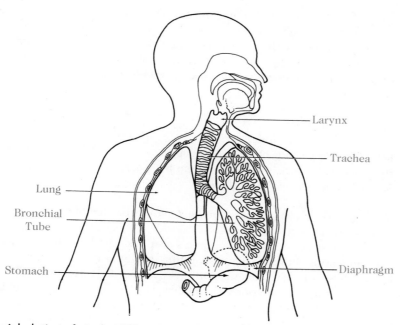

Larynx

Trachea

Lung

Bronchial
Tube

Stomach

Diaphragm

Deep inhalation of air should be controlled by the diaphragm—a muscular partition between the chest and the abdomen.

PROPER CONTROL OF JAW, TONGUE, AND LIPS

The "troublesome *T*'s" of tight jaw, tight tongue, and tight lips cause mumbled, muffled speech sounds that are hard to hear and understand. Pronunciation, enunciation, and clarity of sound depend on your jaw being flexible and your tongue and lips being loose and alive.

Practice freely flexing your jaw by saying "idea," "up and down," and "the sky is blue." Now say those same expressions with a tightly clenched jaw. Notice how clenching your jaw muffles the sounds. For more jaw-flexing practice, count from 91 to 99, and say "fine," "yes," "no," "pay," "buy," and "like" over and over.

For practice in freeing your tongue and making it come alive, say "either," "left," and "wealth." Try to say the same words holding your tongue still. This exercise shows the importance of your tongue being loose and alive for good enunciation. Now count from 21 to 29 and let your tongue move freely and loosely. Say "health," "thin," "think," "alive," and "luck." Practicing these and similar words will increase the flexibility and mobility of your tongue.

Avoid the troublesome *T*'s.

Keep a flexible jaw for clear sounds.

Keep your tongue free and alive for good enunciation.

Good enunciation also depends on freely moving lips.

To free your lips—important controllers of voice quality—say "when," "where," "be," and "back." See what happens to your enunciation when you try to say these words without moving your lips. Other words that are good to practice to free your lips are "west," "window," "puff," "lisp," and "lips."

Here are some sentences you can use to practice keeping your jaw, tongue, and lips flexible:

> Loose lips sink ships.
> Shave a single shingle thin.
> Peter Piper picked a peck of pickled peppers.
> Hickory dickory dock, the mouse ran up the clock.
> She sells seashells by the seashore.

Your jaw, your tongue, and your lips should be flexible for your voice quality to be at its best.

You can improve your voice by practicing breathing and keeping your jaw, tongue, and lips flexible.

Proper control of the physical aspects of speaking is basic to high-quality oral communication. Practice deep breathing until it comes naturally to you. Practice keeping your jaw, tongue, and lips flexible. This practice will result in greater capability to use your voice effectively. The next section builds on these basic skills with suggestions for refining the use of your voice.

USING YOUR VOICE EFFECTIVELY

Once you have control of the basic sound-making mechanisms, you are ready to improve the use of your voice. The important considerations in this improvement are pitch, volume, speed, emphasis, enunciation, and pronunciation. These aspects of using your voice effectively can each be improved with self-analysis using a tape or video recorder, or by obtaining feedback from a family member, a friend, or others.

PITCH

Pitch is the highness or lowness of a voice.

Pitch refers to the highness or lowness of your voice. A voice that is too high or too low will be distracting to your listener or audience. There are two important aspects of pitch. One is to find your natural pitch, and, assuming it is not too shrill or too deep, to use it. The second is to vary your pitch while speaking to provide interest and emphasis.

FIND YOUR PITCH AND USE IT. To determine your natural pitch, yawn deeply three times. Then say aloud, "My natural pitch is . . . ." Yawn deeply, and say these words again. Note that your pitch (your voice sound) became lower—deeper, richer, and fuller. Yawn and repeat the words one more time for a total of three times. Let your voice rest for at least one minute. Now, once again say, "My natural pitch is . . . ." With this exercise you will have found your natural pitch.

> Determine your natural pitch.

To avoid damage to your vocal cords, it is important to find your natural pitch and use it. If, because of nervousness or stage fright, you speak in a pitch higher than your natural pitch, you will strain your vocal cords. If you force yourself to speak in a pitch that is artificially lower than your natural pitch, you will also strain your vocal cords. Strained vocal cords can result in a hoarse, raspy voice; or you may even lose your voice for a time.

> Use your natural pitch to avoid damaging your voice.

If you think your pitch is too high or too low, consult a speech correction specialist. Most colleges have one or more speech correction specialists. With exercises prescribed by a professional, your natural pitch can be changed to a more attractive, pleasant level.

> With proper exercises you can lower or raise your natural pitch.

VARY YOUR PITCH WHILE SPEAKING. The second aspect of improving the use of your voice is to learn to vary your pitch while speaking. The sparkling, interesting, enthusiastic speaker varies the pitch of his or

Interesting speakers use variations in pitch effectively.

Avoid being monotonous by varying your pitch.

her voice while speaking. Variation in the use of high and low sounds avoids the dullness of a monotone voice—a voice with a sameness in pitch level. Nothing will lose an audience faster than a monotone voice, regardless of the quality of the content of the message.

Varying your pitch adds life to your voice.

You can make your presentation style interesting and even exciting by using variations in pitch effectively. As you speak, think of your voice soaring up mountains and gliding down through valleys. Emphasize the ending of a declarative sentence with a definite drop in pitch. Make a question clear and forceful by raising your pitch at the end of the question.

Pitch can be used to give meaning to what you are saying.

There are other, more sophisticated uses of pitch variation that you can adopt. Comparisons can be indicated by using the same pitch level, while contrasts can be indicated with differing pitch levels. For example, equal comparisons can be shown as follows: "The market is *up* (moderate pitch), and its gains are *solid* (moderate pitch)." On the other hand, differing pitch levels can emphasize contrasts as follows: "While the market is *up* (high pitch), its gains are *not solid* (low pitch)." You can show finality by dropping the pitch. Doubt or hesitation is shown by raising the pitch.

Giving attention to varying your pitch while speaking is one of the most important ways to improve the effectiveness of your voice. Variation of pitch holds your listeners' attention and helps them understand the meaning of your messages.

VOLUME

Improve your voice through proper volume control.

A major aspect of using your voice effectively is volume control. Proper volume control enables you to be heard appropriately by your listeners—essential for effective oral communication. Volume control also enables you to vary your emphasis—essential for dynamic, forceful oral communication.

USE THE APPROPRIATE VOLUME LEVEL. The first goal of volume control is to be heard appropriately by every member of the audience—whether the audience is 1 person or 500 persons. While you want to speak with sufficient force to be heard, you will not want to speak too loudly. If your audience thinks you are shouting, you will have established a communication barrier.

Be sure you are being heard, but don't shout.

As you know, an important responsibility of a sender in the communication process is to obtain feedback. You can obtain feedback on the adequacy of your volume level by asking if you are being heard clearly or if you are too loud. Another source of feedback is the nonverbal signals you get from your listeners. Does your audience seem to be getting restless? Are people straining to hear you? Is anyone cupping a hand behind an ear or covering both ears? If any of the feedback indicates your volume level needs to be adjusted, do so immediately.

VARY YOUR VOLUME FOR EMPHASIS.

The second goal of voice volume control is to vary your volume level for emphasis. You can communicate strength, power, forcefulness, and excitement through louder speech. You can create a mood of sorrow, seriousness, respect, and sympathy through a lowering of your voice volume. Both ways can be used to attach importance and emphasis to what you are saying.

Give emphasis by varying your volume.

You can maintain the attention of an audience regardless of its size through variation in the volume of your voice. In a one-to-one situation, your volume variation should be subdued; with a larger group, the volume variation can range from simply being heard clearly to a moving, high-volume level.

SPEED

Variation in the speed of your oral communication provides interest and emphasis. The monotone voice we all try to avoid is not only at the same pitch and the same volume level, it is also at the same speed. It is recommended that for large audiences you vary your rate of speaking from 75 to 150 words a minute. For one-to-one conversations and small groups, your rate should range from 75 to 250 words a minute.

Improve your speech through speed control.

If you want to stress selected parts of your messages, slow your speed at those points. For less-important material speak at a faster rate. Excitement can be conveyed with a high rate of speed, while seriousness can be communicated with a slow rate. The important point in regard to speed is to vary your rate as you speak.

Vary your rate of speaking for emphasis.

EMPHASIS PRACTICE

You can give emphasis to your oral communication by varying your pitch, volume, and speed. The following exercise will help you vary your emphasis and give different meanings to the same words. Say each of the following sentences out loud giving emphasis to the italicized word:

Practice giving emphasis.

> *You* can change your life. (You have the power.)
> You *can* change your life. (It is possible.)
> You can *change* your life. (It can be different.)
> You can change *your* life. (The life you own.)
> You can change your *life*. (The life you are living.)

Did you vary the emphasis in each sentence by using different pitches? volumes? speeds? Probably you used a combination of these techniques. Now repeat each sentence in the exercise and emphasize the italicized words by varying your pitch. Next, say the sentences and vary your volume by saying the italicized words more loudly. Finally, repeat the sentences and vary your rate by saying the italicized word slowly and the rest of the words quickly.

From your use of the different emphasis techniques, you can easily see the powers you have in the variation of your voice. You can generate interest and communicate different meanings. You can strengthen the forcefulness, powerfulness, and effectiveness of your oral communication by using variations in your voice.

ENUNCIATION

Sound each part of each word clearly and accurately.

For effective use of your voice, sound each of the parts of words clearly and accurately. The manner in which you sound the parts of words is called enunciation. An example of correct enunciation is sounding clearly the *g*'s in words ending in *ing*. Say "talk*ing*" instead of "talk*in*," "*going to*" instead of "*gonna*," and "study*ing*" instead of "study*in*."

To improve your enunciation, examine your own sound-making patterns (or ask others to assist you) and correct any errors detected. One way to correct errors in enunciation is to slow down your rate of saying individual words. Give each word its fair share of time so that each part of it can be sounded properly. High-quality enunciation reflects favorably on your intelligence and credibility.

PRONUNCIATION

Join sounds together correctly for proper pronunciation.

The way in which you join sounds to say a word is called pronunciation. You can make sounds distinctly (enunciate clearly) and still not pronounce a word correctly. The dictionary is your best source of information for correct pronunciation of individual words. Generally speaking, the first word pronunciation given in a dictionary is the preferred pronunciation. The second pronunciation is also considered correct but is used less frequently.

As in the case of high-quality enunciation, the correctness of your pronunciation reflects on your intelligence and credibility. Good oral communicators pronounce words correctly. They say "library" instead of "libary," "was" instead of "wuz," "again" instead of "agin," "just" instead of "jist," and "our" instead of "ar." If you are not sure how to pronounce a word, do not use it until you check a dictionary or find out from another person how to pronounce it correctly.

ANALYSIS

You can improve the effectiveness of your voice by analyzing its qualities and the way in which you use it. There are several ways you can perform this analysis. You can record your voice on a tape recorder for self-analysis. You can ask a family member who speaks effectively and correctly to analyze your oral communication. You can ask an instructor at school for feedback, or you can seek a professional speech correction service.

Since most of your communication will be oral communication, it will serve your personal and career interests well to use your voice effectively. Based on high-quality speaking skills, you can build your ability to relate to others clearly, forcefully, and persuasively.

Analyze your voice to improve its effectiveness.

STRENGTHENING YOUR PRESENCE

You can further improve your oral communication by strengthening your personal presence. Your presence is your poise and bearing. It includes your tangible and intangible nonverbal communication. Some refer to an effective presence as *charisma*—a personal magnetism and grace that causes others to react positively and favorably toward the person possessing this quality. The important aspects of charisma are confidence, enthusiasm, sincerity, friendliness, eye contact, body actions, and appearance.

Improve your oral communication by strengthening your poise and bearing.

CONFIDENCE

Whether you are talking to one person or several, the amount of confidence you possess will be sensed by your receiver(s). For a strong presence in support of your oral communication, you need the right amount of confidence—neither too little nor too much.

Your listeners sense your self-confidence.

TOO LITTLE CONFIDENCE. In one-to-one situations, too little confidence is referred to as nervousness; and, when speaking to larger groups, it is called stage fright.

When communicating orally, too little confidence causes discomfort in both yourself and your audience. Your discomfort may be reflected in a shaking voice, shaking hands, perspiration, inability to think clearly, and other

Too little confidence results in nervousness and poor oral communication.

unpleasant mental, emotional, and physical symptoms. With too little confidence in yourself, you are not able to say what you want to say in the way you want to say it. Your effectiveness in achieving your oral communication goals is reduced or eliminated. The oral communication is not a pleasant, productive experience for you or your audience.

TOO MUCH CONFIDENCE.   On the other hand, too much confidence can also inhibit oral communication effectiveness. Your audience will respond negatively to overconfidence by rejecting you personally and by rejecting your message. The overconfident speaker projects a know-it-all attitude and a lack of concern for the audience.

Too much confidence causes a negative, know-it-all attitude and conveys a lack of concern for your audience.

AN EFFECTIVE LEVEL OF CONFIDENCE.   What many oral communicators fail to realize is that too little confidence or too much confidence is primarily caused by self-centeredness. If speakers concentrate only on themselves to the exclusion of consideration of their receivers, they will be perceived as having either too little confidence or too much confidence. The principal way to achieve an appropriate, effective amount of confidence is to keep the emphasis on your listeners and to use the you-viewpoint. You won't be too concerned about yourself if you are thinking about the needs, concerns, and interests of others.

Achieve the appropriate level of self-confidence by concentrating on the audience and using the you-viewpoint.

For some individuals, a lack of sufficient confidence is caused by negative thinking and unrealistic expectations for their oral communication. It is important for these persons to accept that they do not necessarily have to be admired or respected by everyone in their audience. In addition, they must realize that it is normal to misspeak occasionally; they must not allow those errors to reduce their confidence level.

Have realistic expectations for your oral communication.

In addition to placing your listeners first, there are other ways of developing an effective level of confidence. These include careful preparation of your oral presentation, diligent practice, and attention to your personal appearance. Ways to maintain confidence while communicating orally include maintaining eye contact with your audience; talking in a strong, clear voice with sufficient volume; and observing and reacting to the feedback you receive from your audience.

Improve your confidence through preparation, practice, and attention to personal appearance.

ENTHUSIASM

Enthusiasm is contagious if it is genuine. If you are enthusiastic about the ideas in your oral communication, your listener or audience will become enthusiastic and positive about those ideas. Dullness can put receivers to sleep. Enthusiasm can excite them, build their interest, and keep them alert.

An enthusiastic speaker holds the listener's attention and gets a positive reaction.

You can project your enthusiasm if you speak with energy and animation. Variations in pitch, volume, and speed will assist in showing enthusiasm. Facial

Show enthusiasm by speaking with energy and animation.

expressions—smiles, raised eyebrows, wide open eyes—indicate enthusiasm. Energetic and definite gestures and body movements also help. Eyes that are alive and sparkling show enthusiasm.

You can build a positive, enthusiastic presence by realizing its importance and practicing it every time you have an opportunity—in conversations, oral reports, discussions, and speeches.

SINCERITY

An oral communicator will be more effective if the audience perceives that the speaker is sincere. Believability and credibility rest heavily on sincerity. Insincerity is reflected by flippancy, inappropriate nonverbal signals (for example, a smirking facial expression), and an apparent lack of concern for the audience and its reception of the message.

Being sincere strengthens credibility.

If you want to be able to inform, persuade, and/or convince a person or an audience, you must believe in what you are saying. You must believe it is worthy enough to take your receiver's time and your time to talk about it. Sincerity is closely related to your belief in the importance of the content of the message.

Believe in the importance of what you are saying.

Also, sincerity is related to your personal presence: you must appear to be sincere. Your verbal and nonverbal signals should reflect sincerity. This does not mean that you cannot have any humor in your oral communication. It does mean the humor should not detract from your sincerity. You will communicate sincerity if the general tone of your oral presentation conveys that your message is important. Your message should be presented in a warm, friendly, and caring manner.

Your bearing must reflect your sincerity.

FRIENDLINESS

The speaker who can project a congenial, pleasant, cordial, caring image—a warm friendliness—can relate more effectively to a listener or to an audience. As with other personal aspects of oral communication, the appearance of friendliness must be supported primarily by your true friendly feelings toward other people.

Friendliness builds positive relationships with listeners.

Knowing that you can increase your effectiveness significantly with friendliness should motivate you to develop your ability to be sincerely friendly and gracious. A smiling face, an unhurried approach, and a concern for feedback exhibit friendliness and an honest caring for your receivers. As with confidence, enthusiasm, and sincerity, concentrating on the needs and interests of your audience will help convey your friendliness.

Show friendliness by feeling friendly and exhibiting it.

The speaker who projects warm friendliness relates more effectively to the audience.

EYE CONTACT

Good eye contact reflects confidence, interest, honesty, and sincerity.

Eye contact with your receivers is such an important nonverbal signal that it will be discussed separately from other body actions. Appropriate eye contact reflects confidence, interest, honesty, and sincerity. A lack of eye contact reflects a lack of confidence and interest and, therefore, may project an image of weakness, insincerity, and dishonesty. While the amount of eye contact possible and appropriate in different oral communication situations will vary, a good target is to have eye contact with your receivers about 75 percent of the time.

Try to have eye contact with your listeners about 75 percent of the time.

In one-to-one conversations, you should build effective communication bridges with relaxed, comfortable eye contact. In one-to-group situations, you

Although good eye contact takes practice and effort, it is critically important.

should look into the eyes of every member of the audience, lingering long enough so that each person feels you are talking to him or her individually. The impression you should convey is that you are indeed talking to each one personally, and although you need to talk to others in the audience too, you will return to the individual again.

Good eye contact takes practice and effort. Its benefits are so rewarding to the oral communicator that it is critically important for you to work on it. If you fail to achieve the 75-percent goal in your early efforts, do not be discouraged. Keep practicing until you fully realize the benefits of good eye contact with your receivers.

The benefits of good eye contact are rewarding.

BODY ACTIONS

In addition to eye contact, other important nonverbal signals during oral communication fall under the heading of body actions. These nonverbal signals include facial expressions, posture, gestures, and other body movements. Each of these topics will be reviewed briefly here. They are dealt with in more detail in Chapter 17, "Listening and Nonverbal Messages."

There are other important body actions.

Facial expressions will be read as your true feelings.

FACIAL EXPRESSIONS. Regardless of the words you are saying, your eyes and your face appear to your audience to convey your true feelings. If you are sincere and feel friendly toward your receivers, show those feelings in your facial expressions. As you practice an oral communication, look in the mirror to see if you appear to be interested, enthusiastic, and friendly. If not, practice the necessary facial expressions until your nonverbal signals are comparable to your true feelings and your verbal message.

Show that you are interested, enthusiastic, and friendly.

Use gestures to generate interest and convey meaning. Your gestures should be natural.

GESTURES. Gestures of the hands, arms, shoulders, and head while communicating orally are important supporting nonverbal signals. Sitting behind a desk like a statue or standing immobile behind a podium results in a dull, uninteresting appearance. You should use gestures to strengthen your verbal messages. The gestures should be natural, not contrived. Raising the arms with

Gestures are important supporting nonverbal signals. The ones you choose to use should be natural, not contrived.

palms facing upward, for example, can accent a verbal message that asks the rhetorical question, What is the answer? Pointing to an item on an audiovisual aid helps stress the point being made. Gestures should be varied, not repetitious. The two most important points relative to gestures are that they should be used and they should be natural.

POSTURE. An upright, correct posture will improve your appearance and give you a feeling of confidence. You will not want to appear pompous or stiff, but rather natural and comfortable. If you are standing during an oral communication, keep your weight evenly distributed on your feet. Do not lean on a podium, table, or chair. If sitting, sit erectly and comfortably. Do not slouch or hang one leg over a chair arm. Correct posture reflects your confidence and respect for your audience.

Good posture improves your appearance and gives you confidence.

OTHER BODY MOVEMENTS. Walking, leaning, turning, and other body movements are nonverbal signals to your receivers. Some body movement is important to hold attention and to relax your muscles. These movements should be graceful, unhurried, and natural. You can draw an audience's attention to a visual aid by turning your body to it or walking to it. You can signal the end of a one-to-one conversation by moving your chair back and standing up. Body movements are important, and their use during oral communication should be considered carefully. As with facial expressions, you can observe and practice your body movements in front of a mirror until they convey the nonverbal message you want them to convey.

Other important body movements can be useful.

APPEARANCE

The final personal aspect to be considered in strengthening your presence during oral communication is your appearance. Your personal appearance can be a barrier to effective oral communication, or it can be an asset. It is an important part of the total communication environment, particularly as a first impression.

Strengthen your presence with a good personal appearance.

You have to accept and work with the raw material of your own basic appearance. What you do with what you have is what will influence your audience. The clothing you select should be appropriate for the occasion and the audience, and you should be neatly groomed. Good appearance not only sets a favorable stage for oral communication, but it also serves to increase your confidence.

Use what you have to best advantage by wearing appropriate clothing and being neatly groomed.

This chapter has concentrated on improving your oral communication through recommendations for improving your voice qualities, for using your voice effectively, and for strengthening your presence. By following these recommendations, you can become an effective oral communicator. Effective oral communication is rewarding, enjoyable, and well worth your efforts in improving yourself.

DISCUSSION QUESTIONS

1. Discuss how important oral communication is to supervisors, managers, and executives.
2. Name five examples of jobs in business that require an extensive use of oral communication. For each job give an example of oral communication that is commonly required.
3. Describe each of the following types of oral communication in business: (a) one-to-one, (b) one-to-small group, and (c) one-to-large group. Include in your descriptions examples of each of these types of oral communication and the requirements for effective communication for each.
4. Name a leading businessperson or governmental official, and describe the types of oral communication in which he or she participates.
5. Discuss the important physical aspects of a good speaking voice.
6. Describe how you can strengthen your oral communication by varying your pitch.
7. Using your voice effectively involves proper volume control. How can you (a) determine appropriate volume level, and (b) vary your volume for emphasis?
8. Discuss how you can use the speed of your oral communication to provide interest and emphasis.
9. Discuss the relative merits of poor-quality and good-quality enunciation and pronunciation.
10. What role does personal presence play in the effectiveness of a person's oral communication?
11. Discuss the causes of too little confidence and too much confidence. How does a speaker maintain an effective level of confidence while speaking?
12. What roles do enthusiasm, sincerity, and friendliness play in effective oral communication?
13. Describe the benefits of appropriate eye contact and the impact of poor eye contact.
14. Discuss how you can strengthen your personal presence through your appearance.
15. Name a successful leader and describe his or her personal presence and how it affects the message he or she wants to convey.

APPLICATION EXERCISES

1. Reflect on your experiences with oral communication over the past week. Select one example of excellent oral communication and one example of poor oral communication. Share these examples in class. Analyze the importance of effective oral communication in human relationships.

2. Name a prominent world or local figure who frequently and publicly uses oral communication. Analyze his or her pitch, volume, and speed, and indicate the person's strengths and weaknesses in the use of these voice qualities.

3. Record your voice on a cassette tape recorder. Listen carefully to the recording; analyze your voice qualities in regard to pitch, volume, and speed. Write a brief report of your findings including the following: (a) The way your voice sounds to you, (b) the strengths of your voice, (c) the weaknesses of your voice, and (d) a plan for improving your voice.

4. Practice ridding yourself of the troublesome *T*'s of tight jaw, tight tongue, and tight lips by repeating aloud the following words:

finally	wonderful	slippery
brought	waterfall	seventy-seven
preliminary	valley	lilac
yell	backslide	whether
neither	shipping	whenever
limited	number	tribulation

5. Interview a successful manager and ask him or her to tell you the most important qualities in an effective oral communicator. Specifically, ask the following two questions: To be an effective oral communicator, (a) what voice qualities should a person possess? and (b) what personal presence qualities? Share your findings with the class.

6. Give emphasis to the important points in the following paragraph by varying (a) your pitch, (b) your volume, (c) your speed, and (d) your pitch, volume, and speed in appropriate combinations.

If you want to provide leadership to others, your degree of success will relate directly to your ability to speak clearly, intelligently, and persuasively in a confident, convincing manner. Your effectiveness will depend on the quality of your voice and the strength of your presence.

7. Describe how the meaning changes in the following sentence when the emphasis is moved from word to word.
   a. *Most* of your communication in business will be oral.
   b. Most of *your* communication in business will be oral.
   c. Most of your *communication* in business will be oral.
   d. Most of your communication *in* business will be oral.
   e. Most of your communication in *business* will be oral.
   f. Most of your communication in business *will be* oral.
   g. Most of your communication in business will be *oral.*

8. The purpose of this exercise is to increase effective eye contact. Select a member of your class and talk to each other for a few minutes. The goal will be to have effective eye contact with your partner at least 75 percent of the time. After the exercise, the whole class will discuss what took place.

9. Prepare and present to the class a three-minute speech on a topic of your choice.

10. Prepare and present to the class a five-minute speech on one of the chapters in this textbook.

COMMUNICATING ORALLY

L E A R N I N G   O B J E C T I V E S

Your learning objectives for this chapter include the following:

- To understand the dynamics of interpersonal oral communication
- To learn how to communicate successfully in one-to-one oral communication situations
- To develop the ability to be an effective small group leader and participant
- To develop the ability to prepare and deliver an effective presentation to a large group

Communicating orally is both challenging and rewarding. An understanding of the dynamics of interpersonal oral communication is necessary if you are to be effective. Also, if you are to improve your effectiveness, it is important to follow the keys for planning and presenting oral communication. It will be helpful to you in your study to think in terms of the three basic kinds of oral communication: one-to-one, one-to-small group, and one-to-large group.

The dynamics of interpersonal oral communication are discussed in the next section. This material is followed by keys for successful oral communication.

Oral communication is dynamic.

You can improve your effectiveness in oral communication.

471

THE DYNAMICS OF INTERPERSONAL ORAL COMMUNICATION

An oral communication situation is complex.

When people communicate with each other, the communication situation is not static—the communication environment, the sender, and the receiver(s) are continually changing. The communication situation becomes increasingly complex when the communication is oral.

The human variables in interpersonal communication include both emotional and nonemotional factors.

The important *human* variables in oral communication, which are continually changing and adding to the complexity of the situation, include such things as moods, interests, alertness, knowledge, status, trust, respect, power, confidence, honesty, needs, concerns, roles, beliefs, values, and opinions. Other important variables in interpersonal oral communication are the oral communication abilities of the senders and receivers.

Environmental variables include number of people, formality, and purpose.

The important *environmental* variables, which differ from situation to situation, include the number of people participating, the formality or informality of the situation, and the purpose of the communication.

ONE-TO-ONE ORAL COMMUNICATION

Most critical business decisions are made in one-to-one oral communication.

One-to-one oral communication is probably the most important form of communication used in business. More critical business decisions are made in conversations between two people than in any other communication format. Important types of one-to-one oral communication are face-to-face meetings, telephone conversations, and dictation.

KEYS FOR SUCCESSFUL FACE-TO-FACE COMMUNICATION

The keys for successful face-to-face communication are based on an understanding of the dynamics of interpersonal oral communication. The situation is continually changing and evolving during a meeting with another person. The success of an oral communication in this dynamic situation depends on using care in sending the oral message, obtaining and using feedback, and eliminating any communication barriers that threaten the conversation. Here are the keys for successful face-to-face oral communication.

BE CLEAR AND CONCISE.   Use the principles of business communication so that your comments will be clear and concise. Think before you speak. Structure your sentences so that the receiver will understand them. Most receivers react favorably to the ideas of a sender who is concise and to the point. They do not want to hear extensive details that are not necessary for their understanding. The stronger, more effective message is short and simple. In applying this key, use care not to appear abrupt.

LISTEN CAREFULLY.   When people are conversing they often think about what they are going to say next instead of listening to what the other person has to say. By giving your full attention, you hear what the other person is saying and can participate effectively in the conversation. If you listen carefully, you also make the other person feel that he or she is intelligent and interesting. Another important aspect of effective listening is not interrupting. Wait until you are sure the other person is through speaking before you start to talk.

OBSERVE NONVERBAL BEHAVIOR.   Regardless of the verbal responses your receiver makes, his or her nonverbal behavior should be taken as the real message. You may tell an employee that you have decided to give a desirable assignment to a coworker. If the employee becomes teary-eyed

Send messages carefully, use feedback, and eliminate barriers.

Follow these keys for successful face-to-face communication:

- *Be clear and concise* so your messages are understandable and strong.

- *Listen carefully* to participate effectively.

- *Observe nonverbal behavior;* it is often the real message.

Your conversations will produce more effective results if you give your full attention to those speaking to you.

while saying "fine, good," you know that it is not really fine and good. React to the nonverbal signals as well as to the verbal signals in face-to-face conversations.

- *Ask questions* to encourage effective conversation.

ASK QUESTIONS.   One of the best ways to encourage another person to communicate is to ask questions. Carefully structured questions can elicit information you both want discussed. For example, if you are trying to help a subordinate improve the quality of his or her work, you can ask, "What can I do to help you do a better job?" This question will bring out the things you and the subordinate can do to improve the work. Receiver centered questions will encourage involvement in the conversation. While you do not want the entire conversation to be an interrogation, carefully selected questions will stimulate response.

- *Maintain eye contact* to convey positive feelings.

MAINTAIN APPROPRIATE EYE CONTACT.   It has been said that the eyes are the mirror of the soul. Among humans, the eyes communicate a great deal. Shifting eyes with limited eye contact can communicate dishonesty, fear, or a lack of confidence—all barriers to effective communication. Good eye contact conveys strength and sincerity. It makes people feel that you think they are important. Good eye contact is essential in face-to-face communication. In our culture, a realistic goal is to maintain eye contact about 75 percent of the time. Let the circumstances determine when you will have eye contact.

- *Use the receiver's name* to show respect.

USE THE RECIEVER'S NAME.   A person's name is his or her most important possession. Find out what name a person likes to be called, and then use that name in conversation. You show care, concern, and respect for others when you use their names. In turn, they will show their appreciation by responding favorably.

- *Smile* to create a favorable environment.

SMILE APPROPRIATELY.   When you smile at another person, you are saying "I like you." And everyone wants to be liked. A hostile atmosphere in a face-to-face conversation will cause many communication barriers. A warm, friendly environment improves oral communication.

- *Be appropriately assertive* to handle difficult topics.

BE APPROPRIATELY ASSERTIVE.   It is possible to disagree without being disagreeable. Assertiveness does not mean aggressiveness; assertiveness does not alienate others. Be assertive by stating your views clearly and in a straightforward manner appropriate to the circumstances. For example, if you feel you deserve an above average increase in salary, start a conversation with your boss by stating your view clearly: "Because of my performance this past year, I think that I deserve an above average raise. Can we discuss this?"

- *Control emotional reactions* to build good business relations.

CONTROL EMOTIONAL REACTIONS.   In business relationships people are expected to be calm, cool, controlled, and collected. Successful businesspersons do not argue; they discuss. In addition, avoid sarcastic remarks or inappropriate laughter that may embarrass others. Treat others as you would like to be treated, and your face-to-face conversations will be productive.

OTHER KEYS FOR SUCCESSFUL FACE-TO-FACE CONVERSATIONS. Other keys for successful face-to-face conversations are honesty, objectivity, sincerity, and reasonableness. Effective human interpersonal relations and communications are dependent on these attributes.

* *Be honest, objective, sincere, and reasonable.*

KEYS FOR SUCCESSFUL TELEPHONE CONVERSATIONS

Most of the keys for successful face-to-face conversations apply to telephone conversations as well. Only two do not apply directly—observing nonverbal behavior and maintaining appropriate eye contact. Even the suggestion to smile pleasantly applies to telephone conversations because the tone of your voice is more pleasant when you are smiling than when you are not.

The telephone is important for sending and receiving business messages. For some message receivers, in fact, the entire image of the company rests on their experience with you on the telephone. It is important, therefore, to use the telephone and telephone system efficiently, to be considerate of callers, to plan calls carefully, and to be businesslike. These keys for successful telephone conversations are fully discussed in the following paragraphs.

Telephone messages may be your most important oral communication.

Follow these keys for successful telephone conversations:

USE THE INSTRUMENT AND SYSTEM PROPERLY. Hold the telephone mouthpiece one to two inches from your mouth and talk directly into it. Keep the earpiece pressed gently against your ear to hear the caller. Of course, you should be careful not to drop the telephone because of the loud sound that would be transmitted to the caller. Remember that both the mouthpiece and the earpiece must be covered if you do not want your caller to hear you talking.

* *Use the telephone properly* for efficiency.

Be sure to learn how to use the telephone system in your organization. Know how to transfer calls efficiently, arrange conference calls, set up call backs, and use other special features of your system. Employees who are not able to use the company telephone system properly will be perceived as inefficient, as will the organization.

BE CONSIDERATE OF YOUR CALLER. Time passes very slowly while holding a telephone and waiting for an answer, waiting for a call to be transferred, or waiting for someone to return to the phone. Fifteen seconds may seem like one to three minutes. Because the caller's perception of time is distorted, you must try to minimize his or her waiting time. Answer your phone on the first ring if possible. Transfer calls quickly and efficiently.

* *Be considerate* of your caller by being prompt and courteous.

Learn how to use the company telephone system.

If you have to leave the telephone for more than 30 seconds during a conversation, return to the phone to let the caller know you are still there and will be back to the conversation as soon as possible. Keep a pencil and notepad close to the telephone so that you do not waste the caller's time looking for these items if they are needed. Showing consideration for the caller in these ways will improve the effectiveness of your communications.

In addition, it is recommended that you place your own calls. Having another person place your calls and then keeping the party called waiting while you get on the line makes it appear that you feel your time is more valuable than the other party's. Such a procedure is inconsiderate and gets the call off to a bad start.

Finally, be sure to use courteous words. Because you cannot be seen, your voice has to carry the whole message and convey its tone. Use cordial terms such as *please*, *thank you*, and *appreciate*.

PLAN YOUR CALLS CAREFULLY. Before placing a telephone call, determine its specific purpose and outline its major points. Know what your opening remarks will be and have in mind any other comments you plan to make. It is often a good idea to do this planning on paper. Remember, a telephone call is a message—it is an oral letter, memo, or report. Planning is needed to make the call successful. Base your planning on both the purpose of the message and an analysis of the individual you are calling.

• Plan your calls as you would plan any important message.

BE BUSINESSLIKE. When answering the telephone, identify yourself immediately by giving the name of your organizational unit and your own name. For example, say, "Information Systems Department, John Sims." When you are placing a call, the telephone will most likely be answered initially by a receptionist, switchboard operator, or secretary. Either ask, "May I speak to Miss Norma Williams, please?" or say, "Norma Williams, please." It may be appropriate to respond to the initial answer to your call with more information such as, "My name is John Sims, and I am calling Norma Williams about a new teleconferencing system."

• Be businesslike for effective telephone communication.

During telephone conversations, take special care to enunciate clearly, use businesslike language, and keep messages short and simple. As is true of all communication, telephone messages will be more effective if they are receiver centered. Visualize the person on the other end of the line and adapt the message to that person.

KEYS FOR SUCCESSFUL DICTATION

Dictation is an efficient, effective way to transfer your thoughts to letter, memo, or report form. If you have never dictated material, you will need to practice in order to do it comfortably; but it is easy to learn to dictate, and dictation will increase your productivity.

Dictation is efficient and easy.

Dictation can be to a person (a secretary) or to a machine (a desktop, portable, or centralized recorder). Each mode has advantages and disadvantages. The advantage of dictating to a person is that you can secure feedback to assure accuracy of the content and format of the message. The disadvantage of dictating to a person is that two people's time must be scheduled. The main advantage of dictating to a machine is that a person can dictate at his or her convenience without taking a secretary's time. Two disadvantages are that more detailed instructions must be dictated and that immediate feedback is not available.

Dictation is an important form of oral communication. Most of the keys for successful face-to-face and telephone conversations also apply to dictation. There are additional considerations, however, that are specific to dictation. These keys for successful dictation are presented in the following sections.

Most of the keys given earlier apply to dictation.

It is easy to learn to dictate efficiently, and dictation will increase your productivity.

Follow these keys for
successful dictation:
- *Organize for dictation* by gathering and numbering related materials.

ORGANIZE FOR DICTATION.

Gather the material related to your dictation, including incoming mail to be answered and any notes you have on messages to be dictated. In addition, gather any other information needed to support your dictation—including information from the files, other employees, or other sources. Continue organizing for dictation by clipping the materials related to each letter, memo, or report. To assist in communication with your transcriber, assign a number to each separate set of dictation materials.

- *Plan each message* by reviewing the dictation materials.

PLAN EACH MESSAGE.

Review each numbered set of dictation materials and plan your message. This review may be simply a mental process or may be an outline of the message written on the dictation materials or on separate notepaper. Do not write the message before you dictate; if you do that, you lose the advantages of dictating. As with all messages, determine the purpose, analyze the receiver, and plan the message using the you-viewpoint.

- *Begin dictation* by giving essential directions.

BEGIN DICTATION.

At the beginning of the message, identify yourself (if dictating to a machine) and give the transcriber the necessary instructions for the message. For example, say, "Operator, this is Vincent Aldridge in the Sales Department. My extension is 4198. Dictation No. 1 is a letter. Please use the block form with mixed punctuation for this dictation. I need an original for Miss Denise Brock and two copies. One copy will go to Mrs. Marian Randolph, and the other copy is for the file. Get their addresses from the No. 1 set of materials." Give similar necessary information at the beginning of each separate item dictated. As you work over a period of time with the same transcriber or word processor, you may be able to shorten these preliminary instructions.

DICTATE THE MESSAGE. Enunciate each sound clearly as you dictate. Speak in a strong voice and pronounce each word clearly. Clear enunciation is especially important when using a dictation machine because it may not reproduce sounds perfectly.

Dictate the message following your mental or written outline. Because you are composing the message as you dictate, you will have to concentrate on making the message flow coherently. Do the best you can, but keep in mind that revision is easy with today's dictation and word processing equipment. Generally, revision is the most important step in developing powerful business messages. Your need to revise will decrease as you acquire dictating experience.

If you are dictating to a secretary, it will be necessary to pace the dictation speed to assure that he or she is able to record the material accurately. However, if you are dictating to a machine, dictation speed is not as important because the transcriber can start and stop the dictation while transcribing.

You can listen to what you have dictated to a machine, or you can have read back what you have dictated to a secretary. This can be one form of preliminary revision or a way to find your place if you have been interrupted. You will want to minimize this practice, however, because it can significantly lengthen the time spent dictating.

GIVE INSTRUCTIONS. As you dictate, give complete and clear instructions regarding the message content and format. The amount of instruction will depend on your transcriber's skills and knowledge of your work. In addition to the instructions at the beginning of each dictation, you may have to give these kinds of instructions: class of mail service, punctuation, spelling of proper names and unusual words, capitalization, paragraphing, and any other necessary special information.

Here is an example of what your dictation of a letter might be like (your instructions are shown in italics):

> Dear Miss Brock *B-r-o-c-k colon:* Thank you for your letter of June 6 *period.* As you requested *comma,* I am sending the *initial cap* Silversmith *S-i-l-v-e-r-s-m-i-t-h initial cap* Weathervane *W-e-a-t-h-e-r-v-a-n-e comma, initial cap* Model 516 *5-1-6 comma,* by *initial caps* Air Parcel Post *period. Paragraph* Thanks *comma,* Miss Brock *comma,* for your order *period.* We look forward to having the opportunity of serving you again soon *period.* Sincerely *comma, Type this letter for my signature and title. Note that a copy is being sent to Mrs. Marian M-a-r-i-a-n Randolph R-a-n-d-o-l-p-h. End of Dictation No. 1.*

• *Dictate the message* clearly and coherently at the appropriate speed.

• *Give instructions* on content and format as you dictate.

• *Revise as necessary* to develop the most effective message.

REVISE AS NECESSARY. If your office uses word processing equipment, revising the transcripts of your dictated material is relatively easy. Only the changes you make have to be keyboarded again. As mentioned, revision can be the key step in the development of a clear, forceful, and effective message. Do not hesitate to revise your messages as necessary. In fact, you may revise some important messages several times before you are fully satisfied with their quality.

• *Approve the final version* for accuracy and appearance.

APPROVE FINAL VERSION. As dictator of the message, you are responsible for the accuracy and appearance of the final version of a document. Your signature on a letter or your initials on a memo indicate that you have approved the material for mailing. This means, of course, that you should carefully read the material before you sign it. Many dictators read their messages twice—once for content and once for accuracy. If you find errors, the material must be marked and sent back for correction before it is mailed. For clear communication with your transcriber, you should mark errors using the standard proofreaders' symbols given in Appendix B.

ONE-TO-SMALL GROUP ORAL COMMUNICATION

Small groups are formed to share information or solve problems.

Small group meetings in business are quite common. Small groups—usually referred to as committees—are formed for one of two basic purposes: to share information or to solve problems. Because of the interactions within small groups, the quality of the thinking that emerges from their meetings is almost always higher than what one person can achieve alone.

TYPES OF SMALL GROUPS

Committees are standing or ad hoc.

Small groups are generally of two types: standing committees or ad hoc (a Latin term pronounced "add hock") committees. A standing committee has a continuing purpose and usually meets at regularly scheduled times. Standing committees in business have titles such as Finance Committee, Personnel Policy Committee, Social Committee, and Board of Directors. An ad hoc committee is a small group formed for a specific short-term purpose. It usually meets over a brief period of time and then is disbanded. Ad hoc committees in businesses have titles such as Task Force on Budget Reduction, Centennial Planning Committee, and Reorganization Committee.

SIZE OF SMALL GROUPS

Small groups are defined as having 3 to 20 members. The most cost-effective size for meetings is thought by many to be 5 to 7 members. Because most small group meetings are operated democratically and votes are taken on issues, it is best to have an odd number of members in order to avoid tie votes.

During your career you will have many opportunities to be a group leader or a group participant. If you follow proven keys for successfully leading and participating in small groups, you can increase your personal effectiveness and the effectiveness of those groups.

Small groups have 3 to 20 members.

KEYS FOR SUCCESSFUL SMALL GROUP LEADERSHIP

Small group meetings in business are costly both in time and money. It is important that such meetings be conducted efficiently and effectively. The person primarily responsible for the success of a small group meeting is the group leader. The keys for successful small group leadership are presented in the following paragraphs.

Small group meetings are costly.

A group leader is primarily responsible for the efficiency and effectiveness of a meeting. Following the keys for small group leadership will help a group leader achieve success.

Follow these keys for successful small group leadership:

- *Determine the purpose* and communicate it to participants.

- *Plan the meeting agenda* carefully and logically.

- *Prepare the meeting facility* properly and well in advance.

- *Lead the group discussion* to achieve the group's purpose.

DETERMINE THE PURPOSE OF THE GROUP. The purpose for forming the group should be clearly understood and communicated to all members. Is it an information-receiving group or a problem-solving group? What is the scope of its responsibility and authority? While the group will refine its purpose in its early meetings, the group leader is responsible initially for providing as much definition of the group's purpose as possible.

PLAN THE MEETING AGENDA. The group leader must prepare the meeting agenda carefully. The topics to be discussed should be listed in some logical order that will best serve the purpose of the group. For an informal meeting, the leader may simply have mental notes on the agenda that are shared with the participants at the outset of the meeting. For a formal meeting, copies of a written agenda should be distributed to the participants in advance of the meeting so that the members can prepare themselves. A sample agenda for a Personnel Policy Committee meeting is shown in Illustration 19-1.

PREPARE THE MEETING FACILITY. The group leader is responsible for arranging for the meeting room and being sure it is properly prepared for the meeting. In preparing a meeting facility, the leader needs to consider the following: an adequate number of chairs for participants; a table or tables, if needed; comfortable room temperature; the necessary audiovisual equipment; and, if appropriate, pencils, notepads, refreshments, and extra copies of the agenda and related materials. The preparation of the meeting facility should be completed well in advance of the meeting. In addition, it is wise to check on the facility an hour before the meeting starts to be sure all is in order. The leader should arrive a few minutes early for the meeting to make a final check of the meeting facility.

LEAD THE GROUP DISCUSSION. During the meeting the primary role of the leader is to assist the group in achieving its purpose. This means keeping the discussion focused on the group tasks—not allowing the discussion to stray to unrelated topics. It means moving from one item on the agenda to the next after adequate discussion.

When speaking to a small group, the group leader must be prepared to be interrupted with questions or comments. A good group leader actually talks very little during group discussion. Rather he or she encourages participation, controls excessive talkers, and summarizes periodically. A good group leader is a catalyst—one who causes the group participants to work together effectively.

An effective leader secures group decisions after adequate discussion. Group decision making may be by consensus or by vote, depending on the subject matter and the formality of the group. The formality of the group also determines the procedures that will be followed. Formal groups will likely use parliamentary procedure as described in *Robert's Rules of Order* or a similar guide. Informal groups will give less attention to procedure and more attention to achieving the group purpose by whatever approach seems most expedient.

Illustration 19-1 Sample Meeting Agenda

```
                        PAULEY FOODS COMPANY

                    Personnel Policy Committee

     Agenda for Meeting, 9 a.m., Wednesday, March 12, 199-
          Room 203, Corporate Headquarters Building

        1.  Call to Order

        2.  Minutes of February 12 Meeting

        3.  Report of Salary Subcommittee

            a.  Cost-of-Living Proposal

            b.  Status of Merit Policy Survey

        4.  Report of Fringe Benefit Committee

            a.  Increase in Insurance Costs

            b.  Recommendation on Group Life Policy

        5.  Old Business

        6.  New Business

        7.  Information Items

            a.  New Policy Booklets Availability

            b.  Report on Number of Grievances

            c.  Affirmative Action Report

        8.  Announcement of Next Meeting

        9.  Adjournment
```

- *Resolve group conflict* by clarifying the issue or using other proven technique.

RESOLVE GROUP CONFLICTS. Many times participants in group meetings take opposing positions. If the group leader does not resolve these conflicts within the group, the meeting's progress may be inhibited. The first task in conflict resolution is to be sure the basic issue in the disagreement is clear. Sometimes clarifying the issue resolves the conflict. If the conflict continues after the issue is clarified, the leader has several options: (1) a group vote can be taken, leaving the decision to majority rule; (2) the discussion can be postponed, giving time for reflection; (3) the conflict can be submitted to an arbitrator, such as a superior officer in the company; (4) a compromise can be sought through group discussion; or (5) the leader may simply move on to the next agenda item after deciding the conflict is not worthy of the group's time.

- *Encourage participation* by ensuring equality, curtailing those who talk too much, and motivating those who talk too little.

ENCOURAGE APPROPRIATE PARTICIPATION. The group leader is responsible for eliciting the best contributions possible from each participant. If the group is a committee formed of employees from different levels in an organization, there is the possibility that some higher-level people might intimidate some of the lower-level people. This must be avoided if at all possible. While formed into a group with a specific purpose, all employees should be considered equal in order to obtain effective contributions from all participants.

The leader usually faces two challenges in achieving appropriate participation by members of the group. One challenge is to politely curtail those who talk too much, and the other is to encourage those who talk too little.

Ways to control those who talk too much are (1) at the end of a sentence, thank the excessive talker and then ask other participants for their opinions on the topic; (2) stress to the whole group that it is important for everyone to have an equal chance to comment; (3) suggest that the group is beginning to cover the same territory again and that it needs to move on; and (4) remind the whole group (never an individual publicly) that participation should be uniform.

The following are effective ways to encourage those who talk too little: (1) ask them directly by name for their viewpoints; (2) accept any comments that they make even if they are not of the highest quality; (3) ask them direct questions, drawing on their particular expertise relative to the topic; and (4) thank them for their contributions.

- *Be time conscious* at the beginning of, during, and at the ending of the meeting.

BE TIME CONSCIOUS. The group leader should start the meeting on time (not waiting for latecomers) and adjourn the meeting on time. Periodically, the leader may need to remind the group that it has time constraints. Comments on time must be made judiciously, however, or they will curtail desirable discussion. The leader, probably in cooperation with the group, should make judgments on how much time will be devoted to each topic and when the meeting will adjourn. Some of these decisions can be made at the beginning of the meeting; others may be made while the meeting is in progress. The leader should end the meeting positively by summarizing what has been accomplished.

MAINTAIN APPROPRIATE RECORDS. The group leader should maintain a record of the group's accomplishments. If a detailed record is desired, the leader should have a secretary elected or appointed for recording and distributing minutes of the meetings. A group may have the secretary keep records on newsprint or flip charts during the meeting so that all members can see and agree on the actions being recorded. Suggestions for preparing records for group meetings are given in Chapter 15, pages 394–397.

> • *Maintain appropriate records* yourself or elect or appoint a secretary to do it.

If formal minutes or other records of the group's activity are kept, they should be distributed promptly to members following each meeting. This procedure will enable members to note any corrections for the record while the meeting is still fresh in mind.

KEYS FOR SUCCESSFUL SMALL GROUP PARTICIPATION

An effective small group leader will also be an effective small group participant. There are, however, a few additional considerations for those serving as participants. The following keys for successful small group participation will increase your effectiveness in meetings.

> Follow these keys for successful small group participation:

PREPARE TO PARTICIPATE. Every member of a small group should learn as much as possible about the group's purpose. If an agenda is provided in advance, information can be gathered on each topic to assure intelligent participation. All available background information should be gathered and studied for the first and succeeding meetings of the group.

> • *Prepare to participate* by gathering and studying information.

PARTICIPATE APPROPRIATELY. The knowledge of all the participants in a group is essential for group success. All group members should talk during group meetings, but not talk too much. The basic principle of business communication—keep it short and simple—should be followed. Also, participants must maintain objectivity in their comments and control their emotions. Meetings are not the place to argue, but rather to discuss.

> • *Participate appropriately* by giving businesslike input.

LISTEN EFFECTIVELY. Committee meetings or other small group meetings can challenge listening skills. Group members will spend most of their time listening to other participants' comments and must strive to keep their concentration. Members should not have side conversations, gaze into space, or exhibit other behavior that detracts from the effectiveness of their participation as listeners. More than once participants have been surprised when, without warning, a speaker asked them what they thought. Listeners must be ready to change to speakers at any time.

> • *Listen effectively* by not losing your concentration.

The knowledge that you and the other participants have is essential for group success.

• *Be courteous* by being fair to others.

BE COURTEOUS.   In small group meetings it is important for all participants to respect the rights and opinions of others. Opinions should be expressed tactfully, avoiding any indication of self-righteousness. By accepting different viewpoints and by being willing to discuss them, participants can help encourage open, free discussion. Members should avoid interrupting speakers or using sarcasm, and should use humor carefully. In successful small group meetings, members treat each other the way they would like to be treated.

ONE-TO-LARGE GROUP ORAL COMMUNICATION

The purpose of one-to-large group oral communication is to inform or to persuade.

Many people in business are required to make oral presentations to large groups—20 or more people—from time to time. The purpose of these oral presentations will be either *to inform* the audience of certain facts or *to persuade* the audience to accept a point of view or take a certain action. Your career and your organization will benefit if you can achieve these two purposes effectively in your one-to-large group oral communication.

TYPES OF ORAL PRESENTATIONS

There are several different types of oral presentations in business: briefings, oral reports, talks, and speeches. The length of these presentations can vary from less than a minute to an hour or more. The ideal length for a long presentation is 20 minutes or less.

Depending on your position, you may be asked to brief a group of employees on, say, the status of union negotiations. Or you may be asked to give an oral report to company officers on the market research your department has been conducting. You might be requested to give a 20-minute talk to a college group on the rewards of your profession. Or you may be asked to give a 30-minute speech to a financial officers association on financing overseas production facilities. Assuming you have the time, knowledge, and expertise needed, you will want to respond positively to these requests. Making such presentations will generally serve you and your organization well.

Other types of oral presentations that businesspeople are commonly asked to make are introductions, greetings, and recognitions. You may be asked to introduce a speaker, extend a welcome and greetings to a visiting group, or give recognition or an award for outstanding service.

A final way of looking at the different types of oral presentations is by the way they are delivered to the audience. There are four basic types of delivery: manuscript, memorized, impromptu, and extemporaneous.

A *manuscript oral presentation* is written word for word and then read to the audience. This type of presentation is used when precise wording is required, as in a presidential address. Such a presentation is a difficult type of delivery to do well and should be avoided except in very special circumstances.

A *memorized oral presentation* is one in which the speaker has memorized the content verbatim. While this is a way of avoiding notes, it, too, is a difficult presentation to do well. It is likely to appear canned, and there is the danger of forgetting parts of the presentation. A better method is to memorize parts—for example, the opening and closing remarks—rather than trying to memorize the entire presentation.

An *impromptu oral presentation* is one a person is required to give without special preparation. This request to talk comes as a surprise. For example, in a meeting of the company's sales force, you may be asked by your boss, "Owen, would you say a few words to the group about your experience in the Indiana territory?" While you must remain calm and think quickly in this situation, following the suggestions in the remainder of this chapter will help you do a good job.

An *extemporaneous oral presentation* is a briefing, talk, oral report, or speech that is carefully prepared and delivered from notes or an outline. This is the most effective delivery style and the one recommended. The extemporaneous presentation does not require reading from a script, memorizing, or speaking without preparation. It is a more spontaneous and a more natural

Oral presentations include briefings, oral reports, talks, and speeches.

Other types of oral presentations are introductions, greetings, and recognitions.

A manuscript oral presentation is read to the audience.

A memorized oral presentation is learned verbatim.

An impromptu oral presentation is one that has to be given without preparation.

An extemporaneous oral presentation is prepared and given from notes.

way to relate to an audience because it permits good eye contact, it allows free movement, and it permits the speaker to respond to audience feedback. The extemporaneous oral presentation method is the basis for the discussion in the rest of this chapter.

Effective one-to-large group oral communication depends on careful preparation and good delivery techniques. Keys for successfully preparing and delivering an oral presentation are given in the following paragraphs.

KEYS FOR SUCCESSFULLY PREPARING AN ORAL PRESENTATION

Successful oral presentations are well prepared.

Follow these keys for successfully preparing an oral presentation:

• *Determine your purpose* and state it clearly.

The foundation for a successful oral presentation is adequate preparation. Adequate preparation will give you confidence and will assure your audience of an interesting and informative presentation. What is adequate preparation? Some speakers say they spend 40 hours in preparation for each hour of oral presentation. As an average, that is probably a good guideline.

DETERMINE YOUR PURPOSE.   The first key is to determine the purpose of the oral presentation. It will fall into one of two categories: *to inform* or *to persuade*. Stating the purpose clearly and simply will assist you in focusing on the remaining part of the preparation. Your statement of the purpose of an oral presentation should be in terms of the expected result. Here are some example purpose statements:

1. To inform the employees of Joe Acala's contributions during his 20 years of service
2. To inform the audience of recent market research for a product line
3. To persuade employees to give to the United Appeal fund
4. To persuade management to purchase new equipment for the department

When the primary purpose of an oral presentation is *to inform*, you want the audience to learn, to understand, or to know more about the topic. That is the expected result. When the primary purpose is *to persuade*, you want the audience either to adopt your viewpoint or take specific action; that is the expected result.

• *Analyze your audience* for a you-viewpoint presentation.

ANALYZE YOUR AUDIENCE.   The second step to preparing an oral report is to decide exactly who will be in the audience. Then you analyze each member's knowledge, interests, opinions, and emotional state. What do they know about the topic? What is the audience's vocabulary level? What are their concerns, needs, and motivations relative to the topic? What opinions do they hold about the topic? What is their emotional reaction to the topic? See Chapter 1 (pages 12–14) for a complete review of the way to analyze receivers.

The most effective messages are those based on an analysis of the receivers. Nowhere is this truer than a message in an oral presentation. Therefore, you will want to build your oral presentation on an analysis of the audience. Plan to provide information that is not already known. Choose your words to fit your listeners' vocabulary. Consider carefully the audience motivation for listening to the presentation. Why is it important personally to your listeners? Prepare to offset any potential negative emotional reaction to your presentation.

GATHER SUPPORTING INFORMATION. When you have stated your purpose and analyzed the audience, you are ready to gather ideas and materials to support the development of your oral presentation. An oral presentation is researched in the same manner as a written presentation.

The kinds of helpful information to gather include definitions, examples, illustrations, explanations, quotations, statistics, testimonials, comparisons, and analogies. This information can come from your personal knowledge and resources, secondary sources, or primary sources.

• *Gather supporting information* for the presentation.

ORGANIZE YOUR PRESENTATION. As you gather supporting information, you will begin to have an idea of the best way to organize the information for presentation. The overall organizational framework you should use for an oral presentation is as follows:

• *Organize your presentation* using a logical organizational pattern.

1. Opening
2. Body
3. Closing

This framework will assist you in following the successful public speaking formula: Tell them what you are going to tell them, tell them, and then tell them what you told them.

In addition to the overall framework of opening, body, and closing, you need to determine a logical organizational pattern or patterns for the body of the presentation. Here are some frequently used patterns:

1. Time sequence. Review pertinent material from oldest to newest or from newest to oldest.
2. Spatial relation. Describe from top to bottom, bottom to top, left to right, right to left, inside to outside, outside to inside, room to room, desk to desk, or from some other spatial flow pattern.
3. Problem-solution. Describe the problem(s) and present the solution(s).
4. Cause-effect. Show the relationship between events.
5. Direct or indirect. Start or end with the main point.
6. Comparison or contrast. Show the similarities and dissimilarities of the subject matter.
7. Topics-subtopics. Organize the subject according to its logical parts.

A combination of these organizational patterns may be used within the body of an oral presentation. Use the patterns that you think will best serve your audience.

The supporting information you gather should be arranged following the organizational patterns you have selected. Once the information is organized, you can determine the types of audiovisual aids that will best strengthen the presentation.

• *Prepare audiovisual aids* to strengthen the message.

Audiovisual aids should be clear, simple, and cost-effective.

PREPARE AUDIOVISUAL AIDS.   Audiovisual aids can be used to strengthen the message—make it more interesting, understandable, and comprehensive. The use of these aids can spark audience attention and add desirable variety.

When deciding on audiovisual aids, ask yourself the following questions: Will this aid make my message clearer? Will it be simple enough to be

Once your information is organized, you can determine the types of audiovisual aids that will best strengthen your presentation.

understood? Will it be worth the time it will take to develop it? Will it enhance my message? If your answer to any of these questions is "no," you should not use the aid.

Some speakers hand out copies of their speeches to the audience as a visual aid. This type of handout violates every one of the criteria implied by the preceding questions. Be sure the audiovisual aid you select will enhance your remarks rather that detract from them.

There is a great variety of audiovisual aids to choose from. Chapter 16 will be helpful to you in preparing visuals. A brief review of some of the best audiovisuals is presented here.

PROJECTED MATERIAL. The most common and the most helpful audiovisual aids are those that project information onto a large screen that can be seen by every member of the audience. Probably the simplest, most flexible, least costly, and most effective technique is to project information using a transparency on an overhead projector. Other types of projection include opaque, slide, video, motion picture, filmstrip, and microcomputer screen. Each technique can be an effective complement to an oral presentation.

> You can project material in a variety of ways.

FLIP CHARTS AND POSTERS. Easels are available for displaying flip charts or posters. These visual aids can be easily produced at a low cost or prepared professionally at a higher cost. They can be effective if they are kept very simple and if they can be read by every member of the audience. Flip charts are good for topical outlines of a presentation. Posters can be used effectively for charts, graphs, tables, drawings, and pictograms.

> You can display material on an easel.

CHALKBOARD. Many well-equipped meeting rooms now have chalkboards for speakers' use. Also, you can arrange for portable chalkboards. Chalkboards have the advantage of permitting the visual aid to be developed as the presentation is being made.

> You can use chalkboards to develop a visual aid while you speak.

HANDOUTS. Handouts can be used effectively to present an outline of your presentation to an audience. Also, illustrative material can be distributed in this manner. Handouts that are too extensive will detract from a presentation. If you are going to hand out a copy of your talk or speech at the end, let the audience know this in advance. They can concentrate better on your comments if they do not have to worry about taking notes. Pass out any complex supplementary material you think the audience should have at the end of the presentation rather than before or during it.

> Use simple handouts before and during your presentation and detailed ones afterwards.

MODELS AND PHYSICAL OBJECTS. In business presentations you will many times have a product to display either in actual or in model form. This kind of visual aid can strengthen a sales presentation to the extent that the sale might be impossible without it. Again, it is important that any physical objects or models used as visual aids be large enough so that every member of the audience can see them.

> Models and physical objects can strengthen a presentation.

AUDIO TAPES AND RECORDINGS. Variety and impact are made possible by supplementing your oral presentation with an audio aid. When speaking on noise reduction in a factory, it could be effective to have recordings of

> Audio aids should be used selectively.

factory sounds in different settings with different sound treatment. Because audio aids are, in a sense, disembodied sounds, limited use of them is appropriate. An audience can tire quickly of simply listening to sound and not having visual stimuli.

- **Prepare your presentation** by organizing supporting data.

PREPARE YOUR PRESENTATION. You know your purpose. You have analyzed your audience. You have gathered and organized supporting data. You have prepared your audiovisual aids. You are now ready to put all this information together in a coherent oral presentation.

Plan to use an extemporaneous delivery technique.

Different speakers approach this task differently. You will recall that the extemporaneous delivery technique has been recommended for business presentations. So you must prepare notes to prompt you and guide you through the presentation. These notes may be on 5″ × 8″ cards, on sheets of paper in large print, or in some other form. Some speakers write their entire presentation and then make notes from the manuscript. After reading through the manuscript a few times, they put it aside (maybe even throw it away) so that they will not be tempted to read it to the audience. Other speakers simply make an outline and then make notes from the outline, never writing the entire presentation. However you arrive at your fully developed presentation, here are suggestions for each of the major parts.

The opening is crucial.

THE OPENING. An effective opening to an oral presentation is crucial. The audience evaluates your credibility and capability as a speaker in the first few minutes; and, regardless of what you do later, it is almost impossible to change that evaluation. A good first impression will serve you and your audience well throughout a presentation.

After thanking the person who introduced you, use your opening to get the audience's attention and interest. Effective ways to open a presentation include the use of a surprising statement, a quotation, an anecdote, a humorous story, a question, a statement of a problem, an impressive statistic, a visual aid, a reference to the situation, or an illustration. Whatever way you choose to open a presentation, be sure that you know the opening well and that it relates closely to your topic.

Use the opening to lead into the body of your presentation. Include a preview or overview of the main part of the talk and a transition statement. The opening should set the mood for the presentation and establish rapport between you and the audience. The opening is so crucial to the success of your presentation that you should give it careful attention in your preparation.

The body contains most of the information.

THE BODY. Most of the information you present to the audience will be contained in the middle of the presentation—in the body. Using the organized information developed earlier, plan this portion of your oral presentation carefully. Follow the selected organizational pattern(s) and make final decisions on how you will logically present and use the audiovisual aids.

Successful oral presentations depend on careful preparation and good delivery techniques.

As you develop the body of an oral presentation consider these guides:

In the body build on the opening, emphasize the main points, keep the content simple, and involve your listeners.

1. Maintain the listener's attention and interest developed in the opening. Continue to keep your presentation audience centered. Use the you-viewpoint. Use many examples and illustrations to create images in the minds of your listeners.

2. Emphasize your main points. Use the emphasis techniques given in Chapter 2—short sentences, repetition, specificity, mechanical means, and pointing out what is important. You might say, "This is my most important point . . . ," "Listen to this . . . ," "This, then, is the critical issue." You can use audiovisual aids to give emphasis.

3. Keep your presentation simple. Deal with a few main points. Audiences cannot comprehend complex, detailed information. That kind of information should be presented in written form so that it can be studied and reread. Match your vocabulary to that of your audience. Provide a smooth transition from one point to the next. Limit uninterrupted talking (talking without any audience activity) to no more than 20 minutes.

4. Involve your listeners in the presentation. One way to involve listeners was mentioned earlier—helping them to form images that support your points. More direct ways of getting audience involvement include asking questions and conducting discussions. Encouraging members of the audience to ask

questions is another way. Finally, there are many ways to have the audience participate directly in activities related to the topic such as small group discussions, exercises, and demonstrations. Providing for listener involvement in some manner is important to your success.

THE CLOSING.   In the closing, definitely let the audience know that you are ending; summarize the main points of your presentation; specify what the audience should do; and part with the audience on a positive, professional note.

Use both verbal and nonverbal signals to let the audience know you are ending the oral presentation. Ways you can do this include saying "In summary . . . ," "In closing . . . ," "To review . . . ," or "In conclusion . . ." A more subtle way is to pause and lower the pitch of your voice to show finality. Making a significant change in your stance relative to the podium is another way.

In summarizing the main points of your presentation, you can repeat them, have a visual aid summary, or ask the audience to review them with you. The summary should be a very simple statement designed to tie together all the main points.

Specifying what the audience is to do is tied closely to the summary. You may tell your listeners how to use the information you have given them or what action to take based on your persuasion.

Your final goal in the closing will be to part from your audience on a positive, professional note. You want your listeners to remember you and your presentation. You can use some of the suggested opening techniques for the closing. The suitable techniques include a surprising statement, a quotation, an anecdote, a humorous story (carefully used), or an illustration. The closing is an important point of emphasis for your presentation. Be positive and optimistic. Be professional. Most important of all, use the you-viewpoint in the closing.

REHEARSE YOUR PRESENTATION.   Using the notes and audiovisual aids you have developed, rehearse your oral presentation. Some speech authorities recommend that you rehearse a presentation aloud on your feet at least six times as though you were in the real-life situation.

Feedback on your rehearsal will be important to you. To get feedback, rehearse in front of a mirror or before friends, relatives, or colleagues. You can use an audio or a video recorder for this purpose as well. This practice affords the opportunity for revising content and fine tuning your delivery. It also gives you experience in handling your audiovisual aids efficiently. It is the only way you can be sure of the length of your presentation.

Rehearsing your oral presentation is essential to its success. Practice will increase your familiarity with the material and your confidence in delivering it.

Margin notes:

Summarize your main points in the closing and specify what the audience is to do.

• *Rehearse your presentation* aloud using your notes and audiovisual aids.

Get feedback on your rehearsal.

KEYS FOR SUCCESSFULLY DELIVERING AN ORAL PRESENTATION

All the material you studied in Chapter 18, "Improving Your Oral Communication," applies to the delivery of an oral presentation. You will want to use your voice effectively and project a strong presence. You will want to vary your pitch, volume, and speed for emphasis while speaking. You will want to enunciate sounds clearly and pronounce words correctly. Your poise and bearing should convey confidence, enthusiasm, sincerity, and friendliness. You should try to have eye contact with the audience at least 75 percent of the time. You will want to use natural gestures. Your appearance should be appropriate for the audience and the situation.

Use all the information in Chapter 18 to strengthen the delivery of presentations.

You have prepared your oral presentation and now you are ready to deliver it. Here are keys to guide you in successfully delivering your oral presentation.

Follow these keys for successfully delivering your presentation:

START POSITIVELY. Several hours before you are to speak, check the speaking location to orient yourself and to determine if everything you need is in place (or will be before your presentation). Check the podium and make sure it is the right height for you. Learn how to operate the equipment controls and the power supply and locate the room thermostat. Determine who can help if things go wrong.

- *Start positively* by checking the facility, being prepared, and giving the opening confidently.

Arrive five to ten minutes prior to the time you are to speak so you can make a final check of the facilities and the equipment. The lighting, room temperature, public address system, audiovisual equipment, podium, and seating arrangement should support and strengthen your presentation. Be sure your notes and visual aids are with you.

When the program starts and while you are being introduced, look pleasantly and confidently at the audience. After your introduction, walk with authority to the podium. Arrange your notes and audiovisual aids. Look at the audience, and give the opening of your presentation. It is good to memorize at least the first part, if not all, of the opening. In this way you can concentrate on the audience and your delivery and not have to worry about checking your notes for the content of the opening.

Remember that your delivery is part performance and part content. Both must be well prepared for a successful delivery.

HANDLE STAGE FRIGHT. One way to handle stage fright is to realize that even the most practiced and professional speakers have some "racehorse" nervousness before speaking to an audience. One night while Johnny Carson was standing in the wings ready to go on the "Tonight Show," his pulse rate was taken. This seasoned performer's heart rate was an excited 180 beats a minute! Don't be surprised if your own heart rate is accelerated.

- *Handle stage fright* by thinking positively, talking to yourself, and concentrating on the you-viewpoint.

Another way of dealing with nervousness that seems as if it will detract from a successful delivery is to talk to yourself. As you go to the podium tell yourself that you are glad to be there and glad that the audience is there. Remind yourself that you know more about your presentation than anyone in the audience. You have prepared thoroughly and look forward to this opportunity to share information with your audience or persuade it to some action.

Finally, an important way to handle stage fright is to concentrate on the you-viewpoint. Keep the audience's needs, interests, and concerns at the center of your attention. Keep reminding yourself that you are there to benefit the audience and that you can do it.

- *Use audiovisual aids effectively* based on your preparation.

USE AUDIOVISUAL AIDS EFFECTIVELY. You have chosen visuals that complement your presentation and have designed them so that the audience can read or hear everything in them. You have practiced handling them efficiently. To use them effectively during your delivery, simply take advantage of your careful preparation.

- *Evaluate audience feedback* and make necessary adjustments.

EVALUATE AUDIENCE FEEDBACK. Maintain good eye contact with the members of the audience so that you can secure feedback on how the presentation is progressing. As you will recall, during interpersonal oral communication the situation is constantly changing.

Assess your listeners' changing reactions and make necessary adjustments to keep their attention and interest. Are you sure they can all hear you? If not, speak louder. Can they all see the visual aids? If not, make adjustments. Is their interest waning? If so, change your pace, pick up your enthusiasm, and start involving them in some way. Do they seem not to understand a point? If so, ask them questions about it, repeat it in other words, or ask a volunteer to explain his or her understanding of the point. Do members of the audience show signs of discomfort? Do they appear to be too hot or too cold? If so, ask them about it and have the necessary adjustment made. Using the feedback you get from an audience can strengthen the effectiveness of an oral presentation.

- *End positively* using a clear, strong voice.

END POSITIVELY. Endings, like beginnings, are important. They are points of emphasis. You have prepared the content for the closing of your oral presentation. During your delivery of that closing, use a clear, strong voice. Your poise and bearing should be at their best. Even if the body of your presentation did not meet your highest expectations, you can recoup a great deal with an effective closing. At this point eye contact with the audience should be at the 100 percent level. You should be focusing exclusively on your audience and using the you-viewpoint.

A question-and-answer session following a presentation can be used to enhance your relationship with the audience.

After the closing there may be a question-and-answer session. This is common in business oral presentations. This is an excellent opportunity to relate positively to the audience. You can clarify your points, you can re-emphasize points, and you can directly answer any concerns of the audience.

Take advantage of your careful preparation and use your visual aids effectively.

In your preparation, you may have been able to anticipate many of the questions and thus have the answers ready.

Use all your knowledge about interpersonal oral communication during the question-and-answer session. Listen carefully, answer concisely, respect opposing viewpoints, and control your emotions.

A CONCLUDING COMMENT ON ORAL COMMUNICATION

Following the keys for successfully preparing and delivering oral presentations can make your one-to-large group oral communication a most enjoyable and rewarding experience. With practice and additional opportunities to speak, you

Business career success depends on effective oral communication.

will get better and better. Chances are your business career success will grow as you grow in your ability to make effective oral presentations.

This chapter has dealt with the keys for successfully planning and presenting oral communications. These keys concentrated on improving your effectiveness in one-to-one, one-to-small group, and one-to-large group oral communication in business settings. Using the information given in Chapters 18 and 19 can enhance your success as an effective oral business communicator.

DISCUSSION QUESTIONS

1. Discuss the human and environmental variables in an interpersonal oral communication situation.

2. Describe each of the following keys for successful face-to-face oral communication and give an example of its implementation: (a) Observe nonverbal behavior, (b) ask questions, (c) be appropriately assertive, and (d) control emotional reactions.

3. What are the four keys for successful telephone conversations?

4. Describe how a person should organize for dictation.

5. Explain the important procedures a dictator should follow while dictating.

6. Why should a dictator feel free, in most offices today, to revise his or her messages?

7. Discuss the nature of small group meetings.

8. The keys for successful small group leadership can be categorized as things to do before meetings, during meetings, and after meetings. Describe the keys for each category.

9. What are the responsibilities of a small group participant?

10. Discuss the purposes of presentations to large groups.

11. Discuss the keys for successfully preparing an oral presentation.

12. How do you decide on the content and nature of audiovisual aids for use with a presentation to a large group?

13. Discuss the important functions of the opening, the body, and the closing of an oral presentation.

14. Describe how a person who is speaking to a large group can handle stage fright effectively.

APPLICATION EXERCISES

1. Select a national leader and analyze his or her oral communication delivery techniques in (a) news conferences and (b) speeches.

2. Analyze the last three face-to-face conversations you have had. Indicate the strengths and weaknesses of your oral communication performance in these conversations. Suggest improvements that should be made in your next face-to-face conversations.

3. In each of several face-to-face conversations, concentrate on using at least three of the keys for successful face-to-face oral communication. Report your experiences to the class using all or some of these keys. Were you successful with each attempt?

4. For your most recent successful telephone conversation, indicate why telephoning was an especially appropriate technique for this oral communication.

5. Dictate a letter and either transcribe it or have it transcribed. Use one of the letter case problems in this textbook.

6. Interview a manager and ask for his or her opinion on the effectiveness of committees in business organizations. Share your findings with the class.

7. Prepare a three-minute (or longer, as specified by your instructor) extemporaneous oral presentation for the class on a topic of your choice. Be sure to use all the keys given in this chapter for successfully preparing an oral presentation.

8. Deliver the oral presentation that you prepared for Exercise 7. Be sure to use all the keys for successfully delivering an oral presentation.

9. In a small group of five or seven students choose a leader and an observer. Discuss the problems of handling stage fright before and during a presentation to a large group. In this exercise, practice either the keys for successful leadership or the keys for successful participation, depending on your role in the group. After the group discussion, the observer should report to the class on the group's findings and its successes and failures in achieving effective and efficient group discussion.

10. Introduce another member of the class to the class. Use the overall framework of opening, body, and closing for your introduction.

11. In one minute, convince the members of the class that they should study business communication. Have an opening, body, and closing in your remarks.

12. Welcome members of the class (a) to the first class meeting, (b) to the final examination, (c) to the first day of oral presentations, or (d) to some other interesting class meeting.

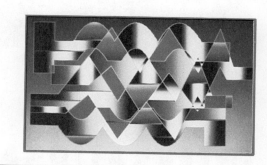

PART SIX

SPECIAL COMMUNICATION APPLICATIONS

CHAPTER 20

INTERNATIONAL BUSINESS COMMUNICATION

LEARNING OBJECTIVES

Your learning objectives for this chapter include the following:

▬ To develop an understanding of the challenges of international business communication

▬ To learn how to communicate successfully in the international business environment

▬ To become aware of key resources in international business communication

International business opportunities are increasing.

Increased profit is motivation for increased world trade.

International business success depends on effective cross-cultural communication.

The rapidly increasing involvement of American businesses in international trade and the growing number of job opportunities in multinational businesses are reasons for you to develop skill in international business communication.

The motivation for American firms to expand their involvement in world trade is increased profits. Businesses increase profits in their foreign operations by achieving increased productivity of high-quality products at lower costs. Also, American companies increase profit margins through exporting their products to other countries or importing foreign products for resale in the United States.

Success in international business communication depends on understanding other cultures and on skill in using the techniques of cross-cultural communication. *Cross-cultural* communication is the transmission of information between members of two different cultures, for example, between Americans and Japanese.

A company and its employees can benefit from a properly managed international business operation. The success of managers in such cross-cultural situations depends on their ability to communicate effectively. There is little doubt that most students studying this chapter will be involved sometime during their careers in international business communication.

This chapter discusses the challenges of international business communication, ways to communicate successfully in the international business environment, and key resources in international business communication.

THE CHALLENGES OF INTERNATIONAL BUSINESS COMMUNICATION

The challenges of international business communication are identical to those of domestic communication—analyzing receivers and using the you-viewpoint—with one major difference. That difference is found in the striking variation among cultures throughout the world. This variation among cultures includes differences in languages, values and attitudes, symbols and gestures, laws, religions, politics, educational levels, technological development, and social organizations.

Cultural variations cause communication challenges.

As many as 20,000 different cultures exist in the world. The cultural diversity even within some countries is striking. This diversity, while possibly more subtle than that between two countries, must be considered when analyzing receivers.

There are cultural differences within countries.

Americans (a term used throughout the world to refer to citizens of the United States) recognize cultural differences within their own country. These differences include variations in behavior between the faster-paced North and the slower-paced South. Persons from Chicago talk faster than persons living in Alabama. The more formal, more reserved people of Maine can be contrasted to the less formal, less reserved people of southern California.

In Kentucky, for example, someone might say, "I would be proud to carry you to the office." For that person the word *proud* would mean "glad" and the word *carry* would mean "transport." Although this would be readily understood by others from the same state, people from some other areas of the country could easily be confused.

The amount of cultural diversity within the United States, however, is small in comparison with the cultural diversity throughout the world. A direct message composed in businesslike terms sent to a German businessperson may be extremely successful for you and your company. The same message sent to a

Japanese businessperson—because of its directness—may fail miserably. The difference in the success of the two communications lies in the cultural differences of the two countries. The next sections describe examples of cultural differences and the challenges these differences present to the business communicator.

Great cultural differences are found between countries.

LANGUAGE DIFFERENCES

More than 3,000 different languages are spoken throughout the world. More than 200 different languages are spoken in India alone. Considering all the various dialects in the world, some linguists estimate that there are at least 10,000 different variations of languages. If you are not skilled in the use of your receiver's primary language, you are facing your first major challenge in international business communication.

There are 3,000 languages and 10,000 dialects in the world.

American auto companies have experienced many difficulties because of lack of knowledge of another culture's language. Chevrolet's Nova was not received well in Spanish-speaking countries. Its name sounded like *no va*, which in Spanish means "it doesn't go." Ford's Comet was named Caliente for the Mexican market. Unfortunately, even though *caliente* means "hot" in a literal translation, it also is a slang word for *streetwalker* in Mexico, and poor sales resulted there.[1]

Word choice can be a problem.

There are other examples of a word being appropriate in one country and not in another. A U.S. trade magazine promoting gift sales in Germany used the English word *gift* in its title. Unfortunately, the word *gift* in German means "poison." The trade magazine did not effectively achieve its objective of selling gifts in Germany. A foreign airline inappropriately selected *EMU* for its name in Australia. An emu is an Australian bird that cannot fly. Finally, *Esso* means "stalled car" in Japanese—hardly an appropriate name for gasoline and oil products being sold in Japan.

Even the way parts of speech are used in different languages varies culturally. In Japanese, the verb is at the end of a sentence. This enables the Japanese to begin to express a thought and watch the receiver's reaction. Depending on how the receiver is reacting to the message, the verb may be changed, thereby changing the whole meaning of the sentence. For example, a Japanese might start to say, "Please go away from me now" and change it to "Please stay with me now" by changing the verb, which is said last.

Languages are structured differently.

An American company caused itself considerable communication problems in Germany by insisting that all its employees call each other by their first names. This made the Germans uncomfortable, because they do not call even close business associates with whom they have worked for years by their first names. In Germany, the use of first names is reserved for intimate friends and relatives. Forcing the Germans to adopt an American custom caused stress that seriously reduced the quality of communication in the German-based American operation.

The degree of formality will vary.

---

[1] David A. Ricks, *Big Business Blunders* (Homewood, Illinois: Dow Jones-Irwin, 1983), 38-39.

NONVERBAL COMMUNICATION DIFFERENCES

A sender's nonverbal signals—facial expressions, body movements, and gestures—influence the receiver's understanding and acceptance of a message. In international business communication, nonverbal signals vary as much as spoken languages do.

Cultural differences in nonverbal signals are extensive.

The cultural diversity in nonverbal communication can be shown by an examination of worldwide differences in the way people greet each other. As can be noted in Illustration 20-1, nonverbal greetings vary from a bow to a handshake to a hug to an upward flick of the eyebrows depending on the country and the culture involved.

Acceptable greetings vary markedly.

Country	Nonverbal Method of Greeting
Argentina	Shaking hands while slightly nodding heads (After long absences, women kiss each other on the cheek and men may embrace.)
Australia	Warm handshake between men (A man shakes hands with a woman only if she extends her hand first.)
Belgium	Shaking hands with everyone, using a quick shake with light pressure
Chile	A handshake and a kiss to the right cheek
China	A nod or slight bow (In addition, a handshake is also acceptable.)
Fiji	A smile and an upward flick of the eyebrows (A handshake is also appropriate.)
France	A handshake (A firm, pumping American handshake is considered impolite.)
Greece	An embrace and a kiss on both cheeks or a handshake
India	The *namaste*—bending gently with palms together below chin
Japan	A bow, as low and as long as the other person's
Portugal	A warm, firm handshake for everyone
Saudia Arabia	A handshake (Frequently males will also extend the left hand to each other's right shoulders and then kiss the left and right cheeks.)
Thailand	The *wai*—placing both hands together in prayer position at chest and bowing slightly
USSR	A handshake and sometimes, among older people, the traditional three kisses on the cheek.
United States	A warm, firm, pumping handshake

Source: Adapted with permission from the **Culturgrams** series, 1988 ed. (Provo, Utah: David M. Kennedy Center for International Studies, Brigham Young University).

Illustration 20-1   Cultural Differences in Greetings

Misunderstanding
nonverbal messages can
cause problems.

Not understanding cultural differences in nonverbal messages causes communication problems. For example, if in Germany an American were to signal *one* by holding up the index finger, it would be understood as *two*. Germans signal *one* by holding up the thumb and *two* by extending the thumb and index finger. An American ordering a train ticket in Germany by raising the index finger, therefore, would likely get two tickets instead of one.

Also in Germany, smiles are mostly reserved for close friends or relatives. Because Germans are more reserved than Americans, the American who laughs often and smiles at everyone would overwhelm many Germans. Such unacceptable nonverbal behavior by an American would definitely interfere with any accompanying verbal communication.

Some nonverbal signals
are considered impolite
or vulgar.

In Japan it is considered impolite or vulgar for people to cross their legs by placing one foot or ankle on the knee of the other leg. The preferred way of sitting in Japan is with both feet on the floor with knees held fairly close together. It is acceptable to cross the legs by placing one knee directly over the other, or to cross the ankles.

Others are simply quite
different.

In Italy a person waves goodbye by raising one hand with the palm facing the body and waving the hand back and forth to and from the body. In Korea, it is acceptable for men to hold hands in public, but it is frowned on to touch the opposite sex in public. In Lebanon, while *yes* is signaled by nodding the head as Americans do, *no* is indicated by an upward movement of the head or raised eyebrows. In France, continual eye contact with someone with whom you are speaking is appropriate. In most Asian countries, however, limited eye contact, with the eyes diverted most of the time, is more acceptable.

A person involved in cross-cultural communication must be aware of the wide variation throughout the world in the meaning of nonverbal signals. These differences in nonverbal signals, however, are only illustrative of much more important underlying cultural differences in the way people think and feel.

OTHER CULTURAL DIFFERENCES

Underlying the cultural variations in verbal and nonverbal communication are many other deep-seated cultural differences that affect communication. The most important differences are in the ways people in other cultures think and feel. These differences are grounded in such things as values, attitudes, religions, political systems, and social orders. Your understanding of these other cultural differences is vital to your success in cross-cultural communication. A few examples of some of them will illustrate this point.

The way people think and
feel is the most important
cultural difference.

The friendly, outgoing, competitive, informal American who primarily uses the direct plan for communicating may not be received well in Asian or some European countries. In most of these countries people are more reserved and less direct in their human relations than are Americans. Most Japanese, for example, need to build a personal relationship of trust and friendship

Most cultures are more
reserved than is the
American culture.

before entering an important business relationship. On the other hand, most Americans are willing to do business with a limited or nonexistent personal relationship with their customers or vendors. In successfully relating to the Japanese, therefore, Americans must be willing to build the necessary personal relationships first. This requires more patience than most Americans normally need to use in their business dealings in the United States.

A simple example of cultural diversity that affects business communication is business hours. You cannot, for instance, telephone a business if that business is not open. Illustration 20-2 shows this variation.

Business hours and days limit contact time.

Country	Business Office Hours
Australia	8:30 a.m. to 5:30 p.m.
Brazil	8 a.m. to 12 noon; 2 p.m. to 6 p.m.
China	8 a.m. to 12 noon; 1 p.m. to 5 p.m.
Greece	8 a.m. to 1:30 p.m.; 5:30 p.m. to 8:30 p.m.
Hong Kong	9 a.m. to 5 p.m. and 9 a.m. to 1 p.m. (on Saturday)
Northern Ireland	9 a.m. to 5 p.m.
Italy	8 or 9 a.m. to 1 p.m.; 3:30 or 4 p.m. until 7 or 8 p.m.
Norway	8 a.m. to 4 p.m.
Romania	7 a.m. to 3 or 4 p.m.
Spain	9 a.m. to 1:30 p.m.; 5 p.m. to 8 p.m.
USSR	8 a.m. to 5 p.m.
United States	8 a.m. to 5 p.m.
Zimbabwe	8 a.m. to 5 p.m.

Source: Adapted with permission from the **Culturgrams** series, 1988 ed. (Provo, Utah: David M. Kennedy Center for International Studies, Brigham Young University).

Illustration 20-2 Common Business Office Hours Around the World

Note in Illustration 20-2 that many countries in warmer climates close offices in the middle of the day. That time is used for the main meal and resting, or a siesta. There is, of course, also variation in business hours due to time differences in international time zones. The six- to nine-hour difference in time between European or Asian countries and the United States allows little or no overlap in normal business hours.

It is also interesting to note that the days of the week that businesses operate vary around the world. In the United States, most business offices operate Monday through Friday with Saturday and Sunday off. In Korea the workweek is Monday through Saturday and possibly Sunday. In contrast, the workweek in Saudi Arabia and other Islamic countries is Saturday through Wednesday with Thursday and Friday off. Friday is the Islamic day of rest and worship.

Days in the workweek vary.

The cultural diversity described in this section is indicative of some of the challenges of international business communication. Guidelines for meeting these and other cross-cultural communication challenges are given in the next section.

COMMUNICATING SUCCESSFULLY IN THE INTERNATIONAL BUSINESS ENVIRONMENT

You can be successful in cross-cultural communication if you follow proven guidelines. Use of the information given previously on business communication foundations and principles will be essential to your success. In addition, follow the special guidelines for international business communication given in this section.

Goal: Communicate without cultural prejudice.

Goal of Cross-Cultural Communication

To achieve normal business communication without cultural prejudice.

Your goal for effective cross-cultural communication is to achieve normal business communication without cultural prejudice. This means having the ability to communicate comfortably in a natural fashion while eliminating barriers that might be caused by cultural differences.

GUIDELINES FOR SUCCESSFUL CROSS-CULTURAL COMMUNICATION

The guidelines for successful cross-cultural communication are presented in three groupings. These consist of basic guidelines for cross-cultural communication, guidelines for cross-cultural communication in English, and guidelines for using an interpreter or translator. The basic guidelines will assist you in gaining the necessary general information and perspective for cross-cultural communication in the international business environment. The guidelines for communicating cross-culturally in English are provided because most of the world's business is conducted in English. Finally, the guidelines for using an interpreter or translator cover those special situations where a bilingual person is employed to bridge the language barrier.

BASIC GUIDELINES FOR CROSS-CULTURAL COMMUNICATION.
The basic guidelines presented in this section should be followed to prepare for cross-cultural communication in the international business environment.

GUIDELINE 1: REVIEW THE FOUNDATIONS AND PRINCIPLES OF BUSINESS COMMUNICATION.
In any cross-cultural communication situation, the basic business communication knowledge you have already gained will apply. A review of that knowledge should be your first step in preparing to participate in communication in the international business environment.

Use foundations and principles of business communication.

As you will recall, the goals of business communication include receiver understanding, necessary receiver response, a favorable relationship between you and your receiver, and goodwill for your organization. These goals will be a part of your international business communication effort.

In addition, the communication process will be the same—you need to analyze your receiver and use the you-viewpoint, select the appropriate form of message, provide for feedback, and remove communication barriers. Finally, application of the KISS principle of business communication (keep it short and simple) will enhance your effectiveness in international business communication.

GUIDELINE 2: ANALYZE YOUR OWN CULTURE.
A starting point in relating effectively to others is to know your own culture. Then understanding how others view your culture is vital for success in cross-cultural communication.

Understanding your own culture is essential.

Oh, wad some Pow'r the giftie gi'e us
To see oursels as ithers see us!

Robert Burns, "To a Louse on a Lady's Bonnet," 1786.

People throughout the world have to use comparisons, evaluations, and categories to assimilate and understand the messages they receive. They use stereotypes of other peoples to help them understand the messages those peoples are sending them. While individuals within one culture vary considerably, many of them will hold common values; have similar tastes in food and clothing; and possess similar attitudes, opinions, and beliefs.

The American culture, for example, comprises a distinct group of people who live in the United States. The people of the world call them *Americans*. Interestingly enough, even the people who live in Canada and Mexico call the people who live in the United States *Americans* while referring to themselves as *Canadians* or *Mexicans*.

Americans tend to be:

• friendly and informal

• time conscious, impatient, and independent

• direct in eye contact and space conscious

• supportive of an individual's rights and needs

• materialistic and capitalistic

The American culture differs from others.

Cultural relativism refers to varying standards of right and wrong.

Be open to and accepting of other cultures.

The American stereotype, which is largely accurate and useful, depicts persons who prefer to communicate in the English language. Although they primarily use the direct plan of communication (versus the indirect plan), they tend to do so politely. Americans are generally friendly and informal. They are likely to greet you by your first name and shake your hand with a firm grip and pumping action. They have a strong sense of humor and laugh and smile frequently.

Americans are time conscious and efficiency oriented. They tend to be impatient. They do not need to have personal friendship as a basis for business relationships. They have limited respect for rank and authority.

Eye contact while conversing is a sign of strength and honesty to Americans. They have a greater need for personal space than do some other peoples—at least two to three feet minimum distances between themselves and others. Americans tend to limit personal touching of each other in public.

Americans value highly an individual's freedom to achieve. They tend to put an individual's needs above an organization's needs. They believe rather firmly that the "American way" is the "right way."

Americans value material possessions and have many more of them than do most peoples of the rest of the world. Americans support an open economy, are predominantly Christian, and believe in democracy.

The foregoing is a limited analysis of the American culture. It can be seen, however, how this stereotype can be helpful to you in cross-cultural communication. As you examine other cultures, you will quickly note that—while there is much in common—there are sharp differences in values, tastes, and attitudes. For example, Japanese have greater respect for rank and authority and greater loyalty to organizations than do Americans. Latin Americans and peoples of the Middle East need and desire much less personal space than do Americans. Germans and many other Europeans are more reserved and formal than Americans.

Cultural relativism is the term used to describe the fact that different cultures have somewhat different standards of right and wrong. As people grow up in their culture, they tend to suppose that the ways they do things are normal and that the ways of other cultures are not, since these other ways strike them as peculiar and strange. As you study other cultures, however, you can realize that there is not necessarily one right or wrong way to do something—merely many different, but equally correct, ways. Understanding the practices of your own culture will enable you to understand and relate more successfully to the practices of other cultures.

GUIDELINE 3: DEVELOP THE ABILITY TO BE OPEN TO AND ACCEPTING OF OTHER CULTURES.   As you studied the American culture in the previous section, you began to sense that it represents one way to believe and to do things. It is important to accept that this is not the only way. This understanding is essential in order to communicate successfully with people of other cultures who believe and do things differently. With your involvement in the international business environment, you will want to adopt an open, accepting attitude toward the differences in others.

Cross-cultural involvement can be an exciting, new adventure. You may be (or have been) apprehensive the first time you meet with persons from another culture. You may feel deficient in some ways and superior in some other ways. You will no doubt have many mixed emotions. The guideline that directs you to be open to and accepting of other cultures will serve you well in the international business environment.

How can you be open and accepting? Be open to learning about the other culture with which you are dealing. Be open to different foods, to different ways of doing things, to different beliefs—beliefs, for example, about the value of time (a clock "runs" in the United States; it "walks" in Spanish-speaking Latin America). Be accepting of other peoples' needs for indirectness in communicating (as in Asia) and for the use of titles and last names instead of first names (as in Europe). Be open to and accepting of the different ways people of other cultures think and feel.

Be patient, but do not be condescending. Be tolerant of differences. Do not rush to an early judgment about the way a conversation or business deal is going. You may be misreading a communication situation because of cultural differences. Ask questions. Ask if you are being understood. Obtain feedback.

Successful cross-cultural communication depends on the ability to be open and accepting of other cultures—their foods, beliefs, and ways of doing things.

Be open to and accepting of differences.

Your success in cross-cultural communication will depend largely on your ability to be open to and accepting of differences in others. Only that way can you communicate in the you-viewpoint without cultural prejudice.

GUIDELINE 4: LEARN ALL YOU CAN ABOUT THE OTHER CULTURE AND APPLY WHAT YOU LEARN. This is the *key guideline* for effective cross-cultural communication. There is, of course, much to be learned about another culture. Do not let the volume of information overwhelm you. Anything you learn will be helpful and will strengthen your ability to communicate. The last section of this chapter provides several good sources of information for learning about other cultures.

Key Guideline:

• Learn about the other culture.

A basic recommendation in learning about another culture is to learn as much as you can of that culture's language. Ideally, you would be able to speak and write the other culture's language fluently. That may not be possible. In any case, learn as much as you can. Learn at least greetings, courtesy words, and the basic positive and negative signals. Learn the few basic phrases that represent typical words used in regard to the subject of your communication. For example, learn how to say "We want to do business with you," if that is appropriate.

• Use what you learn.

You should not only learn as much as possible of the other culture's language, but you should also use what you know in your oral and written messages. Your receivers will appreciate your efforts. They will be understanding and accepting of any deficiencies in your use of their language.

A second aspect of learning about another culture is to learn as much as possible about the people of that culture. This aspect of learning includes a wide range of information from how the people think to the foods they eat. For example, there is considerable evidence that Americans think in an explicit, linear manner while Asians think in an implicit, intuitive manner. Americans are more likely to think in terms of facts and dichotomies—black-white, right-wrong, good-evil, and true-false. Asians, in contrast to Americans, are likely to think in terms of feelings, relationships, and continuums.

In addition to the way people think, understanding other aspects of the culture you are studying is also important. You should try to learn about how the people relate to each other, what their preferences are in foods and how they eat, what their preferences are in apparel, what hours comprise their workday, how they negotiate, what their business ethics are, what topics of discussion are acceptable and what topics are unacceptable, and what gestures are acceptable and what gestures are unacceptable. The list goes on and on. You should try to learn about their religion, politics, educational system, economy, government, and history.

When you have acquired information about the other culture, analyze it in the following ways: How is it similar to your culture? How is it different? How can you best bridge these differences? By applying the information gained in this analysis—and with practice—you can become an effective cross-cultural communicator.

The preceding four basic guidelines are important for success in any cross-cultural communication in the business environment. There are two other categories of guidelines. The category to apply depends on whether your cross-cultural communication will be in English or in two languages.

GUIDELINES FOR CROSS-CULTURAL COMMUNICATION IN THE ENGLISH LANGUAGE.

Fortunately for Americans, most international business communication is conducted in the English language. This is true throughout the world.

While the extensive use of English as the primary cross-cultural language is fortunate for Americans, it is important to recognize that for most persons in the world, English is a second language. Non-Americans' facility with the English language and their understanding of its context will limit communication effectiveness. Some Americans mistakenly equate a lack of ability to speak English fluently with a lack of intelligence in non-Americans. That serious error becomes a communication limitation for the Americans because they will analyze their receivers incorrectly. These guidelines will assist you in overcoming any such limitations.

GUIDELINE 5: WHEN COMMUNICATING IN ENGLISH WITH MEMBERS OF ANOTHER CULTURE, KEEP YOUR MESSAGE SHORT AND SIMPLE. This guideline reminds you to use the KISS principle of business communication (keep it short and simple) when communicating in English with people from another culture. Use short words and short sentences. In addition, it is especially important to avoid jargon, slang, and colloquial expressions such as "the bottom line," "operating by the seat of your pants," and "do you read me?" Most of your receivers will have learned only formal English in their schools.

Use the KISS principle in cross-cultural communication in English.

Except for the use of technical words appropriate for your receiver, the readability level of your message should be at about eighth- to tenth-grade level. Be sure to provide for feedback so that you can confirm receiver understanding of the message.

GUIDELINE 6: IN ORAL COMMUNICATION, ENUNCIATE SOUNDS AND PRONOUNCE WORDS PRECISELY. If the communication in English is oral, be sure to enunciate sounds and pronounce words precisely. Try to overcome any accents or speech mannerisms that may be distracting and may create communication barriers. While you will not want the slowness to appear exaggerated, speak somewhat more slowly. Be sure not to speak more loudly than necessary for normal hearing.

Pronounce words precisely.

GUIDELINES FOR CROSS-CULTURAL COMMUNICATION USING AN INTERPRETER OR TRANSLATOR.

If English is your only language and your receiver does not know English, then you must use an interpreter for oral communication and a translator for written communication. All the previous guidelines apply when using an interpreter or a translator. There are four additional guidelines that should be followed.

When cross-cultural oral communication requires using an interpreter, certain guidelines should be followed.

GUIDELINE 7: WHEN USING AN INTERPRETER, USE SHORT, SIMPLE PHRASES AND SENTENCES. Avoid long introductory phrases, parenthetical elements, interjections, and complex and compound sentences. As you prepare to use an interpreter, give special attention to the parts of your message that may be difficult to convey. Develop clear illustrations of these difficult parts to help ensure your receiver's understanding.

Avoid talking with your interpreter. Talk to your receivers keeping your interpreter in the corner of your eye. Permit your interpreter to explain your remarks if necessary, and encourage your receivers to ask questions if you sense you are not being understood clearly. Remain calm and poised. Concentrate on your receivers' interests and not on yourself or your interpreter.

GUIDELINE 8: PRACTICE WITH YOUR INTERPRETER. If possible, learn your interpreter's preferred ways of operating—in complete thought units, in short phrases, or word by word. You and your interpreter will be a

Use short, simple sentences when using an interpreter.

Avoid talking "to" the interpreter.

Practice using an interpreter.

team. As practice improves any team effort, you will want to rehearse your cooperative effort with an interpreter.

GUIDELINE 9: SELECT ONLY TRANSLATORS WHO ARE QUALIFIED TO TRANSLATE THE TYPE OF WRITTEN MESSAGE YOU ARE SENDING. Most people who have read instructions accompanying foreign-made products know the difficulty of translating from one language to another—generally, languages cannot be translated verbatim. The translator must be qualified in the subject matter so that the *meaning* of the message is conveyed to the receiver, not just the words. As you will recall, insufficient knowledge resulted in the naming of American cars Nova and Caliente for Spanish-speaking markets.

Translators must know the subject matter.

GUIDELINE 10: PROVIDE FOR BACK TRANSLATION OF YOUR WRITTEN MESSAGES. Check for translation errors; i.e., have a second translator translate the message back into English for verification of its meaning. Back translation is a technique for obtaining essential feedback. Many errors have been caught this way.

Back translation catches errors.

COMMUNICATING SUCCESSFULLY WITH MAJOR TRADING PARTNERS OF THE UNITED STATES

Brief examples of analyses of other cultures will help show the value of the previous guidelines. For these examples, the cultures of four major trading partners of the United States will be examined—Japan, Germany, Canada, and Mexico.[2]

Examples from other cultures show how guidelines are used.

COMMUNICATING SUCCESSFULLY WITH JAPANESE BUSINESSPERSONS.
Americans in business can improve communication with the Japanese by taking into consideration Japanese cultural attributes. Remember that these are only stereotypes and that individuals within cultures vary considerably. These generalizations, nonetheless, can help Americans work more effectively with the Japanese in many business enterprises.

JAPANESE CULTURAL ATTRIBUTES. Japanese tend to be modest, respectful of superiors, loyal to their organizations, contemplative and holistic in their thinking, and traditional in terms of their society. They are achievement oriented. They value human relationships above business relationships and practice situational ethics, i.e., moral judgments based more on the merits of the situation than on some absolute ethical standard. Their privacy is important

Japanese are considered modest, respectful, and contemplative.

[2]Source: These cultural analyses were adapted with permission from publications available from the David M. Kennedy Center for International Studies, Brigham Young University, Provo, Utah.

to them, and direct questioning about their personal lives is resented. "Losing face" is their worst catastrophe. The shame of losing face reflects not only on the individual but also on the family.

Communicating with the Japanese calls for diplomacy.

COMMUNICATING WITH THE JAPANESE.   When communicating with the Japanese, American businesspersons should be gracious and diplomatic. In business meetings in Japan, bowing when greeting your hosts and then shaking hands are important gestures. Do not be surprised if the Japanese, who value punctuality less than Americans do, are somewhat late for the start of a meeting. Because status and hierarchy are important in Japan, an exchange of business cards upon meeting will be helpful to them in sorting out relationships. The American belief in the equality of all does not prevail in Japan.

Primarily use the indirect plan of communication with the Japanese.

During meetings, confrontations should be avoided. The Japanese will prefer indirectness in approaching business transactions. They may seem to agree with you in order to avoid offending you. Do not be misled by this courtesy to believe that the agreement is set. The agreement will not be finalized until you get it in writing. Japanese businesspersons will want to spend most of the meeting time clarifying the relationships of the trading partners and discussing the details of the business arrangement. Many times the actual terms will be agreed to in informal social gatherings. Patience is the watchword. If sufficient trust in the Americans and their firm is developed through these negotiations, final approval of the transaction may be achieved. It is important for the Americans not to feel compelled to win points in the negotiations. The Japanese will prefer to share equally the points of agreement. Courtesy and humility should be an American's bywords in communicating with the Japanese.

In business meetings in Japan, American businesspersons should bow when greeting their hosts and then shake hands.

COMMUNICATING SUCCESSFULLY WITH GERMAN BUSINESSPERSONS.

The German cultural attributes are quite distinctive.

GERMAN CULTURAL ATTRIBUTES.

As compared with Americans, German businesspeople are more formal, reserved, and restrained. Germans tend to be inquisitive and want to hear the supporting evidence for a new idea or procedure. They enjoy vigorous discussion based on logical reasoning. They value intelligence and education. Like Americans, Germans value individualism and the success of the individual.

Germans are basically conservative and prefer discipline and order to informality and change. They may seem to move slowly in their business operations, but they are strong and enduring. Germans take a more serious approach to their business affairs than do Americans. Smiles and laughter are likely to be reserved for celebrations with intimate friends and loved ones. Germans are punctual. They believe it is offensive to waste another's time by being late.

Germans approach relationships and communication directly. While some Americans might think they are too outspoken or blunt, Germans would see their behavior as simple honesty. Germans have opinions about most things and express those opinions freely. They reserve compliments for only the most outstanding achievements. Germans are a determined people who set goals and tenaciously accomplish them.

COMMUNICATING WITH GERMANS.

This generalized thumbnail sketch of German businesspeople provides important information which, if used by American businesspeople, will avoid some communication barriers. Fortunately, Americans have much in common culturally with Germans. Building on these commonalities and adapting to the differences are the marks of a good cross-cultural communicator.

When communicating with German businesspersons, Americans should generally be formal, serious, impersonal, and thorough. In meeting with Germans, titles and last names should be used; and greetings should include firm handshakes with all those present. Avoid questions such as How are you? and What do you do? Such questions may be considered too personal. As time passes and the Germans become better acquainted with you, you can establish relaxed, friendly, and personal relationships.

If you are presenting new information or a business proposal, be prepared to answer questions about it. Germans will demand supportive evidence based on solid research or logical reasoning. You may want to present your proposal privately to the top German executive for approval first. Then that executive can either present the proposal to other Germans on your behalf or endorse your presentation after you have made it. This approach can increase the credibility of your proposal with other Germans and reduce the amount of time spent justifying it.

Directness can be used effectively in communicating with German businesspeople in the same way that it can be used with Americans. Avoid humor at business meetings with Germans; it will be distracting. Also, avoid giving

Germans are generally reserved, inquisitive, and conservative.

Communicating with Germans calls for formality and seriousness.

You can use the direct plan of communication with Germans.

minor compliments; they will be perceived as frivolous and will make your sincerity questionable. Be businesslike, and focus on the agreed upon goals of the meeting.

At the end of the meeting you will likely know where you stand with your German receivers. Be on time for your meetings, adjourn them precisely at the agreed time, and be sure to shake hands with everyone as you say good-bye.

COMMUNICATING SUCCESSFULLY WITH CANADIAN BUSINESSPERSONS.
The Canadian culture, while similar to the United States' culture, has some diversity based on the origins of its citizens.

CANADIAN CULTURAL ATTRIBUTES.
The Canadian people's ancestry is basically French and English, although some Canadians have their origins in Germany, the Netherlands, and Ireland. Canadians value their diversity. Twenty-eight percent of all Canadians are of French origin, and 81 percent of the population of the province of Quebec speak French as their first language. While French is the official language of Quebec, the English language is used in parts of Montreal, eastern Quebec, and throughout the rest of Canada.

Eighty-eight percent of the population belong to the Roman Catholic Church. The Canadian economy is strong, and the standard of living is virtually the same as that of the United States. Offices are usually open from 9 a.m. to 5 p.m. or 8 a.m. to 4 p.m., Monday through Friday.

Canadians generally are more reserved and formal than the people of the United States. Most are friendly, kind, open, and polite. They follow more formal rules of etiquette than do Americans. The use of courtesy titles and last names is common, and coats and ties are required for dining in some restaurants. In addition, Canadians dress well and conservatively for formal and semiformal occasions such as business meetings; they dress casually at other times. Western Canadians are likely to be less formal and reserved than eastern Canadians.

Canadians are a conservative, law-abiding people. Their conversations are to the point, intelligent, and polite. As in the United States, eye contact is important. Greetings include a firm handshake and a sincere "hello." Many other cultural attributes are shared by the people of Canada and the people of the United States.

COMMUNICATING WITH CANADIANS.
Successful communication with Canadian businesspersons requires using basically the same approaches as used in the United States. Some important differences, however, should be noted.

When communicating with Canadians, businesspersons from the United States should be more formal and reserved than when dealing with those from the United States. Until told differently, last names and titles should be used. Politeness and courtesy are essential. Directness can be used, but the "hard sell" approach will not appeal to most Canadians. Be sincere, warm, and friendly. Your dress should be formal business attire.

Although Canada is officially a bilingual country, French should be spoken, if possible, when doing business in Quebec. Fortunately for most

---

Canada is bilingual.

Canadians are somewhat more reserved, formal, and conservative than are U.S. citizens.

Canada shares many cultural attributes with the U.S.

Communicating with Canadians calls for politeness and courtesy. The direct plan can be used.

U.S. businesspersons, English is used in the rest of Canada and can be spoken in Quebec if necessary. In Canada some words are used differently than in the United States. For example, school grades are called marks in Canada, tennis shoes are called running shoes, and sofas are called chesterfields. Some words are pronounced differently, such as, aboot for about, vahz for vase, and tomahto for tomato.

Communicating successfully with Canadians is important. Canada is the United States' largest trading partner. A recent agreement will gradually eliminate all trade barriers between the two countries by 1999, so contact and communication with Canadians will increase for American businesspersons.

Some language variations exist between Canada and the U.S.

COMMUNICATING SUCCESSFULLY WITH MEXICAN BUSINESSPERSONS.   The Mexican culture is quite different from the United States' culture.

MEXICAN CULTURAL ATTRIBUTES.   Mexicans are a very warm, friendly, gracious people. They greet another person with a handshake and stand very close while talking, possibly touching the other person or his or her clothing.

Their time is your time. In fact, while they know most Americans will be punctual for appointments, Mexicans give time much less importance. They rank people at a much higher level than time and may be quite late for appointments. They mean no disrespect by this behavior.

While an American defines success in terms of efficiency, achievement, money, and material possessions, a Mexican may be more likely to define success as adapting to the status quo and to the position into which he or she was born.

Mexican graciousness reflects itself in several ways. Their messages are generally indirect and elaborate. Sometimes favorable relationships of the moment are more important than the truth. Mexican businesspeople may seem to make a business commitment that they later do not keep. Their intention was not to deceive you; rather, their commitment was to be courteous to you and to make the current moment pleasant.

Business transactions in Mexico may depend on the development of personal favors and friendships. In order to receive a benefit—something as simple as a public service—some businesspeople have reported that they had to pay money or give gifts to key people. This method of getting things done in Mexico is not considered dishonest because the services provided are not illegal. American businesspersons have considerable difficulty with this way of operating.

Mexicans achieve self-esteem primarily through their friendships and personal relationships rather than through promotions or recognition for job performance. Mexicans will not necessarily be loyal to their employers and their jobs, but rather to superiors at work whom they like. They gain self-esteem through the ways their friends treat and respect them. They tend to trust only their friends.

Mexicans are considered warm, gracious, and person oriented.

Communicating with
Mexicans calls for
personal relationship
development.

COMMUNICATING WITH MEXICANS.   Many American firms have been disappointed in their business dealings in Mexico because they did not understand the differences between the cultures. In attempting to communicate effectively with Mexicans, it should be emphasized that building personal relationships and friendships will be important. Close friends in Mexico are more open with each other than Mexicans are with strangers or acquaintances.

Primarily use the indirect
communication plan with
Mexicans.

Use indirectness in communicating with Mexican businesspersons. In your meetings, plan to visit socially at first in order to accommodate their need for indirectness. Expect your Mexican counterpart to stand or sit very close to you and maybe to touch you while talking with you. Expect your Mexican associate to be very gracious, courteous, and respectful. To build the necessary relationship, you must be the same. Your meetings with Mexican businesspersons will likely start quite late, well after the appointment times.

Because commitments made early in your relationship may not be followed through on, patience must be the foundation of your business venture in Mexico. If Mexicans are working for your organization, realize that they may value job performance less than you might expect in the United States. These kinds of situations will improve as you build a trusting and mutually respectful personal relationship with your Mexican business associates.

In many ways there are greater differences between the cultures of Mexico and the United States than there are between the United States and Japan or Germany. Both the Japanese and Germans are achievement oriented—more like Americans; therefore, this common underlying philosophical goal facilitates communication. Mexicans are changing as their country increases its industrial development.

COMMUNICATING SUCCESSFULLY WITH INTERNATIONAL BUSINESSPERSONS

Your expectations in dealing with people of another culture must be tempered by your knowledge of that culture. Asians truly are more intuitive than are Americans. Canadians and Germans are more reserved and formal. Mexicans value time differently and find their sense of achievement in the amount of respect they receive from their friends.

Respect other cultures.
When in Rome, do as the
Romans do.

There is no need to offend or alienate another person by not respecting his or her beliefs. The Americanized adage that will serve international business communicators best is When in Rome, do as the Romans do.

When they are in Rome, they do there as they see done.

Robert Burton, Anatomy of Melancholy, Vol. 3, 1621.

As the guidelines for successful cross-cultural communication given earlier in this chapter indicate, you must know yourself, be open, learn all you can about the other culture, apply what you learn, and keep your messages short and simple. The key guideline is to learn all you can about the other culture and then use that knowledge in your communication. The last section of this chapter provides sources of information for enhancing your cross-cultural communication.

SOURCES OF INFORMATION ON INTERNATIONAL BUSINESS COMMUNICATION

This chapter has provided basic information on the challenges of international business communication and on communicating successfully in the international business environment. As you prepare yourself further in this area, you will find that an increasing amount of high-quality information is available for study and reference.

Basic to your study should be a review of one or more of the several good international business textbooks now on the market. For more specific information on cross-cultural business communication, the following books are recommended:

Further information is available:

Copeland, Lennie, and Lewis Griggs. *Going International*. NY: Random House, 1985.

• in specialized books

Do's and Taboos Around the Word. Compiled by The Parker Pen Company. Elmsford, NY: The Benjamin Company, Inc., 1985.

Gudykunst, William B., and Young Yun Kim. *Communicating with Strangers: An Approach to International Communication*. Reading, MA: Addison-Wesley Publishing Co., 1984.

Hall, Edward T. *Beyond Culture*. NY: Doubleday and Co., Inc., 1977.

Ricks, David A. *Big Business Blunders*. Dow Jones-Irwin, Homewood, IL, 1983.

Terpstra, Vern and Kenneth David. *The Cultural Environment of International Business*. Cincinnati: South-Western Publishing Co., 1985.

The following organizations are good sources of information on communication generally and international business communication specifically:

Association for Business Communication
English Building
608 South Wright Street
Urbana, IL 61801

• from professional organizations

International Association of Business Communicators
Suite 940, 870 Market Street
San Francisco, CA 94102

A key to success in cross-cultural communication is learning all that you can about the other culture. A good source of extensive publications on other cultures and how to relate effectively to them is the following center:

- from international
centers

David M. Kennedy Center for International Studies
Publication Services, 280 HRCB
Brigham Young University
Provo, UT 84602
Telephone No.: (801) 378-6528

International business
offers opportunities for
achievement and success.

Many institutions of higher education are giving increased attention to preparing businesspersons for effective leadership and service in the international business environment. Most of these programs include information on cross-cultural communication.

There are many employment opportunities available to you today in the international business environment. Travel and work in another culture are broadening and exciting. International business experience not only provides excellent opportunities for achievement and success in your chosen field, but it also prepares you better to communicate effectively and achieve success in your own culture.

DISCUSSION QUESTIONS

1. Why should students study international business communication?
2. Discuss the variations among cultures throughout the world.
3. What are some differences in languages used throughout the world that would cause difficulties in cross-cultural communication?
4. Give three examples of cultural differences in nonverbal signals.
5. Give one example of a culture difference for each of the following categories: behaviors, values, business hours, and workdays.
6. What is the goal of cross-cultural communication? Discuss the meaning of this goal.
7. Analyze the American culture and list several of its attributes.
8. What does "being open to and accepting of other cultures" mean?
9. Explain what one should try to learn about another culture in preparation for cross-cultural communication.
10. Explain the guidelines for cross-cultural communication in the English language.
11. How can you use an interpreter effectively?
12. What precautions should you take to assure that translations are accurate?

13. Cite five features of the Japanese culture that are distinctively different from the American culture.

14. What are five features of the German culture that are different from the American culture?

15. Discuss the similarities and differences between the Canadian and U.S. cultures.

16. What basic advice regarding cross-cultural communication would you give to a manufacturer who wanted to operate a plant in Mexico?

17. In addition to applying the basic foundations and principles of business communication, what is the single, most important thing you can do to enhance your cross-cultural communication?

18. Explain what cultural relativism means.

APPLICATION EXERCISES

1. Gather information at the library that will enable you to analyze a culture other than those cultures (American, Japanese, German, Canadian, and Mexican) analyzed in this chapter. Give particular attention in your analysis to the way the people of the culture think and how that would affect their communication with Americans.

2. Interview a foreign student or businessperson currently residing in your geographic area and ask the following questions: (1) How do the people of your country perceive Americans? (2) What was the most difficult adjustment you had to make when you moved to this culture? (3) What advice would you give to me if I were going to go to your country to live and work? Report the results of your interview to the class.

3. Develop a list of at least three advantages and three disadvantages of using stereotypes to assist you in strengthening your ability to communicate cross-culturally. Debate the value of the use of stereotypes in cross-cultural communication.

4. Interview a foreign language instructor and ask how studying a foreign language can strengthen your effectiveness as an international businessperson.

5. Analyze the distinctive features of your regional culture. Give attention to language, nonverbal signals, and the ways people think and feel. Compare your culture to those in other regions of your country.

6. Gather three evidences of the extent of international business activity that is currently taking place.

7. Do you match the American stereotype presented in this chapter? How are you similar? How are you different?

THE JOB SEARCH AND RESUME

Your learning objectives for this chapter include the following:

- To become familiar with the sources of information about jobs and job requirements
- To learn how to analyze your qualifications for employment
- To learn to prepare general and personalized resumes

Employment communication is your most important communication.

Your most important business communication will be about your employment. During your life, you will spend most of your waking hours at work. Your work should be enjoyable, challenging, and rewarding. When you have completed this chapter and the next one, you should have a plan for successfully obtaining employment—employment that best matches your interests and qualifications.

The job campaign involves several steps.

To obtain employment, you will need to conduct a job campaign. This campaign will include (1) finding positions for which you can apply, (2) determining your qualifications, (3) developing a resume, (4) writing application letters, (5) interviewing for positions, and (6) conducting follow-up communications.

The first three steps in the job campaign will be discussed in this chapter and the last three steps will be discussed in Chapter 22.

OBTAINING EMPLOYMENT OPPORTUNITIES

Finding positions for which you can apply generally requires an organized effort. The first step in your job campaign involves determining which jobs are available and what the job requirements are for those positions.

Many career-related positions are solicited. **Solicited positions** are specific positions for which employers are seeking applicants—positions listed with school or college placement offices, advertised in newspapers or journals, or announced through private or government placement agencies.

Positions that are available but are unlisted or unadvertised are called **unsolicited positions**. These positions may be an important part of your job campaign. Unsolicited positions, if available, are obtained by direct contact with a company of your choice. You will learn of the availability of many of these positions through your network of friends, relatives, and acquaintances.

An effective job campaign requires careful, documented research. You will want to use all appropriate sources of information about the availability of jobs and about their requirements. The following sections discuss possible sources.

Determining job availability and requirements is the first step.

Positions are either **solicited** *or* **unsolicited**.

SCHOOL OR COLLEGE PLACEMENT OFFICE

The most valuable source of information about jobs will likely be your school or college placement office. Whether you are a current student looking for your first career position or a graduate seeking a change in employment, the placement office can provide many services.

Among the placement services offered by most school or college placement offices are job-related publications, listings of job openings, arrangements for on-campus interviews with company representatives, maintenance of a credentials file, advice on resume and application letter preparation, and guidance or training for a job interview. These services are free or offered at minimal cost. The placement office should be one of the first places you visit as you start your job campaign.

Among the publications available at the placement office, one of the most helpful is the *College Placement Annual*. This publication contains positions available across the nation. It lists the positions for which employers are seeking applicants and the educational requirements for those jobs. The employers are listed by geographical location, by occupational specialties, and by company name. From this list of employers, you can develop a prospect list of job opportunities in your field. The person to contact within each

Your school or college placement office is a valuable source of information and services.

Job-related publications aid the job campaign.

company is listed; this enables you to develop a mailing list for your job campaign.

Several other job-related publications will be available at the placement office. These will likely include trade association publications, government publications, and individual company publications.

Two major services of placement offices are listings of specific job openings and, in larger schools and colleges, arrangements for on-campus interviews with company representatives. Generally, the listings of job openings are published periodically. Placement offices will post these listings on campus and may mail them to graduates. If you find a position opening that interests you, request that the placement office assist you with contacting the employer by sending your credentials or by arranging an on-campus interview.

To take advantage of your school's placement services, register with that office. This registration will involve a careful, accurate, thorough, and neat completion of your credentials file. The credentials file contains information about your education and experience. In addition, it contains the letters of reference that you request be placed there.

Completing your credentials file will serve you in at least two ways. One, it will motivate you to gather and record important data about yourself; these data will be helpful to you when in preparing your resume. Two, the credentials file will be duplicated and, with your permission or at your request, provided to potential employers.

Many positions are obtained through the services of a placement office. It should be your first source of information when you initiate a job search.

NEWSPAPER AND JOURNAL ADVERTISEMENTS

The classified advertisement sections of newspapers and many trade or professional journals are other sources of information about job openings. You can obtain trade or professional journals for your field at your school library or public library.

While journal job advertisements are generally national in scope, newspaper job advertisements are a good source of information about specific positions in a given geographic area. Most classified advertisements of position openings also carry information about the job requirements and salary levels. By studying advertisements, you can determine what jobs are available in a geographic area, the salaries offered, and whether you can meet the job requirements. Most newspapers have several editions, and the job opening advertisements may vary from edition to edition. If you wish to relocate to Chicago, for example, be aware that the edition of the *Chicago Tribune* distributed within Chicago will likely contain a more comprehensive listing of job openings than the edition distributed elsewhere.

PRIVATE OR GOVERNMENT EMPLOYMENT AGENCIES

Private employment agencies bring together job seekers and employers. Their services will be similar to those offered by your school or college placement office. Private employment agencies are in business both to provide these specialized services and to make a profit. Therefore, either the employee or the employer will have to pay the significant fee charged. Before using a private employment agency, be sure that you understand clearly what services are provided, how much the fee will be, and who is to pay the fee.

Another category of private employment agency is the nonprofit service of some professional organizations. Many professional organizations publish job opening announcements, assist in linking job seekers and employers at professional conferences, and maintain a credentials file service. These services are usually offered at low cost or no cost to members. To determine what services are available to you from professional organizations, ask a professional in your field.

Public employment agencies are also found at all levels of government: federal, state, regional, and local. There is usually no charge for their services.

At the federal government level, the U.S. Office of Personnel Management administers an extensive employment service. There are hundreds of area federal employment offices throughout the United States that are sources of job opportunities within the U.S. government. You can locate your nearest federal employment office by contacting any federal government agency in your area. Also, at the federal level, there are job opportunities available in the United States Army, Navy, Marines, Coast Guard, and Air Force. These branches of the military service have recruiters in most local communities.

State governments also provide employment services. These services are more extensive than the employment services provided by the federal government. They include employment opportunities both in the private sector and in the state government. Most states have regional employment offices throughout the state to serve local geographic areas. Usually, you can locate these services by looking under the name of your state in the telephone book or by contacting any state government office.

Local and regional government agencies provide employment services to link potential employees with positions within their agencies. Cities, counties, and regional service units are all sources of jobs. Usually, you can locate their employment or personnel offices by looking in the telephone book under the name of the government unit—city, county, or region.

> Private agencies can be sources of jobs.

> They charge the employee or the employer a significant fee for their services.

> Some professional organizations can assist in your job search.

> Government employment agencies can be sources of jobs.

> Federal employment offices provide information on jobs with the federal government.

> State government employment services list jobs in the private sector and in state government.

> Local and regional employment offices provide information on jobs within their agencies.

OTHER SOURCES OF JOB INFORMATION

Friends, relatives, and acquaintances are important sources of job leads.

Other possible sources of information on available jobs and their requirements are friends, relatives, and acquaintances. In an aggressive, vigorous job campaign, you will want to seek assistance from all sources. You may even want to advertise your job interests and qualifications in a newspaper or journal in order to obtain job leads.

ANALYZING YOUR QUALIFICATIONS

Analyze your qualifications.

In your job campaign, because the product you are selling is *you*, you need to know yourself well. While you will want to sell yourself honestly and fairly, concentrate on your most positive features—your accomplishments, education, experience, positive attitudes, and potential.

Analyzing your qualifications is an important part of your job campaign. It is the step that precedes preparing your resume—a list of your qualifications in their most positive light. Your resume will be your primary tool in securing interviews.

From your examination of the job market, you will know what kinds of jobs are available in your field; and you will know their requirements. You will know the type of job you want. Your job campaign may be aimed at one particular solicited job—salesperson for ABC Insurance Agency—or it may involve sending unsolicited applications to a large number of potential employers. In either case, you will need to analyze your qualifications in relation to each job and its requirements.

The job requirements are the framework for your analysis.

Start the analysis of yourself by brainstorming.

In analyzing your qualifications, start by brainstorming (alone or possibly with friends and relatives) to list facts about yourself. The most important facts are evidences of your accomplishments—achievements, honors, and knowledge. Think of your accomplishments as you list the facts that show the record of your education and experience. In addition, you should list personal information about yourself. Finally, list persons who can serve as your references.

Here is an idea to use as you begin to brainstorm. Take four blank sheets of paper and label them at the top as follows: Write "Personal Information" on the first page at the top, "Education" on the next, "Experience" on the third, and "References" on the last. At a good time of the day for you, find a quiet place and start thinking of facts about yourself. Suggestions for the kinds of facts to list are in the following sections.

PERSONAL INFORMATION

Start with personal information because it will be the easiest category. List your personal data in random fashion. Do not try to organize or evaluate this information at this point.

List personal information.

List information on the personal information sheet including your name, temporary and/or permanent address, telephone number(s), age or birthdate, and place of birth. Also, include your marital status, height, weight, health data, interests and hobbies, community service activities, public-speaking experience, church activities, and organization memberships. As appropriate, include accomplishments, offices held, experience gained, and honors or awards.

In addition, list your special talents or skills (such as ability to letter, keyboard, use software, program a computer, or speak or write foreign languages), and personal attributes (such as enthusiasm, positiveness, initiative, drive, sincerity, dependability, sense of humor, or adaptability). Include in your personal data listing your salary expectations, job campaign and career objectives, whether you are willing to relocate, and any other personal information that might be of interest to an employer.

Stress facts and accomplishments.

Some of this personal information will be used in preparing your resume. Other parts of it will assist you in choosing specific jobs, writing application letters, answering questions during interviews, and completing employment forms.

Some information will be used for a resume; some for other purposes.

EDUCATION

On the sheet of paper labeled "Education," list information about the schools you have attended. Even more important, list those facts that show what you have learned, evidences of achievement, honors, and extracurricular activities.

List educational information.

For each school, list its name, its location, the dates you attended, your major, your minor, your grade point average in your major and overall, and the diplomas or degrees you received. Indicate any special groupings of courses that especially qualify you for the position or positions in your job campaign, and list any honors or awards received (such as outstanding student, membership in honorary organizations, dean's honor listings, certificates of recognition or appreciation, or scholarships). Specify any special research reports you have prepared. Indicate all extracurricular activities (such as professional organizations, fraternity or sorority activities, intramural or intercollegiate athletics, or special service activities). List any other educational information about yourself that might be of interest to an employer.

List all schools, key facts, and your achievements.

EXPERIENCE

List all prior job experience.

List all your work experience—part time and full time—on the third sheet. Keep in mind two basic categories as you reflect on each job you have held: (1) responsibilities and (2) accomplishments such as achievements, knowledge or skills acquired, and contributions while performing the job. Most persons only list their job responsibilities on their resumes. While employers are interested in the responsibilities you have had, they are more interested in how successfully you fulfilled those responsibilities. You should list all factual evidences of successful job performances.

For each job, concentrate on responsibilities and accomplishments.

List each job held, including any military service. For each, list your job title, employer and location, and dates of employment. Indicate responsibilities and give evidence of achievements. Specify what you learned while performing the job, any innovations you developed to improve job performance, sales quotas or other goals met, letters or other commendations received regarding your performance, promotions, or increases in responsibilities. List reasons why you held each job, reasons why you left each job, and salaries received.

Include volunteer work.

Add any other work experience information you think might be helpful in your job campaign. You may include jobs held as a volunteer worker. These jobs will be especially important if you have little paid work experience to list.

REFERENCES

List references who will give you favorable recommendations.

References should be individuals who know you or your work well and who are willing to write letters or talk to potential employers on your behalf. You should have at least three references and may have several more if you have been employed many years. You can select those persons as references who know your character or who are former employers, current employers, professors, and coworkers. Potential employers consider former or current employers the best types of references. At this point simply list those potential references who will give you a favorable recommendation. Depending on the job you are seeking, you may use all or part of this list.

Former and current employers are the most important references.

Request permission from references to list them.

Before using anyone as a reference, verify that person's willingness to write a letter of recommendation or speak with a potential employer. While you will need to deal honestly with any unfavorable information in your background, you are not required to list references who will hurt your chances for employment.

List complete information for each reference.

For each potential reference, list the person's title, name, position, organization, business address, and business telephone number.

When you have completed the thorough analysis of your qualifications, you will be ready to prepare your resume—the key written document in your job campaign.

PREPARING YOUR RESUME

A **resume**, also referred to as a *personal data sheet* or *vita*, is a summary of your qualifications. It should be a clear, concise, positive review of who you are and what you have to offer an employer.

Resume: A summary of your qualifications.

You will be judged on the appearance of your resume; it is a potential employer's first impression of you. Your resume should be typed or printed on white, buff, or some other light color paper. This paper should be high-quality, clean, $8\frac{1}{2}$- by 11-inch paper. Be sure your resume is neat, unwrinkled, and error free. The quality and clarity of its content will be a potential employer's second impression of you.

The primary purpose of a resume, along with an application letter, is to obtain a job interview. Fewer than one in ten applications for employment result in an interview. Your resume must be better than your competitors' resumes in both appearance and content if it is to open the door for you.

The primary purpose of your resume is to get you a job interview.

There are two basic types of resumes: personalized and general. A personalized resume is prepared for a specific job application. It is individually keyboarded and printed, and it contains information to show specifically how you qualify for that one job. For example, it may list the courses you had in college that particularly apply to the responsibilities of the specific job.

Resumes can be **personalized** or **general**.

A general resume is a description of your qualifications that can be used for any job and sent to any employer. It is appropriate for use in applying for unsolicited jobs. For example, if you are applying for management trainee positions in several different companies representing different industries, you can use a general resume that is printed in quantity and sent to all the prospective employers.

Use general resumes for unsolicited jobs.

While you will likely prepare and use a general resume for your first career job, a personalized resume is more powerful and should be used for solicited job applications. If you use word processing to prepare your resume, it is easier to personalize and update it.

Use personalized resumes for specific jobs.

There are two basic formats of resumes: reverse chronological and functional. A reverse chronological resume is more traditional. Within each section, it presents the most recent information first. For example, in the section containing your experience, your current or most recent position is described first. The listing then describes each previous position with the first position you held listed last. The same reverse chronological approach is used in the sections for education, publications, community service, or any other section containing information accumulated over time. (An example of a reverse chronological resume is shown in Illustration 21-1 on pages 542-543.)

The basic resume formats are **reverse chronological** and **functional**.

A functional resume does not indicate your qualifications chronologically. Instead, it provides information to show qualifications according to functions. The headings used for functions may include Capable Manager, Effective Communicator, Profit Producer, and Quality Controller. (An example of a resume in functional format is shown in Illustration 21-2 on page 544.)

Most managers prefer
reverse chronological
resumes.

Managers who review resumes and make decisions on who will be granted an interview prefer reverse chronological resumes; therefore, they are more appropriate for most job campaigns.

The format you choose depends on the job you are seeking. If you are applying for a position in a conservative industry, such as banking, public accounting, or manufacturing, you should use the traditional reverse chronological resume. If you are applying for a position in advertising, sales promotion, or entertainment, you may want to choose the nontraditional functional format. The functional format for a resume works well for an individual who has held several jobs and needs to combine them to make the presentation more concise or more favorable.

Be sure your resume is
high quality.

Regardless of the type or format of resume you use, your resume should be a carefully prepared, attractive, high-quality representation of you. As has been indicated, it is the primary sales tool you will use to obtain an interview.

With the information you developed when you analyzed your qualifications, you are now ready to prepare your resume. While following the principles of business communication, exercise creativity in presenting the best possible picture of yourself. The following are the common major sections of a resume:

There are six major
sections of resumes.

1. Opening
2. Education
3. Experience
4. Activities, Honors, or some other appropriate title
5. Personal Information
6. References

Use the sections that fit
your background.

You may not need or want all these sections in your resume. Also, you may want to arrange them in some other order. For example, if your experience is your strong point, it should be presented immediately following the opening. If you are a recent college graduate and have limited experience, have the education section follow the opening.

OPENING

The **opening** includes a
heading, an objective,
and a summary of
qualifications.

The opening of your resume should include a heading with your name, address, and telephone number; your job and/or career objective; and a summary of your qualifications. A resume title may be used. The purposes of the opening are to get potential employers to read the remainder of the resume, to inform them briefly of your interests and qualifications, and to make it easy for them to contact you.

HEADING. A resume heading with your name, address, and telephone number is essential. Include both your permanent and temporary school addresses and telephone numbers. You may or may not include a title for your resume. You can be conservative or quite creative in the development of the heading, but remember that the majority of potential employers prefer a conservative and traditional resume.

It is possible to use a general or a personalized heading for your resume. A variety of headings are shown here:

The heading must include your name, address, and telephone number.

1.

RESUME

LAURA J. WITCOMB
Address: 1223 Murphy Street
Dell City, NM 21271-1223
Phone: (606) 555-2743

2.

Qualifications of Samuel P. Rutledge
for the
Position of Accountant
with the
Ranage Retail Stores

School Address: P.O. Box 826, College, VA 77193-0826
Telephone: (932) 555-9173

Permanent Address: 9917 Sumter Drive, Milroy, WA 77193-9917
Telephone: (932) 555-6713

3.

MARY JO BUTTERWORTH

1910 Magnolia Drive
Somerset City, OK 31206-1910
(500) 555-1933

4.

DORIS A. BOYD
Applicant for
Information Processing Manager
Hale and Oates Company, Inc.

Address: 33165 Sunderland Avenue
Alpena, FL 12712-3316

Telephone No: (617) 555-1731

CAREER AND/OR JOB OBJECTIVE. Most employers like to see a career and/or job objective in the opening of a resume so they can tell if their interests match yours. While this is an optional part of a resume, it is

A career or job objective can gain favorable attention.

another opportunity in your job campaign to get the favorable attention of your receiver. Here are examples of career and job objectives:

1.   Career Objective

To secure an entry-level position in sales that will lead to higher level positions in sales management.

2.   Job Objective

To obtain a summer internship in accounting to better prepare me for a professional career.

3.   Objective

A management position with a progressive company that will afford opportunities for advancement.

4.   Objective

To be appointed to serve as President of the Salem Valley Savings and Loan Association.

SUMMARY OF QUALIFICATIONS.   This section provides a very brief abstract of your qualifications. It is a recent addition to resumes and is gaining the support of busy managers. You may find it advantageous. From this information managers can quickly tell if you seem to offer the qualities they are seeking. Prepare your Summary of Qualifications after you have completed the remainder of the resume, so that it is comprehensive and high-quality. In the summary it is important to convey a sense of accomplishment. Some examples of summaries of qualifications follow:

Convey a sense of accomplishment in your qualifications summary.

1.   Summary of Qualifications

Bachelor of Science in Business with an area in business administration that includes 28 hours of computer information systems course work. Seven years of part-time work in a variety of jobs from janitor to night motel manager-bookkeeper. Work effectively with people and possess productive work habits.

2.   General Qualifications

Nine years of successful experience in three retail sales positions. Surpassed quotas consistently and was promoted to greater responsibility. Associate of Arts degree in retail sales management. Listed on Dean's Honor Roll last four quarters.

EDUCATION

Following your resume opening, present your strongest qualifications. If you are, or will soon be, a recent college graduate and have limited experience, your education and related activities will be your strongest qualifications. That information should follow the opening. If you have been employed for many years and can relate that employment to the job you are seeking, your Experience section should follow the opening.

Education is the next major section for recent graduates.

If you have or will soon be graduated from a postsecondary institution, you may want to review your high school record in the Education section. If your high school record is fairly recent and shows considerable accomplishment, include it. If not, omit it. List your major and overall grade point averages if they are B level or higher. Be sure to emphasize your educational achievements.

Titles that you might use for the education section are "Education," "Educational Qualifications," "Schools Attended," "Training for . . .," "Specialized Education," "Academic Preparation," "Professional Education," "Educational Data," and "Educational Preparation." Remember that all headings at the same level should have parallel construction.

Use reverse chronological order to list the name and location of each school attended and the dates of attendance. Also, for each school show your degrees, major, and other selected information to reflect your achievements and extent of learning. Here are examples:

Use reverse chronological order for presenting your education.

1.

EDUCATION

1986-1990	University of Minnesota, Minneapolis, Minnesota; Degree: Bachelor of Science; Major: Business Administration (AACSB Accredited Program); GPA 3.3 (4.0 = A); Named to Dean's Honor Roll last five semesters.

2.

Educational Qualifications

1988-90	Clermont Community College, Clermont, Indiana; Degree: Associate of Arts; Major: Office Administration; Courses that especially prepared me for your executive secretary position: word processing, information systems, keyboarding, administrative supervision, records management, and office administration.
1982-86	Marshall High School, Marshall, Texas. Diploma: College Preparatory; Graduated tenth in class of 100; Senior Yearbook Editor, Band, Basketball, Latin Club (President), Hi-Y (Treasurer), and Student Council (Secretary).

3. EDUCATION: <u>Smith College</u>, Smith, Arizona (1988-90)
                   Degree: Bachelor of Science in Business
                   Major: Marketing

                   Overall Grade Point Average: 3.21 (4.0 = A)
                   Grade Point Average in Major: 3.57
                   Dean's List

                   <u>Arlington Community College</u>,
                   Arlington, Washington (1986-88)
                   Degree: Associate of Arts
                   Major: Retail Sales Management

                   Overall Grade Point Average: 3.01
                   Grade Point Average in Major: 3.17

                   All undergraduate education was financed by part-
                   time employment and student loans.

EXPERIENCE

Experience is rated highly by employers.

For applicants other than new graduates, employers rate work experience as the most important information in a resume. More decisions to grant or not to grant interviews are based on the quality of work experience than on any other basis.

Although all your work experience is important, the work experience that prepared you for the position or positions you are seeking is especially important and should be highlighted. Your experience indicates your record of responsibility and accomplishments, provides the primary sources for references, and reflects your personality and personal preferences. When analyzing your qualifications, you developed the information needed for the experience section of your resume. Now you must decide how to present it most effectively.

Focus on your accomplishments.

Your accomplishments should be the focal point of your experience presentation, including what you learned from the experience, your achievements, and your contributions to each position. Your responsibilities for each position should also be briefly listed. For each position you should include dates of employment, job title, employer, and employer's address.

Titles you might use for this section include "Experience," "Work Experience," "Qualifications," "Career Related Experience," "Experience That Has Prepared Me for . . .," "Experience in Sales Promotion," "Business Experience," "Skills Developed through Experience," and others.

Examples of different ways to present the same information in both the reverse chronological and the functional formats are as follows:

Present your experience using the reverse chronological or the functional format.

1.
EXPERIENCE

<u>Night Manager</u>　　　Twilight Motel, Beale, Pennsylvania (1987-90)

Responsibilities:　　Supervised four employees, greeted guests, and maintained financial and guest accounting records.

Achievements:　　Learned to work effectively with a variety of people, gained skill in positively meeting difficult customer needs, developed new guest accounting records that saved an average of two hours of clerical time each night.

<u>Part-time Employee</u>　　Various employers in the Beale area (1983-87)

Responsibilities:　　Worked as motel desk clerk, research assistant, appliance salesperson, and janitor.

Achievements:　　Was promoted from motel desk clerk to night manager, learned research techniques while assisting professor in business communication research study, led appliance sales force of four in sales during three of six months of employment, and learned to appreciate the importance and value of all kinds of work.

2.
SKILLS DEVELOPED THROUGH EXPERIENCE

<u>Managerial Skills</u>　　As a motel night manager, developed skill in motivating employees performing a variety of jobs. Assumed additional responsibilities readily. Improved employee productivity. Observed other managers and practiced their effective behavior.

<u>Communication Skills</u>　　Learned to communicate clearly and concisely with employees and customers in many different situations. Developed ability to provide written and oral reports for financial and customer accounting data.

<u>Accounting Skills</u>　　Developed thorough knowledge of double-entry bookkeeping system. Became proficient in completing trial balances, balance sheets, profit and loss statements, and other statements.

3.   WORK EXPERIENCE

1987 to Present	Twilight Motel, Beale, Pennsylvania
Position:	Night Manager
Duties:	Supervised four employees, met and greeted guests, maintained financial and guest accounting records.
Achievements:	Learned to work effectively with a variety of people, gained skill in positively meeting difficult customer needs, developed new guest accounting records that saved an average of two hours of clerical time each night.
1983-1987	Various Employers, Beale, Pennsylvania
Positions:	Motel desk clerk, research assistant, appliance salesperson, and janitor.
Duties:	Registered motel guests; assisted in questionnaire design and mailing, tabulated survey results, and helped write report for major business communication research project; sold kitchen appliances in store; and cleaned University Art Center Annex daily.
Achievements:	Was promoted from motel desk clerk to night manager, learned research techniques while assisting professor in major business communication research study, led appliance sales force of four in sales during three of six months of employment, and learned to appreciate the importance and value of all kinds of work.

ACTIVITIES, HONORS, OR OTHER APPROPRIATE TITLES

Special sections may be included if your background justifies them.

Include additional sections in your resume if your background justifies them. Any additional section included should be one that employers would consider positively. For example, if you were involved extensively in extracurricular activities during college, include a separate section on these activities immediately following the education section. Your background may justify a separate section on honors, special skills, community services, published works, public presentations, military service, organization memberships, or any number of other possible categories. If you have a few each of various kinds of activities, you may combine them into one section labeled simply "Activities." The important point is that you should not leave out any vital information that would enhance your resume.

Examples of these special entries in resumes are:

1.   HONORS

   Outstanding Employee, Bowling Green (Idaho) Steel Company, 1990
   Citizens' Sparkplug Award, Bowling Green Club, 1989
   Outstanding Young Woman in Idaho, 1989
   Dean's Honor List, Fredricksburg State College, 1989-90
   State Academic Scholarship to Fredricksburg State College, 1988-92

2.   EXTRACURRICULAR ACTIVITIES

President, Phi Sigma Omicron Social Fraternity	1988-89
Treasurer, Phi Sigma Omicron Social Fraternity	1987-88
Manager, Phi Sigma Omicron House	1987-89
Coach, Chugger's Basketball Team	1987-89
Business Manager, State University News	1986-88
Photographer, State University News	1985-86

3.   ORGANIZATION MEMBERSHIPS

   Administrative Management Association (Chapter Secretary, 1988-89)
   Information Processing Association
   Association for Data Processing Management
   Civitan Club (Club President 1987-88, Area Governor 1988-89)

4.   SPECIAL SKILLS

   Know microcomputer software including LOTUS 1-2-3, WordPerfect, and dBase III. Speak and write Spanish. Speak and understand limited German and French. Keyboard at 75 words per minute. Know how to use most modern office equipment.

PERSONAL INFORMATION

The Personal Information section is optional. Civil rights laws provide that employers are not to discriminate among applicants on the basis of race, religion, age, sex, marital status, or national origin. Employers cannot ask for this information, but applicants are not prohibited from providing such information in their resumes if they desire. In recent studies, employers have indicated that they have little interest in seeing personal information in resumes.

You may want to provide selected personal information if you believe it will strengthen your application. In addition to the personal information covered by civil rights legislation, other items that could be included are such

*Present only the **personal information** that will strengthen your application.*

things as health, height, weight, hobbies, skills, interests, and avocations. Many employers want to know if you are willing to relocate. You can place that information in the Personal Information section or as the last item in the Summary of Qualifications section.

Omit from your resume any information you think a given employer would prefer not to have. Omit a photograph of yourself from the resume. Today, very few applications include photographs; and, because reactions to personal appearances are so varied, it is better not to take a chance on getting a negative reaction.

Do not include a photograph.

The Personal Information section should be placed near the end of the resume because it is less important than other information. A common location for personal information is just before the section on references. References are traditionally listed in the last section of a resume. Here are two examples of Personal Information sections:

Place personal information near the end of your resume.

1.   PERSONAL INFORMATION

    Birthdate: August 25, 1972   Birthplace: Murray, Indiana

    Health: Excellent   Height/Weight: 5'11"/160 lb

    Interests: Camping, Basketball, Photography, and Cooking

2.   PERSONAL DATA

    Have extremely good health. Enjoy outdoor activities, including camping, basketball, and photography. Am considered a gourmet cook. Energetic. Have sense of humor. Enjoy life. Willing to relocate.

REFERENCES

References are vital.

A vital part of your resume is a listing of carefully chosen references. Though you want to list only those references who will give you positive recommendations, you should list every previous employer if possible. You may also want to list college professors, high school teachers, and—in special circumstances—coworkers. You may list different references for different job applications. Let the nature of the job and its requirements determine the references you think would be the most helpful to the potential employer. Then use those persons for that application.

You are encouraged to provide full information on your references in this section of your resume. Providing the business telephone numbers of your references for the potential employer's convenience, for example, may make the difference in whether you get an interview. If a potential employer finds your qualifications of interest and can easily pick up the phone, call, and receive a favorable recommendation from one or more of your references, you are likely to get an interview. For each reference, list courtesy title, name, position, organization, business address, and business telephone number. Here is the way a reference section might appear:

REFERENCES

Dr. A. D. Gilliam, Professor
Department of Accounting
Middle State College
Middleton, CA 42178-2546
(202) 555-9322

Ms. Shirley Overcast
Communications Consultant
Avery Corporation
1710 Maryvale Avenue
Atlanta, MI 72111-1710
(619) 555-7817

Miss Rita Barnett, Manager
Atlanta Office
Carr and Barnett, CPAs
1234 Womble Street
Atlanta, MI 72111-1234
(619) 555-7853

Mr. Charles Davenport, Manager
Steak Stockade
1700 Main Street
Middleton, CA 42178-1700
(202) 555-1212

In certain unusual circumstances you may want to replace the names of references with "References Available Upon Request." For example, you may have to keep your job search secret for some reason. Such omission of references is not recommended as a regular practice because it will likely decrease your chances for getting an interview. Most employers like to make at least a preliminary telephone check with references prior to offering an interview.

SAMPLE RESUMES

Two complete resumes will be shown as samples. One is in the traditional, reverse chronological format; the other is in the functional format.

In Illustration 21-1, the traditional reverse chronological format for a general resume is shown. As you have learned, most employers prefer this format. It gives the information they need in a familiar sequence. It helps them compare resumes. If they have to search too hard to find a vital bit of information about you, your application may go into the "reject" pile. Illustration 21-1 is just one of many versions of this traditional format.

In Illustration 21-2, the functional format is shown for a personalized resume. This format is more creative in a sense. It is appropriate if you have already provided all the standard information to the employer in an application form. It can be used to apply for positions that require more creativity, such as advertising, design, or copy writing. Some individuals use a combined version of the functional and reverse chronological formats.

Illustration 21-1　A General Resume in Reverse Chronological Format, Page 1.

This attractive general resume is in reverse chronological order.

The opening is complete and balanced.

The career objective reflects short- and long-range goals.

The summary of qualifications emphasizes accomplishments.

Education is this applicant's strongest qualification and is given first. Both vital data and achievements are included.

The work experience presentation emphasizes both duties and achievements.

RESUME

SARAH LYNNE BRAME

Address:　2701 Fern Valley Drive　　Telephone:　(713) 555-6172 (Office)
　　　　　Houston, TX　77044-6521　　　　　　　　(713) 555-1259 (Home)

CAREER OBJECTIVE

To secure a position in the field of accounting leading to opportunities for increased responsibility and advancement.

SUMMARY OF QUALIFICATIONS

Bachelor of Science in Business degree from AACSB accredited school with major in accounting. A variety of part-time and summer employment includes two summer accounting internships and other work experience through which excellent work habits were developed.

EDUCATION

1986-90　Texas Southern University, Houston, Texas

　　　　　Degree:　Bachelor of Science in Business
　　　　　Major:　Accounting (AACSB accredited program)
　　　　　Grade Point Average:　3.3 (Based on 4.0 = A)
　　　　　Financed college with scholarships, part-time work, and stu-
　　　　　　dent loans.
　　　　　Extracurricular Activities:　Accounting Club (Vice-President,
　　　　　　1989-90), Phi Beta Lambda, Beta Sigma Gamma, intramural
　　　　　　athletics.

1982-86　Maryville High School, Maryville, Texas

　　　　　Diploma:　General College Preparatory
　　　　　Rank in Graduating Class:　15th of 194
　　　　　Extracurricular Activities:　Yearbook staff, basketball (four
　　　　　　years), Hi-Y Club, Future Business Leaders of America
　　　　　　(President, 1985-86).

EXPERIENCE

Accounting Intern, Howe & McBride, CPAs, White Rock, Texas,
　　　　　　Summers 1988-89

Duties:　　　　Assisted CPAs with bookkeeping records for small busi-
　　　　　　　　nesses, public and private organizations' audits, and
　　　　　　　　clients state and federal income tax returns.

Achievements:　Learned to apply accounting theory. Became effective
　　　　　　　　team member. Developed human relations skills. Created
　　　　　　　　and implemented bookkeeping services on microcomputer.

Illustration 21-1   A General Resume in Reverse Chronological Format, Page 2.

SARAH LYNNE BRAME   Page 2

EXPERIENCE (Continued)

Fast Food Service Worker, Roberson Burgers, Pasadena, Texas,
                          Summers, 1986-87

Duties: Worked in all capacities, including counter server, cook,
                 salad chef, dining room attendant, and janitor. In 1987
                 served as assistant manager and filled in frequently for
                 manager.

Acheivements: Acquired excellent work habits. Developed human rela-
                 tions skills. Learned management skills of planning,
                 organizing, directing, and controlling.

Various Part-Time Jobs, Pasadena and Houston, Texas,
                        Academic Years 1984-90

Duties: At college--groundskeeping, lifeguarding, and filing and
                 typing in the Dean's office. In the neighborhood--lawn
                 mowing, babysitting, and car washing.

Achievements: Gained valuable work experience in a variety of settings.
                 Paid significant part of own expenses since 16 years old.

SPECIAL SKILLS

Know computer software including word processing, spreadsheets, and file
management. Speak and write Spanish. Have strong communication skills.

PERSONAL INFORMATION

Health, excellent. Born, 1968. Interests--golfing, sailing, swimming,
reading, and jogging. Community service--volunteer in the Big Sister
program for five years and hospital Candy Striper for two years. Willing to relocate.

REFERENCES

Mr. Raymond C. Sullivan   Dr. B. C. Grogan, Professor
Managing Partner   Department of Accounting
Howe and McBride, CPAs   School of Business Administration
19500 Fescue Lane   Texas Southern University
White Rock, TX 75205-7311   Houston, TX 77044-6553
(214) 555-4196   (713) 555-9366

Mrs. Linda Spann, Manager   Dr. Phyllis George, Dean
Roberson Burgers   School of Business Administration
1001 North 12th Street   Texas Southern University
Pasadena, TX 77507-3156   Houston, TX 77044-6553
(409) 555-4185   (713) 555-1234

The format is easy to read.

Note parallelism among individual items.

Special skills are emphasized in a separate section.

Including personal information is optional. This resume is strengthened with its inclusion.

Complete information is given on references.

Illustration 21-2   A One-Page Personalized Resume in Functional Format

This resume is personalized, functional, attractive, and balanced.

The creative opening includes essential data.

QUALIFICATIONS OF JUSTIN CHARLES MOHR
FOR CREATIVE ADVERTISING AND SALES PROMOTION WORK WITH
THE SIMS ADVERTISING AGENCY

710 Pine Street   (804) 555-4198
                    Petersburg, Virginia   23805-0098

OBJECTIVE

A position with the Sims Advertising Agency in advertising and sales promotion work that will afford opportunities for creative contributions and advancement.

QUALIFICATIONS

The functional format combines education and experience information and presents it concisely by functions. Selected items are emphasized by underlining.

CREATIVE   Competent professional photographer who has sold over 25 pictures to advertising agencies for ad campaigns. Experienced copywriter who has written over 250 ads for student newspapers and the Hahn (Ohio) Press.

KNOWLEDGEABLE   Bachelor of Arts degree with major in Advertising and Marketing from Virginia State University. Associate of Arts degree with major in Business Administration from Hanover Community College. Overall GPA 3.4 (scale of 4.0 = A). Won Advertising Club Award for Most Creative Sales Campaign Proposal.

ORGANIZED   President, Advertising Club at Virginia State University, 1988-90. Increased membership by 80 percent (29 to 52). Established committee system, which facilitated significant increases in professional activity and learning. Advertising Manager at Hahn Press (1986-88). Increased ad sales by 22 percent.

Using reference quotes is creative.

"Justin is a go-getter. He did an outstanding job as our Advertising Manager. He is personable and warm--possesses good human relations skills."
--Ms. Gayle Meeks
  Managing Editor
  Hahn Press

". . . one of the most outstanding students and student leaders I have seen. He is quick to learn . . . sees practical application easily."
--Dr. Randy Burton
  Professor, Advertising
  Virginia State University

REFERENCES

Complete information is given on references.

Ms. Gayle Meeks   Ms. Judy Entrup, Inst.   Dr. Randy Burton
Managing Editor   Department of Business   Professor, Advertising
Hahn Press   Hanover Community College   Department of Marketing
P.O. Box 1923   1200 Maple Street   Virginia State University
Hahn, OH 43472-3112   Hanover, IN 47243-4434   Petersburg, VA 23803-2233
(419) 555-1923   (812) 555-7853   (804) 555-4185

Your resume may be one page or longer, depending on the amount of education, experience, and other activities. Be sure to number the second and succeeding pages of long resumes.

While there is no magic number of pages for resumes, many business-persons prefer that they be two pages or less for new college graduates with limited experience. Resumes should be long enough to include all vital information and provide attractive open space for easy readability. In addition, they should be written as concisely and clearly as possible.

There is no magic number of pages for a resume.

You should make effective use of blank space and other techniques for emphasis. Some of these techniques include the use of capital letters, bold-facing, underscoring, italics, lines, and different type sizes. Be sure that the information is not overcrowded or appears so dense as to discourage its being read. Complete sentences are not required; phrases are appropriate to save space. A note of caution: Avoid the use of personal pronouns.

Use emphasis techniques, including blank space, effectively.

Though there are many helpful examples available, you should never copy another resume. Following the guidelines given in this chapter should enable you to create your own distinctive resume.

Avoid personal pronouns.

DISCUSSION QUESTIONS

1. Describe the information and services offered by school or college placement offices.

2. How can the classified advertisement sections of newspapers be of value in a job campaign?

3. Describe the private employment agencies that are available for job applicants.

4. Describe the public employment agencies found at various levels of government.

5. Discuss the approach that a person should take in analyzing his or her qualifications.

6. What are examples of personal information you should list when analyzing your qualifications?

7. How will you use personal information about yourself in a job search?

8. When analyzing your qualifications, what educational data should you list for each school you have attended?

9. To prepare yourself to write the experience section of a resume, what information will you need about your past employment?

10. Whom should you choose to be your references and what information do you need for each?

11. How can you assure that your resume has an excellent appearance?

12. Discuss the relative merits of: (a) personalized resumes and (b) general resumes.

13. When should you use (a) the reverse chronological resume format and (b) the functional resume format?

14. Describe briefly the content of each of the six major sections of information that should be considered for resumes.

APPLICATION EXERCISES

1. Project to a time near your graduation. Using actual information and assuming the course work, activities, and experience you will have between now and then, analyze your qualifications following the recommendations given in this chapter.

2. Using the information gathered in Application Exercise 1, prepare a general resume in reverse chronological format.

3. Prepare a personalized resume in reverse chronological format for an application for a job in your field based on an analysis of the job and its requirements and the information obtained in Application Exercise 1.

4. Prepare a general resume in functional format based on the information obtained in Application Exercise 1.

5. Prepare a personalized resume in functional format for an application for a job in your field based on an analysis of the job and its requirements and the information obtained in Application Exercise 1.

6. Visit a school or college placement office and gather data on the information and services available to assist you in a job campaign.

7. Gather information from a local, regional, state, or federal employment office on its services and job availability.

8. Determine the services available from a private employment agency in your local area. What is the cost of these services?

9. Review the employment section of a local or regional newspaper and assess the employment opportunities and salaries in your field.

10. Interview two executives to learn what qualities they would look for in an applicant who (a) is a new college graduate and (b) has a college education and ten year's experience.

CHAPTER 22

EMPLOYMENT COMMUNICATION AND INTERVIEWING

LEARNING OBJECTIVES

Your learning objectives for this chapter include the following:

— To learn to write letters of application for solicited and unsolicited positions
— To learn how to prepare yourself for an interview
— To learn to compose a variety of other messages related to employment

After completing the first three steps in your job campaign covered in Chapter 21—locating positions for which you can apply, determining your qualifications, and developing a resume—you are now ready for the next three steps. You are ready for writing application letters, interviewing for positions, and conducting follow-up communications. These steps are covered in this chapter.

WRITING APPLICATION LETTERS

Once your resume is completed, you are ready to write a more personal selling tool—an application letter. An application letter is a sales letter—with you as the product. Follow the guidelines for persuasive messages given in Chapter 12

Sell yourself in an application letter.

for developing application letters. An application letter and your resume make up the application package for your job campaign.

Application letters may be either general or personalized.

Application letters can be either general or personalized, as are resumes. Again, the choice depends on whether you are seeking a solicited or an unsolicited position. In some situations you may be able to combine a general resume and a personalized application letter into an effective application package.

The major parts of an application letter are: opening, summary of qualifications, and request for interview.

There are three major parts in a well-designed application letter—an opening that gets favorable attention, a summary of qualifications that is related to job requirements, and a request for an interview. The primary purpose of an application letter is to motivate a potential employer to read your resume. Then, you hope the employer's reading of your letter and resume will result in your getting an interview. The three major parts of an application letter are discussed in the following sections.

GAINING ATTENTION IN THE OPENING

The opening should gain favorable attention and provide transition.

In the opening, you want to gain the favorable attention of your reader—get him or her to read the remainder of the application letter. Also, you want to provide information on why you are writing—provide orientation and transition for the reader. You can indicate, for example, that you are applying for a position that is listed with your placement bureau, is advertised in the newspaper, is recommended by a current employee of the employer, or is unsolicited. Provide for this transition in the first sentence or no later than the second sentence.

There are creative and traditional attention-getting openings for application letters. Your analysis of your reader and the position you are seeking will guide you in determining what kind of opening you should use. Here are example openings:

1. Are you interested in a hard worker with a solid record of accomplishment for your management trainee program?

2. Please compare my qualifications with the job requirements for the auditor's position that you advertised in the May issue of the AAA JOURNAL. I think we will both be glad you did.

3. Creative! Knowledgeable! Organized! Just what you want and need in a new employee for the staff of Brun's Advertising Agency.

4. Mrs. Cassandra Rodreguis, Manager of your Purchasing Office, recommended that I apply for the position you have open in the Division of Operations Research. Please note how well my qualifications, as described in the enclosed resume, match the job requirements of your opening.

CONVINCING AN EMPLOYER THAT YOU FIT THE JOB

The purpose of the second major part of an application letter is to convince a potential employer that you fit the job requirements of the position you are seeking. This is the most important part of your letter. In it, you should show how employing you will benefit the employer. As in a resume, you will want to emphasize your accomplishments.

Show the employer how you fit the job.

In this section of an application letter: (1) specify the job requirements; (2) review your education, experience, and other qualifications relative to the job requirements; and (3) refer to your enclosed resume (this reference may be elsewhere in the letter). The order of content may vary in different application letters. The intent, however, is to compose a clear, concise, concrete, and convincing paragraph or two that will motivate the employer to look closely at your resume. Here are examples of the second part of an application letter:

Specify job requirements, review qualifications, and refer to resume.

1. Your Director of Employment position requires someone who knows personnel management theory and how to practice it. Mr. Jones, I am that person. I believe that my education, experience, and personal qualities, as shown on the enclosed resume, qualify me for your opening.

    Upon graduating from Sagamon State College with a major in personnel administration, I was employed as Assistant Personnel Manager by the Thompson Manufacturing Corporation. Four years of experience with Thompson gave me the opportunity to apply the theories I had learned, to become thoroughly acquainted with state and federal laws governing personnel relations, and to make innovative changes in the operation of the office. While at Thompson, I designed and administered a comprehensive training program for all nonexempt personnel. The program was credited with increasing production 27 percent this past quarter.

2. Franklin salespersons are known throughout the industry for their integrity and productivity. My education and work experience, as detailed on the enclosed resume, have all been directed at preparing me to join Franklin's sales force.

    My education consists primarily of four years of marketing, general business administration, and general education courses at Western State University. The Bachelor of Science in Business degree I will receive in May will assure you that I have both a broad business education and a specialized knowledge of sales. My grade point average of 3.3 (scale of 4.0 = A) reflects the success I have had in the classroom.

Mrs. Samuels, the experience I offer Franklin complements my education and has prepared me further for sales work. During the summers of 1988 and 1989 I sold encyclopedias door to door. My ranking of first in sales in the Northeastern District (a seven-state area) and fifth in the nation during the summer of 1989 indicate my productivity level. During the academic year, I sold furniture part-time, earning a major share of my educational expenses.

In addition, I believe I have the personal qualities that would fit your organization. I am an energetic, goal-oriented worker who enjoys meeting and helping people. I can work effectively with others on group projects and can work effectively alone in one-on-one sales situations.

PROMOTING ACTION IN THE CLOSE

Motivate the employer to read your resume.

Ask directly for the interview in the close.

Make it easy to call or write you.

Be flexible about your availability.

Now you are ready to try to motivate the employer to take action—to read your resume and grant you an interview. In practically every application letter, you will be trying to get an interview. The way to get an interview is to ask directly for it. This request should be made in a positive, pleasant manner; do not push or beg.

In the close of your application letter you should make it easy for an employer to grant you an interview by providing your telephone number and by offering to be at the employer's office at his or her convenience. Even if you do have some limitations on your flexibility—such as another interview scheduled for one day next week—you can usually work those things out if the employer calls you. Here are examples of appropriate closings for application letters:

1. If my qualifications appear to meet your needs, please call me at (601) 555-1300 so that we can arrange an interview. I would enjoy meeting with you to discuss the possibility of joining your staff.

2. If this brief description of my qualifications and the additional information on the accompanying resume demonstrate that I meet your requirements, may I have an interview? My school day ends at 3 p.m. After that time you can reach me at (601) 555-1300. I could arrange a visit to your office at any time convenient for you.

3. May I have an interview to discuss this opportunity with you, Mr. Malinauskas? The prospect of joining the Washington Agency is exciting to me. Please write me or call me at (477) 555-7192 to set up an appointment.

SAMPLE APPLICATION LETTERS

The application letters you use in your job campaign must meet the same high standards as resumes for neatness, clarity, and conciseness. Application letters should be brief, generally no more than one page. Analyze your reader, use the you-viewpoint, use the principles of business communication, and follow the guidelines given in Chapter 12 for persuasive messages.

Use $8\frac{1}{2}$- by 11-inch paper for application letters. The paper should be the same color and quality as was used for your resume. An application letter should be addressed to a specific person and individually prepared. Never photocopy a general application letter for distribution to prospective employers. If you are sending out several letters, word processing equipment can be helpful in preparing them so that variable information may be inserted.

Illustration 22-1 shows a general letter that could be addressed to personnel officers at several companies. It is directed at obtaining an unsolicited job.

Illustration 22-2 is an example of a personalized letter sent in response to a solicited job announcement. Personalized letters are usually more powerful than general letters; in a personalized letter you can show specifically how you will benefit the employer.

Application letters should be high quality and brief—generally no more than one page.

General letters can be designed for unsolicited applications.

Personalized letters should be used for solicited applications.

INTERVIEWING FOR A JOB

The goal of your job campaign has been to get an interview. The interview can be one of the most important experiences in your life, because it can determine the course of your career.

The decision as to whether you will be offered the job will be made as a result of the interview. Your decision as to whether you will accept an offer may be made at this time also. A job interview is obviously a critical juncture in your job campaign. You will want the interview to go as well as possible. When you find out you are going to have an interview, start your final preparation for it.

Your job campaign goal has been to get an interview.

The interview is the critical step in your job campaign.

PREPARING FOR A JOB INTERVIEW

You have already done a great deal of preparation for your job interviews. You have examined the job market and job requirements, analyzed your qualifications, prepared your resume, and written application letters. Through this

Illustration 22-1   General Prospecting Application Letter for Management Trainee Position

This general prospecting letter could be sent to several companies.

The letter is addressed to the appropriate individual.

The opening gains favorable attention and provides reader information on why you are writing.

The review of qualifications emphasizes accomplishments and positive personal attributes.

Limited work experience is presented positively.

The close motivates employer to grant an interview; it includes a reference to the resume.

1250 Siskiyou Boulevard
Ashland, OR 97520-3355
March 15, 199-

Mr. Joshua Burchell, Personnel Manager
Yukimura Electronics, Inc.
227 West 27th Street
New York, NY 10001-0786

Dear Mr. Burchell

Is your company looking for a management trainee who has a thorough knowledge of management theory, appreciates the value of work, and possesses desirable personal qualities including honesty and ambition? If so, please consider my application for employment with you.

In my Southern Oregon State University education I had 43 hours of business administration courses and 54 hours of general education courses. My 3.5 grade point average (4.0 = A) overall and 3.7 average in my management major provide evidence that I took college work seriously and that I worked hard. The College of Business Administration at Southern Oregon State University is rated highly. It is one of only 200 colleges in the nation whose programs meet the accreditation standards of the American Assembly of Collegiate Schools of Business.

My extracurricular activities completed my college coursework. As an active member of Beta Gamma Sigma Honor Society, I served as chairperson of the Membership Committee. I also served as president of the Management Club. The knowledge and work habits I developed in these leadership roles would serve your company well.

In addition, I believe I have other personal qualities you want. I am in excellent health, like to work with people, want to excel, and am interested in advancement. My record of summer and part-time enployment reflects a willingness to work hard to achieve goals.

If these highlights of my qualifications and the additional information in the enclosed resume describe what you want in your management trainees, please call me at (503) 555-3312 to arrange an interview. I can come to your office at any time convenient to you.

Sincerely

J. Scott Robinson

J. Scott Robinson

Enclosure

Illustration 22-2   A Personalized Application Letter for an Assistant Loan Officer
                    Position

3550 Mulberry Drive
Muncie, IL 61857-8762
February 1, 199-

Ms. Katrin Davenport, President
Clinton State Bank
1615 Paris Pike
Seymour, IL 61875-0981

Dear Ms. Davenport

On the suggestion of Dr. Larry Lovins, Professor of Finance, I
am submitting an application for the position of Assistant Loan
Officer. My qualifications include an excellent education in
finance, a solid record of experience, and a well-rounded personality that includes many of the characteristics desirable in
an employee of Clinton State Bank. I believe I am qualified to
be your assistant loan officer, and this position is exactly the
type of job I am seeking.

If you are familiar with the finance program at Muncie State College, you know that the training I would bring to you is of the
highest quality. Dr. Lovins and the business faculty not only
demand that their students learn the sound basics of banking, but
also insist that their students incorporate 12 credit hours of
internship to make certain that they learn to apply the knowledge
they have gained. Membership in the Finance Club (which I served
as vice-president and treasurer) offered an opportunity to gain
further insights into the world of banking. My education and
work experience are described in detail on the enclosed resume.

In addition to the necessary financial knowledge, Clinton State
Bank's assistant loan officer should possess certain personal
qualities--qualities such as honesty, friendliness, dependability, and a genuine concern for serving others. I believe
that I can offer these qualities, and more. My record during my
banking internship reflects my respect for these attributes.
Furthermore, part-time work in a variety of positions during college has enabled me to develop an appreciation of the importance
of hard work, punctuality, productivity, and integrity.

May I have an interview for the Assistant Loan Officer position,
Ms. Davenport? I can be reached at (619) 555-1762 and will be
available for an appointment at your convenience.

Sincerely

David B. Fox

David B. Fox

Enclosure

This personalized
letter is designed
for one specific job
application.

It is addressed to
the appropriate
person.

The positive opening
provides transition
and gains favorable
attention.

A reference to the
resume is included.

The applicant's
qualifications that
relate directly to the
job are reviewed
and emphasized.

The close promotes
employer action.

Preparing for an
interview includes:

- Reviewing information
  gathered to this point

- Anticipating questions

process you have learned more about yourself. In addition, you have organized this information so that you can talk about it efficiently and logically. All this is important preparation for representing yourself in an interview. There are additional things you need to do in preparation for job interviews.

BE READY TO ANSWER QUESTIONS. The next thing you should do is prepare to answer questions about yourself. You need to anticipate all the questions that might be asked in an interview and prepare generally—in advance—the answers you will give. Examples of the questions you may be asked are as follows:

1. Why do you want to work for our company?
2. Tell me about yourself.
3. I see you took a course in information processing. What was that course about?
4. What do you consider your strengths?
5. What do you consider your weaknesses?
6. What kind of work do you like best?
7. What work do you like to do least?
8. What did you do on your job at...?
9. What do you want to be doing five years from now?
10. Do you like to work alone or with other people?
11. Why did you choose this field of work?
12. What kind of supervisor do you like to work for?
13. Tell me about your education at...
14. What courses did you like best? Why?
15. What courses did you like least? Why?
16. Do you consider yourself ambitious?
17. Why should we hire you for this position?
18. What do you think should determine the progress a person makes in a company?
19. What does *teamwork* mean to you?
20. Do you have plans to get additional education?
21. What are the main things you have learned from your work experience?
22. How important is money to you?
23. Do you have any hobbies?
24. Tell me about your extracurricular activities while you were in school.
25. What salary do you expect to receive in this job?

These are questions that have been asked in many interviews. Have your answers ready for these questions and any others that you can anticipate.

Be honest, sincere, positive, and enthusiastic when answering. Be yourself, be polite, and be attentive. Your answers should be brief, but not just *yes* or *no*. For example, in answering the question "Do you have plans to get additional education?" you might say, "Yes, I think it is important to keep up-to-date. I am interested in taking short continuing education courses and, in a few years, working on an MBA degree."

BE PREPARED TO DISCUSS SALARY.

The salary question—the last one in the list of example questions—is an important one. Be sure to be ready to answer it. The employer may have set a salary or a salary range for the position. You should try to get that information before the interview if you can. Also, you should try to learn before the interview what salaries are being paid for similar jobs. Newspaper employment ads many times carry this information. Your school or college placement office is another good source of salary information. Be ready to answer in a straightforward objective manner. You might say, "Apparently the starting salaries for this kind of position range from $_____ to $_____. In comparing my qualifications with others in the job market, I would hope to start at $_____."

* Discussing salary, if appropriate

DEVELOP QUESTIONS TO ASK.

You should have some key questions of your own for the interviewer. Do not just concentrate on questions of personal benefit to you such as ones about fringe benefits, retirement programs, vacation policies, and salary. Probably all that information will be given to you without your asking. Your questions might be about such subjects as job duties, employee evaluation system, management philosophy, company progress and plans, promotion policies, and employee development programs.

* Asking questions

RESEARCH THE COMPANY.

Learn as much as you can about the company prior to the interview. Secure descriptive materials on the company and its industry from the company, your placement bureau, the library, the Chamber of Commerce, the Better Business Bureau, a trade association or some other source. Study these materials carefully. A thorough preparation of this kind will help you in the interview in two basic ways: it will aid your communication with the interviewer, and it will set you apart from the other interviewees who learn nothing about the company prior to an interview.

* Learning all you can about the company

PREPARE YOURSELF PERSONALLY.

Choose your clothes carefully, and give attention to personal grooming. Choose clothes that are similar to the ones worn by those who hold the type of job you are seeking. Plan your schedule so that you arrive early. Allow time for heavy traffic, a flat tire, or other delay. Plan to take two additional copies of your resume with you in case they are needed. Take a copy of your transcript and any appropriate examples of your work. Take a pen and a small notebook for use immediately after the interview. Write the names of the people you meet and record notes about the position.

Talk (mentally) to yourself. Build your confidence by telling yourself that you have done all you can to prepare for the interview. You have anticipated questions and have prepared answers, you have learned about the company, and you have prepared yourself personally. You are ready for the interview.

* Organizing yourself personally; building your confidence

PARTICIPATING IN AN INTERVIEW

An interview should be viewed as an opportunity to share your qualifications with someone who is interested. View the interview as important, but not so important that you become overly nervous. Some "racehorse" nervousness is natural and helpful to you; but too much nervousness will make a poor impression.

Greet your interviewer warmly and call him or her by name, pronouncing it correctly. Let the interviewer take the lead. If an offer is made to shake hands, do so with a firm grip and a smile. Sit when asked to do so. See your role as primarily responding to questions in a businesslike fashion. Keep good eye contact with the interviewer; 75 percent of the time is a good goal.

The interviewer may intentionally challenge you by asking difficult questions or by appearing disinterested or even irritated. Be calm, positive, gracious, and friendly.

During the interview avoid appearing overly aggressive or conceited, meek and mild, negative about past employers or other topics, unenthusiastic, too interested in money, too ambitious, humorless, too vague with answers, or unappreciative of the interviewer's time.

Be alert for signals that the interview is ending. The interviewer may slide her or his chair back, stand up, or send you verbal signals. When the interview is over, express appreciation for the time and information given you. Indicate that you look forward to hearing from the interviewer. Shake hands, and warmly tell the interviewer good-bye.

After the interview, evaluate how you did. Make written notes of those things that went well and those that you will change the next time you interview. Make a record of the information you learned about the job for comparison with other job opportunities. Record the correct spellings of the names and titles of those who interviewed you, and note what you will want to say in your follow-up communication.

Some nervousness is natural and helpful.

Greet interviewer warmly; let the interviewer take the lead.

Show your knowledge and interest.

Be friendly, positive, and levelheaded.

End the interview appropriately.

After the interview, evaluate.

PREPARING OTHER EMPLOYMENT COMMUNICATION

Employment related communication may involve telephone calls, letters, or in-person contacts.

Employment communication is not limited to resumes, application letters, and interviews. Other employment communication can include telephone calls, letters, and in-person contacts. You may need to follow up on a pending application or communicate your acceptance of an invitation for an interview. You may want some kind of follow-up contact after an interview. It will be necessary to communicate your rejection or acceptance of a job offer. If you accept a job, you may need to resign from another job. Finally, you should express appreciation to all those who assisted you in your job campaign. Suggestions for composing these communications are given in the following sections.

FOLLOWING UP AN APPLICATION

If you think it has been too long since you heard about your application with an employer, you may want to initiate a follow-up contact. Remember many unsolicited applications are not acknowledged. Your follow-up contact, depending on the circumstances, can be by letter, by telephone, or in person. Such a letter would be neutral news for the employer; and, consequently, the direct plan should be used. Here is an example of such a follow-up letter:

You may want to follow up an application.

> In February I sent you an application for a position in your marketing department. As I am very much interested in employment with B. J. Harold and Company, I am wondering if I could furnish any additional information that would be helpful to my application.
>
> I want to assure you that I remain an active candidate and will appreciate your giving me an interview.

ACCEPTING AN INTERVIEW INVITATION

Most of the time interview invitations will be by telephone. Be prepared to receive this kind of call any time during your job campaign. Your communication accepting an interview should use the direct plan (for good news) and should (1) express appreciation, (2) indicate availability, and (3) convey a positive and optimistic attitude. Here is an example of the content for either a written or an oral message:

Be prepared to accept an interview invitation.

> Thank you for the opportunity to interview for the accounting position. I am very much interested in meeting with you to discuss the position and my qualifications.
>
> Because of my work and class schedules, the best dates for me for the interview are March 7, 9, or 10. I appreciate your offer that I give you three alternative dates. Any one of them will be fine with me.
>
> I am looking forward to visiting your offices and learning more about the auditing position.

FOLLOWING UP AN INTERVIEW

Following up an interview is appropriate.

A letter of appreciation is appropriate after an interview. This letter should be sent within one or two days following the interview. If you think you are still interested in the position, you should express that interest in the letter. If you are definitely not interested in the position, a letter of appreciation for the interview is still appropriate. In this case, in fairness to the employer, you should withdraw your candidacy. The letter in which you express your continuing interest should use the direct plan while the letter in which you withdraw your candidacy should use the indirect plan. Both of these letters should be brief, cordial, businesslike, and typewritten. Examples of each follow:

1. Thank you for talking with me last Tuesday about the operations management position. The interview was enjoyable and informative. Your explanation of the job responsibilities and the plant tour made me even more interested in the position. I am confident that, as operations manager, I could make major contributions to Fitch, Inc.

   I hope to hear from you soon.

2. Thank you for the informative interview yesterday and all the courtesies you extended me. My visit to the Abrams Publishing Company offices was most pleasant.

   The position of assistant business manager would be challenging. Because of its orientation to computer systems analysis and my primary interest in accounting work, however, I believe it is best to withdraw my candidacy. I am sure that working with the people I met at Abrams would have been most enjoyable.

   I appreciate the time you have given me. I hope to see you at the next AMS Seminar.

ACCEPTING EMPLOYMENT

Use the direct plan when accepting employment.

The communications offering employment and accepting employment most likely will be by telephone, followed by confirming letters. A letter accepting employment is a good news communication and should use the direct plan: (1) the offer should be accepted, (2) any essential information about assuming the position should come next, and (3) an expression of appreciation should close the letter.

A confirming acceptance letter might look like this:

> I am pleased to confirm my acceptance of the sales position with Bailey's Frozen Foods.
>
> It is my understanding that this position pays a salary of $300 a week and 10 percent commission on sales. I am to assume the position August 1.
>
> Thank you for this opportunity. I am eager to begin work with you.

REJECTING EMPLOYMENT

As is the case with accepting employment, the first communications offering employment and rejecting employment most likely will be by telephone. An indirect bad news letter following up an oral employment rejection may be appropriate. If so, it would be very similar to the letter withdrawing a candidacy shown previously.

Employment rejection messages should use the indirect plan.

EXPRESSING APPRECIATION TO REFERENCES AND OTHERS

When you have accepted an employment offer and completed a successful job campaign, share the good news with your references. Also, it will be important to notify any placement service and any others who assisted you. These expressions of appreciation for assistance may be by telephone, by letter, or in person.

Thank those who helped in your job campaign.

RESIGNING FROM A JOB

Once your job campaign is completed, it may be necessary to resign from your present position. It is best for your resignation not to be a surprise for your employer. If you can, let your employer know that you have applied for another position while you are searching. Most resignations will be oral and in person. The employer may then request that you put your resignation

Most resignations will use the indirect plan.

in writing. In most cases this would be a bad news letter that should be written using the indirect plan. Here is an example:

> Thank you for the support and the opportunities you have provided me at Surnegar's.
>
> I have developed professionally over the past three years as assistant personnel manager. Although my tenure has been enjoyable, I now must resign effective June 30 and go on to another challenge.
>
> In my new position as personnel manager for Dreyer's, Inc., I am sure we will have continuing contact. I look forward to that. Best wishes for continued success with your work.

A CONCLUDING COMMENT

Best wishes for success in all of your job campaigns. Following the suggestions in Chapters 21 and 22 has enabled many to secure rewarding positions that match well with their aptitudes and interests.

DISCUSSION QUESTIONS

1. Discuss the nature of application letters.
2. Describe briefly the purposes of each of the three major parts of an application letter.
3. Describe how the early stages of the job campaign help to prepare you for an interview.
4. From the 25 example questions you may be asked in an interview that are given in this chapter, select 5 and develop answers for them.
5. How should you answer the question, "What salary do you expect for this job?"
6. What are ways to secure information about a company to which you are applying for a position?
7. How should you prepare yourself personally for an interview?
8. What is appropriate and inappropriate behavior during an interview?

9. What are the major types of follow-up employment communication?

10. To whom should you express appreciation when you have accepted an employment offer?

APPLICATION EXERCISES

1. Prepare a personalized application letter to accompany the resume you prepared for Chapter 21. The reader of your letter will be a hiring official in your field at a company of your choice.

2. Prepare a general prospecting application letter to accompany your general resume. Your readers will be personnel officers in companies with positions in your field.

3. List your answers to the 25 example interview questions given in this chapter.

4. Assume you submitted an application for a job opening in your field six weeks ago. You are interested in the position and have not heard from the employer since the acknowledgement of the receipt of your application letter and resume. Write a letter following up on this application. Assume that you are able to add some additional information that developed in the past six weeks that might help your candidacy.

5. Assume you graduated from college five years ago and have been employed as an assistant cashier in a bank since graduation. Your experience in this position has been excellent. The cashier, your immediate supervisor, gave you increasing amounts of responsibility, and you grew professionally. In fact, you did so well that you were the successful candidate for a cashier's position in a bank that is a major competitor of your current employer. Your supervisor is aware that you have accepted the new position and has asked that you put your resignation in writing. Write two letters (a) a letter accepting the new position and (b) a letter resigning from your present position. Create any facts necessary for complete letters.

6. Write a letter to a reference of your choice expressing your appreciation for his or her assistance in your recent successful job campaign. Assume that your new position is appropriate for your field of study.

WORD USAGE

The words listed in this Appendix are many of those that can pose problems for writers. Some words are included because they are misused; some are included because they are often confused with other words. The words are listed alphabetically according to the first word in each pair.

ABOVE BELOW	Avoid using these words in business writing. Instead, use *preceding* to indicate what came before and *following* to indicate what will come after.
ADVICE ADVISE	Advice is a noun; advise is a verb. When you advise, you give advice.
AFFECT EFFECT	Although both words may be either a verb or a noun, *affect* is most often used as a verb showing change or influence; *effect* is most often used as a noun denoting a result or an outcome.
ALL READY ALREADY	Refers to a state of complete readiness. Refers to time.
ALL RIGHT ALRIGHT	The word *alright* is considered inappropriate for business writing; use *all right*.
ALL TOGETHER ALTOGETHER	Refers to physical or figurative unity or closeness. Means entirely or wholly.
AMONG BETWEEN	When referring to three or more, use *among*; when referring to two, use *between*. The appropriate conjunction to use with between is "and."
AMOUNT NUMBER	*Amount* is used with "mass" nouns—things that can be measured but cannot be counted; *number* is used with "count" nouns.
ANXIOUS EAGER	Use anxious when you wish to show anxiety or great concern. Eager, which has a positive connotation, is usually a better choice.
ANY ONE ANYONE	Stresses *one* of a group of persons or things. Stresses *any* and refers only to persons.
ANY WAY ANYWAY	Emphasizes *any*; no preference for method. Means in any case.

ASSURE ENSURE SURE	All three refer to making something certain. Use *assure* when indicating you are placing a person's mind at rest, use *ensure* when indicating you are making safe from harm, and use *insure* when indicating you are guaranteeing the safety of life or property.
BAD BADLY	*Bad* is used with "sense" verbs (feel, hear, see, smell, taste, touch, etc.) and is an adjective—it modifies a noun. *Badly* is an adverb; it modifies a verb, adjective, or another adverb.
BRIEF SHORT	Used only when referring to time. Used when referring to time or to measurement.
BRING TAKE GET	*Bring* denotes movement toward the speaker or writer or the place she or he occupies, *take* denotes movement away from the person or place, and *get* refers to gaining possession.
CAN MAY	Refers to ability to do something. Refers to permission to do something.
CAPITAL CAPITOL	Use the *al* ending when referring to assets or uppercase letters; use the *ol* ending when referring to a state or national government building.
COMPARE CONTRAST	Refers to an examination of similarities *and* differences. Refers to an examination of differences.
COMPLEMENT COMPLIMENT	Means to complete or to enhance. Means to praise.
CONTINUAL CONTINUOUS	Means recurring activity with pauses or breaks. Means uninterrupted activity.
COUNCIL COUNSEL	Refers to an advisory group. Refers to advice or one who gives it.
CONTACT CALL/WRITE	*Contact* is very informal and should be avoided in business communication. Writers should use specific words such as telephone, call, and write or the more general "let us know."
DATA DATUM	*Datum* is the singular form of a noun meaning fact; the plural form of the word is *data*. In business writing, data may be followed by either a singular or a plural verb form.
FARTHER FURTHER	Refers to distance—*far*ther. Means additional or advanced.

FEWER
LESS

Fewer applies to things that can be counted; it is used with references to people and to modify other plural nouns. *Less* is most often used to modify plural nouns involving time, distance, weight, and money.

IF
WHETHER

Used to establish or describe a condition.
Used with implicit or explicit alternatives.

IT'S
ITS

Is the contraction for *it is*.
Is the possessive form of the pronoun it.

LAST
LATEST

Last refers to something final, something at the end.
Latest refers to something recent, the most current of a series.

LAY
LIE

Means to put or to place.
Means to recline or to rest.

LOSE
LOOSE

Is a verb; it is the opposite of find.
Is an adjective used to describe fit; it is the opposite of tight.

ME
MYSELF

Me is the objective case of the personal pronoun *I*.
Myself is a reflexive pronoun. It should be used in business writing only when you have been identified earlier in the sentence.

MEDIA
MEDIUM

Media is the plural; it refers to several mass communication methods. Each mass communication method (TV, radio, etc.) is a *medium*.

PERSONAL
PERSONNEL

Means private or relating to a person.
Refers to a group of workers or employees.

PRECEDE
PROCEED

Means to go or to come before.
Means to go forward with or continue some action.

PRINCIPAL
PRINCIPLE

Refers to a leader or to something *chief* or *primary*.
Refers to a rule or a basic truth.

SET
SIT

Means to place or to put.
Means to lie or to rest.

SOME TIME
SOMETIME

Refers to a specific time.
Refers to an indefinite time.

STATIONARY
STATIONERY

Means in a fixed position.
Means writing paper.

THAN
THEN

Used as part of a comparison.
Used with reference to time.

THAT WHICH WHO	*That* is used to refer to persons, animals, or things; it introduces restrictive clauses. *Which* is used to refer to animals or things; it introduces nonrestrictive clauses. *Who* is used to refer only to persons; it may be used to introduce either a restrictive or a nonrestrictive clause.
THOROUGH THROUGH THRU	*Thorough* refers to the fullest level of detail. *Through* is used to show movement into and out of, to specify methods, or to show completion. *Thru* is informal and should not be used in business writing.
TO TOO	Indicates movement or direction. Means also or to an excessive degree.
WHO WHOM	*Who* is a pronoun used in questions to indicate what or which person or persons. *Whom* is an objective case pronoun; it is used as an object of a verb or a preposition.

EDITING SYMBOLS

Defined		Examples

Paragraph   ¶   ¶ Begin a new paragraph at this point.

Insert a character   ∧   Insᵉrt a letter here.

Delete   ℒ   Delete ~~these words.~~ Disregard

Do not change   *stet or*   the previous correction.

Transpose   *tr*   To transpose is to around turn.

Move to the left   ⌐   Move this copy to the left.

Move to the right   ⌐   Move this copy to the right.

No paragraph   *No* ¶   *No* ¶ Do not begin a new paragraph

Delete and close up   ℛ   here. Delete the hyphen from

     pre-empt and close up the space.

Set in caps   *Caps or* ≡   a sentence begins with a capital

Set in lower case   *lc*   letter. This Word should not

Insert a period   ⊙   be capitalized. Insert a period⊙

Quotation marks   ⌄″ ⌄″   Quotation marks and a comma

Comma   ⌄   should be placed here he said.

Insert space   #   Space between these words. An

Apostrophe   ⌄   apostrophe is whats needed here.

Hyphen   =   Add a hyphen to Afro American.

Close up   ‿   Close up the extra spa ce.

Use superior figure   ⌄   Footnote this sentence. Set

Set in italic   *Ital. or* ___   the words, <u>sine qua non</u>, in italics.

Move up   ⌐⌐   This word is too ⌐low.⌐ That word

Move down   ⌐⌐   is too ⌐high.⌐

PROOFREADING PROCEDURES

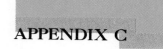

Source: Document Design Center 3333 K Street, NW Washington, DC 20007 (202) 342-5000

EVERYONE'S A PROOFREADER: HOW TO CHECK YOUR DOCUMENTS

by Carolyn Boccella Bagin and Jo Van Doren

> *The man who makes no mistakes does not usually make anything.*
>
> —E.J. Phelps

For most people in our profession, proofreading is drudgery. Hardly anyone notices the perfect proofreading job, but everyone spots the lone, unsightly error after you've gone to press. Uncaught, proofreading mistakes can be embarrassing and sometimes costly. That's why you should make everyone responsible for proofreading the documents you produce. As Phelps implies, if you write documents, you make mistakes. The key is catching them before they cost you money.

Over the years, we've gathered many proofreading hints to help make the job go more smoothly. Since this topic has been popular with our readers, we've updated the article from *Simply Stated No. 65* to give you techniques that you can use every day.

GET SOME HELP WITH THE JOB

1. Never proofread your own copy, if you can help it. You'll tire of looking at the document in its different stages of development and you'll miss new errors.
2. Keep the nature of the document in mind. Interoffice memos need a different level of attention than contracts, books, or clients' publications. Typeset mistakes are more expensive to fix than word-processed ones.

3. If you work with several proofreaders, consider having them initial the copy they check. You might find that your documents have fewer errors because your proofers feel accountable for the ones they miss.

4. Learn from your staff's mistakes. Take notes on what you've missed before—especially those mistakes that have cost time and money to fix. Make sure no one makes the same mistake twice.

5. Use a partner to proof numbers that are in columns. Read the figures aloud and have your partner mark the corrections and changes on the copy being proofread.

6. Not everyone knows and uses traditional proofreading marks. If your staff doesn't know them, create a simple marking system that all of your people can understand. Make a style sheet as a desk reference to avoid confusion.

7. Keep a notebook of unusual spellings, changes in usage, clients' preferences and quirks, common acronyms of your trade, and abbreviations. Before you know it, you'll have a handy reference guide to pass along to new staff members.

WHAT IF YOU DO IT YOURSELF?

8. The hardest thing in proofing your own copy is concentrating on your goal—and not reading for content. If you proofread your own copy, make a line screen for yourself or roll the paper so that you view only one line at a time. This will stop you from skimming the material for content and will help you focus on the proofing task.

9. First read everything in the copy straight through from beginning to end. Then read your document again several times, looking for different types of errors each time.

    For instance, read all of the headings, then check them against the table of contents. Next, read through again for punctuation. Try another round to check if the spacing is consistent. Continue the process until you've covered everything.

10. Read your copy backwards to catch spelling errors. Reading sentences out of sequence will let you concentrate on individual words.

TIMING IS EVERYTHING

11. If you can, alter your routine. Don't proofread at the same time every day. Varying your schedule will help you approach the task with a keener eye.

12. If time allows, put your material aside for awhile. After a break, reread the last few lines to refresh your memory.

TECHNIQUES THAT WORK

13. Read the pages of a document out of order. Changing the sequence helps you review each page as a unit.
14. Look at copy upside down to help check spacing and placement inconsistencies.
15. If you are interrupted in the middle of a proofing task, mark your place with a pencil, paper clip, or colored sheet.
16. If you don't have a style sheet for the format, make notes before you check a lengthy document. You'll need to rely on more than just your memory to check for consistency.

ERRORS TEND TO HIDE IN PARTICULAR PLACES

17. Mistakes cluster. If you find one typo, look carefully nearby for others.
18. Inspect the beginnings of pages, paragraphs, and sections. Some people skim these spots and miss hidden typos. Double-check page and line breaks.
19. Beware of changes in typeface—especially in headings and titles. If you change to italics, boldface, or underlined copy, read those sections several times.
20. Copy printed in all upper-case letters is particularly difficult to proof because the letters have a uniform outline.
21. Check all titles, subtitles, and page numbers against your table of contents and index. Mistakes with numbers are easy to make and difficult to catch.
22. Read sequential material carefully. Check that all numbers or letters are in order. Look for duplications in lists, outlines, or tables.
23. Double-check references such as, "see the chart below," or "go to page 10." After several drafts, referenced material may have moved several pages away.
24. Bibliographies are especially troublesome for some proofers. Make sure your entries are in alphabetical order. Then check the authors' names and titles to verify spelling. Next, match each citation against your style sheet to ensure that the order of items listed is correct. Then examine the punctuation in each citation; skim to make sure quotation marks are paired and commas and periods are in place.
25. Examine numbers and totals. Refigure all calculations and look for misplaced commas and decimal points. If numbers are displayed in columns, make sure that they are properly aligned.
26. Scrutinize features that come in sets—brackets, parentheses, quotation marks, and dashes. It's easy to miss the second half of the pair.

GUIDELINES FOR USING UNBIASED LANGUAGE[1]

The guidelines that follow illustrate that many alternatives to language stereotyping are available. Other alternatives will undoubtedly be devised as continuing progress is made in viewing women and men as equals.

ALTERNATIVES TO MASCULINE PRONOUNS

The following examples show how to implement guidelines for assuring unbiased language by providing alternatives to the generic use of masculine pronouns.

GUIDELINE 1: ELIMINATE THE PRONOUN.

Avoid	Use
If credit is given too freely, the seller will increase *his* sales; but *he* will decrease the percentage of accounts receivable *he* collects.	If credit is given too freely, the seller will increase sales but decrease the percentage of accounts receivable collected.
The student should determine which principle of business communication gives *him* the most difficulty and then practice using it.	The student should determine which principle of business communication gives the most difficulty and then practice using it.

GUIDELINE 2: CHANGE FROM SINGULAR TO PLURAL.

Avoid	Use
When an individual travels by plane, *he* is able to work en route.	When individuals travel by plane, they are able to work en route.
Class participation aids the student in developing *his* ability to communicate.	Class participation aids students in developing their abilities to communicate.

---

[1]This section is adapted from *Guidelines: Fair and Balanced Treatment of Minorities and Women*, (Cincinnati, Ohio: South-Western Publishing Co., 1976), pp. 1-16.

GUIDELINE 3: USE GENDERLESS WORDS. For example, use *person, one, individual,* or *you.*

Avoid	Use
The expert witness was expected to testify as a reasonable *man.*	The expert witness was expected to testify as a reasonable person.
If *he* is not sure *he* wants what *he* is buying, *he* should not buy it.	If you are not sure you want what you are buying, you should not buy it.
The employee will receive all the benefits to which *he* is entitled when *he* retires.	The employee will receive all the benefits to which an individual is entitled at retirement.

GUIDELINE 4: USE JOB TITLES OR FUNCTIONS INSTEAD OF THE PRONOUN.

Avoid	Use
Secondly, *he* could earn as much as $720 a year without loss of family benefits.	Secondly, the head of a household could earn as much as $720 a year without loss of family benefits.
He adds the balances.	The accountant adds the balances.

GUIDELINE 5: CHANGE THE PRONOUN TO AN ARTICLE.

Avoid	Use
When a taxpayer sells *his* residence, taxes must be paid on any capital gains.	When a taxpayer sells a residence, taxes must be paid on any capital gains.
A taxpayer must file *his* 199– return by April 15, 199–.	A taxpayer must file the 199– return by April 15, 199–.
A life insurance policy owner may change *his* beneficiary at any time.	A life insurance policy owner may change a beneficiary at any time.

GUIDELINE 6: CHANGE TO THE PASSIVE VOICE.

Avoid	Use
The retailer was advised that *he* should advertise the merchandise on the radio.	The retailer was advised that the merchandise should be advertised on the radio.
The auditor issued *his* report.	The report was issued by the auditor.
He must inform the employees about the new work schedule.	The employees must be informed about the new work schedule.

GUIDELINE 7: ADD NAMES TO ELIMINATE THE GENERIC USE.

Avoid	Use
The Vice President of Sales scheduled a meeting with *his* salespeople.	The Vice President of Sales, Linda Stevens, scheduled a meeting with her salespeople.

GUIDELINE 8: REPEAT THE NOUN INSTEAD OF USING THE PRONOUN.

Avoid	Use
A farmer harvested 10,000 bushels of wheat. If the price of wheat is $6 a bushel, *he* may sell all *his* wheat; but if it is only $3 a bushel, *he* may sell only enough to meet *his* current cash needs.	A farmer harvested 10,000 bushels of wheat. If the price of wheat is $6 a bushel, the farmer may sell all the wheat; but if it is only $3 a bushel, the farmer may sell only enough to meet current cash needs.
If a manager is promoted, *he* will gain added responsibility and rewards.	If a manager is promoted, that manager will gain added responsibility and rewards.
When a property owner is renting an apartment—unless there is prior notice—the tenant must give *him* permission to enter the apartment.	When a property owner is renting an apartment—unless there is prior notice—the tenant must give the property owner permission to enter the apartment.

GUIDELINE 9: INCLUDE THE FEMININE PRONOUN.

For example, use *she or he* or *his or her*. Where possible, however, use other alternates to avoid awkward wording.

Avoid	Use
If the student has a computer, *he* should use it for this report.	If the student has a computer, he or she should use it for this report.
The salesperson can call on *his* clients.	The salesperson can call on his or her clients.

ALTERNATIVES TO THE GENERIC *MAN*

The following examples offer alternatives to the generic use of the word *man*.

GUIDELINE 10: USE APPROPRIATE SUBSTITUTES FOR THE GENERIC *MAN.*

Avoid	Use
man, men, mankind	human(s), human being(s), person(s), people, individual(s), humanity, human race, women and men, men and women
The prudent *man* would make appropriate adjustments in speed due to weather conditions.	The prudent person would make appropriate adjustments in speed due to weather conditions.
Men care for the environment because they care about the future of mankind.	People care for the environment because they care about the future of humanity.

ALTERNATIVES TO MASCULINE MARKERS

Whenever possible, find up-to-date substitutes for words with "man" suffixes and prefixes, and use up-to-date occupational titles.

GUIDELINE 11: USE UP-TO-DATE SUBSTITUTES FOR "MAN" SUFFIXES AND PREFIXES.

Avoid	Use
businessman	businessperson, business executive, merchant, industrialist, entrepreneur, manager
chairman	chairperson, moderator, chair, group leader, presiding officer
congressmen	members of Congress, Congressional representatives, congressmen and women
manmade	manufactured, hand-built, handmade, machinemade
manpower	human resources, human energy, work force personnel
salesmen	salespeople, salespersons, sales agents, sales associates, sales representatives, sales force
spokesman	representative, spokesperson, advocate, proponent
statesman	political leader, public servant
workmen	workers

GUIDELINE 12: USE UP-TO-DATE SUBSTITUTES FOR OCCUPATIONAL TITLES.[2]

Avoid	Use
cameraman	camera operator
deliveryman	delivery driver, delivery clerk, deliverer
draftsman	drafter
foreman	supervisor
maid	houseworker
pressman	press operator
repairman	repairer
salesman	sales agent, sales associate, sales representative, salesperson
serviceman	servicer, service representative
stock boy, stock man	stock clerk
yardman	yard worker, gardener

ALTERNATIVES TO SEX ROLE STEREOTYPING

Try to use the many available alternatives to words or constructions that stereotype roles in our society.

GUIDELINE 13: AVOID NOUNS THAT UNNECESSARILY IDENTIFY GENDER.

Avoid	Use
poetess	poet
sculptress	sculptor
authoress	author
usherette	usher
co-ed	student
housewife	homemaker

---

[2]Examples from U.S. Department of Labor, "Job Title Revisions to Eliminate Sex-and-Age-Referent Language" from the *Dictionary of Occupational Titles*, 3rd Edition (Washington: U.S. Government Printing Office, 1975).

GUIDELINE 14: AVOID ADJECTIVES THAT IDENTIFY GENDER FOR SUCH GENERIC TERMS AS DOCTOR.

Avoid	Use
lady or female doctor	doctor
male nurse	nurse
Sharon O'Brien is a highly successful lady advertising executive.	Sharon O'Brien is a highly successful advertising executive.

GUIDELINE 15: AVOID THE USE OF MALE AND FE-MALE PRONOUNS OR OTHER LANGUAGE THAT IN-DICATES THAT A PARTICULAR JOB (OR ROLE) IS ALWAYS OR USUALLY HELD BY A FEMALE OR BY A MALE.

Avoid	Use
executive . . . he lawyer . . . he secretary . . . she nurse . . . she	(Techniques for avoiding the use of pro-nouns)
Housewives are complaining about higher prices.	Consumers (homemakers, customers, shoppers) are complaining about higher prices.

GUIDELINE 16: AVOID LANGUAGE THAT IS DEMEAN-ING, PATRONIZING, OR LIMITING. Avoid words and phrases that demean or patronize:

- —womanish, acted like a woman, just like a woman
- —the weaker sex, weak as a girl, weak sister
- —the fair sex, the distaff side
- —woman's work
- —man-sized job, separate the men from the boys
- —took it like a man, a manly act of courage
- —sissified
- —old-maidish, spinsterish
- —woman driver
- —the little woman, the better half, the ball and chain
- —nagging mother-in-law

Avoid	Use
Helga Oberschmidt performs her job as well as any man.	Helga Oberschmidt is a competent per-sonnel manager.

Use the words girl and lady carefully:

Avoid	Use
the girls, the ladies (adult females)	the women
the ladies and the men	the women and the men, the ladies and the gentlemen, the girls and the boys
the girls in the office	the women in the office
The executive vice-president called a meeting of all the men and girls in the accounting department.	The executive vice-president called a meeting of the men and women in the accounting department.
	or
	The executive vice-president called a meeting of the employees in the accounting department.
I'll have my girl look up the information for you.	I'll have my secretary (assistant, person's name) look up the information for you.

Use care to portray women in appropriate roles:

Avoid	Use
man and wife	husband and wife, man and woman, couple
Bill Dewey is a successful banker; his wife, Beverly, is a striking brunette.	The Deweys are an attractive couple. Beverly is a striking brunette, and Bill is a handsome blond.
Judy Kawahara, wife of chemist Yoshi Kawahara and a noted chemist in her own right, spoke to the group.	Noted chemist, Judy Kawahara, spoke to the group.
The new sales manager, Martha Valdez, is an attractive mother of three and wife of city councilman, Jose Valdez.	Martha Valdez, the new sales manager, has been a successful salesperson with Federated Department Stores for 15 years.
City council member Jose Valdez, a somber, brown-eyed father of three, was reelected to his third term.	Valdez was reelected to his third term.

Role Reversal Drives Home Point

Yoshi Kawahara, husband of chemist Judy Kawahara and a noted chemist in his own right, spoke to the group.

The new sales manager, Jose Valdez, is a handsome father of three and husband of city councilwoman, Martha Valdez.

Use courtesy titles (Mr., Ms., Miss, Mrs.) carefully. If it is necessary to use a courtesy title for a woman, use Ms., Miss, or Mrs., if the person's preference is known. If the preference or the marital status is not known and the courtesy title cannot be omitted, use Ms. In some cases, you can simply avoid using the courtesy title.

Avoid	Use
Samuels and Miss Jones	Samuels and Jones, Mr. Samuels and Ms. Jones (preference unknown)
Faulkner, Fitzgerald, and Miss Porter are widely read authors.	Faulkner, Fitzgerald, and Porter are widely read authors.
Gentlemen: Dear Sirs: (letter salutations)	Ladies and Gentlemen or Dear (Name of Group) (i.e., Dear Centertown Rotarian). Or avoid salutation by using simplified block letter style.

Maintain balance by alternating the order of gender references: women and men, men and women; he or she, she or he; etc.

TWO-LETTER POSTAL ABBREVIATIONS

U.S. STATE, DISTRICT, AND TERRITORY NAMES

Name	Two-Letter Abbreviation	Name	Two-Letter Abbreviation
Alabama	AL	Montana	MT
Alaska	AK	Nebraska	NE
Arizona	AZ	Nevada	NV
Arkansas	AR	New Hampshire	NH
California	CA	New Jersey	NJ
Colorado	CO	New Mexico	NM
Connecticut	CT	New York	NY
Delaware	DE	North Carolina	NC
District of Columbia	DC	North Dakota	ND
Florida	FL	Ohio	OH
Georgia	GA	Oklahoma	OK
Guam	GU	Oregon	OR
Hawaii	HI	Pennsylvania	PA
Idaho	ID	Puerto Rico	PR
Illinois	IL	Rhode Island	RI
Indiana	IN	South Carolina	SC
Iowa	IA	South Dakota	SD
Kansas	KS	Tennessee	TN
Kentucky	KY	Texas	TX
Louisiana	LA	Utah	UT
Maine	ME	Vermont	VT
Maryland	MD	Virgin Islands	VI
Massachusetts	MA	Virginia	VA
Michigan	MI	Washington	WA
Minnesota	MN	West Virginia	WV
Mississippi	MS	Wisconsin	WI
Missouri	MO	Wyoming	WY

CANADIAN PROVINCES

Name	Two-Letter Abbreviation	Name	Two-Letter Abbreviation
Alberta	AB	Nova Scotia	NS
British Columbia	BC	Ontario	ON
Manitoba	MB	Prince Edward Island	PE
New Brunswick	NB	Quebec	PQ
Newfoundland	NF	Saskatchewan	SK
Northwest Territories	NT	Yukon Territory	YT

SAMPLE PROPOSAL

Source: Adapted with permission from an actual, more detailed proposal provided by Opryland, U.S.A., Nashville, Tennessee.

A Proposed Pilot Study, Cover Letter

Research Services, Inc.

Louisville, KY 42111-1111

October 15, 199–

Mr. Ed F. Jeffrey
Executive Director of Administration
Opryland, U.S.A.
2802 Opryland Drive
Nashville, TN 37314-1234

Dear Mr. Jeffrey

As you requested, here is a "Proposal for A Pilot Study to Test an Expanded Employee Screening System."

The proposed study supports the development of an expanded employee screening system that could reduce turnover and improve job placement. The proposal is comprehensive. It includes Opryland and the various Six Flags Parks. The pilot study basically will evaluate the current system with two major expansions: (1) valid bases for interviewer judgments and (2) appropriate placement tests. While the full development of the screening system is expected to take 3 years, this proposal covers the steps to be taken in the initial study to be conducted the first 14 months.

Your approval of this proposed pilot study is requested. It has, I believe, considerable promise for improving employee productivity at Opryland and the Six Flags Parks.

Sincerely

Gail Henning

Gail Henning
Consultant

ah

The cover letter:

- Transmits the proposal

- Highlights it

- Requests action

A Proposed Pilot Study, Title Page

The title page:

• Gives the name

• Tells to whom submitted

• Tells who is submitting

• Provides cost and time information

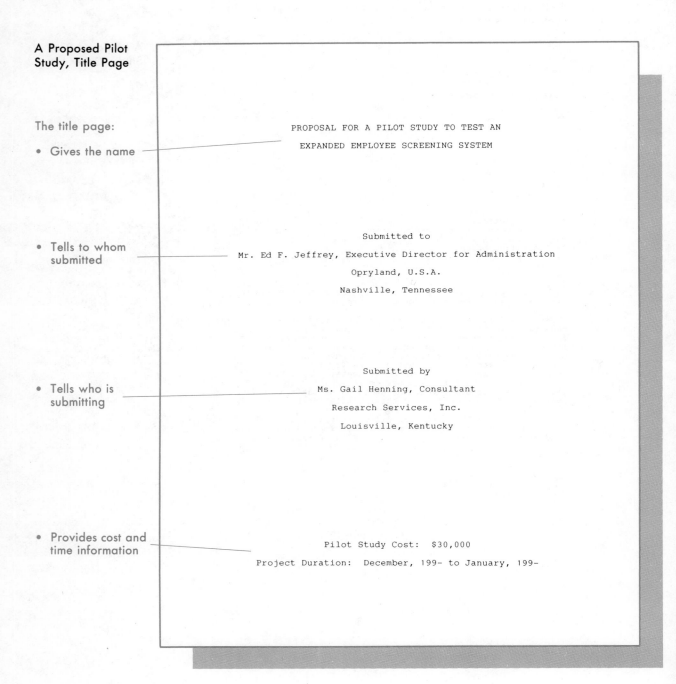

PROPOSAL FOR A PILOT STUDY TO TEST AN

EXPANDED EMPLOYEE SCREENING SYSTEM

Submitted to

Mr. Ed F. Jeffrey, Executive Director for Administration

Opryland, U.S.A.

Nashville, Tennessee

Submitted by

Ms. Gail Henning, Consultant

Research Services, Inc.

Louisville, Kentucky

Pilot Study Cost: $30,000

Project Duration: December, 199– to January, 199–

A Proposed Pilot Study, Table of Contents

TABLE OF CONTENTS

The table of contents lists names and page numbers for all major sections.

ii

A Proposed Pilot
Study, p. 1

PROPOSAL FOR A PILOT STUDY TO TEST AN
EXPANDED EMPLOYEE SCREENING SYSTEM

SUMMARY

The summary gives
a complete overview
of the proposal
contents.

The purpose of this proposal is to reduce employee turnover
through the development and testing of an expanded employee
screening system. The expanded system would add to the current
system valid bases for interview judgments and appropriate placement tests. The design of a pilot study to test the expanded
system would include selecting a random sample of applicants,
screening the applicants, and tracking them on the job. The
pilot study would begin December 199- and conclude January 15,
199-. The cost for this study is projected at $30,000.

PURPOSE

The purpose gives
the nature of and
reasons for the
proposal.

The purpose of this proposal is to develop an expanded employee
screening system designed to (1) reduce turnover and (2) improve
job placement of seasonal employees at Opryland and various Six
Flags Parks. The proposal is that a pilot study be conducted
during 199- to test such an expanded employee screening system.

BACKGROUND

Necessary
background
information is
provided to the
reader.

The current seasonal employee screening system has been effective
in reducing turnover at Opryland and various Six Flags Parks.
This system basically includes the application form, the ideal
leader behavior questionnaire, the management flexibility inventory, and information gained during interviews. An important
part of the current screening system is that the interviewers are
permitted to hire seasonal employees who do not meet cutoff test
scores if, in the interviewer's judgment, the information gained
in the interview indicates a promising employee.

It is believed that the current screening system could be
improved by adding to it (1) the valid bases for interviewer
judgments and (2) appropriate placement tests. An example of an
appropriate placement test would be a short math test to help
decide who should be placed in positions that require handling
money.

A Proposed Pilot
Study, p. 2

2

BENEFITS OF THE STUDY

The proposed pilot study would use an expanded screening system
that includes the interviewer judgment items and standard tests.
The study will:

1. compare those hired who quit and those hired who did not
   quit,
2. provide profiles of high, average, and low performers,
3. guide job placement of seasonal employees,
4. provide improved bases for employee selection, and
5. strengthen our ability to counsel and/or reassign employees.

The full development of the expanded screening system is expected
to take three years. During the first year, several employee
screening items will be developed and tested in the pilot study.
The second year will be devoted to refining the system and the
third year to field testing the final expanded screening system.

This proposal describes the design and procedures for the initial
pilot study.

The benefits to be
gained from the
pilot are clearly
and emphatically
stated.

DESIGN OF THE PILOT STUDY AND EVALUATION PLAN

The following steps would be taken at each participating park:

1. Specify a date on which the pilot study would begin after the
   first 1,000 hirings are completed.

2. Randomly select 300 applicants from the first 1,000 hired
   after the date specified in Step 1.

3. Have each randomly selected applicant complete the screening
   items in the expanded system on a computerized answer sheet.
   The expanded system will include the following:

   a. Rational behavior inventory
   b. A short math test
   c. Judgment items suggested by interviewers
   d. Items related to human relations skills
   e. Leadership opinion questionnaire
   f. Ideal leader behavior questionnaire
   g. Opryland management flexibility inventory
   h. Other items from current screening system

The description of
the proposed pilot
study and its
evaluation plan are
combined in this
section.

**A Proposed Pilot
Study, p. 3**

3

4. Track the following information for each interpretation in
    the study:

    a. Performance appraisal results
    b. Absenteeism
    c. Date of termination
    d. Reason for termination
    e. Rehire status
    f. Employee attitudes (employee perceptions questionnaire)

5. Randomly divide the participants at each park into two
    groups.

6. Use appropriate statistical techniques to identify the best
    predictors of each of the variables listed in Step 4 for one
    of the groups.

7. Use the second group to cross-check the statistical tech-
    niques used in Step 6.

8. Divide the participants, based on all the variables listed in
    Step 4, into three groups:

    a. High performers
    b. Average performers
    c. Low performers

9. Use appropriate statistical techniques to determine how well
    each of the items in the expanded screening system predicted
    employee performance.

QUALIFICATIONS OF KEY PROJECT PERSONNEL

Essential
qualifications of the
personnel who
would do the pilot
study are provided.

Project Manager

Dr. Douglas Williams
Degree: Ph.D., University of Pennsylvania, 19--
Major: Business Statistics
Minors: Management and Personnel
Experience: Assistant Personnel Manager, Opryland; Directed
             several successful research projects

Senior Research Assistant

Dr. Norma Smith
Degree: Ph.D., Indiana University, 19--
Major: Probability Statistics
Minors: Mathematics and Computer Science
Experience: Research Associate, Vanderbilt University; Conducted
             a variety of successful research projects

A Proposed Pilot
Study, p. 4

4

TIME LINE

December 199–

Meet with interviewers from each
participating park to obtain suggested
interviewer judgment items. One
interviewer from each participating
park will meet at Opryland in mid-
December.

January 199–

Develop actual items to be used on
expanded screening system.

January–
November 15, 199–

Start study (date depends on February
199– local park hiring patterns) and
gather specific data.

November 15–
December 15, 199–

Analyze data.

December 15, 199–
January 15, 199–

Revise system for 199– season.

A simple, easy-to-
understand time
schedule is included.

**A Proposed Pilot
Study, p. 5**

The budget for the
pilot study is given.

```
                                                                    5

                              PROJECTED COSTS

Salaries

        Project Manager (10 percent time)              $ 9,000
        Senior Research Assistant (20 percent time)     10,000
        Research Assistant (25 percent time)             5,000
        Temporary Typist (75 hours)                        500

Travel*

        Project Manager
        Senior Research Assistant
        Trips to meet with Six Flags interviewers

Materials                                                5,500

        Computerized answer sheets
        Leadership opinion questionnaires
        Opryland management flexibility inventories
        Ideal leader behavior questionnaires
        Rational behavior inventory
        Employee perceptions questionnaires
        Computer paper
        Duplicating
                                                       ─────────

        Total                                          $30,000


        *Note:  Each park will be responsible for its own travel (except
        that requests for Opryland consultation from Six Flags Parks
        would be paid for by the requesting park).
```

SAMPLE LONG REPORT

Title Page

OPINIONS OF YOUNG ADULTS
ON TELEVISION VIOLENCE AND ITS
EFFECT ON CHILDREN

Prepared for
Dr. Anna Hess
Department of Management

Prepared by
Robert Vineyard
MGT 215-02

School of Business Administration
Tripp Long-Creek College
Forney, Idaho 83115-7201

April 12, 199-

The title page:

- States the subject of the report

- Tells to whom submitted

- Tells who is submitting

- Gives location of organization

- Gives the date of submission

Title Fly

The title fly may be
a blank sheet of
paper or may state
the title of the
report.

OPINIONS OF YOUNG ADULTS

ON TELEVISION VIOLENCE AND ITS

EFFECT ON CHILDREN

Memo of
Authorization

To: Business Communication Students

From: Anna Hess, Professor _AH_

Date: January 3, 199-

Subject: Authorization for Study on Television Violence

You are authorized to study how young adults perceive television
violence affects children. Survey a random sample of Tripp Long-
Creek College students to obtain your data.

Your study will be discussed on the university television channel
this summer. A copy of your report will be sent to Idaho's Commission on Improving the Quality of Living. Your report may be
used as a basis for determining if further studies on television
programming are warranted.

There has been no budget allocation for this project. I recommend that you use telephones to conduct the survey. You may
use the telephone in my office if you do not have one readily
available.

Your report needs to be in my office by April 15 so that I will
have time to review it and forward it to the commission no later
than May 1. You may contact me at any time at extension 4196 for
assistance or further guidance.

gb

The memo of
authorization:

• Gives authority
  for the study

• Tells how results
  of the study will
  be used

• Describes
  available funding

• Gives the date
  that report is due

Letter of Transmittal

Box 1123, University Station
Forney, ID 83115-1123
April 12, 199-

Dr. Anna Hess
Department of Management
School of Business Administration
Tripp Long-Creek College
Forney, ID 83115-7201

Dear Dr. Hess

The letter of
transmittal:

• Transmits the
  report

Here is the report you requested on the opinions of young adults
regarding the effect that television violence has on children.

• Describes the
  purpose and
  procedure

The purpose of this study was to provide you and Idaho's Commission
on Improving the Quality of Living with young adults' opinions
about the effects television violence has on children. To get this
information, a random sample of 434 Tripp Long-Creek College students (about 6 percent of TLC students) were surveyed by telephone.

• Gives the
  highlights of the
  report

The survey results were divided into two groups--students with a
child or sibling under 12 and those not having a child or sibling
under 12. The majority of both groups thought that television has
both positive and negative effects on children and that television
violence does reinforce violence in children's lives. The respondents also thought that parents have the major responsibility for
controlling the child's exposure to television violence.

Based on these findings, I recommend that parents and their children jointly plan a schedule of television programs for viewing. I
also recommend that the commission begin a campaign (1) to inform
parents of the destructiveness of television violence and (2) to
convince networks to limit the amount of violence on television.

• States
  recommendations

• Closes the letter

Thank you for the opportunity to study this problem. If you need
any additional information, I can be reached at extension 2357.

Sincerely

Robert Vineyard

Robert Vineyard
MGT 215-02

Enc.

Table of Contents and List of Illustrations

TABLE OF CONTENTS

The table of contents lists names and page numbers for all major sections.

LIST OF ILLUSTRATIONS

v

Abstract

The abstract briefly summarizes the important parts of the report:

- Purpose and procedure

- Related literature

- Findings

- Analysis

- Recommendations

ABSTRACT

The purpose of the study was to determine how young adults perceive the effects of television violence on children. A telephone survey was administered to 434 of the 7,400 Tripp Long-Creek students to obtain the data.

The related literature shows that television definitely affected children's behavior. Several studies point out the violent content of children's programs. The research of secondary sources revealed that parents are in the best position to control what their children view on television and should assume this responsibility.

The survey revealed that 52.5 percent of the students with a child or sibling under the age of 12 felt television had a moderate effect on children, and 84.9 percent felt it had both positive and negative effects. Of the students without a child or sibling under the age of 12, 56.6 percent felt television had a moderate effect on children, and 88.1 percent felt the effect was both positive and negative. The majority of both groups felt that television does reinforce violence in children's lives and that parents have the major responsibility for controlling the amount of violence that their children see.

An analysis of the primary and secondary findings leads to the conclusion that viewing television violence reinforces violent behavior in children. In addition, parents--not governmental agencies--should control the amount of violence viewed by their children.

Based on these findings, it is recommended that parents monitor the amount of violence their children see on television and inform television programming personnel about their opinions concerning the programs shown. It is also recommended that another survey be conducted to determine how parents should control the amount of violence that their children see on television.

Body

I. INTRODUCTION

The introduction assists the reader in understanding the rest of the report.

Background

Children spend much of their free time watching television. Some of the viewing time is spent on educational programs, and some of the viewing time is spent watching programs containing violence. In recent years there has been much controversy over the amount of television that a child should watch and the types of programs that the child should view. Another area of concern is who has primary responsibility for children's television viewing habits. The opinions of young adults with recent television viewing experience as children should be helpful in studying these problems.

The background describes the problem in general terms.

Statement of the Problem

The problem of this study was to determine the attitudes of young adults regarding the effects of television violence on children under the age of 12.

The statement of the problem identifies the specific problem researched.

Purpose of the Study

The purpose of this study was to provide parents, teachers, adult family members, and other interested parties with young adults' opinions on the effects of television violence on children. The study was also conducted to see if young adults think legislators should take action to control the amount of violence that television stations broadcast.

The purpose of the study tells why the study was conducted.

Scope

The scope of the study included the effects of television on children, the value of regulations to control violence on television, and the responsible parties for controlling television violence.

The scope defines the boundaries of the study.

Limitations for this study include (1) only Tripp Long-Creek College students were surveyed, and (2) time permitted no testing and revising of the questionnaire.

II. RELATED LITERATURE

Violence on television has been a concern for many years. When research about television began, three positions became popular. The first position was that television violence was beneficial because it helped vent hostilities symbolically, and so young viewers were less likely to act violently in real life. The second position was that television violence had no effect. The third position held that television violence could lead to subsequent aggression. Even today, it is considered questionable as to which position is correct.

The related literature reviews research that has been conducted on similar topics.

2

In 1990, the National Advisory Committee on Social Behavior submitted a report to the Surgeon General regarding the effect of television violence on children. The basic conclusion of the report was that television violence does have measurable effects on children. Many young children cannot distinguish between fantasy and reality, and violence they see on television has the same psychological effect as violence they see in the real world. Viewing violence on television has been linked with violent behavior subsequent to viewing. The report concluded that the only way for parents to significantly influence the effect television violence has is to watch television with their children and help them distinguish between fantasy and reality (Gibbs, April 1990, 121).

In a 1989 study by Nathan Goff, it was noted that an average viewer saw violence in seven of every ten programs and eight of every ten cartoons. Mr. Goff felt that parents must be aware of the role television played in their children's lives and act according to their children's best interests (Goff, October 1989, 72).

Some interesting conclusions were drawn by Krause about what types of television violence seem to cause violent behavior in children. Programs that contain more real-life violence have a greater impact on the child's behavior. Programs that do not seem to promote violent behavior include comedies, cartoons, and science fiction. Krause was of the opinion that whether programs do incite violence depends on how deeply they penetrate the child's personal value system (Krause, March 1987, 42-43).

Child Psychology took a nationwide survey entitled, "Does Television Affect Your Child?", which was published in its June issue. The survey received over 5,000 responses from parents; 68 percent of the parents are under 34 years of age. The majority of these parents felt that changes in television violence should be made by the public by deciding whether or not to watch the program (McCann, June 1989, 55).

Although most of the parents felt it was the public's responsibility (contrasted with only 11 percent indicating that it was the federal government's responsibility), 52 percent would have the government offer incentives to stations to keep up the number and the quality of children's programs. Forty-eight percent also believed that children's programs were much too violent.

Studies done on who has the major responsibility for controlling the amount of television a child views all seem to agree that parents are in the best position to monitor their child's viewing habits.

The Television Viewer published the conclusions made from a study conducted by Sara Williams. The study concluded that parents are the single most important contributor to a child's development

Body

3

and, therefore, should direct and moderate their child's viewing habits. Parents should not use television as a baby-sitter. Instead, they should watch television with their child and talk about the programs (Williams, November 18, 1988, 61-64).

Another controversial area that has been thoroughly researched is the amount of violence on television. Elmer Elway spoke to The Association of Concerned Parents about problems associated with violence on television. In his speech he stated, "Research evidence shows that viewing television violence at an early age leads to more aggressive teenage behavior. Many violent crimes are copies of scenes that were shown on television." (Elway, September 3, 1988, 531).

III.   PROCEDURES

Each business communication class had a brainstorming session to develop a list of possible topics to study. The instructors for the five classes compiled the ideas into a single list and allowed students in each class to vote on the topic that would be the best to study. The topic selected was "Television's Effect on Children."

Each student submitted two potential questions for possible use in the questionnaire. From these questions, the instructors compiled a questionnaire that was used to survey the student population at Tripp Long-Creek College.

A statistician developed a sample size for a .05 precision and 95 percent confidence level. The sample of young adults was randomly selected by computer from the total student population at Tripp Long-Creek College.

Copies of the questionnaire were given to students in the classes along with names of three students who would be interviewed by telephone. Information was collected and tabulated by the classes. Each student was given a copy of the survey results to use in preparing his or her individual written report.

The procedures section describes the steps taken in conducting the study.

IV.   FINDINGS

The Business Communication classes surveyed 434 of the 7,400 students registered at Tripp Long-Creek College during the spring term 199-. The sample contained 139 young adults with a child or sibling under the age of 12 and 295 students without a child or sibling under 12.

The findings section presents the results of the study in an objective manner.

Effect of Television on Children

An overwhelming majority of 84.9 percent of the students with children or siblings under 12 as well as 88.1 percent of the students without children or siblings under 12 felt that television has both a positive and a negative effect on children, as shown

Body

4

in Table I. Approximately 4 percent of both groups felt that
television has a positive effect while about 7 percent felt that
television has a negative effect.

TABLE I
OPINIONS OF TLC STUDENTS ON THE EFFECTS OF TELEVISION
ON CHILDREN UNDER THE AGE OF 12

POSSIBLE RESPONSE	Have Child or Sibling under Age of 12		Do Not Have Child or Sibling under Age of 12		All Students Surveyed	
	No.	%	No.	%	No.	%
POSITIVE	6	4.3	11	3.7	17	3.9
POS. & NEG.	118	84.9	260	88.1	378	87.1
NEGATIVE	10	7.2	21	7.1	31	7.1
NO EFFECT	2	1.4	2	0.7	4	0.9
NO OPINION	3	2.2	1	0.3	4	0.9
TOTAL	139	100.0	295	99.9*	434	99.9*

*Rounding error prevents percentages from totalling 100.0.

Television Reinforcement of Violence

As shown in Table II, 82.0 percent of the students with a child
or sibling under 12 agreed that television does reinforce
violence in children's lives. Only 13.7 percent believed that
television does not reinforce violence. Approximately 70 percent
of the students who did not have a child or sibling under 12 felt
that television reinforces violent behavior in children's lives
while 19.0 percent of this group believed that it does not.

TABLE II
OPINIONS OF TLC STUDENTS ON TELEVISION REINFORCING
VIOLENCE IN CHILDREN UNDER THE AGE OF 12

POSSIBLE RESPONSE	Have Child or Sibling under Age of 12		Do Not Have Child or Sibling under Age of 12		All Students Surveyed	
	No.	%	No.	%	No.	%
YES	114	82.0	207	70.2	321	74.0
NO	19	13.7	56	19.0	75	17.3
NO OPINION	5	3.6	31	10.5	36	8.3
INCOMPLETE	3	2.2	1	0.3	2	0.4
TOTAL	139	100.0	295	100.0	434	100.0

Role of the Federal Communication Commission

The majority of students, as reflected in Table III, did not
think that the Federal Communication Commission (FCC) should
interfere by exerting pressures or establishing regulations to

Body

5

limit violent content in television programs. Less than 1 percent of the total population surveyed felt that the FCC should
interfere. More than 94 percent of the students surveyed felt
that the FCC should not be involved in controlling violence on
television.

TABLE III
OPINIONS OF TLC STUDENTS AS TO WHETHER OR NOT THE FCC SHOULD
EXERT PRESSURES OR ESTABLISH REGULATIONS TO CONTROL VIOLENT
CONTENT

POSSIBLE RESPONSE	Have Child or Sibling under Age of 12		Do Not Have Child or Sibling under Age of 12		All Students Surveyed	
	No.	%	No.	%	No.	%
YES	3	2.2	1	0.3	4	0.9
NO	126	90.6	283	95.9	409	94.2
NO OPINION	10	7.2	11	3.7	21	4.8
TOTAL	139	100.0	295	99.9*	434	99.9*

*Rounding error prevents percentages from totalling 100.0.

Parties Responsible for Controlling Violence

When asked who they thought had the major responsibility for controlling the amount of violence seen by children, more than 65
percent of the respondents felt the parents do. As shown in
Table IV, 21.9 percent of the students place the responsibility
on the networks while 4.4 percent place it on the government.

TABLE IV
OPINIONS OF TLC STUDENTS ON WHO HAS RESPONSIBILITY
FOR CONTROLLING TELEVISION VIOLENCE

POSSIBLE RESPONSE	Have Child or Sibling under Age of 12		Do Not Have Child or Sibling under Age of 12		All Students Surveyed	
	No.	%	No.	%	No.	%
PARENTS	88	63.4	196	66.4	284	65.4
NETWORKS	28	20.1	67	22.7	95	21.9
GOVERNMENT	7	5.0	12	4.1	19	4.4
DON'T KNOW	15	10.8	19	6.4	34	7.8
INCOMPLETE	1	0.7	1	0.3	2	0.5
TOTAL	139	100.0	295	99.9*	434	100.0

*Rounding error prevents percentages from totalling 100.0.

V. ANALYSIS

Both the related literature and the survey findings indicate
strong opinions that viewing television violence has an effect on

The analysis presents
relationships that
are significant.

Body

6

children's behavior. TLC students felt strongly (74 percent)
that television reinforces violent behavior in children's lives.
This opinion is supported by studies reported in the secondary
data.

What should be done about this situation? TLC students said
overwhelmingly that it is not a government problem. They say it
is the parents' responsibility to control the amount of violence
seen by their children. While the secondary sources generally
agreed with this position, it is important to note that a 1989
<u>Child Psychology</u> survey found that 52 percent of the respondents
believed that the federal government should offer incentives to
television stations to improve the quantity and quality of television programming for children. This finding suggests that
reducing the amount of violence viewed on television might be
best accomplished by a two-pronged approach--parental and television station control. The TLC students seem to support this
point when 87.3 percent indicated that one or the other--parents
or television networks--has the responsibility for controlling
television violence.

VI. CONCLUSIONS AND RECOMMENDATIONS

<u>Conclusions</u>

The following conclusions are made based on this study:
1. Viewing television violence reinforces violent behavior in
    children.
2. Parents are the most appropriate party to control the amount
    of violence viewed on television by their children.
3. There is only limited perference for governmental or network
    action to control the amount of violence on television.

<u>Recommendations</u>

The following recommendations are made, based on the conclusions
of this study:
1. An educational campaign should be conducted by an appropriate
    group to inform parents of the impact that violence on tele-
    vision has on their children.
2. Parents should be urged in the campaign to monitor closely
    the amount of violence that their children see on television.
3. Another study should be conducted to determine how young
    adults think parents should control the amount of violence
    their children see on television.
4. Networks and advertisers should be informed of the findings
    of this survey concerning violence on television.
5. A state committee composed of concerned parents and govern-
    ment officials should be appointed by the governor to make
    recommendations on the best ways to deal with the problem of
    violence on television and its negative impact on children.

Conclusions are
drawn from the
findings of the
study.

Recommendations
are developed from
the study's
conclusions.

Appendix

APPENDIX

SURVEY INSTRUMENT

An appendix contains material that is indirectly related to the study.

Appendix

8

MGT 215 Survey Questions

Statement to be made at the beginning of telephone conversation:

The Business Communication classes at Tripp Long-Creek College are conducting a telephone survey of students on the topic of television's effect on children. Your responses will be kept confidential. Would you be willing to answer a few questions for this survey? Check the appropriate blank.

1. Do you have a child or a brother or sister under age 12?

    ___ Yes   ___ No

2. In what way does television affect children?

    ___ Positive   ___ Positive and Negative   ___ Negative

    ___ No Effect   ___ No Opinion

3. Do you thing television reinforces violence in our children's lives?

    ___ Yes   ___ No   ___ No Opinion

4. Do you think the FCC should exert any pressures for regulations in controlling violent television program content?

    ___ Yes   ___ No   ___ No Opinion

5. Which of the following has the major responsibility for controlling the amount of violence that children see on television?

    ___ Parents   ___ Networks   ___ Government   ___ Don't Know

Bibliography

BIBLIOGRAPHY

The bibliography is a listing of all references that were used as sources of information in the study.

Bibliography

10

BIBLIOGRAPHY

Elway, Elmer. "Why Television Should Be Banned in Homes with
Children." <u>Proceedings of The Association of Concerned Parents</u>
(September 3, 1988), 531-534.

Gibbs, Joshua. "The Effects of Television on Children." <u>Parents
and Schools</u> (April 1990), 120-121.

Goff, Nathan. "Children's Television Programs Are Horrid."
<u>Children's Social Behavior</u> (October 1989), 67-72.

Krause, Gerald. "Violence Affects Children's Behavior." <u>Child
Psychology</u> (March 1987), 42-43.

McCann, Lois. "Does Television Affect Your Child?" <u>Child
Psychology</u> (June 1989), 55-62.

Williams, Sara. "The Parent's Role in Children's Viewing of
Television Programs." <u>The Television Viewer</u> (November 18, 1988),
61-64.

INDEX

PHOTOGRAPHS

For permission to reproduce the photographs on the pages indicated, acknowledgement is made to the following.

COVER PHOTO: © Marjory Dressler

page iii (middle): Hewlett-Packard Company

page iii (bottom): Courtesy of International Business Machines Corp.

page v (second): Hewlett-Packard Company

page vii (middle): General Instrument Corporation

page viii (top): Photo courtesy of Hewlett-Packard Company

page 94: Photo courtesy of Telex Communications, Inc.

1a: Photo Courtesy of Sperry Corporation

1b: Presentation Graphics, NY, NY

2a: Photo Courtesy of Sperry Corporation

2b: Presentation Graphics, NY, NY

3a: Presentation Graphics, NY, NY

3b: Jack Ward Color Service, Inc., NY, NY

4a: Photo courtesy of International Business Machines Corporation

4b: Photo courtesy of International Business Machines Corporation

page 422: Dominican Tourist Information Center

page 476: Courtesy of AT&T

page 486: Courtesy Honeywell, Inc.

page 490: Houston Instrument, a division of AMETEK

page 493: Printed with permission of Safeway Stores, Incorporated © 1986

page 511: H. Armstrong Roberts

page 514: © Kaz Mori/The Image Bank

page 516: Comstock, Inc.